Volume 5 2016 ISSN No. 2249-2240

GITAM JOURNAL OF GANDHIAN STUDIES

Dedicated to Promote Altruism, Peace & Nonviolence

Published by
GITAM University Press
Visakhapatnam – 530 045 (Andhra Pradesh)

Exclusively distributed by
D.K. Printworld (P) Ltd.
New Delhi - 110 015

GITAM Journal of Gandhian Studies
Volume 5 (2016) Hardbound Rs. 800 $50

ISSN No. 2249-2240

Published by
GITAM School of Gandhian Studies
GITAM University, Rushikonda, Visakhapatnam – 530 045 Andhra Pradesh, India.
Phone: (0891) 284 0317 *Fax:* (0891) 279 0037
e-mail: director_sgs@gitam.edu, b.sambasivaprasad@gmail.com
Web: www.gitam.edu

Printed and exclusively distributed by
D.K. Printworld (P) Ltd.
Regd. office: *'Vedaśrī'*, F-395, Sudarshan Park
ESI Metro Station, New Delhi - 110 015-11
Phones: (011) 2545 3975, 2546 6019
e-mail: indology@dkprintworld.com
Web: www.dkprintworld.com

Notes to Authors

GITAM Journal of Gandhian Studies (GJGS) is a multidisciplinary journal devoted to discussion on Gandhi — his person, philosophy, practices, and their contemporary relevance. It publishes Gandhi's seminal writings and their discussions, original research papers, abstracts of doctoral dissertations and major research project reports, case studies, book reviews and reader's comments. The following are guidelines to authors submitting papers for publication in GJGS.

- The research is original in nature and the paper is neither published nor under consideration for publication anywhere else.
- All the manuscripts should be clearly typed in double space with 12 point font.
- The cover page/letter should contain the title of the paper, author's name, designation, official address, contact phone/fax numbers, e-mail address and an abstract of not more than 150 words.
- The main text should not contain author's name. The footnotes shall be given separately. References should be given at the end of the manuscript and should contain only those cited in the text of the manuscript. References should be given in the following format:

  Bhan, S. (1998). Psychological Manifestations of Communal Violence: A Study of Hindu and Muslim Student Youth. Gandhi Marg, 20(2), 155-163.

  Ellens, J.H. (2002). Psychological Legitimization of Violence by Religious Archetypes. In C.E. Stout (Ed.) The Psychology of Terrorism: vol. 3: Theoretical Understandings and Perspectives (pp. 149-62). Westport, CT: Praeger.

  Ganguli, B.N. (1973). Gandhi's Social Philosophy: Perspectives and Relevance. New Delhi: National Gandhi Museum and Radha Publications.
- The manuscript along with a brief profile of the author, in about 150 words, may be sent to the Executive Editor, GITAM Journal of Gandhian Studies, GITAM School of Gandhian Studies, GITAM University, Rushikonda, Visakhapatnam – 530 045. Ph.: 0891 - 284 0317, Fax 0891 - 279 0037, e-mail: <director_sgs@gitam.edu>, <b.sambasivaprasad@gmail.com>.
- The manuscript should be in MS Word format. All the submitted manuscripts will be sent for peer review.
- The final decision on the acceptance or otherwise of the paper rests with the Editorial Board and it depends entirely on its standard and relevance. The final draft may be subjected to editorial amendment to suit the GJGS requirements. Correspondence and proofs for correction, if required, will be sent to the first named author unless otherwise indicated. Corrected proofs should be returned within ten days.
- The copyright of the contributions published in GJGS unless otherwise stipulated, rests with the GITAM School of Gandhian Studies.

GITAM JOURNAL OF GANDHIAN STUDIES

Volume 5 January – June 2016 Number 1

Contents

GITAM JOURNAL OF GANDHIAN STUDIES

Volume 5 July – December 2016 Number 2

Contents

GITAM JOURNAL OF GANDHIAN STUDIES

Volume 5 | January – June 2016 | Number 1

Contents

Gram Swaraj

M.K. Gandhi

Compiled by
Y.P. Anand
B. Sambasiva Prasad

To the Readers

The source of these selections is *Village Swaraj*, compiled by H.M.Vyas, first published in 1962 by Navajivan Publishing House, Ahmedabad. However, we have not published the book as it is. We have taken the relevant chapters from this work. Some of the topics repeated in this work are avoided in order to save space in this journal. The references found in this book are from journals, such as, *Harijan* and *Young India,* and from various compilations of Gandhiji's "works", such as, *Constructive Programme* (1945), *Key to Health* (1948), and *Khadi: Why and How* (1959). In order to update the references, we have tried to refer all selections to the *The Collected Works of Mahatma Gandhi* (*CWMG*, 1958-94), published by the Publication Division, Ministry of Information and Broadcasting, Government of India, New Delhi. While references to journals *Harijan* and *Young India* have been retained as a part of the references to *CWMG*, references to the older compilations have been normally replaced by the titles and the dates related to the references taken from *CWMG*. In very few cases where the text could not be located in *CWMG*, the reference given in *Village Swaraj* has been retained along with the reference to page number of *Village Swaraj* itself.

In some cases, slight variations were found between the translation from Gujarati/Hindi into English as given in *Village Swaraj* and that given in *CWMG*. In such cases, we have followed the version as given in *CWMG*. Some of the passages found in *Harijan/Young India* are in indirect speech. In such cases we followed the version as given in *Village Swaraj* (direct speech), in order to maintain uniformity and continuation of thought. Further, wherever we find short paragraphs in *CWMG*, we merged them in order to save space.

B. Sambasiva Prasad

Introduction

These selections (of Gandhiji's writings), titled *Gram Swaraj,* have been sourced from the book *Village Swaraj,* compiled by H.M. Vyas, and first published by Navajivan Publishing House, Ahmedabad, in 1962. Chapters 1-3 of *Village Swaraj* being introductory in nature and chapters 7-13 being only more detailed versions of the "Basic Principles of Village Swaraj" have been left out. Thus, in place of 29 chapters in *Village Swaraj,* the collection under *Gram Swaraj* has 19 chapters and all essential subjects have been duly covered.

In *Gram Swaraj,* chapter 1, "Cities and Villages", introduces the basic argument of Gandhiji, that even though bulk of India's population (then 85-90 per cent) lived in its 7,00,000 villages — and according to 2011 data, nearly 70 per cent Indians (833 million out of total population of 1.2 billion) still live in its 6,00,000 villages — rural India was much more impoverished, backward and exploited as compared with urban India.

Chapter 2 deals with the broad concept of "Village Swaraj" including the subject of "The Place of Villages" and the need for "Ideal Villages" as exemplars. Chapter 3, then covers "Basic Principles of Village Swaraj" under twelve subtitles, including very important subjects such as, employment, equality, "Trusteeship", decentralization, *swadeshi,* self-sufficiency, communal harmony, Panchayat Raj, and *Nai Talim* (Gandhiji's charter of "free and compulsory education" for every child up to the age of 14).

Chapters 4 to 8, titled "Agriculture and Cattle Welfare" cover a wide range of subjects related to rural economy, such as the condition of "Kisans", problems related to landownership such as those between landlords and tenants, cooperatives for working cattle and land, scientific treatment of agricultural and other rural wastes and their conversion into valuable compost/manure, and how to deal with the persistent problem of food scarcity.

Chapter 9 covers Gandhiji's well-known programme of "Khadi and Spinning" for the revival of village, as also national economy. Chapter 10 deals with his pursuit of a wide range of "Other Village Industries", such as, pounding/grinding of rice and corn, *ghani* oil, *gur* and *khandsari,* bee-keeping, tanning, soap-making, hand-made paper, and arranging village exhibitions.

Chapter 11 covers the allied subject of "village transport", primarily animal carts at that time. Chapter 12 covers the broader subject of "Currency, Exchange and Tax" as relevant here.

Chapters 13, 14, and 15 cover the interrelated subjects of "Village Sanitation", "Village Health and Hygiene", and "Diet" respectively. Gandhiji's deep and abiding interest in sanitation and health matters is well known but it is generally not known that, based on his studies and experience, he had also written articles/booklets titled "General Knowledge About Health" (from part [-I] dated *Indian Opinion*, 4.1.1913, to the last part [-XXXIV] dated *Indian Opinion*, 16.8.1913; *CWMG* 11 & 12), and then "Key to Health" (18.12.1942) (*CWMG* 77).

Chapter 16 covers the subject of "Village Protection", including Gandhiji's very original ideas about "Peace Brigade", "Police Force", and "Nonviolent Volunteer Corps". Chapter 17, "The Village Worker", gives detailed coverage to Gandhiji's persistent efforts so that selfless and devoted "village workers/volunteers" came forward to pull the Indian villages from the morass and exploitation, which then, and now as well, characterize the life in villages. Chapter 18 briefly relates to "What the Government Can Do", including what the elected ministers should do. The last chapter, "India and the World" concludes the selection with a reminder about what *swaraj* means and how a just and equitable treatment of all Indians including those in villages, alone can let India become an example of a non-exploitative social order for the world.

Before studying Gandhi's vast range of ideas related to "Gram Swaraj" in its all aspects and dimensions, we need to have a quick look at his basic understanding of what *swaraj* means and how villages/villagers were, and are, being discriminated against. There is a vast literature on what Gandhi meant by *swaraj*. A few references are quoted below:

- "It is Swaraj when we learn to rule ourselves. . . . But such *swaraj* has to be experienced, by each one for himself" (*Hind Swaraj*, *CWMG* 10: 39).
- "*Swaraj* is freedom for everyone, the smallest among us, to do as he likes without any physical interference with his liberty" [*Young India* (24.11.1921); *CWMG* 21: 485].
- "To me it has but one meaning: *the eradication of the poverty of India and freedom for every man and woman.* Ask the starving men and

women of India. They say that their *swaraj* is their bread. . . . *Swaraj* should mean this, too, that we become self-supporting" [*Hindi Navajivan* (4.5.1924); *CWMG* 23: 538].

- "[T]he *swaraj* of my dream is the poor man's *swaraj*. The necessaries of life should be enjoyed by you in common with those enjoyed by the princes and moneyed men" (11.3.1931; *CWMG* 45: 280).

And he also related his sense of "freedom" specifically to the state of villages in India, such as:

- "[I]ndependence should be ushered in with the greatest good grace which the poorest villager in the remotest village can at once realize" (Letter to Lord Wavell, 6.4.1946; *CWMG* 83: 371).
- "Independence must begin at the bottom. Thus, every village will be a republic or *panchayat* having full powers. It follows, therefore, that every village has to be self-sustained and capable of managing its affairs even to the extent of defending itself against the whole world. . . . In this structure composed of innumerable villages, there will be ever-widening, never-ascending circles. Life will not be a pyramid with the apex sustained by the bottom. But it will be an oceanic circle whose centre will be the individual always ready to perish for the village, the latter ready to perish for the circle of villages, till at last the whole becomes one life . . . no one is to be the first and none the last" [Independence, *Harijan* (28.7.1946); *CWMG* 85: 32-33].

Brief comments related to the subjects covered under chapters 1 to 19 of *Gram Swaraj* are as follows.

As given in chapter 1, Gandhiji contrasted the condition of villages in India with that of its cities and towns and how the villages were being exploited by the latter. Following references further highlight the inequitable state of villages and the role of freedom struggle in their uplift:

- "Is India living in her 10 or 20 cities, or is she living in her 700,000 villages? What then is the programme that can weld together the 30 crores of people . . . in 700,000 villages? The one and unequivocal answer is the spinning-wheel and *khaddar*. . . . The spinning-wheel can be turned by millions of the villagers of India who have been reduced to pauperism, who have been ground down to dust, not merely under the foreigner's heels but under your heels, under my heels. We the city-dwellers are living upon the labour, upon the wealth of these millions of villagers; . . ." [*Young India* (13.1.1927); *CWMG* 32: 508-09].

- In a speech at Bombay (18.4.1931), he told how the cities should develop in harmony with the villages: "India does not live in its towns but in its villages. But if the cities want to demonstrate that their populations will live for the villagers of India the bulk of their resources should be spent in ameliorating the condition of and befriending the poor. We must not lord it over them, we must learn to be their servants. When the cities realize that they must live for the welfare of the poor, they will make their palaces and institutions and the life of their inhabitants correspond somewhat to our villages" [*Young India* (23.4.1931); *CWMG* 46: 12].

In chapter 2, the Gandhian conception of "Village Swaraj" is explained under its subtitles: "The Place of Villages", "Village Swaraj", and "An Ideal Village". Gandhiji was categorical that India above all meant its villages:

- "I would say that if the village perishes, India will perish too. It will be no more India. Her own mission in the world will get lost. The revival of the village is possible only when it is no more exploited" [*Harijan* (29.8.1936); *CWMG* 63: 241].
- "India lives in her seven lakhs of villages — obscure, tiny, out-of-the-way villages. . . . That is real India, my India, for which I live" (24.3.1946; *CWMG* 83: 315).
- "Just as the universe is contained in the self, so is India contained in the villages" (12.7.1945; *CWMG* 80: 438).
- "If India lives in the villages, then let there be but one ideal village and it can serve as a model for the whole country" (13.7.1945; *CWMG* 80: 438).

After his return to India in 1915, Gandhiji had consistently kept studying and working on the economic, political, social, and any other issues relevant to the uplifting of the life in its villages. He had worked in the villages in Champaran (1917) and then continued thus onwards such as in Kheda, in Wardha and Sevagram, and even while involved in dealing with the communal violence in Bengal and Bihar during 1946-47. He had, therefore, a deep understanding of the problems and their solutions concerning villages in India, or how to bring *swaraj* to the villages. He had initiated the concept of "Constructive Programme" as a concomitant of the freedom movement itself, and finally it included 18 items. While items such as "Khadi" and "Other Village Industries", "Village Sanitation" and "Education in Health and Hygiene", and "Kisans" were related only to the villages, all remaining items too were equally applicable for the villages.

Gandhiji contrasts the condition of Indian villages in earlier times with that in his time thus:

> Sir Henry Maine had left a work on Village Communities . . . had shown . . . that the Indian village life had so much vitality and character that it had persisted all these long years. . . . He had described these villages as so many village republics completely self-contained, having all that one may want — schools, arbitration boards, sanitation boards, and . . . provision for relief of the poor. He had also shown the treasures of art that the genius of the Indian villager had produced. The villager then learnt from his parents by word of mouth all the wisdom. . . . In daily contact with people, he was able to realize the value and possibility of personality."

And then he came to the prevalent state:

> The whole village life was broken. People were dying by millions of . . . diseases, all brought about by insanitation, deep poverty, sloth and idleness. . . . One might search the records of the East India Company to see . . . how ruthlessly the village system was broken . . . how injustice, bribery and corruption reigned . . . the handicrafts of India were ruined.

Hence, Gandhiji invited:

> Any young man who has a character to save venture out to the villages. . . . But he will have to be patient and truthful. . . . There is a Trinity of Evil — insanitation, poverty and idleness . . . you will fight them with broomsticks, quinine and castor oil and, if you will believe me, with the spinning wheel [25.8.1925, *Young India* (17.9.1925); *CWMG* 28: 108-09].

He also insists that the village uplift alone could be the basis of true *swaraj* and democracy:

> Our country was never so unhappy and miserable as it is at present. In the cities people may be getting big profits and good wages, but all that has become possible by sucking the blood of villagers. . . . We must have faith and we must be true to ourselves . . . the main thing necessary is to make the village self-sufficient and self-reliant. . . . I am not preaching isolation. . . . Though the villagers will be self-sufficient so far as it is possible, they will devote their time also to their intellectual development for the creation of the consciousness for he contemplated nonviolent society of the future. . . . When seven lakhs of villages will take up this work in the new spirit we shall not remain a subject nation. Each one of our villages will be independent and self-reliant. That is true swaraj and that is true democracy (1.12.1944; *CWMG* 78: 369-71).

There was an interesting Gandhi–Nehru debate on the role of villages in India. Pandit Nehru had expressed doubts about Gandhiji's views as given in the *Hind Swaraj*. Gandhiji wrote to Nehru regarding this "sharp difference of opinion between us". Extracts from Gandhiji's letter, written on 5.10.1945 (*CWMG* 81: 309), may be seen in two parts under the subtitles "The Place of Villages" and "An Ideal Village" under chapter 2.

Nehru had replied (on 9.10.1945) persisting with his doubts:

> The question before us is not one of Truth versus Untruth and Nonviolence versus Violence. . . . I do not understand why a village should necessarily embody Truth and Nonviolence. A village, normally speaking, is backward intellectually and culturally and no progress can be made from a backward environment. . . .
>
> We have to put down certain objectives like a sufficiency of food, clothing, housing, education, sanitation, etc. which should be the minimum requirements for . . . everyone . . . we must find out specifically how to attain them speedily. Again, it seems to me inevitable that modern means of transport, as well as many other modern developments must . . . be developed. . . . If that be so, inevitably a measure of heavy industry exists. How far that will fit in with a purely village society? Personally, I hope that heavy or light industries should all be decentralized as far as possible, and this is feasible now. . . .
>
> I do not think it is possible for India to be really independent, unless she is a technically advanced country . . . we cannot even advance culturally without a strong background of scientific research. . . . There is in the world today a tremendous acquisitive tendency, both in the individuals and groups and nations, which leads to conflicts and wars. . . . That basis must go and be transformed into one of cooperation, not of isolation. . . . Many of the present overgrown cities have developed evils. . . . Probably, we have to discourage this overgrowth and, at the same time, encourage the village to approximate more to the culture of the town.
>
> . . . how to keep the good in the present, as in the past, is our problem (9.10.1945, Nehru, 507-10).

Gandhiji and Nehru had talks and Gandhiji had then written to Nehru:

> The talks we had yesterday have given me the impression that there is not much difference in our outlook or the way we understand things. I want to tell you how I have understood you. If there is any difference you will let me know.

1. The crucial question according to you, is how to ensure man's mental, economic, political, and moral development. That is my position too.

2. And in doing so every individual should have equal right and opportunity.

3. From this point of view there should be equality between villages and cities. And therefore their food and drink, their way of life, their dress, and their habits should be the same. If such a condition is to be brought about people should produce their own cloth and food and build their own houses. So also they should produce their own water and electricity.

4. Man is not born to live in the jungle; he is born to live in society. If we are to make sure that one person does not ride on another's back, the unit should be an ideal village or a social group which will be self-sufficient, but the members of which will be interdependent. This conception will bring about a change in human relationship all over the world (13.11.1945; *CWMG* 82:71-72).

Thus were their apparent differences and doubts resolved.

Chapter 3 covers a number of important subjects related to village development, such as those of employment, decentralization, self-sufficiency, Panchayat Raj, and *Nai Talim*. These should be studied in detail, particularly about the relevance and application of the Gandhian prescriptions in present times. For example, the present government scheme of "MNREGA" (Mahatma Gandhi Rural Employment Guarantee Act) is a revolutionary step related to the subject of "employment". Gandhiji had worked incessantly for economic revival of *khadi* and other village crafts and industries. As he had argued:

> You cannot build nonviolence on a factory civilization, but it can be built on self-contained villages. . . . Rural economy as I have conceived it eschews exploitation altogether and exploitation is the essence of violence. You have therefore to be rural-minded before you can be nonviolent, and to be rural-minded you have to have faith in the spinning-wheel [25.10.1939; *Harijan* (4.11.1939); *CWMG* 70: 296].

There is a vast Gandhian literature on "Panchayat Raj" and India has also adopted a comprehensive Panchayat Raj system since 1993. We need to study to what extent the present Panchayat Raj laws meet the Gandhian objectives of "Gram Swaraj", for example, as indicated in his article on "Panchayats" [*Young India* (28.5.1931); *CWMG* 46: 239-40]. We also need to study why the "Right to Education" Act (2009) provisions have so far not met the basic postulates of "free and compulsory" education for every child and the "true education" being defined as a harmonious development of head, heart, and hand, under Gandhiji's *Nai Talim*.

Chapters 4-8 cover various subjects related to "Agriculture and Cattle Welfare" including the condition of farmers, land issues, rural wastes and manure, and food shortages. Gandhiji had a deep concern for the well-being of the *kisans* whom he considered to be among the most exploited labour-power. Even while he was in South Africa, he had written under the title "Supreme Virtue of Agriculture", and it included a poem which he wanted the Indians to "ponder over" and "try to act upon it" [*Indian Opinion* (3.12.1910); *CWMG* 10: 376-77]:

O tiller of the soil,
Rightly they call you father of the world;
You, and you alone, provide
For all mankind; —
Cotton, fruits, flowers and grass,
And foodgrains too,
The food that sustains all creatures,
And clothing that is welcome to all.
Braving heat and rain,
Unremitting in toil,
Robust of health,
Ever you move in contentment.
Of worth supreme is the tiller's work,
Work that tends to others' good;
Tireless in your labour,
You teach a good lesson to the world.

Gandhiji saw the national ability to revive the villages from their abysmal state as the core of the *swaraj* in free India:

> We have to tackle the **triple malady** which holds our villages fast in its grip:
>
> 1. want of corporate sanitation; 2. deficient diet; and 3. Inertia. . . . They don't appreciate modern sanitary methods. They don't want to exert themselves beyond scratching their farms or doing such labour as they are used to. These difficulties . . . must not baffle us. . . . We must be patient with the people. . . . The only way is to sit down in their midst and work away in steadfast faith, as their scavengers, their nurses, their servants, not as their patrons, and to forget all our prejudices and pre-possessions [*Harijan* (16.5.1936); *CWMG* 62: 379].

As India approached independence, in his "Talk with Socialists", he gave similar advice:

> [I]f you wish to establish socialism, there is only one way . . . : go and

> live among the poor in the villages, live as they live, . . . use only village-made goods . . . remove illiteracy among the village people, eradicate untouchability, and uplift the women. . . . Make your life an ideal one in this way. . . . Let, therefore, all public workers and all officers of the government forget their quarrels and disputes over ideologies and start learning and teaching spinning, *khadi* work and village industries (27.5.1947; *CWMG* 88: 15).

As early as 1919, soon after he had tried to revive the villages in Champaran, Gandhiji had written a series of four articles (I to IV) under the title, "Father of the World", giving a picture of what the state of the Indian villages then was, what it should be, his experience in Champaran, and the issue of village sanitation, much of which is applicable today also. Extracts from articles I to III are given below (extracts from article IV are given while discussing chapters 13-15):

> The proprietor of thousands of acres is a cultivator; the man who owns only a *bigha* is also a cultivator; he who does not own even a *bigha*, but earns his food by working on another's land, is also called a cultivator and, finally, in Champaran, I have observed thousands of cultivators who were virtually slaves both of the Sahibs and of our people. . . . Even in the Kheda district. . . . The plague has reached villages and . . . other infectious diseases as well. . . . One shudders as one enters a Madras village . . . I could get a fairly clear idea of the stark poverty of the rural population of Madras.
>
> . . . India does not live in her towns. She lives in her villages. . . . Consequently, even if we are able to improve the towns and make them prosperous, these efforts can have very little effect on the villages. . . . But . . . if the living conditions of the farmers are improved and their standards raised, all else will follow [Father of the World-I, *Navajivan* (28.9.1919); *CWMG* 16: 182-3].
>
> Mr. Lionel Curtis . . . says that the villages of India are situated on dunghills. The huts are in ruins and the inhabitants feeble. . . . Cleanliness is non-existent. The general appearance would suggest that no one was responsible for the management of the village.
>
> . . . There ought to be some method in the lay-out of a well-ordered village. The streets should follow a definite pattern . . . In and around the village there should be useful trees and orchards. There should be a *dharmashala*, a school, and a small hospital. . . . Arrangements should be made for the bodily needs of the inhabitants so that the air, the streets, etc., are not polluted. The inhabitants of every village should be able to raise their

> own food and produce their own cloth and should be capable of defending themselves from thieves, marauders or wild beasts. . . . It is only such villages that can be regarded as self-sufficient. And, if all our villages could be so organized, there is little that can afflict the country [Father of the World-II, *Navajivan* (5.10.1919); *CWMG* 16: 213-15].

> When it was decided to open self-sufficient schools in Champaran, I appealed for volunteers . . . to perform only three tasks . . . teach any boys and girls who came, show the villagers how to maintain cleanliness in the streets, in the village and their homes, etc., and give medicine to any patients who might come for it. . . . Dr. Dev and Mr. Soman [volunteers] then took pickaxes . . . to make a sloping platform round the well and to clean the streets. . . . The villagers then sallied forth themselves to do the cleaning and very soon the well and streets of Bhitiharva took on an attractive appearance [Father of the World-III, *Navajivan* (19.10.1919); *CWMG* 16: 242-4].

Chapters 9 and 10 cover "Spinning and Khadi" and "Other Village Industries". Gandhiji had realized in early age itself that India's growing poverty and economic downfall under foreign rule had come about primarily due to the death of India's handicrafts and growing dependence upon imported factory produced cloth and other goods. He wrote in 1909 itself (*Hind Swaraj*, chap. XIX):

> When I read Mr. Dutt's *Economic History of India*, I wept; . . . it is machinery that has impoverished India. . . . It is due to Manchester that Indian handicraft has all but disappeared.

Further, he wanted millowners in India to establish in thousands of households that ancient and sacred handloom [he meant spinning-wheel] and they can buy out the cloth that may be thus woven. He wanted all to "support *swadeshi* and so shall we attain Home Rule".

He wanted handicrafts, small-scale industries, and even some heavy industries, but all appropriate to the needs and resources of the people. Soon after setting up Sabarmati Ashram, he had initiated work on handlooms and then on the spinning wheel and *khadi*. He had set up the All India Spinners Association in 1925. He made hand-spinning and hand-weaving into a universally respected practice as well as an art and science in India's homes, a unique achievement. He had asserted:

> Rural civilization is impossible without the *charkha* and all it implies, i.e., revival of village crafts. Thus the *charkha* is the symbol par excellence of non-violence. . . . The wheel is bound up with my scheme of *swaraj*, indeed with life itself (20.10.1939; *CWMG* 71: 95).

He was clear that in addition to *khadi*, the villages needed a wide and appropriate industrial base for their development. Hence, he also worked incessantly for growth of local industries in varied fields in rural areas such as processing of foodgrains, oilseeds, and other agricultural produce, manufacture of *gur/khandsari* from sugarcane, making of useful products such as honey, soap, hand-made paper, and ink, and tanning processes. In 1934 he had set up the All-India Village Industries Association with J.C. Kumarappa as its main functionary, who set up a vibrant centre of activities related to village industries at Wardha. Kumarappa, Gandhiji's "doctor of rural industries", has left behind a vast literature on the subject including his best-known book, *Economy of Permanence*. [The book, *J.C. Kumarappa*: *Mahatma Gandhi's Economist* by Marl Lindley, Mumbai: Popular Prakashan (2007) provides important source material.]

During discussion with a foreign visitor, Maurice Frydman, Gandhiji had said:

> Therefore we have to concentrate on the village being self-contained, manufacturing mainly for use. Provided this character of the village industry is maintained, there would be no objection to villagers using even the modern machines and tools that they can make and can afford to use [*Harijan* (29.8.1936); *CWMG* 63: 241].

While endorsing a "thought-provoking article", written by Kumarappa and elucidating the case for labour vs capital in India, Gandhiji reproduced extracts from it "with slight unimportant alterations", thus:

> According to the conception of the economic organization on which the A.I.V.I.A. is based, the villager is taken as the centre around whom the universe revolves. . . . Wealth is usually produced by the intelligent use of the means of production and the application of human talent power. . . . Mathematically thus: $W = E + M$. Here W stands for wealth, E for employment of human talent, and M for means in the shape of tools, equipment or capital. . . . When we look around our country we find E in abundance while M is very scarce and, therefore, if our planning is to be effective, we have to lay our foundation stone on labour and not on capital. . . . Most people . . . cannot see that the method of large-scale production can only be employed as a hand-maiden of the cottage and village industries, the former supplying the basic needs of the latter on a service basis [24.9.1939; *Harijan* (18.11.1939); *CWMG* 70: 198-99].

In chapter 11, the subject of village transport is considered briefly. The primary issue then was the organized management of bullocks and animal carts, which were then the primary means of rural transport. Now the subject has to be reviewed in the context of current situation.

Chapter 12 touches upon the subject of currency, exchange, and taxation as applicable in rural India. Here too, the whole set of issues may be reviewed in the context of the current situation.

Chapters 13, 14, and 15 deal with the allied subjects of village sanitation, health and hygiene, and diet, in the varied aspects of which Gandhiji had deep and lasting interest as he considered these to be basic to the well-being of village societies.

In South Africa itself, he had developed a passion to fight the twin "evils" of "insanitation" and "untouchability" and by and by had undertaken to scavenging himself. He used to even look after and treat patients including those suffering from epidemics like plague in South Africa and in India. In 1905 itself he had written on the "Measures to Eradicate Plague in India" that it needed "an improvement in sanitary habits, morality and economic condition of the people" [*Indian Opinion* (17.6.1905); *CWMG* 4: 468-69]. He even said that unless we "rid ourselves of our dirty habits and have improved latrines, *swaraj* can have no value for us" (3.11.1917; *CWMG* 14: 56-58). Along with the struggle for independence, he also led a continuous struggle in South Africa and in India, for sanitation, cleanliness, and efficient management of all types of wastes.

After his return to India, from 1915 itself he actively reviewed the insanitary state wherever he came across it. His stay at Shantiniketan had "taught us that the scavenger's work would be our special function in India". Soon thereafter at the Hardwar Kumbh Mela, his group had offered to cover up excreta with earth and to see to its disposal (*An Autobiography, CWMG* 39: 308-09). The dirt and insanitation at the Kashi Vishwanath Temple at Varanasi made him say in 1916, "Is not this great temple a reflection of our own character?" He had found the city itself "a stinking den" (*CWMG* 13: 212-13, 237-39). Similarly, he commented on Railway authorities' negligence and passengers, dirty habits being responsible for insanitary conditions on railway stations and trains. His "Draft Model Rules for Provincial Congress Committees" made each *panchayat* responsible for the "hygiene and sanitation therein" (*CWMG* 19: 217). And, for the Congress Session in 1921, he insisted for perfect sanitation, so as to be "an object lesson in cleanliness" (*CWMG* 21: 523). And so his propagation of sanitation as a scientific system went on an ever-growing scale, with its application in all fields, such as villages, cities, railways, "ashrams", and Congress sessions.

He called educating villagers in sanitation work and healthy diet as the "only real medical service" (*CWMG* 63: 162). He tried to introduce the hygienic methods of Dr. Poore, who had written books on village sanitation. It turned human excreta into valuable manure. He had followed this method in Sabarmati Ashram for seventeen years. He advised villagers near Wardha to replace open defecation with 6 inches wide and 1 foot deep trenches and cover the excreta with earth to convert it into manure (*CWMG* 60: 299-300). To him, "Sanitation comes first, because it covers most other things" (*CWMG* 84: 109). In Noakhali, while walking from village to village, one day (19.1.1946) he found excreta deliberately put on the narrow path. He himself cleaned it with dry leaves. He also told residents in Noakhali that chronic insanitation was responsible for their diseases and their poverty (*CWMG* 87: 4).

All along he also worked for minimizing the generation of all types of wastes, e.g., in 1919 itself he suggested "Improvement in Method of Cremation" so that the body could be reduced to ashes in a furnace (*CWMG* 16: 218-19). He was unhappy to see masses of flowers being wasted in his welcome and asked for garlands instead being made of handspun yarn (*CWMG* 16: 329). He advised J.C. Kumarappa to take up "the whole subject of economic waste" occurring through preventable diseases, wrong feeding, criminal waste of excreta, etc. (*CWMG* 47: 373-74), and also kept insisting that most the produced wastes could be converted into valuable resources.

As stated earlier, in part IV of his articles titled "Father of the World" he had dealt with the subject of "insanitation" in Indian villages: "Filth is a sign of ignorance and sloth. How, then, are peasants to be rescued from it? . . .

> 1. Many of our diseases originate from our latrines or from our custom of going to the fields for evacuation. . . . If anyone wants to evacuate in the open, it must be a distance of a mile from the village. There must be no habitation in its vicinity, nor any human traffic nearby. The person must dig a hole and after using it must cover the faeces with earth . . . every house should necessarily have a latrine. This should have a bucket. Here also every person should, after use, cover the faeces with earth. . . . Urine too should not be passed in any and every place. . . . There should be ditches for the purpose . . . and the earth will turn it into manure. . . .
>
> 2. No one should spit or clean his nose on the streets. . . .
>
> 3. . . . The well or pond from which drinking and cooking water is taken must be kept clean. . . .
>
> 4. . . . dirt must not be thrown on the street. Disposal of refuse is also a

> science. Glass, iron, etc., should be buried deep. Twigs . . . used for cleaning teeth should be . . . used for fuel. . . . Left-over food, peelings, etc., should be . . . turned into manure. . . . Paper can be made from rags. . . .
>
> 5. Near the village or dwellings, there should be no ditches in which water can collect. Mosquitoes do not breed where water does not stagnate [*Navajivan* (2.11.1919); *CWMG* 16: 271-73].

He had developed lifelong interest in the subject of "Nature Cure" and practised it on some very critical occasions successfully. As already stated, he had written two booklets on sanitation, health and hygiene: "General Knowledge About Health" (parts [I] to [XXXIV]) published in 1913 in South Africa (*CWMG* 11 & 12), and then the "Key to Health" (*CWMG* 77: 1-48), written during the period 28.8.1942 to 18.12.1942 while he was in detention in Aga Khan Palace, Poona.

Gandhiji continues to inspire efforts to deal with the multi-faceted problems of insanitation and ill-health in India, as is seen from the prime minister's speech on the Independence Day (15.8.2014):

> How do we celebrate 150th birth anniversary of Mahatma Gandhi? . . . Mahatma Gandhi had cleanliness and sanitation closest to his heart. Whether we resolve not to leave a speck of dirt in our village, city, street, area, school, temple, hospital, and what have you, by 2019 when we celebrate 150th anniversary of Mahatma Gandhi?

The PM concretized the resolve on 2.10.2014 by launching the *Swachh Bharat Abhiyan* — "Clean India Mission" — to provide sanitation facilities to every Indian, including toilets, solid and liquid waste disposal systems, village sanitation, and safe and adequate drinking water by 2.10.2019. As per 2011 Census, 113 million households in India do not have toilets, which means nearly 50 per cent of households in India (67.3 per cent of rural and 12.6 per cent of urban households) still defecate in the open and are exposed to diseases, harassment, and shame. Let us hope that the government ensures fulfilment of this part of the Gandhian agenda, particularly for the Indian villages. The rest of the agenda related to rural sanitation, health and hygiene, and diet too may then follow.

Chapter 16 refers to Gandhian ideas concerning "Peace Brigade", "Police Force", and "Non-violent Volunteer Corps", for social protection not only in villages but also in cities and towns.

Chapter 17, titled "Village Worker", covers a vital feature of Gandhiji's whole public life and its activities. He believed public issues are best pursued through services rendered willingly by volunteers committed to the pursuit of the aims and causes which serve the interests of the poor and the deprived sections of the society. He himself was such a "worker" par excellence in multiple fields. A study of the whole history of his setting up his first *ashram* in South Africa, i.e., Phoenix Settlement, in 1904 and of growing involvement of him and his co-workers in it as well as in his other movements against racial discrimination in South Africa, can provide a detailed understanding of his whole concept of volunteering for public service.

After his return to India, while fighting against the exploitation of local farmers in Champaran, how he converted it into an opportunity for uplifting the impoverished villagers through his "village workers", remains an ideal example. This is also how he ran his *ashrams*, the various social service organizations he set up, such as All India Spinners' Association, All India Village Industries Association, Hindustani Talimi Sangh, and Harijan Sevak Sangh, and the numerous mass movements he led during 54 years of his public life — all with help of volunteers dedicated to the particular cause. This is also how he pursued his *Constructive Programme*, which finally covered eighteen major subjects, viz., communal unity, removal of untouchability, prohibition, *khadi*, other village industries, village sanitation, new or basic education, adult education, women, education in health and hygiene, provincial languages, national language, economic equality, *kisan*s, labour, *adivasi*s, lepers, and students. He wrote in his "Foreword" to its booklet:

> Given an indomitable will on the part of a band of earnest workers, the programme is as workable as any other and more than the most (13.11.1945; *CWMG* 82: 66-68).

Chapter 18 indicates Gandhiji's views about the duties of the government, and particularly of elected representatives in it, for "Gram Swaraj", and chapter 19 tells how India, if it develops along the Gandhian lines, can become a role model for the development of the whole world.

Finally, I consider it very relevant to refer here to Gandhiji's directives given on/after independence for how free India should develop and realize "Gram Swaraj", and also a recent "Manifesto for Village Development" written by India's former President, A.P.J. Abdul Kalam.

> Gandhiji gave the following *talisman* in August 1947: *Whenever you are in doubt, or when the self becomes too much with you, apply the following test. Recall the face of the poorest and the weakest man whom you may have seen, and ask yourself if the step you contemplate is going to be of any use to him. Will he gain anything by it? Will it restore him to a control over his own life*

and destiny? In other words, will it lead to swaraj for the hungry and spiritually starving millions? Then you will find your doubts and yourself melting away (*CWMG* 89: 125).

Then a day before his martyrdom, he issued a "Draft Constitution of Congress", in which he gave clear directions as to how to attain "Gram Swaraj":

India having attained political independence . . . has still to attain social, moral, and economic independence in terms of its seven hundred thousand villages as distinguished from its cities and towns. . . . For these and other similar reasons, the A.I.C.C. resolves to disband the existing Congress organization and flower into a Lok Sevak Sangh under the following rules with power to alter them as occasion may demand. Every *panchayat* of five adult men or women being villagers or village-minded shall form a unit.

Two such contiguous *panchayat*s shall form a working party under a leader elected from among themselves. When there are one hundred such *panchayat*s, the fifty-first grade leaders shall elect from among themselves a second-grade leader and so on . . . till they cover the whole of India. . . . All second-grade leaders shall serve jointly for the whole of India and severally for their respective areas. The second-grade leaders may elect, whenever they deem necessary, from among themselves a chief who will, during pleasure, regulate and command all the groups. . . .

1. Every worker shall be a habitual wearer of *khadi* . . . and . . . a teetotaller. If a Hindu, he must have abjured untouchability . . . must be a believer in the ideal of inter-communal unity . . . and equality of opportunity and status for all irrespective of race, creed or sex. 2. He shall come in personal contact with every villager within his jurisdiction.

. . . 5. He shall organize the villages so as to make them self-contained and self-supporting through their agriculture and handicrafts. 6. He shall educate the village folk in sanitation and hygiene and take all measures for prevention of ill health. . . . 7. He shall organize the education of the village folk from birth to death along the lines of *Nayee Talim*. . . . 8. He shall see that those whose names are missing on the statutory voters' roll are duly entered therein. . . .

The Sangh shall affiliate the following autonomous bodies:

1. A.I.S.A. 2. A.I.V.I.A. 3. Hindustani Talimi Sangh. 4. Harijan Sevak Sangh. 5. Goseva Sangh. . . . (29.1.1948; *CWMG* 90: 526-28).

Even over 68 years after Independence, the villages in India remain backward and impoverished in comparison with urban India. This issue had been studied by late President A.P.J. Abdul Kalam and he has proposed in his many writings the policies and actions which should be taken so that the villages develop equitably with urban India. In his recent book, *A Manifesto for Change: A Sequel to India 2020* [written with V. Ponraj, Noida: Harper Collins Publishers India (2014)] there is a chapter titled "Manifesto for Village Development" (pp. 83-109).

The chapter starts with Gandhiji's quote, "You cannot build nonviolence on a factory civilization but it can be built on self-contained villages" [*Harijan* (4.11.1939), *CWMG* 70: 296]. He quotes 2011 census data showing that 70 per cent of India still lives in villages. Discussing the present situation, it states:

> The picture emerging makes it clear that India's aspirations are increasingly directed towards the cities. The obvious challenge before our nation is . . . to avoid large-scale migration from rural to urban areas by providing urban amenities in rural areas. What makes this challenge all the more pressing is that about 30 per cent of the population of the country still lives below the poverty-line, and nearly 80 per cent of those below poverty-line are located in rural areas . . . .

It also refers to non-availability of electricity in the villages and how Gandhiji had said, "I would prize every invention of science made for the benefit of all."

It rightly comes to the conclusion:

> The first priority for societal transformation of India is accelerated rural development . . . all developmental activities have to be sustainable and should be activated in 6,00,000 villages which have missed both the Industrial Revolution and Information Technology Revolution and in fact even the first Green revolution in many of the states.

Abdul Kalam's well-known solution for uplifting villages is to implement the Provision of Urban Amenities in Rural Areas (PURA) cluster approach, as proposed by him, for rural development. Under this system, 30-50 villages are connected as a cluster complex with the creation of three connectivities, viz., physical, electronics, and knowledge, these leading to economic connectivity. Along with the Gram Sabhas, PURA would enable working for strengthening agriculture, agro-processing industry, power generation, skill development, health care and sanitation, water harvesting, and all other development indicators. PURA aims at building improved infrastructure, doubling per capita income, and a better quality of life, factors which can lead to reverse migration.

The chapter also discusses the contents of the Constitutional (73rd

Amendment) Act, 1992, which came into force on 24.4.1993 to provide constitutional status to Panchayat Raj Institutions over whole rural India — at three levels: Gram Sabhas (Village level), Panchayat Samitis (Block level), and Zilla Parishads (District level). It proposes an exemplary "Vision Manifesto for Village Panchayats", which covers a long list including revival of all the ponds, tanks, and lakes, encouraging rainwater harvesting in all homes and creating a sustainable water infrastructure; segregating organic and inorganic waste and converting wastes into wealth; ensuring sanitation in all homes; erecting community solar panels; planting trees; respecting our teachers and helping them teach our children well, and encouraging skill development; encouraging sports and games; promoting good hygiene, regular vaccination, and periodic medical check-ups; promoting peace and harmony; ensuring best practices in agriculture including quality seeds and necessary water availability; pooling resources for common requirements; helping people get rid of addictions and vices; encouraging development of core competence of villages and working with industry, academics, government and banks to create young entrepreneurs; and making the village a carbon-neutral village, with a clean and green environment.

To conclude, though India as a whole has been on a continuous trajectory of growth and development since Independence, the fact remains that bulk of India (now 65-70 per cent as against 85-90 per cent in 1947) still lives in its villages and that rural India remains backward, less developed, and much poorer than urban India, and very much lacking in opportunities and "entitlements" as compared with the cities and towns. Gandhiji had realized that "Gram Swaraj" was essential if India were to be really *free* and he worked for the development of rural India in all its dimensions along with the struggle for India's political freedom. After Gandhiji, many eminent leaders, such as Vinoba Bhave, too have worked for the uplift of Indian villages. We all, including the vast structure of the government, academicians, economists, and social organizations need to work for achieving "Gram Swaraj" . . . so that living in villages will not in any way offer less opportunities for attainments in any field than in the cities — at the earliest. There is also a vast variation in the levels of development, availability of resources and talents, and of needs in different regions of rural India. The government must set up suitable institutional systems for a continuous study and review of the needs of each region so as to achieve "Gram Swaraj" of Gandhiji's dream as early as possible in the modern context.

29 May 2016 **Y.P. Anand**

Contents

1

Cities and Villages

There are two schools of thought current in the world. One wants to divide the world into cities and the other into villages. The village civilization and the city civilization are totally different things. One depends on machinery and industrialization, the other rests on handicraft. We have given preference to the latter.

After all, this industrialization and large-scale production are only of comparatively recent growth. We do not know how far it has contributed to our development and happiness, but we know this much that it has brought in its wake the recent world wars. This Second World War is not still over and even before it comes to an end we are hearing of a third world war. Our country was never so unhappy and miserable as it is at present. In the cities people may be getting big profits and good wages, but all that has become possible by sucking the blood of villagers. We do not want to collect lakhs and crores. We do not always want to depend on money for our work. If we are prepared to sacrifice our lives for the cause, money is nothing. We must have faith and we must be true to ourselves. If we have these, we shall be able to decentralize our capital of thirty lakhs in the villages to create national wealth amounting to three hundred crores. To do that, the main thing that is necessary is to make the village self-sufficient and self-reliant. But mind you, my idea of self-sufficiency is not a narrow one. There is no scope for selfishness or arrogance in my self-sufficiency (Address to A.I.S.A. Trustees, 1.12.1944; *The Bombay Chronicle*, 7.12.1944; *CWMG* 78: 369-70).

We may not be deceived by the wealth to be seen in the cities of India. That wealth does not come from England or America. It comes from the blood of the poorest. I claim to be an economist though not of the academic sort. I understand the roots of misery and [poverty] of India. Are you going to stamp out India's starvation by feeding a few hungry mouths? There are said to be 7,00,000 villages in India. Some of them have been simply wiped out. Who has kept count of them? I am a villager. I can recognize at a glance the traces of a ruined village. Where has it gone? Where are the villagers? If anyone raises a doubt about my allegations, I can go round with him and show him the devastation. God will give me the strength for that. The government reports, though an underestimate, of the thousands who have died of starvation and disease in Bengal, Karnataka, and elsewhere are shocking. But this devastation is negligible compared to the wider havoc wrought over India through the centuries.

Why this havoc? It is because the blood of the poorest is being sucked; whoever eats a morsel more than he really needs is sucking the blood of the poor. The money that goes to England and America is not your money, it is the blood of the poorest. I tell you that the pressure from the top crushes those at the bottom. What then is the remedy? All that is necessary is to get off their backs (Speech to Congressmen, Poona, 29.6.1944; *CWMG* 77: 341).

The workers in the mills of Bombay have become slaves. The condition of the women working in the mills is shocking. When there were no mills, these women were not starving. If the machinery craze grows in our country, it will become an unhappy land. It may be considered a heresy, but I am bound to say that it were better for us to send money to Manchester and to use flimsy Manchester cloth than to multiply mills in India. By using Manchester cloth we only waste our money; but by reproducing Manchester in India, we shall keep our money at the price of our blood, because our very moral being will be sapped, and I call in support of my statement the very mill-hands as witnesses. And those who have amassed wealth out of factories are not likely to be better than other rich men. It would be folly to assume that an Indian Rockefeller would be better than the American Rockefeller. Impoverished India can become free, but it will be hard for any India made rich through immorality to regain its freedom. I fear we shall have to admit that moneyed men support British rule; their interest is bound up with its stability. Money renders a man helpless. The other thing which is equally harmful is sexual vice. Both are poison. A snakebite is a lesser poison than these two, because the former merely destroys the body but the latter destroy body, mind, and soul. We need not, therefore, be pleased with the prospect of the growth of the mill-industry (*Hind Swaraj*, 1910, p. 92; *CWMG* 10: 58).

The poor villagers are exploited by the foreign government and also by their own countrymen — the city-dwellers. They produce the food and go hungry. They produce milk and their children have to go without it. It is disgraceful. Everyone must have a balanced diet, a decent house to live in, facilities for the education of one's children and adequate medical relief (*The Hindu*, 26.1.1946; *Harijan*, 31.3.1946, p. 63; *CWMG* 83: 26-27).

The half a dozen modern cities are an excrescence and serve at the present moment the evil purpose of draining the life-blood of the villages. . . . The cities with their insolent torts [*sic*] are a constant menace to the life and liberty of the villagers (*Young India*, 17.3.1927, p. 86; *CWMG* 33: 166).

"It is the city man who is responsible for war all over the world, never the villager" (Bapu in conversation) (*Gleanings*, 1949, p. 17).

I regard the growth of cities as an evil thing, unfortunate for mankind and the world, unfortunate for England, and certainly unfortunate for India. The British have exploited India through its cities. The latter have exploited the villages. The blood of the villages is the cement with which the edifice of the cities is built. I want the blood that is today inflating the arteries of the cities to run once again in the blood vessels of the villages (*Harijan*, 23.6.1946, p. 198; *CWMG* 84: 226).

You have called cities boils or abscesses on the body politic. What should be done with these boils?

If you ask a doctor he will tell you what to do with a boil. It has to be cured either by lancing or by the application of plasters and poultices. Edward Carpenter called civilization a malady which needed a cure. The growth of big cities is only a symptom of that malady. Being a nature-curist, I am naturally in favour of nature's way of cure by a general purification of the system. If the hearts of the city-dwellers remain rooted in the villages, if they become truly village-minded, all other things will automatically follow and the boil will quickly heal. (*Harijan*, 25.8.1946, p. 282; *CWMG* 85: 97-98).

I have believed and repeated times without number that India is to be found not in its few cities but in its 7,00,000 villages. But . . . . We town-dwellers have believed that India is to be found in its towns and that the villages were created to minister to our needs. We have hardly ever paused to inquire if those poor folk get sufficient to eat and clothe themselves with and whether they have a roof to shelter themselves from sun and rain (*Harijan*, 4.4.1936, p. 63; *CWMG* 62: 298).

I have found that the town-dweller has generally exploited the villager, in fact he has lived on the poor villager's subsistence. Many a British official has written about the conditions of the people of India. No one has, to my knowledge, said that the Indian villager has enough to keep body and soul together. On the contrary they have admitted that the bulk of the population live on the verge of starvation and 10 per cent are semi-starved, and that millions have to rest content with a pinch of dirty salt and chilies and polished rice or parched grain. You may be sure that if any of us were to be asked to live on that diet, we should not expect to survive it longer than a month or should be afraid of losing our mental faculties. And yet our villagers go through that state from day-to-day (*Harijan*, 4.4.1936, pp. 63-64; *CWMG* 62: 298).

Over 75 per cent of the population are agriculturists. . . . But there cannot be much spirit of self-government about us if we take away or allow others to take away from them almost the whole of the result of their labour (Speech at Banaras Hindu University, 6.2.1916; *CWMG* 13: 214).

The cities are capable of taking care of themselves. It is the villages we have to turn to. We have to disabuse them of their prejudices, their superstitions, their narrow outlook and we can do so in no other manner than that of staying amongst them and sharing their joys and sorrows and spreading education and intelligent information among them (*Village Swaraj*, p. 26; *Young India*, 30.4.1931, p. 94).

We have got to be ideal villagers, not the villagers with their queer ideas or absence of ideas, about sanitation and giving no thought to how they eat and what they eat. Let us not, like most of them, cook anyhow, eat anyhow, live anyhow. Let us show them the ideal diet. Let us not go by mere likes and dislikes, but get at the root of those likes and dislikes (*Harijan*, 1.3.1935 p. 21; *CWMG* 60: 251-52).

We must identify ourselves with the villagers who toil under the hot sun beating on their bent backs and see how we would like to drink water from the pool in which the villagers bathe, wash their clothes and pots, in which their cattle drink and roll. Then and not till then shall we truly represent the masses and they will, as surely as I am writing this, respond to every call (*Young India*, 11.9.1924, p. 300; *CWMG* 25: 122).

We have got to show them that they can grow their vegetables, their greens, without much expense, and keep good health. We have also to show that most of the vitamins are lost when they cook the leaves (*Harijan*, 1.3.1935, p. 21; *CWMG* 60: 252).

We have to teach them how to economize in time, health, and money. . . . Lionel Curtis described our villages as dung-heaps. We have to turn them into model villages. Our village folk do not get fresh air, though they are surrounded by fresh air; they don't get fresh food, though they are surrounded by the freshest foods. I am talking like a missionary in this matter of food, because my mission is to make villages a thing of beauty (*Harijan*, 1.3.1935, p. 21; *CWMG* 60: 252).

It is profitless to find out whether the villages of India were always what they are today. If they were never better it is a reflection upon the ancient culture in which we take so much pride. But if they were never better, how is it that they have survived centuries of decay which we see going round us and of which Savli is but a type?

The task before every lover of the country is how to prevent this decay or, which is the same thing, how to reconstruct the villages of India so that it may be as easy for anyone to live in them as it is supposed to be in the cities. Indeed, it is the task before every patriot. It may be that the villagers are beyond redemption, that rural civilization has had its day and that the seven hundred thousand villages have to give place to seven hundred well-ordered cities supporting a population not of three hundred millions but thirty. If such is to be India's fate, even that won't come in a day. It must take time to wipe out a large number of villages and villagers and transform the remainder into cities and citizens (*Harijan*, 7.3.1936, p. 30; *CWMG* 62: 248-49).

The village movement is as much an education of the city people as of the villagers. Workers drawn from cities have to develop village mentality and learn the art of living after the manner of villagers. This does not mean that they have to starve like the villagers. But it does mean that there must be a radical change in the old style of life (*Harijan*, 11.4.1936, p. 68; *CWMG* 62: 319-20).

The only way is to sit down in their midst and work away in steadfast faith, as their scavengers, their nurses, their servants, not as their patrons, and to forget all our prejudices and prepossessions. Let us for a moment forget even *swaraj*, and certainly forget the "haves" whose presence oppresses us at every step. They are there. There are many who are dealing with these big problems. Let us tackle the humbler work of the village which is necessary now and would be even after we have reached our goal. Indeed, the village work when it becomes successful will itself bring us nearer the goal (*The Bombay Chronicle*, 11.5.1936; *Harijan*, 16.5.1936, p. 112; *CWMG* 62: 379).

The village communities should be revived. Indian villages produced and supplied to the Indian towns and cities for all their wants. India became impoverished when our cities became foreign markets and began to drain the villages dry by dumping cheap and shoddy goods from foreign lands (*Harijan*, 27.2.1937, p. 18; *CWMG* 64: 118).

It is only when the cities realize the duty of making an adequate return to the villages for the strength and sustenance which they derive from them, instead of selfishly exploiting them, that a healthy and moral relationship between the two will spring up, and if the city children are to play their part in this great and noble work of social reconstruction, the vocations through which they are to receive their education ought to be directly related to the requirements of the villages (*Harijan*, 9.10.1937, p. 293; *CWMG* 66: 169).

We are inheritors of a rural civilization. The vastness of our country, the vastness of the population, the situation, and the climate of the country have, in my opinion, destined it for a rural civilization. Its defects are well known but not one of them is irremediable. To uproot it and substitute for it an urban civilization seems to me an impossibility, unless we are prepared by some drastic means to reduce the population from three hundred million to three or say even thirty. I can therefore suggest remedies on the assumption that we must perpetuate the present rural civilization and endeavour to rid it of its acknowledged defects (*Young India*, 7.11.29, p. 364; *CWMG* 42: 108).

2
Village Swaraj

The Place of Villages

To serve our villages is to establish *swaraj*. Everything else is but an idle dream (*Young India*, 26.12.29, p. 420; *CWMG* 42: 317).

If the village perishes India will perish too. It will be no more India. Her own mission in the world will get lost (*Harijan*, 29.8.1936, p. 226; *CWMG* 63: 241).

We have to make a choice between India of the villages that are as ancient as herself and India of the cities which are a creation of foreign domination. Today the cities dominate and drain the villages so that they are crumbling to ruin. My *khadi* mentality tells me that cities must subserve villages when that domination goes. Exploiting of villages is itself an organized violence. If we want *swaraj* to be built on nonviolence, we will have to give the villages their proper place (*Harijan*, 20.1.1940, p. 423; *CWMG* 71: 103).

I believe that if India, and through India the world, is to achieve real freedom, then sooner or later we shall have to go and live in the villages — in huts, not in palaces. Millions of people can never live in cities and palaces in comfort and peace. Nor can they do so by killing one another, that is, by resorting to violence and untruth. I have not the slightest doubt that, but for the pair, truth and nonviolence, mankind will be doomed. We can have the vision of that truth and nonviolence only in the simplicity of the villages. That simplicity resides in the spinning-wheel and what is implied by the spinning-wheel. It does not frighten me at all that the world seems to be going in the opposite direction. For the matter of that, when the moth approaches its doom it whirls round faster and faster till it is burnt up. It is possible that India will not be able to escape this moth-like circling. It is my duty to try, till my last breath, to save India and through it the world from such a fate (Letter to Jawaharlal Nehru, 5.10.1945; *CWMG* 81: 319).

Village Swaraj

My idea of Village Swaraj is that it is a complete republic, independent of its neighbours for its own vital wants, and yet interdependent for many others in which dependence is a necessity. Thus every village's first concern will be to grow its own food crops and cotton for its cloth. It should have a reserve for its cattle, recreation, and playground for adults and children. Then if there is more land available, it will grow *useful* money crops, thus excluding *ganja,* tobacco, opium, and the like. The village will maintain a village theatre, school, and public hall. It will have its own waterworks ensuring clean water supply. This can be done through controlled wells or tanks. Education will be compulsory up to the final basic course. As far as possible every activity will be conducted on the cooperative basis. There will be no castes such as we have today with their graded untouchability. Nonviolence with its technique of *satyagraha* and noncooperation will be the sanction of the village community. There will be a compulsory service of village guards who will be selected by rotation from the register maintained by the village. The government of the village will be conducted by the *panchayat* of five persons annually elected by the adult villagers, male and female, possessing minimum prescribed qualifications. These will have all the authority and jurisdiction required. Since there will be no system of punishments in the accepted sense, this *panchayat* will be the legislature, judiciary, and executive combined to operate for its year of office. Any village can become such a republic today without much interference, even from the present government whose sole effective connection with the villages is the exaction of the village revenue. I have not examined here the question of relations with the neighbouring villages and the centre, if any. My purpose is to present an outline of village government. Here there is perfect democracy based upon individual freedom. The individual is the architect of his own government. The law of nonviolence rules him and his government. He and his village are able to defy the might of a world. For the law governing every villager is that he will suffer death in the defence of his and his village's honour.

. . . there is nothing inherently impossible in the picture drawn here. To model such a village may be the work of a lifetime. Any lover of true democracy and village life can take up a village, treat it as his world and sole work, and he will find good results. He begins by being the village scavenger, spinner, watchman, medicine man, and school-master all at once.

If nobody comes near him, he will be satisfied with scavenging and spinning (*Harijan*, 26.7.1942, p. 238; *Sevagram*, 18.7.1942; *CWMG* 76: 308-09).

An Ideal Village

An ideal Indian village will be so constructed as to lend itself to perfect sanitation. It will have cottages with sufficient light and ventilation built of a material obtainable within a radius of five miles of it. The cottages will have courtyards enabling householders to plant vegetables for domestic use and to house their cattle. The village lanes and streets will be free of all avoidable dust. It will have wells according to its needs and accessible to all. It will have houses of worship for all, also a common meeting place, a village common for grazing its cattle, a cooperative dairy, primary and secondary schools in which industrial education will be the central fact, and it will have *panchayat*s for settling disputes. It will produce its own grains, vegetables and fruit, and its own *khadi*. This is roughly my idea of a model village. . . . I am convinced that they can, under intelligent guidance, double the village income as distinguished from individual income. There are in our villages inexhaustible resources not for commercial purposes in every case but certainly for local purposes in almost every case. The greatest tragedy is the hopeless unwillingness of the villagers to better their lot.

The very first problem the village worker will solve is its sanitation. It is the most neglected of all the problems that baffle workers and that undermine physical well-being and breed disease. If the worker became a voluntary *bhangi*, he would begin by collecting night-soil and turning it into manure and sweeping village streets. He will tell people how and where they should perform daily functions and speak to them on the value of sanitation and the great injury caused by the neglect. The worker will continue to do the work whether the villagers listen to him or not (*Harijan*, 9.1.1937, p. 383; *CWMG* 64: 217-18).

In this village of my dreams the villager will not be dull — he will be all awareness. He will not live like an animal in filth and darkness. Men and women will live in freedom, prepared to face the whole world. There will be no plague, no cholera, and no smallpox. Nobody will be allowed to be idle or to wallow in luxury. Everyone will have to do body labour. Granting all this, I can still envisage a number of things that will have to be organized on a large scale. Perhaps there will even be railways and also post and telegraph offices (Letter to Jawaharlal Nehru, 5.10.1945; *CWMG* 81: 319).

3

Basic Principles of Village Swaraj

a. Supremacy of Man: Full Employment

The supreme consideration is man (*Young India*, 13-11-1924, p. 378; *CWMG* 25: 251).

The end to be sought is human happiness combined with full mental and moral development. I use the adjective moral as synonymous with spiritual. This end can be achieved under decentralization. Centralization as a system is inconsistent with a nonviolent structure of society (*Harijan*, 18-1-1942, p. 5; *CWMG* 75: 216).

According to me the economic constitution of India, and for the matter of that of the world, should be such that no one under it should suffer from want of food and clothing. In other words, everybody should be able to get sufficient work to enable him to make the two ends meet. And this ideal can be universally realized only if the means of production of the elementary necessaries of life remain in the control of the masses. These should be freely available to all as God's air and water are or ought to be; they should not be made a vehicle of traffic for the exploitation of others. Their monopolization by any country, nation or groups of persons would be unjust. The neglect of this simple principle is the cause of the destitution that we witness today not only in this unhappy land but in other parts of the world too (*Young India*, 15.11.1928, p. 381; *CWMG* 37: 411-12).

That economics is untrue which ignores or disregards moral values. The extension of the law of nonviolence in the domain of economics means nothing less than the introduction of moral values as a factor to be considered in regulating international commerce (*Young India*, 26.12.1924, p. 421; *CWMG* 25: 475).

Every human being has a right to live, and therefore to find the wherewithal to feed himself and where necessary, to clothe and house himself (Speech at Muir College Economic Society, Allahabad, 22.12.1916; *The Leader*, 25.12.1916; *CWMG* 13: 312).

"Take no thought for the morrow" is an injunction which finds an echo in almost all the religious scriptures of the world. In well-ordered society the securing of one's livelihood should be and is found to be the easiest thing in the world. Indeed, the test of orderliness in a country is not the number of millionaires it owns, but the absence of starvation among its masses (Speech at Muir College, Allahabad, 22.12.1916; *The Leader*, 25.12.1916; *CWMG* 13: 312).

Any plan which exploited the raw materials of a country and neglected the potentially more powerful manpower was lopsided and could never tend to establish human equality. . . .

Therefore, real planning consisted in the best utilization of the whole manpower of India (*Harijan*, 23.3.1947, p. 79; *CWMG* 87: 26-27).

We should be ashamed of resting or having a square meal so long as there is one able-bodied man or woman without work or food (*Young India*, 6.10.1921, p. 314; *CWMG* 21: 239).

Every man has an equal right to the necessaries of life even as birds and beasts have. And since every right carries with it a corresponding duty and the corresponding remedy for resisting any attack upon it, it is merely a matter of finding out the corresponding duties and remedies to vindicate the elementary fundamental equality. The corresponding duty is to labour with my limbs and the corresponding remedy is to non-cooperate with him who deprives me of the fruit of my labour (*Young India*, 26.3.1931, p. 49; *CWMG* 45: 339).

b. Body Labour

How can a man who does not do body labour, have the right to eat? (*From Yeravda Mandir*, p. 51; Letter to Narandas Gandhi, 16.9.1930; *CWMG* 44: 149).

"Earn thy bread by the sweat of thy brow," says the Bible. Sacrifices may be of many kinds. One of them may well be bread labour. If all laboured for their bread and no more, then there would be enough food and enough leisure for all. Then there would be no cry of over-population, no disease, and no such misery as we see around. Such labour will be the highest form of sacrifice. Men will no doubt do many other things either through their bodies or through their minds, but all this will be labour of love, for the common good. There will then be no rich and no poor, none high and none low, no touchable and no untouchable (*Harijan*, 29.6.1935, p. 156; *CWMG* 61: 211-12).

The hungry millions ask for one poem — invigorating food. They cannot be given it. They must earn it. And they can earn only by the sweat of their brow. . . (*Young India*, 13.10.1921, p. 326; *CWMG* 1: 291).

Return to the villages means a definite voluntary recognition of the duty of bread labour and all it connotes (*Harijan*, 29.6.1935, p. 156; *CWMG* 61: 212).

Intellectual work is important and has an undoubted place in the scheme of life. But what I insist on is the necessity of physical labour. No man, I claim, ought to be free from that obligation (*Harijan*, 23.2.1947, p. 36; *CWMG* 86: 437).

God created man to work for his food and said that those who ate without work were thieves (*Young India*, 13.10.1921, p. 325; *CWMG* 21: 289).

c. Equality

True economics never militates against the highest ethical standard just as all true ethics to be worth its name must at the same time be also good economics. An economics that inculcates mammon worship and enables the strong to amass wealth at the expense of the weak, is a false and dismal science. It spells death. True economics, on the other hand, stands for social justice, it promotes the good of all equally including the weakest, and is indispensable for decent life (*Harijan*, 9.10.1937, p. 292; *CWMG* 66: 168).

I want to bring about an equalization of status (*Harijan*, 15.1.1938, p. 416; *CWMG* 66: 341).

My ideal is equal distribution, but so far as I can see, it is not to be realized. I therefore work for equitable distribution (*Young India*, 17.3.1927, p. 86; *CWMG* 33: 167).

Economic equality is the master key to nonviolent independence. Working for economic equality means abolishing the eternal conflict between capital and labour. It means the levelling down of the few rich in whose hands is concentrated the bulk of the nation's wealth on the one hand, and a levelling up of the semi-starved naked millions on the other. A nonviolent system of government is clearly an impossibility so long as the wide gulf between the rich and the hungry millions persists. The contrast between the palaces of New Delhi and the miserable hovels of the poor labouring class nearby cannot last one day in a free India in which the poor will enjoy the same power as the richest in the land. A violent and bloody revolution is a certainty one day unless there is a voluntary abdication of riches and the power that riches give and sharing them for the common good.

I adhere to my doctrine of trusteeship in spite of the ridicule that has been poured upon it. It is true that it is difficult to reach. So is non-violence. But we made up our minds in 1920 to negotiate that steep ascent (*Constructive Programme*: *Its Meaning and Place*, 13.12.1941; *CWMG* 75: 158).

The real implication of equal distribution is that each man shall have the wherewithal to supply all his natural needs and no more. For example, if one man has a weak digestion and requires only a quarter of a pound of flour for his bread and another needs a pound, both should be in a position to satisfy their wants. To bring this ideal into being the entire social order has got to be reconstructed. A society based on nonviolence cannot nurture any other ideal. We may not perhaps be able to realize the goal, but we must bear it in mind and work unceasingly to near it. To the same extent as we progress towards our goal we shall find contentment and happiness, and to that extent too, shall we have contributed towards the bringing into being of a nonviolent society (*Harijan*, 25.8.1940, p. 260; *CWMG* 72: 399).

d. Trusteeship

Indeed at the root of this doctrine of equal distribution must lie that of the trusteeship of the wealthy for the superfluous wealth possessed by them. For according to the doctrine they may not possess a rupee more than their neighbours. How is this to be brought about? Nonviolently? Or should the wealthy be dispossessed of their possessions? To do this we would naturally have to resort to violence. This violent action cannot benefit society. Society will be the poorer, for it will lose the gifts of a man who knows how to accumulate wealth. Therefore the nonviolent way is evidently superior. The rich man will be left in possession of his wealth, of which he will use what he reasonably requires for his personal needs and will act as a trustee for the remainder to be used for the society. In this argument, honesty on the part of the trustee is assumed.

If however, in spite of the utmost effort, the rich do not become guardians of the poor in the true sense of the term and the latter are more and more crushed and die of hunger, what is to be done? In trying to find out the solution of this riddle I have lighted on nonviolent non-cooperation and civil disobedience as the right and infallible means. The rich cannot accumulate wealth without the cooperation of the poor in society. . . . If this knowledge were to penetrate to and spread amongst the poor, they would become strong and would learn how to free themselves by means of nonviolence from the crushing inequalities [which have brought them to the verge of starvation] (*Harijan*, 25.8.1940, p. 260; *CWMG* 72: 400-01).

e. Decentralization

I suggest that, if India is to evolve along nonviolent lines, it will have to decentralize many things. Centralization cannot be sustained and defended without adequate force. Simple homes from which there is nothing to take away require no policing; the palaces of the rich must have strong guards to protect them against dacoity. So must huge factories. Rurally organized India will run less risk of foreign invasion than urbanized India, well equipped with military, naval, and air forces (*Harijan*, 30.12.1939, p. 391; *CWMG* 71: 56).

You cannot build nonviolence on a factory civilization, but it can be built on self-contained villages. . . . Rural economy as I have conceived it, eschews exploitation altogether, and exploitation is the essence of violence (*Harijan*, 4.11.1939, p. 331; *CWMG* 70: 296).

f. Swadeshi

Swadeshi is that spirit in us which restricts us to the use and service of our immediate surroundings to the exclusion of the more remote (Speech at Missionary Conference, Madras, 14.2.1916; *The Hindu*, 28.2.1926; *CWMG* 13: 219).

If we follow the *swadeshi* doctrine, it would be your duty and mine to find out neighbours who can supply our wants and to teach them to supply them where they do not know how to, assuming that there are neighbours who are in want of healthy occupation. Then every village of India will almost be a self-supporting and self-contained unit exchanging only such necessary commodities with other villages as are not locally producible. This may all sound nonsensical. Well, India is a country of nonsense. It is nonsensical to parch one's throat with thirst when a kindly Mohammedan is ready to offer pure water to drink. And yet thousands of Hindus would rather die of thirst than drink water from a Mohammedan household. These nonsensical men can also, once they are convinced that their religion demands that they should wear garments manufactured in India only and eat food only grown in India, decline to wear any other clothing or eat any other food (Speech at Missionary Conference, Madras, 14.2.1916; *The Hindu*, 28.2.1926; *CWMG* 13: 222-23).

A true votary of *swadeshi* will never harbour ill-will towards the foreigner, he will not be moved by antagonism towards anybody on the earth. Swadeshism is not a cult of hatred. It is a doctrine of selfless service that has its roots in the purest *ahimsa*, i.e., love (The Law of Swadeshi, *Young India*, 18.6.1931, p. 149; *CWMG* 46: 256-57).

g. Self-Sufficiency

The unit should be an ideal village or a social group which will be self-sufficient, but the members of which will be interdependent (Letter to Jawaharlal Nehru, 13.11.1945; *CWMG* 82: 72).

Every village's first concern will be to grow its own food crops, and cotton for its cloth (*Harijan*, 26.7.1942, p. 238; *CWMG* 6: 308).

The central fact of *khaddar* is to make every village self-supporting for its food and clothing (*Young India* 17.7.1924, p. 234; *CWMG* 24: 390).

Self-sufficient *khadi* will never succeed without cotton being grown by spinners themselves or practically in every village. It means decentralization of cotton cultivation so far at least as self-sufficient *khadi* is concerned (*Harijan*, 27.7.1935, p. 188; *CWMG* 61: 286).

Every village has to be self-sustained and capable of managing its affairs even to the extent of defending itself against the whole world (*Harijan*, 28.7.1946, p. 236; *CWMG* 85: 32).

h. Cooperation

As far as possible every activity will be conducted on the cooperative basis (*Harijan*, 26.7.1942, p. 238; *CWMG* 76: 308).

The system of cooperation was far more necessary for the agriculturists than for the mat-weavers. The land as he maintained, belonged to the state; therefore, it yielded the largest return when it was worked cooperatively. Let it be remembered that cooperation should be based on strict nonviolence (*Harijan*, 9.3.1947, p. 58; *CWMG* 86: 462).

i. Satyagraha

Nonviolence with its technique of *satyagraha* and non-cooperation will be the sanction of the village community (*Harijan*, 26.7.1942, p. 238; *CWMG* 76: 308).

j. Equality of Religions

Every religion has its full and equal place. We are all leaves of a majestic tree whose trunk cannot be shaken off its roots which are deep down in the bowels of the earth. The mightiest of winds cannot move it (*Harijan*, 28.7.1946, p. 236; *CWMG* 85: 33).

k. Panchayat Raj

The government of the village will be conducted by the *panchayat* of five persons annually elected by the adult villagers, male and female, possessing minimum prescribed qualifications. . . . Since there will be no system of punishments in the accepted sense, this *panchayat* will be the legislature, judiciary, and executive combined to operate for its year of office (*Harijan*, 26.7.1942, p. 238; *CWMG* 76: 308).

Every *panchayat* of five adult men or women being villagers or village-minded shall form a unit.

Two such contiguous *panchayat*s shall form a working party under a leader elected from among themselves.

When there are one hundred such *panchayats*, the fifty–first-grade leaders shall elect from among themselves a second-grade leader and so on, the first grade leaders meanwhile working under the second-grade leader. Parallel groups of two hundred *panchayats* shall continue to be formed till they cover the whole of India, each succeeding group of *panchayats* electing second-grade leader after the manner of the first. All second-grade leaders shall serve jointly for the whole of India and severally for their respective areas. The second-grade leaders may elect, whenever they deem necessary, from among themselves a chief who will, during pleasure, regulate and command all the groups.
(*Harijan* 15.2.1948, p. 32; *CWMG* 90: 527).

l. Nai Talim

By education I mean an all-round drawing out of the best in a child and man — body, mind, and spirit. Literacy is not the end of education nor even the beginning. It is only one of the means whereby men and women can be educated. Literacy in itself is no education. I would therefore begin the child's education by teaching it a useful handicraft and enabling it to produce from the moment it begins its training. Thus every school can be made self-supporting, the condition being that the state takes over the manufactures of these schools (*Harijan*, 31.7.1937, p. 197; *CWMG* 65: 450).

4

Agriculture and Cattle Welfare-I: Kisan

Our villagers depend on agriculture and cattle for ploughing. I am rather ignorant in this respect for I have no personal experience. But there is not a single village where we have no agriculture or cattle. There is the buffalo, but except in Konkan and a few other places it is not much used for agriculture. . . . Our worker will have to keep a careful eye on the cattle wealth of his village. If we cannot use this wealth properly India is doomed to disaster and we also shall perish. For these animals will then, as in the West, become an economic burden to us and we shall have no option before us save killing them (Discussion with Shrikrishnadas Jaju, 8.10.1944; *CWMG* 78: 162).

From the very beginning it has been my firm conviction that agriculture provides the only unfailing and perennial support to the people of this country. We should take it up and see how far we can go with it as basis. I would not at all mind if some of our young men serve the country by training themselves as experts in agriculture in the place of *khadi*. The time has now come for us to pay attention to agriculture. Till now I believed that improvement in agriculture was impossible unless we had the administration of the state in our own hands. My views on this are now undergoing modification. I feel that we can bring about improvements even under the present conditions, so that the cultivator may be able to make some income for himself from the land even after paying his taxes. Jawaharlal says that any extra income to the peasant through the improvement of agriculture will be swallowed up under one pretext or the other by the alien government. But I feel that even if it were so, it should not hinder us from acquiring and spreading as much knowledge about agriculture as possible. It may be that the government will take away any additional income that may come to the villagers through improvements in agriculture. If they do, we can protest and teach the people to resist and make it clear to the government that it cannot loot us in this manner. . . . I therefore hold that we must hereafter find workers who will interest themselves in agriculture (Discussion with Shrikrishnadas Jaju, 11.10.1944; *CWMG* 78: 178-79).

I am, therefore, thinking of ways and means of improving the condition of the people through a rehabilitation of agriculture, cattle-breeding, and all other village industries. My problem will be solved, if I succeed even in half a dozen villages, for as is the part so is the whole (Discussion with Shrikrishnadas Jaju, 12.10.1944; *CWMG* 78: 187).

Bread labour is a veritable blessing to one who would observe non-violence, worship Truth, and make the observance of *brahmacharya* a natural act. This labour can truly be related to agriculture alone. But at present at any rate, everybody is not in a position to take to it. A person can therefore spin or weave, or take up carpentry or smithery, instead of tilling the soil, always regarding agriculture, however, to be the ideal (Letter to Narandas Gandhi, 16.9.1930; *CWMG* 44: 150).

Years ago I read a poem in which the peasant is described as the father of the world. If God is the Provider, the cultivator is His hand. What are we going to do to discharge the debt we owe to him? So long we have only lived on the sweat of his brow. We should have begun with the soil but we could not do so. The fault is partly mine.

There were people, remarked Gandhiji, who said that no basic reform in agriculture was possible, without political power. They dreamt in terms of industrialization of agriculture by large-scale application of steam and electricity. He warned them that trading in soil fertility for the sake of quick returns would prove to be a disastrous, short-sighted policy. It would result in virtual depletion of the soil. Good earth called for the sweat of one's brow to yield the bread of life.

People might criticize that approach as being slow and unprogressive.

It did not hold out promise of dramatic results. Nevertheless, it held the key to the prosperity of both the soil and the inhabitants living on it. Healthy, nourishing food was the alpha and omega of rural economy.

The bulk of a peasant's family budget goes to feed him and his family. All other things come afterwards. Let the tiller of the soil be well fed. Let him have a sufficiency of fresh, pure milk and ghee and oil, fish, eggs, and meat if he is a non-vegetarian. What would fine clothes, for instance, avail him, if he is ill-nourished and underfed?

The question of drinking-water supply and other things would come next. A consideration of these questions would naturally involve such issues, as the place of plough cattle in the economy of agriculture as against the tractor plough and power irrigation, etc. and thus, bit by bit, the whole picture of rural economy would emerge before them. In this picture, cities would take their natural place and not appear as unnatural, congested spots or boils on the body politic as they were today.

We stand today in danger of forgetting the use of our hands. To forget how to dig the earth and tend the soil is to forget ourselves. To think that your occupation of the ministerial chair will be vindicated if you serve the cities only, would be to forget that India really resides in her 7,00,000 village units. What would it profit a man if he gained the world but lost his soul in the bargain? (*Harijan*, 25.8.1946, pp. 281-82; *CWMG* 85: 96-97).

The moment you talk to them and they begin to speak, you will find wisdom drops from their lips. Behind the crude exterior you will find a deep reservoir of spirituality. I call this culture. You will not find such a thing in the West. You try to engage a European peasant in conversation and you will find that he is uninterested in things spiritual. In the case of the Indian villager, an age-old culture is hidden under an encrustment of crudeness. Take away the encrustation, remove his chronic poverty and his illiteracy, and you have the finest specimen of what a cultured, cultivated, free citizen should be (*Harijan*, 28.1.1939, p. 439; *CWMG* 68: 266).

We have to teach them how to economize time, health, and money. Lionel Curtis described our villages as dung-heaps. We have to turn them into model villages. Our village-folk do not get fresh air though they are surrounded by fresh air; they don't get fresh food though they are surrounded by the freshest foods. I am talking like a missionary in this matter of food, because my mission is to make villages a thing of beauty (*Harijan*, 1-3-1935, p. 21; *CWMG* 60: 252).

We have to tackle the triple malady which holds our villages fast in its grip: (i) want of corporate sanitation; (ii) deficient diet; and (iii) inertia. . . . They are not interested in their own welfare. They don't appreciate modern sanitary methods. They don't want to exert themselves beyond scratching their farms or doing such labour as they are used to. These difficulties are real and serious. But they must not baffle us. We must have an unquenchable faith in our mission. We must be patient with the people. We are ourselves novices in village work. We have to deal with a chronic disease. Patience and perseverance, if we have them, overcome mountains of difficulties. We are like nurses who may not leave their patients because they are reported to have an incurable disease (*The Bombay Chronicle*, 11.5.1936; *Harijan*, 16.5.1936, p. 111; *CWMG* 62: 379).

The greatest education in the villages consists in the villagers being taught or induced to work methodically and profitably all the year round whether it be on the land or at industries connected with the villages (*Harijan*, 6.3.1937, p. 29; *CWMG* 64: 427).

I make bold to say that in spite of the crudeness which one sees among the villagers, class considered, in all that is good in human nature they compare favourably with any villagers in the world. This testimony is borne out by the majority of travellers who from the time of Huen Tsang down to the present times have recorded their impressions. The innate culture that the villages of India show, the art which one sees in the homes of the poor, the restraint with which the villagers conduct themselves, are surely due to the religion that has bound them together from time immemorial (*Harijan*, 6.3.1937, p. 29; *CWMG* 64: 426-27).

The *kisan* or the peasant, whether as a landless labourer or a labouring proprietor, comes first. He is the son of the soil which rightly belongs or should belong to him, not to the absentee landlord or zamindar. But in the nonviolent way the labourer cannot forcibly eject the absentee landlord. He has so to work as to make it impossible for the landlord to exploit him. Closest cooperation amongst the peasants is absolutely necessary. To this end, special organizing bodies or committees should be formed where there are none and those already in existence should be reformed where necessary. The *kisans* are for the most part illiterate. Both adults and young persons of school-going age should be educated. This applies to men as well as women. Where they are landless labourers their wages should be brought to a level that would ensure a decent living which should mean balanced food, dwelling houses, and clothing, which should satisfy health requirements (Hints for Constructive Workers, *Sevagram*, 22.10.1944; *The Bombay Chronicle*, 28.10.1944; *CWMG* 78: 219-20).

If I have my say, our Governor-General and our Premier would be drawn from the *kisans*. In my childhood I had learnt in the school books that the *kisans* are heirs to the kingdom of the earth. This applies to those who labour on the land and eat from what they produce. Such *kisans* to be worthy of high offices might be illiterate, provided they have robust common sense, great personal bravery, unimpeachable integrity, and patriotism above suspicion. As real producers of wealth, they are verily the masters while we have enslaved them. It has been suggested to me that the higher secretariat, posts should also be manned by *kisans*. I would endorse this suggestion provided they are suitable and have knowledge of the work expected of them. When *kisans* of this type are forthcoming I would publicly ask ministers and others to make room for them (*Village Swaraj*, pp. 96-97; *Harijan*, 8.2.1948, p. 21).

5

Agriculture and Cattle Welfare-II: Land Problem

Ownership of Land

Land and all property is his who will work it. Unfortunately the workers are or have been kept ignorant of this simple fact (*Harijan*, 2.1.1937, p. 375; *CWMG* 64: 192).

I believe that the land you cultivate should belong to you, but it cannot be your own all at once, you cannot force it from the zamindars. Non-violence is the only way, consciousness of your own power is the only way (*Village Swaraj*, p. 97; *Harijan*, 20.5.1939, p. 133).

No man should have more land than he needs for dignified sustenance. Who can dispute the fact that the grinding poverty of the masses is due to their having no land that they can call their own?

But it must be realized that the reform cannot be rushed. If it is to be brought about by nonviolent means, it can only be done by education both of the haves and the have-nots. The former should be assured that there never will be force used against them. The have-nots must be educated to know that no one can really compel them to do anything against their will, and that they can secure their freedom by learning the art of nonviolence, i.e. self-suffering (*Harijan*, 20.4.1940, p. 97; *CWMG* 71: 424-25).

Landlord and Tenant

I would tell you that ownership of your land belongs as much to the ryots as to you and you may not squander your gains in luxurious or extravagant living but must use them for the well-being of ryots (Answers to Zamindars, 23.7.1934; *Amrita Bazar Patrika*, 2.8.1934; *CWMG* 58: 247).

I do not believe that the capitalists and the landlords are all exploiters by an inherent necessity, or that there is a basic or irreconcilable antagonism between their interests and those of the masses. . . . What is needed is not the extinction of landlords and capitalists, but a transformation of the existing relationship between them and the masses into something healthier and purer (Discussion with Students, 21.7.1934; *Amrita Bazar Patrika*, 3.8.1934; *CWMG* 58: 217-18).

My objective is to reach your hearts and convert you so that you may hold all your private property in trust for your tenants and use it primarily for their welfare. I am aware of the fact that within the ranks of the Congress a new party called the Socialist Party is coming into being, and I cannot say what would happen if that party succeeds in carrying the Congress with it. But I am quite clear that if a strictly honest and unchallengeable referendum of our millions were to be taken, they would not vote for the wholesale expropriation of the propertied classes. I am working for the cooperation and coordination of capital and labour and of landlords and tenants (Answers to Zamindars, 25.7.1934, *Amrita Bazar Patrika*, 2.8.1934; *CWMG* 58: 247).

But I must utter a note of warning. I have always told mill-owners that they are not exclusive owners of the mills. Workmen are equal sharers in ownership. In the same way, I would tell you that the ownership of your land belongs as much to the ryots as to you and you may not squander your gains in luxurious or extravagant living, but must use them for the well-being of ryots. Once you make your ryots experience a sense of kinship with you and a sense of security that their interests as members of the family will never suffer at your hands, you may be sure that there cannot be a class war between you and them (*Amrita Bazar Patrika*, 2.8.1934; *CWMG* 58: 247).

I do not want to destroy the zamindar, but neither do I feel that the zamindar is inevitable. . . . I expect to convert the zamindars and other capitalists by the nonviolent method, and therefore there is for me nothing like an inevitability of class conflict. For it is an essential part of nonviolence to go along the line of least resistance. The moment the cultivators of the soil realize their power, the *zamindari* evil will be sterilized. What can the poor zamindar do when they say that they will simply not work the land unless they are paid enough to feed and clothe and educate themselves and their children in a decent manner? In reality the toiler is the owner of what he produces. If the toilers intelligently combine, they will become an irresistible power. That is how I do not see the necessity of class conflict. If I thought it inevitable, I should not hesitate to preach it and teach it (*Harijan*, 5.12.1936, pp. 338-39; *CWMG* 64: 72-73).

A model zamindar would therefore at once reduce much of the burden the ryot is now bearing, he would come in intimate touch with the ryots and know their wants and inject hope into them in the place of despair which is killing the very life out of them. He will not be satisfied with the ryots' ignorance of the laws of sanitation and hygiene. He will reduce himself to poverty in order that the ryot may have the necessaries of life. He will study the economic condition of the ryots under his care, establish schools in which he will educate his own children side by side with those of the ryots. He will purify the village well and the village tank. He will teach the ryot to sweep his roads and clean his latrines by himself doing this necessary labour. He will throw open without reserve his own gardens for the unrestricted use of the ryot. He will use as hospital, school, or the like most of the unnecessary buildings which he keeps for his pleasure. If only the capitalist class will read the signs of the times, revise their notions of God-given right to all they possess, in an incredibly short space of time the seven hundred thousand dung-heaps which today pass muster as villages can be turned into abodes of peace, health, and comfort. I am convinced that the capitalist, if he follows the Samurai of Japan, has nothing really to lose and everything to gain. There is no other choice than between voluntary surrender on the part of the capitalist of superfluities and consequent acquisition of the real happiness of all on the one hand, and on the other, the impending chaos into which, if the capitalist does not wake up betimes, awakened but ignorant, famishing millions will plunge the country and which not even the armed force that a powerful government can bring into play can avert (*Young India*, 5.12.1929, p. 396; *CWMG* 42: 240).

The zamindars would do well to take the time by the forelock. Let them cease to be mere rent collectors. They should become trustees and trusted friends of their tenants. They should limit their privy purse. Let them forgo the questionable perquisites they take from the tenants in the shape of forced gifts on marriage, and other occasions, or *nazrana* on transfer of holdings from one *kisan* to another or on restoration to the same *kisan* after eviction for nonpayment of rent. They should give them fixity of tenure, take a lively interest in their welfare, provide well-managed schools for their children, night-schools for adults, hospitals and dispensaries for the sick, look after the sanitation of villages and in a variety of ways make them feel that they, the zamindars, are their true friends taking only a fixed commission for their manifold services. In short they must justify their position. They should trust Congressmen. They may themselves become Congressmen and know that the Congress is a bridge between the people and the government. All who have the true welfare of the people at heart can harness the services of the Congress. Congressmen will on their part see to it that *kisans* scrupulously fulfil their obligations to the zamindars. I mean not necessarily the statutory, but the obligations which they have themselves admitted to be just. They must reject the doctrine that their holdings are absolutely theirs to the exclusion of the zamindars. They are or should be members of a joint family in which the zamindar is the head guarding their rights against encroachment. Whatever the law may be, the *zamindari* to be defensible must approach the conditions of a joint family.

I like the ideal of Rama and Janaka. They owned nothing against the people. Everything including themselves belonged to the people. They lived in their midst a life not above theirs, but in correspondence with theirs. But these may not be regarded as historical personages. Then let us take the example of the great Caliph Omar. Though he was monarch of a vast realm created by his great genius and amazing industry, he lived the life of a pauper and never considered himself owner of the vast treasures that lay at his feet. He was a terror to those officials who squandered people's money in luxuries (*Young India*, 28.5.1931, pp. 120-21; *CWMG* 46: 234-35).

To the landlords I say that if what is said against them is true, I would warn them that their days are numbered. They could no longer continue as lords and masters. They have a bright future if they become the trustees of the poor *kisans*. He has in mind not trustees in name but in reality. Such trustees would take nothing for themselves that their labour and care did not entitle them to. Then they would find that no law would be able to touch them. The *kisans* would be their friends (*Village Swaraj*, p. 102; *Harijan*, 4.5.1947, p. 134).

It can, however, be asked whether the present *rajas* and others can be expected to become trustees of the poor. . . . If they do not become trustees of their own accord, force of circumstances will compel the reform unless they court utter destruction. When Panchayat Raj is established, public opinion will do what violence can never do. The present power of the zamindars, the capitalists, and the *rajas* can hold sway only so long as the common people do not realize their own strength. If the people non-cooperate, what can a *raja*, a zamindar or a capitalist do? In Panchayat Raj only the *panchayat* will be obeyed and the *panchayat* can work only through the law of its making (*Harijan*, 1.6.1947, p. 172; *CWMG* 88: 2).

Real socialism has been handed down to us by our ancestors who taught: "All land belongs to Gopal, where then is the boundary line? Man is the maker of the line and he can therefore unmake it." Gopal literally means shepherd; it also means God. In modern language it means the state, i.e., the people. That the land today does not belong to the people is too true. But the fault is not in the teaching. It is in us who have not lived up to it. I have no doubt that we can make as good an approach to it as is possible for any nation, not excluding Russia, and that without violence. The most effective substitute for violent dispossession is the wheel with all its implications. Land and all property is his who will work it. Unfortunately the workers are or have been kept ignorant of this simple fact (*Harijan*, 2.1.1937, p. 375; *CWMG* 64: 192).

In the nonviolent order of the future, the land would belong to the state, for had it not been said *sabhi bhumi gopalki*? Under such dispensation, there would be no waste of talents and labour. This would be impossible through violent means. It was therefore a truism to say that the utter ruin of the landowners brought about through violence would also involve the ruin of the labourers in the end. If the landowners, therefore, acted wisely, no party would lose (*Harijan*, 9.3.1947, p. 58; *CWMG* 86: 462).

6

Agriculture and Cattle Welfare-III: Cooperation

The most important question for consideration . . . was whether cow farming should be in the hands of individuals or done collectively. I myself had no hesitation in saying that she could never be saved by individual farming. Her salvation, and with her that of buffalo, could only be brought about by collective endeavour. It is quite impossible for an individual farmer to look after the welfare of his cattle in his own home in a proper and scientific manner. Amongst other causes lack of collective effort has been a principal cause of the deterioration of the cow and hence of cattle in general. The world today is moving towards the ideal of collective or cooperative effort in every department of life. Much in this line has been and is being accomplished. It has come into our country also, but in such a distorted form that our poor have not been able to reap its benefits. *Pari passu* with the increase in our population land-holdings of the average farmer are daily decreasing. Moreover, what the individual possesses is often fragmentary. For such farmers to keep cattle in their homes is a suicidal policy; and yet this is their condition today. Those who give the first place to economics and pay scant attention to religious, ethical or humanitarian considerations proclaim from the house-tops that the farmer is being devoured by his cattle due to the cost of their feed which is out of all proportion to what they yield. They say it is folly not to slaughter wholesale all useless animals. What then should be done by humanitarians is the question. The answer obviously is to find a way whereby we may not only save the lives of our cattle but also see that they do not become a burden. I am sure that cooperative effort can help us in a large measure. The following comparison may be helpful:

1. Under the collective system no farmer can keep cattle in his house as he does today. They foul the air and dirty the surroundings. There is neither intelligence nor humanitarianism in living with animals. Man was not meant to do so. The space taken up by the cattle today would be spared to the farmer and his family, if the collective system were adopted.
2. As the number of cattle increases, life becomes impossible for the farmer in his home. Hence he is obliged to sell the calves and kill the male buffaloes or else turn them out to starve and die. This inhumanity would be averted, if the care of cattle were undertaken on a cooperative basis.
3. Collective cattle farming would ensure the supply of veterinary treatment to animals when they are ill. No ordinary farmer can afford this on his own.
4. Similarly one selected bull can be easily kept for the need of several cows under the collective system. This is impossible otherwise except for charity.
5. Common grazing ground or land for exercising the animals will be easily available under the cooperative system, whereas today generally there is nothing of the kind for individual farmers.
6. The expense on fodder will be comparatively far less under the collective system.
7. The sale of milk at good prices will be greatly facilitated, and there will be no need or temptation for the farmer to adulterate it as he does as an individual.
8. It is impossible to carry out tests of the fitness of every head of cattle individually, but this could easily be done for the cattle of a whole village and would thus make it easier to improve the breed.
9. The foregoing advantages should be sufficient argument in favour

> of cooperative cattle farming. The strongest argument in its favour is that the individualistic system has been the means of making our own conditions as well as that of our cattle pitiable. We can only save ourselves and them by making this essential change.

I firmly believe too that we shall not derive the full benefits of agriculture until we take to cooperative farming. Does it not stand to reason that it is far better for a hundred families in a village to cultivate their lands collectively and divide the income therefrom than to divide the land anyhow into a hundred portions? And what applied to land applies equally to cattle.

It is quite another matter that it may be difficult to convert people to adopt this way of life straightaway. The straight and narrow road is always hard to traverse. Every step in the programme of cow service is strewn with thorny problems. But only by surmounting difficulties can we hope to make the path easier. My purpose for the time being is to show the great superiority of collective cattle farming over the individual effort. I hold further that the latter is wrong and the former only is right. In reality even the individual can only safeguard his independence through cooperation. In cattle farming the individual effort has led to selfishness and inhumanity, whereas the collective effort can abate both the evils, if it does not remove them altogether (*Harijan*, 15.2.1942, p. 39; *Sevagram*, 8.2.1942; *CWMG* 75: 295-97).

"Should peasants pool together their land and divide the crop in proportion to the area of the fields they hold?"

My notion of cooperation is that the land would be held in cooperation by the owners and tilled and cultivated also in cooperation. This would cause a saving of labour, capital, tools, etc. The owners would work in cooperation and own capital, tools, animals, seeds, etc., in cooperation. Cooperative farming of my conception would change the face of the land and banish poverty and idleness from their midst. All this is only possible if people became friends of one another and as one family. When that happy event takes place, there would be no ugly sore in the form of a communal problem. (Speech at Prayer Meeting, 15.2.1947; *Harijan*, 9.3.1947, p. 59; *CWMG* 86: 468).

The system of cooperation is far more necessary for the agriculturists than for the mat weavers. The land belonged to the state; therefore, it yields the largest return when it is worked cooperatively. Let it be remembered that cooperation should be based on strict nonviolence. There is no such thing as success of violent cooperation. Hitler was a forcible example of the latter. He also talked vainly of cooperation which was forced upon the people and everyone knew where Germany had been led as a result.

It would be a sad thing if India also tried to build up the new society based on cooperation by means of violence. Good brought about through force destroyed individuality. Only when the change is effected through the persuasive power of nonviolent non-cooperation, i.e., love, could the foundation of individuality be preserved and real, abiding progress be assured for the world. (*Harijan*, 9.3.1947, p. 58; *CWMG* 86: 462-63).

7

Agriculture and Cattle Welfare- IV: Manure

Compost Manure

An All India Compost Conference was held in New Delhi during the month (December 1947) to consider the question of compost development on the widest scale possible. It was the conception of Shrimati Mirabehn and was presided over by Dr. Rajendraprasad. Sardar Datar Singh, Dr. Acharya, and other eminent men in the line took part in it. Several important resolutions were passed by it on schemes for towns and villages. A subcommittee consisting of Shrimati Mirabehn, Shri Shivakumar Sharma, Dr. B.N. Lai, and Dr. K.G. Joshi (with Dr. B.N. Lai as convener) was appointed to prepare a skeleton scheme for the provinces. The resolutions emphasized the necessity of "the agricultural utilization of town sewage, sullage, and sludge, the utilization of the by-products of the slaughter house and other trade wastes (for example, wool waste, mill waste, leather waste, etc.) and for the composting of other materials like water-hyacinth, cane-trash, press-mud, forest leaves, etc."

These resolutions are good and useful if they do not remain merely on paper. The chief thing is whether they would be reduced to practise throughout India. To do so will tax the resources of many Mirabehns. Given the willing cooperation of the masses of India, this country can not only drive out the shortage of food, but can provide India with more than enough. This organic manure ever enriches, never impoverishes the soil. The daily waste, judiciously composted, returns to the soil in the form of golden manure causing a saving of millions of rupees and increasing manifold, the total yield of grains and pulses. In addition, the judicious use of waste keeps the surroundings clean. And cleanliness is not only next to godliness, it promotes health (*Harijan*, 28.12.1947, p. 484; *CWMG* 90: 269-70).

One potent way of increasing production is proper manuring.

Artificial manures . . . are harmful to the soil. . . . The compost manure emit no bad odour. It would save lakhs of rupees and also increase the fertility of the soil without exhausting it (*Village Swaraj, p.* 109; *Harijan*, 28.12.1947, p. 488).

Manure Pits

I know that the pits such as Mr. Brayne suggests are generally recommended. In my opinion, however, superficial burial recommended by Poore is more scientific and more remunerative. The cost of digging is lessened and that of removal avoided altogether or certainly lessened. Add to this the fact that the excreta are turned into manure in almost a week's time, for the reason that the bacteria, which live within six or nine inches of the surface of the earth, and the air and the rays of the sun act upon the excreta and turn them into sweet manure much more quickly than when the refuse is buried deep.

But the chief thing to remember is not the various methods of disposing of refuse, so much as the necessity of burying all the refuse for the double purpose of promoting the villagers' health and their material condition through the better yield of their crops which the manure must produce. It should be remembered that organic rubbish other than excreta must be separately buried. Attention to hygiene is undoubtedly the first step to village reconstruction (*Harijan*, 1.3.1935, p. 20; *CWMG* 60: 269-70).

Night-soil as Manure

G.I. Fowler states, in his *Wealth and Waste*, that a proper disposal of human excreta would realize Rs. 2 per head per year. In the vast majority of cases, all this rich manure is being wasted and disease invited. He quotes Prof. Brultini, from his volume *The Use of Waste Materials*, who says that "nitrogen derived from the 282,000 residents of Delhi is sufficient to fertilize a minimum of 10,000 and a maximum of 95,000 acres". Because we do not know how to treat our scavengers, Delhi of ancient fame has pestilential spots of which we have to feel ashamed. If we all become scavengers, we would know how to treat ourselves and how to turn what today is poison into rich food for plant life. Thirty crores of the population of India should mean, according to Dr. Fowler, an annual gain of 60 crores of rupees to the country if we would but make a wise use of human excreta (*Harijan*, 15.3.1935, p. 36; *CWMG* 60: 303).

Preparation of Compost Manure

[There is in Indore an Institute of Plant Industry. It issues from time to time leaflets for those whom it is designed to serve. The first one of these describes the utility and the method of preparing compost manure from farm wastes. As it is valuable for Harijans and village workers who handle cattle-dung and night-soil, I copy below practically the whole of the leaflet incorporating footnotes into the running description of the process] (*Harijan*, 17.8.1935, p. 213; *CWMG* 61: 338). [The leaflet referred herein is not reproduced in *CWMG*. It appeared in *Harijan* issues of 17.8.1935 and 24.8.1935, and its text, as given in *Village Swaraj*, is reproduced below in two parts corresponding to the two issues of *Harijan*.]

It has long been recognized that adequate and systematic recuperation of organic matter in Indian soils must be part of any successful scheme for intensive agriculture. It is also equally understood that the available sources of farm yard manure cannot supply the quantities needed, apart from the fact that during the making a large portion of the nitrogen is lost and the final product takes a very long time to attain the most efficient physical condition. Green manuring is perhaps a possible substitute, but under monsoon conditions it is uncertain in most parts of India. The decomposition of green manure in the soil also interferes for the time being with the natural processes of recuperation of available plant food in the soil which lay a very substantial part in the maintenance of soil fertility in tropical regions. It is clearly the best course to relieve the soil of the burden of manufacturing humus and enable it to concentrate solely upon the work of recuperation and crop growth. The simplest way of doing this is to prepare humus as a by-product during the routine of farm work, utilizing all agricultural wastes which are not needed as fuel or fodder.

It should be emphasized at this stage that any substitute for farm yard manure must closely resemble humus in its composition, and the Indore method aims at and achieves this. The object of the Indore method thus differs radically from that of processes where the aim is to produce a highly nitrogenous active manure whose special utility is similar to that of artificials.

The work carried out at the Institute of Plant Industry at Indore, which was the final outcome of twenty years' attempts by Mr. Albert Howard in this direction, has now proved definitely that these principles can very easily be put into actual practice. The Indore method of compost making supplies a practical technique and opens new avenues for development. The unlimited resources of natural wastes both from the farm and the towns can thus be tapped for use in agriculture. A copious supply of manure is made possible without having recourse to any unnatural measures such as encroaching upon the use of dung as fuel and the export of oilcakes, at the same time securing economy in the use of artificials which give their best results when reinforced with organic matter.

The problems and underlying principles involved have been discussed and the elaboration of the Indore method described in the *Utilization of Agricultural Waste* (Howard and Wad, Oxford University Press, 1931). This article gives only a brief working outline of the process as applicable to the Indian cultivator's conditions.

The value of farm-yard manure is appreciated in the case of irrigated crops in India, but periodic moderate dressings to fields under dry cultivation are equally essential. The Indore compost method quickly produces larger amounts of richer manure, which is moreover, actively useful to crops immediately on application, which is not always the case with farm-yard manure. Indore compost is ready for use after three months, when properly prepared, and is then a dark-brown or coffee-coloured amorphous substance, containing about 20 per cent of partially decomposed coarse material readily crushed between the fingers, the rest being fine enough when wet (and the colloidal particles therefore swollen) to pass through a sieve of 6 meshes per linear inch. The nitrogen content varies from .8 per cent to 1.0 per cent or more according to the nature of the wastes used. About fifty cartloads of compost per pair of bullocks can easily be made each year by the use of only one-fourth of the fresh dung along with 100 to 125 cartloads of farm wastes of all kinds and half of the quantity of urine-soaked earth which is available from the cattle-shed. The remaining half is also a good manure and can be added directly to fields. If more residues are available, all the dung and urine earth can be utilized to make about 150 cartloads of compost. The cost of making is 8½ annas per cartload of ripe compost at Indore rates of wages (men 7 annas, women 5 annas per day of eight hours).

Outline of Indore Method

The main feature of the process is to decompose rapidly a mixture of otherwise useless farm wastes with fresh dung, wood ash, and urine earth in pits. The pits should not be deeper than 2 ft and should be 14 ft in breadth. A convenient length is 30 ft. This suits both large- and small-scale work; for instance a portion 3 ft in length can be filled in 6 days with bedding from under 2 pairs of bullocks. The adjacent portion is next filled, each being subsequently treated as a separate unit. The material is uniformly moistened with a slurry of water containing small quantities of dung, wood ash, urine earth, and fungus starter from an active pit. Actively decomposing compost soon becomes white with fungus growth. This material is then used to start vigorous decomposition in a fresh charge. For the first time when no starter is available fungus growth is stimulated by the addition of a small quantity of green leaves to the bedding when made. Full activity is attained in the starter after three to four generations. The activity is then kept up by regulating moisture and air by means of surface waterings and turnings assisted by a second addition of starter, this time taken from a pit more than thirty days old. The mass soon becomes very hot and remains so for a long time. The systematic handling secures a good mixture (as shown by its uniform appearance) and a copious air supply at every stage. Moderate watering begins decomposition at once, which continues without a break to the end, producing a very uniform final product.

The Making of Pits

Select a well-drained area near the cattle-shed and if possible near a source of water supply. Dig out one foot of earth and spread it on all sides to make a pit, 30′ × 14′ × 2′; such pits should be arranged in pairs, the long side being east to west. The distance between two pits in a pair should be six feet and the pairs themselves should be 12 ft apart. The final heaps and monsoon heaps are made on these broad spaces which are also useful for removal of manure by carts directly from each heap.

Earth and Urine

The urine passed by cattle is rich in valuable manurial matter and this is mostly wasted in the usual method of making farm-yard manure. A *pakka*-floor in the cattle-shed is both costly and unsuitable for the bullocks. A soft, warm, and dry bed on which cattle may rest and sleep can be made cheaply of loose earth. Convenient sources are threshing-floor sweepings, silt from choked drains, and earth from silage pits. A flat 6″ layer is sufficient to absorb all urine without nuisance, if wet patches are scrapped daily and thinly covered by a little fresh earth and with uneaten fodder from the manger over it. This urine earth should be removed and replaced every four months by a fresh layer. The finer portion should be reserved for compost making and the bigger lumps directly added to fields. It is a rapidly acting manure specially suitable as a top-dressing for any irrigated crop [*Village Swaraj*, pp. 111-15; *Harijan*, 17.8.1935, pp. 213-15).

Cow-dung and Ash

Only a quarter of the daily supply of fresh dung is needed; this is applied as liquid "slurry", being mixed with water; the rest can be made into fuel if required. Wood ashes from the kitchen and other places should be carefully collected and stored under cover.

Farm Wastes or Kuchra

Every type of vegetable waste not otherwise needed on the farm can be made into compost, e.g. weeds, stalks of cotton, pigeon pea, sesamum, safflower, niger, linseed, rapeseed, black and green gram, sugar-cane trash, stools of juar, maize and sugar-cane, fallen leaves of trees and uneaten residues of grass, straw, juar, and other fodders. Hard materials require cracking. This has been successfully done, even on soft unmetalled roads in Sind, by simply spreading such material on a cart track and periodically removing crushed portions and replacing them by unbroken stuff. Very hard residues like stumps and roots require (in addition to cracking) soaking in water for at least two days, or burial with moist earth for two to three months before they can be successfully utilized. The latter can be done easily during the monsoon period. Green materials must be partially dried and then stacked. Small amounts of various kinds of residues should be stacked together, while separate *ganjisy,* i.e., stacks, must be made for larger quantities of any single material. At the time of removing to the compost pit care must be taken to get a mixture of all types, no single material ever exceeding 1/3 of the total amount thus removed. The very hard-soaked or softened residues should be used only in very small quantities at a time. This is really automatically achieved by the proportions of different residues normally available if they are stored and used in quantities which will ensure a steady supply all round the year. The quality of the compost can be further improved by using for it a *kharif*-sown catch-crop of *sann* or other legume harvested green, and stacked after withering. The land will be clear in time to sow a *rabi* crop which will also benefit by the *sann* having been grown.

Water

It is a saving of labour and an advantage if household waste water is led to a small pit or sunk tub near the compost area and utilized every day. Any kind of water which has long been lying stagnant is harmful. Additional water required must be secured by other means. Between 50 to 60 four-gallon kerosene tins of water are necessary to prepare one cartload of compost according to season.

The Process in Detail

Filling the pits with bedding: Take a *pal* or a stretcher made of a piece of gunny sacking 4′ × 3′ the longer edges being fastened to two bamboos each 7′ 6″ long. Up to one *palful* of farm wastes for each bullock and one and a half *pals* for each buffalo should be spread every day on the floor of the cattle-shed on which the cattle rest and sleep. The material thus gets impregnated with urine as well as mixed and crushed by the animals. The bedding in the rainy season is made by sandwitching a layer of green withered stuff between two of dry wastes specially reserved for the purpose. Fresh dung left over after making the slurry can either be made into *kurdas*, i.e., dried dung cakes, or spread over the bedding in lumps not bigger than a small orange. The portion of the urine earth and fungus starter also left over after making the slurry is then scattered over the bedding next morning when it is removed by spades and *pals* from end to end of the floor to be directly dropped in pits and spread in thin layers by rakes. Every such layer is then moistened uniformly by the slurry containing ash, dung, earth, and fungus starter in small amounts. After the removal of all bedding the floor is swept of all finer portions which are then added to the pit as a surface layer. The top layer is wetted by sprinkled water and soaking is completed by further sprinklings in the evening and next morning. A pit, or a portion of it according to the quantity of waste material available, must be filled to the top in six days. A fresh charge in another portion or pit should then be begun. Trampling while charging is harmful as air is excluded.

During the monsoon rains the pits get full of water. When the rains begin the contents should be removed and heaped on ground level taking advantage of the routine turnings. During the rains fresh compost should be made on the ground in heaps 8 × 8 × 2′ with vertical sides, and closely grouped together on the broad spaces so that they are protected from cold winds.

Turning and Watering of Compost

The surface of the decomposing compost is kept moist by weekly sprinkling of water. It is necessary to restore moisture and air in the interior at intervals and hence three turns have to be given, accompanied by watering to make up for lost moisture. In wet weather the quantity of these waterings may be lessened or no water may be added, but the water during the first filling or stacking must be added in all seasons.

First Turn after about Fifteen Days

Remove the undecomposed surface layer from the whole pit and use it as part filling for a fresh pit. Scatter compost about thirty days old over the exposed surface and sprinkle water over the top till well moistened for about six inches. During this first turning the pit is divided lengthwise and the half on the windward side is left undisturbed. The other half is then thrown over it (a wooden rake is convenient for this). The material should not be taken off layer after layer but as far as possible from the top to the bottom of the pit by a vertical or slanting stroke. Every layer of the turned material, about six inches thick, must be soaked with sprinkled water. In the monsoon the whole heap may be turned to avoid too much height.

Second Turn after One Month

The material in one half of the pit is simply raked as above on to the other vacant side of the pit with adequate watering, the same care to mix it from top to bottom being taken.

Third Turn at the End of Two Months

The compost is similarly transferred by shovels to the surface on the broad spaces and watered. The material from two pits can be conveniently shovelled on to the space between to make one heap 10′ broad and 3½′ high; the length is immaterial and several pits or heaps can thus be stored together. If convenient the manure after moistening well may be directly carted from pits to the field. The heap should be made on the spot where the product is to be used, thus saving valuable time at the sowing season. All heaps should be dressed to vertical sides and flat tops to prevent excessive drying which stops decomposition.

Good compost gives no smell at any stage and the appearance is uniform throughout. If smell or flies appear it is a sign that more air is wanted and the pit should therefore be turned and a little ash and dung added.

The quantities required in individual cases can easily be found out by simple calculations with the help of the following data:

Quantities Required for Forty Animals

Filling into pits every day for six days:

Bedding and sweepings removed to the pit in one day; 40 to 50 *pal*s after scattering on it 4 *tagari*s, i.e., sheet iron basins being 18″ diameter by 6″ depth, of fungus starter, 15 of urine earth, and excess of dung if not used as fuel.

Slurry: For one day's output from cattle-shed 20 kerosene tins (4 gallons) of water, 5 *tagari*s of dung, 1 *tagari* of ash, 1 *tagari* of urine earth, and 2 *tagari*s of fungus starter.

Water: For one day's output from cattle-shed 6 tins immediately after filling, 10 tins in the evening and 6 next morning.

Surface waterings: 25 tins each time.

Water at turning time: First turn 60 to 100 tins, Second turn 40 to 60 tins, third turn 40 to 80 tins according to season.

Fungus starter at the time of First turn: 12 *tagari*s.

TABLE

Volume (in double handfuls) and weights (in lbs.) of the contents of a *tagari* or basket

Material	*Volume in Double-handfuls*	*Weight (lb).*
Fresh dung	6 to 7	40
Urine earth	20 to 21	22
Wood ashes	15	20
Fungus starter	5	20
For First turn starter	6	20

TIME TABLE OF OPERATIONS

Days	*Events*
1	Filling begins
6	Filling ends
10	Fungus established
12	First watering
15 } 16	First turn and addition of one month old compost
24	Second watering
30 } 32	Second turn
38	Third watering
45	Fourth watering
60	Third turn
67	Fifth watering
75	Sixth watering
90	Compost ready for use

When circumstances do not permit the adoption of the Indore process in full detail its advantages may be partially secured in the following way:

The mixed waste is used as bedding for cattle and the requisite amounts of fung, unrine earth, and ash scattered over it next morning before removal as already described. The material is then carried to the margin of a field where the manure is to be used, or to some other suitable well-drained place, and stored in heaps not more than 3" high and 8" broad, and of any convenient length. After the rains have set in the fungus will establish itself in about a month. One full turn is then given choosing a cloudy or moderately rainy day. Another turn or two after an interval of a month will cause the material to rot by the end of the season, given a favourable distribution of rainfall.

A year of waiting is, of course, necessary before the manure is ready and possibly longer if the rains fail seriously.

The resulting manure, though probably rather inferior to compost made in the standard way, will be undoubtedly better than ordinary farm-yard manure, for even by this modified process hard, woody waste can be rotted easily, thus giving a far larger quantity of manure than is produced in existing village practice (*Village Swaraj*, pp. 115-22; *Harijan*, 24.8.1935, pp. 218-19, 224).

Village Crops

Every village's first concern will be to grow its own food crops and cotton for its cloth. It should have a reserve for its cattle, recreation, and playground for adults and children. Then if there is more land available, it will grow *useful* money crops, thus excluding *ganja*, tobacco, opium, and the like (*Harijan*, 26.7.1942, p. 238; *CWMG* 76: 308).

8

Agriculture and Cattle Welfare-V: The Problem of Scarcity of Food

Food Shortage

India is not unfamiliar with starvation and death of tens of thousands, if not millions, due to famine, natural or man-made. I claim that in a well-ordered society there should always be pre-arranged methods of successful treatment of scarcity of water and food crops. This is, however, not the occasion for describing a well-ordered society and for showing how it would deal with the matter. Our concern, for the present, is to see whether we can, with a fair hope of success, deal with the present food crisis.

I think we can. The first lesson we must learn is of self-help and self-reliance. If we assimilate this lesson, we shall at once free ourselves from disastrous dependence upon foreign countries and ultimate bankruptcy. This is not said in arrogance but as a matter of fact. We are not a small place, dependent for our food supply upon outside help. We are a subcontinent, a nation of nearly 400 millions. We are a country of mighty rivers and a rich variety of agricultural land, with inexhaustible cattle-wealth. That our cattle give much less milk than we need is entirely our own fault. Our cattle-wealth is any day capable of giving us all the milk we need. Our country, if it had not been neglected during the past few centuries, should today not only be providing herself with sufficient food, but also be playing a useful role in supplying the outside world with much-needed foodstuffs of which the late war has unfortunately left practically the whole world in want. This does not exclude India. The distress is growing instead of showing signs of decreasing. My suggestion does not include ungrateful rejection of free supply that any foreign country may wish to offer us. All I say is that we must not go begging. It demoralizes. Add to this the difficulty of internal transport of foodstuffs from one place to another. We have not the requisite facility for rapid movement of grains and other foodstuffs from place to place. Further add to this the remote possibility of delivery of uneatable stuff. We dare not lose sight of the fact that we have to deal with human nature. In no part of the world it is to be found perfect or even very nearly so.

Next, let us see what possible foreign aid we can get. I am told, not more than 3 per cent of our present wants. If this information is correct and I have had it checked by several experts who confirm the figure, I am sure the case for reliance on outside help falls to the ground. The slightest dependence on outside help is likely to deflect us from exploring to the fullest extent our immense internal possibilities in the shape of utilizing every inch of arable land for growing crops for daily food in the place of growing money crops. We must reclaim waste land which is capable of being placed under immediate cultivation.

Centralization of foodstuffs, I apprehend, is ruinous. De-centralization easily deals a blow to black marketing, saves time and money in transport to and fro. Moreover, the villager who grows India's cereals and pulses knows how to save his crops against rodents. The movement of grain from station to station makes it liable to be eaten by rodents. This costs the country many millions and deprives it of tons of grain, every ounce of which we badly need. If every Indian were to realize the necessity of growing food wherever it can be grown, we should most probably forget that there was scarcity of foodstuffs in the land. I have by no means dealt fully with the fascinating and absorbing subject of growing more food, but I hope I have said enough to stimulate interest and turn the wise towards the thought of how every individual can help in the laudable enterprise.

Let me now show how to deal with the 3 per cent of grain we might possibly get from outside. Hindus observe a fast or a semi-fast every eleventh day per fortnight. Muslims and others are not prohibited from denying themselves especially when it is for the sake of the starving millions. If the whole nation realized the beauty of this partial self-denial, India would more than cover the deficit caused by the voluntary deprivation of foreign aid.

Personally I hold that rationing has very limited use, if any. If the producers were left to themselves, they would bring their produce to the market and everyone would get good and eatable grain, which today is not easily obtainable.

I shall close this hurried review of the food crisis by drawing attention to President Truman's reported advice to the American people that they should eat less bread, and thus save the much-needed grain for starving Europe. He added that Americans would not lose in health by the recommended act of self-denial. I tender my congratulations to President Truman on this philanthropic gesture. I must decline to endorse the suggestion that at the back of this philanthropy there is the sordid motive of deriving a pecuniary advantage for America. A man must be judged by his action, not the motive prompting it. God alone knows men's hearts. If America would deny herself for the sake of hungry Europe, should we fail to do this little act of self-denial for ourselves? If many must die of starvation, let us at least earn the credit of having done our best in the way of self-help which ennobles a nation (*Harijan*, 19.10.1947, pp. 376-77; *CWMG* 89: 293-95).

In Times of Scarcity

He who saves gains as much, that is to say, he produces as much. Hence those who feel for the poor, those who would be one with them must curtail their wants. There are many ways. I shall only mention some here. There is much, too much food eaten and wasted by the well-to-do.

Use one grain at a time. *Chapati*, rice and pulses, milk, *gur*, *ghee*, and oil are used in ordinary households besides vegetables and fruit. I regard this as an unhealthy combination. Those who get animal protein in the shape of milk, cheese, eggs or meat need not use pulses at all. The poor people get only vegetable protein. If the well-to-do give up pulses and oils, they set free these two essentials for the poor who get neither animal protein nor animal fat. Then the grain eaten should not be sloppy. Half the quantity suffices when it is eaten dry and not dipped in any gravy. It is well to eat it with raw salads such as onion, carrot, radish, salad leaves, tomatoes. An ounce or two of salads serves the purpose of eight ounces of cooked vegetables. *Chapati*s or bread should not be eaten with milk.

To begin with, one meal may be raw vegetables and *chapati* or bread, and the other cooked vegetables with milk or curds.

Sweet dishes should be eliminated altogether. Instead, *gur* or sugar in small quantities may be taken with milk or bread or by itself.

Fresh fruit is good to eat, but only a little is necessary to give one to the system. It is an expensive article, and an over-indulgence by the well-to-do has deprived the poor and the ailing of an article which they need much more than the well-to-do.

Any medical man who has studied the science of dietetics will certify that what I have suggested can do no harm to the body, on the contrary it must conduce to better health.

This is only one way of saving foodstuff. It is obvious. But by itself it cannot produce much visible effect.

Grain dealers have to shed their greed and the habit of making as much profit as possible. They must be satisfied with as little as possible. They run the risk of being looted, if they do not gain the credit of being keepers of grain for the sake of the poor. They should be in touch with the people in their neighbourhood. . . .

By far the most important part of the work consists in educating the villagers to keep what they have and to induce cultivation of fresh crops wherever water is available. This requires widespread and intelligent propaganda. It is not generally known that bananas, potatoes, beetroot, yam, and *suran,* and in a measure pumpkin are a food crop easily grown. They can take the place of bread in time of need.

There is too scarcity of money. There may be grain available but no money to buy it with. There is no money because there is no employment. This has to be found. Spinning is the readiest and the handiest. But local needs may supply other sources of labour. Every available source has to be tapped so that there is no want of employment. Only the lazy ones need and must starve. Patient handling will induce even this class to shed their laziness (*Harijan*, 25.1.1942, p. 12; *CWMG* 75: 233-34).

In the circumstances (of food crisis) the following things should be attended to at once:

1. Every person should confine his daily wants regarding food to the minimum, consistent with his or her health requirements; and where, as in cities, milk, vegetables, oil, and fruit are available, grains and pulses should be reduced as they easily can be. Starch can be derived from starchy roots such as carrots, parsnips, potatoes, yam, bananas; the idea being to exclude from present

diet and conserve those grains and pulses which can be kept and stored. Vegetables too should not be eaten as an indulgence or for pleasure, when millions are denied the use of these things altogether and are now threatened with starvation due to shortage of cereals and pulses.

2. Everyone who has access to any water should try himself or herself to grow some edible for personal or general use. The easiest way to do so is to collect clean earth, mix it with organic manure where possible — even a little bit of dried cowdung is good organic manure — and put it in any earthen or tin pot and throw some seeds of vegetables such as mustard and cress, etc., and daily water the pots. They will be surprised how quickly the seeds sprout and give edible leaves which need not even be cooked but can be eaten in the form of salad.
3. All flower gardens should be utilized for growing edibles. And in this connection I would suggest to the Viceroy, Governors, and high officials to take the lead. I would ask the heads of agricultural departments at the Centre and Provinces to flood the country with leaflets in the provincial languages telling laymen how and what to grow easily.
4. Reduction should be taken up not merely by the civilian population but equally, if not predominantly, by the military. I say "predominantly" for the military ranks, being under rigid military discipline can easily carry out measures of economy.
5. All exports of seeds, such as oil seeds, oils, oilcakes, nuts, etc., should be stopped, if they have not been already. Oilcakes, if the seeds are sifted of earth and foreign matter, are good human food with rich protein content.
6. Deep wells should be sunk by the government wherever possible and required, whether for irrigation or for drinking purposes.
7. Given hearty cooperation by government servants and the general public, I have not the slightest doubt that the country can tide over the difficulty. Just as panic is the surest way to defeat, so also will be the case when there is widespread distress impending and prompt action is not taken. Let us not think of the cause of the distress. Whatever the cause, the fact is that if the government and the public do not approach the crisis patiently and courageously, disaster is a certainty. . . .
8. Above all, black marketing and dishonesty should disappear

altogether and willing cooperation between all parties should be the order of the day in so far as this crisis is concerned (*Harijan*, 24.2.1946, p. 19; *Sevagram*, 14.2.1946; *CWMG* 83: 127-28).

Food Shortage and Overpopulation

If it is contended that birth control is necessary for the nation because of overpopulation, I dispute the proposition. It has never been proved. In my opinion, by a proper land system, better agriculture, and a supplementary industry, this country is capable of supporting twice as many people as there are in it today (*Young India*, 2.4.1925, p. 118; *CWMG* 26: 450).

This little globe of ours is not a toy of yesterday. It has not suffered from the weight of overpopulation through its age of countless millions. How can it be that the truth has suddenly dawned upon some people that it is in danger of perishing of shortage of food unless birth rate is checked through the use of contraceptives? (*Harijan*, 14.9.1935, p. 244; *CWMG* 61: 417).

9

Khadi and Spinning

Khadi connotes the beginning of economic freedom and equality of all in the country. . . . It must be taken with all its implications. It means a wholesale *swadeshi* mentality, a determination to find all the necessaries of life in India and that too through the labour and intellect of the villagers. . . . The latter will be largely self-contained and will voluntarily serve the cities of India and even the outside world in so far as it benefits both the parties.

This needs a revolutionary change in the mentality and tastes of many. Easy though the nonviolent way is in many respects, it is very difficult in many others. It vitally touches the life of every single Indian, makes him feel aglow with the possession of a power that has lain hidden within himself, and makes him proud of his identity with every drop of the ocean of Indian humanity. . . .

Khadi to me is the symbol of unity of Indian humanity, of its economic freedom and equality and, therefore, ultimately in the poetic expression of Jawaharlal Nehru, "the livery of India's freedom".

Moreover, *khadi* mentality means decentralization of the production and distribution of the necessaries of life. Therefore, the formula so far evolved is, every village to produce all its necessaries and a certain percentage in addition for the requirements of the cities. . . .

Having explained the implications of *khadi*, I must indicate what Congressmen can and should do towards its promotion. Production of *khadi* includes cotton growing, picking, ginning, cleaning, carding, slivering, spinning, sizing, dyeing, preparing the warp and the woof, weaving, and washing. These, with the exception of dyeing, are essential processes. Every one of them can be effectively handled in the villages and is being so handled in many villages throughout India which the A.I.S.A. is covering. . . .

If Congressmen will be true to their Congress call in respect of *khadi*, they will carry out the instructions of the A.I.S.A. issued from time to time as to the part they can play in *khadi* planning. Only a few broad rules can be laid down here:

1. Every family with a plot of ground can grow cotton at least for family use. Cotton growing is an easy process. In Bihar the cultivators were by law compelled to grow indigo on 3/20 of their cultivable land. This was in the interest of the foreign indigo planter. Why cannot we grow cotton voluntarily for the nation on a certain portion of our land? The reader will note that decentralization commences from the beginning of the *khadi* processes. Today cotton crop is centralized and has to be sent to distant parts of India. Before the war it used to be sent principally to Britain and Japan. It was and still is a money crop and, therefore, subject to the fluctuations of the market. Under the *khadi* scheme cotton growing becomes free from this uncertainty and gamble. The grower grows what he needs. The farmer needs to know that his first business is to grow for his own needs. When he does that, he will reduce the chance of a low market ruining him.
2. Every spinner would buy — if he has not his own — enough cotton for ginning, which he can easily do without the hand-ginning roller frame. He can gin his own portion with a board and an iron rolling pin. Where this is considered impracticable, hand-ginned cotton should be bought and carded. Carding for self can be done well on a tiny bow without much effort. The greater the decentralization of labour, the simpler and cheaper the tools. The livers made, the process of spinning commences. . . . Imagine the unifying and educative effect of the whole nation simultaneously taking part in the processes up to spinning! Consider the levelling effect of the bond of common labour between the rich and the poor! . . .

If Congressmen will put their heart into the work, they will make improvements in the tools and make many discoveries. In our country there has been a divorce between labour and intelligence. The result has been stagnation. If there is an indissoluble marriage between the two, and that in the manner here suggested, the resultant good will be inestimable.

In this scheme of nation-wide spinning as a sacrifice, I do not expect the average man or woman to give more than one hour daily to this work (*Constructive Programme*: *Its Meaning and Place*, 13.12.1941; *CWMG* 75: 150-52).

The message of the spinning wheel is much wider than its circumference. Its message is one of simplicity, service of mankind, living so as not to hurt others, creating an indissoluble bond between the rich and the poor, capital and labour, the prince and the peasant (*Young India*, 17.9.1925, p. 321; *CWMG* 28: 188).

I stand by what is implied in the phrase, "Unto This Last". . . . We must do even unto this last as we would have the world do by us. All must have equal opportunity. Given the opportunity, every human being has the same possibility for spiritual growth. That is what the spinning-wheel symbolizes (*Harijan*, 17.11.1946, p. 404; *CWMG* 86: 21).

I can only think of spinning as the fittest and most acceptable sacrificial body labour. I cannot imagine anything nobler or more national than that for say one hour in the day we should all do the labour that the poor must do, and thus identify ourselves with them and through them with all mankind. I cannot imagine better worship of God than that in His name I should labour for the poor even as they do. The spinning-wheel spells a more equitable distribution of the riches of the earth (*Young India*, 20.10.1921, p. 329; *CWMG* 21: 308).

I feel convinced that the revival of hand-spinning and hand-weaving will make the largest contribution to the economic and the moral regeneration of India. The millions must have a simple industry to supplement agriculture. Spinning was the cottage industry years ago and if the millions are to be saved from starvation, they must be enabled to reintroduce spinning in their homes, and every village must repossess its own weaver (*Young India*, 21.7.1920, p. 4; *CWMG* 18: 72).

If he (the reader) would visualize the picture of the Indian skeleton, he must think of the 80 per cent of the population which is working its own fields, and which has practically no occupation for at least four months in the year, and which therefore lives on the borderland of starvation. This is the normal condition. The ever recurring famines make a large addition to this enforced idleness. What is the work that these men and women can easily do in their own cottages so as to supplement their very slender resources? Does anyone still doubt that it is only hand-spinning and nothing else? (*Young India*, 3.11.1921, p. 350; *CWMG* 21: 391).

Cottage manufacture of yarn and cloth cannot be expensive even as domestic cookery is not expensive and cannot be replaced by hotel cookery. Over twenty-five crores of the population will be doing their own hand-spinning and having yarn thus manufactured woven in neighbouring localities. This population is rooted to the soil, and has at least four months in the year to remain idle.

If they spin during those hours and have the yarn woven and wear it, no mill-made cloth can compete with their *khadi*. The cloth thus manufactured will be the cheapest possible for them (*Young India*, 8.12.1921, p. 405; *CWMG* 21: 547).

What is claimed for spinning is that:

1. It supplies the readiest occupation to those who have leisure and are in want of a few copper coins.
2. It is known to the thousands.
3. It is easily learnt.
4. It requires practically no outlay of capital.
5. The wheel can be easily and cheaply made. Most of us do not yet know that spinning can be done even with a piece of tile and splinter.
6. The people have no repugnance to it.
7. It affords immediate relief in times of famine and scarcity.
8. It alone can stop the drain of wealth which goes outside India in the purchase of foreign cloth.
9. It automatically distributes the millions thus saved among the deserving poor.
10. Even the smallest success means so much immediate gain to the people.
11. It is the most potent instrument of securing cooperation among the people (*Young India*, 21.8.1924, p. 277; *CWMG* 25: 22).

The disease of the masses is not want of money so much as it is want of work. Labour is money. He, who provides dignified labour for the millions in their cottages, provides food and clothing, or which is the same thing, money. The *charkha* provides such labour. Till a better substitute is found, it must, therefore, hold the field (*Young India*, 18.6.1925, p. 211; *CWMG* 27: 255).

Idleness is the great cause, the root of all evil, and if that root can be destroyed, most of the evils can be remedied without further effort. A nation that is starving has little hope or initiative left in it. It becomes indifferent to filth and disease. It says of all reforms, "to what good?" That winter of despair can only be turned into the "sunshine of hope" for the millions only through the life-giving wheel, the *charkha* (*Young India*, 27.8.1925, p. 299; *CWMG* 28: 123).

The spinning-wheel is an attempt to produce something out of nothing. If we save sixty crores of rupees to the nation through the spinning-wheel, as we certainly can, we add that vast amount to the national income. In the process we automatically organize our villages. And as almost the whole of the amount must be distributed amongst the poorest of the land, it becomes a scheme of just and nearly equal distribution of so much wealth. Add to this immense moral value of such distribution, and the case for the *charkha* becomes irresistible (*Young India*, 17.2.1927, p. 52; *CWMG* 33: 93).

Indeed, in some places, there are to be found weavers who are classed as untouchables on account of their occupation. They are mostly weavers of coarsest *khadi* without any pattern. This class was fast dying out when *khadi* came to the rescue and there was created a demand for their coarse manufacture. It was then discovered that there were numerous Harijan families that even subsisted on spinning. Thus *khadi* is doubly the poor man's staff of life. It helps the poorest, including the Harijans, who are the most helpless among the poorest. They are so because many occupations which are available to the others are not available to the Harijans (*Harijan*, 27.4.1934, p. 85; *CWMG* 57: 441).

To those also who aspire to observe *brahmcharya*, I do present the spinning-wheel. It is not a thing to be despised, for it is experience here that speaks. A person who wants to subdue his passions has the need to be calm. All commotion within him ought to cease; and so quiet and gentle is the motion of the spinning-wheel, that it has been known to still the passions of those who have turned it in the fullness of faith . . . human passions are fleeter even than the wind, and to subdue them completely requires no end of patience. All that I claim is that in the spinning-wheel they will find a powerful means of cultivating steadiness (*Young India*, 27.5.1926, p. 190; *CWMG* 30: 451-52).

Spinning would spell the creation of so much fresh industry, the organization of crores into a joint co-operative effort, the conservation and utilization of the energy of the millions, and the dedication of crores of lives to the service of the motherland. The carrying out of such a gigantic task would, further, give us a realization of our own strength. It would mean our acquiring a thorough mastery of the detail and innumerable knotty problems which it presents, e.g. learning to keep account of every pie, learning to live in the villages in sanitary and healthy conditions, removing the difficulties that block the way and so on. For, unless we learn all this, we would not be able to accomplish this task. The spinning wheel, then, provides us with a means for generating this capacity in us (*Young India*, 27.5.1926, p. 190; *CWMG* 30: 452-53).

The only universal industry for the millions is spinning and no other. That does not mean that other industries do not matter or are useless. Indeed, from the individual standpoint, any other industry would be more remunerative than spinning. Watch-making will be no doubt a most remunerative and fascinating industry. But how many can engage in it? Is it of any use to the millions of villagers? But if the villagers can reconstruct their home, begin to live again as their forefathers did, if they begin to make good use of their idle hours, all else, all the other industries will revive as a matter of course (*Young India*, 30.9.1926, p. 341; *CWMG* 31: 463).

This revival (of *charkha*) cannot take place without an army of selfless Indians of intelligence and patriotism working with a single mind in the villages to spread the message of the *charkha* and bring a ray of hope and light into their lustreless eyes. This is mighty effort at cooperation and adult education of the correct type. It brings about a silent and sure revolution like the silent but sure and life-giving revolution of the *charkha*.

Twenty years' experience of *charkha* work has convinced me of the correctness of the argument here advanced by me. The *charkha* has served the poor Muslims and Hindus in almost an equal measure. Nearly five crores of rupees have been put into the pockets of these lakhs of village artisans without fuss and tom-toming.

Hence I say without hesitation that the *charkha* must lead us to *swaraj* in terms of the masses belonging to all faiths. The *charkha* restores the villages to their rightful place and abolishes distinctions between high and low. (*Harijan*, 13.4.1940, p. 85; *Sevagram*, 9.4.1940; *CWMG* 71: 410-11).

The spinning-wheel is a symbol not of commercial war but of commercial peace. It bears not a message of ill-will towards the nations of the earth but of goodwill and self-help. It will not need the protection of a navy threatening a world's peace and exploiting its resources, but it needs the religious determination of millions to spin their yarn in their own homes as today they cook their food in their own homes. I may deserve the curses of posterity for many mistakes of omission and commission but I am confident of earning its blessings for suggesting a revival of the *charkha*. I stake my all on it. For every revolution of the wheel spins peace, goodwill, and love (*Young India*, 8.12.1921, p. 406; *CWMG* 21: 548).

It is my claim that as soon as we have completed the boycott of foreign cloth, we shall have evolved so far that we shall necessarily give up the present absurdities and remodel national life in keeping with the ideal of simplicity and domesticity implanted in the bosom of the masses. We will not then be dragged into an imperialism which is built upon exploitation of the weaker races of the earth, and the acceptance of a giddy materialistic civilization protected by naval and air forces that have made peaceful living almost impossible. On the contrary, we shall then refine that imperialism into a commonwealth of nations which will combine, if they do, for the purpose of giving their best to the world and of protecting, not by brute force but by self-suffering, the weaker nations or races of the earth. . . . Such a transformation can come only after the complete success of the spinning-wheel. India can become fit for delivering such a message, when she has become proof against temptation and therefore, attacks from outside, by becoming self-contained regarding two of her chief needs — food and clothing (*Young India,* 29.6.1921, p. 206; *CWMG* 20: 296).

When once we have revived the one industry, all the other industries will follow. . . . But I would make the spinning-wheel the foundation on which to build a sound village life, I would make the wheel the centre round which all other activities will revolve (*Young India*, 21.5.1925, pp. 176-77S; *CWMG* 27: 130-31).

The ideal of *khadi* has always been as a means, par excellence, for the resuscitation of villages and there — through the generation of real strength among the masses — the strength that will *ipso facto* bring *swaraj* (*Village Swaraj*, p. 139; *Swaraj through Charkha* 1945, p. 8).

My experience tells me that if *khadi* is to become universal, both in cities and in villages, it should be made available only in exchange of yarn. Today one anna's worth of yarn in the rupee is demanded. But this is only the beginning. When people have understood and learnt how to spin, then *khadi* will be given only in full exchange for yarn spun. I hope that as days go by everyone will himself insist on buying *khadi* only in exchange of yarn. If this does not happen and if they give yarn grudgingly *swaraj* through nonviolence is impossible (Why Khadi For Yarn and Not

For Money?, July 1945; *Gram Udyog Patrika*, pp. 352-54; *CWMG* 81: 55).

If more mills are increased and the number of cities is increased it will not make India prosperous. On the other hand, it will make crores die of starvation and of the many diseases produced by starvation. If city people are pleased with such a spectacle I have nothing to say. Then it will be the reign of violence, not of nonviolence and truth, and I will admit that in that case *khadi* will have no place, it can have no place. Then military training will be compulsory whether we like it or not. But what I am talking about relates to the crores of the starving people. If they are to live, and live well, the *charkha* will have to be central and spinning undertaken voluntarily also by those who do not need to spin (Why Khadi For Yarn and Not For Money?, July 1945; *Gram Udyog Patrika*, pp. 352-54; *CWMG* 81: 56-57).

Our work had a very humble beginning. When I started *khadi* I had with me, apart from Maganlalbhai and others who had elected to live and die with me, Vitthaldasbhai and a few sisters. . . . We have travelled a long way since then and today about two crores of people have come under the influence of the *charkha*. So far, we have maintained that the *charkha* has the power to bring us freedom. With its help we have been able to provide the village people with a large amount of money. But can we still hold, as we have always maintained, that *swaraj* is impossible without the *charkha?* So long as we do not substantiate this claim the *charkha* is really no more than a measure of relief, to which we turn because we can do nothing else about it. It would not then be the means of our salvation.

Second, we have failed to carry our message to the crores of our people. They have neither any knowledge of what the *charkha* can do for them nor even the necessary curiosity for it. The Congress did accept the *charkha*. But did it do so willingly? No, it tolerates the *charkha* simply for my sake. The Socialists ridicule it outright. They have spoken and written much against it. We have no clear or convincing reply to offer to them. How I wish I could convince them that the *charkha* is the key to *swaraj*! I have not been able to justify the claim all these years.

Now for my third point: nonviolence is not something of the other world. If it is, I have no use for it. I am of the earth and if nonviolence is something really worthwhile I want to realize it here on this earth while I am still alive. The nonviolence is one which the masses can follow in practice. And how else can it be realized except in a society which has compassion and other similar virtues as its characteristics?

If you go to the house of one who has use for violence you will find his drawing room decorated with tigers' skins, deers' horns, swords, guns, and such like. I have been to the Viceregal Lodge, I also saw Mussolini. In the houses of both I found arms hanging on the walls. I was given a salute with arms, a symbol of violence.

Just as arms symbolize violence the *charkha* symbolizes nonviolence, in the sense that we can most directly realize nonviolence through it. But it cannot symbolize nonviolence so long as we do not work in accordance with its spirit. The sword in Mussolini's hall seemed to say "Touch me and I will cut you". It gave a vivid picture of violence. It seemed to ask you to touch it and realize its power. So also we must illustrate the power of the *charkha* so that a mere look at it may speak to us about nonviolence. But we are bankrupt today. What is our answer to Socialists? They complain that we have been harping on the *charkha* for years and yet we have achieved nothing.

The *charkha* was there during Muslim rule also. Dacca was famous for its muslins. The *charkha* then was a symbol of poverty and not of nonviolence. The kings took forced labour from women and depressed classes. The same was later repeated by the East India Company. Kautilya mentions in his *Arthashastra* the existence of such forced labour. For ages the *charkha* was thus a symbol of violence and the use of force and compulsion. The spinner got but a handful of grain or two small coins, while ladies of the court went about luxuriously clad in the finest of muslins, the product of exploited labour.

As against this, I have presented the *charkha* to you as a symbol of nonviolence. I shall now pass to my fourth point. We have not yet proved that there can be no *swaraj* without the *charkha*. It cannot be proved so long as you do not explain it to Congressmen. The *charkha* and the Congress should become synonyms.

The task of proving the superiority of nonviolence is a difficult one. We have to fathom its depths if we are to realize its truth. I have always supported all that I have said so far. The world is going to put me to the test. It may declare me a fool for my tall talk about the *charkha*. The task of making the *charkha*, which for centuries had been a symbol of poverty, helplessness, injustice and forced labour, the symbol now of mighty nonviolent strength, of the new social order and of the new economy, has fallen on our shoulders. We have to change history. And I want to do it through you.

I hope you follow what I am saying. But if in spite of it you do not believe that the *charkha* has the power to achieve *swaraj*, I will ask you to leave me. Here you are at the crossroads. If you continue with me without faith you will be deceiving me and doing a great wrong to the country. I beg of you not to deceive me in the evening of my life.

It is I who am responsible for defects in our working so far. The fault is mine because I have remained the head even when I was conscious of its defects. But let bygones be bygones. Do we honestly believe today that the *charkha* is the emblem of nonviolence? How many of us are there who believe so from the depths of our heart?

Now we have the tri-colour flag. What is it but a piece of *khadi* of specific length and breadth? You can well have another piece in its place. But behind that *khadi* cloth lie encased your feelings. It is a symbol of *swaraj*, a symbol of national emancipation. We cannot forget it. We will not remove it. We are prepared to die for it. So also the *charkha* should be an emblem of nonviolence.

What does the *charkha*, as an emblem of nonviolence, signify in the economic sphere? Call it self-sufficiency or what you like. In the name of national reconstruction and self-sufficiency millions are being bled white in Western countries, as also in other countries for their sake. Ours is not a self-sufficiency of that pattern. The *charkha* is the way to get rid of exploitation and domination. I am not so much concerned with words as with the thing itself. . . .

We are familiar with the controversy in our religion as to whether God has a form or no. The believers in form prefer to worship God through an emblem. So if nonviolence is to be pursued as an ideal, the *charkha* must be acknowledged as its true form and emblem, and kept ever before view. Whenever I think of nonviolence the picture of the *charkha* comes before me. . . . We cannot visualize nonviolence in the abstract. So we choose an object which can symbolize for us the formless. That is what the *charkha* does for me and that is why I worship it. . . . Unless you understand and imbibe this spirit behind my worship of the *charkha* you will not gain an understanding of nonviolence even for a hundred years. That capacity for nonviolence which I find in the *charkha* can also be perceived by you only if you approach it with a heart like mine. That is why I say: Follow me or leave me. If you want to come with me, I will give you a scheme and do everything possible. If you have not understood what I mean I am prepared to sit and discuss it with you the whole day. But if you say that you have grasped my meaning when you really have not, you will be deceiving both yourselves and me. Ours is not an association for making profit. We do not seek loaves and fishes. There are a thousand fields in which we can serve the country. Why then remain in *charkha* work and sail under false colours? Please do not therefore remain with me under an illusion. Let me go my way alone. But if it were found that I was myself suffering from an illusion and that my belief in the *charkha* was mere idol-worship, either you may burn me to ashes with the wood of the *charkha*, or I myself would set fire to the *charkha* with my own hands.

If the Charkha Sangh has to go, let us wind it up with our own hands. That will put an end to all our struggle like sun clearing the mist. Then the *charkha* which has for the moment put us into a labyrinth of difficulties will be left in the hands of a few who believe in it, and may in their hands prove to be a mighty weapon. If you regard it as sheer folly I certainly have no ambition to run an idiots' association and thus degrade the country. On the other hand, if you can demonstrate nonviolence through the *charkha*, it will not merely move but sweep forward. You will not then have to worry about keeping it alive.

I repeat that you either leave me alone or digest what I say and follow me. I have brought this new idea to you after two years of penitential thinking. I do not know if I have succeeded in conveying my idea to you. If I have been able to carry conviction please do one thing. Those of you who want to remain with me give me in writing that you regard the *charkha* from today as the emblem of nonviolence. You have to make your decision today. If you do not or cannot regard the *charkha* as the emblem of nonviolence and yet remain with me, then you will thereby put yourself in an awkward plight and also drag me down with you (Speech at A.I.S.A. Meeting-III, 3.9.1944; *CWMG* 78: 75-79).

One epoch of *khadi* has ended. *khadi* has achieved something for the benefit of the poor. Now we have to demonstrate how the poor can be self-supporting (*Village Swaraj*, p. 145; *Ideology of the Charkha* 1959, p. 94).

I saw that our work would be incomplete, so long as we did not carry the message of the *charkha* to every home (Speech at A.I.S.A. Meeting-I, 1.9.1944; *CWMG* 78: 63).

The *charkha* is the symbol of nonviolent economic self-sufficiency. If we and the people grasp this significance of the *charkha* not a pice need be spent on propaganda for the *charkha*. . . . Nor need we look to the rich for alms. We shall without effort become the centre of hope, and the people will come to us of their own accord. They will not go elsewhere to seek work. Every village will become the nerve-centre of independent India. India will then not be known by her cities like Bombay and Calcutta, but by her 400 millions inhabiting the seven lakhs of villages. The problems of Hindu–Muslim differences, untouchability, conflicts, mis-understandings and rivalries will all melt away. This is the real function of the

Sangh. We have to live and die for it (Speech at A.I.S.A. Meeting-I, 1.9.1944; *CWMG* 78: 66).

The pursuit of the *charkha* must become the mainspring of manifold other activities like village industries, Nai Talim, etc. If we are able to adopt the *charkha* intelligently we can revive the entire economic life of our villages once more (Speech at A.I.S.A. Meeting-I, 1.9.1944; *CWMG* 78: 66).

With its help we have been able to provide the village people with a large amount of money. But can we still hold, as we have always maintained, that *swaraj* is impossible without the *charkha*? So long as we do not substantiate this claim the *charkha* is really no more than a measure of relief, to which we turn because we can do nothing else about it. It would not then be the means of our salvation (Speech at A.I.S.A. Meeting-III, 3.9.1944; *CWMG* 78: 75).

Now I feel that *khadi* alone cannot revive the villages. Village uplift is possible only when we rejuvenate village life as a whole, revive all village industries and make the entire village industrious (Discussion with Shrikrishnadas Jaju, 12.10.1944; *CWMG* 78: 187).

Khadi is not an occupation or craft merely to earn a livelihood. None of us should harbour this idea (Discussion with Shrikrishnadas Jaju, 13.10.1944; *CWMG* 78: 192).

Our reason for putting forward *khadi* is that it is the only way to redeem the people from the disease of inertia and indifference, the only way to generate in them the strength for freedom. If other crafts are also thus revitalized, our villages could be made self-sufficient and self-reliant (Discussion with Shrikrishnadas Jaju, 13.10.1944; *CWMG* 78: 193).

But what we are required to prove above all is need for *khadi* to establish a strong, nonviolent village economy (Discussion with Shrikrishnadas Jaju, 14.10.1944; *CWMG* 78: 198).

. . . Charkha Jayanti will be truly observed when the *charkha*, which is the symbol of freedom and *ahimsa*, hums in every home. What can the observance signify if a few poor women, or even a million poor women, spin to earn a pittance? What great work will have been accomplished? This is possible even under a tyrannical regime and is indeed the normal thing in the capitalist system. The doles given to the poor help in sustaining the affluence of the millionaires, even if such doles be in the form of wages.

The observance will have meaning only when both the rich and the poor understand that all created alike by God, that all must work to attain glory and that the freedom of all will be protected not by guns but by the ball of yarn, not by violence but by nonviolence (*Harijan*, 22.9.1946, p. 320; *CWMG* 85: 321).

Ponder and realize what wealth this would mean to India, if 300 crores worth of cloth was produced by their own hands in the villages. There was a veritable mint of gold for them and if *khadi* became universal, the villages would rise to unknown heights. Today our masses were poverty-stricken, without the lustre of hope or intelligence in their eyes. The pure hands of the spinners could create this miracle for them and everyone could help. They should have understanding hearts and seeing eyes to detect the beauty in *khaddar* even if it is coarse and not be allured by mill finery which could never clothe their nakedness in the true sense of the term. The only way to clothe their nakedness and drive away hunger was for them to grow their own food and make their own cloth. If this happy consummation could be achieved, the eyes of the whole world would be turned towards India (*Harijan*, 22.9.1946, p. 322; *CWMG* 85: 327-28).

When the *charkha* class is in progress, all else appears insignificant to me. For in every thread drawn I see Rama. I see *swaraj* in it. The thought of 20 crores of our people spinning fills me with boundless joy. How long it will be before that number of people take to spinning is another matter. But not to believe this possible will only show our ignorance and lack of faith. Is it impossible for the whole or even half of the population of the country to spin for half an hour everyday? If we cannot make even this small sacrifice for the country, what can we be worth? (*Harijan*, 22.9.1946, p. 322; *CWMG* 85: 335).

10

Other Village Industries

Why Village Industries

I recall a conversation I had with Fazalbhai in 1920, when I was on the eve of launching movement for *swadeshi*. He characteristically said to me: "If you Congressmen become advertising agents of ours, you will do no good to the country except to put a premium on our wares and raise the prices of our manufactures." His argument was sound. But he was nonplussed when I informed him that our object was to encourage hand-spun and hand-woven *khadi* which had been woefully neglected and which needed to be revived if the starving and unemployed millions were to be served. But *khaddar* is not the only such struggling industry. I therefore suggest you direct your attention and efforts to all the small-scale minor unorganized industries that are today in need of public support. They may be wiped out if no effort is made on their behalf. Some of these are being pushed back by large-scale industries which flood the markets with their manufactures. It is these that cry for your help (Interview to All-India Swadeshi League Deputation, 17.6.1934; *Cent Per Cent Swadeshi*, 1938, p. 4; *CWMG* 58: 88-89).

I have no doubt in my mind that we add to the national wealth, if we help the small-scale industries. I have no doubt also that true *swadeshi* consists in encouraging and reviving these home industries. That alone can help the dumb millions. It also provides an outlet for the creative faculties and resourcefulness of the people. It can usefully employ hundreds of youths in the country who are in need of employment. It may harness all the energy that at present runs to waste. I do not want any one of those who are engaged in more remunerative occupations to leave them and take to the minor industries. Just as I did with regard to the spinning wheel. I would ask only those who suffer from unemployment and penury to take to some of these industries and add a little to their slender resources. It will thus be seen that the change in activity that I have suggested to you does in no way conflict with the interests of major industries. I want to say only this much: Treat you national servants well, restrict your activities to the minor industries and let the major ones help themselves as they are doing today. Minor industries, I conceive, will not replace major ones but will supplement them (Interview to All-India Swadeshi League Deputation, 17.6.1934; *Cent Per Cent Swadeshi*, 1938, p. 5; *CWMG* 58: 89).

We may profess to gratuitously help textile, sugar and rice mills and, respectively, kill the village spinning-wheel, the handloom and their product, *khadi*, the village cane-crusher and its product, the vitamin-laden and nourishing *gur* or molasses, and the hand-pounder and its product, unpolished rice, whose pericarp, which holds the vitamins, is left intact by these pounders. Our clear duty is, therefore, to investigate the possibility of keeping in existence the village wheel, the village crusher and the village pounder, and, advertising their products, discovering their qualities, ascertaining the condition of the workers, and the number displaced by the power-driven machinery and discovering the methods of improving them, whilst retaining their village character, to enable them to stand the competition of the mills. How terribly and criminally we have neglected them! Here, there is no antagonism to the textile or the sugar or the rice mills. Their products must be preferred to the corresponding foreign products. If they were in danger of extinction from foreign competition, they should receive the needed support. But they stand in no such need. They are flourishing in spite of foreign competition. What is needed is protection of the village crafts and the workers behind them from the crushing competition of the power-driven machinery, whether it is worked in India or in foreign lands. It may be that *khadi, gur,* and unpolished rice have no intrinsic quality and that they should die. But, except for *khadi,* not the slightest effort has been made, so far as I am aware, to know anything about the fate of the tens of thousands of villagers who were earning their livelihood through crushing cane and pounding rice (*Harijan,* 10.8.1934, p. 204; *CWMG* 58: 293-94).

I have ruled out organized industries, *not* because they are not *swadeshi,* but because they do not need special support. They can stand on their own legs and, in the present state of our awakening, can easily command a market (*Harijan,* 28-9-1934, p. 259; *CWMG* 59: 87).

In a nutshell, of the things we use, we should restrict our purchases to the articles which villages manufacture. Their manufactures may be crude. We must try to induce them to improve their workmanship, and not dismiss them because foreign articles or even articles produced in cities, that is, big factories, are superior. In other words, we should evoke the artistic talent of the villager. In this manner we shall repay somewhat the debt we owe to them. We need not be frightened by the thought whether we shall ever succeed in such an effort. Within our own times we can recall instances where we have not been baffled by the difficulty of our tasks when we have known that they were essential for the nation's progress. If, therefore, we as individuals believe that revivification of India's villages is a necessity of our existence, if we believe that thereby only can we root out untouchability and feel one with all, no matter to what community or religion they may belong, we must mentally go back to the villages and treat them as our pattern, instead of putting the city life before them for imitation. If this is the correct attitude, then, naturally, we begin with ourselves and thus use, say, hand-made paper instead of mill-made, use village reed, wherever possible, instead of the fountain pen or the penholder, ink made in the villages instead of the big factories, etc. I can multiply instances of this nature. There is hardly anything of daily use in the home which the villagers have not made before and cannot make even now. If we perform the mental trick and fix our gaze upon them, we immediately put millions of rupees into the pockets of the villagers, whereas at the present moment we are exploiting the villagers without making any return worth the name. It is time we arrested the progress of the tragedy (*Harijan,* 30.11.1934, p. 332; *CWMG* 59: 414).

Bit by bit village people are being confined only to the hand-to-mouth business of scratching the earth. Few know today that agriculture in the small and irregular holdings of India is not a paying proposition. The villagers live a lifeless life. Their life is a process of slow starvation. They are burdened with debts (*Harijan*, 16.11.1934, p. 316; *CWMG* 59: 355).

Extinction of village industries would complete the ruin of the 7,00,000 villages of India (*Harijan*, 16.11.1934, p. 316; *CWMG* 59: 355).

Mechanization is good when the hands are too few for the work intended to be accomplished. It is an evil when there are more hands than required for the work, as is the case in India (*Harijan*, 16.11.1934, p. 316; *CWMG* 59: 356).

But if the cloth manufactured in mills displaces village hands, rice mills and flour mills not only displace thousands of poor women workers, but damage the health of the whole population in the bargain. Where people have no objection to taking flesh diet and can afford it, white flour and polished rice may do no harm, but in India, where millions can get no flesh diet even where they have no objection to eating it, if they can get it, it is sinful to deprive them of nutritious and vital elements contained in whole wheat meal and unpolished rice. It is time medical men and others combined to instruct the people on the danger attendant upon the use of white flour and polished rice (*Harijan*, 16.11.1934, p. 316; *CWMG* 59: 356).

The way to take work to the villagers is not through mechanization but that it lies through revival of the industries they have hitherto followed (*Harijan*, 16.11.1934, p. 316; *CWMG* 59: 356).

Hence the function of the All India Village Industries Association must, in my opinion, be to encourage the existing industries and to revive, where it is possible and desirable, the dying or dead industries of villages according to the village methods, i.e. the villagers working in their own cottages as they have done from times immemorial. These simple methods can be considerably improved as they have been in hand-ginning, hand-carding, hand-spinning, and hand-weaving (*Harijan*, 16.11.1934, p. 316; *CWMG* 59: 356-57).

Khadi is the sun of the village solar system. The planets are the various industries which can support *khadi* in return for the heat and the sustenance they derive from it. Without it, the other industries cannot grow. But during my last tour I discovered that, without the revival of the other industries, *khadi* could not make further progress. For villagers to be able to occupy their spare time profitably, the village life must be touched at all points (*Harijan*, 16.11.1934, p. 317; *CWMG* 59: 357).

Involuntary and voluntary idleness of villagers make them a perpetual prey of exploiters, foreign and indigenous. Whether the exploiter is from outside or from the Indian cities, their state would be the same, they would have no *swaraj*. So I said to myself, "Let these people be asked to do something else; if they will not interest themselves in *khadi*, let them take up some work which used to be done by their ancestors, but which has of late died out." There were numerous things of daily use which they used to produce themselves not many years ago, but for which they now depend on the outer world. There are numerous things of daily use to the town-dweller for which he depends on the villagers but which he now imports from cities. The moment the villagers decided to devote all their spare time to doing something useful and town-dwellers to use those village products, the snapped link between the villagers and the town-dwellers would be restored (*Harijan*, 7.12.1934, p. 340; *CWMG* 59: 408-09).

I am not asking the city-dwellers to go to and live in the villages. But I am asking them to render unto the villagers what is due to them. Is there any single raw material that the city-dwellers can obtain except from the villager? If they cannot, why not teach him to work on it himself, as he used to before and as he would do now but for our exploiting inroads? (*Harijan*, 7.12.1934, pp. 340-41; *CWMG* 59: 410).

We shall have to see that the villagers become first of all self-contained and then cater to the needs of the city-dwellers (*Harijan*, 7.12.1934, p. 341; *CWMG* 59: 411).

Village industries come in as a hand-maid to *khadi*. They cannot exist without *khadi*, and *khadi* will be robbed of its dignity without them. Village economy cannot be complete without the essential village industries such as hand-grinding, hand-pounding, soap-making, paper-making, match-making, tanning, oil-pressing, etc. Congressmen can interest themselves in these and, if they are villagers or will settle down in villages, they will give these industries a new life and a new dress. All should make it a point of honour to use only village articles whenever and wherever available. Given the demand there is no doubt that most of our wants can be supplied from our villages. When we have become village-minded, we will not want imitations of the West or machine-made products, but we will develop a true national taste in keeping with the vision of a new India in which pauperism, starvation, and idleness will be unknown (*Constructive Programme: Its Meaning and Place*, 13.12.1941; *CWMG* 75: 152-53).

The revival of village industries is but an extension of the *khadi* effort. Hand-spun cloth, hand-made paper, hand-pounded rice, home-made bread and jam are not uncommon in the West. Only, there they do not have one-hundredth of the importance they have in India. For, with us, their revival means life, their destruction means death, to the villagers, as he who runs may see. Whatever the machine age may do, it will never give employment to the millions whom the wholesale introduction of power machinery must displace (*Harijan*, 4.1.1935, p. 372; *CWMG* 60: 55).

The pursuit of the *charkha* must become the mainspring of manifold other activities like village industries, *Nai Talim*, etc. If we are able to adopt the *charkha* intelligently we can revive the entire economic life of our villages once more (Speech at A.I.S.A. Meeting-I, 1.9.1944; *CWMG* 78: 66).

Our worker should be able to identify himself with all that requires to be done in the village, that is, with the entire life of the village and yet feel as light as ever (Discussion with Shrikrishnadas Jaju, 7.10.1944; *CWMG* 78: 157).

I regard it (*charkha*) as the centre of village uplift. In addition, the worker will have to see what other village crafts can prosper in his village. The first in order among these crafts will be the bullock oil-press. Our worker would have to know its technique which has now been scientifically improved at Maganwadi. . . . Another industry which may be introduced is hand-made paper. This has to be learnt not with the view of supplying paper to the whole country but in order to make the village self-sufficient and capable of earning a little income. . . . Next to oil and hand-made paper we must revive the hand-*chakki* (grinding stone) — a vital thing in every village. Otherwise flour-mills which have been a source of anxiety to me for several years will be our fate. Similarly in regard to rice. . . . We must get our people in the villages to take to hand-pounding of rice or hand-*chakki*s for husking paddy, for it is a well-established fact that the white polished rice put out by mills is harmful to health (Discussion with Shrikrishnadas Jaju, 8.10.1944; *CWMG* 8: 161-62).

The village worker should acquire all-round knowledge about building up the whole village. There will be some sewing work in the village, smithy, carpentry, leather work, agriculture, etc. The village worker should seek to bring about cooperation among the workers in these various occupations so as to make them serve as harmonious parts of one whole and thus organize the villages (Discussion with Shrikrishnadas Jaju, 8.10.1944; *CWMG* 78: 163).

Now we have to do the work anew with the objective of all-round village uplift. Let us see how far we can go. Even if our present activities have to be slackened or reduced to nought for some time on account of these changes, it does not matter. We have created some sentiment about *khadi* among the people. But if there is some error in what we told the people about the significance of *khadi* we must pause. If ours was a wrong claim we must declare our error openly and withdraw our claim.

I would ask city-dwellers to produce their own *khadi*. I would forgo the temptation to supply *khadi* to them. We shall go and settle in the villages. In case workers want to leave us on account of this change we shall let them go. Unless our head and heart are converted to this extent we cannot achieve the desired result. We of the A.I.S.A. will merely direct policy. But decentralizing our work as much as possible we shall free ourselves from day-to-day *khadi* work completely. Thereafter we shall concentrate our energy and attention on the other activities or crafts carried out in the vicinity of the village we settle in. Only then will the real substance of our work be realized. . . . Today our main concern should be to lay the foundation for this work as deep as possible (Discussion with Shrikrishnadas Jaju, 12.10.1944; *CWMG* 78: 183-84).

I am therefore, thinking of ways and means of improving the condition of the people through a rehabilitation of agriculture, cattle-breeding and all other village industries. My problem will be solved if I succeed even in half a dozen villages, for "as is the part so is the whole" (Discussion with Shrikrishnadas Jaju, 12.10.1944; *CWMG* 78: 187).

Begin with Yourself

Correspondents have been writing, and friends have been seeing me, to ask me how to begin the village industries work and what to do first.

The obvious answer is, "Begin with yourself and do first that which is easiest for you to do."

This answer, however, does not satisfy the enquirers. Let me, therefore, be more explicit.

Each person can examine all the articles of food, clothing, and other things that he uses from day to day and replace foreign makes or city makes, by those produced by the villagers in their homes or fields with the simple inexpensive tools they can easily handle and mend. This replacement will be itself, an education of great value and a solid beginning. The next step will be opened out to him of itself. For instance, say, the beginner has been hitherto using a toothbrush made in a Bombay factory. He wants to replace it with a village brush. He is advised to use a *babul* twig. If he has weak teeth or is toothless, he has to crush one end of it, with a rounded stone or a hammer, on a hard surface. The other end he slits with a knife and uses the halves as tongue-scrapers. He will find these brushes to be cheaper and much cleaner than the very unhygienic factory-made toothbrush. The city-made toothpowder he naturally replaces with equal parts of clean, finely-ground, wood-charcoal and clean salt. He will replace mill-cloth with village-spun *khadi*, mill-husked rice with hand-husked, unpolished rice, and white sugar with village-made *gur*. These I have taken merely as samples . . . to deal with the difficulties that have been mentioned by those who have been discussing the question with me (*Harijan*, 25.1.1935, p. 400; *CWMG* 60: 108-09).

Dairying

Criminal negligence is the only cause of the miserable condition of our cattle. Our *pinjrapoles*, though they are an answer to our instinct of mercy, are a clumsy demonstration of its execution. Instead of being model dairy farms and great profitable national institutions, they are merely depots for receiving decrepit cattle. . . . Whilst professing the religion of cow protection, we have enslaved the cow and her progeny, and have become slaves ourselves (*Young India*, 6.10.1921, p. 318; *CWMG* 21: 249).

An ideal *goshala* would supply the city of its domicile with cheap and wholesome milk from cattle of its own keeping and cheap and lasting footwear not out of slaughtered hide but of the hide of dead cattle. Such a *goshala* will not be on one or two acres of ground in the heart of a city or in its immediate neighbourhood, but it would have, at some distance but within easy reach, fifty to a hundred acres of ground where a modern dairy and a modern tannery would be conducted on strictly business but on national lines. Thus there would be no profits and no dividends to be paid and there would be also no loss incurred. In the long run such institutions dotted all over India would be a triumph of Hinduism and would be proof of Hindu earnestness about cow, that is, cattle protection and it would provide decent employment for thousands of men including educated men; for both dairy and tannery work requires expert scientific knowledge. Not Denmark but India should be a model State for the finest dairy experiments and India should not to her shame have to export nine crore rupees worth of dead cattle hide annually and for her own consumption use slaughtered cattle hide. If such a state of things is a shame for India it is a greater shame for Hindus. I wish that all the *goshala* committees will fake to heart the remarks I made in reply to the Giridih address and make their *goshala*s into ideal dairies and tanneries and a refuge for all worn out and maimed cattle (*Young India*, 22.10.1925, p. 361; *CWMG* 28: 369).

Every *goshala* or *pinjrapole* should have a tannery adequate to its needs attached to it. In other words, the manager in charge of every such institution should have a thorough knowledge of the immediate steps necessary for utilizing the remains of dead cattle. If this is done, the question, viz., how many heads of cattle should a particular *goshala* contain, won't arise at all.

I do not know what the rate of mortality of cattle in *goshalas* is, nor is it relevant to my proposition. So long as there is a single head of cattle in a *goshala*, its manager ought to know how to dispose of its remains after it is dead, just as he is expected to know how to look after it while it is alive.

Such humanitarian institutions for the protection of cattle as I have described should normally take charge of the remains of the cattle that might die in the village. Therein lies the interest of the cattle, the depressed classes and the general public alike. In villages where there are no *goshalas* or the concomitant tanneries, some local person who believes in cow protection should take it upon himself to get the carcasses removed to the nearest tannery or get the preliminary processes performed upon it and send the useful parts there.

The establishment of such tanneries as I have described does not require much capital outlay. Only some initial expenditure would be needed to train up workers for this work (*Young India*, 3.11.1927, p. 367; *CWMG* 33: 393-94).

Hand-pounding of Rice and Hand-grinding of Corn

In my writing on cent per cent *Swadeshi*, I have shown how some aspects of it can be tackled immediately with benefit to the starving millions both economically and hygienically. The richest in the land can share the benefit. Thus if rice can be pounded in the villages after the old fashion, the wages will fill the pockets of the rice pounding sisters and the rice-eating millions will get some sustenance from the unpolished rice instead of pure starch which the polished rice provides. Human greed, which takes no account of the health or the wealth of the people who come under its heels, is responsible for the hideous rice mills one sees in all the rice-producing tracts. If public opinion was strong, it would make rice mills an impossibility by simply insisting on unpolished rice and appealing to the owners of rice mills to stop a traffic that undermines the health of a whole nation and robs the poor people of an honest means of livelihood (*Harijan*, 26.10.1934, p. 292; *CWMG* 59: 226).

I regard the existence of power wheels for the grinding of corn in thousands of villages as the limit of our helplessness. I suppose India does not produce all the engines or grinding machines. . . . The planting of such machinery and engines on a large scale in villages is also a sign of greed. Is it proper to fill one's pockets in this manner at the expense of the poor? Every such machinery puts thousands of hand-*chakki*s out of work and takes away employment from thousands of housewives and artisans who make these *chakki*s. Moreover, the process is infective and will spread to every village industry. The decay of the latter spells too the decay of art. If it meant replacement of old crafts by new ones, one might not have much to say against it. But this is not what is happening. In the thousands of villages where power machinery exists, one misses the sweet music in the early morning of the grinders at work (*Harijan*, 10.3.1946, p. 34; *CWMG* 83: 196).

Machine Oil and Ghani Oil

Shri Jhaverbhai has found out why the machine oil is at all cheaper than the *ghani* oil. He gives three reasons, two of which are unavoidable. They are capital and the ability of the machine to extract the last drop of oil and that too in a shorter time than the *ghani*. These advantages are neutralized by the commission the owner of the oil mill has to pay to the middleman. But Shri Jhaverbhai cannot cope with the third reason, adulteration, unless he also takes to it. This naturally he will not do. He therefore suggests that adulteration should be dealt with by the law. This can be done by enforcing the Anti-adulteration Act if there is one or by enacting it by licensing oil mills.

Jhaverbhai has also examined the cause of the decline of the village *ghani*. The most potent cause is the inability of the oilman to command a regular supply of seeds. The villages are practically denuded of seeds after the season. The oilman has no money to store the seeds, much less to buy them in the cities. Therefore he has disappeared or is fast disappearing. Lakhs of *ghani*s are today lying idle causing a tremendous waste of the country's resources. Surely it is the function of the state to resuscitate the existing *ghani*s by conserving seeds in the places of their origin and making them available to the village oilman at reasonable rates. The government loses nothing by giving this aid. It can be given, so Shri Jhaverbhai contends, through cooperative societies or *panchayat*s. If this is done, Shri Jhaverbhai is of opinion, based on research, that *ghani* oil can compete with the machine product and the villager can be spared the infliction of the adulterated oil he gets today. It should be borne in mind that the only fat the villager gets, when he gets any, is what the oils can give him. To ghee he is generally a stranger (*Harijan*, 2.9.1939, p. 253; *CWMG* 70: 121).

Gur and Khandsari

Take the sugar industry. The largest major industry next to the textile is that of the manufacture of sugar. It stands in no need of our assistance. Sugar factories are fast multiplying. Popular agencies have done little to help the growth of this industry. It is indebted for its growth to favourable legislation. And today the industry is so prosperous and expanding that the production of jaggery is becoming a thing of the past. It is admittedly superior to refined sugar in nutritive value. It is this very valuable cottage industry that cries out for your help. This by itself furnishes large scope for research and substantial help. We have to investigate the ways and means of keeping it alive. This is but an illustration of what I mean (Interview to All-India Swadeshi League Deputation, 17.6.1934; *CWMG* 58: 89).

The advantages, attributed to toddy, are all available from other foodstuffs. Toddy is made out of *khajuri* juice. Fresh *khajuri* juice is not an intoxicant. It is known as *nira* in Hindustani and many people have been cured of their constipation as a result of drinking *nira*. I have taken it myself though it did not act as a laxative with me. I found that it had the same food value as sugar-cane juice. If one drinks a glass of *nira* in the morning instead of drinking tea, etc., he should not need anything else for breakfast. As in the case of sugar-cane juice, palm juice can be boiled to make palm jaggery. *Khajuri* is a variety of palm tree. Several varieties of palm grow spontaneously in our country. All of them yield drinkable juice. As *nira* gets fermented very quickly, it has to be used up immediately and therefore on the spot. Since this condition is difficult to fulfil except to a limited extent, in practice, the best use of *nira* is to convert it into palm jaggery. Palm jaggery can well replace sugar-cane jaggery. In fact some people prefer it to the latter. One advantage of palm jaggery over sugar-cane jaggery is that it is less sweet and therefore one can eat more of it. The All-India Village Industries Association has done a great deal to popularize palm jaggery, but much remains to be done. If the palms that are used for making toddy are used for making jaggery, India will never lack sugar and the poor will be able to get good jaggery for very little money. Palm jaggery can be converted into molasses and refined sugar. But the jaggery is much more useful than refined sugar. The salts present in the jaggery are lost in the process of refining. Just as refined wheat flour and polished rice lose some of their nutritive value because of the loss of the pericarp, refined sugar also loses some of the nutritive value of the jaggery. One may generalize that all foodstuffs are richer if taken in their natural state as far as possible (*Key to Health*, 18.12.1942; *CWMG* 77: 15-16).

Bee-keeping

Bee-keeping seems to me to possess immense possibilities. Apart from its village value, it may be cultivated as a hobby by moneyed young men and women. They will add to the wealth of the country and produce the finest health-giving sugar for themselves. If they are philanthropically inclined, they can distribute it as health-giving food among sickly Harijan children. There is no reason why it should be a luxury of the rich or an expensive medicinal vehicle in the hands of the *hakims* and *vaidyas*. No doubt, my hope is based on inferences drawn from meagre data. Experiments that may be made in villages and in cities by young men and women should show whether honey can become a common article of food or has to remain an uncommon article, which it is today (*Harijan*, 1.2.1935, p. 407; *CWMG* 60: 149).

Tanning

It is estimated that rupees nine crores worth of raw hide is annually exported from India and that much of it is returned to her in the shape of manufactured articles. This means not only a material, but also an intellectual drain. We miss the training we should receive in tanning and preparing the innumerable articles of leather we need for daily use.

Tanning requires great technical skill. An army of chemists can find scope for their inventive talent in this great industry. There are two ways of developing it. One for the uplift of Harijans living in the villages and eking out a bare sustenance, living in filth and degradation and consigned to the village ghetto, isolated and away from the village proper. This way means part reorganization of villages and taking art, education, cleanliness, prosperity, and dignity to them. This means also the application of chemical talent to village uplift. Tanning chemists have to discover improved methods of tanning. The village chemist has to stoop to conquer. He has to learn and understand the crude village tanning, which is still in existence but which is fast dying owing to neglect, not to say want of support. But the crude method may not be summarily scrapped, at least not before a sympathetic examination. It has served well for centuries. It could not have done so, if it had no merit. The only research I know in this direction is being carried on in Santiniketan, and then it was started at the now defunct Ashram at Sabarmati. I have not been able to keep myself in touch with the progress of the experiment at Santiniketan. There is every prospect of its revival at the Harijan Ashram, which the Sabarmati Ashram has now become. These experiments are mere drops in the ocean of possible research.

Cow-preservation is an article of faith in Hinduism. No Harijan worth his salt will kill cattle for food. But, having become untouchable, he has learnt the evil habit of eating carrion. He will not kill a cow but will eat with the greatest relish the flesh of a dead cow. It may be physiologically harmless. But psychologically there is nothing, perhaps, so repulsive as carrion-eating. And yet, when a dead cow is brought to a Harijan tanner's house, it is a day of rejoicing for the whole household. Children dance round the carcass, and as the animal is flayed, they take hold of bones or pieces of flesh and throw them at one another. As a tanner, who is living at the Harijan Ashram, describing the scenes at his own now forsaken home, tells me, the whole family is drunk with joy at the sight of the dead animal. I know how hard I have found it working among Harijans to wean them from the soul-destroying habit of eating carrion. Reformed tanning means the automatic disappearance of carrion-eating.

Well, here is the use for high intelligence and the art of dissection. Here is also a mighty step in the direction of cow-preservation. The cow must die at the hands of the butcher, unless we learn the art of increasing her capacity of milk-giving, unless we improve her stock and make her male progeny more useful for the field and carrying burdens, unless we make scientific use of all her excreta as manure and unless, when she and hers die, we are prepared to make the wisest use of her hide, bone, flesh, entrails, etc.

I am just now concerned only with the carcass. It is well to remember here that the village tanner, thank God, has to deal only with the carcass, not the slaughtered animal. He has no means of bringing the dead animal in a decent way. He lifts it, drags it, and this injures the skin and reduces the value of the hide. If the villagers and the public knew the priceless and noble service the tanner renders, they will provide easy and simple methods of carrying it, so as not to injure the skin at all.

The next process is flaying the animal. This requires great skill. I am told that none, not even surgeons, do this work better or more expeditiously than the village tanner does with his village knife. I have inquired of those who should know. They have not been able to show me an improvement upon the village tanner. This is not to say that there is none better. I merely give the reader the benefit of my own very limited experience. The village tanner has no use for the bone. He throws it away. Dogs hover round the carcass, whilst it is flayed, and take away some, if not all, of the bones. This is a dead loss to the country. The bones, if powdered fine, apart from their other uses, make valuable manure. What remains after the dogs have taken away their share is transported to foreign countries and returns to us in the shape of handles, buttons, etc.

The second way is urbanizing this great industry. There are several tanneries in India doing this work. Their examination is outside the scope of this article. This urbanization can do little good to the Harijans, much less to the villages. It is a process of double drain from the villages. Urbanization in India is slow but sure death for her villages and villagers. Urbanization can never support 90 per cent of India's population, which is living in her 7,00,000 villages. To remove from these villages tanning and such other industries is to remove what little opportunity there still is for making skilled use of the hand and the head. And when the village handicrafts disappear, the villagers working only with their cattle on the field, with idleness for six or four months in the year, must, in the words of Madhusudan Das, be reduced to the level of the beast and be without proper nourishment, either of the mind or the body, and, therefore, without joy and without hope.

Here is work for the cent per cent Swadeshi-lover and scope for the harnessing of technical skill to the solution of a great problem. The work fells three apples with one throw. It serves the Harijans, it serves the villagers, and it means honourable employment for the middle-class intelligentsia who are in search of employment. Add to this the fact that intelligentsia have a proper opportunity of coming in direct touch with the villagers (*Harijan*, 7.9.1934, pp. 236-37; *CWMG* 58: 417-19).

Soap

They (villagers) would prepare their own soap from *sajji*-clay. That soap will not have the luring fragrance of soaps turned out in the factories of Tata and Godrej. Its packing also will not be so attractive. But it will have the quality of self-sufficiency even like *khadi* (*CWMG* 78: 193).

Hand-made Paper

I was told that, if there were enough orders, the paper could be supplied at the same cost as the mill-made article. I know that hand-made paper can never supply the daily-growing demand for paper. But lovers of the seven hundred thousand villages and their handicrafts will always want to use hand-made paper, if it is easily procurable. Those who use hand-made paper know that it has a charm of its own. Who does not know the famous Ahmedabad paper? What mill-made paper can beat it in durability or polish!

The account-books of the old style are still made of that paper. But it is probably a perishing industry like many such others. With a little encouragement, it ought never to perish. If there was supervision, the processes might be improved and the defects that are to be noticed with some of this hand-made paper may be easily removed. The economic condition of the numberless people engaged in these little-known trades is well worth investigating. They will surely allow themselves to be guided and advised and feel thankful to those who would take interest in them (*Harijan* 14.9.1934, p. 241; *CWMG* 58: 444-45).

Ink

The ink with which I am writing comes from Tenali. It supports about twelve workers. It is making headway against odds. I had three more specimens sent to me by different makers, all no doubt struggling like the Tenali group. They interested me. I entered into correspondence with them. But I could do no more for them. A Swadeshi organization will examine the samples of these inks in a scientific manner and guide them and encourage the most promising ones. It is a good and growing industry, requiring expert chemical knowledge (*Harijan*, 14.9.1934, p. 241; *CWMG* 58: 444).

Village Exhibitions

If we want the villages to survive and become strong and prosperous the exhibition should be free from all pomp and ostentation characteristic of the cities. There should be no place for city games and entertainments. The exhibition should not under any circumstances be reduced to a show or a source of revenue. It should not become an attraction for traders. No goods should be sold, not even *khadi* or other products of village industry. The exhibition should become a place of education. It should be interesting and should be such that, having seen it, a villager should be inspired to learn some craft or other. There should be people to explain to the visitors the shortcomings of the villages in general and how to remove them. They should be shown what progress has been made since the work for the uplift of villages was first taken up. There should also be someone to instruct the villagers in the ways in which village life can be made artistic. Let us now see how the exhibition can be made to conform to these requirements.

1. There should be two models of villages: one showing an average village as it is today and the other showing the village as it will look after the reform. The reformed village will be clean, with dwellings, village paths, general surroundings, fields, and the condition of the livestock greatly improved. There should be maps and charts and books to show how different industries are carried on and developed.

2. Guidance should be provided on how the various village industries are run and where the necessary tools for them are to be had or manufactured. There should also be demonstrations of the working of the various industries. Along with this we should show the following things:

   (a) Ideal village diet

   (b) The difference between cottage industry and machine industry

   (c) An object lesson in animal husbandry

   (d) A model latrine

   (e) An art section

   (f) Organic manure vs chemical fertilizers

   (g) The utilization of hides and bones of dead cattle

   (h) Folk music and folk dances

   (i) Village sports, gymnastics, and wrestling

   (j) Nayee Talim

   (k) Village herbs

   (l) Village maternity home

If further things can be added keeping in view the guidelines enunciated above, this may be done. The things I have enumerated should be taken only as illustrations. I have not included here the various village crafts, of which the *charkha* is the first. Without them the exhibition should be considered as of no value. (Village Industries Exhibition: What It Should Be Like, *Hindustan*, 2.9.1946; *CWMG* 85: 236-38).

11

A Plea for the Village Cart

Shri Ishvarbhai S. Amin of Baroda sent me a long note on animal power vs machine power. From it I copy the following relevant portion:

> Animal power is not costlier than machine power in fields or short distance work and hence can compete with the latter in most cases. The present-day tendency is towards discarding animal power in preference to machine power.
>
> Take for example a bullock-driven cart, costing Rs. 100 and Rs. 200 for the bullocks. The bullocks can drive the cart at least 15 miles per day with a load of 16 Bengal maunds on rough sandy village roads. This service will cost . . . in total Rs 1/6 per day. A one-ton motor lorry will cost for 15 miles . . . Rs. 2/12, i.e., Rs. 1/6 per cartload of 16 Bengal

> maunds. . . . A motor lorry may compete when it has to carry loads at a stretch for a long distance on a good metal road, where bullock carts seem too slow and uneconomical. . . . It is the slowness only which goes against the bullock cart. . . . If a farmer has his own cart and travels in it, he has not to spend anything in the form of ready money but uses the produce of his own field in producing power by feeding bullocks. Really grass and grain should be looked upon by the farmer as his petrol, and the cart the motor lorry, and bullocks the engine converting grass into power. The machine will neither consume grass nor will it yield manure, an article of vast importance. Then the villager has to have his bullocks; in any case he has his grass. And if he has a cart, he is maintaining the village carpenter and the blacksmith; and if he is keeping a cow, he is maintaining a hydrogenation plant converting vegetable oil into solid butter or ghee and also at the same time a bullock manufacturing machine — thus serving a twofold purpose.

The invasion of the motor lorry may or may not succeed. It would be wisdom if intelligent workers will study the pros and cons and definitely guide the villagers. Shri Ishvarbhai's note should provoke the thought of all village workers in the direction indicated in it (*Harijan*, 3.7.1937, p. 168; *CWMG* 65: 364-65).

Motor vs. Cart

Gram Udyog Patrika for August (1946) examines the respective merits of motor vans and carts for village propaganda. Those who will read the whole argument should send for the *Patrika*. I give below the most important part of the argument:

> We have been asked whether District Boards and other such local bodies, who wish to set apart a certain amount of money for village work, will do well to invest in motor vans for propaganda work of various kinds in villages. . . . The question is whether speeding up matters by the use of motor vans which can visit more than one village in a night will suit the purpose.
>
> In all our expenditure, especially when that expenditure is undertaken expressly for the benefit of the village people, it is necessary to see that the money spent goes back to the villager. District and Local Boards obtain their money from the people, and their purchases must be such as will help to circulate money among the people. . . .
>
> What the villager needs above all is profitable employment. We steadily deprive him of employment by buying imported articles, and by way of compensation give him lectures, magic lantern shows and tinned music all at his expense, and pat ourselves on the back that we are working for

> his welfare. Can anything be more absurd?
>
> Compare with this what happens if in the place of the motor-van the much despised bullock-cart were used. . . . It can reach the most remote villages which a motor-lorry cannot do. It costs only a fraction of the money required for a van, so that many bullock-carts can be bought, if necessary, to serve groups of villages in the district. The money spent on them goes to the village carpenter, blacksmith, and cart-driver. Not a pie of it need go out of the district. . . .
>
> Rural work and motor vans appear, therefore, to go ill together. What is required is steady, constructive effort, not lightning speed and empty show. We would commend to Local Boards and public institutions genuinely interested in village welfare to start by using only village-made goods, to study the conditions which are steadily producing poverty in the villages, and concentrate on removing them one by one. When every side of village life needs intensive, well-considered effort, it seems a waste of public money to throw it away on methods which attempt to bring about village uplift overnight.

It is to be hoped that those who interest themselves in village welfare will take to heart the obvious argument advanced in favour of the cart. It will be cruel to destroy the village economy through the very agency designed for village welfare (*Harijan*, 16.9.1939, p. 276; *CWMG* 70: 118-19).

Bullocks as Means of Transport

The bullocks are the means of transport everywhere in our villages and have not ceased to be such even in a place like Simla. The railway train and the motor-car go there, but all along the mountain road I found bullocks trudging up and down dragging heavily-laden carts. It seems as if this means of transport is part of our lives and our civilization. And the bullock has to endure if our handicraft civilization is to endure. . . . You have to find out whose animals are the best and to discover how he manages to keep them so well. You will find out whose cow gives the largest amount of milk and discover how he keeps her and feeds her. You may fix some prize for the best bullock and the best cow in the village. . . . I am telling you that without model cattle we cannot have a model village (*Harijan*, 15.9.1940, p. 282; *CWMG* 72: 432).

12

Currency, Exchange, and Tax

Under my system, again, it is labour which is the current coin, not metal. Any person, who can use his labour has that coin, has wealth. He converts his labour into cloth, he converts his labour into grain. If he wants peraffin oil, which he cannot himself produce, he uses his surplus grain for getting the oil. It is exchange of labour on free, fair, and equal terms — hence it is no robbery. You may object that this is a reversion to the primitive system of barter. But is not all international trade based on the barter system? (*Harijan*, 2.11.1934, p. 302; *CWMG* 48: 166).

Then every village of India will almost be a self-supporting and self-contained unit exchanging only such necessary commodities with other villages where they are not locally producible (Speech on Swadeshi at Missionary Conference, Madras, 14.2.1916; *The Hindu*, 28.2.1916; *CWMG* 13: 223).

My experience tells me that if *khadi* is to become universal, both in cities and in villages, it should be made available only in exchange of yarn. Today one anna's worth of yarn in the rupee is demanded. But this is only the beginning. When people have understood and learnt how to spin, then *khadi* will be given only in full exchange for yarn spun. I hope that as days go by everyone will himself insist on buying *khadi* only in exchange of yarn (Why Khadi For Yarn and Not For Money? July 1945; *Gram Uduog Patrika*, vol. 1, pp. 352-54; *CWMG* 81: 55).

Labour, as a matter of fact, is as much money as metallic coin. In the same way as money, labour is also put in a particular concern. Just as without money your labour will be useless, so also all the money of the world will be useless if there is no labour (*Harijan*, 2.2.1934, p. 6; *The Bombay Chronicle*, 3.2.1934; *CWMG* 57: 57).

Self-sufficiency does not mean narrowness. To be self-sufficient is not to be altogether self-contained. In no circumstances would we be able to produce all the things we need nor do we aim at doing so. So though our aim is complete self-sufficiency, we shall have to get from outside the village what we cannot produce in the village; we shall have to produce more of what we can in order thereby to obtain in exchange what we are unable to produce (Discussion with Shrikrishnadas Jaju, 10.10.1944; *CWMG* 78: 171).

Just as gold and silver emerge as coin from the mint, so *khadi* alone should emerge from a yarn bank (*Harijan*, 7.7.1946, p. 209; *CWMG* 84: 381).

In my part of India shells and seedless dried almonds were used as coins accepted by the people and the state treasury. They had no intrinsic value. They were a measure of people's deep poverty. They could not afford the lowest metal coin. Five shells would buy them a little vegetable or a needle. I have suggested a measure which will not be a mere token but which will have always an intrinsic value which will also be its market value. In that sense it will be an ideal measure. For the present and by way of experiment I have suggested a warp length of a single thread of yarn as the lowest measure and to be used in dealings principally with the spinners and generally with *khadi* lovers. The spinners can have all their daily wants supplied as against fixed quantity of yarn. Stores will need to be maintained by the A.I.S.A. in combination with the A.I.V.I.A. and ultimately with those who will give their cooperation. As I conceive it, the system can be worked only if it is decentralized. This is not its demerit but merit (*Harijan*, 18.1.1942, p. 5; *Sevagram*, 13.1.1942; *CWMG* 75: 215).

Payment (of tax) in labour invigorates the nation. Where people perform labour voluntarily for the service of society, exchange of money becomes unnecessary. The labour of collecting the taxes and keeping accounts is saved and the results are equally good (*Harijan*, 25.3.1939, p. 65; *CWMG* 69: 53).

13
Village Sanitation

Divorce between intelligence and labour has resulted in criminal negligence of the villages. And so, instead of having graceful hamlets dotting the land, we have dung-heaps. The approach to many villages is not a refreshing experience. Often one would like to shut one's eyes and stuff one's nose; such is the surrounding dirt and offending smell. If the majority of Congressmen were derived from our villages, as they should be, they should be able to make our villages models of cleanliness in every sense of the word. But they have never considered it their duty to identify themselves with the villagers in their daily lives. A sense of national or social sanitation is not a virtue among us. We may take a kind of a bath, but we do not mind dirtying the well or the tank or the river by whose side or in which we perform ablutions. I regard this defect as a great vice which is responsible for the disgraceful state of our villages and the sacred banks of the sacred rivers and for diseases that spring from insanitation (*Constructive Programme: Its Meaning and Place*, 13.12.1941; *CWMG* 75: 153).

The things to attend to in the villages are cleaning tanks and wells and keeping them clean, getting rid of dung-heaps. If the workers will begin the work themselves, working like paid *bhangis* from day to day and always letting the villagers know that they are expected to join them so as ultimately to do the whole work themselves, they may be sure that they will find that the villagers will sooner or later cooperate. . . .

Lanes and streets have to be cleansed of all the rubbish, which should be classified. There are portions which can be turned into manure, portions which have simply to be buried and portions which can be directly turned into wealth. Every bone picked up is valuable raw material from which useful articles can be made or which can be crushed into rich manure. Rags and waste-paper can be turned into paper, and excreta picked up are golden manure for the village fields. . . . Village tanks are promiscuously used for bathing, washing clothes, and drinking and cooking purposes. Many village tanks are also used by cattle. Buffaloes are often to be seen wallowing in them. The wonder is that, in spite of this sinful misuse of village tanks, villages have not been destroyed by epidemics. It is the universal medical evidence that this neglect to ensure purity of the water supply of villages is responsible for many of the diseases suffered by the villagers.

This, it will be admitted, is a gloriously interesting and instructive service, fraught with incalculable benefit to the suffering humanity of India. I hope it is clear from my description of the way in which the problem should be tackled, that, given willing workers who will wield the broom and the shovel with the same ease and pride as the pen and the pencil, the question of expense is almost wholly eliminated. All the outlay that will be required is confined to a broom, a basket, a shovel and a pickaxe, and possibly some disinfectant. Dry ashes are, perhaps, as effective a disinfectant as any that a chemist can supply. But here let philanthropic chemists tell us what is the most effective and cheap village disinfectant that villagers can improvise in their villages (*Harijan*, 8.2.1935, p. 416; *CWMG* 60: 190-92).

14

Village Health and Hygiene

In a well-ordered society the citizens know and observe the laws of health and hygiene. It is established beyond doubt that ignorance and neglect of the laws of health and hygiene are responsible for the majority of diseases to which mankind is heir. The very high death rate among us is no doubt due largely to our gnawing poverty, but it could be mitigated if the people were properly educated about health and hygiene.

Mens sana in corpore sano is perhaps the first law for humanity. A healthy mind in a healthy body is a self-evident truth. There is an inevitable connection between mind and body. If we were in possession of healthy minds, we would shed all violence and, naturally obeying the laws of health, we would have healthy bodies without an effort (*Constructive Programme: Its Meaning and Place*, 13.12.1941; *CWMG* 75: 156).

It is necessary to understand the meaning of the word health . . . "In Health" means body ease. He is a healthy man whose body is free from all disease; he carries on his normal activities without fatigue. Such a man should be able with ease to walk ten to twelve miles a day, and perform ordinary physical labour without getting tired. He can digest ordinary simple food. His mind and his senses are in a state of harmony and poise (*Key to Health*, 18.12.1942; *CWMG* 77: 1).

The fundamental laws of health and hygiene are simple and easily learnt. The difficulty is about their observance. Here are some:

Think the purest thoughts and banish all idle and impure thoughts.

Breathe the freshest air day and night. Establish a balance between bodily and mental work.

Stand erect, sit erect, and be neat and clean in every one of your acts, and let these be an expression of your inner condition.

Eat to live for service of fellow-men. Do not live for indulging yourselves. Hence your food must be just enough to keep your mind and body in good order. Man becomes what he eats.

Your water, food, and air must be clean, and you will not be satisfied with mere personal cleanliness, but you will infect your surroundings with the same threefold cleanliness that you will desire for yourselves (*Constructive Programme: Its Meaning and Place*, 13.12.1941; *CWMG* 75: 156).

Nature Cure for Disease

The practice of nature cure does not require high academic qualifications or much erudition. Simplicity is the essence of universality. Nothing that is meant for the benefit of the millions requires much erudition. The latter can be acquired only by the few and therefore can benefit the rich only. But India lives in her seven lakhs of villages — obscure, tiny, out-of-the-way villages — where the population in some cases hardly exceeds a few hundreds, very often not even a few scores. I would like to go and settle down in some such village. That is real India, my India, for which I live. You cannot take to these humble people the paraphernalia of highly qualified doctors and hospital equipment. In simple, natural remedies and Ramanama lies their only hope (*Harijan*, 7.4.1946, p. 69; *CWM* 83: 315).

I hold that where the rules of personal, domestic and public sanitation are strictly observed and due care is taken in the matter of diet and exercise, there should be no occasion for illness or disease. Where there is absolute purity, inner and outer, illness becomes impossible. If the village people could but understand this, they would not need doctors, *hakims* or *vaidyas*. . . . Nature cure implies an ideal mode of life and that in its turn presupposes ideal living conditions in towns and villages. The name of God is, of course, the hub round which the nature cure system revolves (*Harijan*, 26.5.1946, p. 153; *CWMG* 84: 180).

Nature cure implies that the treatment should be the cheapest and the simplest possible. The ideal is that such treatment should be carried out in the villages. The villagers should be able to provide the necessary means and equipment. What cannot be had in the villages should be procured. Nature cure does mean a change for the better in one's outlook on life itself. It means regulation of one's life in accordance with the laws of health. It is not a matter of taking the medicine free from the hospital or for fees. A man who takes free treatment from the hospital accepts charity. The man who accepts nature cure never begs. Self-help enhances self-respect. He takes steps to cure himself by eliminating poison from the system and takes precautions against falling ill in the future. . . . Right diet and balanced diet are necessary. Today our villages are as bankrupt as we are ourselves. To produce enough vegetables, fruits, and milk in the villages, is an essential part of the nature cure scheme. Time spent on this should not be considered a waste. It is bound to benefit all the villagers and ultimately the whole of India (*Harijan*, 2.6.1946, p. 165; *CWMG* 84: 203).

As I conceived nature cure for the villagers, it should confine itself to such remedies as are available in the villages and should do without the aid of electricity and ice. This would be the limit of this treatment. Such work can only be for a person like me who has become a villager and whose heart is in the villages even though he be living in a city (*Harijan*, 11.8.1946, p. 257; *CWMG* 85: 118).

This thing [my nature cure] is meant for villagers, for the villages. Therefore there is no place here for a microscope or an X-ray plant. Nor is there any place in nature cure for quinine, emetin, penicillin, and such other drugs. Village sanitation, domestic cleanliness, personal hygiene, and health care have the first place and also full scope, the underlying idea being that this done there can be no disease. And in case disease has occurred, Ramanama is the basic remedy besides observance of the laws of nature. As long as the practitioner has not personally experienced the efficacy of Ramanama, the latter treatment cannot be applied universally. Hence, the treatment in the form of Ramanama cannot all of a sudden become universal. However, the endeavour is to cure disease with the help of whatever energy we can churn out of the five elements, viz., earth, water, ether, fire, and air. And this is where, I think, nature cure ends. Hence the experiment that is being now conducted at Uruli Kanchan is one of instructing the villagers in the art of health care and curing those who are sick with the help of the five elements. This includes the use of herbs locally available in Uruli, whenever the need is felt. It also covers restrictions as to diet [Letter to D.D. Joshi, 1.8.1946; *CWMG* 85: 105-06 (its another translation from Gujarati is in *Harijan*, 11.8.1946, p. 260)].

The science of natural therapeutics is based on a use, in the treatment of disease, of the same five elements which constitute the human body (*Key to Health*, 18.12.1942; *CWMG* 77: 25-26).

Earth

Just lays great emphasis on the use of earth. I felt that I ought to give it a trial. For constipation, Just advises cold mud-poultices on the lower abdomen. I made a mud-poultice by mixing clean, dry earth with water, packed it in a piece of thin cloth and kept it on the abdomen throughout the night. The result was most satisfactory (*Key to Health*, 18.12.1942; *CWMG* 77: 26).

The mud poultice should be three inches broad, six inches long and half an inch thick (*Key to Health*, 18.12.1942; *CWMG* 77: 26).

It is my experience that a mud-poultice applied to the head, relieves headache in most cases. I have tried it in hundreds of cases. Headache may be due to several causes, but whatever the cause, as a general rule, an application of mud-poultice relieves it for the time being.

Mud-poultices cure ordinary boils. I have applied mud to discharging abscesses as well. For these cases I prepare the poultice by packing the mud in a clean piece of cloth dipped in potassium permanganate lotion, and apply it to the abscess after washing clean with permanganate lotion. In the majority of cases this treatment results in complete cure. I do not remember a single case in which it has failed me. Mud application immediately relieves the pain of a wasp sting. I have used it in many cases of scorpion sting, though with much less success. (*Key to Health*, 18.12.1942; *CWMG* 77: 27).

In high fever, an application of mud-poultice on the head and abdomen is very useful. Although it does not always bring down the temperature, it does invariably soothe the patient and make him feel better, so that the patients themselves ask for these applications.

I have used it in several cases of typhoid fever. The fever no doubt runs its own course but mud applications seem to relieve restlessness and abate the suffering (*Key to Health*, 18.12.1942; *CWMG* 77: 27).

In Sevagram we have made free use of hot mud-poultices as a substitute for antiphlogistine. A little (mustard) oil and salt is added to the mud and it is heated sufficiently long to ensure sterilization (*Key to Health*, 18.12.1942; *CWMG* 77: 27).

It is safe to use soft alluvial clay, which is neither gritty nor sticky. One should never use earth taken from manured soil. Earth should be dried, pounded, and passed through a fine sieve. If there is any doubt as to its cleanliness, it should be well heated and thus sterilized (*Key to Health*, 18.12.1942; *CWMG* 77: 27-28).

Just writes that clean earth may be eaten in order to overcome constipation. Five to ten grams is the maximum dose. The rationale is said to be this. Earth is not digested. It acts as roughage and must pass out. The peristalsis thus stimulated pushes out the faecal matter as well. I have not tried it myself. Therefore those who wish to do so, should try it on their own responsibility. I am inclined to think that a trial or two is not likely to harm anyone (*Key to Health*, 18.12.1942; *CWMG* 77: 28).

Water

Hip bath and sitz bath are the most important of Kuhne's contributions to hydrotherapy. He has devised a special tub for use though one can do without it. Any tub thirty to thirty-six inches long according to the patient's height generally serves the purpose. Experience will indicate the proper size. The tub should be filled with fresh cold water so that it does not overflow when the patient sits in it. In summer the water may be iced, if it is not cold enough to give a gentle shock to the patient. Generally, water kept in earthen jars overnight answers the purpose. Water can also be cooled by putting a piece of cloth on the surface of the water and then fanning it vigorously. The tub should be kept against the bathroom wall and a plank put in the tub to serve as back rest. The patient should sit in the tub keeping his feet outside. Portions of the body outside water should be kept well covered so that the patient does not feel cold. After the patient is comfortably seated in the tub, gentle friction should be applied to his abdomen with a soft towel. This bath can be taken for five to thirty minutes. When it is over, the body should be rubbed dry and the patient put to bed.

Hip bath brings down the temperature in high fever, and given in the manner described above, it never does any harm, and may do much good. It relieves constipation and improves digestion. The patient feels fresh and active after it. In cases of constipation, Kuhne advises a brisk walk for half an hour immediately after the bath. It should never be given on a full stomach.

I have tried hip baths on a fairly large scale. They have proved efficacious in more than 75 cases out of 100. In cases of hyperpyrexia, if the patient's condition permits of his being seated in the tub, the temperature immediately invariably falls at least by two to three degrees, and the onset of delirium is averted. (*Key to Health*, 18.12.1942; *CWMG* 77: 28-29).

Now about the sitz or friction bath. The organ of reproduction is one of the most sensitive parts of the body. There is something illusive about the sensitiveness of the glans penis and the foreskin. Anyway, I know not how to describe it. Kuhne has made use of this knowledge for therapeutic purposes. He advises application of gentle friction to the outer end of the external sexual organ by means of a soft wet piece of cloth, while cold water is being poured. In the case of the male the glans penis should be covered with the foreskin before applying friction. The method advised by Kuhne is this: A stool should be placed in a tub of cold water so that the seat is just about the level of the water in the tub. The patient should sit on the stool with his feet outside the tub and apply gentle friction to the sexual organ which just touches the surface of the water in the tub. This friction should never cause pain. On the contrary the patient should find it pleasant and feel rested and peaceful at the end of the bath. Whatever the ailment, the sitz bath makes the patient feel better for the time being. Kuhne places sitz baths higher than hip baths. I have had much less experience of the former than of the latter. The blame, I think, lies mostly with myself. I have been lax. Those whom I advised sitz baths, have not been patient with the experiment, so that I cannot express an opinion on the efficacy of these baths, based on personal experience. It is worth a trial by everyone. If there is any difficulty about finding a tub, it is possible to pour water from a jug or a *lota* and take the friction bath. It is bound to make the patient feel rested and peaceful. As a general rule people pay scant attention to the cleansing of the sexual organ. The friction-bath will easily achieve that end. Unless one is particularly careful, dirt accumulates between the foreskin and the glans penis. This must be removed. Insistence on keeping the sexual organ clean and patiently following the treatment outlined above will make the observance of *brahmacharya* comparatively easier. It will result in making the local nerve endings less sensitive and unwanted seminal emissions less likely. To say the least it is very unclean to allow seminal emissions to occur. Greater insistence on cleanliness should and will cause a feeling of revulsion against the process and make one much more particular than otherwise in taking all the precautions to avoid them (*Key to Health,* 18.12.1942; *CWMG* 77: 30-31).

Wet-sheet packs are also useful in the treatment of prickly heat, urticaria, other forms of skin irritation, measles, smallpox, etc. I have tried them on a fairly large scale for these ailments. For smallpox and measles cases, I added enough potassium permanganate to the water to give it a light pink colour. The sheet used for these patients should afterwards be sterilized by soaking it in boiling water and leaving it in it till it cools down sufficiently and then washed with soap and water.

In cases where circulation has become sluggish, the leg muscles feel sore and there is a peculiar ache and feeling of discomfort in the legs, an ice massage does a lot of good. This treatment is more effective in summer months. Massaging a weak patient with ice in winter might prove a risky affair.

Now a few words about the therapeutics of hot water. An intelligent use of hot water gives relief in many cases. Application of iodine is a very popular remedy for all sorts of injuries and the like. Application of hot water will prove equally effective in most of these cases. Tincture of iodine is applied on swollen and bruised areas. Hot water fomentations are likely to give equal relief, if not more. Again, iodine drops are used in cases of earache. Irrigation of the ear with warm water is likely to relieve the pain in most of these cases. The use of iodine is attended with certain risks. The patient may have allergy towards the drug. Iodine mistaken for something else and taken internally might prove disastrous. But there is no risk whatsoever in using hot water. Boiling water is as good a disinfectant as tincture of iodine. I do not mean to belittle the usefulness of iodine or suggest that hot water can replace it in all cases. Iodine is one of the few drugs which I regard most useful and necessary, but it is an expensive thing. The poor cannot afford to buy it and moreover its use cannot be safely entrusted to everybody. But water is available everywhere. We may not despise its therapeutic value because it is obtained so easily. Knowledge of common household remedies often proves a godsend in many a crisis. (*Key to Health,* 18.12.1942; *CWMG* 77: 32-33).

Steam is a more valuable therapeutic agent. It can be used to make the patient sweat. Steambaths are most useful in cases of rheumatism and other joint pains. The easiest as well as the oldest method of taking steam bath is this: Spread a blanket or two on a sparsely but tightly woven cot and put one or two covered vessels full with boiling water under it. Make the patient lie flat on the cot and cover him up in such a way that the ends of the covering blankets touch the ground and thus prevent the steam from escaping and the outside air from getting in. After arranging everything as above, the lid from the vessels containing boiling water is removed and steam soon gets on to the patient lying between the blankets. It may be necessary to change the water once or twice. Usually in India people keep an *angithi* under pots to keep the water boiling. This ensures continuous discharge of steam, but is attended with risk of accidents. A single spark might set fire to the blankets or to the cot and endanger the patient's life. Therefore it is advisable to use the method described by me even though it might seem slow and tedious.

Some people add *neem* leaves or other herbs to the water used for generating steam. I do not know if such an addition increases the efficiency of steam. The object is to induce sweat and that is attained by mere steam. In cases of cold feet or aching of legs, the patient should be made to sit with his feet and legs immersed up to the knees in as hot water as he can bear. A little mustard powder can be added to the water. The foot bath should not last for more than fifteen minutes. This treatment improves the local circulation and gives immediate relief. In cases of common cold and sore throat a steam kettle which is very much like an ordinary tea kettle with a long nozzle can be used for applying steam to the nose or throat. A rubber tube of required length can be attached to any ordinary kettle for this purpose. (*Key to Health*, 18.12.1942; *CWMG* 77: 33-34).

Akash

Akash might be taken for the empty space surrounding the earth and the atmosphere round it (*Key to Health*, 18.12.1942; *CWMG* 77: 34).

Sky or the ether is the abode of the atmosphere. One can pump out air, say, from an empty bottle and create a vacuum, but who can pump out the vacuum itself? That is *akash*. This *akash* we have to make use of to maintain or to regain health (*Key to Health*, 18.12.1942; *CWMG* 77: 35).

The more we utilize this great element *akash* the healthier we will be. The first lesson to be learnt is this, that we should not put any partition between ourselves and the sky — the infinite — which is very near and yet very far away. If our bodies could be in contact with the sky without the intervention of houses, roofs, and even clothes, we are likely to enjoy the maximum amount of health. This is not possible for everyone. But all can and should accept the validity of the statement and adapt life accordingly. To the extent that we are able to approach the state in practice, we will enjoy contentment and peace of mind (*Key to Health*, 1812.1942; *CWMG* 77: 35).

This train of thought will make the thinker keep his surroundings as open as possible. He will not fill the house with unnecessary furniture and will use the minimum of clothes that are necessary. Many households are so packed with all sorts of unnecessary decorations and furniture which one can very well do without, that a simple living man will feel suffocated in those surroundings. They are nothing but means of harbouring dust, bacteria, and insects (*Key to Health*, 18.12.1942; *CWMG* 77: 36).

One should make it a point to sleep in the open. Sufficient covering should be used to protect oneself against the inclemencies of the weather — against cold and dew. In rainy season an umbrella-like roof without walls should be used for keeping the rain out. For the rest, the starlit blue canopy should form the roof so that whenever one opens one's eyes, one can feast them on the ever-changing beautiful panorama of the heavens. One will never tire of the scene and it will not dazzle or hurt one's eyes. On the contrary, it will have a soothing effect on one. To watch the different starry constellations floating in their majesty is a feast for the eyes. One who establishes contact with the stars as living witnesses to all his thoughts will never allow any evil or impurity to enter his mind and will enjoy peaceful, refreshing sleep.

Let us descend from the *akash* above to the *akash* within and immediately about us. Thus the skin has millions of pores. If we fill up the empty space within these pores, we simply die. Any clogging of the pores, therefore, must interfere with the even flow of health. Similarly we must not fill up the digestive tract with unnecessary foodstuffs. We should eat only as much as we need and no more. Often one overeats or eats indigestible things without being aware of it. An occasional fast, say once a week or once a fortnight, will enable one to keep the balance even. If one is unable to fast for the whole day, one should miss one or more meals during the day. That Nature abhors a vacuum is only partially true. Nature constantly demands a vacuum. The vast space surrounding us is a standing testimony of the truth (*Key to Health*, 18.12.1942; *CWMG* 77: 36-37).

Sun

Sunbath is as useful as ordinary water bath though the two cannot replace one another. In cases of debility and slow circulation, exposure of the uncovered body to the morning sun acts as an all-round general tonic and accelerates the metabolism. The morning sun has the largest amount of ultra-violet rays which are a most effective component of the sun's rays. If the patient feels cold, he should lie in the sun covered up and gradually expose more and more of his body as he gets used to it. One can also take the sunbath pacing up and down in the sun without any clothes on, in a private enclosure or in any other place away from public gaze. If such a place is not within easy reach, one can just cover up the private parts by tying up a piece of cloth or a *langoti* and expose the rest of his body to the sun (*Key to Health,* 18.12.1942; *CWMG* 77: 37).

I know of many persons who have been benefited by sunbaths. It is a well-known treatment for tuberculosis. . . . Sun treatment often results in the cure of intractable ulcers (*Key to Health,* 18.12.1942; *CWMG* 77: 38).

Air

This fifth element is as important as the four already discussed in the foregoing pages. The human body which is composed of the five elements cannot do without any one of them. Therefore no one should be afraid of air. Generally, wherever our people go, they make devices to keep out the sun and the air and thus jeopardize their health. If one cultivates the habit of living in the open in the midst of plenty of fresh air, right from childhood, the body will become hardened and one will never suffer from cold in the head and the like ailments (*Key to Health,* 18.12.1942; *CWMG* 77: 38).

The Extent of Medical Aid

With the commencement of the activities of the A.I.V.I.A., medical aid finds a prominent, if not almost an exclusive, place on the programme of many workers. The aid consists in distributing among the villagers free medicines, Allopathic, Ayurvedic, Unani or Homoeopathic, or all combined. Druggists selling these medicines are quite ready to oblige workers approaching them for a few medicines, which cost them a trifle and which, in their opinion, may, if they look at the gift selfishly; bring them more buyers. The poor patients become the victims of well-intentioned but ill-informed or over-enthusiastic workers. More than three-fourths of these drugs are not only useless but imperceptibly, if not perceptibly, harmful to the bodies into which they are put. Where they do bring some temporary relief to the patients, their substitutes are as a rule to be found in the village bazaar. . . .

Therefore, A.I.V.I.A. is leaving medical relief of the kind I have described severely alone. Its primary care is education in matters of health as well as of economy. Are not both interrelated? Does not health mean wealth for the millions? There bodies, not their intellects, are the primary instruments of wealth. The Association, therefore, seeks to teach people how to prevent disease. It is well known that the food of the millions is very deficient in its nourishing value. What they do eat they misuse. Their knowledge of hygiene is practically nil. Village sanitation is as bad as it well can be. If, therefore, these defects can be put right and the people imbibe the simple rules of hygiene, most of the ailments they suffer from must disappear without further effort or any outlay of money. Hence the Association does not contemplate opening dispensaries. Investigations are now being made to find out what the villages can supply in the shape of drugs. Satisbabu's cheap remedies are an effort in that direction. But incredibly simple though they are, he is experimenting with a view to making drastic reduction in the number of these remedies, without diminishing their efficacy. He is studying the bazaar drugs and testing them and comparing them with the corresponding drugs in the British pharmacopoeia. The desire is to wean the simple villagers from the awe of mysterious pills and infusions (*Harijan*, 5.4.1935, p. 59; *CWMG* 60: 384-85).

Where cases of fever, constipation or such common diseases come to village workers for help, they will certainly have to render such help as they can. Where one is certain of the diagnosis, there is no doubt that the village bazaar medicine is the cheapest and best. If one must stock drugs, castor oil, quinine and boiling water are the best medical agents. Castor oil may be locally procurable. The *senna* leaf may serve the same purpose. Quinine one should use sparingly. Every fever does not require quinine treatment. Nor does every fever yield to quinine. Most fevers will disappear after a fast or a semi-fast. Abstention from cereals, pulses and milk, and taking fruit juices or boiling raisin water, even boiling *gur* water with fresh lemon juice or tamarind, is a semi-fast. Boiling water is a most powerful medical agent. It may move the bowels, it will induce perspiration and therefore abate fever; it is the safest and cheapest disinfectant. In every case where it is required to be drunk, the water must be allowed to cool till it is fairly bearable to the skin. Boiling does not mean mere heating. The water begins to bubble and evaporate after it is on the boil.

Where the workers do not know for certain what to do, they must allow the local *vaidya* to have full sway. Where he is non-existent or unreliable and the workers know a philanthropic doctor nearby, they may invoke his assistance. But they will find that the most effective way of dealing even with disease is to attend to sanitation. Let them remember that nature is the finest physician. They may be sure that nature is repairing what man has damaged. She appears to have become powerless when man continuously hampers her. Then she sends death — her last and peremptory agent to destroy what is beyond repair — and provides a fresh garment for the wearer. Sanitary and hygienic workers are therefore the best helpers of the best physician every person has, whether he knows it or not (*Harijan,* 11.5.1935, p. 100; *CWMG* 61: 49-50).

Medical relief as part of village work or social service plays an important part in many reports I receive from numerous organizations. This relief consists of medicines supplied to patients who from far and near flock to any person who advertises himself as distributor of such relief. It means no trouble on the part of the medicine man. He need not have much or any knowledge of diseases and the symptoms. Medicines he often receives free from obliging chemists. Donations are always to be had from indiscriminate donors whose conscience is satisfied if they can distribute their charity in aid of suffering humanity.

This social service has appeared to me to be the laziest form of service and often even mischievous. It works mischief when the patient is expected to do nothing save to swallow the drug given to him. He is none the wiser for having received the medicine. If anything, he is worse off than before. The knowledge that he can get for nothing, or for a trifle, a pill or a potion that will correct certain irregularities will tempt him to repeat them. The fact that he gets such aid free of charge will undermine his self-respect which should disdain to receive anything for nothing.

There is another type of medical relief which is a boon. It is given by those who know the nature of diseases, who will tell the patients why they have their particular complaints and will also tell them how to avoid them. Such servants will rush to assist at all odd hours of the day or night. Such discriminating relief is an education in hygiene, teaching the people how to observe cleanliness and to gain health. But such service is rare. In the majority of cases mention of medical relief in reports is a piece of advertisement leading to donations for other activities requiring perhaps as little exertion or knowledge as medical relief. I would therefore urge all workers in the social field, whether urban or rural, to treat their medical activity as the least important item of service. It would be better to aviod all mention of such relief. Workers would do well to adopt measures that would prevent disease in their localities. Their stock of medicines should be as small as possible. They should study the bazaar medicines available in their villages, know their reputed properties, and use them as far as possible. They will find as we are finding in Sindi (a village near Wardha) that hot water, sunshine, clean salt, and soda with an occasional use of castor oil or quinine answer most purposes. We make it a point to send all serious cases to the Civil Hospital. Patients flock to Mirabehn and receive lessons in hygiene and prevention of diseases. They do not resent this method of approach instead of simply being given a powder or a mixture (*Harijan*, 9.11.1935, p. 308; *CWMG* 62: 103-04).

15
Diet

Whilst it is true that man cannot live without air and water, the thing that nourishes the body is food. Hence the saying, food is life.

Food can be divided into three categories: vegetarian, flesh, and mixed. Flesh foods include fowl and fish. Milk is an animal product and cannot by any means be included in a strictly vegetarian diet. It serves the purpose of meat to a very large extent. In medical language it is classified as animal food. A layman does not consider milk to be animal food. On the other hand, eggs are regarded by the layman as a flesh food. In reality, they are not. Nowadays sterile eggs are also produced. The hen is not allowed to see the cock and yet it lays eggs. A sterile egg never develops into a chick. Therefore he who can take milk should have no objection to taking sterile eggs.

Medical opinion is mostly in favour of mixed diet although there is a growing school, which is strongly of the opinion that anatomical and physiological evidence is in favour of man being a vegetarian. His teeth, his stomach, intestines, etc., seem to prove that nature has meant man to be a vegetarian.

Vegetarian diet, besides grains, pulses, edible roots, tubers, and leaves, includes fruits, both fresh and dry. Dry fruit includes nuts like almond, pistachio, walnut, etc. I have always been in favour of pure vegetarian diet. But experience has taught me that in order to keep perfectly fit, vegetarian diet must include milk and milk products such as curds, butter, ghee, etc. This is a significant departure from my original idea. I excluded milk and ghee from my diet for six years. At that time I felt none the worse for the denial. But in the year 1918, as a result of my own ignorance, I was laid up with severe dysentery. I was reduced to a skeleton, but I stubbornly refused to take any medicine and with equal stubbornness refused to take milk or buttermilk. But I could not build up my body and pick up sufficient strength to leave the bed. I had taken a vow of not taking milk. A medical friend suggested that at the time of taking the vow, I could have had in mind only the milk of the cow and buffalo, why should the vow prevent me from taking goat's milk? My wife supported him and I yielded. Truly speaking, for one who has given up milk, though at the time of taking the vow only the cow and the buffalo were in mind, milk should be taboo. All animal milks have practically the same composition, though the proportion of the components varies in each case. So I may be said to have kept merely the letter, not the spirit of the vow. Be that as it may, goat's milk was produced immediately and I drank it. It seemed to bring me new life. I picked up rapidly and was soon able to leave the bed. On account of this and several similar experiences, I have been forced to admit the necessity of adding milk to the strict vegetarian diet. But I am convinced that in the vast vegetable kingdom there must be some kind, which, while supplying those necessary substances which we derive from milk and meat, is free from their drawbacks, ethical and other.

In my opinion there are definite drawbacks in taking milk or meat. In order to get meat we have to kill. And we are certainly not entitled to any other milk except the mother's milk in our infancy. Over and above the moral drawback, there are others, purely from the point of view of health. Both milk and meat bring with them the defects of the animal from which they are derived. Domesticated cattle are hardly ever perfectly healthy. Just like man, cattle suffer from innumerable diseases. Several of these are overlooked even when the cattle are subjected to periodical medical examinations. Besides, medical examination of all the cattle in India seems to be an impossible feat, at any rate for the present. I am conducting a dairy at the Sevagram Ashram. I can easily get help from medical friends. Yet I cannot say with certainty that all the cattle in the Sevagram Dairy are healthy. On the contrary, a cow that had been considered to be healthy by everybody was found to be suffering from tuberculosis. Before this diagnosis was made, the milk of that cow had been used regularly in the Ashram. The Ashram also takes milk from the farmers in the neighbourhood. Their cattle have not been medically examined. It is difficult to determine whether a particular specimen of milk is safe for consumption or not. We have to rest content with as much safety as boiling of the milk can assure us of. If the Ashram cannot boast of fool-proof medical examination of its cattle, and be certain of the safety of its dairy products, the situation elsewhere is not likely to be much better. What applies to the milch cattle applies to a much greater extent to the animals slaughtered for meat. As a general rule, man just depends upon luck to escape from such risks. He does not seem to worry much about his health. He considers himself to be quite safe in his medical fortress in the shape of doctors, *vaidyas*, and *hakims*. His main worry and concern is how to get wealth and position in society. This worry overshadows all the rest. Therefore so long as some selfless scientist does not, as a result of patient research work, discover a vegetable substitute for milk and meat, man will go on taking meat and milk.

Now let us consider mixed diet. Man requires food which can supply tissue-building substances to provide for the growth and daily wear and tear of the body. It should also contain something which can supply energy, fat, certain salts, and roughage to help the excretion of waste matter. Tissue-building substances are known as proteins. They are obtained from milk, meat, eggs, pulses, and nuts. The proteins contained in milk and meat, in others words the animal proteins, being more easily digestible and assimilable, are much more valuable than vegetable proteins. Milk is superior to meat. The medicos tell us that in cases where meat cannot be digested, milk is digested quite easily. For vegetarians milk, being the only source of animal proteins, is a very important article of diet. The proteins in raw eggs are considered to be the most easily digestible of all proteins.

But everybody cannot afford to drink milk or eat eggs. Nor are they available in every place. I would like to mention here a very important fact with regard to milk. Contrary to the popular belief, skimmed milk is a very valuable article of diet. There are times when it proves even more useful than whole milk. The chief function of milk is to supply animal proteins for tissue-building and tissue-repair. Skimming, while it partially removes the fats, does not affect the proteins at all. Moreover the available skimming instruments cannot remove all the fat from milk. Neither is there any likelihood of such an instrument being constructed.

The body requires other things besides milk, whole or skimmed. I give the second place to cereals — wheat, rice, *juwar, bajri*, etc. These are used as the staple diet. Different cereals are used as staple in different provinces of India. In many places, more than one kind of cereals are eaten at the same time; for instance, small quantities of wheat, *bajri* and rice are often served together just for the sake of taste. This mixture is not necessary for the nourishment of the body. It makes it difficult to regulate the quantity of food intake, and puts an extra strain upon digestion. As all these varieties supply starch mainly, it is better to take one only at a time. Wheat may well be described as the king among cereals. If we glance at the world map we find that wheat occupies the first place. From the point of view of health, if we can get wheat, rice and other cereals become unnecessary. If wheat is not available and *juwar*, etc., cannot be taken on account of dislike or difficulty in digesting them, rice has to be resorted to.

The cereals should be properly cleansed, ground on a grinding-stone, and the resulting flour used as it is. Sieving of the flour should be avoided. It is likely to remove the *bhusi* or the pericarp which is a rich source of salts and vitamins, both of which are most valuable from the point of view of nutrition. The pericarp also supplies roughage, which helps the action of the bowels. Rice grain being very delicate, nature has provided it with an outer covering or epicarp. This is not edible. In order to remove this inedible portion, rice has to be pounded. Pounding should be just sufficient to remove the epicarp or the outer skin of the rice grain. But machine-pounding not only removes the outer skin, but also polishes the rice by removing its pericarp. The explanation of the popularity of polished rice lies in the fact that polishing helps preservation. The pericarp is very sweet and unless it is removed, rice is easily attacked by certain organisms. Polished rice and wheat without its pericarp, supply us with almost pure starch. Important constituents of the cereals are lost with the removal of the pericarp. The pericarp of rice is sold as rice polishings. This and the pericarp of wheat can be cooked and eaten by themselves. They can be also made into *chapati*s or cakes. It is possible that rice *chapati*s may be more easily digestible than whole rice and in this form a lesser quantity may result in full satisfaction.

We are in the habit of dipping each morsel of the *chapati* in vegetable or *dal* gravy before eating it. The result is that most people swallow their food without proper mastication. Mastication is an important step in the process of digestion, especially that of starch. Digestion of starch begins on its coming into contact with saliva in the mouth. Mastication ensures a thorough mixing of food with saliva. Therefore starchy foods should be eaten in a relatively dry form, which results in a greater flow of saliva and also necessitates their thorough mastication.

After the starch-supplying cereals come the protein-supplying pulses — beans, lentils, etc. Almost everybody seems to think that pulses are an essential constituent of diet. Even meat-eaters must have pulses. It is easy to understand that those who have to do hard manual work and who cannot afford to drink milk, cannot do without pulses. But I can say without any hesitation whatsoever that those who follow sedentary occupations as, for instance, clerks, businessmen, lawyers, doctors, teachers, and those who are not too poor to buy milk, do not require pulses. Pulses are generally considered to be difficult to digest and are eaten in a much smaller quantity than cereals. Out of the varieties of pulses, peas, gram, and haricot beans are considered to be the most and *mung* and *masoor* (lentils) the least difficult to digest.

Vegetables and fruits should come third on our list. One would expect them to be cheap and easily available in India. But it is not so. They are generally considered to be delicacies meant for the city people. In the villages fresh vegetables are a rarity and in most places fruit is also not available. This shortage of greens and fruit is a slur on the administration of India. The villagers can grow plenty of green vegetables if they wish to. The question of fruit cannot be solved so easily. The land legislation is bad from the villagers' standpoint. But I am transgressing.

Among fresh vegetables, a fair amount of leafy vegetables must be taken every day. I do not include potatoes, sweet potatoes, *suran*, etc., which supply starch mainly, among vegetables. They should be put down in the same category as starch-supplying cereals. A fair helping of ordinary fresh vegetables is advisable. Certain varieties such as cucumber, tomatoes, mustard cress, and other tender leaves need not be cooked. They should be washed properly and then eaten raw in small quantities.

As for fruits, our daily diet should include the available fruits of the season, e.g., mangoes, *jambu*, guavas, grapes, pawpaws, limes — sweet or sour — oranges, *mosambi*, etc., should all be used in their season. The best time for taking fruit is early in the morning. A breakfast of fruit and milk should give full satisfaction. Those who take an early lunch may well have a breakfast of fruit only.

Banana is a good fruit. But as it is very rich in starch, it takes the place of bread. Milk, banana, and leafy vegetable make a perfect meal.

A certain amount of fat is also necessary. This can be had in the form of ghee or oil. If ghee can be had, oil becomes unnecessary. It is difficult to digest and is not so nourishing as pure *ghee*. An ounce and a half of *ghee* per head per day should be considered ample to supply the needs of the body. Whole milk also is a source of *ghee*. Those who cannot afford it should take enough oil to supply the need for fat. Among oils, sweet oil, groundnut oil, and coconut oil should be given preference. Oil must be fresh. If available, it is better to use hand-pressed oil. Oil and *ghee* sold in the bazaar are generally quite useless. It is a matter of great sorrow and shame. But so long as honesty has not become an integral part of business morals, whether through legislation or through education, the individuals will have to procure the pure article with patience and diligence. One should never be satisfied to take what one can get, irrespective of its quality. It is far better to do without ghee and oil altogether rather than to eat rancid oil and adulterated *ghee*. As in the case of fats, a certain amount of sugar is also necessary. Although sweet fruits supply plenty of sugar, there is no harm in taking one to one and a half ounces of sugar, brown or white, in the day. If one cannot get sweet fruits, sugar may become a necessity. But the undue prominence given to sweet things nowadays is wrong. City folk eat too much of sweet things. Milk puddings, milk sweets and sweets, of other kinds are consumed in large quantities. They are all unnecessary and are harmful except when taken in very small quantities. It may be said without any fear of exaggeration that to partake of sweetmeats and other delicacies, in a country where the millions do not even get an ordinary full meal, is equivalent to robbery.

What applies to sweets applies with equal force to *ghee* and oil. There is no need to eat food fried in ghee or oil. To use up ghee in making *puri*s and *laddu*s is thoughtless extravagance. Those who are not used to such food cannot eat these things at all. For instance, Englishmen on their first coming into our country cannot eat our sweets and fried foodstuffs. Those that do eat them, I have often seen, fall ill. Taste is acquired, not born with us. All the delicacies of the world cannot equal the relish that hunger gives to food. A hungry man will eat a dry piece of bread with the greatest relish, whereas one who is not hungry will refuse the best of sweetmeats.

Now let us consider how often and how much one should eat. Food should be taken as a matter of duty — even as a medicine — to sustain the body, never for the satisfaction of the palate. Thus pleasurable feeling comes from satisfaction of real hunger. Therefore we can say that relish is dependent upon hunger and not outside it. Because of our wrong habits and artificial way of living, very few people know what their system requires. Our parents who bring us into this world do not, as a rule, cultivate self-control. Their habits and their way of living influence the children to a certain extent. The mother's food during pregnancy is bound to affect the child. After that, during childhood the mother pampers the child with all sorts of tasty foods. She gives the child a little bit out of whatever she herself may be eating and the child's digestive system gets a wrong training from its infancy. Habits once formed are difficult to shed. There are very few who succeed in getting rid of them. But when the realization comes to man that he is his own bodyguard and his body has been dedicated to service, he desires to learn laws of keeping his body in a fit condition and tries hard to follow them. 9 September 1942.

We have now reached a point where we can lay down the amount of various foods required by a man of sedentary habits, which most men and women who will read these pages are.

Cow's milk	2 lb
Cereals (*wheat, rice, bajri*) in all	6 oz
Vegetables leaf	3 oz
Others	5 oz
Raw	1 oz
Ghee	1½ oz
Or butter	2 oz
Gur or white sugar	1½ oz

Fresh fruit according to one's taste and purse. In any case it is good to take two sour limes a day. The juice should be squeezed and taken with vegetables or in water, cold or hot.

All these weights are of raw stuff. I have not put down the amount of salt. It should be added afterwards according to taste.

Now, how often should one eat? Many people take two meals a day. The general rule is to take three meals: breakfast early in the morning and before going out to work, dinner at midday and supper in the evening or later. There is no necessity to have more than three meals. In the cities some people keep on nibbling from time to time. This habit is harmful. The digestive apparatus requires rest (*Key to Health*, 18.12.1942; *CWMG* 77: 6-13).

16

Village Protection

Peace Brigade

Some time ago I suggested the formation of a Peace Brigade whose members would risk their lives in dealing with riots, especially communal. The idea was that this Brigade should substitute the police and even the military. This reads ambitious. The achievement may prove impossible. Yet, if the Congress is to succeed in its nonviolent struggle, it must develop the power to deal peacefully with such situations. . . .

Let us therefore see what qualifications a member of the contemplated Peace Brigade should possess.

1. He or she must have a living faith in nonviolence. This is impossible without a living faith in God. A nonviolent man can do nothing save by the power and grace of God. Without it he won't have the courage to die without anger, without fear, and

without retaliation. Such courage comes from the belief that God sits in the hearts of all and that there should be no fear in the presence of God. The knowledge of the omnipresence of God also means respect for the lives of even those who may be called opponents or *goonda*s. This contemplated intervention is a process of stilling the fury of man when the brute in him gets the mastery over him.

2. This messenger of peace must have equal regard for all the principal religions of the earth. Thus, if he is a Hindu, he will respect the other faiths current in India. He must therefore possess a knowledge of the general principles of the different faiths professed in the country.
3. Generally speaking this work of peace can only be done by local men in their own localities.
4. The work can be done singly or in groups. Therefore no one need wait for companions. Nevertheless one would naturally seek companions in one's own locality and form a local brigade.
5. This messenger of peace will cultivate through personal service contacts with the people in his locality or chosen circle, so that when he appears to deal with ugly situations, he does not descend upon the members of a riotous assembly as an utter stranger liable to be looked upon as a suspect or an unwelcome visitor.
6. Needless to say, a peace bringer must have a character beyond reproach and must be known for his strict impartiality.
7. Generally there are previous warnings of coming storms. If these are known, the Peace Brigade will not wait till the conflagration breaks out but will try to handle the situation in anticipation.
8. Whilst, if the movement spreads, it might be well if there are some wholetime workers, it is not absolutely necessary that there should be. The idea is to have as many good and true men and women as possible. These can be had only if volunteers are drawn from those who are engaged in various walks of life but have leisure enough to cultivate friendly relations with the people living in their circle and otherwise possess the qualifications required of a member of the Peace Brigade.
9. There should be a distinctive dress worn by the members of the contemplated Brigade so that in course of time they will be recognized without the slightest difficulty.

These are but general suggestions. Each centre can work out its own constitution on the basis here suggested (*Harijan*, 18.6.1938, p. 152; *CWMG* 67: 125-27).

My Idea of a Police Force

Even in a nonviolent state a police force may be necessary. This, I admit, is a sign of my imperfect *ahimsa*. I have not the courage to declare that we can carry on without a police force as I have in respect of an army. Of course, I can and do envisage a state where the police will not be necessary; but whether we shall succeed in realizing it, the future alone will show.

The police of my conception will, however, be of a wholly different pattern from the present-day force. Its ranks will be composed of believers in nonviolence. They will be servants, not masters, of the people. The people will instinctively render them every help, and through mutual cooperation they will easily deal with the ever-decreasing disturbances. The police force will have some kind of arms, but they will be rarely used, if at all. In fact, the policemen will be reformers. Their police work will be confined primarily to robbers and dacoits. Quarrels between labour and capital and strikes will be few and far between in a nonviolent state, because the influence of the nonviolent majority will be so great as to command the respect of the principal elements in society. Similarly there will be no room for communal disturbances (*Harijan*, 1.9.1940, p. 265; *Sevagram*, 28.8.1940; *CWMG* 72: 403).

Nonviolent Volunteer Corps

Some time ago an attempt was made, at my instance, to form *shanti dal*s but nothing came of it. This lesson, however, was learnt, that the membership, in its very nature, of such organizations could not be large. Ordinarily, the efficient running of a large volunteer corps based on force implies the possibility of the use of force in the event of breach of discipline. In such bodies little or no stress is laid on a man's character. Physique is the chief factor. The contrary must obtain in nonviolent bodies in which character or soul force must mean everything and physique must take second place. It is difficult to find many such persons. That is why nonviolent corps must be small, if they are to be efficient. Such brigades may be scattered all over; there may be one each for a village or a *mohalla*. The members must know one another well. Each corps will select its own head. All the members will have the same status, but where everyone is doing the same work there must be one person under whose discipline all must come, or else the work will suffer. Where there are two or more brigades the leaders must consult among themselves and decide on a common line of action. In that way alone lies success.

If nonviolent volunteer corps are formed on the above lines, they can easily stop trouble. These corps will not require all the physical training given in *akhadas*, but a certain port of it will be necessary.

One thing, however, should be common to members of all such organizations and that is implicit faith in God. He is the only Companion and Doer. Without faith in Him these Peace brigades will be lifeless. By whatever name one calls God, one must realize that one can only work through His strength. Such a man will never take another's life. He will allow himself, if need be, to be killed and thereby live through his victory over death.

The mind of the man in whose life the realization of this law has become a living reality will not be bewildered in a crisis. He will instinctively know the right way to act.

In spite, however, of what I have said above, I would like to give some rules culled from my own experience:

1. A volunteer may not carry any weapons.
2. The members of a corps must be easily recognizable.
3. Every volunteer must carry bandages, scissors, needle and thread, surgical knife, etc., for rendering first aid.
4. He should know how to carry and remove the wounded.
5. He should know how to put out fires, how to enter a fire area without getting burnt, how to climb heights for rescue work and descend safely with or without his charge.
6. He should be well acquainted with all the residents of his locality. This is a service in itself.
7. He should recite Ramanama ceaselessly in his heart and persuade others who believe to do likewise.

. . . Man often repeats the name of God parrot-wise and expects fruit from so doing. The true seeker must have that living faith which will not only dispel the untruth of parrot-wise repetition from within him but also from the hearts of others (*Harijan*, 5.5.1946, p. 113; *CWMG* 84: 66-67).

17
The Village Worker

The Ideal Village Worker

I propose to speak to you about the ideal of work and life that you have to keep in view and work towards.

You are here not for a career in the current sense of the term. Today man's worth is measured in rupees, annas, pies,and a man's educational training is an article of commerce. If you have come with that measure in mind, you are doomed to disappointment. At the end of your studies you may start with an honorarium of ten rupees and end with it. You may not compare it with what a manager of a great firm or a high official gets.

We have to change the current standards. We promise you no earthly careers, in fact we want to wean you from ambition of that kind. You are expected to bring your food-bill within Rs. 6 a month. The food-bill of an I.C.S. may come to Rs. 60 a month, but that does not mean that he is or will be on that account physically or intellectually or morally superior to you. He may be for all his sumptuous living even inferior in all these respects. You have come to this institution because, I presume, you do not value your qualifications in metal. You delight in giving your service to the country for a mere pittance. A man may earn thousands of rupees on the Stock Exchange but may be thoroughly useless for our purposes. He would be unhappy in our humble surroundings and we should be unhappy in his. We want ideal labourers in the country's cause. They will not bother about what food they get, or what comforts they are assured by the villagers whom they serve. They will trust to God for whatever they need, and will exult in the trials and tribulations they might have to undergo. This is inevitable in our country where we have 7,00,000 villages to think of. We cannot afford to have a salaried staff of workers who have an eye to regular increments, provident funds, and pensions. Faithful service of the villagers is its own satisfaction.

Some of you will be tempted to ask if this is also the standard for the villagers. Not by any means. These prospects are for us servants and not for the village folk our masters. We have sat on their backs all these years, and we want to accept voluntary and increasing poverty in order that our masters' lot may be much better than it is today. We have to enable them to earn much more than they are earning today. That is the aim of the Village Industries Association. It cannot prosper unless it has an ever-increasing number of servants such as I have described. May you be such servants. (*Harijan*, 23.5.1936, p. 19; *The Bombay Chronicle*, 11.5.1936; *CWMG* 62: 381-82).

Requisite Qualifications

[The following qualifications are prescribed by Gandhiji, as essential for every *satyagrahi*.]

1. He must have a living faith in God, for He is his only Rock.
2. He must believe in truth and nonviolence as his creed and therefore have faith in the inherent goodness of human nature which he expects to evoke by his truth and love expressed through his suffering.
3. He must be leading a chaste life and be ready and willing for the sake of his cause to give up his life and his possessions.
4. He must be a habitual *khadi*-wearer and spinner. This is essential for India.
5. He must be a teetotaller and be free from the use of other intoxicants in order that his reason may be always unclouded and his mind constant.
6. He must carry out with a willing heart all the rules of discipline as may be laid down from time to time. The qualifications are not to be regarded as exhaustive. They are illustrative only.
7. He should carry out the jail rules unless they are specially devised to hurt his self-respect.

The qualifications are not to be regarded as exhaustive. They are illustrative only (*Harijan*, 25.3.1939, p. 64; *CWMG* 69: 70).

His Duties

1. Every worker shall be a habitual wearer of *khadi* made from self-spun yarn or certified by the A.I.S.A. and must be a teetotaller. If a Hindu, he must have abjured untouchability in any shape or form in his own person or in his family and must be a believer in the ideal of inter-communal unity, equal respect, and regard for all religions and equality of opportunity and status for all irrespective of race, creed, or sex.
2. He shall come in personal contact with every villager within his jurisdiction.
3. He shall enroll and train workers from amongst the villagers and keep a register of all these.

4. He shall keep a record of his work from day to day.
5. He shall organize the villages so as to make them self-contained and self-supporting through their agriculture and handicrafts.
6. He shall educate the village folk in sanitation and hygiene and take all measures for prevention of ill health and disease among them.
7. He shall organize the education of the village folk from birth to death along the lines of Nayee Talim, in accordance with the policy laid down by the Hindustani Talimi Sangh.
8. He shall see that those whose names are missing on the statutory voters' roll are duly entered therein.
9. He shall encourage those who have not yet acquired the legal qualification, to acquire it for getting the right of franchise. (*Harijan*, 15.2.1948, p. 32; *CWMG* 90: 528).

Village Work

The centre of the village worker's life will be the spinning wheel. . . . The idea at the back of *khadi* is that it is an industry supplementary to agriculture and coextensive with it. . . . The spinning wheel cannot be said to have been established in its own proper place in our life, until we can banish idleness from our villages and make every village home a busy hive. . . .

The worker will not only be spinning regularly but will be working for his bread with the adze or the spade or the last, as the case may be. All his hours minus the eight hours of sleep and rest will be fully occupied with some work. He will have no time to waste. He will allow himself no laziness and allow others none. His life will be a constant lesson to his neighbours in ceaseless and joy-giving industry. . . . Our compulsory or voluntary idleness has to go. If it does not go, no panacea will be of any avail, and semi-starvation will remain the eternal problem that it is. He who eats two grains must produce four. Unless the law is accepted as universal, no amount of reduction in population would serve to solve the problem. If the law is accepted and observed, we have room enough to accommodate millions more to come.

The village worker will thus be a living embodiment of industry. He will master all the processes of *khadi*, from cotton-sowing and picking to weaving, and will devote all his thought to perfecting them. If he treats it as a science, it won't jar on him, but he will derive fresh joy from it every day, as he realizes more and more its great possibilities. If he will go to the village as a teacher, he will go there no less as a learner. He will soon find that he has much to learn from the simple villagers. He will enter into every detail of village life, he will discover the village handicrafts and investigate the possibilities of their growth and their improvement. He may find the villagers completely apathetic to the message of *khadi*, but he will, by his life of service, compel interest and attention. Of course, he will not forget his limitations and will not engage in, for him, the futile task of solving the problem of agricultural indebtedness.

Sanitation and hygiene will engage a good part of his attention. His home and his surroundings will not only be a model of cleanliness, but he will help to promote sanitation in the whole village by taking the broom and the basket round.

He will not attempt to set up a village dispensary or to become the village doctor. These are traps which must be avoided. I happened during my Harijan tour to come across a village where one of our workers who should have known better had built a pretentious building in which he had housed a dispensary and was distributing free medicine to the villages around. In fact, the medicines were being taken from home to home by volunteers and the dispensary was described as boasting a register of 1,200 patients a month! I had naturally to criticize this severely. That was not the way to do village work, I told him. His duty was to inculcate lessons of hygiene and sanitation in the village folk and thus to show them the way of preventing illness, rather than attempt to cure them. I asked him to leave the palace-like building and to hire it out to the Local Board and to settle in thatched huts. All that one need stock in the way of drugs is quinine, castor oil, iodine, and the like. The worker should concentrate more on helping people realize the value of personal and village cleanliness and maintaining it at all cost.

Then he will interest himself in the welfare of the village Harijans. His home will be open to them. In fact, they will turn to him naturally for help in their troubles and difficulties. If the village folk will not suffer him to have the Harijan friends in his house situated in their midst, he must take up his residence in the Harijan quarters.

A word about the knowledge of the alphabet. It has its place, but I should warn you against a misplaced emphasis on it. Do not proceed on the assumption that you cannot proceed with rural instruction without first teaching the children or adults how to read and write. Lots of useful information on current affairs, history, geography, and elementary arithmetic, can be given by word of mouth before the alphabet is touched.

The eyes, the ears, and the tongue come before the hand. Reading comes before writing, and drawing before tracing the letters of the alphabet. If this natural method is followed, the understanding of the children will have a much better opportunity of development than when it is under check by beginning the children's training with the alphabet.

The worker's life will be in tune with the village life. He will not pose as a litterateur buried in his books, loath to listen to details of humdrum life. On the contrary, the people, whenever they see him, will find him busy with his tools — spinning wheel, loom, adze, spade, etc. — and always responsive to their meanest inquiries. He will always insist on working for his bread. God has given to everyone the capacity of producing more than his daily needs and, if he will only use his resourcefulness, he will not be in want of an occupation suited to his capacities, however poor they may be. It is more likely than not that the people will gladly maintain him, but it is not improbable that in some places he may be given a cold shoulder. He will still plod on. It is likely that in some villages he may be boycotted for his pro-Harijan proclivities. Let him in that case approach the Harijans and look to them to provide him with food. The labourer is always worthy of his hire and, if he conscientiously serves them, let him not hesitate to accept his food from the Harijans always, provided that he gives more than he takes. In the very early stages, of course, he will draw his meagre allowance from a central fund where such is possible. . . . Remember that our weapons are spiritual. It is a force that works irresistibly, if imperceptibly. Its progress is geometrical rather than arithmetical. It never ceases so long as there is a propeller behind. The background of all your activities has, therefore, to be spiritual. Hence the necessity for the strictest purity of conduct and character.

You will not tell me that this is an impossible programme, that you have not the qualifications for it. That you have not fulfilled it so far should be no impediment in your way. If it appeals to your reason and your heart, you must not hesitate. Do not fight shy of the experiment. The experiment will itself provide the momentum for more and more effort. (*Harijan*, 31.8.1934, pp. 229-30; *CWMG* 58: 305-09).

Items of Village Work

The very first problem the village worker will solve is its sanitation. It is the most neglected of all the problems that baffle workers and that undermine physical well-being and breed disease. If the worker became a voluntary *bhangi*, he would begin by collecting night-soil and turning it into manure and sweeping village streets. He will tell people how and where they should perform daily functions and speak to them on the value of sanitation and the great injury caused by the neglect. The worker will continue to do the work whether the villagers listen to him or no (*Harijan*, 9.1.1937, p. 383; *CWMG* 64: 218).

If rural reconstruction were not to include rural sanitation, our villages would remain the muck-heap that they are today. Village sanitation is a vital part of village life and is as difficult as it is important. It needs a heroic effort to eradicate age-long insanitation. The village worker who is ignorant of the science of village sanitation, who is not a successful scavenger, cannot fit himself for village service.

It seems to be generally admitted that without the new or basic education the education of millions of children in India is well-nigh impossible. The village worker has, therefore, to master it, and become a basic education teacher himself.

Adult education will follow in the wake of basic education as a matter of course. Where this new education has taken root, the children themselves become their parents' teachers. Be that as it may, the village worker has to undertake adult education also.

Woman is described as man's better half. As long as she has not the same rights in law as man, as long as the birth of a girl does not receive the same welcome as that of a boy, so long we should know that India is suffering from partial paralysis. Suppression of woman is a denial of *ahimsa*. Every village worker will, therefore, regard every woman as his mother, sister or daughter as the case may be, and look upon her with respect. Only such a worker will command the confidence of the village people.

It is impossible for an unhealthy people to win *swaraj*. Therefore we should no longer be guilty of the neglect of the health of our people. Every village worker must have a knowledge of the general principles of health.

Without a common language no nation can come into being. Instead of worrying himself with the controversy about Hindi-Hindustani and Urdu, the village worker will acquire a knowledge of the *Rashtrabhasha*, which should be such as can be understood by both Hindus and Muslims.

Our infatuation about English has made us unfaithful to provincial languages. If only as penance for this unfaithfulness the village worker should cultivate in the villagers a love of their own speech. He will have equal regard for all the other languages of India, and will learn the language of the part where he may be working, and thus be able to inspire the villagers there with a regard for their own speech.

The whole of this programme will, however, be a structure on sand if it is not built on the solid foundation of economic equality. Economic equality must never be supposed to mean possession of an equal amount of worldly goods by everyone. It does mean, however, that everyone will have a proper house to live in, sufficient and balanced food to eat, and sufficient *khadi* with which to cover himself. It also means that the cruel inequality that obtains today will be removed by purely nonviolent means (*Harijan*, 18.8.1940, pp. 252-53; *CWMG* 72: 380-81).

A Talk to Village Workers

Khadi will certainly occupy the centre of the village industries. But remember that we have to concentrate on making the villages self-sufficing in *khadi*. Out of self-sufficing *khadi* will follow commercial *khadi* as a matter of course. . . .

You will of course take up any other industry available in villages and for which you can find a market, care being taken that no shop has to be run at a loss and no article produced for which there is no market. Give eight hours of your day to any home craft you like and show to the villagers that as you earn your wage, even so can they earn it by eight hours' work. . . .

You will also not take a companion to work with you. Our policy is to send a single worker to a village or group of villages. That will enable him to bring his resourcefulness into full play. He may pick out any number of companions from the village itself. They will work under his direction, but he will be mainly responsible for the village under his charge.

Let us not be tempted by the allurements of the machine age, let us concentrate on rendering our own body-machines perfect and efficient instruments of work, and let us get the best out of them. This is your task. Go ahead with it, without flinching (*Harijan*, 2.11.1935, p. 302; *CWMG* 62: 59-60).

Fear Complex

Many workers are so frightened of village life that they fear that if they are not paid by some agency they will not be able to earn their living by labouring in villages, especially if they are married and have a family to support. In my opinion this is a demoralizing belief. No doubt, if a person goes to a village with the city mentality and wants to live in villages the city life, he will never earn enough unless he, like the city people, exploits the villagers. But if a person settles in a village and tries to live like the villagers, he should have no difficulty in making a "living by the sweat of his brow". He should have confidence that if the villagers who are prepared to toil all the year round in the traditional unintelligent manner can earn their living, he must also earn at least as much as the average villager. This he will do without displacing a single villager, for he will go to a village as a producer, not as a parasite.

If the worker has the ordinary size family, his wife and one other member should be full-time workers. Such a worker won't immediately have the muscle of the villager, but he will more than make up for the deficiency by his intelligence, if only he will shed his diffidence and fear complex. He would be doing productive work, and not be a mere consumer, unless he gets an adequate response from the villagers so as to occupy the whole of his time in serving them. In that case he will be worth the commission on the additional production of the villagers induced by his effort. But the experience of the few months that the village work has gone on under the aegis of the A.I.V.I.A. shows that the response from the villagers will be very slow and that the worker will have to become a pattern of virtue and work before the villagers. That will be the best object-lesson for them which is bound to impress them sooner or later provided that he lives as one of them and not as a patron seated amongst them to be adored from a respectful distance.

The question, therefore, is: what remunerative work can he do in the village of his choice? He and the members of the family will give some time to cleaning the village, whether the villagers help him or not, and he will give them such simple medical assistance as is within his power to give. Every person can prescribe a simple opening drug or quinine, wash a boil or wound, wash dirty eyes and ears, and apply a clean ointment to a wound. I am trying to find out a book that will give the simplest directions in the ordinary cases occurring daily in the villages. Anyway these two things must be an integral part of village work. They ought not to occupy more than two hours of his time per day. The village worker has no such thing as an eight hours' day. For him the labour for the villager is a labour of love. For his living, therefore, he will give eight hours at least in addition to the two hours. It should be borne in mind that under the new scheme propounded by the A.I.S.A. and A.I.V.I.A. all labour has an equal minimum value. Thus a carder who works at his bow for one hour and turns out the average quantity of cards will get exactly the same wage that the weaver, the spinner or the paper-maker would, for the given quantity of their respective works per hour. Therefore, the worker is free to choose and learn whatever work he can easily do, care being always taken to choose such labour whose product is easily saleable in his village or the surrounding area or is in demand by the Associations.

One great need in every village is an honest shop where unadulterated foodstuffs and other things can be had for the cost price and a moderate commission. It is true that a shop, be it ever so small, requires some capital. But a worker who is at all known in the area of his work should command sufficient confidence in his honesty to enable him to make small wholesale purchases on credit.

I may not take these concrete suggestions much further. An observant worker will always make important discoveries and soon know what labour he can do to earn a living and be at the same time an object-lesson to the villagers whom he is to serve. He will therefore have to choose labour that will not exploit the villagers, that will not injure their health or morals but will teach the villagers to take up industries to occupy their leisure hours and add to their tiny incomes. His observations will lead him to direct his attention to the village wastes including weeds and the superficial natural resources of the village. He will soon find that he can turn many of them to good account. If he picks up edible weeds, it is as good as earning part of his food. Mirabehn has presented me with a museum of beautiful marble-like stones which serve several useful purposes as they are, and I would soon convert them into bazaar articles if I had leisure and would invest into simple tools to give them different shapes. Kakasaheb had, given to me, split bamboo waste that was destined to be burnt, and with a rude knife he turned some of it into paper knives and wooden spoons both saleable in limited quantities. Some workers in Maganwadi occupy their leisure in making envelopes out of waste paper blank on one side.

The fact is the villagers have lost all hope. They suspect that every stranger's hand is at their throats and that he goes to them only to exploit them. Divorce between intellect and labour has paralysed their thinking faculty. Their working hours they do not use to the best advantage. The worker should enter such villages full of love and hope, feeling sure that where men and women labour unintelligently and remain unemployed half the year round, he, working all the year round and combining labour with intelligence, cannot fail to win the confidence of the villagers and earn his living honestly and well by labouring in their midst.

"But what about my children and their education?" says the candidate worker. If the children are to receive their education after the modern style, I can give no useful guidance. If it be deemed enough to make them healthy, sinewy, honest, intelligent villagers, any day able to earn their livelihood in the home of their parents' adoption, they will have their all-round education under the parental roof and withal they will be partly earning members of the family from the moment they reach the years of understanding and are able to use their hands and feet in a methodical manner. There is no school equal to a decent home and no teachers equal to honest virtuous parents. Modern high school education is a dead weight on the villagers. Their children will never be able to get it, and thank God they will never miss it if they have the training of the decent home. If the village worker is not a decent man or woman, capable of conducting a decent home, he or she had better not aspire after the high privilege and honour of becoming a village worker (*Harijan*, 23.11.1935, pp. 324-25; *CWMG* 62: 131-33).

Village Workers Questions

I

[The village workers gave a list of questions to Gandhiji and requested him to enlighten them.]

The first question was about the duties of the village workers. The only duty of the village worker was to serve the villagers, said Gandhiji, and he could best serve them if he kept the eleven vows [nonviolence, truth, non-stealing, *brahmacharya*, non-possession, body-labour, control of the palate, fearlessness, equal respect for all religions, *swadeshi* (restricting oneself to the use and service of one's nearest surroundings in preference to those more remote) and spirit of unexclusive brotherhood] in front of him as a beacon-light.

The second question was about the livelihood of the village worker. How was he to earn it? Was he to draw an allowance from an institution, or to earn it by labouring for it, or to depend upon the village for it? The ideal way, said Gandhiji, was to depend upon the village. There was no shame therein, but humility. There was no scope for self-indulgence either, for he could not think of a village which would encourage or tolerate self-indulgence. All that the worker need do was to work for the village all his working hours, and to collect whatever grain and vegetables he needed from the village. He might collect a little money too (for postage and other monetary expenditure) if he should need it, though Gandhiji did not think he could not do without it. The village would willingly support him if he had gone there at the invitation of the village. He could conceive an occasion when the villagers might not be able to tolerate his views and withdraw their support, as, for instance, they did when he admitted untouchables in the Satyagraha Ashram in 1915. Then he should work for his living. It was no use depending on an institution.

The third question was about body-labour. The village worker was in the village to do as much body-labour as possible and to teach the villagers to outgrow idleness. He might do any kind of labour, but give preference to scavenging. Scavenging was certainly a productive labour. He liked some of the workers' insistence on devoting at least half an hour to work entirely of service and of a productive kind. Scavenging certainly came under that category. Also grinding; for money saved is money got.

The fourth question was about maintaining a diary. Gandhiji had no doubt that the village worker must be prepared to account for every minute of his waking hours and must fill them with work and mention it distinctly in his diary. A real diary was a mirror of the diarist's mind and soul, but many might find it difficult to make a truthful record of their mind's activities. In that case they might confine themselves to a record of their physical activities. But it should not be done in a haphazard way. Simply saying, "Worked in the kitchen" would not do. One may have whiled away one's time in the kitchen. Specific items of work should be mentioned.

The fifth question was about work among Dublas who work more or less as serfs in certain parts of Gujarat. Service of Dublas, said Gandhiji, meant readiness to share their toil and their hardships, and to get into touch with their masters and to see that they dealt with them justly and kindly.

Summing up, Gandhiji said:

The village worker will leave politics alone. He may become a Congress member, but he may not take part in an election campaign. He has his work cut out for himself. The Village Industries Association and the Spinners' Association were both created by the Congress and yet they work independently of the Congress. That is why they and their members steer clear of all Congress politics. That is the nonviolent way.

He will also leave village factions alone. He must go and settle there determined to do without most of the things he does not do without in a city. If I sit down in a village I should have to decide what things I should not take with me in the village, however inherently harmless those things may be. The question is whether those things will sort well or ill with the life of an ordinary villager. He will be incorruptible and stand like a rock against the inroad of temptations and save the village from them. Even one pure soul can save a whole village, as one Vibhishana saved Lanka. Sodom and Gomorrah were not destroyed so long as there was one pure soul left in them. That is why I said long ago that I would far rather that India perished than sacrifice truth in order to save it (*Harijan*, 29.2.1936, pp. 18-19; *CWMG* 62: 202-04).

II

[In answer to a question if a village worker can allow himself milk, fruit, and vegetables which villagers cannot afford, Gandhiji wrote:]

The main thing to be borne in mind by the village worker is that he is in the village for the villagers' service, and it is his right and his duty to allow himself such articles of diet and other necessaries as would keep him fit and enable him to fulfil his function. This will necessarily involve the acceptance of a higher standard of living by the village worker, but I have an impression that the villagers do not grudge the worker these necessary things. The worker's conscience is the test. He must be self-restrained, he will eat nothing in order to indulge his palate, he will go in for no luxuries, and will fill all his waking hours with work of service. In spite of this, it is likely that a handful of people will cavil at his mode of life. We have to live that criticism down. The diet I have suggested is not quite unobtainable in a village, with a certain amount of labour. Milk can generally be obtained, and there are numerous fruits, e.g. *ber, karamda, mhora* flower, which are easily available, but which we count of no value because they are so easily available. There are all kinds of leaves available which grow wild in our villages, which we do not use because of sheer ignorance or laziness (if not snobbery). I am myself using numerous varieties of these green leaves which I had never tried before, but which I find I should have used. It is quite possible to make a cow in a village pay for her upkeep and maintenance. I have not tried the experiment but I think it should be possible. I have also an impression that it is not impossible for the villagers to obtain and live on the same articles of diet as the village workers and thus to adopt the same standard of life (*Harijan*, 24.8.1935, p. 223; *CWMG* 61: 358-59).

III

In almost all villages there are parties and factions. When we draft local help, whether we wish it or not, we become involved in local power politics. How can we steer clear of this difficulty? Should we try to bypass both parties and carry on work with the help of outside workers? Our experience has been that such work becomes entirely contingent upon outside aid and crumbles down as soon as the latter is withdrawn. What should we do then to develop local initiative and foster local cooperation?

A. Alas for India that parties and factions are to be found in the villages as they are to be found in our cities. And when power politics enter our villages with less thought of the welfare of the villages and more of using them for increasing the parties' own power, this becomes a hindrance to the progress of the villagers rather than a help. I would say that whatever be the consequence, we must make use as much as possible of local help and if we are free from the taint of power politics, we are not likely to go wrong. Let us remember that the English-educated men and women from the cities have criminally neglected the villages of India which are the backbone of the country. The process of remembering our neglect will induce patience. I have never gone to a single village which is devoid of an honest worker. We fail to find him when we are not humble enough to recognize any merit in our villagers. Of course, we are to steer clear of local politics and this we shall learn to do when we accept help from all parties and no parties, wherever it is really good. I would regard it as fatal for success to bypass villagers. As I knew this very difficulty I have tried rigidly to observe the rule of one village, one worker except that where he or she does not know Bengali, an interpreter's help has been given. I can only say that this system has so far answered the purpose. I must, therefore, discount your experience. I would further suggest that we have got into the vicious habit of coming to hasty conclusions. Before pronouncing such a sweeping condemnation as is implied in the sentence that "work becomes entirely contingent upon outside aid and crumbles down as soon as the latter is withdrawn", I would go so far as to say that even a few years' experience of residence in a single village, trying to work through local workers, should not be regarded as conclusive proof that work could not be done through and by local workers. The contrary is obviously true. It now becomes unnecessary for me to examine the last sentence in detail. I can categorically say to the principal worker: "If you have any outside help, get rid of it. Work singly, courageously, intelligently with all the local help you can get and, if you do not succeed, blame only yourself and no one else and nothing else" (*Harijan*, 2.3.1947, p. 44; *CWMG* 86: 449-50).

Conversation with Trainees

Q. Do the village folk come to see you?

A. They do, but not without fear, and perhaps even suspicion. These also are among the many shortcomings of villagers. We have to rid them of these.

Q. How?

A. By gently insinuating ourselves into their affections. We must disabuse them of the fear that we have gone there to coerce them, we must show them by our behaviour that there is no intention to coerce, nor any selfish motive. But this is all patient work. You cannot quickly convince them of your bona fides.

Q. Don't you think that only those who work without any remuneration or allowance can inspire confidence in them, i.e. those who accept nothing whether from any association or from the village?

A. No. They do not even know who is and who is not working for remuneration. What does impress them is the way in which we live, our habits, our talks, even our gestures. There may be a few who suspect us of a desire to earn; we have to dispel their suspicion no doubt. And then do not run away with the feeling that he who accepts nothing from an association or from the villages is by any means an ideal servant. He is often a prey to self-righteousness which debases one.

Q. You teach us village crafts. Is that to give us a means of earning our livelihood or to enable us to teach the villagers? If it is for the latter object, how can we master a craft in the course of a year?

A. You are being taught the ordinary crafts, because unless you know the principles you will not be able to help people with suggestions. The most enterprising among you would certainly earn a living by following a craft. . . . The things we teach here are such that you are likely to be able to bring to the villagers better knowledge of them. We have improved grinding stones and rice-husking stones and oil-presses. We are carrying on experiments in improving our tools and we have to take the improvements to them. Above all there is truth and honesty in business that we have to teach them. They adulterate milk, they adulterate oil, they will adulterate truth for petty gain. It is not their fault, it is ours. We have so long ignored them and only exploited them, never taught them anything better. By close contact with them we can easily correct their ways. Long neglect and isolation has dulled their intellect and even moral sense. We have to brighten them up and revive them all along the line (*Harijan*, 25.7.1936, p. 187; *CWMG* 63: 159-60).

Danger from Within

No movement or organization having vitality dies from external attack. It dies of internal decay. . . . What is necessary is character above suspicion, ceaseless effort accompanied by ever-increasing knowledge of the technique of the work and a life of rigorous simplicity. Workers without character, living far above the ordinary life of villagers, and devoid of the knowledge required of them for their work, can produce no impression on the villagers whether Harijan or other.

As I write these lines instances of those workers who for want of character or simple living damaged the cause and themselves recur to my mind. Happily, instances of positive misconduct are rare. But the greatest hindrance to the progress of the work lies in the inability of workers of quality to support themselves on the village scale. If every one of such workers puts on his work a price which village service cannot sustain, ultimately these organizations must be wound up. For the insistence of payments on the city scale except in rare and temporary cases would imply that the gulf between cities and villages is unbridgeable. The village movement is as much an education of the city people as of the villagers. Workers drawn from cities have to develop village mentality and learn the art of living after the manner of villagers. This does not mean that they have to starve like the villagers. But it does mean that there must be a radical change in the old style of life. While the standard of living in the villages must be raised, the city standard has to undergo considerable revision, without the worker being required in any way to adopt a mode of life that would impair his health (*Harijan*, 11.4.1936, p. 68; *CWMG* 62: 319-20).

Our Villages

A young man who is trying to live in a village and earn his livelihood has sent me a pathetic letter. He does not know much English. I am therefore giving the letter below in an abridged form:

Three years ago when I was 20 years old I came to this village life after spending 15 years in a town. My domestic circumstances did not allow me to have college education. The work you have taken up for village revival has encouraged me to pursue village life. I have some land. My village has a population of nearly 2,500. After close contact with this village I find the following among more than three-fourths of the people:

1. Party feelings and quarrels
2. Jealousy
3. Illiteracy
4. Wickedness
5. Disunion
6. Carelessness
7. Lack of manners
8. Adherence to the old meaningless customs
9. Cruelty.

This is an out of the way place. No great man has ever visited such remote villages. The company of great ones is essential for advancement. So I am afraid to live in this village. Shall I leave this village? If not, what guidance will you give me?

Though no doubt there is exaggeration in the picture drawn by the young correspondent, his statement may be generally accepted. The reason for the tragic state is not far to seek. Villages have suffered long from neglect by those who have had the benefit of education. They have chosen the city life. The village movement is an attempt to establish healthy contact with the villages by inducing those who are fired with the spirit of service to settle in them and find self-expression in the service of villagers. The defects noticed by the correspondent are not inherent in village life. Those who have settled in villages in the spirit of service are not dismayed by the difficulties facing them. They knew before they went that they would have to contend against many difficulties including even sullenness on the part of villagers. Only those, therefore, who have faith in themselves and in their mission will serve the villagers and influence their lives. A true life lived amongst the people is in itself an object-lesson that must produce its own effect upon immediate surroundings. The difficulty with the young man is, perhaps, that he has gone to the village merely to earn a living without the spirit of service behind it. I admit that village life does not offer attractions to those who go there in search of money. Without the incentive of service village life would jar after the novelty has worn out. No young man having gone to a village may abandon the pursuit on the slightest contact with difficulty. Patient effort will show that villagers are not very different from city-dwellers and that they will respond to kindliness and attention. It is no doubt true that one does not have in the villages the opportunity of contact with the great ones of the land. With the growth of village mentality the leaders will find it necessary to tour in the villages and establish a living touch with them. Moreover, the companionship of the great and the good is available to all through the works of saints like Chaitanya, Ramakrishna, Tulsidas, Kabir, Nanak, Dadu, Tukaram, Tiruvalluvar, and others too numerous to mention though equally known and pious. The difficulty is to get the mind tuned to the reception of permanent values. If it is modern thought — political, social, economical, scientific — that is meant, it is possible to procure literature that will satisfy curiosity. I admit, however, that one does not find such as easily as one finds religious literature. Saints wrote and spoke for the masses. The vogue for translating modern thought to the masses in an acceptable manner has not yet quite set in. But it must come in time. I would, therefore, advise young men like my correspondent not to give in but persist in their effort and by their presence make the village more livable and lovable. That they will do by serving the villages in a manner acceptable to the villagers. Everyone can make a beginning by making the villages cleaner by their own labour and removing illiteracy to the extent of their ability. And if their lives are clean, methodical and industrious, there is no doubt that the infection will spread in the villages in which they may be working (*Harijan*, 20.2.1937, p. 16; *CWMG* 64: 387-88).

Pilgrimage to Villages

[Shri Sitaram Sastry has organized "pilgrimages of workers" who conveyed the message of village service among their surroundings. Sastry sent a brief report of the second pilgrimage to Gandhiji. Reacting upon this Gandhiji wrote:]

This is a step in the right direction. I would suggest that the pilgrims should avoid all travelling by rail, motor, or even village carts. If they will adopt my advice, they will observe that their work will be more effective and that the expenses will be practically nil. No more than two or three should form a party. I would expect villagers to house and feed the parties. Small parties will be no tax on the resources of villagers, as large ones are likely to be. The work of the parties should be more in the nature of sanitary service, survey of village conditions, and instruction of the villager as to what they can do without much, if any, outlay of money to improve their health and economic conditions (*Harijan*, 22.3.1935, pp. 42-43; *CWMG* 60: 328-29).

New Ways for Old?

Workers must not, without considerable experience, interfere with the old tools, old methods, and old patterns. They will be safe if they think of improvements, retaining intact the old existing background. They will find that it is true economy (*Harijan*, 29.3.1935, p. 49; *CWMG* 60: 354).

All-round Village Service

A *Samagra Gramasevak* must know everybody living in the village and render them such service as he can. That does not mean that the worker will be able to do everything single-handed. He will show them the way of helping themselves and procure for them such help and materials as they require. He will train up his own helpers. He will so win over the villagers that they will seek and follow his advice. Supposing I go and settle down in a village with a *ghani* (village oil-press), I won't be an ordinary *ghanchi* (oil-presser) earning 15-20 rupees a month. I will be a Mahatma *ghanchi*. I have used the word "Mahatma" in fun but what I mean to say is that as a *ghanchi* I will become a model for the villagers to follow. I will be a *ghanchi* who knows the *Gita* and the Koran. I will be learned enough to teach their children. I may not be able to do so for lack of time. The villagers will come to me and ask me: "Please make arrangements for our children's education." I will tell them: "I can find you a teacher but you will have to bear the expenses." And they will be prepared to do so most willingly. I will teach them spinning and when they come and ask me for the services of a weaver, I will find them a weaver on the same terms as I found them a teacher. And the weaver will teach them how to weave their own cloth. I will inculcate in them the importance of hygiene and sanitation and when they come and ask me for a sweeper, I will tell them: "I will be your sweeper and I will train you all in the job." This is my conception of *Samagra Gramaseva* (*Harijan*, 17.3.1946, p. 42; *CWMG* 83: 46).

18

Government and the Villages

What the Government Can Do?

It is legitimate to ask what Congress ministers will do for *khaddar* and other village industries now that they are in office. . . . Whether a minister is separately appointed or not, a department for the work is surely necessary. In these times of scarcity of food and clothing, this department can render the greatest help. The ministers have experts at their disposal through the A.I.S.A. and the A.I.V.I.A. It is possible to clothe today the whole of India in *khadi* on the smallest outlay and in the shortest time possible. Each Provincial government has to tell the villagers that they must manufacture their own *khaddar* for their own use. This brings in automatic local production and distribution. And there will undoubtedly be a surplus for the cities at least to a certain extent which, in its turn, will reduce the pressure on the local mills. The latter will then be able to take part in supplying the want of cloth in other parts of the world.

How can this result be brought about?

The governments should notify the villagers that they will be expected to manufacture *khaddar* for the needs of their villages within a fixed date after which no cloth will be supplied to them. The governments in their turn will supply the villagers with cotton seed or cotton wherever required, at cost price and the tools of manufacture also at cost, to be recovered in easy instalments payable, in, say, five years or more. They will supply them with instructors wherever necessary and undertake to buy surplus stock of *khaddar*, provided that the villagers in question have their cloth requirements supplied from their own manufacture. This should do away with cloth shortage without fuss and with very little overhead charges.

The villages will be surveyed and a list prepared of things that can be manufactured locally with little or no help and which may be required for village use or for sale outside, such for instance, as *ghani*-pressed oil and cakes, burning oil prepared through *ghanis*, hand-pounded rice, *tad gud*, honey, toys, mats, hand-made paper, village soap, etc. If enough care is thus taken the villages, most of them as good as dead or dying, will hum with life and exhibit the immense possibilities they have of supplying most of their wants themselves and of the cities and towns of India. Then there is the limitless cattle wealth of India suffering from criminal neglect. Goseva Sangh, as yet not properly experienced, can still supply valuable aid.

Without the basic training the villagers are being starved for education. This desideratum can be supplied by the Hindustani Talimi Sangh (*Harijan*, 28.4.1946, p. 104; *CWMG* 84: 44-45).

If I Were the Minister

My views expressed remain unaltered. One thing has created a misunderstanding. Some friends have read compulsion in that note. I am sorry for the obscurity. In it I had answered the question as to what representative governments could do if they wished. I had, I hope pardonably, assumed that such government's notices too could not be interpreted as compulsion. For every act of a bona fide representative government would assume consent of the voters represented. The voters would mean the whole populace, whether registered as voters or not. With that background, I wrote that the government should notify to the villagers that mill cloth would not be supplied to the villagers after a certain fixed date, so as to enable them to wear *khadi* prepared by themselves.

Whatever the meaning of my above article of 28th April last, I want to state that any scheme adopted about *khadi* without the willing cooperation of those concerned must mean death to *khadi* as a means for attaining *swaraj*. Then the taunt that *khadi* was a return to the darkness and slavery of the Middle Ages would be true. But I have held the contrary view. Whilst *khadi* under compulsion was a badge of slavery, *khadi* intelligently and voluntarily prepared, primarily for one's own use, was easily the badge of our freedom. Freedom is nothing if it is not all-round self-help. I, for one, would have nothing to do with *khadi*, if it were not a free man's privilege as well as duty.

A friendly critic asks whether *khadi* thus prepared could also and at the same time be for sale. Yes, if sale is its secondary use; not if manufacture for sale is its only or even primary use. That we began with sale of *khadi* shows temporary necessity as well as our limited vision.

Experience is a great teacher. It has taught us many things. Not the least is its primary use. But it is by no means the last. But I must leave this fascinating field of speculation and proceed definitely to answer the question put in the heading.

My first business, as the minister in charge of revival of the villages as the centre of all governmental activity would be to find out from among the Permanent Service honest and incorruptible men capable for the work. I would put the best among them in touch with the A.I.S.A. and the A.I.V.I.A., creations of the Congress, and bring in a scheme for giving the village-crafts the greatest encouragement. I would stipulate, there should be no compulsion on the villagers, that they must not slave for others and that they should be taught to help themselves and rely upon their own labour and skill for the production of articles of food, cloth, and other necessaries. The scheme would thus have to be comprehensive. I would instruct my first man, therefore, to see the Hindustani Talimi Sangh and see what it has to say.

Let us assume that the scheme, thus produced, contains a clause, saying that the villagers themselves declare that they would not want mill cloth, say, after one year from a fixed date, that they require cotton, wool, and necessary implements and instruction, not as a gift but to be paid for on the easiest terms. The scheme provides too that it will not apply at once to the whole of any province but only to a part to begin with. The scheme further tells one that the A.I.S.A. will guide and assist the working of the scheme.

Being convinced of its soundness, I would give it legal form in consultation with the law department and issue a notification, fully describing the genesis of the scheme. The villagers as well as the mill-owners and others would have been party to it. The notification will show clearly that it is the people's measure, though bearing the government stamp. The government money will be used for the benefit of the poorest villagers, making the largest return possible to the people concerned. It will, therefore, be probably the most profitable investment in which expert assistance will be voluntary and overhead charges the least item. The notification will give in detail, the whole cost to the country and the return to the people. The only question for me as minister is whether the A.I.S.A. has the conviction and capacity to shoulder the burden of creating and guiding a *khadi* scheme to success. If it has, I would put my little barque to sea with all confidence (*Harijan*, 1.9.1946, p. 288; *CWMG* 85: 210-12).

19
India and the World

When India becomes self-supporting, self-reliant, and proof against temptations and exploitation, she will cease to be the object of greedy attraction for any power in the West or the East and will then feel secure without having to carry the burden of expensive armament. Her internal economy will be India's strongest bulwark against aggression (*Young India*, 2.7.1931, p. 161; *CWMG* 47: 90).

My notion of *purna swaraj* is not isolated independence but healthy and dignified independence. My nationalism, fierce though it is, is not exclusive, is not devised to harm any nation or individual. Legal maxims are not so legal as they are moral. I believe in the eternal truth of *sic utere tuo ut alienum non laedas* (use thy own property so as not to injure thy neighbour's) (*Young India*, 26.3.1931, p. 51; *CWMG* 45: 343).

A free, democratic India will gladly associate herself with other free nations for mutual defence against aggression and for economic co-operation. She will work for the establishment of a real world order based on freedom and democracy, utilizing the world's knowledge and resources for the progress and advancement of humanity (*Harijan*, 23.9.1939, p. 278; *CWMG* 70: 411).

It only means that the Western nations have to use their skill. If they want to use their skill abroad, from philanthropic motives, America would say, "Well, we know how to make bridges, we won't keep it a secret, but we say to the whole world, we will teach you how to make bridges and we will charge you nothing." America says, "Where other nations can grow one blade of wheat, we can grow two thousand." Then, America should teach that art free of charge to those who will learn it, but not aspire to grow wheat for the whole world, which would spell a sorry day for the world indeed (*Harijan*, 2.11.1934, p. 302; *CWMG* 48: 165).

[Africans wanted to know what India could give them and how they could achieve cooperative industrialization in order to be saved from the terrible exploitation under which they were suffering.]

The commerce between India and Africa will be of ideas and services, not of manufactured goods against raw materials after the fashion of Western exploiters. Then India can offer you the spinning wheel. If I had discovered it when I was in South Africa, I would have introduced it among the Africans who were my neighbours in Phoenix. You can grow cotton, you have ample leisure and plenty of manual skill. You should study and adopt the lesson of the village crafts we are trying to revive.

Therein lies the key to your salvation (*Harijan*, 24.2.1946, p. 18; *CWMG* 83: 12-13).

Has the spinning-wheel a message for America? Can it serve as a counter weapon to the atom bomb?

I do feel that it has a message for USA and the whole world. . . . I have not the slightest doubt that the saving of India and of the world lies in the wheel. If India becomes the slave of the machine, then, I say, Heaven save the world (*Harijan*, 17.11.1946, p. 404; *CWMG* 86: 20-21).

I feel in the innermost recesses of my heart, . . . that the world is sick unto death of blood-spilling. The world is seeking a way out, and I flatter myself with the belief that perhaps it will be the privilege of the ancient land of India to show that way out to the hungering world (Broadcast to America, 13.9.1931; *The New York Times*, 14.9.1931; *CWMG* 48: 8-9).

If India fails, Asia dies. It has been aptly called the nursery of many blended cultures and civilizations. Let India be and remain the hope of all the exploited races of the earth, whether in Asia, Africa or in any part of the world (*Harijan*, 5.10.1947, p. 354; *CWMG* 89: 221).

We do not want to cut adrift from the whole world. We will have a free interchange with all nations, but the present forced interchange has to go. We do not want to be exploited, neither do we want to exploit any other nation. Through the scheme we look forward to making all children producers, and so to change the face of the whole nation, for it will permeate the whole of our social being. But that does not mean that we cut adrift from the whole world.

There will be nations that will want to interchange with others because they cannot produce certain things. They will certainly depend on other nations for them, but the nations that will provide for them should not exploit them.

But if you simplify your life to an extent that you need nothing from other countries, you will isolate yourselves from them; whereas I want you to be responsible for America also.

It is by ceasing to exploit and to be exploited that we can be responsible for America. For America will then follow our example and there will be no difficulty in a free interchange between us (*Harijan*, 12.2.1938, p. 2; *CWMG* 66: 354-55).

I know that the work (of shaping the ideal village) is as difficult as to make of India an ideal country. . . . But if one man can produce one ideal village, he will have provided a pattern not only for the whole country, but perhaps for the whole world. More than this a seeker may not aspire after (*Harijan*, 4.8.1940, p. 235; *Sevagram*, 30.7.1940; *CWMG* 72: 335-36).

In free India whose interest shall be supreme? If a neighbouring state is in want, would India adopt an attitude of isolationism, saying that her own needs must come first?

A truly independent and free India would rush to the help of her neighbours in distress.

A man whose spirit of sacrifice does not go beyond his own community, himself becomes, and makes his community, selfish. The logical sequel of self-sacrifice is that the individual sacrifices himself for the community, the community for the district, the district for the Province, the Province for the nation, and the nation for the world. A drop from the ocean perishes without doing any good. As a part of the ocean it shares the glory of carrying on its bosom whole fleets of mighty ships (*Harijan*, 23.3.1947; *CWMG* 87: 23).

Let no one commit the mistake of thinking, that Rama-rajya means a rule of the Hindus. My Rama is another name for Khuda or God. I want *Khudai raj*, which is the same thing as the Kingdom of God on Earth. . . . The establishment of such a *rajya* would not only mean welfare of the whole of the Indian people but of the whole world (*Harijan*, 23.3.1947; *CWMG* 87: 23).

I would like to see India free and strong so that she may offer herself as a willing and pure sacrifice for the betterment of the world. The individual, being pure, sacrifices himself for the family, the latter for the village, the village for the district, the district for the province, the province for the nation, the nation for all (*Young India*, 17.9.1925, p. 321; *CWMG* 28: 190).

Through *swaraj* we would serve the whole world (*Young India*, 16.4.1931, p. 79; *CWMG* 45: 399).

There is no limit to extending service to our neighbours across our state-made frontiers. God never made those frontiers (*Young India*, 31.12.1931, p. 427; *CWMG* 48: 409).

Refernces

CWMG (1958-1994). *Collected Works of Mahatma Gandhi* (100 vols.). Delhi: Publications Division, Ministry of Information of Broadcasting, Government of India.

Gandhi, M.K. (1910). *Indian Home Rule (Hind swaraj)*. Phoenix, Natal: International Printing Press.

———. (1922). *Speeches and Writings of M.K.Gandhi*, With an Introduction by C.F. Andrews. Madras: G.A. Natesan & Co.

———. (1935). *From Yeravda Mandir: Ashram Observances*. Tr. Valji Govindji Desai. Ahmedabad: Jivanji Desai.

———. (1945). *Constructive Programme: Its Meaning and Place*. Ahmedabad: Navajivan Publishing House.

———. (1948). *Key to Health*. Tr. Sushil Nayar. Ahmedabad: Navajivan Publishing House.

———. (1962). *Vilage Swaraj*. Compiled by H.M. Vyas. Ahmedabad: Navajivan Publishing House.

Mira. (1949). *Gleanings Gathered at Bapu's Feet*. Ahemedabad: Navajivan Publishing House.

Nehru, Jawaharlal. (1958). *A Bunch of Old Letters*. Bombay: Asia Publishing House.

Truth through Nonviolence*

P. Venkata Rayudu

"Woman is the incarnation of ahimsa." — *M.K. Gandhi*

Abstract: What is reality? How do we know? Answers to these foundational questions of ontology and epistemology, based on Mahatma Gandhi's "experiments with truth", are: reality is nonviolent (in the sense of not-inconsistent), and nonviolence (in the sense of respecting-meaning) is the only means of knowing (Gandhi, 1940). Be that as it may, science is what we think of when we think of reality and knowing. How does Gandhi's nonviolence, discovered in his spiritual quest for Truth, relate to the scientific pursuit of truth? Here we show that Gandhian nonviolent knowing of nonviolent reality is an abstraction of both individual knowing (looking, reasoning) and collective scientific knowing (measurements, calculations). Specifically, Gandhi's truth-through-nonviolence is a law-like summation of the methods of physics ("do not disturb" of measurements) and of mathematics ("do not tear" of calculations) that are used to know. Moreover, physics (with its lawful behaviour of bodies) and biology (in preserving the meaning of genetic code) do affirm that the defining attribute of reality is nonviolence. In light of these correspondences, the Mahatma's derivation of a universal method of knowing (nonviolence of preserving-structure) from a universal truth (nonviolence of consistent-becoming) constitutes a science-supported general theory of reality and knowing.
Keywords: *Ahimsa,* biological reproduction, calculation, cognition, epistemology, Mahatma Gandhi, measurement, nonviolence, ontology, reality, science.

Introduction

Truth and nonviolence are, in the words of Gandhi, "as old as hills"

---

* I am grateful to Prof. K. Ramakrishna Rao, for his generous encouragement, guidance, and support. I dedicate this paper to the memory of my younger brother P.V.V. Subrahmanyam.

(Gandhi, 1936). They are also light years apart, rarely making contact in ordinary or scientific conceptual space. This state-of-affairs changed for good, thanks to Gandhi's reflective life of experimentation (Gandhi, 1940). In an intellectual tour de force, Mahatma Gandhi brought to figural salience, for all to see, the propinquity between truth and nonviolence: "*Ahimsa* is the means; Truth is the end" (Gandhi, 1955: 35). The simple terms with which Gandhi expressed the conceptual kinship between *Truth* and *Nonviolence* helped one and all to see the quintessence of his thinking; but the surface simplicity, not unlike that of Einstein's $E = mc^2$, is not that revealing of the metaphysical depths of the Mahatma's meditations. Simply put, what does it mean to say, as Gandhi often said, "the way to Truth lies through *ahimsa*". Our attempts to unravel led us to recognize Gandhi's insights into Truth and *ahimsa* as reflective of an understanding of reality and knowing that subsumes scientific accounts spanning across physics, biology, cognition, and mathematics. We begin, so as to facilitate proper appreciation of the vast reach of Gandhian thought, with an overview of Gandhi's nonviolence. Next we examine Truth, meaning, as Gandhi noted, "that which is" (*CWMG*, 48: 405), which helps us see the nonviolence of knowing — of looking, reasoning, physical measurements, and mathematical calculations — in accord with Gandhi's conceptualization.

Gandhi's Nonviolence

There are two conceptualizations of nonviolence: (1) nonviolence before Gandhi, and (2) nonviolence after Gandhi. The *ahimsa* of ancient India, as it was preached and practised, was that of individual virtue valued and promoted on moral grounds. It is the nonviolence of "do not kill", of "go vegan", and of love and peace. Gandhi transformed this moral principle into a mode of action that both individuals and institutions can use as a means to achieve just ends (Rao, 2011). Gandhi's practical applications of nonviolence, which have been instrumental in bringing about India's Independence, have been duly recognized as a work of genius (Gardner, 1993). No less a work of genius is his prophetic interpretation of *ahimsa* as an ideal means of knowing.

Gandhi found *ahimsa* in searching for Truth (in the sense of SATYA or reality): He said: ". . . I do claim to be a passionate seeker after Truth. . . . In the course of that search, the discovery of nonviolence came to me" (CWMG, 72: 230-31). First, Gandhi recognized the nonviolent nature of reality, which he articulated by pointing out that the violence of history is not an invariant attribute of reality for the simple reason that history is but a record of changes and not that of invariance: "History, as we know it, is a record of the wars of the world. History, then, is a record of an interruption of the course of nature" (Gandhi, 1910: 75). Changes can be readily seen, but perceiving invariance calls for added reflection. If violence were the law of nature, Gandhi argued, we would not be:

> Why can we not see that if the sum-total of the world's activities was destructive, it would have come to an end long ago? . . . *ahimsa*, sustains this planet of ours. — *CWMG*, 90: 195

Having thus appreciated the nonviolence of reality, Gandhi realized that the way to reality is through nonviolence.

How does one go from recognizing an attribute (nonviolence) of an object (reality) to realizing that that attribute (nonviolence) can be used to find the object (reality)? Using an attribute of an object to locate the object (be it in material or mental realms) is a working method of knowing. We use, for example, the colour of a car to find the car in a parking lot. From this perspective, it seems plausible to go from recognizing nonviolence as an attribute of reality to realizing that nonviolence can be used to know reality, as Gandhi did. Looking beyond plausibility, what exactly is the cognitive trajectory from "reality is nonviolent" to "nonviolence is how we know"? Let us look at few more readily relatable situations that can inform our question. Police, for example, question an English criminal in English and a Telugu criminal in Telugu. We use eyes with photoreceptors to see, while we use nose with chemical receptors to smell. Stones with weight are used to measure weights, while sticks with length are used to measure lengths. Dots of a graph are listed using maps from a dot, while arrows are listed using maps from an arrow. This matching of how [we know] to what [we are trying to know] is suggestive of the sensibility of approaching nonviolent reality nonviolently. That there is more to knowing than mere matching of means to ends can also be seen in the above examples. Both the photoreceptors that are used to see and the surfaces that are seen "trade" in light, but one detects while the other reflects. In a similar vein, in an interrogation both police and criminal may speak in English, but there is a difference: the English of the police is that of questions, while the English of the criminal is that of answers. Drawing parallels, we ask: granted nonviolence is the "language" of both reality and knowing, how is the nonviolence of knowing "tuned" to the nonviolence of reality? In searching for an answer, to our pleasant surprise, we noticed the likeness between Gandhi's spiritual yearning for truth and the scientific struggle to make sense.

The main thesis of the present paper is: Gandhi's nonviolence of knowing, notwithstanding its spiritual genesis, is an abstraction of both individual knowing (looking, reasoning) and the collective knowing of science (measurements, calculations). Gandhi's truth through nonviolence — a derivation of the "how" of knowing from the "what" of reality — gives us one more reason, a reason for scientists, to acknowledge his genius. In the following we provide an overview of reality and knowing so as to facilitate a clear understanding of how Gandhi, starting at the *AHIMSA* of ancient Indian thought and via "falsehood is violence" (Rao, 2012), arrived at his original NONVIOLENCE of truth-through-nonviolence.

Nonviolent Reality

Reality can be approached by contrasting it with fiction. Anything and everything can happen in fiction, which makes it inconsistent. Reality is not fiction, i.e., not-inconsistent. It is not a place where anything happens; reality is a *space of consistent-happenings*: solids stay put, while liquids flow down, and gases, unlike both solids and liquids, diffuse out. Violence, naïvely speaking, is where anything can happen (which is why violence is not the default setting for solving problems). From this viewpoint, violence, not unlike fiction, is inconsistent. The inconsistency of violence, which is "anything can happen in violent situations", can sustain nothing. Negating violence gives nonviolence: nonviolence understood as consistent-becoming or becoming consistent with being. Nonviolence understood as consistent-becoming is thus the defining attribute of reality, or as Gandhi understood: "*Ahimsa* is the supreme law or *dharma*" (Gandhi, 1948: 301).

Turning our attention to biology, we do find violence — violence implicit in *survival of the fittest* — treated as a trait of nature. But if one were to focus away from the change of speciation and focus on the invariance of reproduction within a species, then one finds biological processes such as translation and transcription, which embody nonviolence in their commitment to "do not mutate". Summing up, physics (with its lawful motions and transformations of bodies) and biology (in preserving the meaning of genetic code during reproduction) constitute an unequivocal proclamation of the nonviolent character of nature.

Nonviolence of Knowing

The nonviolence of reality is nonviolence defined as not-inconsistent. What about the nonviolence of knowing? The nonviolence of knowing is a positive reading of nonviolence: nonviolence defined as respecting or preserving.

There are few books, some papers, and some more notebooks on my desk. How did I know? I looked and the act of looking brought about the knowledge of things that are on the desk. My looks, when I look to see what is out-there, do not change the way things are. So is the case with reasoning, which is another means of knowing at the level of individual. In drawing conclusions, the acts of reason do not change the given premises. In addition to looking and reasoning that we, the individuals, routinely deploy to know, there is the collective knowing of science. At the level of science, measurements, and calculations constitute the acts of knowing. The disciplined nature of knowing, i.e., the "do not change" of looking and reasoning that is obvious at the level of individual knowing is taken as the defining condition on knowing. So we try to make sure that the act of measurement does not change that which is measured.

Knowing can be thought of as making explicit something that is implicit in a given situation without disturbing. The defining condition on knowing, then, is *being respectful of the given* as we bring into focus that which we are trying to see. In practice, however, measurements are not completely non-invasive (e.g. inserting micro-electrodes into brains to measure neural activity). Hence, the "do not disturb" is an ideal to which physical measurements aspire to. The ideal "do not disturb" of physical knowing becomes, in the following, the actual "do not tear" of mathematical knowing.

Mathematical knowing involves calculations such as establishing isomorphisms (as a way of knowing unknown objects in terms of known objects), determination of functional relationships (such as that between radius and area), evaluating functions (to find, for example, the area of a circle, given its radius), solving equations (for, say, the point of intersection between two lines), assigning truth values to statements and characterizing truth value objects of various domains of discourse, abstracting concepts (e.g. GROUP), and interpreting theories (e.g. group theory). Beneath this bewildering diversity of mathematical calculations — making unknown known — is a simple method of respecting-meaning or preserving-structure. More explicitly, mathematical objects (such as groups or graphs) are thought of as structures and the way we get to know about mathematical objects is by way of probing with morphisms, which, in geometric terminology, "do not tear" apart the structure of objects (Lawvere and Schanuel, 2009: 133-37, 149-51 and 210). Structure-preserving morphisms can be thought of as transformations preserving positive properties (e.g. cats have tails, in contrast to negative properties such as "do not have horns"). This instrument of preserving-meaning, with violence as "distortion of meaning" (Rao, 2012), exemplifies Gandhi's assertion that nonviolence is the only means of knowing. The extensive mathematical reach of the nonviolence of knowing springs from an elemental equation: "falsehood is violence" that Gandhi insisted on (Rao, 2012). We can measure, to give a familiar illustration, the unknown size of a room using sticks of known lengths. Being truthful about the lengths of measuring sticks is a necessary condition for knowing the true size of the room. Putting it all together, we find the Mahatma's truth-through-nonviolence validated in cognition, in physics, and in mathematics — in their respective struggles to know.

Concluding Remarks

We showed how the time-tested concept of *AHIMSA* — deeply rooted in ancient Indian spirituality of Jainism, Buddhism, and Patañjali's *Yoga-Sutras* — speaks to the core concerns of science in general and science of knowing in particular. Our work began as a simple-minded study to understand Gandhi's experimental finding: "the only means for the realization of Truth is *ahimsa*" (Gandhi, 1940: 615). Upon grasping its import, we examined scientific practices across a range of disciplines — physics, mathematics, and cognition — to see how we acquire knowledge. We find that Gandhi's insight into knowing is a sublime abstraction — in true scientific spirit — of the scientific methods of knowing (measurements, calculations, and reasoning).

In closing, we address various criticisms of truth-through-nonviolence. One criticism is that it is a category mistake to characterize reality as nonviolent or to read nonviolence into knowing. In response, it might seem like a category mistake to say that reality is nonviolent or to say that nonviolence is an ideal means of knowing, especially, when one's thinking is wedded to a conceptualization of violence engendered by, say, watching news, by the violence of wars and terrorism. Our thesis on nonviolence is rather removed from the imagery of bombs and bloodshed, though not unrelated; the relevant contrast here is with *violation* as in "falsehood is violence", "violence is denial of *dharma*", and "distortion of meaning" (Rao, 2012). In this sense, the nonviolence we are explicating is reminiscent of obeying laws and of being respectful. In a sense, all that we are reading into Gandhi's nonviolence is a rational interpretation — in the terminology of cognition, physics, and mathematics — of Gandhi's conviction that (1) there is a method within the madness all around, (2) nonviolence is its name, and (3) it could be harnessed to make the chaos we are suspended in little more manageable: "Non-violence is the supreme law. . . . I have not yet come across a situation . . .

that I had no remedy in terms of non-violence" (*CWMG*, 68: 202). There is also the criticism that "nonviolence is a natural means of knowing" is at best a tautology since the truth that one finds in it is none other than the fact that we have no choice but to be truthful in finding truth. Without disagreeing, we add that the specific incarnations of truth-through-nonviolence in different ways of knowing — cognition, physical measurements, and mathematical calculations — are not obvious until explicitly stated and hence worth documenting. Another criticism is that the application of nonviolence — as a means of knowing — is limited to frameworks with definite subject–object divide. Yes, truth-through-nonviolence is classical. It is not clear how nonviolence informs the study of consciousness, specifically where there is no clear separation between observation and [observed] experience (Rao, 2005); so is the case with quantum mechanics in view of its observation problem (Gomatam, 1999). Nevertheless, there is hope (outstanding-work): "If there is a fundamental distinction between man and beast, it is the former's progressive recognition of the law and its application" (*CWMG*, 63: 321) and "I see new implications about them. I see them in a newer light every day and read in them a newer meaning" (Gandhi, 1955: 6). This is not surprising since Gandhi's truth-through-nonviolence is a concise statement of the determination of the "how" of epistemology by the "what" of ontology.

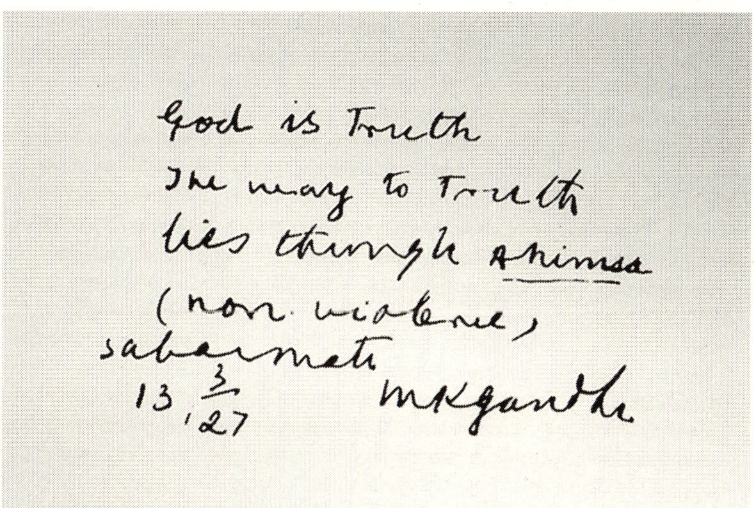

Gandhi's nonviolence: The way to Truth lies through *Ahimsa*.
(*Source*: gandhiserve.org)

References

CWMG. (1958-1994). *Collected Works of Mahatma Gandhi* (100 vols.). Delhi: Publications Division, Ministry of Information and Broadcasting, Government of India.

Gandhi, M.K. (1910). *Indian Home Rule* [*Hind Swaraj*]. Phonix, Natal: International Printing Press.

———. (1936). *Harijan*, 28 March.

———. (1940). *The Story of My Experiments with Truth*. Tr. Mahadev Desai. Ahamedabad: Navajivan.

———. (1948). *Non-Violence in Peace and War*, vol. 1. Ahmedabad: Navajivan Publishing House.

———. (1955). *Truth Is God*. Compiled by R.K. Prabhu. Ahmedabad: Navajivan Publishing House.

Gardner, H. (1993). *Creating Minds: An Anatomy of Creativity Seen Through the Lives of Freud, Einstein, Picasso, Stravinsky, Eliot, Graham, and Gandhi*. New York: Basic Books.

Gomatam, R.V. (1999). Quantum Theory and the Observation Problem. *Journal of Consciousness Studies*, 6(11-12), 173-90.

Lawvere, F.W. and Schanuel, S.H. (2009). *Conceptual Mathematics: A First Introduction to Categories*. Cambridge: Cambridge University Press.

Rao, K.R. (2005). Perception, Cognition and Consciousness in Classical Hindu Psychology, *Journal of Consciousness Studies*, 12(3), 3-30.

———. (2011). *Gandhi and Applied Spirituality*. New Delhi: Matrix Publishers.

———. (2012). Violence and Nonviolence in Gandhi's Philosophy of Life. *GITAM Journal of Gandhian Studies*, 1(1), 131-47.

From Gandhirama to Gandhi Mandir in Visakhapatnam*

K. Ramakrishna Rao

While greeting and welcoming all of you to this inaugural event of the second edition of Gandhirama, I express my special gratitude to Sri Venkaiah Naidu, Hon'ble Minister of Urban Development and Parliamentary Affairs, Government of India, New Delhi, for taking time to be with us this morning.

It was about four years ago, when I was the Chairman of the Indian Council of Philosophical Research, I conceived the idea of Gandhirama. I sat with some of my friends and scholar colleagues who shared my enthusiasm to promote Mahatma Gandhi's thought and practices. These included Dr. Srivatsa Goswami, Dr. Y.P. Anand, Prof. Ashok Vohra, Shri Rajiv Chandran, Dr. Kapila Vatsyayan, Shri Abid Hussain, and a few others. Together we discussed the various facets of Gandhirama and then went on to organize the first international convention, Gandhirama-2012 at Jawaharlal Nehru University in New Delhi during 17-22 August 2012.

Dubbed as Gandhi Festival and a Feast of Ideas it was more successful than we expected. Besides the ICPR, the ICCR, the ICSSR, and IGNCA joined us in this effort. In addition, the UNESCO and the UN gave their endorsement. We had several distinguished Gandhian scholars making significant presentations. Dr. Sathasivan Cooper of South Africa, President of the International Union of Psychological Sciences, a freedom fighter in South Africa, who was in jail with Nelson Mandela, gave the keynote address. We had exhibited movies on Gandhi and rare clippings of videos of his activities.

Now, the second edition of Gandhirama is an improved and expanded version with increased participation and added attractions. We are again helped by various organizations. In addition to the hosts GITAM University and Andhra University, we have as collaborators Indira

---

* Presidential opening remarks, delivered on the occasion of Gandhirama second edition, held at GITAM University, Visakhapatnam, during 16-21 January 2016.

Gandhi National Centre for the Arts, Mahatma Gandhi Museum and Library. We received support from Adi Kavi Nannaya University and a host of other organizations. GITAM University administration, faculty, and students extended their full cooperation. Again, all the members of the Organizing Committee of Gandhirama and especially Prof. Haribabu, Prof. Laskshmi Prasad, Dr. Savita Singh, Prof. Ashok Vohra, and Prof. Y.P. Anand helped in all possible ways. Thanks to all of them, we are able to put up this impressive show in the cause of peace and nonviolence. Above all, it is the personal interest and constant guidance of Dr. M.V.V.S. Murthi garu without whose direct involvement all this would not have been possible.

A special feature of the present Gandhirama is the focus on youth. We brought together a large number of students from across the country (for example 35 students from North Eastern Hill University, Shillong) and endeavoured to involve them in a truly unique Gandhian Mela with symposia, workshops, discussions, exhibitions, cultural events, film screenings, and other entertainment programmes, all focused on Gandhiji. We have here an exciting opportunity for our young leaders of the future to interact with outstanding Gandhian scholars and devout disciples of the Mahatma. We thus endeavour to expose them to the person and philosophy of Gandhi as an icon of hope and an inspiration for change in a world overshadowed by terror and conflict.

We have at this edition of Gandhirama several erudite presentations and significant discussions on the many-sided splendour of Mahatma Gandhi and the contemporary relevance of his ideas. We have special panels to discuss topics like "Religious Fundamentalism, Political Extremism and Gandhi's Nonviolence" and Swachh Bharat Abhiyan.

My interest in Gandhi is not recent. It has been long-standing. I was sixteen years old when the Mahatma was assassinated. I was in the final year in high school, a student leader. I still recall very vividly the pain and trauma we experienced at the time and how we were glued to All India Radio sharing the nationwide grief. The grief gradually gave away to a deep interest not only in Mahatma as a person and leader who helped us to become politically free, but as a thinker who held ideas that would change the world some day.

This interest led me to take up Gandhi as the subject for my Ph.D. dissertation. I had the benefit of studying Gandhi in India with Professor Satchidananda Murty at Andhra University here in Visakhapatnam and later at the University of Chicago in USA with Professor Richard McKeon. The result was my book *Gandhi and American Pragmatism: An Inter-Cultural*

Study (Oxford & IBH, 1968). Again, among my recent books is *Gandhi and Applied Spirituality* (Indian Council of Philosophical Research, 2011). During the next few months my latest book *Gandhi's Dharma* will appear.

Thus Mahatma Gandhi has been in mind in several of my academic incarnations in a span of sixty plus years, which covered parapsychology, Indian psychology, consciousness studies, and Yoga. The interest is more than acquiring scholarship. It is almost a passion — a passion that led me among other things (a) to conceive events like Gandhirama, (b) be a part of the Centre for Gandhian Studies at GITAM University, (c) start the *GITAM Journal of Gandhian Studies*, and (d) help organize several forums to discuss and disseminate Gandhi's ideas.

Now, I have a new dream flowing from my interest in Gandhi. I shared it with our President Dr. M.V.V.S. Murthi garu and my friend and fellow-traveller Dr. Savita Singh. I want to share that vision with you this morning briefly and seek your support and blessings, especially from those sitting on the dais. The dream pictures a beautiful structure on the top of Kailasagiri, here in Visakhapatnam, to be called Mahatma Gandhi Mandir, which will house among other things a museum and a library, and function as a perennial centre to creatively promote Gandhiji's thought and practices. Let me make it very clear at the outset that I do not mean by Mandir a temple or a shrine, but an institution, a Gandhian icon and an academic monument to inspire, project, and promote the paradigm of nonviolence.

Mahatma Gandhi Mandir will have standing photographic exhibits, multimedia interactive space, ideas park, a museum with sculptures, frescoes, and mural replicas. In addition, it will have a children's corner, prayer and meditation centre, Shilpgram, Kola Manch, and weekly light and sound programmes. All these focus on educating the public and create Gandhi consciousness in the minds of visitors. More importantly the Mandir will be the seat of research and serve as the centre for spreading Gandhi *shruti*, *smriti*, and *samskriti*. In addition, we hope to have Gandhi *stūpa* with the statue of Mahatma erected on an architecturally designed platform.

Delhi has most of the memorials, libraries, and other activities relating to Mahatma Gandhi. These include Gandhi Smriti and Darshan Samiti, the establishment at Birla Bhavan, Gandhi Museum and Library. Gujarat comes next with Sabarmati Ashram and other Gandhian legends. There are very few such in south India and none in Visakhapatnam and Andhra Pradesh. Gandhi belongs to the entire nation, nay the world. Therefore, in order to spread the message of Mahatma we need to build and promote such Mandirs in all parts of the country. It is in this context that I have this dream of Mahatma Gandhi Mandir on Kailasagiri. It can be a Gandhi bridge between North and South, East and West; and a path of peace and harmony for all mankind.

My vision of a spectacular Mahatma Gandhi Mandir in Visakhapatnam is to have a centre that functions as a splendid place to perennially preserve Gandhi *shruti* (thought), actively promote Gandhi *smriti* (*dharma*) and widely spread Gandhi *samskriti* (culture). I see our Prime Minister Shri Narendra Modiji laying the foundation stone shortly, and fancy that it will be open when we celebrate Gandhi's 150th Birth Anniversary in October 2019. When all this happens it would indeed be the culmination and fitting finale of Gandhirama and grand beginning of an unending movement to spread the philosophy and practices of nonviolence.

Now, my vision does not end there. Shri Venkaiah Naidu garu is here today as the Chief Guest for Gandhirama. In the context of Mahatma Gandhi Mandir, I picture him as the Chief with his headgear representing the entire Gandhi tribe building the Mahatma Gandhi Mandir in Visakhapatnam. Then, I see Dr. Mahesh Sharma resourcefully guiding us giving inspirational counselling. I visualize these Hon'ble Members on the dais lending their helping hands; and Dr. M.V.V.S. Murthi coordinating and giving the ground crew the marching orders. On my part, I am faithfully yours. We will then move on effortlessly from this *konda* (hill), Rushikonda, where we are now meeting, to the other *konda*, Kailasagiri, where we will have Mahatma Gandhi Mandir.

As a rational man and as a psychologist with some expertise, I ask myself: Why is this passion in me for Gandhi? And why is it that I have these dreams and fantasies? Let me try to introspect and share some of my thoughts.

As I drive to work from my home at Daspalla Hills to GITAM campus in Rushikonda on the beach road, I have noted during the past several months how the roads are getting cleaner and the surroundings greener changing from week to week. The beach front of Visakhapatnam now has a truly smart city look. I would like to think that all this cleaning and greening is to welcome all of you to this international gathering on Gandhi and to showcase Visakhapatnam as the preferred destiny of Gandhian scholars and peace workers like you who have come from far and wide to participate in Gandhirama. However, I realize that all this is being done in the context of holding the International Fleet Review (IFR) to welcome the naval forces belonging to many nations. These forces and ships are meant to defend our freedom and make us to live in peace.

It is just a happy and unplanned coincidence that we are holding Gandhirama in Visakhapatnam two weeks ahead of IFR and we are the unintended beneficiaries of the IFR munificence. I think it is quite fair and appropriate that we bask in the IFR shine because Gandhirama is also for promoting a secure and peaceful world. There is, however, a world of difference between the two. One seeks peace through the display of force as a deterrent. The other seeks peace through nonviolence. I do not see the two events as conflicting. They are in significant ways complementary, like the ministries of Defence and Culture in our government.

I am realistic enough to realize that we cannot wish away conflicts, violence, and wars. History has shown us that they are ubiquitous. At the same time, we also know that violence is no real and permanent solution to resolve conflicts. Violence breeds more violence. Therefore, we need to explore other methods and new weapons and fight different kinds of wars based on nonviolence — wars against poverty, disease, illiteracy, economic exploitation, and personal greed. The Mahatma has bequeathed to us an important legacy we must treasure as a new resource to promote peace. Gandhiji offered *satyagraha* as the moral equivalent of war. Perpetual peace would be impossible on the model of violence. It is something conceivable from the perspective of Gandhian paradigm of nonviolence. We are at a point in human history where we need to pursue both strategies with the objective of achieving increasing dependence on nonviolent modes of peace and decreasing reliance on conventional ways based on violence. In this sense, the holding of IFR and Gandhirama in Visakhapatnam at about the same time is a good augury. They are complementary events, reinforcing each other, though it is unlikely to be seen as such by most people unless we make this explicit.

The relevance of Mahatma Gandhi's message of nonviolence to the troubled world today traumatized by terror is all too obvious. However, less understood and more significant are the philosophy behind Gandhi's message and the methods he experimentally designed and actually practised in life, which are derived from his basic philosophical premises and his understanding of human nature. I may summarize them in a few sentences.

Change begins with oneself. So do social development, political freedom, and perpetual peace. *Self* is different from the ego. The ego divides people, because it is the principle behind separation. *Self* is the spiritual component of humans. The ego is the culmination of the animal instincts within us. Man is a unique combination of the divine and the brute. The goal is to suppress the brute and realize the divine within. In order to achieve this one has to control the ego. Gandhiji felt that elimination of the ego is possible by reducing oneself to zero or nothingness. One can accomplish this by cultivating altruism, engaging in *karma-yoga,* doing selfless service, and involving oneself in objective and nonviolent search for truth. Various methods Gandhiji championed such as *satyagraha* flow from the above premises.

We revere Mahatma, as the Father of the Nation because he was the principal architect of Indian freedom struggle. Besides paying our due respects on his birth and death anniversaries, the successive governments of India since Independence did little to implement various constructive programmes the Mahatma has championed as essential ingredients in the country's peaceful development.

In this context, it is very refreshing to note that Shri Narendra Modi, ever since he became the prime minister, has repeatedly asserted that he was inspired by Gandhiji's teachings and saw their relevance to the country and the world. He asserted unequivocally that he and his government have "no tolerance for intolerance", reflecting the pluralistic perspective, the Anekantavada, of Mahatma Gandhi. Modiji did not stop with eloquent speeches; he actually planted new ideas to implement several of the items in Mahatma's constructive programmes by some well thought-out initiatives. These include Swachh Bharat, clean India mission, and Saansad Adarshgram Yojana. In a message at the time of releasing the guidelines for Saansad Adarshgram Yojana on 11 October 2014, Modiji wrote:

> I have been deeply inspired by the ideology of Mahatma Gandhi. He had the foresight to realize that you do not only need electricity poles to bring light to a village but that true enlightenment will come from shaping values, community spirit and promoting good education. I too believe that inspiring values of national pride, patriotism, unity, self-confidence are as important as developing infrastructure.

What specially attracted me is Modiji's design to connect tradition with modernity and adapt Gandhian ideas to changing conditions in society and the world at large. It is necessary to recognize that Gandhiji's ideas are not cast in concrete. They are in a significant sense organic and meant to grow. What is permanent in Gandhi are the principles such as cultivating love, practising nonviolence, and pursuing truth. However, the methods and practices are experimental and are likely to change with time to suit the circumstances. Take for example the fact that the Mahatma was opposed to India's partition at the time of Indian Independence in 1947.

However, when the partition did take place, his attention had shifted to focus on how the two countries should live in peace, helping and supporting each other. In fact, he even thought of moving to Pakistan to build a permanent peace bridge between the two sister nations.

During his time, Gandhi was opposed to rapid industrialization and growing migration to urban areas. He articulated well his reasons for it and the principles behind *gram swaraj*, his call for the urban elite to return to their rural roots, his advocacy of *charkha*, spinning, and *swadeshi*. Now, since Gandhi's time, industrialization has become indispensable for development, and development necessary to provide for increasing production to help people to live in comfort and happiness. Similarly, globalization has taken over and urbanization appears to be irreversible. What would Gandhi do under these changed conditions? Recall Gandhi was opposed to war. But when wars did break out, he did try to find ways of helping. In fact, he enlisted himself in the medical core to serve the injured during the First World War.

It is in this context I look at the new initiatives of Government of India and the prime minister's efforts to adapt Gandhian thought to current needs. I see a new hope with a sense of justified optimism. However, I do recognize that what we have are ideas and preliminary plans. We need to wait for their development, implementation, and consequent results. All that we can say at this time is that we seem to be on the right track and hope that we will move without serious hurdles to reach the goal of Rama-Rajya that Mahatma had visualized.

Further progress depends on two more things. First, there is need to increase people's awareness of Gandhi and relevance of his ideas to the world now at crossroads. Second, we need discussion, research, and further development of Gandhian thought. It is our belief that Gandhirama is a right step toward these goals.

I hope we will have a fruitful week of Gandhirama, experiencing Mahatma and gaining insights into Gandhi consciousness. Once again, I extend to all of you a hearty welcome. I look forward to inviting all of you when we lay the foundation stone for Mahatma Gandhi Mandir!

Gandhirama-2016
Abstracts

Triumph of Ancient Indian Philosophy and Modern Constitution

Sankarshan Acharya
Professor, University of Illinois, e-mail: <acharya.sankarshan@gmail.com>

This paper is not only about truth and nonviolence for coexistence of humans. It also presents a profound truth discovered through decades of research about the ancient human/Indian philosophy that perhaps subconsciously had inspired even Gandhi. A rational process of discovery of ancient Indian philosophy indicates that this philosophy is the crux of the modern constitution and rules of law, which are needed to (a) create equal opportunity for all humans to prosper by own diligence and perseverance, and (b) maintain social stability.

Gandhi's Sarvadharma Samabhava and Religious Harmony: Issues and Challenges

Afzal Ahmad
Research Scholar, Department of Philosophy, University of Delhi,
e-mail: <afzalahmad333@gmail.com>

Gandhi believed in the fundamental unity of all religions. In his speeches and writings he proclaimed the truth of the universality of all religions and actually practised and proved this truth in his life. A detailed study of the sacred scripture of different religions led him to the conclusion that the underlying principles behind every religion are the same and they differ only in their rituals and practices. According to him, co-operation and dialogue among various religions is the key to achieve religious harmony.

He believed that the concepts of truth, nonviolence, love, benevolence, justice, and universal brotherhood form the basis of every religion, and thereby, the world. Truth, nonviolence, and righteousness were the supreme manifestation of religion to Gandhi and he wanted the religion of truth, *ahimsa,* and righteousness to govern all spheres of life. *Ahimsa* teaches us to entertain the same respect for the religious faiths of others as we accord to our own. These concepts are also important for the proper functioning of human life. Thus for Gandhi, religion is a moral principle aimed at the welfare of humanity.

This paper is an attempt to analyse the relevance of Gandhi's views on religion and its implication in the present context especially conflict resolution and attainment of peaceful society. The notion of *sarvadharma samabhava,* i.e., equal treatment to all religions as espoused by Gandhi is an effective tool to counter the increasing tensions among different religious groups. The proposed paper will also deal with the issues of religious harmony in the contemporary world order through Gandhian perspective.

Gandhi, Islam, and Muslim Politics in Pre-Independence India: Implications for Muslim Politics in Post -Independence India

Anwar Alam
Professor, Department of International Relations, Zirve University, Gaziantep, Turkey, e-mail: <alam.anwar@gmail.com>

At a time when there is a global demonization of Islam for its supposed connectivity with violence, it is pertinent to revisit Gandhi's approach towards Islam and its implications for understanding the nature and concern of "Muslim Politics" that was conducted during the inter-war periods. As Gandhi conducted his "moral-ethical politics" within the frame of his religious world view mediated through Sanatan Hindu tradition, how does he approach and understand Islam and its dominant symbols and traditions including Prophet Muhammad? How and where does Islam figure in his conception of Hinduism? Whether his approach towards Islam has implications in generating a negative response among a section of Muslim community leading to the Partition of the country? In particular, was Jinnah's "Islamic politics" a direct response to Gandhi's religious politics mediated through Hindu traditions, as claimed by the left-liberal intelligentsia? Or whether the "phenomenon of Jinnah" or "Pakistan" symbolizes a construction of Islam that rejected India's plural traditions, despite having flourished within the liberal-plural traditions of Indian society, has an autonomous roots within the Islamic traditions that flourished upon the threat perception of Muslim's fear of insecurity of Islam in the emerging structure of nation state. This paper reflects upon this set of questions and argues that it was not the Gandhian Hinduism or religious inspired politics but "secular distrust" between a section of Hindu and Muslim elites that resulted in the eventual Partition of the country. The paper further argues that Gandhi's understanding of religion that broadly informs the mainstream understanding of secularism in India has to a large extent been a factor in containing the emergence of sustained, if not sporadic, Islamic militancy within the country despite the favourable conditions for the development of the same.

Gandhi's Approach to His Favourite Bhagavadgita: Hermeneutical Disaster, Profoundly Insightful, or Invitation for Our Creative Reconstitution of Its Significance Today

Douglas Allen

Professor, University of Maine, e-mail: <douglas_allen@umit.maine.edu>

M.K. Gandhi repeatedly avows that the *Bhagavadgita* is his favourite text, his moral and spiritual guide to daily living. In his formulations, Gandhi is consistent with most previous interpretations of *karma-yoga*. What renders Gandhi's approach to the *Gita* so idiosyncratic, controversial, and seemingly bizarre is his claim that it is also a gospel of nonviolence. How is this possible?

Critics assert that Gandhi's nonviolent interpretation is a hermeneutical disaster and has nothing to do with a rigorous objective interpretation of the meaning of the text. Others most frequently use Gandhi's own writings on the *Gita* to assert that Gandhi is offering an allegorical, highly symbolic reading that cannot be taken literally. Such allegorical, mythic, and symbolic interpretations of Gandhi's approach are invaluable, but they do not address Gandhi's most important moral, spiritual, and hermeneutical claim in his nonviolent interpretation of the *Gita*.

What has generally been overlooked is Gandhi's surprisingly complex, nuanced, and insightful methodological claims about texts, contexts, the interpretation of meaning, and a dynamic, open-ended approach to formulating and applying the values and principles of the *Bhagavadgita*. Gandhi grants that earlier formulators and interpreters of the *Gita* did not view it as a gospel of nonviolence. The *Gita* is a gospel of nonviolence for Gandhi (and for us today) because he claims that we can purify and develop the text, in more moral and spiritual ways. We can and must do a rereading of the *Gita*, reformulating it, reapplying it, in dynamic, open-ended, experiments with truth. This involves embracing traditional insights of *karma-yoga* and other paths, but addressing our contextual situatedness living in a contemporary world of such violent relations toward our self, other beings, and nature.

How can Gandhi inspire us to do this, and what are key moral and spiritual issues and obstacles to such a significant project?

The Concept of Ahimsa in Gandhian and Buddhist Philosophy

Abhinav Anand
Research Scholar, e-mail: <anandabhinav2009@gmail.com>
&
A.K. Behura
Associate Professor, Department of Humanities and Social Sciences,
Indian School of Mines, Dhanbad, e-mail: <ajitbehura@gmail.com>

Both Buddha and Gandhi are known for peace and harmony. The famous traditional proclamation *ahimsa paramo dharmah, ahimsaiva param tapah* shows the depth of *ahimsa* in Indian Ethical Tradition. The concept is very much central to the writings of Gandhi and Buddhist philosophy. Both Buddha and Gandhi emphasized universal compassion and love as *ahimsa* and taught it as the paramount virtue which morally sustains life. In both traditions, *ahimsa* is generally understood, preached, and practised as an ethical virtue. Gandhi himself acknowledged the influence of Buddhist thought in his philosophy. Gandhi said that he has nothing new to teach to the world, because truth and nonviolence are as old as hills. During the Vedic period or in the pre-Buddhist era, the practice of killing animals for sacrificial purposes was prevalent and thus a distressed Buddha preached *ahimsa* as the highest virtue. Similarly Gandhi chooses nonviolence as a means for freedom when many others affirmed violent approach in national movement. The richness of both the thoughts on *ahimsa* can be articulated at one platform. This paper would analyse the concept of *ahimsa* in Indian ethics, especially in the ethics of Buddha and Gandhi and its application to the contemporary world crisis.

Gandhian Concept of "Trusteeship": Gandhian Thesis of Social Ownership

Y.P. Anand
Former Director, National Gandhi Museum and Library, Rajghat, New Delhi.
e-mail: <ypanandindia@yahoo.co.in>

In Gandhi's time, two main systems of economic order prevailed — the capitalistic, and, the communistic/socialistic (a form of "state" capitalism). As predicted by him, the latter order has not lasted and now nearly whole world is governed by some form of capitalistic market economy, with varying measures of state regulation. Gandhi had seen how the concept of ownership of private property, wealth, and other assets was leading to increasing levels of appropriation and inequality, violence, exploitation, alienation, and socially and environmentally wasteful and unsustainable consumption. His basic premise was that everything on earth was from God and, hence, for the people as a whole. All that wealth, now "owned", did not belong to any individual or group or "class"; what belonged to anyone was the right to an honourable and need-based livelihood, no better than that available to all others and the rest of it belonged to the community. Thus, Gandhi wanted the present "owners" to outgrow their greed and sense of possession and to voluntarily convert themselves into "trustees" of their possessions, retaining their stewardship in order to use their talents to increase the social wealth. Gandhi's concept of "trusteeship" was founded on Indian philosophy (*tena tyaktena bhunjitha — Ishopanishad*) as well as on considerations of political economy, and developed over time into a comprehensive thesis of an alternative nonviolent, equitable, and sustainable economic order, as also seen from its most definitive format, "Practical Trusteeship Formula", which was approved by Gandhi but was published in 1952. It has remained a subject of research and discussion in India and abroad even after his martyrdom and a vast literature had grown around it. The paper attempts to give a historical review of the studies and praxis on the subject in the past and its relevance in the present context, particularly in India.

Swachh Bharat Abhiyan (Clean India Mission)

Y.P. Anand

Former Director, National Gandhi Museum and Library, New Delhi,
e-mail: <ypanandindia@yahoo.co.in>

Swachh Bharat Abhiyan is one of the major initiatives of the Government of India led by Shri Narendra Modi, inspired by Mahatma Gandhi. Gandhiji had realized early in his life that the prevalent poor state of sanitation and cleanliness in India and particularly the lack of adequate toilets, in the then largely rural India, needed as much attention as was being devoted toward the attainment of *swaraj*. He said that unless we "rid ourselves of our dirty habits and have improved latrines, *swaraj* can have no value for us". Along with the struggle for India's Independence, he led a continuous struggle for sanitation, cleanliness, and efficient management of all categories of wastes throughout his public life in South Africa and later in India. He dealt with nearly all aspects of sanitation — technical, social, and economic — and their different dimensions — personal, domestic, and corporate.

Prime Minister Modi in his speech on the Independence Day (15 August 2014) raised the question:

> How do we celebrate 150th birth anniversary of Mahatma Gandhi? . . . Mahatma Gandhi had cleanliness and sanitation closest to his heart. Whether we resolve not to leave a speck of dirt in our village, city, street, area, school, temple, hospital, and what have you, by 2019 when we celebrate 150th anniversary of Mahatma Gandhi? This happens not just with the government, but with public participation. That is why we have to do it together.

This resolve was concretized when on 2 October 2014, the prime minister launched a nationwide sanitation campaign, Swachh Bharat Abhiyan (Clean India Mission) to provide sanitation facilities to every Indian, including toilets, solid and liquid waste disposal systems, village sanitation, and safe and adequate drinking water supply by 2 October 2019.

It is in this context that the Gandhian movement for cleanliness, an important ingredient in Mahatma's Constructive Programme, becomes a reference point for the attainment of the Swachh Bharat targets by 2019. The panel discussion focuses on the various dimensions of cleanliness, various levels and actors involved, the multiple targets to be achieved, and the ways of reaching those goals.

Adverse Effect of Industrialization on Elders: A Gandhian Remedy

M. Arulappan
General Fellow (ICPR), Department of Philosophy, Pondicherry University,
e-mail: <tmsarul@rediffmail.com>

People are sceptical about the feasibility of Gandhian principles in globalized modern world. The rationale behind is that Gandhian principles demand self-discipline in every activity that is undertaken by the individuals. The present study focuses on the issue of overemphasis on industrialization in the name of modernization and its adverse effect on elders. Industrialization leads to modernization, modernization causes urbanization, and urbanization is the cause for social mobilization in the society. Therefore people migrating from rural areas to urban areas is an inevitable phenomenon of the industrialized modern world. Industrialization brings with it the material prosperity and materialistic comforts, at the same time, there are also adverse social changes that take place. One of them is social and emotional alienation of elders.

Gandhiji is not completely against industrialization or modernization but he strongly opposed the adverse attitude which is to be cultivated through this overemphasis on industrialization, such as mechanization of human life which is against the very nature of human being. It makes human being to be mechanical and artificial in his or her attitude towards not only others but to his or her family members too. This attitude results in the adverse effect on the elders. The elders are alienated from the family. They are made to become homeless and destitute in their last part of life. There is an increase in homes for the destitute and the elders in India.

The economic independence of elders could be one of the remedies to the problem of social alienation but the emotional alienation will be always there in the mind of elders. This paper inquires into the question: Could Gandhian principle of *ahimsa* bridge the gap between the elders and their near and dear ones which not only preaches the virtue of nonviolence but also teaches us the practice of values like love and tolerance towards others?

Gandhian Empathy: Psychological Reflections

N.V. Ashwini
Assistant Professor, Jain University, e-mail: <ashwiniganig@gmail.com>
&
Deepti Swamy
Lecturer, Jain University, e-mail: <deeptiswamy.8911@gmail.com>

When the entire world is riddled with instances of war, strife, and abuse, empathy is being championed as an elixir for the malady. It is regarded as one of the most important factors influencing the quality of interpersonal relationships across domains. It refers to the ability of human beings to enter the subjective world of others and feel/think from others' perspective. It is therefore not surprising that "Mirror Neurons" — responsible for empathy among human beings — are referred to as "Gandhi Neurons".

This study attempts to understand and analyse the dimensions of Gandhian Empathy from a psychological perspective and uses Gandhiji's autobiography as the content source. The objectives of the study is three-fold. First, it attempts to understand the dispositional and situational aspects of Gandhian Empathy. Second, it tries to understand cognitive and affective aspects of Gandhian Empathy. Third, it aims to understand how Gandhiji was able to convert the experience of empathy to its actual manifestation in championing the cause of truth and nonviolence.

For the current study, Gandhiji's Autobiography (*My Experiments with Truth*) was chosen for the fact that it is a primary source and offers personal narrative of Gandhiji's own experiences and thoughts. The fact that Gandhi's name is synonymous with the term empathy shows that he was able to successfully utilize empathy, which underlies his major philosophical and political concepts. Understanding Gandhian empathy will therefore enable one to train and help people to become more empathetic by nature.

Concept of Universal Religion in Swami Vivekananda and Mahatma Gandhi

An Introspection

Harsha Badkar
Associate Professor & Head, Department of Philosophy, Wilson College, Mumbai,
e-mail: <harsha_badkar@yahoo.com>

The purpose of this paper is to put forth the basic similarity between the religious views of Swami Vivekananda and Mahatma Gandhi and suggest that their approach to religion has the potential to bring about peace and harmony in the world which is torn apart due to the dogmatic approach towards religion. Through this paper I want to suggest that Gandhi's concept of *sarva dharma samabhava* (equal respect for all religions) was influenced by Vivekananda's Concept of Universal Religion and that his interpretation of the word Secularism guided by Vivekananda is the only solution to the problems created by fundamentalist approach to religion.

There are certain striking similarities between Swami Vivekananda and Mahatma Gandhi which are both interesting and instructive to reflect upon the bond that existed between them. Swami Vivekananda was the spiritio-religious emancipator, whereas Mahatma Gandhi was the socio-political emancipator of India. Though the realms of both the stalwarts remain different, the crux of their ideology remains the same, i.e., secular religion. The common factor between the two is their contribution of putting "the Indian way" at the centre stage of world thought through its spiritual and religious treasure. They took inspiration from Indian philosophical traditions, especially Vedanta, on the basis of which they presented a new design for life: a model of love, compassion, goodwill, and universal brotherhood.

Both of them accepted religion as one of the most important aspects of human life. It was Vivekananda who impressed the whole world with his views on religion and influenced majority of the social leaders of his time including Gandhi. Gandhi himself acknowledged the impact of Vivekananda on his life. Though both of them believed in the concept of Nationalism, the path adopted by Vivekananda was spiritual, whereas Gandhi adhered to socio-political movement which was inevitably related to religion. The spiritual leadership provided by Vivekananda served as the base for Gandhi's political movement. Gandhi believed that religion has an impact on each and every aspect of human life and therefore it cannot be separated from politics. He introduced the concept of "spiritualization of politics" and attempted to develop the political theory and strategy on the strong foundation of religion.

As "reason" played a pivotal role in both their philosophies of human life guided by religious ideology, both Swami Vivekananda and Gandhi are accepted as the contemporary Indian philosophers. Till date, both serve as powerful guiding force to young India. Far before, it became absolutely necessary to avoid religious conflict and establish peace and harmony in the world for the survival of humanity in the twenty first century. Both these thinkers have provided us with a novel approach to religion through which, rather than being the dividing factor, religion can become a uniting force of the society.

Humanism: The Thread that Binds Gandhi and M.N. Roy

Harsha Badkar

Associate Professor & Head, Department of Philosophy, Wilson College, Mumbai, e-mail: <harsha_badkar@yahoo.com>

M.N. Roy was the constant critic of Gandhi. He was very much against the concept of spiritualization of politics, as he strongly opposed the affiliation of religion and politics prescribed by Gandhi. His approach to politics was thoroughly rational. He was so much against Gandhian philosophy that while rejecting the parliamentary democracy as the ideal form of government, he did not even mention or consider Gandhian model of village *panchayat* as a plausible alternative. But, later, when Gandhi did not accept any powerful position post-Independence, Roy appreciated his attempts to solve the communal problem in Bengal. It is at this stage that he started realizing his mistake and confessed that he had failed to detect the secular approach beneath the religious idiom, and the essentially "moral, humanist, and cosmopolitan" character of Gandhi's message.

Through this paper, I am planning to deal with the possible affinity between the views of Gandhi and Roy in spite of the apparent conflict of approach between the two. Thus I will try to bring out some of the similarities between them which are so striking that they can overshadow the differences. I aim to suggest that Humanism as an ideology is the common thread that can bind the two seemingly contradictory ideologies of Gandhi and Roy. It is the genuine concern for the "welfare of all" that comes to the forefront through Gandhi's Sarvodaya and Roy's Radical Humanism.

Religion as Religious Consciousness: Gandhi's Tolstoyan View

Prashant Bagad
Assistant Professor, Department of Humanities and Social Sciences, IIT Kanpur, e-mail: <pbagad@iitk.ac.in>

In his *Hind Swaraj*, Gandhi considers religion in at least three major senses: (1) religion as sect; (2) religion as a set of values underlying several different religions; and (3) religion as a personal quest. Gandhi places great emphasis on the third sense. I propose to delineate in this paper that strand in Gandhi's short, polemical masterpiece *Hind Swaraj*. Anthony Parel contends that "religion" in *Hind Swaraj* stands for *dharma* in the theory of *purushartha*s. On Parel's view, Gandhi thinks it is the integrated and harmonious pursuit of the *purushartha*s that is lacking in modernity. Though I agree with this reading, I think it misses a crucial dimension of Gandhi's thought.

My contention is that Gandhi uses the word "religion" in the sense in which Tolstoy uses the notion of "religious consciousness" in his *What is Art?* Religion, for Gandhi, is not merely a set of ethical rules encoded in scriptures or statements of individual or social authorities/institutions. Gandhi's Tolstoyan addition seems to be that a human being or a society should be driven by religious consciousness, which is, "an understanding of the meaning of life which is the highest that has been reached by the people of that society and which defines the highest good for which that society *strives*". As a good artwork contains within itself a confluence of several complementary as well as conflicting currents of thought but displays a striving for the finest thought, a good life, Gandhi seems to suggest, is a perpetual quest for the best and highest understanding and practice of a true, humane objective of life; it is not merely an unanimated series of instances of rule-following.

Exploring Gandhi's Karma as Dharma

Balamurali Balaji
Founder-Director, Centre for Information Techonology & Gandhian Philosophy of Nonviolence & Peace, Mettur, e-mail: <bbmurali_2000@yahoo.com>

Based on the premises of *karma-yoga*, one could comprehend how Mahatma Gandhi led his life with the great virtues, dedicated to service, by pure and perfect action, leading to the realization of the Self, the final attainment of the soul. It is the *moksha*, the eternal state of a being in the form of soul, surrendering at the feet of God, the almighty. There is nothing more one could give back to the creator of the universe. *Rishi*s and *yogi*s have the similar way of living by surrendering their *bhakti* to see God through their insight and intuition. They did wonders, it is believed, to mankind with their mystic powers obtained through *tapas*, penance, and hymns. Out of such ancestral beginnings, Indian culture evolved through other forms of self-realization practices such as fasting, strict vegetarianism, worshipping by performing rites and rituals. Gandhi was the most successful in creating a desirable effect in large scale by means of fasting to achieve the goals of changing the lives of millions in a country.

This paper explores how Gandhi led a life of *karma* that fulfils his *dharma* of nonviolence. It ponders over the question of "how to choose one's *dharma*", the roots of dharmic needs and understanding of one's *karma* that finally makes the human life more meaningful and enlightened among the other species. It recounts *dharma* in Vedic terms and highlights how Gandhi's *dharma* of nonviolent actions surpassed the other forms of *karma*.

Gandhi and Corporate Leadership

Balamurali Balaji
Founder-Director, Centre for Information Techonology & Gandhian Philosophy of Nonviolence & Peace, Mettur, e-mail: <bbmurali_2000@yahoo.com>

It will be rather intriguing to understand the relevancy of Gandhism in the modern corporate world that otherwise talks of stocks, prices, sell-outs, and buy-ins everyday. If Gandhiji was alive today, how would he fit himself in corporate suits to make important decisions on crucial problems what the modern business houses face everyday? Could he do fair for the bucks and perks the companies spare? Could he be capped as a true leader in the corporate sector? Do the political principles he stated be appropriate in current day's technology-enabled business world? How far the Barrister could achieve in business with the strategies he followed in freeing the nation from the slavery?

The successes and failures of a great company lie in their strategies and the management principles and leadership skills. And these have almost become *mantras* as pronounced by *gurus* of management. Nevertheless, the corporate leaders need to possess great qualities to perform these *mantras* as sacred ceremonies to stay in business. Many *gurus* of corporate leadership have made up their minds that management is purely a science and leadership is a skill that need to be practised, not divine or simply preached, to attain success. The use of technology in business has fuelled this spirit to a greater extent.

After giving some serious study on management and leadership, one could understand how Gandhian ideology is near perfect strategy for leading and managing the corporate. Management *gurus* and authors never failed to point out the ideologies that Gandhiji formulated with respect to leadership wisdom. The current ethics of leadership could very well be traced and equated with Gandhian methods, characteristics, and ideals.

We would have to go through the whole history to study Gandhian methods and leadership principles to come out with the truth behind his successful leadership. In those days, political leadership was different from corporate leadership. There were very few management- and leadership-related books and resources during the beginning of the last century and most of the practices and leadership skills were formulated only in the later part of the twentieth century. But today, a thorough and definite understanding of Management and Leadership is on hand and it has become a *mantra* and ritual to perform business dutifully.

Gandhian Perspective of Rama-rajya: Reflections from Ramayana

D.S.V.S. Balasubrahmanyam
Lecturer, SRR & CVR Government Degree College, Vijayawada,
e-mail: <dsvsbs2004@gmail.com>

The purpose of state is to ensure well-being of its citizens in terms of social, political, cultural, religious, and spiritual progress. All the political thinkers though diverge as to the mechanisms to achieve this goal, unanimously accept this avowed purpose of the state. To ascertain what constitutes welfare of citizens, one has to first determine what human nature is. After all, what is good for us depends on what we are. This paper attempts to look into the fabric of Gandhian political thought to understand his conception of Rama-rajya as the ideal state, spirituality as the essential nature of human beings and how *Ramayana* influenced these conceptions. The concept of justice in *Ramayana*, which is the central notion in the public administration of Rama-rajya, has direct bearing on Gandhian political views. This paper observes that service of spiritually enlightened, morally upright, naturally cooperating, and a socially coherent citizen is the highest goal of Gandhi's Rama-rajya.

Relevance of Gandhi's Concept of Nonviolence in the Contemporary World

Rima P. Basheer
Research Scholar, Department of Philosophy, Pondicherry University,
e-mail: <rimabasheer@gmail.com>

The contemporary world and our own country are encountering violence of various forms because of unemployment, inflation, and violence against women and differences of opinion among the people. In such a situation the question in everybody's mind is whether the concept of non-violent philosophy of Gandhi is relevant or not. Unfortunately Indians themselves forgot and discarded Gandhi's ideals. Gandhi's concept of nonviolence is the outcome of his vast experiences and experiments which he did in laboratory of his own life. Nonviolence is a crucial and important Gandhian principle. In fact, Gandhi's ethics came to be known as ethics of a*himsa*. As a matter of fact Gandhi was undoubtedly the greatest ethical and religious thinker. In all his writings and speeches, he gave more importance to nonviolence and Truth. He sincerely believed that violence would bring the doom to the mankind. But people who have difference of opinions with Gandhi believe that Gandhi was not much harmful to his opponents while he being alive but he is more harmful after his death. The reason behind this is that the world is finding itself involved in violence, economic meltdown, starvation, unemployment, and hatred. And the need for adopting Gandhi's philosophy is being felt more eagerly everywhere. According to Gandhi, one should be brave and not a coward. He should present his views, suggestions, and thoughts without being violent. One can wage a war with the weapons of truth and nonviolence. Hence I make an attempt to signify the relevance of Gandhi's teaching by one of his most important theories of nonviolence. In this theory, I try to project the basic ideology of nonviolence and its significant relevance to the contemporary India.

Gandhian Philosophy, Mentoring and Youth Civic Engagement in India: Indicators of Positive Self-Development

Rachana Bhangaokar
Assistant Professor, Department of Human Development & Family Studies, MS University of Baroda, e-mail: <kulrachana@gmail.com>

Mahatma Gandhi remains an influential proponent of peace and nonviolence (*ahimsa*) across the world. Gandhi emphasized the spirit of practice more than the form, specifying that the spirit be consistent with the basic belief in truth, peace, and nonviolence. A qualitative study was carried out to describe the civic engagement experiences of thirteen youth and nine mentors volunteering at Gandhian institutions in programmes for social and community development in different parts of Gujarat. The participants were selected purposively using the snow-ball technique and in-depth interviews were carried out. Civic engagement within a Gandhian paradigm brought a unique dimension of tolerance, love, and friendship to the process of volunteering and self-development for the participants. Shared understanding of Gandhian ideas, beliefs, and practices included accepting each other peacefully with a sentiment of surrender and spirituality. In the process, youth became mindful of their selves and could focus inwardly on becoming better human beings. Mentors focused on "being" Gandhians rather than "creating" Gandhians and practised the principles of simplicity, compassion, kindness, and equanimity in their own lives, inspiring youth without direct preaching or coercion. The study found that youth civic engagement within the clear frames of Gandhian philosophy has tremendous potential for positive self- transformation. In a world, inching closer to violence every day, Gandhian mentors can build bridges for more youth to engage with the spirit of Gandhian philosophy and embrace peace and nonviolence in their lives.

Swaraj: An Evolving Concept

P.R. Bhat
Professor, Indian Institute of Technology, Bombay, e-mail: <parameshwar1951@gmail.com>

Hind Swaraj was published first in 1909 and its English version was brought out later. The response of M.K. Gandhi to many of the issues were speculative since India has not yet achieved freedom. This was the period when Gandhiji was working on the concept of self-rule. "Self-rule" before Independence and after Independence was expected to undergo some change. We are attempting to work out this modified concept of self-rule in this essay. Self-rule is taken to be rule by individuals. There seems to be a need to modify "self-rule" replacing self with "we". The ontology of "we" is different from the ontology of "I". Gandhi's "experiment with truth" is collective experiment in society. *Satyagraha* too is a social experiment. The place of *satyagraha* in democracy can be brought out better if we replace "I" with "we" in democracy. One way to understand "we" is to speak of participation of political parties in democracy. Another way of understanding "we" is to think of community at the level of village, township, etc., and think of a nation as a community. Since Gandhiji believed in secularism, community cannot be interpreted on religious lines. The paper concludes by claiming that electronic democracy effectively using social media would achieve Gandhiji's *swaraj*.

Vinoba Bhave's Reading of Gandhian Ethics

Kavita Bhatt
UGC Post-Doctoral Fellow, Department of Philosophy, HNB Garhwal University,
e-mail: <mrs.kavitabhatt@gmail.com>

It is a globally accepted fact that Gandhian insight into the moral vision has an originality and a freshness at the same time is very influential in nature for attracting the attention of the people around. His ethics is mainly dominated by the views regarding truth and nonviolence as the end and means. In any ethical philosophy that aims at describing the nature and standards of morality, the problems regarding means and end become very significant. Gandhi's thought about end and means is intimately related one with the other in a common sense assertion; but he goes beyond; when he accepts that means and end are convertible terms in his philosophy of life. And, this spirit was captured by Vinoba Bhave. He elaborated the Ekadash Vratas of Gandhi in a pragmatic sense. These are NonViolence, Truth, Non-Stealing, Brahmacharya, Asangrah, Physical Labour, Control of Taste, Fearlessness, Universal Religion, Equality, Swadeshi, and Untouchability. For clarity and preciseness, the present paper is divided into two parts. The first part will explain Gandhian views of morality primarily in terms of truth and nonviolence and second, associated with love, equality, and commitment to truth (*satyagraha*). All these concepts of morality are found in the writings of Gandhi with reference to certain life situations, but it is difficult to find a systematic theoretical assertion of morality in the classical sense. Vinoba Bhave made an attempt to reformulate Gandhian moral views in his own innovative way — Ekadash Vrata. And, this will be the theme of the second part of the paper. While concluding the present paper, we shall try to explore the relevance of the moral views of Vinoba Bhave with reference to Gandhi.

Ahimsa: Nonviolent World Order

Shatakshy Bhatt
Indraprastha College, Delhi, e-mail: <shatakshy.bhatt@gmail.com>

Ahimsa is a virtue. It is not only a negative virtue of non-killing or non-injury but a positive virtue of doing well to others, i.e., softness, tenderness, and supreme sacrifice. Mahatma Gandhi was not the founder of *ahimsa* but he was the first to apply it on large mass in the political field. He said that *himsa* (violence) is slavery. Nonviolence does not mean passivity in the face of danger/evil. It is the "Soul Force". It is, in short, *satyagraha* which means "resistance to evil" (zest for truth). Nonviolence is a perfect state and it is the goal towards which all mankind moves naturally though unconsciously.

Irom Chanu Sharmila also known as "Iron Lady of Manipur" is a civil rights activist and a political rights activist. She considers hunger strike as the most nonviolent way of protesting like Mahatma Gandhi, her idol.

Ahimsa, the key tenant of Gandhi's belief would rid a person of anger, obsession, and destructive impulses. The commitment to work for peace by peaceful means through training, strategic planning, constructive programmes, and personal discipline implies a revolution of the human spirit, and points to the possibility of a shift in human consciousness in which *ahimsa* becomes a way of life.

Is *ahimsa* a way of life in the present world scenario? Can *ahimsa* be made the way of life today? These are some questions that need consideration.

Relevance of Gandhiji in the Twenty-first Century

Prakruthi Burra
BITS, Pilani, Hyderabad Campus, e-mail: <burraprakruthi@gmail.com>

Is Mahatma Gandhi relevant to the world of today? Will he continue to be important in the future?

These seemingly simple questions encompass in their ambit many other significant questions, beliefs, value systems, and ethical and moral standards. First, the study of Gandhi is not just about the study of his life, work, and ideas, equally important is the ever-evolving application of his ideology to new challenges and situations — economic, social or political.

Second, a person can be relevant to one's own self, a locality, a nation or for humanity itself. Gandhiji can of course be profitably studied and followed in each of these facets. His life is as much an embodiment of the ancient Hindu saying *tat tvam asi* as it is of the Sermon on the Mount.

Third, relevance of his life can be remote, or immediate. Perhaps Albert Einstein had this in mind when he said of Gandhi "Generations to come, it may be, will scarce believe that such one as this ever in flesh and blood walked upon this earth", making Gandhiji's relevance immortal.

Gandhiji's relevance to present-day's turbulent world cannot be **over** emphasized. Humanity is in dire need of his wise and practical message on many fronts. The paper is an endeavour to recall, present, and rededicate one's self to Gandhiji's multifaceted message and to share it with others.

Reflections on Nandigram: A Gandhian Solution to the Development vs Displacement Debate in West Bengal

Shiladitya Chakraborty

Assistant Professor, Department of Political Science, University of Kalyani, e-mail: <shiladitya_chak@yahoo.co.in>

The tendency to equate economic growth with industrialization had in the recent past started a violent and bloody movement in Nandigram in West Bengal. The movement in Nandigram rapidly acquired explosive proportions with the intellectuals, civil society, and anti-left political parties throwing in their weight behind the displaced peasants. This movement ultimately became an albatross around the neck of the Left leadership and sank their political fortunes in West Bengal. In fact, the Nandigram tragedy is only one episode among a series of agitations that have exploded in various parts of India thereby renewing the development vs displacement debate in recent times. The killing of protesting peasants in Nandigram by the trigger happy police not only exposed the political myopia and inhuman indifference of the arrogant Left Front government but showed that the political process in India was increasingly getting governed by the logic of market which sees displacement only as an appendix to development. What we need today is a Gandhian model of economic development which is based on altruism and egalitarianism. This article would focus on the reasons behind the inception of a violent movement in Nandigram, the fundamental flaws in the development model, and policy of rehabilitation of the erstwhile Left Front government in West Bengal, and end by providing a Gandhian solution to this dilemma.

Mahatma Gandhi on Enlightenment of Women

Tapati Chakravartty
Assistant Professor, Department of Philosophy, S.S.L.N.T. Mahila Maha Vidyalaya, Dhanbad, e-mail: <tapati_phil@yahoo.com>

What we need is a mass upsurge by mankind — radical at the core and also freedom in content, not a battle by women against men i.e., a honest justice to women in all facets of life. Women vs man, is totally a false dilemma. The issue is that of enlightenment vs ignorance — against all forms of injustice — for both men and women. In Mahatma Gandhi's words — "I am firmly of the opinion that India's salvation depends on the sacrifice and enlightenment of her women"' (*Harijan*, 27-6-1936, p. 153).

Souls have no sex; as such in the world of spirit there is no gender differentiation or female discrimination as we find in a corporal order that is bred by a masculine civilization. For this very reason though we regard women as fairer but also consider them to be weaker than man and — this haunts our value system in which we poetize, romanticize, and even enslave women-kind. Mahatma Gandhi has stressed on the point as he was convinced:

> The soul in both is the same. The two live the same life, have the same feeling. Each is a compliment of the other. The one cannot live without the other's active help. — *Selections from Gandhi*, N.K. Bose, p. 271

Moreover, Gandhiji also pointed out:

> But somehow or other man has dominated woman from ages past, and so woman has believed in the truth of man's interested teaching that she is inferior to him. — ibid.

So a woman as equal to man has had her ups and downs in the zigzag stream of pre-history and history. She has been a slave, a subordinate and mostly praised into the prison-house of domestic drudgery. Mahatma Gandhi asserted: I passionately desire the utmost freedom for our women" [*Young India*, 21-7-21].

What is required is, freedom on both sides must become a natural norm. The right to work and life should belong to both and this perfect equality springs from the socialist philosophy which sets its face against all manner of oppression.

Psychological Perspectives of Nonviolence

Sudarsan Raju Chandolu
Principal, JJR College of Education, Visakhapatnam,
e-mail: <drcsrpublications@gmail.com>

Not only in India, the importance of nonviolence is essential throughout the world for peace and happiness of human life. Therefore, the United Nations General Assembly on 10 November 1998, proclaimed the first decade of the twenty-first century and the third millennium, the years 2001 to 2010, as the International Decade for the Promotion of a Culture of Peace and Nonviolence. Nonviolence is the practice of being harmless to self and others under every condition. It comes from the belief that hurting people, animals or the environment is unnecessary to achieve an outcome and refers to a general philosophy of abstention from violence based on moral, religious or spiritual principles. Nonviolence refers more specifically to the absence of violence and is always the choice to do no harm or least harm, and passivity is the choice to do nothing. Hence, the nonviolent approach to social struggle represents a radical departure from conventional thinking about conflict, and yet appeals to a number of commonsense notions. The principal aim of this paper is to find out the most important psychological factors of violence and the remedies to overcome the violence and to usher in world peace. In this connection a theoretical approach has been carried out from the earlier studies of violence and peace, and how the philosophers guide the route from violence to peace.

Globalization and Nonviolent World Order: Relevance of Gandhi in the Twenty-first Century

Subhash Chandra
Associate Professor, Intercultural Open University,
e-mail: <schandra101@gmail.com>

At the turn of the twenty-first century, the world was immediately gripped by conflicts, violence, and war on terrorism. In reflection, the twentieth century was a period marked by tremendous technological and economic progress — but it was also the most violent century in human history. It is a matter of great concern for all the people, particularly educators and social scientists to think together and work together towards peace building for the welfare of mankind. Human values are eroding at a very fast rate resulting in a declining quality of life of the people. At the dawn of the new millennium, what is required most is "Gandhian Philosophy of Nonviolence" for creating a peaceful society and making a new world order.

This paper is based upon Gandhian philosophy of holistic human development and nonviolence movement for creating a nonviolent world in twenty-first century. The main objectives of the paper are to explore how Gandhian principles of *satyagraha* and *ahimsa* (nonviolence) can best contribute in developing a nonviolent world order in the era of globalization. The paper also tries to explore "the Gandhian philosophy of compassion, forgiveness, friendship, tolerance, equality, etc.," for making sustainable peace and nation building. The paper provides a framework of Gandhian vision for developing nonviolent world order based on Gandhian philosophy of nonviolence and Gandhi's top seven values for changing the world order in the twenty-first century.

Gandhi and Khadi

Nekkalapudi Pujith Chowdary
e-mail: <pujithchowdarynekkalapudi@gmail.com>
&
Sri Sai Sailesh
GITAM Institute of Management, GITAM University, Visakhapatnam
e-mail: <saileshv1995@gmail.com>

The objective of this paper is to study the central ideas of *swaraj* and development of village industries in Mahatma Gandhi's concept of *khadi*. *Khadi* had great importance to Gandhi as a symbol of nationalism, *swaraj* (self-rule), freedom, equality, and self-reliance. It was Gandhi's belief that the reconstruction of society and effective *satyagraha* against foreign rule can be possible only through *khadi*. He also recommended *khadi* as the central core of reconstructive activities. He believed that there could be no *swaraj* without universal and voluntary acceptance of *khadi*. In his own words, "I am a salesman of *swaraj*. I am a devotee of *khadi*. It is my duty to induce people, by every honest means, to wear *khadi*."

In India, *khadi* is not just a cloth, it is a whole movement started by Gandhi. The *khadi* movement in 1918 promoted an ideology, an idea that Indians could be self-reliant on cotton and be free from the high-priced goods and clothes which the British were selling them. The British used to buy cotton from India at cheap prices and export them to Britain where they were woven into clothes. These clothes were then brought back to India to be sold at hefty prices. The *khadi* movement was aimed at boycotting foreign goods including cotton and promoting Indian goods. Gandhi began promoting the spinning of *khadi* for rural self-employment and self-reliance instead of using clothes manufactured industrially in Britain. Gandhi believed in production for masses rather than mass production. The spinning wheel was at one time the symbol of India's poverty and backwardness. Gandhi turned it into a symbol of self-reliance and nonviolence. The proposed paper will also deal with the condition of *khadi* in the contemporary globalised world.

Gandhi's Innovation in Ethics: Satyagraha as a Method of Rational Proof

J. Gray Cox
Professor, College of the Atlantic, Bar Harbor, Maine, e-mail: <gcox@coa.edu>

As Alasdair MacIntyre has argued in *After Virtue*, the threat of relativism plagues the Western tradition in ethics because it lacks a framing metaphysics and epistemology that allows for grounding prescriptive knowledge in morals. As a result, unresolvable debates between rival ethical principles and traditions leave people at odds with incommensurable views. Gandhi's method of *satyagraha* offers a way out of this impasse because (1) it adopts a dialogical, conflict resolution and negotiation approach to differences and ethical questions rather than a monological, deductive, foundationalist approach, (2) it frames its metaphysics and epistemology in emergentist terms — understanding objectivity, truth, and meaning as occurring in matters of degree and lesser or fuller completeness rather than in absolute, universal, and dichotomous ways, and (3) introduces a method of testing truths through practices of self-sacrifice in dialogical engagements with others. The aim of this paper is to clarify the nature of Gandhi's innovation in ethical reasoning and to explain its potential for resolving the impasse faced by Western ethics.

Gandhi and Vivekananda on Peace: A Comparative Study

Gauri Ramakrishna Dangre
Student, Mumbai University, e-mail: <gauridangre91@gmail.com>

The concept of peace was explored by two great thinkers of modern India. The present paper will explore the genesis of peace as stated by Mahatma Gandhi and Swami Vivekananda.

Mahatma Gandhi and Swami Vivekananda are two most notable thinkers who worked for the welfare of the society, masses, and their country and countrymen.

Gandhi looks at peace as nonviolence, force of love, tolerance of all. Gandhi quoted:

> I have found people who envy my peace. That peace comes from prayer; I am not a man of learning but I humbly claim to be a man of prayer. I am indifferent as to the form. Everyone is a law unto Himself in the respect.

Swami Vivekananda quoted:

> Blessedness, eternal peace, arising from perfect freedom, is the highest concept of religion underlying all the ideas of God in Vedanta — absolutely free existence, not bound by anything, no change, no nature, nothing that can produce a change in him.

This paper will inquire into differences between both the thinkers where Gandhi's field was politics and that of Vivekananda was religion, i.e., Vedanta. Though their paths were different, both of them aimed to achieve peace for the people and society and world at large, for which they have struggled throughout their life. The paper will also throw light on the relevance of Gandhian and Vivekananda's views in today's world.

Gandhi's Concept of Nonviolence and Its Practicality in the Present Context

Anjali Das
Srihati Bathan High School, Howalkuchi, e-mail: <anjalidas0190@gmail.com>

Nonviolence is the central concept of Gandhi's philosophy. The word nonviolence is a translation of the Sanskrit word *ahimsa*. Gandhi stated that in its positive form *ahimsa* means "largest love", "the greatest charity". He stated that *ahimsa* binds us to one another and also to God. *Ahimsa* is a unifying agent. Gandhi wrote, "*ahimsa* and love are one and the same thing". According to Gandhi the more we try to practise nonviolence and compassion and the more we can increase them. As a result we can elevate ourselves morally. When we do so, we become more happy and more contented. Gandhi puts utmost emphasis upon the ideal of nonviolence. For him without nonviolence truth cannot be realized. His truth is identical with God. Therefore the realization of God is possible only through the practice of nonviolence or *ahimsa*. The concept of nonviolence means love towards all living creatures. This nonviolence is not only extended to mean love towards human being but to all sentient creatures in the world. *Ahimsa* should be practised at the mental level also. So nonviolence means noninjury to others not only in the physical sense but in the mental sense also. Hence the concept of nonviolence according to Gandhi has a very significant application. He said if *ahimsa* is better practised in one's domestic life it becomes easier for him to attain success in his relationship with others. An attempt will be made to discuss Gandhi's concept of nonviolence and its practicality in the present context.

Ecological Responsibility: A Gandhian Perspective

Jaharlal Debbarma
Research Scholar, Centre for Buddhist Studies, University of Hyderabad,
e-mail: <debbarma.jauhar@gmail.com>
&
Beroleeka Debbarma
Department of Philosophy, North Eastern Hill University

Globalization and the advancement of modern science and technology have helped in the growth of industrialization resulting in uncontrolled emission of carbon dioxide to the atmosphere. It has led to a great environmental crisis today. The exploitation and pollution of the planet has brought ecological catastrophes and has put the eco-system and human existence in jeopardy. With ego-centric, individualistic, and consumerist attitude of the people this crisis has worsened. Gandhi's ideas of *satya* (Truth), *ahimsa* (nonviolence), *satyagraha* (insistence on truth), on technology and development, self-sufficiency and *gram-swaraj*, etc., disclose his deepest environmental concern. This paper tries to see how far this ecological crisis can be minimized if one applied Gandhian principles in his day-to-day life.

A Critical Analysis of Gandhi's Concept of Satyagraha

Jayashree Deka
Department of Philosophy, University of Hyderabad,
e-mail: <deka.jayashree@gmail.com>

The aim of this paper is to explain Gandhi's concept of *satyagraha* and to analyse how he applied his concept of *satyagraha* in various conflict resolutions. Through the application of the method of *satyagraha* Gandhi tried to resolve various troubles prevailed not only in India but also in South Africa. He resolved the racial discrimination against black people by the white people in South Africa through the application of the method of *satyagraha*. He also applied the method of *satyagraha* to make India free from the British rule. In this paper, I am trying to critically analyse how Gandhi succeeded in resolving various social problems through his concept of *satyagraha*.

Gandhian Approach to a Nonviolent World Order

Sailaja Gullapalli
Research Associate, Gandhi Smriti and Darshan Samiti,
e-mail: <sailajagullapalli@gmail.com>

Ahimsa (nonviolence) is one of the basic prerequisites for a peaceful life of the mankind. The basic premise is that human beings have an element of divinity imbedded in them and it is this feature that calls for both inner and outer peace. While all the religions and philosophies have vehemently insisted on truth and nonviolence, Mahatma Gandhi, with his spiritual approach, called them as his twin principles that are as old as hills. While it is much easier to resort to violence, being nonviolent and adhering to nonviolence is a much difficult task. Keeping in view the contemporary world and its perennially disturbed state, it is necessary to revisit Gandhi's views and thoughts on this virtue. The twentieth century has seen two world wars and the ensuing destruction. The same has been the case with the modern world where there are many issues which have become a source of conflict and continue to perturb peaceful conditions.

It is in this context that Gandhi's views on nonviolence and his vision for a peaceful world order need to be reviewed. Gandhi's approach was pacifist rather than confrontational as evident from his thoughts and praxis. This paper intends to examine the concept of a nonviolent world order within the framework of the international relations and how Gandhi's views have great relevance in this context.

Contemporary Relevance of Gandhian Tools of Conflict Management

Alok Kumar Gupta
Associate Professor, Centre for Political Studies, Central University of Bihar, Patna,
e-mail: <alokgupta@cub.ac.in>

Gandhi, who became an icon for the erstwhile freedom fighters during the nationalist movement to liberate the Indians from the shackles of foreign powers, continues to be an icon for the youth, the young, and the grown-up Indians, with ever-increasing relevance not only in the Indian context but also for the world community at large. It is more so when more than half the world and nearly 60 per cent of the world community resides in the "Zone of Chaos", where inter-state wars, intra-state wars, low-intensity conflicts of various kinds are widely prevalent. It seems the "Zone of Peace" in the world is shrinking fast. The rigmarole effect of "economic recession" that set rolling on the American soil has forced the thinking being on this earth about an "alternative model of economy". Probably, the answer as well as the solace lie in the Gandhian model of "self-sufficient village economy" (*Gram Swaraj*).

The whole world seems to be conflict-ridden of different hues. Nepal, Myanmar, Pakistan, Bangladesh, Sri Lanka, Maldives in our own vicinity are itsy-bitsy; so also Syria, Sudan, Somalia, Kosovo, Israel, Palestine, Iraq, are the names but a few about which lesser said is better. We all know and have been reading about Tahrir Square, Shahbagh Movement, Azad Maidan, Arab Spring which are just the trailer of role that technology and military hardware can play towards contributing to conflict in the world and killing humanity. The contemporary world presents a backdrop where "peace" seems to be extremely sought-after necessity; yet it is too rare and fast eloping from our midst. Since the beginning of recorded history, around 3600 BCE, over 14,500 major wars have killed about four billion people. The wars that took place in the twentieth century killed around 200 million people; in the Second World War 66 million died, compared to 15 million in the First.

The arms approach to peace has proved disastrous. Arms kill to arrive at peace. Diplomacy, war, negotiations, reconciliations, and several other mechanisms to arrive at peace and endeavours towards containment of conflict also seem to have been failing and have proved a costly affair without much success. Therefore, it makes it imperative to search for an alternative method for conflict prevention, conflict management, conflict resolution, and conflict transformation so that there is sustainable peace which shall be the path to a just society. It is in this context that Gandhi,

Gandhism, Gandhian Thought, and the tools such as truth (*satya*), non-violence (*ahimsa*), *satyagraha* (passive resistance), as devised by the "Father of the Nation" Mahatma Gandhi, becomes of great relevance and perhaps the only means and mechanism to arrive at sustainable peace and economic development. Therefore, I propose to explore and discuss the contemporary relevance of Gandhian tools of conflict management and suggest why and how it could be applied.

Gandhi on Freedom: A Retrospective Analysis

Merry Halam
Handique Girls' College, Guwahati, e-mail: <merryhalam@gmail.com>

Gandhiji had struggles during a major part of his life for the freedom of India from British domination. But his conception of freedom is not merely freeing India from the English yoke but also freeing India from any yoke whatsoever. He said that when the British leave the country, freedom would of course reach New Delhi, but until it goes to every hut, and every villager feels freedom in his/her own life, it would not be of much meaning. What he meant was that until the common man of India lives a life of dignity and fearlessness, India would not achieve the freedom of his concept.

Moreover, his concept of freedom like other fields of human life is circular and not pyramidal, because he sees life as a circle. For him the individual is the centre. In his own words, "Life will not be a pyramid with the apex sustained by the bottom, but it will be an oceanic circle whose centre will be the individual" (*Harijan*, 1956). In this structure, the outermost circumference will not wield power to crush the inner circle but will give strength to all within and derive its own strength from it.

The paper would, therefore, analyse the concept of freedom according to Gandhi. In the process, it would try to emphasize the political, economic, social, and individual aspects of freedom as discussed by him. Finally, attempts would be made to relate Gandhi's conception of freedom with the present world order, where freedom is still a dream for millions.

Strategies of Nation Building through Gandhian Approach

S. Indira
Associate Professor, Department of Philosophy, Pondicherry University, Puducherry, e-mail: <indira611@gmail.com>

In the contemporary world man has been able to make tremendous strides in all fields like space research, nuclear energy, medical and bio-sciences and also advancement in technology. It became a significant feature in the progress of the twenty-first century. However this progress has not been accompanied by the progress or harmony among the human relations. They become strained day-by-day. Initially they may start with difference of opinion but ultimately they may lead to conflicts and conflagrations. In this context, I wish to present a paper on "Strategies of Nation Building through Gandhian Approach". Gandhi envisioned for an egalitarian society of the twenty-first century without any conflict, war, and violence. He envisioned for a world of talent, knowledge, and wisdom that is used for the friendship and fellowship within the nation and also among the nations of the world. Gandhiji made use of truth and nonviolence as the twin powerful instruments to make the desired world. He insisted on the means to be moral because means justify the end and they are two faces of the same reality. They are the identical terms. His conviction about morality is the basis of things and truth is the substance of all morality. He aspired that the modern civilization must have the roots of moral conviction. It should be free from any kind of evils like religious creed, political, social, and economic vices.

Gandhi's Critique of Modernity: An Exploration of the Five Great Vows

Reetu Jaiswal
Research Scholar, University of Delhi, e-mail: <jaiswal.reetu@yahoo.com>

Modernity as an idea and phenomenon is characterized by a number of features such as rationalism, imperialism, industrialism, individualism, universalism, democracy, control over nature, scientific developments, and globalization. Though it emerged against the existing evils of society, for instance suppression, slavery, authoritarianism, etc., it produced numerous complexities with its origin and dissemination. Mahatma Gandhi is one of the resolute critics of modernity in the twentieth century. According to him, modern civilization lacks moral and spiritual depth, and therefore, is a great threat to humanity. Gandhi was influenced by the Vedas, the *Gita*, and the *Ramayana*. He had a strong belief in "Five Great Vows": *satya, ahimsa, asteya, aparigraha,* and *brahmacharya*. Modernity advanced the universal concept of truth, ignoring its plurality and diversity. It relies merely on the faculty of reason and ignores the role of intuition and emotions. Gandhi accepts that truth could be found only in the experience of one's life. Modern values are violent in nature. The scientific experiments, the role of state, medical science, lawyers, are all the means of exploitation and violence. It is not found on the need of people, but on the greed to get more production, more power, and more capital. It is based on the unchecked and ever-increasing covetousness of the human race where human life has become completely mechanical. This paper will attempt to present Gandhi's critique of modernity vis-à-vis an exploration of the five great vows.

The Gandhian Concept of Truth

Abha Jha
Assistant Professor, Depatment of Philosophy, Ranchi College,
e-mail: <abha.jhaphilosophy@gmail.com>

Mahatma Gandhi was influenced by Vedantic doctrine "All life is one". He believed in the unity of human life, this unity is a synthetic whole and can neither be divided in spheres like social, religious, political, moral or ethical, nor can be distinguished in levels like individual or collective. The seemingly separate segments are in fact different facets of human life and are related to each other and react upon one another. According to Gandhi, the Supreme Being God, who is the creator of all, is the power behind the above unity. For Gandhi, He is also the Truth and it is His voice within every one that inspires to follow the vision of truth. This way Gandhi taking God, the supreme creator, declares Him "the Truth" and the basis as well as the symbol of unity. He accepted, if it is possible for the human tongue to give the fullest description of God, that for himself, God is Truth. Even Gandhi went one step further and said that Truth is God. According to him, there is never a double meaning to truth and even atheists had not demurred to the necessity or power of truth and in their passion for discovering truth, the atheists have not hesitated to deny the very existence of God — from their own point of view rightly. And it was because of this reasoning, rather than say that God is Truth, he said that "Truth is God".

Gandhian Economics: Unheard Presage of a Sage

Pragya Jha
Department of Philosophy, Indraprastha College, University of Delhi,
e-mail: <jjhappragya@gmail.com>

1947-77 were the years when the country was fabricating itself into an unsolved conundrum. On one side the organization of the states was at its apogee and on the other side was the economy of the country which was in complete disdain. Many scholars claim that the Indian economical growth was better in this period than under colonial rule but then there is this saying that the whole world did better post-1950.

The paper deals particularly with the man who was considered as the Father of the Nation, yet whose economical perspectives were not taken into any account. Was this just a by-product of different economical tastes of Gandhi–Nehruvian policy? If considered how far the Gandhian policy would have gone? — These are the questions, inquired into in this paper.

The *idée fixe* with the heavy industry led the labour-intensive industry to peril and the same happened to the Nehru–Indira socialism version; yet such a model was followed unquestioned for decades. All this leads to a single dish on the porcelain that is as to what led to the neglect of Mahatma's policies and what would be the prima facie of the Indian states if it happened the way he wanted it to happen.

The paper deals with the increasing fascination of the foreign companies with the Indian handicraft and there yet another start of serving us our *swadeshi* objects, their growth models, and the repetition of the raw material-finished good corollary of the colonial era.

Gandhiji, Ramana Maharishi, and Philosophy of Self

Gautam Kalotra
Assistant Professor, Department of Philosophy, Panjab University, Chandigarh,
e-mail: <gkalotra63@gmail.com>

This paper will be an approach to understand two great personalities of the contemporary times — Gandhiji and Ramana Maharishi. Though they never met, they established the philosophy of Self. I find their approaches similar. Gandhiji holds spiritual philosophy of Self in socio-political domain. On the other hand, Ramana Maharishi expresses everything in Self and Self-Inquiry. I would like to quote a famous incident in the life of Dr. Rajindra Prasad, when he expressed his desire to be in Peace,

Gandhiji advised Dr. Prasad to visit Ramana Maharishi's *ashram*, but requested him not to ask any questions to Maharishi. In year 1938 Dr. Prasad visited Ramanashramam; on the last day of his visit, he asked Ramana Maharishi whether, he would like to send any message to Gandhiji. Ramana Maharishi replied that the same Self is here and it is working there and hence there is no need for a message. Though Ramana Maharishi hardly speaks, he emphasizes upon Self-Inquiry. Gandhiji on the other hand, believed in Self as kingdom (*swaraj*). Hence, the philosophy of both of them is the paradigm of Self. No doubt, world history looks at Gandhiji being a part of freedom struggle, but in the very core of his heart he was a true spiritual leader and practitioner. Gandhiji was a real *karmayogi*. Both Gandhiji and Ramana Maharishi are the two sides of the same coin — silence as Self and Self as kingdom (*swaraj*).

The Pragmatic Implications of Gandhian Insights of Ahimsa

Indoo Pandey Khanduri
Associate Professor, Department of Philosophy, HNB Garhwal University,
e-mail: <indoo_khanduri@rediffmail.com>; <indookhanduri@gmail.com>

The objective of this paper is to discuss the pragmatic implications of Gandhian insights of *ahimsa* with reference to individual personality traits and satisfaction, surrounding in terms of peaceful and harmonious environment and society for inculcating a creative vision and directions towards a better living condition. For clarity and comprehensibility, the present paper is divided into three parts. In the first part, we shall discuss the concept of *ahimsa* in ancient Indian writings of Vedas, Upnishads, and Jainism for understanding its dynamics as the soul-force suitable to modern world order having conflict situation. In other words, it will constitute a brief historical background of Gandhian notion of *ahimsa*. In the second part of the paper, Gandhian notion of *ahimsa*, in terms of its presuppositions, meaning, and structure is discussed. In the third part, we shall make an attempt to reflect upon the practical implications of practising *ahimsa* from the individual, surroundings, and social points of view. For individual, the practice of *ahimsa* involves the assumption of love for all at core of heart, along with tolerance, sacrifice, courage, and standing for justice. From the surrounding point of view, the practice of *ahimsa* implies a peaceful and harmonious environment for avoiding differences and conflicts. For society, rising above from selfish motive, the practice of *ahimsa* inculcates the vision and creativity for inculcating, nourishing, and growing better living conditions. Thus, apart from being a means to the ends — Truth, the Gandhian insights into the practice of *ahimsa*, has multifarious pragmatic implications.

Gandhi:
The Human Rights Advocate Nonpareil

Poosarla Bayola Kiran
e-mail: <bayola13@gmail.com>

The Universal Declaration of Human Rights, 1948, is widely accepted to be the most important milestone in the recognition of human rights. The idea of a human right is multi-faceted, and being so, generations of human rights have been identified and brought to the fore. Much prior to this declaration, Mahatma Gandhi had propounded the idea of human rights in a simple but very effective way. He was, of course, a lawyer, trained in the best traditions of British jurisprudence and a member of the Inner Temple. More importantly, he was a compassionate human being, who chose to use the law not for his personal benefit, but for unshackling the shackled and for uplifting the downtrodden. In doing so, he synthesized the best of oriental and occidental philosophies and ideologies. The unique methods he adopted for achieving his noble ideals, i.e., *satyagraha*, nonviolence, civil disobedience, and non-cooperation, have shown all oppressed people the most effective path for attaining and preserving of their human rights. Every champion of human rights, right from Martin Luther King Jr. to Aung San Suu Kyi has followed his footsteps. The present paper aims at highlighting the seminal contribution of Gandhian ideology to the concept of human rights. It also focuses on the dynamic nature of human rights, i.e., the ever evolving idea of human rights and the continuing relevance of Gandhian tradition to the concept.

Gandhi's Moral Revolution

Nishikant Kolge
Assistant Professor, Department of History, Tripura University,
e-mail: <kolge270477@gmail.com>, <nishikantkolge@tripurauniv.in>

Critics of Gandhi, particularly those who call themselves Marxist or leftist in political thought and movement, have often criticized Gandhi's political philosophy and his general outlook on life as medieval, reformist, and even reactionary. Most of them describe Gandhi's leadership of Indian liberation movement and his introductions of nonviolence in politics as an effective strategy to consolidate the power of a bourgeoisie allied to feudal and imperialist class interests. R. Palme Datt, a well-known Marxist scholar writes: "All the hopes of the bourgeoisie (the hostile might say, the hopes of imperialism) were fixed on Gandhi as the man to ride the waves, to unleash just enough of the mass movement in order to drive a successful bargain, and at the same time to save India from revolution." Therefore, most Marxist scholars described Gandhi as "counter-revolutionary" and Gandhism as a philosophy of "counter-revolution". However, there have been substantial efforts from the side of Gandhian scholars to defend Gandhi, his role in India's struggle for political independence against British and his introduction of nonviolence in politics. In Gandhi's defence, they generally argue that Gandhi introduced nonviolence in politics because he did not want India's political independence to be the effort of a small group of elite, legally and constitutionally trained, upper-middle-class Indian men only. He wanted people from different class, section, and gender should earn this independence. A Gandhian scholar writes:

> Gandhi had learnt from experience that in violent revolutions there is no real involvement of the widest sections of the people; a minority participates in a revolution and the microscopic minority that wields power installs a dictatorship "in the name of the people". Vast masses remain mere passive spectators both of the revolution and of the phase of reconstruction. — *Comparing Study of Gandhi and Marx*, p. 50

Though, it is a noteworthy defence of Gandhi's position on such an important issue, it presupposes that like Marxist scholars, Gandhi too believed that revolution means "replacement of old ruling class by new ruling class". They give credit to Gandhi for introducing nonviolence as a method for peaceful replacement of old ruling class by new ruling class, hence making it possible for the large section of the society to be part and parcel of this process. However, in order to have comprehensive understanding of Gandhi's revolution, it is important to question such presupposition and ask some basic questions, i.e., what does revolution mean? How does Gandhi understand revolution? How is it different from Marxist scholars' understanding? Therefore, the first section of this paper attempts to answer above raised questions and argues that for Gandhi revolution means "complete reversal of the existing moral values". The second section of this paper attempts to explain what Gandhi means by complete reversal of the existing moral values.

Gandhi's Moral Psychology on Truth

Manik Konch
Research Scholar in Philosophy, Department of Humanities and Social Sciences, IIT Bombay, e-mail: <kkonch.2@gmail.com>

Truth is often defined as other-worldly and as an abstract theoretical concept. It is spiritual. Gandhi is a critic of this spiritual conception of truth. According to him, truth is experienced in the act of truth seeking. In other words, truth as a normative concept is very much a part of moral experience. This normative conception of truth could be unfolded with the help of the analysis of the moral attitude of truth seeking. Gandhi is a moral exampler who has displayed moral attitude of truthfulness in his everyday life. The paper discusses the act of truth seeking by bringing some of the important episodes from Gandhi's life and tries to elucidate the moral psychology of Gandhi on truth.

Significance of Gandhian Concept in Shaping Indian Teachers

P. Kowsalya
Research Scholar, School of Education, Pondicherry University, e-mail: <pkowsalya1988@gmail.com>

On analysing Mahatma Gandhi's views and vision of what constituted a truly civilized and free India, it was not surprising that he developed firm views on education. Education not only moulds the new generation, but reflects a society's fundamental assumption about itself and the individual. Gandhi's conception of basic education was concerned with learning that was generated within everyday life which is the basis on which informal educators work. It can also be seen as education focused on the individual but reliant on cooperation between individuals. There is a familiar relationship between educators and student/learners. According to Gandhi, "A teacher is one who establishes rapport with the taught, becomes one with them, and learns more from them than he teaches them". This paper focuses on the significance of teacher updating and enhancing techno skills and knowledge in understanding the changing needs and capacities of a diversified learning community. It also underlines Gandhian views on the method of teaching which is none other than "Learning By Doing", "Vocational Training", and "Basic Craft". With reference to Gandhian Philosophy of Education it tries to bring out the values of teacher–pupil relationship. This paper suggests professional ethics and discipline to be followed by Indian teachers of today to create global citizens of tomorrow. The above-mentioned points will be discussed briefly one by one in this paper which give a wholesome idea of Gandhiji's role in shaping Indian teachers.

Trusteeship in the Philosophy of Mahatma Gandhi

V. Venkata Krishnarjun
Research Scholar, Department of Philosophy, S.V. University, Tirupati,
e-mail: <vv_krishnarjun@yahoo.com>

Trusteeship essentially means having faith and confidence in a process of taking responsibility for assets and social values, and administering their rightful and creative usage for the benefit of others — now and in coming generations. The term "trusteeship" was first used in relation to property and its ownership. In our country the word "trustee" is used in connection with temples and *mutts* and "trustee" means a person who manages the property of the temple without any selfish interest. Gandhi's understanding of trusteeship is basically a principle of economic conscience, a dynamic model of the concept of economic organization and moral imperatives.

Gandhi conceived trusteeship as a system wherein the individual considers that part of his wealth in excess of his needs as being held in trust for the larger good of society and acts accordingly. Gandhiji invented and preached trusteeship, as a technique of social change. Trusteeship can be viewed as an attitude to life. Trusteeship means personal gain together with social gain. Trusteeship can provide a way to avoid not just violence between humans but also between humans and their environment, and has to be the ethic for the next century.

Gandhi's Concept of Education and Its Relevance in the Twenty-first Century

Neenu Kumar
Aditi Mahavidyalaya, University of Delhi, e-mail: <kumar.neenu@gmail.com>

Gandhi's views on education were not only relevant in his times but they also provided a blueprint for the future generations. Retrospectively, during his lifetime, Gandhi wanted education not merely to educate but he wanted education to develop the integral personality of man. He wanted to utilize education as a constructive agency for the development of the society. Educators such as Tagore, Dewey, Gandhi, and others felt that a child's personality should be allowed to unfold in a conducive atmosphere and education could play an important role towards achieving that. External education is neither *sat* (true) nor *asat* (untrue). It is an amalgam of both as also different from them. Gandhi felt that education, which cannot instill feelings of service and sacrifice, is of no consequence. According to Tagore also an education which cannot generate humanistic emotions and "ensure that students in thought, emotion and action, attain truth and achieve the fullest development in all the various manifestations of the human spirit", is worthless. Gandhi felt that formal education should be substantiated by vocational training so as to make it job-centric for the youth. His policy of education was not only value based but also mass oriented. Manual work is coupled with intellectual exercise, which is at the heart of learning at all stages. Gandhi's philosophy of education is taken a step forward by Narendra Modi. He envisions an education system where students can be the harbingers of change. He wishes this change to be positive and constructive. This in accordance with Vivekananda's views who says:

> The ideal of all education, all training, should be this man-making. . . . The man who influences, who throws his magic, as it were, upon his fellow-beings, is a dynamo of power, and when that man is ready, he can do anything and everything he likes; that personality put upon anything will make it work.

Gandhian Economics: Its Relevance to Modern Times

Tanuja Kumari
Assistant Professor, Department. of History, S.S.L.N.T.M. College, Dhanbad, e-mail: <tanujadhanbad10@gmail.com>

Gandhiji's economic thoughts are relevant in modern times. They are based upon egalitarianism, simplicity, and ascetism. They are reflected in Dr. J.C. Kumarappa's *Gandhian Economic Thought*, Shriman Narayan's *Relevance of Gandhian Economics*, a number of pamphlets and articles, and also in Gandhiji's *Hind Swaraj*.

Gandhian economic thought is based upon truth, nonviolence, dignity of labour, and simplicity. Gandhiji believed in making the villages self-sufficient and this leads to the decentralization of power. He believed in labour-intensive methods of production in a country with surplus labour. Gandhiji said that industrialization cannot remove poverty of India. He stressed upon the development of village industries and believed that large-scale production was laid on violence. Gandhiji desired production by the masses but not mass production. He strongly believed in the development of cottage industries. For him village *swaraj* was the ideal condition for the economic set-up of India. He wanted to make each and every village of India self-sufficient and capable of managing its affairs independently. Gandhiji gave us the doctrine of trusteeship as an alternative to Marxian socialism. Gandhiji wanted the capitalists to become trustees of the nation by carrying on with their businesses with integrity and efficiency and for the welfare of the people. The modern economist may dismiss Gandhiji's economic thoughts as being utopian in nature. However, it should be remembered that Gandhiji was a practical idealist. We observe nowadays that due to mad race of industrialization and urbanization, pollution and degradation of the environment are taking place. If Gandhiji's ideal of self-sufficient village economy is followed, environmental pollution will not be a cause of concern, especially when we are talking about global warming and green-house gas effect. Gandhiji had a futuristic approach towards the economics of India or rather we can say for the whole world. Gandhi was a man of the future.

Philosophical Outlook of Gandhi

A. Malliga
Post-Doctoral Fellow, Department of Philosophy, Pondicherry University, Puducherry, e-mail: <malligaa45@gmail.com>

Gandhi was not a philosopher in the academic sense. He never put forth anything like "Gandhism" and he never claimed to have introduced any new principle or doctrine. He never wanted to leave behind him any sect to be followed. But rather he had simply tried to apply the eternal truths to daily life and problems. There is no "ism" in his philosophy, since he had no training in philosophical discipline he plod through the problems of life, paying little attention to academicians subtle distinctions. He was a self-styled philosopher, a philosopher of life. Philosophy without life is like a body without life. The traditional philosophy was primarily speculative in nature, and hence the problems of life were to a great extent neglected there. Gandhi, the humanist reluctant to be an ivory tower thinker, paid attention to the problems arising out of harsh realities of life. The "eternal truths" of the great teachers of the world appealed to him for their practical values. He followed and transmuted, and applied them to life in his own way. P.T. Raju aptly observes, "Mahatma Gandhi infused life into some of them (Indian Philosophical concepts) by coming across them in the very course of his life, which is a struggle for the discovery of truth. In this voyage of life he brought to bear a new philosophical outlook that formed an integral part of his thought and was interwoven into it. As an ardent social thinker he viewed life in its totality; the problems of life as a whole. He made no watertight compartments of the various fields of life. To him the problems of life — ethical, economic, religious, social, political, etc., — formed an organic whole. He treated it in its entirety."

Gandhiji and Women Empowerment

B.V.L.A. Manga
Reader, Department of Political Science, Maharajah College, Vizianagaram, e-mail: <bovela2003@yahoo.co.in>

Today the empowerment of women has become one of the most important concerns of twenty-first century. Democracy has meaning and reality only where people at large sensitized to their rights, duties, and obligations and encouraged to exercise them. Mahatma Gandhi said that women are more fit than men to make exploration and take bolder steps in decision-making or whatever field they are entrusted with. He opined that there is no occasion for women to consider themselves, subordinate or inferior to men. In fact, a woman is a personification of self-sacrifice but unfortunately it is unacknowledged and undervalued. This paper examines the importance and relevance of Gandhiji's views on issues directly or indirectly influencing the status of women. Empowerment of a woman as an ideal scenario is best understood as a life-changing experience of her, irrespective of her socio-economic cultural, health (differently-abled) conditions, where they considered in exercising own choices towards various issues without fear or favour; where she is the mistress of her choices, her freedom of expression, movement, employment, reproduction, freedom over her own body relationship, etc., without endangering or giving cause for finding fault with her on account of this personal choice; with access to all services as a human person, etc. However the fact remains that this is a restrictive reality.

At this juncture this paper focuses on Gandhi's work which awakens women, and makes them shed their deep-rooted sense of inferiority and raise them to dignity and self-esteem. In line to achieve the twin goals of gender equality and woman empowerment, even today Gandhian literature will continue to be a prescription for many years to come. At this critical and crucial juncture in Indian history, it is befitting to recall Mahatma's observation that progress of the country is impossible without the empowerment of one half of the population.

Gandhi's Educational Thought: An Index of Human Values

Susila Mary
Asian Christian Studies, Department of Philosophy, Pondicherry University, e-mail: <s.susila.1213@gmail.com>

"Raise up nonviolent society" provides the basis to Gandhiji's Educational Philosophy. Education is the process by which society deliberately transmits its accumulated knowledge, skills, and values from generation to generation. Education is the means of the "social continuity of life" (John Dewey, *Democracy and Education: An Introduction to the Philosophy of Education*, 1916, p. 3). A nation is advanced in proportion as education and intelligence spread among the masses. Gandhiji wanted free and compulsory primary education between the ages of 7-14 for the whole mass of Indian population.

He introduced craft in his scheme to encourage dignity of labour and to break down the barriers between the intellectuals and the manual workers. In Basic Education all subjects must be taught through a chosen craft, using the correlational approach. The scheme seems to have a psychological basis. This will integrate all knowledge and encourage self-activity rather than rote memory. Mother-tongue of the child should be the medium of instruction.

According to Gandhi, education is "an all round drawing out of the best in child and man — body, mind, and spirit". Purity of personal life is one indispensable condition for building sound education. For Gandhiji *ahimsa* was the searchlight by means of which he examined all aspects of education as well as social problems. Gandhi integrated politics and education at the philosophical level. Child-centred approach to education and making craft the centre and medium of educational experience are the unique contributions of Gandhi to modern educational thought.

Truth or Consciousness: The Sure Way to Peace and Harmony

Susila Mary
Asian Christian Studies, Department of Philosophy, Pondicherry University, Puducherry, e-mail: <s.susila.1213@gmail.com>

The author delineates the core of religion for Mahatma Gandhi as TRUTH which is the only surest way to peace and harmony. The individual is regarded not as a mere aggregate of physical or chemical elements but as an inherently divine being engrossed in the quest of Truth. The goal of life as visualized by Gandhi was a synthesis of material and the moral progress of man, a synthesis of individual and the social culminating in the collaboration of different cultures and religions. At the root lies independent authority of consciousness.

Religion for Gandhi was ethical religion. It was synonymous with allegiance to a moral law and a religious man must be one who pursues a moral end and try to mould his action in accordance with such a law. All moral acts have certain characteristics such as voluntary, promoted by moral instinct, free from fear and universal. Following the Kantian principle of moral law, being the nature of a categorical imperative, this view maintains that a citizen obeys the law having its "seat in the soul". Gandhi stands for the sanctity of human conscience of a moral man in pursuit of a social good. The way to achieve *moksha* is to do good deeds, to have compassion for all living beings.

Gandhi's philosophy was a unique blend of spirituality and practicality. He attempted to compare the various religions and show how all the religions are only so many roads, leading to the realization of one God. They are all sparks of the same Truth. The sum total of these sparks is indescribable, as-yet-unknown Truth, which is God.

Management Guru: The Gandhian Model

Geeta Mehta

Adjunct Professor, Somaiya Vidyavihar, Mumbai, e-mail: <mehtageeta40@hotmail.com>

Gandhi achieved greatness through his efforts. The three facets of his life shaped his management qualities.

1. His family life: His joint family life taught him to stay with the people of different likings and temperament from childhood.

   In London the club of vegetarians formed the company of the people of his liking. His larger family in South Africa consisted of Phoenix Ashram and Tolstoy Farm.

   It started with Sabarmati Ashram and then Sevagram Ashram involving the lovers of nonviolence having social service and independence of India as their mission.

2. The second factor which influenced his leadership and management power was legal profession. Deep interest in legal

profession helps one to understand human nature thoroughly. It opens up good as well as bad facets of human nature before the advocate.

His motto was "we must not think of starting mass civil disobedience unless we are sure of peace being retained". He viewed management as a synthesis and not analysis. His holistic view of management made him to develop the idea of production by masses rather than mass-production.

3. Journalism was the third factor in shaping Gandhi's personality as a Management *guru*. Gandhi was a fervent thinker, a prolific writer, an eloquent speaker, and an excellent communicator. All these factors led to synthetic personality in his case. One of the components of his management skills is transparency. Though the field of his operation was complex and vast, he still demonstrated an exceptional managerial prowess and unique managerial fitness.

A Study of Socio-Political Thinking of M.K. Gandhi in Pursuit of Peace

Shilpita Mitra
Assistant Professor, Department of Philosophy, University of Calcutta,
e-mail: <shilpita.mitra1@gmail.com>

Education means change and development of an individual. Right education eradicates the evils of the society and maintains a spiritual realization of an individual. Like Buddha's call for fellow feeling and compassion in the sixth century BCE. Gandhiji woke up and unified India with nonviolent resistance to attain new heights. The uniqueness of Gandhiji lies in the fact that he effortlessly merged with the people of his country.

Gandhiji's deep concern for the well-being of the masses is the pivot on which his social and political philosophy revolves. To succeed in life, an individual needs a social system which should be able to remove the impediments on the way of his development towards his goal and provide facilities which may help him reach his target. Gandhiji therefore attempted to construct such social order based on *satyagraha, swadeshi,* and trusteeship which he called "Sarvodaya Samaj". As he writes in "Ethical Religion", man becomes great exactly in the degree in which he works for the welfare of his fellowmen.

Gandhism is not a set of doctrines but a way of life which provides ancient solutions for modern problems. Our country today with the help of new legislations and schemes is providing opportunities to the underprivileged so that a classless society can be formed. To Gandhi, the individual alone is the one supreme consideration and all other things are valuable not in themselves, but only as related to the personality of the individual. Though an individual may aim at the personal good, he cannot realize it in isolation from the good of others. The good of the individual is not what is private to him: it is what is good to him as a member of the community of persons. It is good to others as well, for they are also rational and moral agents like him. There is reciprocal relationship between the individual and society. A society cannot advance unless the units composing it advance, and, conversely, no individual can advance without the society of which he is a part also advancing.

Gandhi's concept of truth as being both absolute and relative makes him a great conflict resolver. He viewed truth as the goal and *ahimsa* as the path to the goal. His views regarding the nature of truth are the key to what he has to say about resolving conflicts. The concept of purification of the human personality accompanies this process. Does the Mahatma's framework of thought admit of genuine deep-rooted conflicts fed by long conditioning? In other words, has Mahatma Gandhi really given a formula of conflict resolution to apply regardless of time and place? Is he relevant today in this respect or was his method bound up with his own charismatic personality; making it non-repeatable and historically unique? Are Gandhi's beliefs about man to be accepted in totality if his path is to be followed? Can one spell out the essential and non-essential aspects of his thought if it is to be employed for conflict resolution in the present world? This paper includes discussion of some of these questions in the context of conflict resolution.

In the twenty-first century, the global agenda must contain the goal of saving environment urgently, lest it is too late because the existence of all the beings whether sentient or insentient is at stake. Further, collective cooperation is the only way out in an ever-increasing interdependent world of today. Ultimately it is a matter of human well-being and ethics to attain all this. Gandhian traits and tools are the best guide. Gandhi provides a broad framework of speculation and dialogue; as none is perfect in this world. Particularly his passion for harmony with nature, belief in soul force, spiritualism, control of lust and desires, rise of all, simple life, and finally, conversion of words into deeds, are best suited to serve the cause of saving the environment. Therefore the need is not to worship, but rather to follow Gandhi.

So, an obvious question comes up. To what extent are Gandhi's thoughts and actions relevant for the twenty-first-century world?

Of late, there has been a lot of debates about Gandhi, the person. Most books, films, and plays in recent years have focused on Gandhi, the father, husband, and friend than the great statesman. Some see a great design in this trend. Gandhi always meant different things to different people — in his lifetime as well as after. Even today, Gandhi makes an appearance at rallies, be it against globalization or for environmental protection.

At the end of the last millennium, Gandhi was rated, invariably, as the world's most admired human being of the twenty-first century. The present-day world is confronted with the unprecedented crisis due to various political problems which are mounting tensions and wars and which have great impact on the world.

As a result I have tried in my humble way to focus on the outstanding contribution of Gandhi to the twenty-first century. Gandhi's dedication is multi-faced. His presentation of Truth and nonviolence to the human civilization which would invariably result in peace has become more significant and of greater relevance than before. The real human happiness lies in the experience of real peace. Thus Gandhi advocated the principle of nonviolence as the only way of achieving peace. Its application results in the moral reordering of the world in order to usher in a new peaceful world order. In this project it has been my endeavour to show from the socio-political aspect how the establishment of global peace is essential in the world of today to create a sense of mutual tolerance, respect, and goodwill.

Gandhian Approach to Justice

P.K. Mohapatra

National Fellow, ICPR, Bhubaneswar, e-mail: <mohapatra97@gmail.com>

Gandhi was interested in "*how* should we be just?" rather than "what *is* justice?". Rather than seeking a profound definition of justice he was more passionately seeking justice to prevail in the lives of men. That is why we do not see much of doctrinairing in his thoughts. His ideas grew out of practical situations, from what he experienced and tested and found to be practicable. Ideas must be put to actions, and applications of ideas are what he called "experiments". Like scientists he would be prepared to reject a hypothesis (a view on justice or a method of protest, say) if it happens to be not workable. He was open and willing to change his stand or modus operandi if a situation so demands. The testing ground of his view on justice was experience — not theory, precedence or conformity to abstract principles. The justice that Gandhi sought and fought for was justice that was missing in British India, in the pernicious practice of apartheid in South Africa; it was justice that was lost in casteism, untouchability, and communal hatred.

Removal of these evils was the primary agenda in Gandhi's struggle for freedom and justice. You get justice if you *deserve* it, you deserve it only by *being just*. This was Gandhi's message and objective. And this objective was best achieved through *satyagraha* and *ahimsa* — the two concepts that came to be identified with Gandhi, Gandhism, and Gandhian Philosophy.

Mahatma Gandhi on Truth and Nonviolence

G.C. Narasimhulu
Post-Doctoral Fellow – UGC, Department of Philosophy, S.V. University, Tirupati, e-mail: <narasimhulu1983@gmail.com>

Ahimsa and truth are so intertwined that it is practically impossible to disentangle and separate them. They are like two sides of a coin, or rather a smooth unstamped metallic disc. Who can say, which is the obverse, and which the reverse? Nevertheless, *ahimsa* is the means and Truth is the end. If we take care of the means, we are bound to reach the end sooner or later. When once we have grasped this point, final victory is beyond question. Whatever difficulties we encounter, whatever apparent reverses we sustain, we may not give up the quest for truth which alone is being God himself.

Ahimsa is not the goal. Truth is the goal. But we have no means of realizing truth in human relationship except through the practice of *ahimsa*. A steadfast pursuit of *ahimsa* is inevitably bound to truth not to violence. That is why I swear by *ahimsa*. Truth came naturally to me. *Ahimsa* I acquired after a struggle.

But *ahimsa* being the means, we are naturally more concerned with it in our everyday life. It is *ahimsa*, therefore, that our masses have to be educated in. Education in truth follows from it as a natural end.

Ahimsa is my God, and Truth is my God. When I look for *ahimsa*, Truth says "Find it out through me". When I look for Truth, *ahimsa* says, "Find it out through me".

Peace Problems and Conflict Resolution in Mahatma Gandhi

G.C. Narasimhulu
Post-Doctoral Fellow – UGC, Department of Philosophy, S.V. University, Tirupati,
e-mail: <narasimhulu1983@gmail.com>

The quest for peace is an eternal pursuit for human fulfilment. Peace or absence of antagonistic, violent, or establishing conflict is essential for existence to become life, for survival to become human. Human beings can become human and humane only in conditions of peace. Creativity, spirituality, individual and collective achievements attain grandeur and glory only when there is peace. All human beings do not think alike or feel alike. They have therefore no escape from having to encounter differences. Differences can lead to intolerance; intolerance to confrontation, and hostile confrontation can, does often, lead to conflict. The objects that set one on the path of confrontation and conflict are therefore very important in understanding "conflict". So are the means — tactics and instruments that one uses to engage in conflict. Both these affect the individual as well as the group or society in which, or on behalf of which he or she wants to engage in conflict. They act and interact on the individual as well as the institutions that he fashions or lives under, and the "forces" that they generate and employ for bringing about change or resisting change. The problems that arise from these interrelationships cannot be solved by saying that conflicts are inevitable in the life of the individual and society.

The Gandhian technique of conflict resolution is known by its Gujarati name of *satyagraha* which has variously been interpreted as "passive resistance", "nonviolent resistance", "nonviolent direct action", and even as "militant nonviolence". "Satyagraha", Gandhi explained, is "literally holding on to Truth and it means, therefore, Truth-force. Truth is soul or spirit. It is therefore known as Soul-force".

Debating Religiosity: A Gandhian Model for a World of Peaceful Coexistence

Adarasupally Nataraju
Dean, Sarvepalli Radhakrishnan School of Philosophy, Assam University, Silchar,
e-mail: <adinatraj@gmail.com>

True religiosity is distinct from popular religion with its tradition, authority, and divisive features. Making such a distinction probably would solve many a contemporary problem related to religion. Gandhi's philosophy has inspired millions across the continents in moving towards peaceful coexistence. Metaphysical presuppositions that Gandhi uses in developing activistic tools in transforming the social order and transforming human lives are: (a) devoid of all differences whatsoever, whether within itself, or from the things of the same class, or from things of other classes — Brahman is the immanent and transcendental principle, and (b) the welfare of an individual is connected with all living forms of life since the material cause is a unitary substance. The highest intuitive Truth of Vedanta — oneness of human life — was brought into everyday life in addressing human suffering. This paper will further explore Gandhi's philosophy in expounding Gandhi's understanding of Vedanta for future generations and would try to prove beyond doubt that an individual's welfare is invariably connected with that of collective welfare. For this, I would rely upon Advaitic notion of "Oneness of Life" principle and "Unified Field Theory" of modern physics.

I would like to start with a hypothesis that an individual's freedom or *moksha* is incomplete as long as there are suffering millions. To put it in other words — an individual's material as well as spiritual welfare are incomplete without the welfare of all the life forms on the earth. The general understanding of the thesis of the *lokasangraha* or *Bhutahita* from the *Bhagavadgita* ethics is that working for the welfare of society around would bring in purity of the inner soul — *citta shuddhi*. The action, thus performed, was a purificatory exercise. However, what needs to be understood is that social service acts not only as a tool for the purification of *citta* but there is no escape form it even after attaining *jivan mukti* since the completeness of freedom or *mukti* is not possible if there exists even a single soul that is bound. Like in Quantum Physics, though particles are separated in space, and are not connected materially, they influence each other, so also an individual's freedom is affected by the suffering millions. Freedom needs space to exist; it does not exist in vacuum. Since there is limitedness to space (this idea has reference to Einstein — our general understanding that space is unlimited is questioned, there is a possibility that space may be limited), freedom also becomes limited. The interconnectedness of the freedom of all the life forms is what I derive from the Advaita theory of "Oneness of Life"— *ekam eva advitiyam brahma, neha nanasti kincana*. Thus, it becomes imperative for a human to work for collective human welfare. I strongly believe that this kind of an understanding was the working force behind the work of Gandhi. Among the contemporary thinkers in India, the position of Gandhi can never be underestimated. His understanding of Vedanta was on par with any other Vedantin of his era.

In this paper I would relocate Gandhi's ideas for the welfare-of-all in the context of true religiosity and also discuss the Advaita ethics in transforming human lives and attaining freedom.

Religious Philosophy of Gandhi

Yugendar Nathi
Junior Research Fellow, Department of Philosophy, Osmania University, Hyderabad, e-mail: <yugendarnathi@gmail.com>

Religion, according to Gandhi, is more or less, a way of life, and as such is the personal concern of the individual who has to choose his way of life. Gandhi believes that different religions are the different ways of apprehending the Truth. The basic conviction of Gandhi is that there is one reality — that of God, which is nothing else but Truth. His religious ideas are also derived from that conviction. If Truth is God, sincere pursuit of Truth is religion. Religion is ordinarily defined as devotion to some higher power or principle, Gandhi is not against such a description of religion, he only qualifies it further by saying that higher principle being truth, devotion to Truth (or God) is religion.

Gandhi believes that true religion has to be practical. Therefore, he says that religion should pervade every aspect of our life. Religion is the belief that there is an ordered moral government of the universe, and this belief must have practical bearings for all aspects of life. According to Gandhi there is no difference between religious ideal and metaphysical or moral ideal, the religious way is also the way of truth — *sathyagraha*. This paper discusses about Gandhi's ideas of God, religion, the way of religion, and the religious harmony in the world.

The Evolution of Human Rights in India and M.K. Gandhi's Role: An Analysis

Namita Nimbalkar
Assistant Professor, Department. of Philosophy, University of Mumbai, e-mail: <namita.nimbalkar@gmail.com>

The notion of "Human Rights" was less known till the second half of the nineteenth century in India. With the spread of Western education, impact of science and technology, an awareness of atrocities committed on different sections of the society was felt. Many social reforms took place. However, with the advent of Mohandas Karamchand Gandhi on the Indian scene, the rights of man came into prime focus.

The influence of three places had great impact on Gandhi in shaping his views on Human Rights. While studying law in London he was mesmerized by its free spirit of man and society. In South Africa, he started the movement of civil rights against discrimination meted out to natives and Indians and was fairly successful in his nonviolent struggle, also known as *satyagraha*. In India, Gandhi strived to win independence with his philosophy of nonviolence.

The present paper will discuss the different writings of Gandhi written to awaken the masses of their rights. The paper will also discuss the emphasis laid by Gandhi on performance of "duties" first in order to enjoy "rights".

Significance of Satyagraha in Gandhian Education

P. Nithiya

ICPR General Fellow, Department of Philosophy, Pondicherry University, Puducherry, e-mail: <nisezhe@gmail.com>

In this paper, I am going to discuss about *satyagraha* in Gandhian education and also I have made an attempt to analyse how he practised his philosophical principles like *satyagraha*, truth, and nonviolence in education. The word *satyagraha* means adherence to truth. In Gandhian sense, education aims at the achievement of truth content of *satyagraha*. His *satyagraha* puts education on a different path with regard to its relation to truth. Gandhiji looked to education as an instrument for socio-economic progress, material advancement, political evolution, and moral development for individuals in society. Wholesome knowledge, according to Gandhi, involves the development of the mind depending upon a thorough knowledge of fundamental truths for which a strong conscience is a basic requirement. The path of truth should be the determined aim of education. Truth is the beginning because that alone validates the principles of education. Truth is the end because all education has discovery of truth as the final end. Truth has to be achieved through the process of education in which nonviolence becomes the practice. An education geared to *satyagraha* through nonviolence can be developed by presenting the educational aims with direct or indirect bearing on *ahimsa*. Gandhian education has *ahimsa* as a principal content that needs to be communicated to students in a variety of ways. His education subsumes *satyagraha* as a principle and a force that has an encompassing potential to penetrate every minute detail of education and bring in a powerful transformation.

Living in Harmony with Nature: A Gandhian Response

Ranjan Kumar Panda
Associate Professor, HSS Department, IIT Bombay,
e-mail: <ranjan.panda@iitb.ac.in>
&
Khangembam Romesh Singh
Post-Doctoral Fellow, HSS Department, IIT Bombay,
e-mail: <khromesh@gmail.com>

We live in a rapidly changing world where one encounters ever-increasing loss of natural resources and loss of human values. Most of the irreparable damages to natural resources are caused by expanding modernization, industrialization, massive construction projects, mining, etc. These activities are integral parts of economic growth in the larger framework of globalization which also has caused wearing down of our environment in the form of pollution of air, water, and soil. Such a living has apparently changed our lifestyle and has made us victims of many lifestyle diseases. We have started living apparently in the *culture of silence* where certain forms of life are accepted without questioning them, and recognizing its impact on the intrinsic values of life. The silence prevails due to the "vanishing ethics" from everyday life. People have started de-recognizing the norms and virtues that are supposed to be the guiding force of thoughtful living. The voice of conscience is suppressed against the material needs and gratification of sensuous desires. People are bugged to the materiality of life. Hence, these losses have damaged the living environment, not only physically but also morally. It is a challenge how to overcome this environmental crisis. Gandhi's response helps us to conceptualize a new paradigm of human nature and engagement that will help us to restore not only the human dignity but also lay down a perspective of addressing the environmental virtues. This perspective neither advocates any kind of monistic ideas nor pragmatic concerns; rather tries to value the environmental virtues and character traits that deeply relate the person with *the other*, as an essential element of *unification* of life that shows the primacy of normative engagement that renovates values and unfolds the ground of living in harmony.

Nonviolence: A Gandhian Perspective

Ratikanta Panda

Department of H&SS, IIT Bombay, e-mail: <ratikantaiitb@gmail.com>

Mohandas Karamchand Gandhi is one of those few luminaries who have made original contribution in not only raising the stature of one's culture and civilization in the eyes of the world, but also providing it strength and stability to sustain that raising for ages to come. Having given to the freedom fighters the weapons of *satyagraha* and *ahimsa*, he devised the system of peaceful revolution for the first time in the world. *Ahimsa* (nonviolence) is in fact the biggest achievement of Gandhi in the war-ridden world. With this weapon of *ahimsa* he mobilized around twenty million people of India against their British rulers. Not only that he successfully used these weapons, but proved them as an answer to war-ridden cultures of early twentieth century. Nonviolence involves non-exploitation or equality. There cannot be nonviolence in a society if it is affected by gross inequality and exploitation. Absolute nonviolence is impossible as long as we exist physically. Our survival will be untenable by accepting absolute nonviolence. The realization of absolute nonviolence is impossible. We accept relative nonviolence and put no limit to its application. The more it fits the scope of application the greater will be realization of justice. Further instead of giving nonviolence any extra-mundane justification, Gandhi brings out its relevance in our social relationships. Thus the aim of this paper is to reflect on Gandhian view on nonviolence and it also highlights its implications in the present-day society.

Smart Cities or Sarvodaya Cities

S.S. Rama Rao Pappu

Professor, Miami University (USA), e-mail: <pappuss@miamioh.edu>

"Smart" is the buzzword these days. We have in the West "smart phones", "smart cars, "smart meters" , even "smart water", and IBM says it is now working on a "smart planet". Recently, with the announcement of India's central government that they are building 100 smart cities, Indians are suddenly excited about "smart cities". I have asked a few Indian city dwellers how a "smart city" looks like, and they told me that a smart city will have metro trains, superfast express ways, 100-story high-rise buildings, movie screen ads at every junction, etc. In other words, a smart Indian city looks more like an American city like New York or Chicago. But New York is not a smart city, and they seek the help of IT companies how to run their trains more efficiently, how to conserve energy, how to reduce the pollutants, and a million other problems; in short, how to make living in New York more tolerable. A smart city does not bring any new values, it only makes urban living more tolerable. I shall argue here that Internet, big data, cloud computing, etc., do not solve the human problems of people living in India's cities, and unless we start from ground-up, the sort of life India's urban masses cherish will only be a dream. Gandhi would argue that human problems must have human solutions, not technological solutions. In fact, all the issues that Gandhi raised in his famous manifesto "A Critique of Modern Civilization" will apply more strongly to the Smart City concept.

However, we are not just stuck with Smart Cities, because Gandhian philosophy of Sarvodaya gives us an alternative city and village planning, namely what I call "Sarvodaya Cities". With the same money, we can build not 100 Smart Cities but thousands of Sarvodaya Cities which have the following characteristics:

a. It is a fact of Indian life that urbanization is taking place at an enormous pace. Each of the 100 cities chosen by the central government must be divided into 10, 15 or 20 manageable "Sarvodaya Cities" so that there is adequate people's participation in the promotion of the welfare of each.

b. The growth and welfare of each such Sarvodaya city must come "bottom–up", i.e., from the local people; instead of "top–down" — like the central government or IT companies dictating the "dos" and "donts". Afterall, what do the central bureaucrats sitting in New Delhi or the IBM professionals sitting in Washington have any idea of what constitutes the welfare of some local people, say in Visakhapatnam?

c. The people who will be elected to the Sarvodaya cities should not be elected on party lines. The only "party" that will be recognized is the "*sarvodaya* party" and the "*sarvodaya* platform" which should be one based on Gandhian principles of Truth, nonviolence, fraternity, and self-sacrifice.

d. The good of the individual should not be different from the good of the community. The feelings one should cultivate should not be "how better off I am in the system, but how much welfare WE have accomplished". Taking Bhutan's much publicized state policy "not GNP, but GNH" (not gross national product, but gross national happiness), each community should assess how much the community has developed in promoting the welfare of all.

e. Private property will be permitted, but it should be based on Gandhi's concept of trusteeship theory of property. Where the welfare of the community is involved, individuals should give up their property for the common good (similar to Vinoba Bhave's Bhoodan Movement).

f. Humanity, not efficiency, should be the driving force behind the Sarvodaya cities.

The ultimate test "which city is the most livable" can be assessed by individuals who have lived both in a smart city like say "New Delhi/ New York" and "Pedda Waltair" in Visakhapatnam (before it became part of a mega city), most people (like me who lived in Pedda Waltair, New Delhi and New York) would say Pedda Waltair is a more livable place than New Delhi.

The Moral Philosophy of Sankaradeva and M.K. Gandhi: An Approach

Jagadish Patgiri
Department of Philosophy, Cotton College, Guwahati,
e-mail: <jagadishpatgiri@gmail.com>

Srimanta Sankaradeva (CE 1449–1568), a saint-scholar, playwright, social-religious reformer, is a renowned figure in the cultural and religious history of Assam and India. His literary and artistic contributions are living traditions in Assam today. Sankaradeva laid the foundation of building of Assamese literature and culture. He started Bhakti movement. His religion Mahapurushia Dharma was part of his Bhakti movement. He took great role for unification specially in Assam. For him it was successful for good relationship between Ahom Kingdom and Koch King Kingdom. He created new religious feeling that gave shape to a set of new values and social synthesis.

Mahatma Gandhi is an international figure though an Indian, his role in the Western world is well known. Throughout the world his philosophical views on morality, religion, social philosophy, economics, politics, etc., are scattered along with his works.

M.K. Gandhi, whom we revere as "Father of the Nation" and whose birthday October 2nd is observed as "International Nonviolence Day" was born in 1869 at Porbandar town in Gujarat. He was influenced particularly by the *Bhagavadgita* from Hindu thought, the sermon on the Mount from Christianity, and the writings of Tolstoy, Ruskin, Emerson, and Thoreau. His moral and religious life was primarily influenced by his family religion of Vaishnavism, the teachings of the *Bhagavadgita*, Buddhism, Christianity, Islam, and also by Tolstoy's book *The Kingdom of God Is Within You*, and Ruskin's *Unto This Last*. He is honoured as Mahatma, not simply because of his contribution to the political fields of South Africa and India, but because of his inspiring moral and religious activities whose impact on mankind is very unique and tremendous. He is unquestionably regarded as one of the greatest moral thinkers the world has ever produced.

The religion that Sankaradeva preached is practised by a large population, and Shatras (monasteries) that he and his followers established continue to flourish and sustain his legacy. In reverence to his personality, teachings, and humanitarian love, he is a *mahapurusha* (Great Man) as has M.K. Gandhi been popularly known as Mahatma Gandhi.

In this paper an attempt is made to focus on their moral or ethical views and also highlight some sort of similarity and dissimilarity in their concepts.

Breaking the Wires: Women's Status and Role in Society according to Gandhi

Hema Prasad
Research Scholar, Department of Philosophy, Tilka Majhi Bhagalpur University,
e-mail: <prasadhe9@gmail.com>

Mohandas Karamchand Gandhi was one of the few in his generation who had recognized a central role of women folk in the Indian society. My article examines the importance and relevance of his views on issues that directly or indirectly impact the status of women in India. Equality of sexes, marriage, *purdah*, dowry system are some of them. For Gandhi, "When woman, whom we all call *abala* becomes *sabala*, all those who are helpless will become powerful". Women, urban and rural, educated and uneducated, were attracted to his ideas and deeds. Gandhi respected traditions of the society, but not at the cost of loss of individual dignity. He believed that men and women are equal as the same *atma* (soul) dwells in all of them, Gandhi considered woman not only equal to man but in many ways superior to man. To him bravery lay in dying and not killing. Actually Gandhi had tremendous faith in women's inherent capacity for nonviolence.

In this paper, I want to focus on Gandhi's views on women in the context of social, economic, and political issues. Gandhi gave totally a new perspective regarding gender equality and nonviolence. He not only opposed the harmful practices and encouraged regeneration of women but gave the idea that women are not just equal and different but superior to men. Gandhi sympathizes with women, but he does not want to pity them all the time.

Gandhian Economics: An overview

B. Sambasiva Prasad
Centre for Gandhian Studies, GITAM University, Visakhapatnam,
e-mail: <b.sambasivaprasad@gmail.com>

Gandhian economics is spiritual and moral in its approach. Truth and nonviolence constitute the yardsticks of Gandhian economics. According to him, in acquiring wealth the means should be as pure as that of the ends. *Satya, sarvodaya, swarajya,* and *swadeshi* are the pillars at the four corners of Gandhi's economic philosophy. Gandhian economics is value loaded. It addresses the genuine needs of people and does not serve their greed. It emphasizes upon the consumer and not on consumption. Its goal is not mass production, but production for the masses and by the masses. The modern economics which aims at maximizing profits, individual gains, and encourages nothing but wealth generation should be transformed. It should take Gandhian economics as a role model and work on the basis of ethical and spiritual values.

Gandhi's Nonviolent "Army": The Pros and Cons of Using "Army" as a Metaphor for Nonviolent Endeavours

Gail M. Presbey
Professor of Philosophy, University of Detroit Mercy,
e-mail: <presbegm@udmercy.edu>

Gandhi many times referred to himself as the "Commander" of a nonviolent army. In what way is this metaphor helpful? On the one hand, the idea and practice of "Shanti Sena" or nonviolent army seems practical to many, as the "Shanti Sena Network" grows in USA, in collaboration with the Metta Peace Center and the Meta Peace Team, organizations led by Michael Nagler and Peter Dougherty, two winners of the Jamnalal Bajaj Award for promoting Gandhian values. The practical work of a peace team is easy to appreciate. But in what way does it, or does it not, function as an "army"? Gandhi saw military discipline, and the discipline of life in the *ashram*, as related to self-control advocated by study of *yoga*. One overcomes one's own ego's willfulness following what is good instead of what is desired. Two categories of militaristic virtues are to be discussed. The first category has to do with self-discipline of a soldier containing his own passions and avoiding chaos by conforming to rules. Second, and relatedly there are the issues of giving oneself completely to the army commander and entrusting him with one's life, and/or more specifically, being willing to give one's life if one's commander asks for it. Accomplishing such discipline makes the army a formidable force because the general non-armed forces public is both in more chaotic disarray as well as inclined to act selfishly so that they cannot act in as unified a way. Gandhi appreciated both understandings of discipline. But understanding army "discipline" takes on a different light when Michel Foucault's study of discipline is applied to this context.

Does the subject of discipline internalize a standard of thought and action that comes from outside the self? Is this outside standard to be trusted? And should or could it become a nonviolent practice or method? I will suggest that current Shanti Sena practices in the US are more democratic and less militaristic and authoritarian than what Gandhi had described.

Gandhi's Concept of Nonviolence and Its Relevance

Puja Rai

Jawaharlal Nehru University, New Delhi, e-mail: <pujarai.jnu@gmail.com>

Gandhi arrived at his understanding of nonviolence through an assimilation of various philosophical tenets such as Buddhism, Jainism, *Bhagavadgita*, Christianity, etc. He used nonviolence to fight not only colonial rule but also social evils such as racial and caste-based discriminations. He identified two basic expressions of nonviolence — negative form (not injuring any living being) and positive form (the largest love and the greatest charity). For him, nonviolence does not construe indulging in violence but it's also a way of taking positive action to resist oppression or bring about change. The aim of nonviolent conflict is to change one's opponent's heart. The weapon of nonviolence is not the resort of the weak but is the power of the strong. His method of *satyagraha* is based on his notion of nonviolence. Acknowledging the inherent goodness of human beings, Gandhi emphasized the capacity of all human beings to develop their full potential of nonviolence. He saw the path of violence as a downward path away from our humanity and closer to that of brutality while the path of nonviolence was closer to humanness. This paper will attempt to examine the relevance of Gandhi's notion of nonviolence in the contemporary times.

Relevance of Gurajada and Gandhi in twenty-first Century

S. Raminaidu
Research Scholar, Centre for Gandhian Studies, GITAM University,
e-mail: <raminadni@gmail.com>

This paper deals with the views of Gurajada and Gandhi and their relevance in twenty-first century. The new wave of technological civilization is dehumanizing the people day by day. India, the land where from Buddhism spread to other parts of the world is now facing sociological and ethical deterioration. The intellectuals and rational thinkers like Gurajada and Gandhi have blended the minds of their age.

Mahakavi Gurajada Venkata Apparao (1862–1915) is one of the most highly gifted personalities in the field of modern Telugu literature. All his writings, drama, poetry, and stories are simple and his vision was deep into the human nature. *Kanyasulkam* (drama) with the selected episodes from the lives of common people of the day will glow with life and humanity in every page. He invented new metre Mutyala Saralu (a garland of pearls). *"Poornamma"* and *"Kanyaka"* poems stand as great criticism of social customs. *Deshabhakti* (Patriotism) is an inspiring example and a directive principle for a prosperous world.

South Africa was the place from where M.K. Gandhi (1869–1948) turned out to be a leader or Mahatma and gained the hearts of the people by solving their problems. Reaching India back, Gandhi led the freedom movement and brought India free from British yolk by leading the Non-Cooperation Movement, the Civil Disobedience Movement, and the Quit-India Movement. *Ahimsa* was his powerful weapon. Gandhi wrote for women's liberation, removal of untouchability and worked all together for promoting human values in the society. If we rebuild our minds with the values they taught us, we can save our country from the deterioration and can surely make our country surge ahead. Both Gurajada and Gandhi are prophets who want to establish human values in the society.

Gandhi's Constructive Programme

J. Hari Hara Rao
Centre for Gandhian Studies, GITAM University, Visakhapatnam,
e-mail: <hariharaaraojagatha@gmail.com>

Gandhi's constructive programme is a method to achieve *poorna-swaraj,* that is, complete independence. It does not signify political independence but rather an economic and social independence. Mahatma Gandhi started his constructive programme in early 1940s as he had already foreseen political independence of India but the real independence through truth and nonviolence means independence of every unit be it the humbles of the nation, without distinction of race, colour, or creed. Gandhi's constructive programme was really another form of *satyagraha*, which was the only road to economic development for a developing country like India. The constructive programme was conceived as a means as well as an end for the creation of a new civilization. The core of the programme is the synthesis between the material and moral advancement of human society. The objective of constructive programme was to bring about socio-economic changes and reconstruction of social order based on freedom, equality, and respect for individual personality. The ultimate purpose was to build a nonviolent, non-exploitative social and economic order for a society based on the ideas of *sarvodaya*. The present and future crises can be reduced by adopting a fully constructive programme as evolved by Gandhi. Constructive work should became both a lamp and a mirror, it will show us what we are. Gandhi introduced a number of programmes touching social, political, educational, economic, and cultural aspects of man's life. From 1915-45 Gandhi was able to formulate a compact programme of total transformation.

Religious Fundamentalism, Political Extremism and Gandhi's Nonviolence

P.S. Rama Mohan Rao
Former Governor, Tamil Nadu

K. Padmanabhaiah
Former Union Home Secretary, Hyderabad, e-mail: <padam_k@yahoo.com>

H.J. Dora
Former DGP, Andhra Pradesh, e-mail: <hjdora2004@yahoo.co.in>

Today, we live in a troubled world. Irrational violence is becoming increasingly rampant. Violence is of course not a new phenomenon. It has been with us throughout known human history. What is new, however, is how it is currently perpetuated in the name of identities that came into existence primarily to unite people. Identities are now a source to divide rather than bring people together. Religions are believed to focus on the spiritual side of humans, bond them with love and compassion, and lead men and women to peace and harmony. Instead we find in some parts of the world what goes in the name of religious fundamentalism. It has increasingly fanned violence and created terror groups operating in different parts of the world, threatening peace and security. At a lower level, we find intolerance raising its ugly head posing a serious threat to free speech and independent thinking.

In our own country, there has been prolonged violence in the Kahsmir Valley, North-Eastern states and the Naxal-infected areas in Jharkand, Madhya Pradesh, Orissa, Telangana, and Andhra Pradesh. Like fundamentalism in religion, extremism in politics is clearly a root cause of organized violence. In the name of seeking political and social justice, groups are engaged in unjust violence.

In sharp contrast to religious fundamentalism and political extremism stand Gandhi's philosophy and practice of nonviolence. Gandhi believed that all men are inherently good; the manifest evil is a product of circumstances. It is possible to change the person and his attitudes by persuasion and by appealing to one's spiritual side without resorting to any form of violence. Therefore, the right course of action for conflict resolution, according to the Mahatma, is to change the adverse circumstances and harmful attitudes, and not hurt individuals who are their victims. Gandhi felt that violence is utterly inappropriate to achieve this. He developed nonviolent methods to replace those based on violence and attempted to practise them to resolve all kinds of conflicts.

Is Gandhi correct in his assumptions? Do his methods in their original form, or suitably modified, help to contain current conflicts arising from religious fundamentalism and political extremism? The panel provides the framework for discussing these and similar issues by experts with first-hand experience in dealing with these issues.

Gandhian Concept of Justice and the Indian Legal System

J. Uma Rao
Assistant Professor, School of Law, GITAM University,
e-mail: <umasastryburra@gmail.com>

> Democracy must in essence, . . . mean the art and science of mobilizing the entire physical, economic and spiritual resources of all the various sections of the people in the service of the common good of all.
>
> — Mahatma Gandhi

Mahatma Gandhi is universally recognized as one of the greatest political and spiritual leaders. Honoured as the father of the nation, he propounded and put into practice the principle of *satyagraha* — resistance to tyranny through mass nonviolent civil disobedience — and applied it to free India from foreign rule. It is also known to one and all that he spearheaded massive campaigns to build religious and ethnic harmony, alleviate poverty, expand women's rights, and eliminate other social evils and injustices prevalent in the socio-economic environment. But then what of his influence on the present-day scenario? Does his philosophy of *dharma* find place in that all important political and social instruments that we as a nation have framed for ourselves, i.e., the Constitution of India, the fountainhead of all the rights enjoyed by people of the country? Have his Ideals of Justice been incorporated in the justice delivery system? Though converging at many places, there are some unfortunate divergences between Gandhiji's ideology and the constitutional and legal framework of the country at present. These divergences, convergences, and the way ahead are the focus and content of the paper.

Truth through Nonviolence

P.V. Rayudu
Research Fellow, Consciousness Studies Programme of National Institute of Advanced Studies (NIAS), Bangalore, e-mail: <posinavrayudu@gmail.com>

What is reality? How do we know? Answers to these fundamental questions of ontology and epistemology, based on Mahatma Gandhi's "experiments with truth", are: reality is nonviolent (in the sense of not-inconsistent), and nonviolence (in the sense of respecting-meaning) is the only means of knowing. Be that as it may, science is what we think of when we think of reality and knowing. How does Gandhi's nonviolence, discovered in his spiritual quest for Truth, relate to the scientific pursuit of truth? Here we show that Gandhian nonviolent knowing of nonviolent reality is an abstraction of both individual knowing (looking, reasoning) and collective scientific knowing (measurements, calculations). Specifically, Gandhi's truth-through-nonviolence is a law-like summation of the methods of physics ("do not disturb" of measurements) and of mathematics ("do not tear" of calculations) that are used to know. Moreover, physics (with its lawful behaviour of bodies) and biology (in preserving the meaning of genetic code) do affirm that the defining attribute of reality is nonviolence. In the light of these correspondences, Mahatma's derivation of a universal method of knowing (nonviolence of preserving-structure) from a universal truth (nonviolence of consistent-becoming) constitutes a science-supported general theory of reality and knowing.

The Spirit of Swaraj in Frugal Technologies

Vegitha Reddy
e-mail: <vegitha@iitb.ac.in>

Aman Tripathi
e-mail: <aman.tripathi@iitb.ac.in>
&
P.R. Bhat
Professor, e-mail: <p.r.bhat@iitb.ac.in>
Department of HSS, Indian Institute of Technology Bombay, Mumbai

Frugal innovations are ultra-low-cost technologies. However, just because they are inexpensive, this does not mean that their quality is compromised. Rather the emphasis is on making the products more appropriate and holistic. The frugal technologies are socially viable and endeavour to be in the service of all. In this paper we argue that frugal technology when taken in the spirit of *swaraj*, would make it as a means for a just society as was exemplified by the *charkha*. Such a society empowers the poorest of its citizens, gives autonomy to all its members, and is equally in harmony with nature.

Gandhi : The Apostle of Ahimsa: A Critical Estimate

R. Venkat Reddy
Professor, Osmania University, Hyderabad,
e-mail: <rendla_venkatreddy@yahoo.com>

Gandhi's message of *ahimsa* has an important relevance to the present-day world. So, the concept of *ahimsa* and its applications will be discussed in this paper from the Gandhian point of view. The concept of *ahimsa* is one of the distinctive concepts in Indian thought. This concept was later developed and elaborated in the form of various types of doctrines by Buddha, Jaina *tirthankaras*, and others. In the twentieth century Gandhi developed his doctrine of social action around the pivotal concept of *ahimsa. Ahimsa* literally means "non-injury" or "non- killing". It was in this sense that the word was used in ancient Indian philosophy. But, in this paper the word is being used in its Gandhian sense.

The word *ahimsa* has normally a negative import, but in Gandhi it has been given a positive significance. According to him *ahimsa* is "love", love represents the essence of *ahimsa*, and such *ahimsa* is a matter of sincere feeling. However, as a realistic thinker and apostle of *ahimsa*, Gandhi admits the inevitability of violence. Gandhi on the other hand accepts that perfect nonviolence can go only with complete non-possession. Here, Gandhi refers to another important Indian doctrine, i.e., "desire for enjoyment creates bodies for the soul". Gandhi was an absolutist. "The fact is," he says "that a votary of *ahimsa* cannot subscribe to the utilitarian formula. Gandhi feels that violence is in fact an expression of weakness. One who is inwardly strong is not afraid of anything. On the other hand, one who is inwardly weak develops a sort of fear.

According to Gandhi, greatest battles of life can be won by subjecting oneself to conscious suffering. Gandhi sincerely believes that by non-violent suffering, by loving the opponent wholeheartedly one can neutralize the forces of evil. The system of nonviolent actions is the sustainer and promoter of normal and ethical interpersonal relationships in society. It is the system which sustains social equilibrium. Means and ends are convertible terms in Gandhi's philosophy. Gandhi emphasizes the purity of means as much as the purity of the end towards which they were directed.

In conclusion, Gandhi's message of nonviolence, as a pearl for reorganizing human relationship, has a great appeal, especially in the world situation, as it prevails today. On these broad principles, the Gandhian doctrine of *ahimsa* deserves appreciation.

Revisiting Legends-Understanding: The Concept of Gandhian Architecture

Mani Sachdev
e-mail: <manisachdev4@gmail.com>

Sahiba Sachdev
BBD Govt. PG College, Chimanpura

&

Shruti Sachdev
Department of Architecture, School of Arts & Architecture, Gurgaon

The five classic elements — space, earth, water, fire, and air — believed to be the fundamental constituents of the universe, foreground the spirits and essence of Gandhian space. This reflects most clearly in the Sabarmati Ashram — the legacy of the living institution of Mahatma Gandhi — these spaces highlight the austere simplicity of the Mahatma's life.

Witness to historic event, such as the "Dandi March" which led to the nationwide civil disobedience movement against the British, the Sabarmati Ashram remains, till date, a powerful enigma. Consciously constricted asymmetrically with its use of basic material such as stone floors, brick walls, wooden doors, and several pathways, the Ashram on the one hand is analogous to the Indian village and on the other is the epicentre of passionate nationalistic deliberations, which led to mass movements that shocked the British Empire.

This paper aims to study the concept of Gandhi's enigmatic architecture to understand what it was that inspired the legend of the great Indian freedom struggle, so significant for modern Independent India. This paper seeks to trace the roots and study the foundations of his phenomenon, once inhabited by divine soul, which continues to inspire even today.

Refraining as a Form of Social Action: An Inquiry into Gandhian Concept of *Ahimsa*

Arabinda Sahoo
Assistant Professor, National University of Study and Research in Law, Ranchi,
e-mail: <arabindasahoo@gmail.com>

The main aim of this paper is to argue that refraining is a higher form of social action with reference to Gandhian concept of *ahimsa*. The first section deals with Gandhian notion of *ahimsa*. According to Gandhi, *ahimsa* is refraining from the act of inflicting physical and mental pain, i.e., *himsa*. Refraining in this context is very powerful as it requires self-control. Gandhi also says not to contribute anything to *himsa* either by direct physical force or indirectly in defence of anything. That means, to follow *ahimsa* means not to react to *himsa* but letting oneself suffer *himsa*. The agent prepares himself to be passive. This passivity is the consequence of conscious decision of the agent. The second section of the paper discusses refraining as a kind of action. Refraining presupposes the elements of ability, control, and situation where (re)action could have taken place. These elements are too present in physical movement called action. The last section develops the argument that refraining is a powerful tool to stop the reaction, i.e., *himsa* of another agent. Physical positive action may positively contribute to *himsa* but *ahimsa* which is seen as a kind of refrain stops the reaction, i.e., *himsa*.

A Voice of Women: Gandhi and Gilligan

Prasanta Sarkar
Assistant Professor, Department of Philosophy, University of Burdwan,
e-mail: <sarkarp32@gmail.com>

The discussions that take place in feminist philosophy have come from critiquing traditional moral philosophy which undergo patriarchal social thinking. Some feminists have shown that traditional ethics have devalued women; they never raise the issue of suppression, oppression, domination that women have faced in society. Some faults that embedded in it, they found, are like one of non-recognition of works of private realm that usually women do. Actually the aims and objectives of feminist ethics are to revise and reformulate the society that captured by traditional patriarchal thinking and proposed for a society that should be gender neutral. Carol Gilligan, one of the psychologists who is also known as a feminist has raised her voice against patriarchal thought and discovered a language or a voice that women have, called Care, through which feminist goals can be fulfilled. On the other hand, Gandhi has talked about that a society should be more conscious on feminine values and must take feminist strategy to achieve the ideal that a good society needs. He also pointed out that the basis of this society will be love, cooperation, care, sympathy — all those virtues with which women are associated, against independence, autonomy and abstract ideas. The only language that women have, Language of Care, instead of language of justice, irrespective of any gender like men and women if they are able to achieve that, can be considered as feminist. Therefore, our concern here for both Gandhi and Gilligan, it seems to be clear is that a society goes on to sustain properly only when we make room that women deserve for sympathy, emotion, care, and so on and so forth.

Gandhian Constructive Programme: A Means to Protect Human Dignity

S. Abdul Sattar
Professor, e-mail: <sabdulsattar.svu@gmail.com>
&
B. Sreenivasulu Naik
Department of Philosophy, S.V. University, Tirupati
e-mail: <sreenivasulunaik22@gmail.com>

Constructive programme is the basic work advocated by Gandhiji to remove inequalities in the society. The real implication of constructive programme is to distribute wealth equally to all. Equal distribution means each shall have the wherewithal to meet all his normal needs and no more. For example, if one man has a weak digestion and requires, only a quarter of a pound of flour for his bread and another needs a pound, both should be in a position to satisfy their wants. To bring this ideal into being the entire social order has got to be reconstructed on the basis of the fundamental principle of human rights, viz., protecting the dignity of human person. As Gandhiji thinks, a society based on nonviolence cannot nurture any other ideal. We may not perhaps be able to realize the ideal, but we must bear it in mind and work unceasingly to reach it. To the same extent as we progress towards our goal we shall find contentment and happiness.

Gandhiji coined the unique *sarvodaya* a social order aiming at the good of all, but in practice he worked for *antyodaya* a social order striving for the good of the weakest through the means of constructive programme. This was the clear end of his fight for independence and after. It was for achieving such an end that he formulated his constructive programme. An attempt is made in this paper to highlight the principles of constructive programme adopted by Gandhiji with a view to protect human dignity from dehumanization.

Gandhian Perspective on Aharashuddhi and Vedanta

Satyamurti
Reader, Department of Sanskrit, University of Delhi,
e-mail: <satyamurti9@gmail.com>

The Vedanta school of Indian philosophy has developed a systematic method of human resource management through leading a proper lifestyle. The purification of food (*aharashuddhi*) plays a vital role in it. What diet should be taken? When should it be taken? How should it be taken? *Aharashuddhi* subsumes all of these aspects of our diet. The present paper is a modest endeavour to bring the Gandhian perspective on *aharashuddhi* in the light of Vedanta philosophy to the fore. For increasing the work-efficiency and achieving good output, one needs to reveal maximum potentialities inherent in an individual. The Vedanta philosophy strongly believes that by managing oneself, one can do wonders in whatsoever entrepreneurship one starts. Here, our food habits become cardinal in this regard. At many places, Gandhiji has mentioned the importance of right eating. His ideas seem as a reflection of Vedantic approach to *aharashuddhi*.

There are fatal challenges in the modern lifestyle, i.e., unhealthy eating habits, which are directly affecting the work-efficiency of an individual.

In this paper, we have taken a HR Management model for living long and healthy life primarily on the basis of the idea given by Tankacarya, a Vishishtadvaita scholar of CE 600 in his *Brahmasutravakya* 1.1.1.

The HR Management model is as follows:

- Right eating — Good eating habits (*aharashuddhi*) and maintaining proper hygiene
- Stress busting — Conditioning mind through proper stress management
- Exercise — Physical activities as per one's choice including the practice of *pranayama*.

The present paper deals with the first component of this HR model, i.e., right eating. The term *viveka* used in the sentence of Tankacarya signifies right eating habits. The term *viveka* means discrimination between good food and bad food. It is the wisdom to adopt good food and right eating habits and to discard improper food and unhygienic eating habits. This is called *aharashuddhi*, which is extremely important for the purity of body.

Not just the nutrition aspect, but our eating habits and hygienic practices too are extremely important for enhancing quality in diet. Proper hygiene must be maintained in connection with plate, utensils, place, handwash, etc. All these cautions are mentioned in ancient Indian medicine. Ancient Indian tradition prescribes a proper method of having food including *achamana*. If we follow these methods properly and take quality food in appropriate quantity, we would definitely be owning a sound body full of radiance and exuberance. This is the exhaustive description of *aharashuddhi*. This kind of *aharashuddhi* or purification of food purifies one's mind and that leads to indelible memory. There is no need to explain how a sound body, a sharp mind, and indelible memory can do wonders in any entrepreneurship one starts. It is interesting to know these similarities in the ideas of Vedanta and Gandhiji.

The Concept of Dharma: From Gandhian Perspective

R. Savithiri

Research Scholar, Department of Philosophy, Pondicherry University, Puducherry, e-mail: <savithiri86@gmail.com>

According to Gandhi, the word *dharma*, used in Sanskrit, has no English equivalent. According to him, *satya* is practice of truth and it is not an intellectual proposition but a way of life which has to be actualized and embodied directly by each person. There is no place for the reification or codification of *satya*, because truth is not held in some book or set of laws; it lives in oneself, and cannot be separated from oneself. This philosophical distinction is at the heart of Gandhi's notion of *dharma*. *Satya-graha*, insisted by Gandhi, is a civil disobedience method that has to be individually lived, as opposed to being theorized or institutionalized. Gandhi's *dharma* is captured in the term *ahimsa*, which is translated as "non-violence". *Ahimsa* also applies to cultures taken as a whole. *Swadeshi* is another Sansrkit term used by Gandhi for the "from the soil" a native product, similar to the "buy local" movement. He advocated a dharmic society based on traditional decentralized governance built from the bottom–up at the village level. He took the *Bhagavadgita*'s notion of ethics and lived his *dharma* in terms of the battles to be fought.

Spiritual Foundation of Gandhi's Thought

Dilip Shah
Former Professor and Head, Mahatma Gandhi Department of Rural Studies
V.N.S.G. University, Surat, e-mail: <drsmrs2005@yahoo.co.in>

The whole of Gandhian framework and thought is not possible to understand without understanding the evolution and process of spiritual outlook of Mahatma Gandhi. The paper has the following sections with integrated linkages: The first section explains the importance of spiritual foundation for understanding Gandhi's thought and action. The second section deals with the conceptual building of Gandhian practical-spiritual thought. The third section discusses the role of religion in the life of Gandhi. The fourth section explains the different sources of spiritual development of Gandhi including his family background, role of Indian religious books like *Ramacharitamanas*, and dramas like *Harischandra* and *Taramati*. Also discussed in this section are the three vows that Gandhi took before he travelled to England, the religious books that he studied in London like the *Gita* and the Bible. His contacts with Tolstoy and Rajchandra, and his study of the works of Ruskin and Tolstoy are also focused. The fifth section explains the philosophic framework of Gandhi's thought and practice. This section is based on the excellent paper of K. Ramakrishna Rao, who explained the difference between the dialectical materialism of Marx and dialectical spiritualism of Gandhi. The sixth section narrates the day-to-day practice and spiritual development of Gandhi through prayers, *vratas*, and specific code of conduct. The seventh section points out the distinguished characterstics of Gandhi's spiritual philosophy and life, such as human service and self-control as part of spiritual *sadhana*.

The paper concludes with a brief summary on the works of Vinoba Bhave, who was declared as Gandhi's spiritual heir.

Violent Economic Growth and Conflict Resolving Remedies under Gandhian Perspective

Dilip Shah
Former Professor, Mahatma Gandhi Department of Rural Studies, V.N.S.G. University, Surat, e-mail: <drsmrs2005@yahoo.co.in>

This paper is a critical review of Indian economic growth and development. It brings out violent elements emerged out of neo-liberal, market-friendly globalization policy, adopted since 1991–2000. On the basis of analytical evidence and finding, it attempts to suggest specific policy actions which are possible to prevent violent economy without loss of Gandhian framework to a large extent of policy, principles, and values.

The paper is divided into six sections. The first section spells out the specific objectives, sources of data, and central thesis of the study. The second section explains the role and place of nonviolence in Gandhian thought. The third section briefly states Gandhi's concepts of economics, economic progress, development, and sustainable development. The fourth section provides historical account of evolution of India's new economic policy and economic reforms during 1990-91, 2000-01, and 2013-14. The fifth section discusses conflict generating process and outcomes, leading to violence in economy and violent society. The sixth section deals with the details of Gandhian conflict resolving remedies.

The paper concludes with an optimist note that even within Neo-liberal economy today, Gandhian prescriptions are possible to help to reduce elements of violence by way of better pro-poor policy environment.

Satyagraha as the Way of Life

Reeta Kumar Sharma
HOD, Philosophy, S.S.L.N.T.M.M College, Dhanbad, e-mail: <reeta.sharma287@gmail.com>

The practical application of *ahimsa* is *satyagraha*. It is a method of securing a right by personal suffering not by inflicting injury on others. The principles of *satyagraha* and *ahimsa* were applied by Gandhiji in the field of politics, and a number of conditions favour its growth and success. The conditions were absence of armed force in the Indian masses, the cast restrictions in non-kshatriya Hindus, regarding the use of weapon, and the Hindu doctrine of *karma*. Really, *satyagraha* is the need of the hour, because life will be successful and beautiful if the principle of *satyagraha* reflected in everybody's life. It acts as a conflict resolution technique and also it is an instrument for loving people. Evil can be abolished by doing good things in life. We can realize equality among men through the principle of *satyagraha*. *Satyagraha* acts as a spiritual weapon which is the fundamental element to establish morality and values in human life. Through morality and values, we can establish good by avoiding evil. This paper reflects how we accept *satyagraha* as our way of life and then the Gandhian dream of *satyagraha* will come true.

Gandhi's Philosophy of Civilization

Purnendu Shekhar
Associate Professor, P.G. Department of Philosophy, T.M. Bhagalpur University, Bhagalpur, e-mail: <pshekhar26@yahoo.com>

Gandhi's philosophy of civilization has taken its shape in the form of a therapy. In the field of therapy there are four steps: (1) disease, (2) cause/s of disease, (3) treatment/medicines of disease, and (4) aim of treatment/cure. Gandhi has propounded his philosophy of civilization in his famous book *Hind Swaraj* (1909) in a seed form. His other thoughts expressed throughout his life confirm his views on civilization as enshrined in *Hind Swaraj*. According to Gandhi modern civilization is a disease/evil. The causes of this disease include egoism, hedonism, utilitarianism, capitalism, naturalistic evolutionism, communalism, consumerism, rationalism, anarchism, authoritarianism, colonialism, industrialization, dependence on technological advancement, etc. There are two types of treatment which Gandhi provides: (a) universal and most fundamental, and (b) supplementary treatment. *Satya* (Truth) and *ahimsa* (nonviolence) are two fundamental treatments but there are so many other treatments too, Gandhi prescribes in different contexts. They are: *asteya, aparigraha, brahmacharya, swadeshi, sarvadharma samabhava, abhaya, sharirashram, asprishyata-nivarana*, trusteeship, need-based life, purity of means, duty-based conduct, Nayi Taalim/basic education, constructive programmes, community works, etc. Good civilization and *sarvodaya* are cures or aims of his treatment. First, Gandhi eliminates those principles which constitute the root of modern civilization, second, he advocates those principles, values, and activities upon which the good civilization is based. In his *Hind Swaraj*, Gandhi performs his duty as an ethico-spiritual surgeon as it were. His good civilization is based on ethical principles. His civilizational discourse covers almost all aspects of life. In my paper I would focus specially on Gandhi's views concerning religion, morality, politics, society, technological advancement, economy, culture, governance, communal harmony, world peace, professional code of conduct, etc.

Gandhian Philosophy of Education

Sudhanshu Shekhar
Department of Philosophy, T.M. Bhagalpur University,
e-mail:<sudhan.ph@gmail.com>

According to Mahatma Gandhi, education makes a man perfect and true, helps him in his total development, and motivates him for performing his duties with honesty and sincerity. He tries to prove that neither primary education nor higher education is able to make one a perfect and true man. Both of these do not enable us to do our duties well.

Gandhi said that it is not necessary to make this present education compulsory to all. He added that our ancient school system is enough. Character building has the first place in it and that is real primary education. In short, Gandhi believes in the ideals of *sa vidya ya vimuktye* and *vidya dadati vinayam*. According to him the true meaning of education is to develop the noble elements of human body, mind, heart, and soul.

Today, issues raised by Gandhi as mentioned above have assumed greater importance, for the governments of free India have exerted their utmost energy to promote knowledge of letters only besides eulogizing Western madness for scientific advancements. This has caused great harm to the age-honoured conventional know-how of the Indian peasants and craftsmen. Indian farmers today are largely dependent on markets, not only for agricultural implements, but also for seeds and fertilizers. The condition of the people engaged in manufacturing *khadi* and silk clothes too has become precarious.

To sum up, today's education-system is, no doubt, producing students laden with the "burden" of information and "Munnabhais" bent upon achieving success by hook or crook to the utter neglect of healthy competition, but it is failing miserably in "producing" sensitive and creative "man". If the young product of this educational system finds time to go through the *Hind Swaraj* of Gandhi, the half-naked *fakir* of India, even once, nation will be amply benefited.

Satyagraha and Democracy: A Review

Abha Singh
Professor & Head, Post-Graduate Department of Philosophy, A.N. College,
e-mail: <abhasingh126@gmail.com>

The word *satyagraha* has been coined by Gandhi to describe his method of action. It is a Sanskrit word and is a compound of two words — *satya* (truth) and *agraha* (insistence or adherence). Its literal meaning is "holding on to truth", i.e., to endure in the way of truth in spite of all difficulties, dangers, and sufferings. Although "nonviolence" is not included in the compound *satyagraha*, it designates a new way of life based on non-violence. The *satyagrahi*'s object is to convert, not to coerce the wrongdoer. Since the basis of nonviolence is love, it would be more accurate to define *satyagraha* as action based on truth, love, and nonviolence. Therefore, for Gandhi, *satyagraha* is soul-force or spiritual-force. It is the technique to achieve Truth or God.

Satyagraha is a new way of life with a philosophy of action and a technique for social change. Gandhi has called *satyagraha* a science and an art of life. He claims himself, quite rightly, to be the author of *satyagraha*. He said that he was evolving the new way of life by living, as well as preaching it. He never claimed that the evolution of *satyagraha* was ever complete. For him, the concept was still growing and there was nothing like finality. For him, the evolution of *satyagraha* is linked with social evolution itself. Gandhi's life, thought and action can be said to be a running commentary — illustrative, interpretative, and expositional on *satyagraha*.

In the context of the individual, *satyagraha* means a three-dimensional progress in truth, love, and nonviolence. However, in relation to the state, the possible application of the principle of *satyagraha* may be broadly classified into three categories. The first category consists of those relating to the method of resistance to the state by individual or groups who are opposed to it. The second comprises the uses of *satyagraha* within a state by individuals and groups in their mutual dealings. The last category is the application of *satyagraha* by the state in dealing with its subjects and in its relations with other states. The method of *satyagraha*, as suggested by Gandhi, may broadly be classified as non-cooperation, refusal, and resistance.

It is in the field of resistance to the government that Gandhi was engaged in practising *satyagraha* during most of his life. However, Gandhi's resistance was against an oppressive and unrighteous government in South Africa and an alien imperialism in India. Now the question is: Can the same principles and tactics be applied when citizens of a state have to resist their own national government especially when it is a democracy? And here lies the suitability of *satyagraha* in democracy. To my mind, democracy is nearer to *satyagraha* than any other system of government because it depends, to a greater extent, on consent and persuasion for the implementation of all its policies and activities.

All the issues, stated above, would be discussed, in detail, in the paper and an attempt would be made to prove that constitutional democratic methods are half-way between violence and *satyagraha* and a firm alliance between the advocates of democracy and a believer of *sayagraha* promises the safest and swiftest march of humanity towards world peace and elimination of injustice and exploitation.

Mahatma Gandhi and the Peasant Movement in Bihar

Damodar Singh
Professor, Department of History, B.S. College, Danapur,
e-mail: <damodarsingh27@gmail.com>

Mahatma Gandhi, the exponent of the *satyagraha* (nonviolent civil disobedience) movement, staged his first *satyagraha* in Champaran district of Bihar in 1917-18, wherein he took up the cause of the peasants of the area and seemingly passed the litmus test. It served as a launching pad for him to enter into national politics. The event gains all the more significance since it was during this agitation that Gandhi was addressed by the people, for the first time, as *Bapu* (Father) and *Mahatma* (Great Soul). It is also of special interest from Bihar's point-of-view, because after the separation of Bihar from Bengal (1912), this was the first major struggle in the province.

The fluctuation of political opinion during this movement was mirrored in the print media. The press of this period was not always very representative of public opinion, because it was edited by men whose ideas had been formed during the preceding epoch of the national movement. There was a good deal of political demands made in the preceding decades, which were yet to be fulfilled. Nevertheless, most of these editors tried their best to portray the real developments of this movement. Their editorial statements reflected the varying phases of the agitationalist dilemma as it presented itself to the educated middle class. In this paper the event shall be analysed on the basis of records, as available today, from contemporary print media, viz., *Bengal Magazine, Hindu Patriot, The Biharee, Pratap, Bharat Mitra, Amrit Bazar Patrika, Dainik*

Bharat Mitra, Mithila Mihir, Young India, Statesman, and many other magazines.

The historic peasant movement in Champaran district of Bihar in 1917 was, in fact, the culmination of century-old agrarian discontent against the European planters. The root cause of the trouble was the system of indirect cultivation, particularly the unpopular *tinkathia* system, whereby *raiyat*s were bound to grow indigo for the planters on three-twentieth, i.e., 15 per cent of his holdings. The selection of land as well as the price of the indigo thus grown was determined by the European indigo planters, who were buyers of the said crop as well. This, as a net result, only added misery and poverty to the peasants. With the government siding the planters, the poor peasants had nowhere to appeal for redress or help. In this way, for all practical purposes, the *raiyat*s were turned into serfs in this pseudo-feudal system.

In a bid to search someone who could bring them out of quagmire, Raj Kumar Shukla, a peasant of Champaran, contacted Gandhiji, a recent champion of the oppressed Indians' cause in South Africa, at Lucknow in December 1916 and persuaded him to take up the cause of Champaran peasants or at least personally investigate the reality of the situation. Though Gandhiji initially disagreed, but ultimately Raj Kumar Shukla prevailed; and on 15 April 1917 Gandhiji reached Motihari, the headquarters of the district of Champaran, on a fact-finding mission.

The local administration, being suspecting of Gandhi's movements, served a notice, asking him to leave the district by next train available since his presence was a threat to public peace. But so strong was the sense of public responsibility in Gandhiji that he decided to disobey the order and preferred to face the punishment for his defiance of law. As a result, he was tried in the district court on 18 April 1917.

The news of these developments spread like a wild fire, and soon thousands of peasants rallied around Gandhiji. The deadlock was broken when the D.M. withdrew the case; and Gandhiji was at liberty to continue his enquiry, which was definitely not an insignificant victory.

Subsequently, a triumphant Gandhi embarked upon investigating and recording the peasants' grievances. In this mission he was joined by many volunteers of the area, and also young intellectuals from different parts of Bihar as well as from other parts of India, viz., Rajendra Prasad, Mazharul Haque, Anugrah Narain Singh, Shri Krishna Sinha, Mahadeo Desai and many others.

Along with his inquiry, he taught the peasants to come out of fear since the first condition of freedom is freedom from fear. Besides building on the confidence of villagers, he began leading the clean-up of villages, building of schools and hospitals and encouraged the villagers to undo *purdah*, untouchability, and the suppression of women.

Meanwhile, the provincial government appointed a Commission to look into the peasants' grievances, and nominated Gandhi as one of its members. The latter was able to prevail easily upon the commission on the basis of records of about 25,000 peasants he had already collected.

Finally, as a result of the Commission's report — signed on 3 October 1917 and enforced from 1 May 1918 — the *tinkaṭhiya* system, courtesy Gandhiji, was abolished. With it, the main grievance of the peasants were remedied and the planters lost their foothold in Champaran. It also created a mass base for the nationalist movement in Bihar, along with bringing together a group of political activists in Bihar to give proper leadership to the masses.

The contemporary print media provided an interesting record of the whole development. It was the media which kept the issue of poor *raiyat*s alive and kicking, and prompted Gandhiji to take up their cause. During the whole struggle, the print media kept on highlighting the events, and, thereby, it apparently played the role of a catalyst in forcing the British government to concede to Gandhiji's initiative for the issue-based emancipation of the *raiyat*s of Champaran.

Gandhi's Ideas on Education and Its Practice in Present Context

Abani Sonowal
Research Scholar, Department of Philosophy, North Eastern Hill University,
e-mail: <sonobani89@gmail.com>

Education, being a lifelong process, is an essential part of human being. Gandhi, one of the outstanding figures of contemporary Indian philosophy, began his first experiment in education at the Tolstoy's Farm Ashram in South Africa. Gandhi's concept of education has several layers of meaning. These concepts developed out of his experiences with the English educational systems and colonialism. For Gandhi education is the moral development of the person, a process that is by definition "life long". His concept of education was directed toward his alternative vision of the social order. Therefore his basic education was an embodiment of his perception of an ideal society, consisting of small, self-reliant communities with his ideal citizen being an industrious, self-respecting, living in a small cooperative society. By education, he meant all-round drawing out of the best in child and man — body, mind, and spirit. Literacy is not the end of education nor even the beginning. It is only one of the means by which man and women can be educated. By this he tried to bring child's education by teaching it a useful handicraft and enabling it to produce from the moment it begins its training. An attempt will be made to discuss Gandhi's ideas on education and its practice in the present context.

Economic Philosophy of Gandhi

K. Srinivas
Department of Philosophy, School of Humanities, Pondicherry University, Puducherry, e-mail: <ragsri55@yahoo.com>

Not only our country, but the entire world is witnessing an unprecedented economic slowdown. According to economists and market experts, the situation is going to be much worse in coming months and years. Unless we take firm steps to curb inflation, the life of common man would be miserable and pathetic. The popular belief is that there is tremendous progress in almost all fronts of human life. This may be true for a small section of people, but not to all. Deaths due to hunger, lack of proper nourishment, lack of health care are increasing day-by-day. A welfare society is one in which there is promotion and protection of economic and social well-being of all its citizens. Equal opportunities and equal distribution of nation's wealth to all its citizens would be the preamble of any ideal welfare society. Modern economic models, to a great extent, failed to protect the right to livelihood of millions of individuals all over the globe. Exploitation of "individuals and natural resources" has become the order of the day for modern industrialized economy. It contributed to the lopsided development of so-called advanced societies wherein the division between the rich and the poor is widening. In the name of urbanization, the village (rural) economy is completely ignored. Under these circumstances, we have to go back to Gandhian economic model which promotes the socio-economic growth of every individual as a citizen of a welfare society. An attempt is made in this paper to assess whether Gandhian economic model would be a viable alternative to modern economic theories for overall development of nation's economy and well-being of its citizens.

Quintessence of Gandhi's Philosophy in Satyagraha and Ahimsa

Kamala Srinivas
Assistant Professor, Department of Philosophy, SIES College of Arts, Science and Commerce, Mumbai, e-mail: <kamala.srinivas16@gmail.com>

> Philosophy without life corresponding is like a body without life . . . I know that in this land of ours we have enough philosophy but little life. But I know also the laws governing the conduct of man have still to be explored and the condition of exploration is imperative and unalterable.
> — M.K. Gandhi (*Young India*, 14.4.1927, p. 121)

The impact of a personality like Gandhi, which while challenging the Western civilization has experimented with forces that transformed our country from being a socially conservative and politically ineffective nation to a nation alive with a new political vigour and a new social conscience. Twenty-first-century philosophers, research scholars, academicians of India have involved themselves in making significant contributions by understanding Gandhi's philosophy and the application of it for the standard socio-economic problems which have perplexed every person concerned all over the world. The quintessence of Gandhi's philosophy lies in his conviction on truth, nonviolence, integration, social upliftment, and welfare. He infused life into some of them by experiencing and practising them in the very course of his struggle for the discovery of truth. As a result, the conclusions that he arrived in his life are not the results of an "ideal experiment" as Bradley would call it, in which theory is compared with theory, and concept with concept, but the results of actual experiment on his own life. "As Gandhi is not an academic philosopher, he has been unable to give the complete implications of his discoveries. But these implications can be developed, and his philosophy can be presented in a systematic form", says Prof. P.T. Raju in his book *Idealistic Thought of India* (1953).

The paper attempts to focus on the metaphysical side of Gandhi's teaching and understand his guiding ideas in a coherent form. The real clue to his conception of reality is found in the pregnant words, *satyagraha* and *ahimsa* which are translated as truth-force and passive resistance. Further, the paper shall attempt to answer the questions raised with regard to: are *satyagraha* and *ahimsa* morally binding or not? Can Gandhi's idea of reality meet the demands of the moral will? What is moral, can that be considered as natural? Lastly, then isn't it natural on the part of man to be moral?

Value of "Right Means" in Gandhian Morality

Shilpi Srivastava
Assistant Professor, Janki Devi Memorial College, University of Delhi,
e-mail: <simplyshilpi@gmail.com>

The world that we live in today is a fiercely competitive one. From the grades one earns in school and college to the salary and promotion and even the car one buys, one doesn't want to settle for anything less than the best. In such an environment of cut-throat competition, results have become the driving force and the sole criterion to decide the success of an action. In such a scenario, any path that leads to the desired end is seen as the right one. As a result, we find ourselves living in a community that is full of violence, stress, hatred, and distrust.

On the other hand, the principles that Gandhi preached and lived by were in complete contrast. He firmly believed that we only have a control over our means, and none over the ends; and if we are committed to ensure the purity of our means, the end will take care of itself. It would be wrong to say that Gandhi's principles were a natural response of his times, as we are all aware that he had to face serious difficulties throughout his life to abide by them. The freedom struggle is a very relevant example about his commitment to the purity of his means.

In this paper I propose to analyse the importance of "right means" in Gandhi's overall moral scheme. I would also discuss the idea with relation to the philosophy of *Bhagavadgita*, that Gandhi was greatly influenced by, and further discuss that how such an approach can offer a solution to many of our present-day social evils.

The Relevance of Mahatma Gandhi Today

Raviprolu Subrahmanyam
Pinakini Satyagraha Ashramam, Nellore
e-mail: <raviprolusmanyam@gmail.com>, <sraviprolu@icloud.com>

"What is the relevance of Mahatma Gandhi" is the question that is upper most in the minds of all thinking people. This is the question one has to explore objectively and from many points of view. The study of Gandhi should not be confined to the study of his life, works, and ideas. It should involve the application of those ideas to new challenges and situations. In this attempt, one has to find a much explored new ground and try sincerely to uncover the relevant facts without malice to any one.

Gandhism has to be reinjected into the docile and sleepy youth of this nation and also across the globe. The relevance of Gandhi must be explained to the present-day's healthy, charming, intelligent but anguished and confused generation with scientific exploration. Particularly, his views on *satyagraha* are to be explored and taught. It is a fact that nonviolent *satyagraha* sometimes takes a long time to achieve, but definitely, it causes less damage to the people and property and does not leave a trace of hatred and ill-will. Ultimately imbibed with *ahimsa*, it is the pursuit of Truth and Truth is the ultimate winner.

Even though Gandhi was loyal to India, his responsibility as a modern intellectual figure made him speak the "truth" beyond the national and cultural frontiers by picking up the right moral and political alternative and then intelligently representing it where it could do the most good and cause the right change.

Revisiting Gandhi's *Nayi Talim* or Basic Education

Tejashree S. Trimakhe
Department of Philosophy, University of Mumbai, e-mail: <tej1214@gmail.com>

We are living in twenty-first-century India where the problem of unemployment is an issue of concern. Here there is a need to take human resource development seriously. On one hand there is a rise in the tendency towards professional education of engineering and medical studies but on the other hand people are struggling to earn their *roti, kapda,* and *makan*. So just producing doctors and engineers will not serve the higher purpose of making the masses self sufficient. There is a need to ask the question that is our education really practical and applicable.

We should not look at our students as homogeneous. So the level of education must suit student's level of maturity and must have relevance to the experience. Here Gandhi's programme of basic education or Nayi Talim can be seen as an answer and it should be revisited.

The purpose of this paper is to understand the basic tenets of Nayi Talim and its relevance in the present context, where lived experience and man making will be of utmost importance. Education through industry will lead to respect for manual labour, sense of cooperation, feeling of friendship and economic self-reliance, team spirit, and sincerity.

We always strive for excellence be it material or intellectual and always aim for luxuries but we are less considerate about the helpless youth. If we equip our generations with self-supporting primary education many problems would be resolved and our dream of a content, peace loving, and crimeless society can be achieved.

Swaraj: The Just Society

Aman Tripathi
e-mail: <aman.tripathi@iitb.ac.in>

Vegitha Reddy
e-mail: <vegitha@iitb.ac.in>
&

P.R. Bhat
Professor, Department of HSS, Indian Institute of Technology Bombay,
e-mail: <p.r.bhat@iitb.ac.in>

A society endeavours to be harmonious. If it is to be harmonious, it must be just. Justice therefore is a prerequisite for harmony in a society. However, the assumption made in the contemporary perception of justice is that it should necessarily be enforced. But an act of enforcement is an act of violence, the outcome of which is a society that enforces justice and yet cannot achieve harmony. However, in Gandhian perspective we retain the harmony through self-regulation that is inherent in the *swaraj*. *Swaraj* for an individual is a moral standpoint, which is an act of volition that abides by *svadharma* and is not based on external force. It is this spirit of volition that is valued and protected in *swaraj*. Thereby, we achieve a society, which is not only just but also inherently harmonious.

Moral Dynamics of Nonviolence: Richard Gregg's Analysis

M. Varalakshmi
Research Fellow, Centre for Economics and Social Studies (CESS), Hyderabad,
e-mail: <mogantyvl@yahoo.com>

The history of nonviolence evinces us that its mechanism had tremendous influences to win the hearts of people and to restore social and political harmony. Richard Gregg's analysis of nonviolent mechanism is aimed at two things: one, to substantiate Gandhi's nonviolent conflict resolution in order to make it more explicit to Western minds and another, to show how and why human unity can help, solve human conflicts. Gregg coined a word called *moral jiu-jitsu* where a nonviolent resister wins the game through his nonviolent ways where the violent attacker and the nonviolent resister exercise certain power to win over the other. In this process public approbation is one crucial factor. Gregg brings forth these aspects taking cues from various sources; from the historical events, Gandhi's methods and other theoretical perspectives and analyses from sociology and psychology. Gregg further discusses on the wise use of emotional energy and application of the nonviolent power by masses and state and nonviolent resolution as an effective substitute for war. One has to understand Gandhi's method of nonviolence at various levels; emotional, rational, political, social, and spiritual. Gregg has come closer to understand Gandhi's method, for he has understood that Gandhi's nonviolence is rooted in his love for all; even towards the most dangerous animal or a human being. This paper looks into these mechanisms in view of growing violence in the world.

Gandhiji's Conception of Nonviolence and Conflict Resolution

G. Vedaparayana
Professor, SV University, Tirupati, e-mail: <parayanaveda_49@yahoo.com>

Peace is not a commodity available in the market nor is it a tangible thing that one can give to the other. Peace is not the mere absence of war nor is it a truce between two wars. On the contrary, peace is the state of mind and the inward being of the individual. Peace in its holistic sense is the non-existence of violence "within" and "without". It is the absence of conflict in thought, word, and deed and in all the spheres of existence. Peace in its profound sense is possible only when the individual is integrated and holistic. It requires the individual who has realized the supreme truth and is in the practice of nonviolence or love.

This paper proposes to give an exposition of Gandhiji's ideal of nonviolence as an effective means of conflict resolution and establishing peace in the life-world. The paper brings out in brief the philosophical bases of the ideal of love in the Eastern and the Western thought. It elucidates the Buddhist ideal of compassion in particular as the source of the Gandhian principle of nonviolence in precept and praxis. It deals at length with the concept of nonviolence as the means of realizing truth, seeing God face to face, in serving the other without expecting anything in return. The paper concludes with an observation that the Gandhian means of nonviolence remains to be significant as long as humanity is oblivious of the truth and nonviolence as the best possible and meaningful means of resolving conflict in all its dimensions. *Satyagraha* has been proved to be a potent and an indispensible means of establishing peace locally and globally, individually, and socially.

Gandhiji on Truth and the Means of Its Realization

G. Vedaparayana
Professor, SV University, Tirupati, e-mail: <parayanaveda_49@yahoo.com>

This paper in three parts is an attempt at an exposition of the nature and means of realizing truth from the Gandhian perspective. Part one deals with the Gandhian conception of Truth as God, the Eternal Principle that includes the principles of conduct like *brahmacharya* (celibacy) and truth in thought, word, and deed. Part two comprises the exposition of *brahmacharya, anasaktiyoga,* and *satyagraha* adopted by Gandhi as the important means of realizing the Truth. And in part three it is pointed out that in spite of his relentless search after the Truth, what Gandhi could have were only its fleeting glimpses. In conclusion, it is held that Gandhi could not have the full glimpse of the Truth probably because the means he followed were not only inadequate and preliminary, but also misplaced.

Grama Swaraj: A Dream of Gandhi

Sailaja Velpula
Assistant Professor, GITAM School of Law, e-mail: <sailajavelpula1980@gmail.com>

Gandhiji believed that Independence has to begin at the lowest rung and a society must be built in which every village must be self-sustained and capable of managing its own affairs. Gandhi's cherished dream of *swadeshi grama swaraj* is evident in his book *Hind Swaraj* (1909), in which he argues for self-rule/home rule not only by transfer of power from the British to the Indians but also by economic and democratic decentralization. He was very emphatic about individual freedom and empowerment, which can be attained only in autonomous and self-reliant communities which can offer equal opportunity to the people and encourage simple living and high thinking. Unfortunately Gandhiji's dreams of *grama swaraj* had only been paid lip service by successive governments and it is only in the recent past that concrete efforts have been made to translate them into reality.

Under this backdrop, the paper focuses on Gandhian spirit of *grama swaraj* and village self-governance and relevant constitutional provisions. It also highlights Panchayat Raj Institutions as tools for good governance in the light of Balawant Rai Mehata Committee report and the 73rd Constitutional Amendment. Furthermore the paper discusses the present-day adverse impact of globalization over these village communities and onslaught of Multinational Companies on cottage industries and offers possible solutions to protect grassroot economic and political self-reliance, which can serve as the backbone of the economic and social well-being of the nation.

Human Rights: Dream of Gandhi

Chanchala Verma
Assistant Professor, Department of Home Science, SSLNT Mahila College, Dhanbhad, e-mail: <dr.chanchalaverma@gmail.com>

Gandhi has been attributed as being the inspiration or model for various rights, struggles around the world. The term "human rights" has been made familiar by its use in today's international political discourse and the prominence accorded to it by the media. In simple way we can say that a right is something to which we are entitled. In seeking to understand the notion of human rights in the context of the approach and ideology of Mahatma Gandhi, we examine the notion of human rights. As the leader of the national freedom movement, Gandhi's objective was to attain independence, but his other objective was to save Indian society, and more specifically, Hinduism. He insisted that India should show her capacity to reform herself even while asking for freedom. His method of integration of nationalist aspirations within the framework of social reform explains his extraordinary tactics. This was illustrated in Poona in 1931 when he fasted to exact from Ambedkar his withdrawal of the demand of a separate electorate for the untouchables. His thrust was that of a social reformer campaigning amongst the higher castes of the higher community, propagating social acceptance of the untouchables by the community. In this process, he renamed the untouchables as "Harijans" (sons of God). Gandhi's programme of social reform was based on duties rather than on rights. He said very clearly that he did not care for rights, but for duties.

Gandhi takes the attitude of a social reformer calling upon the higher castes to accept the untouchables. He does not say that the untouchables have rights, but says that upper castes have a duty towards them. When he advocates resistance, he adds that it must be done in the manner of satyagraha, that is, not by asking for rights, but by showing the other person what his duty is. It is obvious that Gandhian notions are not sympathetic to human rights unless they are products of duties well performed.

To accept Gandhi's notion that rights and duties are two sides of the same coin would be too simplistic. It can be valid only in an ideal world, but since we live in the grim reality of human fighting not only for resources, but for self-respect and dignity, the notion of rights assumes added significance. The notion of duties has sadly been used by those in position of power either to deny rights to others, or to dole out peaceful favours, eroding not only the dignity of the recipients of such so-called favours, but also eroding the power of the others to work towards standing on their own feet. Gandhi sought to change the heart of the caste Hindus by moral pressure within the framework of Hindu tradition. Thus, Gandhi has in his own ways been responsible for the establishment and ideological sustenance of a large number of organizations that claim to work in the field of human rights.

Gandhian Way of Approaching Globalization

R.Vetrickarthick
Research Scholar
Department of Gandhian Studies and Ramalinga Philosophy, Madurai Kamaraj University, e-mail: <vetrickarthick@yahoo.co.in>
&
A. Ravichandran
Librarian, Gandhi Memorial Museum, Madurai

As we are successfully reaching towards 70th year of Independence, we are about to face a real challenge of our democracy in the name of Globalization. Discovery of sea route on 20 May 1498, caused India 450 years of colonization to French, Dutch, Portuguese, and English. World Wide Web threatens India even bigger slavery of developed nations. Liberalized Indian market paves the way for the Multinational Companies'. domination in India. Economists look at globalization as an unmitigated "good" and their badly flawed models miss the real world problems. As Gandhi told, "The world has enough for everyone's *need*, but not enough for everyone's *greed*". Economists miss the point: the world is finite. We do have very limited resources. We also have limited ability to handle excess pollution. Some of the researchers think, due to globalization social equality can be achieved but they forget the fact that economic equality is actually interlinked. Moreover in developing countries like India, small firms will be forced out of the race from the competitive global market due to financial and technological lacking. Globalization will generate a big gap between the rich and the poor. Developing countries will depend on the developed countries for meeting their goals and needs. Hence countries like India, need to pay a big price for the liberalized market. This paper discusses Mahatma Gandhi's decentralization as an alternative to globalization. This paper also brings out a framework of Mahatma Gandhi's economic model which will be suitable for the developing nations.

Gandhiji and Swami Vivekananda's Views on Education

Sharmila Jayant Virkar
Department of Philosophy, University of Mumbai,
e-mail: <sharmila.virkar@hotmail.com>

Mahatma Gandhi and Swami Vivekananda are the two towering personalities who emphasized education as a means to social change. Education, however, was not equated by them, with literacy. Both Gandhiji and Swamiji brought out effectively their concept of education which is essentially the same. In the first part of the paper, I intend to discuss the definition, meaning, end, purpose or goal of education as conceived by both of them. In the second part, I propose to consider Gandhiji, vis-à-vis Swamiji, on the way education is to be imparted. The issues pertaining to methodology or pedagogy are taken up here. Not only how but also when, to whom, by whom, and most importantly, of what type of education needs to be imparted are also significant questions regarding education. These questions are dealt with in the third part of this essay. In the fourth and concluding part my observations will be stated.

Gandhian Values and Hind Swaraj

Manasvini M. Yogi
Associate Professor, Department of Philosophy, Indraprastha College,
University of Delhi, e-mail: <mmyogi@rediffmail.com>

When one reads *Hind Swaraj* today one feels immediately that Gandhi's critique of modern civilization ignores many of its strengths. He rejects Western civilization and industrialization which is derived mainly from the capitalist ideology.

Gandhi asked questions which are now very important for the underdeveloped countries and the societies which have undergone industrialization. He anticipated the threats to humanity that emanate from technology and, industrialization under the influence of the West and consumerism. He was able to ask these questions, because he tested and judged every aspect of human activity on a scale of some values and ethical norms.

Gandhian values were not derived from any metaphysical system. They were derived from his own philosophical ideas which he arrived at as a result of historical, spiritual, and material knowledge and his experience. Gandhi's values thus reflect his understanding of human nature, of social and production relations, of man's constant struggle against forces which tried to push him down into one kind of oppression or another and of his attempts to rise above his existentialist situation.

Hind Swaraj primarily inquires into the meaning and attainment of freedom and its relevance to the present-day world.

Swaraj: Localization and Globalization: An Extraordinary Journey of an Ordinary Man

Manasvini M. Yogi
Associate Professor
&
Pragati Tripathi
Student
Department of Philosophy, Indraprastha College, University of Delhi
e-mail: <pragatitripathi28@gmail.com>

Swaraj or self-rule was born during the Indian freedom struggle in Gandhi's book named *Hind Swaraj*. To a layman it just meant getting rid of the colony and becoming a nation ruled by its own people but Gandhi sought to clarify that the meaning was much more than simply "wanting English rule without English men". The father of the nation, the greatest soul ever and above all an ordinary man of extraordinary deeds dedicated his entire life for the achievement and establishment of *swaraj*.

The crux of his argument centred on the belief that the socio-spiritual underpinnings of British political, economical, bureaucratic, legal, military, and educational institutions were unjust, exploitative, and alienating.

Now the question must be asked why *swaraj*? The answer lies in the fact that call for *swaraj* represents a genuine attempt to regain control of the "self"— our self-respect, self-responsibility, and capacities for self-realization from institution of dehumanization.

From his very first public appearance in BHU to Quit India movement — Gandhi organized mass mobilizations in such a way that the entire nation came united which lead towards *swaraj*. All these events went viral, moving people from within and out and hence took place the localization and globalization.

I will deal with the above concepts in detail and will creatively analyse the content and the consequences of our current economic, political, social, and educational systems, without reverting to a romanticized past of so-called untouched or pristine tradition.

Book Reviews

K. SRINIVAS, ***Gandhi the Pacifist,*** New Delhi: Suryodaya Books (*publishers*) & D.K. Printworld (*distributors*), 2015, x + 122 pp., Rs. 350

As the author says in his Preface, the very survival of Gandhian thought proves that it is not a rigid set of doctrines but a complete philosophy covering varied aspects of human life and society with an inbuilt elasticity to include changes that come with time. Gandhi, a "practical idealist", applied robust idealism in all fields. The author stresses upon Gandhi's triple methods of action as a radical pacifist — nonviolence, compassion, and love for universal peace and harmony; he equated God and truth and was guided by his "inner voice" in all actions.

This book deals with selected topics related to Gandhian thought. It has seven chapters, followed by Epilogue, Bibliography, and Index. While the first chapter (Prologue) provides a broad coverage and the last (Reappraising Gandhi) gives a book review by the author, chaps. 2 and 3 cover the subject of peace and conflict resolution, chap. 4 that of corruption and human values, and chaps. 5 and 6 that of economics and the socialist views of Gandhi and Marx.

Chapter 1 — Prologue: Considering Gandhi as a philosopher, the author sees him more as a *karmayogi* than as a *darshanika,* and gives a broad overview of the Gandhian thought and action. Gandhi's world view was an outcome of his own intuition and insight. Humanism and practical reason set his ideals. It was a miracle how he led and changed the mindsets of the Indian masses — young and old, men and women, rich and poor, educated and illiterate. His philosophy included his thoughts, words, and actions. In his pursuit of truth, his mind was always open to fresh knowledge. He titled his autobiography as his *Experiments with Truth*. He was always ready to acknowledge his "Himalayan blunders". He emphasized the underlying unity of all religions. As moral beings, we must be ready to suffer in pursuit of justice and equity. Being influenced by Leo Tolstoy and H.D. Thoreau, he stressed the role of the individual in social reconstruction. He had his faith in the innate goodness of human beings, and his entire life was spent in the struggle for India's political freedom and for social emancipation of weaker sections.

He had immense moral courage, and as a votary of fearlessness he had love even for an opponent as all share the same source of divinity. He changed the assertion, "God is Truth" to "Truth is God". All must pursue truth as they could perceive it. His doctrine of truth and love led to his pursuit of nonviolence as it distinguishes man from the brute. He had realized the inevitability of differences and conflicts among human beings and advocated nonviolence and self-suffering as the means for their resolution. Where violence was unavoidable he advocated minimum violence as the preferred choice to cowardice. Nonviolence is a positive and constructive force. It means persuasion, a change of heart, a rational appeal for peaceful coexistence.

Chapter 2 — Peace as an Embodiment of Spirituality: The author writes that according to Gandhi, peace embodies spirituality, spirituality being universal in nature. In the Indian tradition, spirituality and science are correlated, the former being guided by the transcendental aspect of the Being. Violence and peace are antithetical. Peace includes inner peace and denotes tranquillity, blissfulness, and social harmony. The author further says that peace eludes today's society as it gets divided on accidental lines, such as religion and caste, while forgetting the sense of spirit, which unites humankind despite phenomenal divisions. The author says that the qualities of a person with divine character given in the *Gita* constitute spirituality. Gandhi saw that the British were ruling over India by the strategy of divide and rule and appealed to all Indians to unite and fight nonviolently for freedom.

Gandhi firmly believed that all religions teach the same truth and spiritual ideals of nonviolence, compassion, and love. The quote — "Gandhi was first in human history to extend the principle of nonviolence from the individual to the social and political plane" — attributed by the author to "Radhakrishnan", was in fact stated by Martin Luther King Jr. Gandhi considered nonviolence as a force mightier than that of arms. By *satyagraha,* he meant pursuit of truth. A *satyagrahi* resists evil, such as unjust laws, through nonviolence and self-suffering. Strangely, the author then remarks that Gandhi's ideals "cannot be translated into concrete realities easily, especially in social, political, and international realms". Also, that "Gandhi never worked out a systematic philosophy".

Chapter 3 — Conflict Resolution: The author here very well explains why conflicts arise and the Gandhian rationale for their nonviolent resolution.

In any society, people enter into a diversity of relationships, which also often lead to varied conflicts at the individual and social levels. Conflicts are inevitable due to disagreements over values, perceptions, interests, and backgrounds. Even trivial differences may arouse strong feelings. Hence, the parties to a conflict need to look into the others' viewpoints, overcoming resentment and anger. Conflicts, if not resolved thus with a positive approach can prove destructive, and may damage the very basis of a society or a nation. A conflict is aggravated by animosity, fear, anger, and cowardice. Nonviolent resolution of conflicts is the only sane approach.

Gandhi's approach to conflict resolution was aimed at the pursuit of truth, which means looking into each other's viewpoints and excludes deceit, conceit or violence. It demands courage and use of right means for right ends. Then trust and compromise become its constitutive parts and it works at all levels, from the individual to the international. Use of violence degrades human beings to the level of an animal. The author cites examples of successful conflict resolution, both under Gandhi and in other cases. He refers to Juergenmeyer's well-known work, *Gandhi's Way: A Handbook of Conflict Resolution* to emphasize that Gandhi's way is the only legitimate way for resolution of conflicts. It may need patience when the opponent may not cooperate. But then the author, very strangely concludes that the "Gandhian paradigm does not offer solutions to many conflicts", though he also says that "experiments with truth" must continue!

Chapter 4 — *Corruption and Human Values*: As the author writes, dishonesty in a society leads it to corrupt practices. He defines a corrupt practice as any deviation from the normally accepted and socially approved practice. By and large, greed and power make persons corrupt. Corruption may be private or public, the latter being far more dangerous due to its social implications. He mentions about some recent scams in India and about the role of whistleblowers and money and muscle power in areas of public corruption. He claims to examine whether human values can mitigate corruption as envisaged by Gandhi, but only refers to his views on *varna dharma,* which does not seem to be relevant here.

The author also refers to the ten "Ashram Vows" (should be eleven), and the most important of these being *aparigraha,* which he calls "non-stealing", while it should be "non-possession", "non-stealing" being another of the eleven vows (*asteya*). He is right that Gandhi had become seriously alarmed by the presence and growth of corruption soon after India became independent. Corruption in public life "eats away our moral values and reduces us to the level of barbarians".

Chapter 5 — Economic Philosophy: The author defines a welfare state as one where economic and social well-being of all and equal opportunities and distribution of wealth are ensured. However, modern economic models have to a great extent failed to achieve this and the exploitation of people and natural resources is common. Hence, it becomes imperative to go back to the Gandhian economic model, which overcomes drawbacks of both the capitalist and communist models.

The author then analyses the Gandhian model with emphasis on his concepts of "trusteeship", economic equality, and appropriate industrialization. Its first priorities are alleviation of exploitation and poverty, right to employment and equal importance to labour and capital. He summarizes Gandhi's six-point practical "trusteeship" formula as the ideal for a nonviolent and egalitarian society: under it all one owns is held on behalf of the society as a trust, it allows regulation by the state, assures maximum and minimum limits to incomes, and nature of production is determined by social need and not greed. The trustee may lead only a frugal life and use all his wealth, including talents, for social welfare. Gandhi wanted the poor to realize that the rich cannot accumulate wealth without their cooperation. Gandhi's definition of economic equality as "the master-key to nonviolent independence" meant meeting the basic needs of all and elimination of the cruel disparities, and "equal" distribution meant "to each according to his needs". An individual's good lies in social good. The author also discusses Gandhi's views on industrialization as it prevailed in his time. Gandhi was clear that "machinery has a place", but its use must not be exploitative; it should work for the benefit of all. Hence, he worked for decentralization and for development of rural industries.

The author very well sums up that to Gandhi economics and ethics went together and his economic philosophy was meant to eliminate exploitation, poverty, and unemployment, and provide dignified life for all. But strangely, he also comments that, "At the most the Gandhian ideals can be practised at the individual level but not at the social level", while also says that the limits are not in Gandhian philosophy but in our pursuit of greed.

Chapter 6 — Socialist Outlook: Gandhi and Marx: The author gives an insightful analysis of the socialist views of Gandhi and Marx, both visionaries who under their different situations proposed different approaches to put down exploitation of every kind — Gandhi by non-violent *satyagraha* and the thesis of "trusteeship", and Marx by revolt against the exploiters.

Gandhi sharply reacted to the exploitation of people under capitalism. He argued that all wealth belonged to the society as a whole and we are thieves "in a way" if we take anything not needed for immediate use. Nature produces "enough for all our wants" and so if all took just enough none would starve or be a pauper. Economics that hurt the moral well-being of an individual or a community was immoral. Gandhi's socialism meant, "even unto the last". He wanted production to be localized so that means of production remained with the masses. The author rightly calls Gandhi's *sarvodaya* "an important preamble to socialism" as it seeks welfare of all. Gandhi opposed the use of violence to end exploitation and hence also the prevalent form of communism.

Marx's ideology of communism brought about historic changes in the world. His thesis of "historical materialism" identified factors that had led to the evolution of private ownership and modern capitalism and why capitalism would finally collapse due to its inherent contradictions, and finally lead to the higher forms of society — socialism and communism. His concept of social development was dialectical. Marx envisaged dictatorship of the proletariat in a socialist state as a necessary first step towards emergence of a classless society or communism. In a socialist state, private property is converted into a collective product of all and vested in the state. Communism deprives everyone of the power to appropriate the labour of others. However, as seen in practice in Soviet Russia and China, serious contradictions emerged even under communism and these societies have returned to the capitalist mode.

Both Gandhi and Marx had rightly highlighted the negative aspects of capitalism. While Gandhi brought in ethical economics and the concepts of "Unto This Last" and "Trusteeship", Marx had sought much more radical changes with capitalism giving way to socialism/communism. As the author says, history has further evolved after Gandhi and Marx, and the capitalist order has been re-established. Despite some welfare correctives, its basic character persists, leading to wide disparities, self-aggrandizement, consumerism, and luxury coexisting with poverty.

Chapter 7 — Reappraising Gandhi: In this chapter, the author just presents his own review of the book *Reading and Reappraising Gandhi* by Ram Chandra Pradhan, which has five parts apart from appendices. The first part gives an in-depth analysis regarding how a text interprets its subject matter and concludes that it should be rational and historical without it being mythological. The second part of the book very well sums up the ideas of Gandhi's *Hind Swaraj*, which remains so relevant even a century after it was written. The book refers to its well-known interpretation by

Anthony Parel, who had called it a new political philosophy by Gandhi, to Gandhi's civic humanism, and his critique of "modern" civilization, sources of Gandhi's Western and Eastern inspiration, his concept of *swaraj* as self-rule and as home-rule, and the other ideas.

The third part discusses pre-modernity, modernity, and post-modernity. It then covers some key ideas of Gandhi, such as how he was not opposed to science and technology nor necessary social changes. It examines Bhikhu Parekh's views on Gandhi's critique of "modern" civilization in his book *Gandhi's Political Philosophy* and then David Hardiman's views in his book *Gandhi: In His Time and Others*. Gandhi took from modernity what he approved and rejected what he found as anti-humane. It then refers to Ramashray Roy's work *Self and Society: Sounding in Political Philosophy*, and also Lloyd and Susanne Rudolphs' *Postmodern Gandhi*. It takes up Gandhi's concepts of *swaraj* and *swadeshi* and then Gandhi's theory and practice of *satyagraha*.

The fourth part deals with the subject of Gandhi and modern India, specifically in relation to the issues of untouchability, Indian nationalism, and the status of women. It explains how Gandhi and Ambedkar both fought for removal of untouchability but with different emphases and how their approaches may be seen as complementary. Indian nationalism had to be an outcome of people belonging to different religions, regions, and languages. Gandhi brought about the cultural unity by his emphasis on religious tolerance and struggle for freedom, his pursuit of non-violence, and taking nationalism as the basis for universalism. Gandhi worked for gender equality and for the elimination of social evils such as child marriage. Finally, the seminal point of Gandhian political philosophy was the symbiotic relationship between man and his fellow beings and nature. The fifth part quotes the most inspiring sayings of Gandhi on a wide range of subjects.

In the "Epilogue", the author curiously remarks that Gandhian idealism has positive and negative sides. He says that it worked when he led the masses but its application in different fields is not easy as individuals do not easily change their nature or adopt the socially relevant moral behaviour. But he also says that Gandhi was a practical idealist and self-critical and never held to his assertions dogmatically except for the cardinal virtues of truth, compassion, and love.

To sum up, the book covers a wide range of important subjects related to Gandhian thought. However, each such subject has been dealt with more as a self-contained essay rather than as an integral part of the subject of the title of the book itself. The presentation of the whole text could have been made more cohesive.

Y.P. Anand
Former Director
National Gandhi Museum & Library
New Delhi
e-mail:ypanandindia@yahoo.co.in

DR. BINOD, ***The Essence of Gandhian Philosophy: Its Impact on Our Literature,*** New Delhi: Kalpaz Publications, 2015, 286 pp., Rs. 850

Dr. Binod's *The Essence of Gandhian Philosophy: Its Impact on Our Literature* is a stimulating volume that paves the way for further research. It is an interesting exploration into a little researched area — Gandhi as Writer and Gandhi as Writer's Writer, and has received much admiration from eminent scholars, writers, and academicians.

Chapter One — "Gandhi: The Literary and Spiritual Mentor", starts with outlining the huge impact of Gandhi and his philosophy on the masses of India and ends with focusing on the intellectual impact of Gandhi on the Indian writers who translated his philosophy into writing and created a unique literature of the masses. Gandhi was viewed as the divine *avatara* who had descended to free India from British rule. The magical impact of Gandhi's persona and message led to a great spiritual, moral, and artistic flowering in all the literatures of India. The author touches upon the influence of Gandhi on the great nationalist Hindi and Gujarati poets, on the Kannada and Assamese lyricists and prose writers, the novelists and poets of Bengali and Tamil, the dramatists and poets of Marathi, the Malayalam poets and prosodists, the ardent nationalist writers of Punjabi, Oriya and Sindhi literatures. No nook of India could escape the Gandhian whirlwind which transformed dust into gold.

The author next focuses on the impact of Gandhi on Indian English novels and makes it clear that almost all the great Indian English novelists have been deeply influenced by the Mahatma. He rightly describes Gandhi as the pioneer of a new theme and style — thematically, he brought in the focus on the common man which had pervaded contemporary European literature, and stylistically, he imparted to Indian novels the clarity, simplicity, and immediacy which marked his own writing. The chapter concludes with the author reiterating that Gandhi remains an eternal and inescapable motif in Indian thought and literature.

Chapter Two — "Gandhian Impact on the Thematic and Stylistic Pattern" depicts how Gandhi by his public and private life and his own writing created a virtual revolution in the theme and style of Indian literature in general and Indian English literature in particular. Thematically, Gandhi initiated a movement towards a literature of the masses which focused on capturing the living reality. This gave rise to a new Indian ethos which could combat the overwhelming influence of Marxian and Freudian literature. Stylistically, Gandhi advocated a clear and simple style that was totally utilitarian, yet had a beauty of its own. It was the end of the ornate and formal Macaulayan tradition of speech and writing. By his own example, Gandhi proved to be a great formative influence and ushered in a new heroic age or renaissance in Indian thought and writing. The author quotes Gandhi:

> I want art and literature that can speak to millions. . . . For me, all arts must be based on truth. I reject beautiful things, if instead of expressing truth they express untruth. Whatever can be useful to starving millions is beautiful to my mind; let us give today first the vital things of life, and all the graces and ornaments of life will follow. — p. 74

With regard to fictional themes, the 1930s or the dawn of the Gandhian age led to a new flowering of the Indian English novel, creating entire libraries of novels, plays, poems, and stories based on Gandhian issues, ideas, and movements.

Stylistically, the author looks at Gandhi from three different angles. Gandhi as a journalist, who wrote columns in and edited popular newspapers, is the great communicator of truth to the masses. He believed in writing only the truth and his sincerity, authenticity, and conviction ensure that his journalistic writings have permanent appeal and are elevated to the level of classical literature. Ironically, Gandhi himself was of the opinion that his writings should be cremated with his body. Second, as a speaker, Gandhi is totally himself, totally simple, and yet there is an undefined thrill and greatness of thought in his speeches which sets the souls of his listeners on fire. The book contains a very useful and interesting section which compares the speeches of leaders in the pre-Gandhian era with the speeches of great leaders in the post-Gandhian era. The speeches of Pandit Nehru, Sarojini Naidu, Rajaji, and Sardar Patel are analysed to show the Gandhian impact on their style. Third, having made a study of the general prose writings of Gandhiji, Dr. Binod describes him as one of the masters of modern English prose-writing attaching great premium to his qualities of clarity, force, vigour, and inspiring simplicity.

However, two paragraphs in the chapter are not properly placed — one which compares the thoughts of Gandhi and Tolstoy on art and another which speaks of Gandhian influence on bilingual English writers and regional writing.

Chapter Three — "The Core of Gandhian Philosophy" is an important and very useful chapter, however, it could have been better organized and positioned earlier in the book. Nevertheless, the chapter presents the essence of Gandhian thought in a lucid and concise format. The author outlines all the key points of Gandhian ideology starting with a reference to Gandhi's evolution from commoner to Mahatma to Gandhi's staunch Vaishnavite roots, the influence of authors like Ruskin, Thoreau, and Tolstoy on Gandhi, the influence of Gandhi's stay in London and South Africa, the influence of Christianity, Buddhism, and Hinduism on Gandhi's ideal of nonviolence, his *satyagraha*, and *ahimsa*, his championing of the cause of the weaker races and untouchables, and Gandhi's innovations of *swadeshi*, *charkha*, and *swaraj*, etc. Dr. Binod concludes that equating Truth with God, austere living and selfless service constitute the core of Gandhian ideology.

Chapter Four — "Gandhian Philosophy in the Novels of Mulk Raj Anand" puts forth that Mulk Raj Anand, the great Indian English novelist with an avowed social mission, was greatly influenced by Marxist thought. However, the message of Gandhi drew him to stay at Sabarmati Ashram and the direct personal contact with the Mahatma led him to write his first novel and masterpiece *Untouchable* (1935) which champions the cause of the Dalits. Dr. Binod proceeds to offer a detailed analysis of the text quoting poignant passages wherein the untouchable boy Bakha feels that Gandhi alone unites him with the rest of the community and is moved upon hearing Gandhi's desire to be reborn as an untouchable. But Anand's other novels like *The Sword and the Sickle* and *The Big Heart* pit Gandhism vs. Marxism and industrialization, and delineate the struggle of the masses who admire Gandhi but cannot fully grasp his lofty ideal of *ahimsa* as they are surrounded by fierce caste and class wars. Thus, Mulk Raj Anand, while a genuine admirer of Gandhi, remains firm in his Leftist leanings and his quest is more for the establishment of an equal society with no class or caste inequalities rather than replacement of British rule with Indian. Even as he appreciates Gandhian humanism, he is aware of its limitations and attempts to modify Gandhian ideals for their better implementation in the contemporary era.

Chapter Five — "Raja Rao's Kanthapura and the Mahatma" delves into the great Raja Rao's magnum opus *Kanthapura* (1938) which offers a touching panorama of the Gandhian nationalist spirit during the 1930s. The novel is a dramatic monologue filled with ardour for the Mahatma. Its uniqueness lies in its totally native colouring and style; it is a *sthala-purana* mythologizing Gandhi in the Hindu tradition which enables better understanding of Gandhi's persona and message. Again, the language of Raja Rao is a faithful translation of the speech of India's rural folk. In his later novels and short stories too, Raja Rao integrates history, myth, and philosophy, and succeeds in integrating Gandhian nationalism with India's ancient, native cultures, religions and philosophies.

Chapter Six — "Into the World of Narayan and Abbas" deals with two novelists. R.K. Narayan, the acclaimed writer is an unmatched observer of ordinary Indian life, a pure artist. Dr. Binod explores in detail Narayan's Gandhian novel *Waiting for the Mahatma* (1955). Despite his artistic commitment and refusal to side with any ideology, Narayan could not escape the overwhelming Gandhian spirit of his times. *Waiting for the Mahatma* has Gandhi as one of its characters and projects him as a genial, grandfatherly figure. Thus, Narayan takes a risk which no other contemporary novelist dared to take — that of making the towering Gandhi a character in his fiction and making him appear in person. It is the love story of two Gandhian freedom fighters and revolves around issues of love, politics, idealism, and marriage. Gandhi is very much a part of their love story and heartily blesses their union. R.K. Narayan offers a very personal rendering of the impact of Gandhi on the hearts, minds and souls of his hero and heroine. He is able to present both the call to lofty ideals and great sacrifices as also the very human aspect of the Mahatma.

K.A. Abbas the great nationalist novelist hints at the Gandhian freedom struggle in almost all his novels. Yet, it is in his famous *Inquilab* (1955) that he gives the most direct description of the Gandhian movement in the 1930s and 1940s. While dealing with the impact of the Mahatma on the psyche of a young boy, Abbas offers a unique and oft less known Muslim perspective of the Mahatma. He graphically analyses the major events and burning issues of the times, such as, the Jallianwala Bagh episode, the Khilafat movement, the revolutionary activities of Bhagat Singh, the Dandi March, the politics of the Muslim League, and so on. This is a major political and historical novel and Abbas with his unique realism and Urdu flavour depicts the quest for identity, unity, and staunch nationalism of the Muslim community.

Chapter Seven — "Unfavourable Treatment of Gandhian Ideals" is a very useful chapter. Dr. Binod observes that while novelists like Anand, Raja Rao, Narayan, and Abbas capture the positive influence of Gandhi, the post-1947 novelists depict the decline of and loss of faith in Gandhian ideals in independent India. This is a relatively new approach and the author chooses three major novelists to illustrate what he describes as the negative projection of Gandhi in Indian literature.

Khushwant Singh's acclaimed *Train to Pakistan* (1956) which renders poignantly the horrors of Partition not only castigates the hypocrisy of the native ruling class but also blames the miscalculations of Gandhi and his followers for the catastrophe of India's division. Chaman Nahal's *Azadi* (1975) also deals with the bloodshed following Partition and depicts how the commoners felt that their faith in Gandhi and his followers was betrayed. Manohar Malgaonkar stands apart from the novelists of his time in his scathing indictment of the ruling class in the days immediately after independence. His *A Bend in the Ganges* (1964) is set in the 1940s and questions not only the hypocrisy of Gandhi's followers but also the feasibility and practicability of the ideal of nonviolence. Some excerpts from the novel prove that Malgaonkar does not merely criticize Gandhi but also looks at the complex situation from all angles:

> . . . as far as the people of India were concerned, Gandhi's message was merely a political expedient . . . for the bulk of them, it had no deeper significance . . . they had accepted it as an effective weapon against British rule . . . in the wake of freedom . . . what was achieved through nonviolence brought with it one of the bloodiest upheavals of history. . . . In the midst of Gandhi's nonviolence, violence persists. Violence such as no one has ever seen. . . . Yet what was the alternative? Would terrorism have won freedom at a cheaper price. . . . — pp. 222-23

Dr. Binod concludes that irrespective of the success or failure of Gandhi's followers and ideals, the greatness of Gandhi as a man and the perennial relevance of his message cannot be denied.

Chapter Eight — "Gandhian Philosophy Needs Revalidation in the Changed Context" is a study of the Indian English novelists who portray neither a positive nor a negative view of Gandhian ideals. These writers wrote in the 1960s and the 1970s which were times of both national consolidation and turbulence. They emphasize the need to adapt Gandhian ideals to the governance of the free Indian state.

Nayantara Sahgal's *This Time of Morning* (1965) deals with doubts about the Gandhian ideal of *ahimsa* in the aftermath of the Indo-China war, and her *Storm in Chandigarh* (1969) is a study in the swiftness with which Gandhian values are replaced by parochial politics during national crises.

Sahgal's *The Day in Shadow* (1971) is a novel of revolutionary ideas that stresses on the need for a clean sweep from the past:

> It is time to throw away sentiment, the weak, the worn out liberation of the past, time to bury Gandhi, and write a new page of Indian history. . . . Which is the famous workable idea that will lead us out of our tribulations? So where is it, the touchstone that will work today?
>
> — pp. 240-41

Bhabani Bhattacharya depicts the tussle between Gandhian and Nehruvian ideals, proving that the only way out is to reconcile both the Eastern and Western ideals in the Tagorean spirit of integration. Bhattacharya's novels broadly come to the conclusion that the futile Gandhian struggle for freedom still continues, for, 1947 brought freedom only to the elite.

Chapter Nine — "Conclusion" extensively quotes the tributes paid to Gandhiji by Romain Rolland, summarizes the contents of all the previous chapters and concludes by quoting Einstein's praise for Gandhi. What is lacking is a new vision for the future, a critical summing up of the overall influence of Gandhi on Indian literature and a focus on new areas to explore in the field.

The book has deficiencies in proofreading and editing, and flaws in organization with far too many side-headings. The title of the volume *The Essence of Gandhian Philosophy: Its Impact on Our Literature* is somewhat misleading. In many places the focus is on Gandhian philosophy and nationalist movement rather than on the impact of Gandhi on Indian literature. While the title suggests that the author would be dealing with the impact of Gandhi on all of Indian literature, the book actually focuses only on Indian English literature. Again, while the preface states that the book focuses on Gandhian impact on Indian Writing in English, the book actually focuses only on select Indian English novelists.

All the same, the volume is highly informative and points the way to an area which is full of potential for research. The door is opened for others to explore the influence of Gandhi on other genres of Indian English literature apart from the novel, and the influence of Gandhi on various genres of Indian literature in other languages, as also on world literature and non-Indian authors.

Rositta Joseph Valiyamattam
Assistant Professor (English)
GITAM Institute of Management
GITAM University, Visakhapatnam
e-mail:rositta.joseph@gmail.com

D.C. JHA (ed. & comp.), ***Remembering Pyarelal: Mahatma Gandhi's Secretary and Biographer***, New Delhi: KW Publishers, 2014, 2nd edn, 250 pp., Rs. 795

Dr. D.C. Jha, a well-known historian, has written a beautiful account of the life of the unsung hero Pyarelal who was closely associated with Mahatma Gandhi and was shy of being himself brought to limelight. This was probably possible as Dr. Jha himself was very closely associated with Pyarelal. The biography brings out the essence of devotion and dedication towards the great master and his work which is mostly unknown to the present generation. The book carries combination of tributes in English as well as Hindi. To add to its glory Dr. Sushila Nayar, sister of Pyarelal and well-known Physician (after whom there is a famous Medical College in Sevagram) has given a lucid account and her memoires about her brother Pyarelal.

The book is an admirable effort focused on the unconventional manner in which Pyarelal (life-long Secretary and Biographer of Gandhiji) choose to serve his master Mahatma Gandhi. It starts with a list of books by Pyarelal and his sister Dr. Sushila Nayar. The preface of the book covers an editorial obituary entitled "Passing Away of Gandhi's Boswell" on the death of Pyarelal in October 1982.

The introduction rightly begins with "A Most Ignored Man of Our Times". Pyarelal was 19 when he joined the Mahatma Gandhiji's Secretarial Staff. He accompanied Gandhi's small team to the 1931 Round Table Conference in London. After Mahadev Desai's sudden death at Aga Khan's Palace in 1942, Pyarelal became his successor.

The book is conveniently divided into four chapters. The first is titled "Tributes" paid to Pyarelal by friend's colleagues and admirers after he passed away in 1982. It deals with twenty-six dignitaries who knew Pyarelalji starting with Late Smt. Indira Gandhi and ending with the author D.C. Jha. The tribute written by G. Ramchandran on pp. 19-21, (who was then Secretary of the National Gandhi Memorial Trust) appealed to me the most wherein he says ". . . Pyarelal dived deep into his subject and those who dive deep are seldomly noticed." Ramchandran also remembers that once Pyarelal mentioned "people want to compare Gurudev (Tagore) and Bapuji". But they were in fact incomparable. It is like comparing the Himalayas and Indian Ocean. Similarly it was identical to compare a Banyan tree with a Coconut tree.

The second chapter *Shraddhanjaliyan* covers twenty-two individuals conveying their tributes to Pyarelalji in Hindi. The one written by Shri Gulabchand Jain highlights how Pyarelal contributed regularly to the weeklies *Young India* and *Harijan*. He writes that it was surprising that the team making Gandhi film never took any help from Pyarelalji.

Chapter three focuses in Hindi (*Patta Tuta Dal Se*) about Pyarelalji's life by his own sister Dr. Sushila Nayar, who was the force behind the establishment of the Pyarelal foundation. She has written about the unique work her Bhaiji (as she addressed him) did at Noakhali. At this Gandhi's heroic pilgrimage of pain and suffering Pyarelalji was always by the side of Gandhi. Lastly in the Appendix Dr. Jha has put forth his exclusive two page views on Pyarelal's Sister — "remembering Dr. Sushila Nayar" based on his association with Pyarelal's family.

Here is an immensely well-written book about a tireless machine (as the author calls) called Pyarelal, who was 48 years old when Gandhji's assassination took place. The author Dr. Jha himself was associated and had worked with Pyarelal almost for a decade on his project of the multi-volume biography of Mahatma Gandhi. Five black and white photographs depict events from 1930 to 1982 which make us feel nostalgic.

Mahadev Desai and his son Narayan Desai's association with Gandhi has received much focus, while this did not happen with Pyarelalji, hence the above work brings to limelight the lifelong dedication of this Gandhian disciple.

This book is a useful entrant for bilingual students interested in Gandhian studies and institutions which have centres for Gandhian Studies as well as the present-generation seekers of truth.

Neeta M. Khandpekar
Department of History, University of Mumbai
Santacruz (E), Mumbai
e-mail: neeta_khandpekar@yahoo.com

Contributors

Anand, Y.P., worked as the Director, National Gandhi Museum and Library, Rajghat, New Delhi, for ten years from 1996 to 2006. He has written numerous papers and compiled books on various Gandhian subjects. His books include *The Essential Relationship between Netaji Subhas Bose & Mahatma Gandhi* (1997); *Birth of Free India's National Anthem: A Gift from Netaji Subhas Bose* (1997); *Mahatma Gandhi & the Railways* (English and Hindi, 2002); *Mahatma Gandhi and Art* (2003); *Mahatma Gandhi and Satyagraha: A Compendium* (2006); *Albert Einstein and Mahatma Gandhi: The Centenary of Physics, War, Satyagraha and Peace* (2006/2010); *Mahatma Gandhi's Works and Interpretation of the Bhagavad Gita* (in 2 vols.) (2009); *Gitapadarthakosha* (by Mahatma Gandhi), translated into Hindi (2010); and *Historical Background to the Imposition of SALT TAX under the British Rule (1757–1947) & Mahatma Gandhi's SALT SATYAGRAHA (1930-31)* (2014, published by Ministry of Culture). He attended seminars on Gandhian subjects in USA, Canada, and Italy. He is now working on the subject of "Tolstoy and Gandhi". e-mail: <ypanandindia@yahoo.co.in>.

Ramakrishna Rao, K., is a philosopher, psychologist, and educationist with international expertise in the areas of Indian psychology, consciousness, and Gandhian Studies. He published over 200 research papers and sixteen books. His most recent books are *Cognitive Anomalies, Consciousness and Yoga* (Matrix Publishers), a thousand-page volume that brings together the wisdom from different disciplines for building a unified psychological model of the person, and *Gandhi and Applied Spirituality*. Prof. Rao has served as the Executive Director of the Foundation for Research on the Nature of Man in USA. He was the Founder, Head, and Professor of the Department of Psychology and Parapsychology, and Honorary Director of the Institute for Yoga and Consciousness, at Andhra University. He has held various other major executive and advisory positions including Vice-Chancellor of Andhra University, Chairman of the A.P. State Commission of Higher Education, and Chairman of the Indian Council of Philosophical Research. He is currently, the Chancellor of GITAM University and President of the Asian Congress of Philosophy. e-mail: <krrao007@gmail.com>.

Sambasiva Prasad, B., is working in GITAM Centre for Gandhian Studies, GITAM University, Visakhapatnam. Earlier, he was Professor

of Philosophy, at Sri Venkateswara University, Tirupati. His current areas of interest include Gandhian philosophy and Peace Studies. He published about forty research papers in reputed journals and anthologies. Some of them were published in *JICPR, IPQ, Gandhi Marg* and *GITAM Journal of Gandhian Studies.* He has presented about seventy research papers in national and international conferences. He is the Executive Editor of *GITAM Journal of Gandhian Studies* and was the Executive Director of the ICPR projects on "Phenomenology of Violence" and "Application of Gandhian Ideas in the Areas of Peace, Conflict Resolution, Rural Development, and Higher Education".
e-mail: <b.sambasivaprasad@gmail.com>.

Venkata Rayudu, P., is a Research Fellow at the Consciousness Studies Programme of National Institute of Advanced Studies (NIAS), Bangalore. At NIAS, Rayudu is pursuing a unique research programme with the objective of putting in place the foundations of consciousness science, using category theory. Prior to joining NIAS, he worked at the Centre for Gandhian Studies, GITAM University, Visakhapatnam, investigating Gandhi's philosophy of nonviolence from the perspectives of ontology and epistemology. Rayudu is an electrical engineer, whose long-standing commitment to understanding consciousness led him to do extensive research in both theoretical and experimental cognitive neurosciences at Harvard Medical School, National Brain Research Centre, and The Salk Institute for Biological Studies, USA. His research findings were published in journals such as *Nature, Neuroscience, Neuron, Progress in Brain Research,* and *Proceedings of the National Academy of Sciences.*
e-mail: <posinavrayudu@gmail.com>.

GITAM JOURNAL OF GANDHIAN STUDIES

Volume 5 July – December 2016 Number 2

Contents

ON EDUCATION

M.K. Gandhi

Compiled by

Y.P. Anand

B. Sambasiva Prasad

Assisted by

Aruna Pariti

Contents

Introduction

Mahatma Gandhi had shown a lifelong and keen interest in the prevalent state and the requirements of the education system in India. Throughout his public life, starting from his arrival in South Africa in 1893 till his martyrdom in 1948, even while constantly engaged with political and associated activities, he continued to take deep interest in the subject of "education". His views in respect of "education" cover the long-term basic principles which should underlie the educational system and also include features more specifically relevant to his time.

Even during his stay in South Africa (1893–1914) he said that India should have need-based universal education system and praised the scheme to provide compulsory education in Baroda. He referred to "Macaulay's Minutes" (1835) which had led to education being imparted through English medium instead of Indian languages. He stressed the higher aims of education, as education by itself was only a means to an end. He also experimented with providing education to boys and girls at the "Tolstoy Farm".

After his return to India, Gandhi repeatedly commented on the changes necessary in the prevalent system of education. He wanted that education which makes us men and women of character. In 1917, a National School was started at Ahmedabad for education on his lines. He dealt with vital issues such as the medium of instruction, national language, and the education system necessary in India where most people lived in villages. He specifically pointed out the main defects of the existing system of education as emphasis on "head" while ignoring the role of "heart" and "hand", use of foreign medium, and not being related to the Indian needs. He wrote and spoke extensively on how education should be made universal and adapted to the needs of the poor and the rural population.

While Congress ministries were formed in many provinces (1937-39), he worked out a scheme of what the school education should be, so as to cover the issues of head, heart and hand harmoniously, to draw out the best in the student. Under his guidance, an "Educational Conference" held at Wardha worked out the "Wardha Scheme" for the "Basic Education"/"Nayee Talim" as well as "Higher" education. He advocated the use of crafts as the medium of education itself. Later when active freedom struggle was resumed and after independence (1940-48), he continued to propagate his system of "Basic Education", and under his "Constructive Programme" (1941) five out of the 18 items were related to education. He had also set up the Hindustani Talimi Sangh for propagating "Nayee Talim" and "National schools" were being set up. He continued to stress the use of mother tongue as the medium of instruction and of Hindi in Devanagari and Urdu scripts as "national" language.

In the following pages, Gandhi's representative ideas on "education" have been collected from the primary sources and presented under the following chapters:

1. Meaning and Aims of Education
2. Experiments on Education
3. Stages of Education
4. Nature and Working of Universities
5. Medium of Instruction: The Question of Language/The Need for National Language
6. Religious/Ethical Education
7. Adult Education
8. Women's Education
9. Physical Education
10. Education through Prayer, Music, Art, and Culture
11. Libraries and Textbooks
12. Message to Teachers and Students

The *first chapter* on "Meaning and Aims of Education" elaborates upon Gandhi's fundamental conception of education. Under its Section I on "Meaning of Education", as early as in 1909 (in *Hind Swaraj*) he considers education as a "knowledge of letters" as merely an instrument which may be "well used or abused". He emphasizes character building as the "primary education" as was followed in our ancient system, but which he found missing in the Western education system being introduced in India. He says that education truly means the "path of morality". One must not only learn what is good but also act upon that knowledge. He refers to Emerson, Ruskin, Mazzini, and the Upanishads to reiterate that true education consists in "character building", in "a knowledge of duty", and in "serving others".

True education must lead to freedom, to *dharma*. According to the

Bible too, education is to seek "first the Kingdom of God, and His righteousness". To him, education, character and religion are convertible terms. The "Ideal Primary Education" makes the child choose "the good and the true, while rejecting the bad and the untrue". Even the study of Shakespeare and Wordsworth would be in vain if at the same time we do not build character and control our passions. "Literacy in itself is no education" and by "education" he means "an all-round drawing out of the best in child and man — body, mind and spirit". Even for education in "science" he emphasizes "the point of responsibility which science must observe in its application". Again, "Education is the means and culture is the end". Real education consists in drawing "the best out of yourself", it must arm the students to fight against social and other evils. And the "true economics of education" means harmonious combination of the intellect, body, and heart or soul, thus culminating in "making of the whole man".

Under Section II on "Aims of Education", Gandhi says that education is just a means, its aim being "to improve oneself and serve the country", to be "put to good use" and "employed in public cause". Its aim was not mere "employment" but "to develop courage, strength, virtue, the ability to forget oneself in working towards great aims". Its essence was "kindness to all, friends and foes, men and beasts". Its outcome should be "an ideal citizen, an ideal patriot and an ornament to his family, his country and his nation". For example, the aim of the law students was "to serve humanity in order to serve the motherland". He reiterates that the "end of all knowledge must be building up of the character", and true education means "purity of personal life", to know "our true self, God and Truth", to "acquire the power of independent thinking", and "to grow into a courageous, healthy and service-minded persons".

The *second chapter* titled "Experiments on Education" — deals with Gandhi's experiments conducted in South Africa under Section I, and later in India, after his return in 1914, under Section II.

After he took his family to South Africa, he provided education to his sons himself to the best of his abilities and he did not try to send them to the schools for the European children. He discusses this subject in his *Autobiography* and concludes that had he sent them to a school, he "should have deprived them of the object-lesson in liberty and self-respect that I gave them at the cost of literary training". In his very first Ashram at Phoenix, he ran a school for the immigrant children. While his curriculum included various Indian languages and English, as also history of India and religious education, its main aim was "to assist in building moral character of boys".

He carried out further experiments in education for the *satyagrahis*' children at the "Tolstoy Farm". He regarded "character building as the proper foundation for their education", while also arranging literary education, physical education by means of work on the Farm, and vocational training such as in shoemaking and carpentry. The languages taught included Hindi, Tamil, Gujarati, Urdu, English, and Sanskrit. The teachers functioned as the textbooks. Children were also given training of the "spirit": "To develop the spirit is to build character and to enable one to work towards a knowledge of God and self-realization". The Teacher's own character set the example through "discipline and restraint". He did not believe in corporal punishment of the pupils.

After coming to India, he first put his team up at Shantiniketan. There he advised the students to do away with the services of paid cooks and thus provide training in self-help for teachers and students. Tagore said to the boys: "The experiment contains the key to *swaraj*". Gandhi's first experiment in education in India was at the Satyagraha Ashram in Kochrab. He taught reading and writing to children and adults. His experiments grew in scale along with the struggle for freedom.

His views on education (as expressed in "History of the Satyagraha Ashram", 1932) covered student life in three stages. In the first stage till 8 years of age, these included co-education, providing manual training, recognizing special aptitude of each child, teaching first drawing and then alphabet, first reading and then writing, education through mother tongue and teaching Hindi/Urdu as national language, and religious education through teacher's own conduct. In the second stage from 9 to 16 years, co-education as far as possible, continuing manual training along with enhanced literary education, teaching subjects such as history, geography, botany, astronomy, mathematics, Sanskrit/Arabic, English as international language, and education being self-supporting. In the third stage from 16 to 25 years, education may be provided according to the student's wishes and circumstances. Teachers will be persons of character and take a living wage. Special facilities may be provided for women's education as required. Real education came through life itself, after the school.

In January 1917, Gandhi wrote about the decision to start "National Gujarati School" as a national school as the "present education" not being "national", people did not "get from it the benefit they ought to". Its education was meant to be physical, intellectual, and religious; physical — meaning training in agriculture, hand-weaving and other crafts, and drill and preservation of health; "intellectual"— including study of Indian languages, Gujarati as medium of instruction and no English till first three years, study of mathematics and other subjects; and study of religious (ethical) principles for good character. Due to reduced load of learning English, a few years of such education would produce well-informed graduates. After five years a student could be fixed up in some work and paid for it. Expenses would be met by donations.

In his talk (June 1917) with teachers of the National School at Ahmedabad, he explained the objects of the new method of education as special attention to character building, at least 10 per cent of the students going for national service, spreading education in Gujarati with Hindi as national language and English as an optional language, opening such schools in every place as examples for others. He wanted teachers to be proficient in the languages and in weaving and to be ready to work in the Ashram also. Drawing was to be taught for practical purposes including good handwriting. There would be discipline but no compulsion.

Gandhi felt that the current system with English as the medium after first five years, had no relation to the life at home. Education must be given in the mother tongue, be free and imparted by teachers having competence and high character. The precious contents in English should be translated into Indian languages, as was being done in Japan and Germany. In his inaugural speech on "National Higher Education" at the setting up of Gujarat Vidyapith (1920), he asserted, "You have undertaken to secure freedom through the miracle of not learning but of character, . . . with peaceful, spiritual effort" as against the Government's "aggressive, Satanic way".

He saw "national" institutions as "so many oases in the desert", as a part of the freedom struggle. Their final success depended upon the worth of the teachers and on students' "ability, integrity, application, and patriotism". Freedom came from "discipline and humility". During the freedom struggle, Gandhi had also involved students, and this constituted one of the 18 subjects of his "Constructive Programme". His terms for their participation in freedom movement included: they "must not take part in party politics" nor "resort to political strikes" but should copy "the best in their heroes"; they should do "sacrificial spinning in a scientific manner", use *khadi* and village products, not impose any symbols on others, and harbour neither communalism nor untouchability; they should help in village sanitation and education, learn Hindustani as the national language, and even sacrifice their lives in nonviolent quelling of riots.

Gandhi found most of the students and intellectuals to be an "instance of intellectual dissipation rather than intellectual development". His own experiments in education affirmed up his view that "true education of intellect can only come through a proper exercise and training of the bodily organs", and such a "development of mind and body goes hand in hand with a corresponding awakening of the soul", i.e., the heart or spirit. Education must mean a harmonious development of the faculties of body, mind, and soul. Only that will make "the whole man", and "constitutes the true economics of education" and will be "for the common good of all".

Gandhi's conception of true "intellectual development" crystallized into his propagation of the Nayee Talim, also called "basic education" or "Wardha scheme". The view that the child must be educated properly through manual work as a means of intellectual training, matured during his stay in Segaon. Looking to the needs of the villages he asserted that "rural education ought to be made self-supporting if it is to be compulsory". He introduced a seven-years' course of school education, from age 7 to 14, for the child to become "an earning unit". His mind, body, spirit, handwriting, artistic sense and other faculties would be trained around a craft, its being self-supporting being only the logical corollary and not the test of education. Each teacher would have a class of 25 pupils with one craft. Gandhi lamented that village crafts had been ignored and, hence, "we had no Cromptons and Hargreaves". He said that the new scheme would lead to "hope taking the place of despondency, food of poverty, work of unemployment, unity of dissensions".

"Basic education" would be no less than matriculation, and the student would be even a better banker than students who studied in ordinary schools.

He reiterated that "basic education" would "lay the foundation of a juster social order" without an unnatural division between "haves" and "have-nots", and everyone having a right to a living wage and to freedom, all achieved without a class war. As India approached independence, in an "Address to Trainees of Basic Teachers' Camp" (1946), Gandhi asserted that "useful manual labour, intelligently performed, is the means par excellence for developing the intellect", and the soul, and intellect thus developed became an instrument for service. Soon after Independence, while recounting the fundamentals of "basic education", he said that it would be "self-supporting except for the capital which will remain intact", all education being "imparted through the medium of the provincial language" and Hindustani taught as "national language", and no "sectional religious training" but full scope for "fundamental universal ethics".

The *third chapter* entitled "Stages of Education" deals with education from the infant stage up to the adult stage. By infant education Gandhi means training of the infant right from its conception in the womb of the mother. At this stage it is the mother who needs training to mould the child into a good human being. First we should teach the child to distinguish colours and begin teaching the letters of the alphabet only with the help of pictures. "His education should be a form of play". The next stage is the "early childhood education". It goes up to 7 years before the child joins the school, and consists in learning to use in the right way all one's sense organs, including the mind. "That child has made very good progress in his education who can understand the difference between truth and untruth . . . and chooses the good and true." Teaching is not based on "knowledge of the alphabet or of any script". Children "receive elementary education from their mothers". And while preparing herself, the mother "will prepare the children as well". Gandhi agreed with the scientific views of Madame Montessori, but warned that if propagated in their Western garb, they were likely to prove useless, even harmful, for Indian villages.

The next stage of "primary education" begins at the age of 7. It should be given to the child at least for a year without books and even after that, their use should be minimal. Children "must receive their primary education from teachers through the spoken word", and in the first year get knowledge of history and geography through play and as stories. Their hands being engaged in drawing geometrical lines and recognizing pictures, is "the primary education of the hands". Secondary education is the next stage which Gandhi deals with more elaborately. It requires more experimentation, such as, without English as medium of instruction and school buildings being simple and inexpensive. Any "sectional religious education" would mean "negation of education". Students at this stage should work for the revitalization of our rural civilization.

College education is the next stage. Gandhi observes that it should relate to the national necessities. He has also discussed vocational education, rural education, and higher education. For rural education, the curriculum of the Vidya Mandirs and universities may need to be changed and the teachers must understand rural needs, crafts, and professions.

The *fourth chapter*, "Nature and Working of Universities", continues with Gandhi's views on "higher education". He was not opposed to even the highest type of education but wanted the state to pay for it only where it had definite use for it. He found the "so-called education in arts" being given in the colleges as sheer waste as it was leading to "educated unemployment" and its use of foreign language as the medium did "incalculable intellectual and moral injury to the nation". There should be more and more libraries, research institutions and they should produce an army of scientists, engineers, and other experts to serve the nation and to meet social needs.

He had started the National University in Gujarat for the study of vernaculars and Hindustani, to inculcate spirit of independence not only through the usual subjects but also by vocational training for economic independence. He wanted to "revolutionize college education and relate it to national necessities", have degrees for engineers attached to various industries and also have colleges for commerce, arts, medicine, and agriculture. He wanted higher education to be left to private enterprise and state universities as purely examining and regulatory bodies. After India became independent, he wanted a proper background for setting up new universities.

The *fifth chapter* — "Medium of Instruction: The Question of Language/The Need for a National Language" — covers Gandhi's views about multiple issues related to the teaching and use of languages in the whole system of education. He wanted education to be imparted not through the foreign medium of English but through the mother tongue. At an Education Ministers' Conference (1946) he said that he must cling to his mother tongue as to his mother's breast.

In his speech at Banaras Hindu University (1916), he exhorted that "our language is the reflection of ourselves", English could never be India's national language, and the professors at Poona were certain that every Indian student lost at least six years of his life because he got his knowledge through English, and was it not a shame that the researches of Professors Bose and Ray were "not the common property of the masses"? Again, in 1920 he said that the foreign medium had "caused brain fag" and made children "crammers and imitators, unfitted for original work and thought" and prevented growth of our vernaculars. In 1928 he said that the youth could not have "a living contact with the masses" unless they were taught through a medium understood by the people. In 1938, he called it a "false de-Indianizing education" which made graduates "strangers in their own homes". He wanted provincial languages to be given their rightful place, including their use as the languages of the law courts while, "at the centre, Hindustani must rule supreme".

He said in 1917 itself, that India's "national language" had to be easy to learn for government officials, to be able to function as a medium of intercourse throughout India, and be the language of a large number of Indians and had to be easy enough to be learnt by all Indians. Hence, English could not be India's national language, and only Hindi, written in Devanagari or Urdu scripts fulfilled all the requirements. The more common script would in due course become the national script. Later he said that the "Provincial tongues provided the sure foundation on which the edifice of the national tongue should rest. The two were intended to complement, not supplant each other."

He explained that while mother tongue would be used as the medium of instruction, English could be used by a few as a language "of international commerce", "of diplomacy", and of "rich literary treasure". We do not need to learn English "to get at the best of what Shakespeare or Milton wrote", just as non-Bangalis too knew the beauties of Tagore's "matchless productions" and non-Russians of Tolstoy. English, as the world language, had its place as an optional language, not in schools but at the university level.

Gandhi said that every Hindu child must have some knowledge of Sanskrit to understand the teachings of the scriptures such as the *Gita*. It should be used in Hindu religious ceremonies as translation of its verses into regional languages will "diminish the air of solemnity which attaches to them". He had written in 1909 in *Hind Swaraj* that every Hindu, in addition to the provincial language must know Sanskrit, a Muslim Arabic, a Parsee Persian, and all must know Hindi with the option of Nagari or Persian script, and again in his *Autobiography* (1927) that besides the vernaculars, higher education should also have a place for Hindi, Sanskrit, Arabic, and English.

Gandhi had realized that multiplicity of scripts for various Indian languages worked as "an effectual barrier against the acquisition of knowledge". He wrote: "We must promote a common language. The beginning must be made with the script." He insisted that Devanagari was "an easily adaptable universal script for all India". He regarded the suggestion for introduction of Roman script as "a superimposition which can never become popular". Devanagari had "nothing to be ashamed of in point of symmetry and beauty", and its use as the common script would allow picking up "a workable knowledge of the provincial languages" in little time, and "save for the future generations tons of labour and time".

The *sixth chapter* covers Gandhi's views on "Religious/Ethical Education". He had written in *Hind Swaraj* (1909) itself that "we cannot do without it" (religious education). In his speech at Students' Conference, Bhagalpur (1917), he wanted that students must study Shastras and conform their conduct to their ideals as without *dharma* there can be "neither knowledge, nor wealth, nor health, nor anything else" and "life is devoid of all joy". To learn about *dharma* and morals, Gandhi himself took to Tulsidas' *Ramcharitmanas* and the *Gita* with "love and reverence". For Muslim students, the Koran was the best source.

He considered that teaching fundamental ethics was the state's duty but religious education was the sole concern of religious associations. Religious instruction should be "imparted by teachers living the religion themselves" and it should include a study of the tenets of other faiths. To Gandhi, "religion" meant truth and *ahimsa* and only teachers who imbibed these, could give "instruction in the universal essentials of religion", "with reverence and broad-minded tolerance".

In the *seventh chapter* on "Adult Education", Gandhi insists that "mass illiteracy is India's sin and shame and must be liquidated". The literacy campaign must cover both the knowledge of alphabet and useful knowledge, and cover all population, particularly in the villages. It must make people better citizens. Under the scheme of "basic education", adult education too was to be given through the medium of agriculture or a craft. He wanted it to be correlated to villagers' daily needs and have their cooperation. "The meaning of adult education is that we will give them, through their own language, all-round education of a pure and socially useful life."

In the *eighth chapter,* — "Women's Education", Gandhi says that the unjust "immemorial tradition" of "the status of inferiority" made women's illiteracy an even more "potent curse" than men's illiteracy. There was "no disparity in the condition of men and women" in all countries where people lived a decent life. India was much poorer because half of its population remained ignorant. He said in a speech (1916): "We shall accept equality of rights for women, but I think their education should differ from men's, as their nature and functions do." In another speech (1917) he said that it was woman's right to rule the home and man was master outside it. She was her children's educator and hence, "mother to the nation". Therefore, separate arrangements may be made for women's education after a certain age. They should be taught about the management of the home, their pregnancy, and nursing and care of children.

He was opposed to child marriage as a "wicked custom", and wanted that in such cases husbands must act as wife's teachers, even where classes were being conducted for married women. He reiterated in a speech (1918) that education was essential for women to uphold their "natural rights and attain true knowledge of self". He said that "man and woman are of equal rank", but they are not identical but supplementary to each other, and their courses of instruction "are based on a discriminating appreciation of these basic principles" for their fullest growth.

In a speech at Women's Christian College, Madras (1925), Gandhi referred to his having seen the strides made in girls' education in Tranvancore and asked himself, "What will India do with its modern girls?"— and, how would they relate to the needs of Indian villages. He wrote in 1927 that for elementary education, women must learn at least mother tongue, Hindi (if not mother tongue), Sanskrit to understand the *Gita*, elementary arithmetic, composition and music, and child care and processes up to the weaving of cotton.

Regarding "sex education", he thought it necessary to impart young pupils knowledge about "the use and function of generative organs" to a certain extent. He favoured their being taught "the significance and right use of their generative organs", its object being "the conquest and sublimation of the sex passion". Regarding "co-education", he explained (1938) that the question "will regulate itself according to the time and spirit" and that personally he had "an open mind".

In the *ninth chapter* — "Physical Education" — Gandhi considers exercise to be as essential "as are air, water, and food", as "he alone is healthy who has a sound mind in a sound body". He said that, as with the farmer families, nature had so arranged "that we can be continuously taking exercise one way or another". However, in many professions, such as in business, the body movements "are too slight to be of any account". He says that sports did give some exercise to the body but "nothing to improve the mind". Further, the intellectual men "are seldom sportsmen as well". He also considered "walking" as the best form of exercise, but a walk should cover 10 or 12 miles. He says that Thoreau used to walk for 8 hours daily when he wrote his best book and Tolstoy wrote his best books by never sitting at his table before he had plenty of exercise.

It was necessary to introduce in our schools "indigenous games, exercises, and the Western type of drill". Regular exercise was essential for the students. Walking energetically for an hour or half every morning and evening too kept the body healthy and the mind fresh. He also endorsed the old Indian system of *pranayama, asanas*, etc., for students' physical training. He was happy that physical training and games had been made compulsory at the Satyagraha Ashram School.

The *tenth chapter* on "Education through Prayer, Music, Art and Culture" includes his emphasizing at a Students' Meeting that "prayer" was "necessary for the soul", and pointing out the strife and quarrels which arose due to the "absence of the spirit of true prayer". He said: "If you students would base your education on the true foundation of a pure character and pure heart there is nothing so helpful as to offer your prayers every day truly and religiously."

At the Second Gujarat Educational Conference (1917), he said that no place was given to music anywhere and wanted "everything possible to teach music to our boys and girls" to be done. Harmonious music had the power "to soothe the anguish of the soul". It meant rhythm and order. He said in an interview (1924) that he was so fond of music that in a South African Hospital, he felt greatly soothed as a friend's daughter sang the song "Lead Kindly Light" at his request. He found songs of Mirabai to be "so beautiful" because they "come from the heart". He often asserted that "our beautiful music had been neglected in the schools and colleges". He claimed to be an artist himself, "a lover of music as well as other arts"; only his values were different.

He considered the education system to be incomplete without the study of music. "Music brings sweetness to the individual and to the social life of the people." "To make life musical means to make it one with God." There could be no music where there was filth, squalor, and misery. He did not approve of those fighting shy of sending "our sisters and daughters to music schools".

During his discussion with G. Ramachandran (1924), he asserted that, "All true art is thus the expression of the soul" and the outward forms "have value only in so far as they are the expressions of the inner spirit of man". It did not mean that he refused to accept the value of productions of art, generally accepted as such, but only he personally felt "how inadequate those are compared with the eternal symbols of beauty in Nature". He saw and found beauty in Truth or through Truth, in truthful faces, pictures, or songs. He said that to a true artist, only that face is beautiful which, "quite apart from exterior, shines with the Truth within the soul".

He felt that painting, unlike music, could be learnt only by a few who had a natural aptitude for it. However, in painting too, drawing of lines and the figures of objects could be taught to all, and he wanted it to be taught to every child before he/she was taught the alphabet.

Regarding culture, he wanted "the cultures of all the lands to be blown about my house as freely as possible" but he refused to be blown off his feet by any. He contended that "an appreciation of other cultures can fitly follow, never precede an appreciation and assimilation of our own". He insisted that no culture can live if it attempts to be exclusive.

The *eleventh chapter* gives Gandhi's views on "Libraries and

Textbooks". He wanted the library to be planned so as to serve as a lecture hall, a quiet place for students to read and study, and also for research scholars. He wanted a librarian (to be one who) not only preserves books but who also "appreciates them and can select them".

He preferred that the teacher should impart education mostly by word of mouth, which he could do with the help of books and textbooks. It was the duty of the teacher to teach his pupils discrimination. A multiplicity of textbooks also meant depriving the vast majority of poor village children of the means of instruction. He concluded that "books are required more for the teachers than for the taught", and every teacher, "to do full justice to his pupils, will have to prepare the daily lessons from the material available" and "to suit to the special requirements of his class". Gandhi saw that textbooks also seemed to have become "an article of commerce" and it was "a pathetic sight to see boys and girls going to schools loaded with books". He wanted the commercial spirit to be "entirely eliminated and the question approached entirely in the interest of the scholars".

The *twelfth chapter* on "Message to the Teachers and Students" covers Gandhi's "Message to the Teachers" under Section I and "Message to Students" under Section II. He defined a "true teacher" as one who "introduces the pupil to his subjects, creates in him interest for the subject, and enables him to understand it independently". Students' interest "is sustained not by the subject matter but by the teacher". At the opening of a "national" school (1919) he said that "national education" required teachers of good character who took teaching as their *dharma*.

He said that teachers must also give all their time outside the classroom to their students in order to "fashion their hearts rather than their brains". Also, discipline has nothing to do with artificial restraint upon the students' all-round growth. A teacher must "take the place of a mother". He believed in the ancient idea of teachers teaching for the love of it and receiving barest maintenance. He even said that a teacher who had rapport with the taught, became one with them, learnt more from them than he taught them. The primary aim of all education being "the moulding of the character of pupils", a teacher who has character, need never lose heart.

He insisted that students must not be given "corporal punishment". But the teacher may punish himself in some way so that the children, due to their affection for him, change for the better. This was how mothers reformed their children. There is violence in punishing pupils, and a punishment is just only if the pupil himself accepted it as such. Occasions when "even the best of teachers cannot but inflict punishment" should be an exception. A teacher has to develop the technique of teaching students and maintaining discipline without punishment. However, nonviolence did not compel a teacher to keep in his school a student who did not follow the disciplinary rules.

Regarding his "Message to the Students", in his speech at Bihar Students Conference (1917), Gandhi stressed the need for exercise as "the body is the abode of the spirit". Their daily life must be above reproach and they "have to strive for great achievement" in the world. They must be introduced to the theoretical study of politics but not with its "practical activity". He said that it was a student's duty to "study well, safeguarding his health meanwhile and cherishing the aim of using the fruits of his study in the service of the country", to live "a purposeful life and taking care to be mindful of our own interest and to work for others". They should instruct co-passengers in a train and the masses about hygiene and sanitation. They should practise what they learn and what appeared to them to be right.

A student's life should be similar to a *sannyasi*'s. University students would be judged not by their knowledge but solely by their good conduct. He told the students at Mysore (1927) that "real service of the country and of God consists in serving the poor humanity". At a college in Karachi (1934), he said, "if learning is to be put to proper use, if it is to be used only for the sake of service, one should acquire more and more humility". While propagating his scheme of "Basic Education" he said that intelligence could be developed not only through reading books but also by artisan's work being learnt in a scientific manner.

1

Meaning and Aims of Education
Section I — Meaning of Education

What is the meaning of education? It simply means a knowledge of letters. It is merely an instrument, and an instrument may be well used or abused. . . . We daily observe that many men abuse it and very few make good use of it; and if this is a correct statement, we have proved that more harm has been done by it than good.

> . . . To teach boys reading, writing and arithmetic is called primary education. A peasant earns his bread honestly. He has ordinary knowledge of the world. He knows fairly well how he should behave towards his parents, his wife, his children and his fellow villagers. He understands and observes the rules of morality. But he cannot write his own name. What do you propose to do by giving him a knowledge of letters? Will you add an inch to his happiness? Do you wish to make him discontented with his cottage or his lot? And even if you want to do that, he will not need such an education. Carried away by the flood of Western thought we came to the conclusion, without weighing pros and cons, that we should give this kind of education to the people.

Now let us take higher education. I have learned Geography, Astronomy, Algebra, Geometry, etc. . . . In what way have I benefited myself or those around me? Why have I learned these things? Professor Huxley has thus defined education:

> That man, I think, has had a liberal education who has been so trained in youth that his body is the ready servant of his will and does with ease and pleasure all the work that as a mechanism it is capable of; whose intellect is a clear, cold, logic[al] engine with all its parts of equal strength and in smooth working order . . . whose mind is stored with a knowledge of the fundamental truths of nature . . . whose passions are trained to come to heel by a vigorous will, the servant of a tender conscience . . . who has learnt to hate all vileness and to respect others as himself. Such a one and no other, I conceive, has had a liberal education, for he is in harmony with nature. He will make the best of her and she of him.

If this is true education, I must emphatically say that the sciences I have enumerated above I have never been able to use for controlling my senses. Therefore, whether you take elementary education or higher education, it is not required for the main thing. It does not make men of us. It does not enable us to do our duty.

> . . . Our ancient school system is enough. Character-building has the first place in it and that is primary education. A building erected on that foundation will last.
>
> — *Hind Swaraj*, Chapter XVIII, 22-11-1909; *CWMG* 10: 54-55

> In brief, formation of character should have priority over knowledge of the alphabet. If this order is reversed, the attempt would be like putting the cart before the horse and making it push the cart with its nose, and would meet with the same success as the latter course.
>
> — *Navajivan*, 9-9-1928;
> What Do Children Understand? *CWMG* 37: 248

True Value of Education

The real difficulty is that people have no idea of what education truly is. We assess the value of education in the same manner as we assess the value of land or of shares in the stock-exchange market. We want to provide only such education as would enable the student to earn more. We hardly give any thought to the improvement of the character of the educated (*Indian Opinion*; *True Education*, p. 38).

The true occupation of man is to build his character. It is not quite necessary to learn something special for earning [one's livelihood]. He who does not leave the path of morality never starves, and is not afraid if such a contingency arises (Letter to Manilal Gandhi, 27-9-1909, *CWMG* 9: 435).

Learning to live a good life is in itself education. All else is useless. (Letter to Manilal Gandhi, 12-10-1909, *CWMG* 9: 475).

Education Is Not Mere Literacy

The Pall Mall Gazette, a well-known journal in England, has explained the nature of real education. The writer says:

> We hold that real education does not consist merely in acquainting oneself with ancient or modern books. It consists in the habits which one knowingly or unknowingly imbibes from the atmosphere, one's surroundings and the company one keeps and above all in work. It is all very well to acquire a stock of knowledge from good books or from other sources. But the more important thing is to learn humanity. The primary function of teachers is, therefore, not to teach the alphabet, but to inculcate humanity. . . . Aristotle said that virtue is not learnt by reading big volumes. It is by doing good deeds that we learn virtue. Another great writer also says that it is well for one to know what is good, but one will be considered a happy person only if one acts upon that knowledge.

. . . We can readily realize how a country that invests in education with such a noble purpose becomes prosperous. India's star will shine bright when Indian children receive such education. Parents, teachers and pupils ought to ponder over the passage quoted above. It would not do merely to know it, it is necessary to act upon it. That is to say, parents should provide for excellent education, teachers should discharge their responsibility and pupils should recognize that mere literacy is not education.

— *Indian Opinion*, 18-5-1907; What Is Education?, *CWMG* 6: 484-85

Education as Training

I have been reading Emerson, Ruskin and Mazzini. I have also been reading the Upanishads. All confirm the view that education does not mean a knowledge of letters but it means character building, it means a knowledge of duty. Our own word literally means "training". If this be the true view and it is to my mind the only true view, you are receiving the best education — training — possible (Letter to Manilal Gandhi, 25-3-1909; *CWMG* 9: 208).

My experience has proved to my satisfaction that literary training by itself adds not an inch to one's moral height and that character building is independent of literary training (*Young India*, 1-6-1921; The Poet's Anxiety, *CWMG* 20: 162).

Education as Service

Addressing his son Ramdas, Gandhiji explains:

True education lies in serving others, . . . The more mature you grow, the more you will realize this. A great deal of religious obligations on us are fulfilled when we nurse the sick. I am not worried about your bookish learning so long as you perform your duties and observe solemn ethical conduct. For me carrying out the fundamentals of ethics is *duty*.

— Letter to Ramdas Gandhi;
The Making of the Mahatma by Ravji Bhai, p. 97

To do good to others and serve them without any sense of egoism — this is real education (Letter to Manilal Gandhi, 17-9-1909, *CWMG* 9: 417).

Education for Liberation of "Self"

"That is true education which leads to freedom." That alone is true education which enables us to preserve our *dharma*. This is the motto accepted by our university. The idea has appealed to me very much: "That is true education which leads to freedom." That which liberates is education. Liberation is of two kinds. One form of liberation consists in securing the freedom of the country from foreign rule. Such freedom may prove short-lived. The other kind of liberation is for all time. In order to attain *moksha*, which we describe as our *parama dharma*, we should have freedom in the worldly sense as well. He who is ridden with many fears cannot attain the ultimate *moksha*. If one would attain this, would achieve the highest end of human effort, one has no choice but to attain that *moksha* which is nearest to one. That education which delays our freedom is to be shunned, it is Satanic, it is sinful. Whatever the quality of the education given in government schools and colleges, it is to be shunned because the government which imparts it is Satanic and deserves to be shunned (*Navajivan* 18-11-1920; Speech to Students, Ahmedabad, 15-11-1926, *CWMG* 18: 471).

The ancient aphorism, "Education is that which liberates" is as true today as it was before. Education here does not mean mere spiritual knowledge, nor does liberation signify only spiritual liberation after death. Knowledge includes all training that is useful for the service of mankind and liberation means freedom from all manner of servitude even in the present life. Servitude is of two kinds: slavery to domination from outside and to one's own artificial needs. The knowledge acquired in the pursuit of this ideal alone constitutes true study (*Harijan*, 10-3-1946; What After Finishing Studies, *CWMG* 83: 208).

Education as Assimilation

It is the duty of students to assimilate whatever they have learnt. They should have religious and moral instruction, as much of it as they can usefully apply. They need education in such measure that it would not become too much of a useless burden on them. I should like to address a few words exclusively to students. Men and women students, you will benefit from what you have learnt only to the extent that you have assimilated it. That should be the object of this institution too. You should ponder over the element of truth in whatever books of religion you read. If you cling to truth, success is yours. I would advise you, from my experience, to profit well from your education. That will be to your advantage and to your country's as well (*Kathiawar Times*, 17-2-1915; Speech at Prize Distribution to Students in Bombay, 14-2-1915, *CWMG* 13: 23).

Education to Overcome Fear

For us, fear has become synonymous with life. What is the use of that education which does not help us to overcome fear, but which, on the contrary, strengthens it? What kind of an education is it which does not teach us to follow truth and to cultivate devotion for the country?

(*Navajivan*, 8-12-1920; Speech at Students Meeting in Agra, 23-11-1920, *CWMG* 19: 16).

The greatest obstacle in the way of students is fear of consequences mostly imaginary. The first lesson therefore that students have to learn is to shed fear. Freedom can never be won by those who are afraid of rustication, poverty and even death. The greatest fear for students of government institutions is rustication. Let them realize that learning without courage is like a waxen statue beautiful to look at but bound to melt at the least touch of a hot substance (*Young India*, 12-7-1928; Awakening among Students, *CWMG* 37: 47).

In the circumstances in which you pursue your studies, you can only learn to fear man. I would say, on the other hand, that he alone is a real M.A. who has given up the fear of man and has learnt to fear God. Any education you receive will have justified itself only when you have become so strong that you will not beg of anyone for your living. It will have justified itself when the feeling has grown in you that, so long as you are strong of limb, you need not humble yourselves before anyone for a livelihood (*Navajivan*, 5-12-1920; Speech at Students' Meeting, Banaras, 26-11-1920, *CWMG* 19: 27).

Culture of the Heart

There is one thing which, as I am speaking to you, occurs to me, which comes to me from my early studies of the Bible. It seized me immediately. I read the passage:

> But seek ye first the Kingdom of God, and his righteousness; and all these things shall be added unto you.

I tell you that if you will understand, appreciate and act up to the spirit of this passage, you won't even need to know what place Jesus or any other teacher occupies in your heart. If you will do the proper scavenger's work, clean and purify your hearts and get them ready, you will find that all these mighty teachers will take their places without invitation from us. That, to my mind, is the basis of all sound education. Culture of the mind must be subservient to the culture of the heart. May God help you to become pure! (*The Hindu*, 2-12-1927; Speech at Central College, Jaffna, *CWMG* 35: 343).

Education as Contemplation

Education, character and religion should be regarded as convertible terms. There is no true education which does not tend to produce character, and there is no true religion which does not determine character. Education should contemplate the whole life. Mere memorizing and book-learning is not education. I have no faith in the so-called systems of education which produce men of learning without the backbone of character (*Indian Review*, October 1928; Interview with W.W. Hall, *CWMG* 37: 320).

Education of the Whole Child

Education does not mean a knowledge of the alphabet. This type of knowledge is only a means to education. Education implies a child's learning how to put his mind and all his senses to good use. That is to say, he really learns how to use his hands, feet and other organs of action and his nose, ear and other organs of sense. A child who has acquired the knowledge that he should not use his hands for stealing or for killing flies, nor for beating up his companions or younger brothers and sisters, has already begun his education. He has started it, we can say, when he understands the necessity of keeping his body, his teeth, tongue, ears, head, nails, etc., clean and keeps them clean. That child has made good progress in education who does not indulge in mischief while eating and drinking, eats and drinks alone or in society in a proper manner, sits properly and chooses pure foodstuffs knowing the difference between pure and impure foodstuffs, does not eat like a glutton, does not clamour for whatever he sees and remains calm even if he does not get what he wants. Even that child has advanced on the road to education whose pronunciation is correct, who can recount to us the history and geography of the country surrounding him without knowing those terms and who understands what his country means. That child has made very good progress in his education who can understand the difference between truth and untruth, worth and worthlessness and chooses the good and the true, while rejecting the bad and the untrue (*Navajivan*, 2-6-1929; Ideal Primary School for Children, *CWMG* 41: 6).

Education as Self-Discipline

All your scholarship, all your study of Shakespeare and Wordsworth would be in vain if at the same time you do not build your character, and attain mastery over your thoughts and actions. When you have attained self-mastery and learnt to control your passions you will not utter notes of despair. You cannot give your hearts and profess poverty of action. To give one's heart is to give all. You must, to start with, have hearts to give. And this you can do if you will cultivate them (*Young India*, 19-9-1929; Speech to Students, Agra, 13 September 1929, *CWMG* 41: 391).

Development of Body, Mind and Spirit

The English word "education" etymologically means "drawing out". That means an endeavour to develop our latent talents. The same is the meaning of *kelavani,* the Gujarati word for education. When we say that we develop a certain thing, it does not mean that we change its kind or quality, but that we bring out the qualities latent in it. Hence "education" can also mean "unfoldment".

In this sense, we cannot look upon knowledge of the alphabet as education. This is true even if that knowledge gains us the M.A. degree or enables us to adorn the place of a Shastri in some *pathshala* with the requisite knowledge of Sanskrit. It may well be that the highest literary knowledge is a fine instrument for education or unfoldment, but it certainly does not itself constitute education.

True education is something different. Man is made of three constituents, the body, mind and spirit. Of them, spirit is the one permanent element in man. The body and mind function on account of it. Hence we can call that education which reveals the qualities of spirit. That is why the seal of the Vidyapith carries the dictum "Education is that which leads to *moksha*".

Education can also be understood in another sense; that is, whatever leads to a full or maximum development of all the three, the body, mind and spirit, may also be called education. The knowledge that is being imparted today may possibly develop the mind a little, but certainly it does not develop the body and spirit. I have a doubt about the development of the mind too, because it does not mean that the mind has developed if we have filled it with a lot of information. We cannot therefore say that we have educated our mind. A well-educated mind serves man in the desired manner. Our literate mind of today pulls us hither and thither. That is what a wild horse does. Only when a wild horse is broken in we can call it a trained horse. How many "educated" young men of today are so trained?

Now let us examine our body. Are we supposed to cultivate the body by playing tennis, football or cricket for an hour every day? It does, certainly, build up the body. Like a wild horse, however, the body will be strong but not trained. A trained body is healthy, vigorous and sinewy. The hands and feet can do any desired work. A pickaxe, a shovel, a hammer, etc., are like ornaments to a trained hand and it can wield them. That hand can ply the spinning-wheel well as also the ring and the comb while the feet work a loom. A well trained body does not get tired in trudging 30 miles. It can scale mountains without getting breathless. Does the student acquire such physical culture? We can assert that modern curricula do not impart physical education in this sense.

The less said about the spirit the better. Only a seer or a seeker can enlighten the soul. Who will awaken that dormant spiritual energy in us all? Teachers can be had through an advertisement. Is there a column for spiritual quest in the testimonials which they have to produce? Even if there is one, what is its value? How can we get teachers through advertisements who are seekers after self-realization? And education without such enlightenment is like a wall without a foundation or, to employ an English saying, like a white sepulchre. Inside it there is only a corpse eaten up or being eaten by insects (*Navajivan, Education Supplement*, 28-2-1926; What Is Education? *CWMG* 30: 58-59).

By education I mean an all-round drawing out of the best in child and man — body, mind and spirit. Literacy is not the end of education nor even the beginning. It is only one of the means whereby man and woman can be educated. Literacy in itself is no education. I would therefore begin the child's education by teaching it a useful handicraft and enabling it to produce from the moment it begins its training. Thus every school can be made self-supporting, the condition being that the state takes over the manufactures of these schools (*Harijan*, 31-7-1937; Criticism Answered, *CWMG* 65: 450).

Right Learning

"Learning owes its worth to *dharma*". . . . I have discovered in the course of my travels in India that, without *dharma*, learning is barren. This raises the question: "What is right learning?" I have given my reply often enough. We shall settle afterwards the issue of what manner of learning to provide. For the present, we may follow one definite method and include religious instruction in it. Religion is not a matter for reflection but of conduct. It is not a subject for talking about, be it noted. Teachers can create the thing only by their conduct (*Gujarati*, 13-7-1919; Speech at Foundation Laying of Vanita Vishram, Ahmedabad, 26-9-1919, *CWMG* 15: 410-11).

Science and Responsibility

At the time when emphasis in education is put more upon literary knowledge than upon character building, the following from the article of Principal Jacks in the "Sunday School Chronicle" will be read with profit:

Our life presents itself as an endless movement, in which the march of science never quite overtakes the final problem of its own application. The point where responsibility rests upon us all is always just ahead of the last point reached by advancing science. The more the pursuer quickened his pace the more the fugitive quickens his. This inability of science to overtake responsibility is what I mean by its limitations. Applied science will tell you how to make a gun, but it will not tell you when to shoot nor whom to shoot at. You say that moral science will look after that. I answer that moral science in revealing the right use of my gun, inevitably reveals the wrong use also, and since the wrong will often serve my selfish purpose better than the right, my neighbours run a new risk of being shot at and plundered. A bad man armed with moral science is another name for the devil. If Mephistopheles had been examined in moral science in the University of London, he would have carried off all the prizes. At that point moral science and natural science are both in the same boat. How shall we name this fugitive thing which science never catches? I have called it life, others call it spirit or soul or sense, or perhaps the will. I do not think it matters greatly what we call it, so long as we recognize that it exists and that it carries in its arms the fortunes of mankind. Let education look to that. This is the point where all the enterprise of education and all the activities of religion come to their focus — the point of responsibility. If we do it at all other points and leave the point of responsibility uncared for, we shall inevitably come to grief. — *Young India*, 30-9-1926; Notes, *CWMG* 31: 456

Education and Culture

"Culture" means refinement of feelings and "education" means knowledge of literature. Education is a means and culture is the end. The latter is possible even without education. For instance, if a child is brought up in a truly cultured family, it will unconsciously imbibe culture from its environment. In our country at any rate, present-day education and culture have no connection with each other. If the educated still retain some culture, that is in spite of their education. This fact shows that the roots of our culture are deep (Letter to Premabehn Kantak 5-1-1931, *CWMG* 45: 63-64).

Strengthening of Character

In my wanderings among the students I made the discovery at an early stage of the movement that in order to conduct a movement of this kind character must be the foundation. We also found that real education consists not in packing the brain with so many facts and figures, not in passing examinations by reading numerous books but in developing character. I do not know to what extent you students of France lay stress upon character rather than upon intellectual studies, but I can say this that if you explore the possibilities of nonviolence you will find that without character it will prove a profitless study (*Young India*, 1-10-1931; Speech at Meeting of Students, Marseilles, 11-9-1931, *CWMG* 47: 422).

Real Education

Real education has to draw out the best from the boys and girls to be educated. This can never be done by packing ill-assorted and unwanted information into the heads of the pupils. It becomes a dead weight crushing all originality in them and turning them into mere automata (*Harijan*, 1-12-1933; School Books, *CWMG* 56: 295).

Real education consists in drawing the best out of yourself. What better book can there be than the book of humanity? (*Harijan*, 30-3-1934; Speech at Annamalai University, Chidambaram, *CWMG* 57: 170).

Education of the Hand

Literary education should follow the education of the hand — the one gift that visibly distinguishes man from beast. It is a superstition to think that the fullest development of man is impossible without a knowledge of the art of reading and writing. That knowledge undoubtedly adds grace to life, but it is in no way indispensable for man's moral, physical, or material growth (*Harijan*, 8-3-1935; A Baffling Problem, *CWMG* 60: 283).

Fighting Social Evils

All this means education of a character that will revolutionize the mentality of the youth of the nation. Unfortunately the system of education has no connection with our surroundings which therefore remain practically untouched by the education received by a microscopic minority of the boys and girls of the nation. Whilst, therefore, whatever can be done to abate the evil must be done, it is clear to me that this evil and many others which can be named can only be tackled if there is education which responds to the rapidly changing conditions of the country. How is it that so many boys and girls who have even passed through colleges are found unable or unwilling to resist the manifestly evil custom which affects their future so intimately as marriage does? Why should educated girls be found to commit suicide because they are not suited? Of what value is their education if it does not enable them to dare to defy a custom which is wholly indefensible and repugnant to one's moral sense? The answer is clear. There is something radically wrong in the system of education that fails to arm girls and boys to fight against social or other evils. That education alone is of value which draws out the faculties of a student so as to enable him or her to solve correctly the problems of life in every department (*Harijan*, 23-5-1936; Marriage by Purchase, *CWMG* 62: 436).

Making the Whole Man

I hold that true education of the intellect can only come through a proper exercise and training of the bodily organs, e.g., hands, feet, eyes, ears, nose, etc. In other words an intelligent use of the bodily organs in a child provides the best and quickest way of developing his intellect. But unless the development of the mind and body goes hand in hand with a corresponding awakening of the soul, the former alone would prove to be poor lop-sided affair. By spiritual training I mean education of the heart. A proper and all-round development of the mind, therefore, can take place only when it proceeds *pari passu* with the education of the physical and spiritual faculties of the child. They constitute an indivisible whole. According to this theory, therefore, it would be a gross fallacy to suppose that they can be developed piecemeal or independently of one another.

Man is neither mere intellect, nor the gross animal body, nor the heart or soul alone. A proper and harmonious combination of all the three is required for the making of the whole man and constitutes the true economics of education (*Harijan*, 8-5-1937; Intellectual Development or Dissipation? *CWMG* 65: 73-74).

Section II — Aims of Education

". . . it is necessary to consider what the true aim of education is." Huxley has said that education should aim at building character. Our seers aver that, if a man, though well-versed in the Vedas and the Shastras, fails to realize the Self and to make himself worthy of liberation from all bonds, all his learning will have been in vain. They have also said: "He who has known the Self knows all." Self-realization is possible even without knowledge of letters. Prophet Mahomed was illiterate. Jesus Christ never went to school. But it would be foolhardy to assert, therefore, that these great souls had not attained self-realization. Though they never went to our schools and colleges to take any examination, we revere them. They had all that learning and knowledge could bring. They were *mahatmas* (Speech at Bihar Students' Conference, Bhagalpur, 15-10-1917; *CWMG* 14: 133).

Education is just a means. If it is not accompanied by truthfulness, firmness, patience and other virtues, it remains sterile, and sometimes does harm instead of good. The object of education is not to be able to earn money, but to improve oneself and to serve the country. If this object is not realized, it must be taken that the money spent on education has been wasted (*Indian Opinion*, 9-3-1907; James Godfrey, *CWMG* 6: 361).

Public Good

Without the right kind of education, the community will not only remain backward, but become increasingly so. Education in England, the study of English, world history and of the sciences — all these are essential in the world of today. Without them one is crippled. It is also necessary to learn how to put the knowledge thus acquired to proper use. In itself knowledge is only a means. It can be employed for good, for making money, and in the service of public causes. Knowledge is justified only when it is put to good use and employed in the public cause. Otherwise, as we pointed out once earlier and as everyone will readily admit, it is like poison (*Indian Opinion*, 4-4-1908; Hassan Mia's Departure, *CWMG* 8: 171).

Cardinal Virtues

If you practise the three virtues (truth, *ahimsa* and *brahmacharya*), if they become part of your life, so far as I am concerned, you will have completed your education — your training. Armed with them, believe me, you will earn your bread in any part of the world and you will have paved the way to acquire a true knowledge of the soul, yourself and God (Letter to Manilal Gandhi, 25-3-1909, *CWMG* 9: 205-06).

Not Mere Employment

You — the students of Madras as well as students all over India — are you receiving an education which will make you worthy to realize that ideal and which will draw the best out of you, or is it an education which has become a factory for making government employees or clerks in commercial offices? Is the goal of the education that you are receiving that of mere employment whether in the government departments or other departments? If that be the goal of your education, if that is the goal that you have set before yourselves, I feel and I fear that the vision which the poet pictured for himself is far from being realized (Speech at Y.M.C.A., Madras, 27-4-1915; *CWMG* 13: 65).

. . . I am afraid that most of the students never think as to the real aim of education. They attend school merely because that is the normal thing to do. Some do so in order to be able to obtain employment later on. In my humble opinion, to think of education as a means of earning a living betrays an unworthy disposition of mind. The body is the means of earning a living, while the school is a place for building character. To regard the latter as the means of fulfilling one's bodily needs is like killing a buffalo for a small piece of hide. The body should be maintained through bodily work. How can the *atman*, the spirit, be employed for this purpose? "Thou shalt earn the bread by the sweat of thy brow" — this is a *mahavakya* of Jesus Christ. The *Gita* also seems to say the same. . . .

Students, who attend school without taking thought as to the true aim of education, should first make sure what it should be. Such a student may resolve this very day that, henceforth, he will regard school as a place for building character. I am sure that he will effect a change for the better in his character in the course of a month and that his companions will also bear witness to his having done so. The Shastras assert that we become what we think (Speech at Bihar Students' Conference, Bhagalpur, 15-10-1917; *CWMG* 14: 134-35).

Building Character

All education must aim at building character. I cannot see how this can be done except through religion. We are yet to realize that gradually we are being reduced to a state in which we shall have lost our own without having acquired the new. I cannot go more into this, but I have met hundreds of teachers and they sighed in pain as they told me of their experiences. This is an aspect which the Conference cannot but deeply ponder over. If pupils in schools lose their character, everything will have been lost (Speech at Gujarat Educational Conference, Broach, 20-10-1917; *CWMG* 14: 29).

That is certainly what we mean. Even imparting knowledge should aim at character-building. Knowledge is the means and character-building is the end (*Navajivan*, 20-10-1921; My Notes, *CWMG* 21: 327).

National Character

Q: What is your goal in education when India obtains self-rule?

Gandhi said: "Character-building. I would try to develop courage, strength, virtue, the ability to forget oneself in working towards great aims. This is more important than literacy, academic learning is only a means to this greater end. That is why India's great lack of literacy, deplorable as it is, does not appeal to me nor make me feel that India is unfit for self-rule.

One's own inner convictions come first always. But in a nation where character is developed in all individuals, there can be no conflict between the dictates of one's own conscience and those of the state (Carlton

Washburne: *Remakers of Mankind* (1932), pp. 104-05, cited by N.K. Bose in *Selections from Gandhi* (1948), p. 255).

Manliness and Self-Respect

If education is to be bought at the price of manliness and self-respect, the price is too heavy. "Man does not live by bread alone." Self-respect and character are above means of livelihood or a career. I am sorry that so many students have taken their expulsion so much to heart. The parents as well as students must revise their ideas about education. Education is treated merely as a means of earning a livelihood and acquiring a status in society. These are not unworthy ambitions. But they are not everything in life. There are many other honourable means of acquiring wealth and status. There are many independent activities in life which one may undertake without having to contemplate loss of self-respect. And there is no better or cleaner passport to status in society than honesty and selfless service of fellow-beings. If, therefore, after due effort, the college door remains banged in the students' faces, they should not lose heart but seek other means of livelihood. And if the other students will empty the recalcitrant colleges as a matter of respectful protest, they and India will not be losers, but both will be considerable gainers (*Young India*, 1-10-1919; The Punjab Students, *CWMG* 16: 195-96).

Kindness to All

Gandhi said that the essence of all education was kindness — kindness to all, friends, foes, men and beasts. The chief object of education was the building of character which could be done by strict observance of *brahmacharya*. Gandhi then explained to the students the necessity of learning Hindi and spinning and said that if the whole younger generation was educated in the manner in which they were trained in national schools then there would not have been any difficulty in getting *swaraj* (*The Bombay Chronicle*, 17-3-1921; Speech at National College, Bombay, 16-3-1921, *CWMG* 19: 441).

Reaching the Ideal

In my humble opinion, knowledge should never be used for acquiring wealth. Business should be the only means of doing so. The means of livelihood should be labour, i.e., weaving, carpentry, tailoring and such other occupations essential for maintaining human life. I believe that one of the chief reasons for our moral fall is that doctors, lawyers, teachers and others acquire their knowledge mainly for getting money and, in fact, use it for that purpose. What I have set out is, of course, an ideal, which we cannot attain. I have no doubt, however, that the nearer we get to it, the better for us (*Navajivan*, 1-6-1924; Vidyapith and Anandshankarbhai, *CWMG* 24: 174).

Making a True Student

The education that you are receiving is intended for *swaraj*. . . . The outcome of education is that the student becomes an ideal citizen, an ideal patriot and an ornament to his family, his community and his nation (*Navajivan*, 14-9-1924; Speech at Tilak Mahavidyalaya Convocation, Poona, 14-9-1924, *CWMG* 25: 89).

Service of Humanity

In asking them to study the lives of lawyers like Ghose, Mahatma Gandhi asked them not merely to be satisfied with the heritage those great lawyers had left for them, but wished the present generation to do better. They should become the poor man's friend in every sense and then alone would they be able to justify the legal profession. Their end was not to get more than a decent livelihood or how to shine in life, but to serve humanity in order to serve the motherland. They ought not to become lawyers in order to increase cases. The education they received ought not to be prostituted to the base use of earning a livelihood, it ought to be used to promote moral growth to enable them to realize themselves, to understand that there was the Maker who saw everything and registered all thoughts, pure and impure, and the learning they derived should be dedicated to a vigorous self-analysis and not prostituted (*The Hindu*, 16-3-1925; Speech at Law College, Trivandrum, 14-3-1925, *CWMG* 26: 307).

Studies should be undertaken only with the aim of equipping oneself for service. Since, however, service of others gives one the highest joy, one may say that studies are for joy. I have not heard of anyone, however, who found unbroken joy in life through literary pursuits alone without devoting himself to service (Letter to Premabehn Kantak, 3-8-1932; *CWMG* 50: 326).

Fearlessness

Fearlessness is the foundation of all education, the beginning and not the end. If you do not build on that foundation, the edifice of all your education will topple over (*Young India*, 31-3-1927; Speech at Boys' Meeting, Kolhapur, *CWMG* 33: 192).

Purity of Personal Life

Purity of personal life is the one indispensable condition for building a sound education. And my meetings with thousands of students and the correspondence which I continuously have with the students in which they pour out their innermost feelings and take me into their confidence show me quite clearly that there is much left to be desired. I am sure that all of you understand thoroughly what I mean. In our languages, there is a beautiful word, equivalent for the word student, that is, *brahmachari*. *Vidyarthi* is a coined word and a poor equivalent for *brahmachari*. And I hope you know what the word *brahmachari* means. It means searcher after God, one who conducts himself so as to bring himself nearest to God in the least possible time. And all the great religions of the world, however much they may differ, are absolutely one on this fundamental thing that no man or woman with an impure heart can possibly appear before the Great White Throne. All our learning or recitation of the Vedas, correct knowledge of Sanskrit, Latin, Greek and what not will avail us nothing if they do not enable us to cultivate absolute purity of heart. The end of all knowledge must be building up of character (*Young India*, 8-9-1927; Speech at Voorhees College, Vellore, 30-8-1927, *CWMG* 34: 422-23).

Quest for Truth

True education is that which helps us to know the *atman*, our true self, God and Truth. To acquire this knowledge, some persons may feel the need for a study of literature, some for a study of physical sciences and some others for art. But every branch of knowledge should have as its goal knowledge of the self. That is so in the *ashram*. We carry on numerous activities with that aim in view. All of them are, in my sense of the term, true education. Those activities can also be carried on without any reference to the goal of knowledge of the self. When they are so carried on, they may serve as a means of livelihood or of something else, but they are not education. In an activity carried on as education, a proper understanding of its meaning, devotion to duty and the spirit of service are necessary. The first necessarily brings about development of the intellect. In doing any piece of work, however small, we should be inspired by a holy aim and, while doing it, we should try to understand the purpose which it will serve and the scientific method of doing it. There is a science of every type of work — whether it be cooking, sanitation, carpentry or spinning. Everybody who does his work with the attitude of a student knows its science or discovers it (Education, 10-7-1932; *CWMG* 50: 182).

Sparing the Rod

Our aim is not just to impart education to children or teach them discipline, but to build character in them. Education, discipline, etc., are means to that end. If the result of building character in them is that education and discipline are neglected, let that be so. I understand your argument, though. I also see that there is no ill will behind your use of the rod. But there are certainly anger and impatience behind them. May I make a suggestion? Call a meeting of the children. If any of them says, "You may punish us, and in this manner, if we play mischief or disobey you", you may punish them in the manner which they suggest (Letter to Premabehn Kantak, 14-12-1930, *CWMG* 44: 380).

Self-Control

The true aim of education is spiritual development. One should, therefore, go in for such kind of education as will bring it about. It need not be of one fixed type. Hence it is not necessary to say anything on that subject. One should lead a life of self-control (Letter to Bhogilal, 20-2-1933, *CWMG* 53: 366).

Developing Independent Thinking

At present, the minds of the students become dull there. They can only imitate. Instead of this, they must acquire the power of independent thinking. We are born into this world not for indulging in sensuous activities but for sacrifice, for restraint. The purpose of education is that we know God and progress towards the ideal, and get closer to Him. It is the strict law of God that anyone who desires to be close to Him should renounce the world and yet be in it. This is what the first *mantra* of the *Ishopanishad* exhorts us to do. This thing is difficult and yet easy at the same time. It is easy if we believe that we have to live for service. We acquire learning not for sensuous pleasures and for earning but for *mukti*. Education is considered necessary to save ourselves from darkness, sensuous pleasures and capricious behaviour (*Harijanbandhu*, 29-7-1934; Speech at Students' Meeting, Lahore, 13-7-1934, *CWMG* 58: 183).

Wholesome Educational Environment

That boy will grow into a courageous, healthy and service-minded man, provided he gets a wholesome environment. His body as well as his mind will develop in right proportion. He will be free of any fraud or immorality. Staying in the village he will serve the villagers and will be content to live on the subsistence provided by the villagers. Through his service and the knowledge acquired by him he will provide proper guidance to the people around him and thus train more young men. I expect that a student trained under the Nayee Talim would develop on these lines (*Biharni Komi Agman*, p. 238; Talk with Manu Gandhi, 21-4-1947, *CWMG* 87: 326).

2

Experiments in Education

Gandhi is not a man of words but a man of action. This is very much true whether he talks about *satyagraha*, education, or any other issue. Without conducting trials, he would not propagate anything. His experiments were so great that in every sphere of life they become a message for the future generations. He always used to say: "My life is my message". From this it is clear that all that he preached is purely from his experiments. In this chapter, we discuss some of his experiments conducted in the field of education, first while he was in South Africa, where he started his school named after his inspirer Tolstoy (Tolstoy Farm) and later in India at Gujarat after his return in 1914.

Section I — Experiments in Education in South Africa

Trials in South Africa

When I landed at Durban in January 1897, I had three children with me, my sister's son ten years old, and my own sons nine and five years of age. Where was I to educate them?

I could have sent them to the schools for European children, but only as a matter of favour and exception. No other Indian children were allowed to attend them. For these there were schools established by Christian missions, but I was not prepared to send my children there, as I did not like the education imparted in those schools. For one thing, the medium of instruction would be only English, or perhaps incorrect Tamil or Hindi; this too could only have been arranged with difficulty. I could not possibly put up with this and other disadvantages. In the meantime I was making my own attempt to teach them. But that was at best irregular, and I could not get hold of a suitable Gujarati teacher.

I was at my wit's end. I advertised for an English teacher who should teach the children under my direction. Some regular instruction was to be given to them by this teacher, and for the rest they should be satisfied with what little I could give them irregularly. So I engaged an English governess on £7 a month. This went on for some time, but not to my satisfaction. The boys acquired some knowledge of Gujarati through my conversation and intercourse with them, which was strictly in the mother tongue. I was loath to send them back to India, for I believed even then that young children should not be separated from their parents. The education that children naturally imbibe in a well-ordered household is impossible to obtain in hostels. I therefore kept my children with me. I did send my nephew and elder son to be educated at residential schools in India for a few months, but I soon had to recall them. Later, the eldest son, long after he had come of age, broke away from me and went to India to join a High School in Ahmedabad. I have an impression that the nephew was satisfied with what I could give him. Unfortunately he died in the prime of youth after a brief illness. The other three of my sons have never been at a public school, though they did get some regular schooling in an improvised school which I started for the children of *satyagrahi* parents in South Africa.

These experiments were all inadequate. I could not devote to the children all the time I had wanted to give them. My inability to give them enough attention and other unavoidable causes prevented me from providing them with the literary education I had desired, and all my sons have had complaints to make against me in this matter. Whenever they come across an M.A. or a B.A., or even a matriculate, they seem to feel the handicap of a want of school education.

Nevertheless I am of opinion that, if I had insisted on their being educated somehow at public schools, they would have been deprived of the training that can be had only at the school of experience or from constant contact with the parents. I should never have been free, as I am today, from anxiety on their score, and the artificial education that they could have had in England or South Africa, torn from me, would never have taught them the simplicity and the spirit of service that they show in their lives today, while their artificial ways of living might have been a serious handicap in my public work. Therefore, though I have not been able to give them a literary education either to their or to my satisfaction, I am not quite sure, as I look back on my past years, that I have not done my duty to them to the best of my capacity. Nor do I regret not having sent them to public schools. I have always felt that the undesirable traits I see today in my eldest son are an echo of my own undisciplined and unformulated early life. I regard that time as a period of half-baked knowledge and indulgence. It coincided with the most impressionable years of my eldest son, and naturally he has refused to regard it as my time of indulgence and inexperience. He has on the contrary believed that that was the brightest period of my life, and the changes, effected later, have been due to delusion miscalled enlightenment. And well he might. Why should he not think that my earlier years represented a period of awakening, and the later years of radical change, years of delusion and egotism? Often have I been confronted with various posers from friends: What harm had there been, if I had given my boys an academical education? What right had I thus to clip their wings? Why should I have come in the way of their taking degrees and choosing their own careers?

I do not think that there is much point in these questions. I have come in contact with numerous students. I have tried myself or through others to impose my educational "fads" on other children too and have seen the results thereof. There are within my knowledge a number of young men today contemporaneous with my sons. I do not think that man to man they are any better than my sons, or that my sons have much to learn from them.

But the ultimate result of my experiments is in the womb of the future. My object in discussing this subject here is that a student of the history of civilization may have some measure of the difference between disciplined home education and school education, and also of the effect produced on children through changes introduced by parents in their lives. The purpose of this chapter is also to show the lengths to which a votary of truth is driven by his experiments with truth, as also to show the votary of liberty how many are the sacrifices demanded by that stern goddess. Had I been without a sense of self-respect and satisfied myself with having for my children the education that other children could not get, I should have deprived them of the object-lesson in liberty and self-respect that I gave them at the cost of the literary training. And where a choice has to be made between liberty and learning, who will not say that the former has to be preferred a thousand times to the latter? (*An Autobiography*, Part III, Chapter VI, *CWMG* 39: 161-63).

Best Lessons in the Household

I introduced as much simplicity as was possible in a barrister's house. It was impossible to do without a certain amount of furniture. The change was more internal than external. The liking for doing personally all the physical labour increased. I therefore began to bring my children also under that discipline. . . .

We had engaged a servant to look after the house. He lived with us as a member of the family, and the children used to help him in his work. The municipal sweeper removed the night-soil, but we personally attended to the cleaning of the closet instead of asking or expecting the servant to do it. This proved a good training for the children. The result was that none of my sons developed any aversion for scavenger's work, and they naturally got a good grounding in general sanitation. . . .

Children inherit the qualities of the parents, no less than their physical features. Environment does play an important part, but the original capital on which a child starts in life is inherited from its ancestors. I have also seen children successfully surmounting the effects of an evil inheritance. That is due to purity being an inherent attribute of the soul (*An Autobiography,* Part IV, Chapter XXIII, *CWMG* 39: 248-49).

Curriculum

When Gandhi established a school in the Ashram at Phoenix for the benefit of the immigrant children, he had remarked:

The main object of this school is to strengthen the pupils' character. It is said that real education consists in teaching the pupil the art of learning. In other words, a desire for knowledge should grow in him. Knowledge, however, is of many kinds. There is some knowledge which is harmful. If, therefore, the boys' character is not formed well, they will acquire the wrong kind of knowledge. Because of lack of proper planning in education, we observe that some persons grow to be atheists and some, though highly educated, fall a prey to vices. It is therefore the main object of this school to assist in building the moral character of boys. . . .

Boys will be taught their own language, that is, Gujarati or Hindi and, if possible, Tamil, as also English, arithmetic, history, geography, botany and zoology. Advanced pupils will also be taught algebra and geometry. It is expected that they can be brought up to the matriculation level.

For purposes of religious instruction, parents will be allowed to send any religious teacher of their choice. Hindu boys will be taught the fundamentals of the Hindu religion in any manner that may be desired by their parents. Indian Christians will be taught the elements of the Christian religion by Mr. West and Mr. Cordes and the basis of the teachings of Theosophy. For boys of the Muslim faith, we want to arrange for a Maulvi, if possible. They will be permitted to go to Durban on Fridays. We believe that the education of any people is fruitless without religious instruction. Therefore, it is the duty of parents with a religious bent of mind to provide their children with both religious and secular education. We shall find on reflection that what we call secular education is also for strengthening the religious instinct. We think education imparted without any such aim is often harmful.

Boys will be taught the history of ancient and modern India so as to inculcate in them love of India and help them grow patriotic.

Apart from this, there is no other information to be given. We hope that those who want to send their boys will do so indeed. As for the difficulty about the building, it is the duty of the parents to remove it. It is hardly necessary to mention that a report on the school and a statement of accounts will be published regularly (*Indian Opinion*, 9-1-1909; Phoenix School, *CWMG* 9: 138-39).

Tolstoy Farm

I did not believe in the existing system of education, and I had a mind to find out by experience and experiment the true system. Only this much I knew — that, under ideal conditions, true education could be imparted only by the parents, and that then there should be the minimum of outside help, that Tolstoy Farm was a family, in which I occupied the place of the father, and that I should so far as possible shoulder the responsibility for the training of the young. . . .

But I had always given the first place to the culture of the heart or to the building of character, and as I felt confident that moral training could be given to all alike, no matter how different their ages and their upbringing. I decided to live amongst them all the twenty-four hours of the day as their father. I regarded character building as the proper foundation for their education and, if the foundation was firmly laid, I was sure that the children could learn all the other things or with the assistance of friends.

But as I fully appreciated the necessity of a literary training in addition, I started some classes with the help of Mr. Kallenbach and Sjt. Pragji Desai. Nor did I under-rate the building up of the body. This they got in the course of their daily routine. For there were no servants on the Farm, and all the work, from cooking down to scavenging, was done by the inmates. There were many fruit trees to be looked after, and enough gardening to be done as well. Mr. Kallenbach was fond of gardening and had gained some experience of this work in one of the governmental model gardens. It was obligatory on all, young and old, who were not engaged in the kitchen, to give some time to gardening. The children had the lion's share of this work, which included digging pits, felling timber and lifting loads. This gave them ample exercise. They took delight in the work, and so they did not generally need any other exercise or games. . . .

A word about vocational training. It was my intention to teach every one of the youngsters some useful manual vocation. For this purpose Mr.

Kallenbach went to a Trappist monastery and returned having learnt shoemaking. I learnt it from him and taught the art to such as were ready to take it up. Mr. Kallenbach had some experience of carpentry, and there was another inmate who knew it; so we had a small class in carpentry. Cooking almost all the youngsters knew. All this was new to them. They had never even dreamt that they would have to learn these things some day. For generally the only training that Indian children received in South Africa was in the three Rs.

On Tolstoy Farm we made it a rule that the youngsters should not be asked to do what the teachers did not do, and therefore, when they were asked to do any work, there was always a teacher cooperating and actually working with them. Hence whatever the youngsters learnt, they learnt cheerfully (*An Autobiography,* Part IV, Chapter XXXII, As Schoolmaster, *CWMG* 39: 266-68).

Literary Training

Literary training, however, was a more difficult matter. I had neither the resources nor the literary equipment necessary; and I had not the time I would have wished to devote to the subject. . . .

We gave three periods at the most to literary training. Hindi, Tamil, Gujarati and Urdu were all taught, and tuition was given through the vernaculars of the boys. English was taught as well. It was also necessary to acquaint the Gujarati Hindu children with a little Sanskrit, and to teach all the children elementary history, geography and arithmetic. . . .

Of textbooks, about which we hear so much, I never felt the want. I do not even remember having made much use of the books that were available. I did not find it at all necessary to load the boys with quantities of books. I have always felt that the true textbook for the pupil is his teacher. I remember very little that my teachers taught me from books, but I have even now a clear recollection of the things they taught me independently of books.

Children take in much more and with less labour through their ears than through their eyes. I do not remember having read any book from cover to cover with my boys. But I gave them, in my own language, all that I had digested from my reading of various books, and I dare say they are still carrying a recollection of it in their minds. It was laborious for them to remember what they learnt from books, but what I imparted to them by word of mouth, they could repeat with the greatest ease. Reading was a task for them, but listening to me was a pleasure, when I did not bore them by failure to make my subject interesting. And from the questions that my talks prompted them to put, I had measure of their power of understanding (*An Autobiography*, Part IV, Chapter XXXIII, Literary Training, *CWMG* 39: 268-70).

Training of the Spirit

The spiritual training of the boys was a much more difficult matter than their physical and mental training. I relied little on religious books for the training of the spirit. Of course I believed that every student should be acquainted with the elements of his own religion and have a general knowledge of his own scriptures, and therefore I provided for such knowledge as best I could. But that, to my mind, was part of the intellectual training. Long before I undertook the education of the youngsters of the Tolstoy Farm I had realized that the training of the spirit was a thing by itself. To develop the spirit is to build character and to enable one to work towards a knowledge of God and self-realization. And I held that this was an essential part of the training of the young, and that all training without culture of the spirit was of no use, and might be even harmful.

I am familiar with the superstition that self-realization is possible only in the fourth stage of life, i.e., *sannyasa* (renunciation). But it is a matter of common knowledge that those who defer preparation for this invaluable experience until the last stage of life attain not self-realization but old age amounting to a second and pitiable childhood, living as a burden on this earth. I have a full recollection that I held these views even whilst I was teaching, i.e., in 1911-12, though I might not then have expressed them in identical language.

How then was this spiritual training to be given? I made the children memorize and recite hymns, and read to them from books on moral training. But that was far from satisfying me. As I came into closer contact with them I saw that it was not through books that one could impart training of the spirit. Just as physical training was to be imparted through physical exercise, and intellectual through intellectual exercise, even so the training of the spirit was possible only through the exercise of the spirit. And the exercise of the spirit entirely depended on the life and character of the teacher. The teacher had always to be mindful of his ps and qs, whether he was in the midst of his boys or not.

It is possible for a teacher situated miles away to affect the spirit of the pupils by his way of living. It would be idle for me, if I were a liar, to teach boys to tell the truth. A cowardly teacher would never succeed in making his boys valiant, and a stranger to self-restraint could never teach his pupils the value of self-restraint. I saw, therefore, that I must be an eternal object-lesson to the boys and girls living with me. They thus became my teachers, and I learnt I must be good and live straight, if only for their sakes. I may say that the increasing discipline and restraint I imposed on myself at Tolstoy Farm was mostly due to those wards of mine.

One of them was wild, unruly, given to lying, and quarrelsome. On one occasion he broke out most violently. I was exasperated. I never punished my boys, but this time I was very angry. I tried to reason with him. But he was adamant and even tried to over-reach me. At last I picked up a ruler lying at hand and delivered a blow on his arm. I trembled as I struck him. I dare say he noticed it.

This was an entirely novel experience for them all. The boy cried out and begged to be forgiven. He cried not because the beating was painful to him; he could, if he had been so minded, have paid me back in the same coin, being a stoutly-built youth of seventeen; but he realized my pain in being driven to this violent resource. Never again after this incident did he disobey me. But I still repent that violence. I am afraid I exhibited before him that day not the spirit, but the brute, in me.

I have always been opposed to corporal punishment. I remember only one occasion on which I physically punished one of my sons. I have therefore never until this day been able to decide whether I was right or wrong in using the ruler. Probably it was improper, for it was prompted by anger and a desire to punish. Had it been an expression only of my distress, I should have considered it justified. But the motive in this case was mixed.

This incident set me thinking and taught me a better method of correcting students. I do not know whether that method would have availed on the occasion in question. The youngster soon forgot the incident, and I do not think he ever showed great improvement. But the incident made me understand better the duty of a teacher towards his pupils.

Cases of misconduct on the part of the boys often occurred after this, but I never resorted to corporal punishment. Thus in my endeavour to impart spiritual training to the boys and girls under me, I came to understand better and better the power of the spirit (*An Autobiography*, Part IV, Chapter XXXIV, Training of the Spirit, *CWMG* 39: 270-72).

Fasting as Penance

Day by day it became increasingly clear to me how very difficult it was to bring up and educate boys and girls in the right way. If I was to be their real teacher and guardian, I must touch their hearts. I must share their joys and sorrows, I must help them to solve the problems that faced them, and I must take along the right channel the surging aspirations of their youth. . . .

I hold, however, that some occasions do call for this drastic remedy. But it presupposes clearness of vision and spiritual fitness. Where there is no true love between the teacher and the pupil, where the pupil's delinquency has not touched the very being of the teacher and where the pupil has no respect for the teacher, fasting is out of place and may even be harmful. Though there is thus room for doubting the propriety of fasts in such cases, there is no question about the teacher's responsibility for the errors of his pupil (*An Autobiography*, Part IV, Chapter XXXVI, Fasting as Penance, *CWMG* 39: 273-74).

Section II — Experiments in Education in India

Shantiniketan

From Rajkot I proceeded to Shantiniketan. The teachers and students overwhelmed me with affection. The reception was a beautiful combination of simplicity, art and love. . . . I put it to the teachers that, if they and the boys dispensed with the services of paid cooks and cooked their food themselves, it would enable the teachers to control the kitchen from the point of view of the boys' physical and moral health, and it would afford to the students an object-lesson in self-help. One or two of them were inclined to shake their heads. Some of them strongly approved of the proposal. The boys welcomed it, if only because of their instinctive taste for novelty. So we launched the experiment. When I invited the Poet to express his opinion, he said that he did not mind it provided the teachers were favourable. To the boys he said: "The experiment contains the key to *swaraj*. . . ."

Changes like these when once begun always develop. Not only was the Phoenix party's kitchen self-conducted, but the food cooked in it was of the simplest. Condiments were eschewed. Rice, dal, vegetables and even wheat flour were all cooked at one and the same time in a steam cooker. And Shantiniketan boys started a similar kitchen with a view to introducing reform in the Bengali kitchen. One or two teachers and some students ran this kitchen (*An Autobiography*, Part V, Chapter IV, Shantiniketan, *CWMG* 39: 302-03).

Satyagraha Ashram, Kochrab

The Ashram experiment in education was a trial for us as nothing else was.

We saw at once that the women and children in the Ashram should be taught to read and write, and a little later on that there should be similar facilities for even the illiterate men that came to the Ashram. Those who had already joined the Ashram could not undertake to teach. If capable teachers were to be attracted to the Ashram, the rule of *brahmacharya* had to be relaxed in their case. The Ashram was therefore divided into two sections, the teachers' quarters and the Ashram proper. . . .

Then again there were differences of opinion as regards the method of education which gave rise to difficulties in administration. There were bitter discussions, but at last all calmed down and learned the lesson of forbearance. This was in my view a triumph of truth, the goal of all Ashram endeavour. Those who held divergent views harboured no evil intentions in their minds, and were indeed grieved at the divergence. They wished to practise truth as they saw it. . . .

I have my own perhaps peculiar views on education which have not been accepted by my colleagues in full, and here they are:

1. Young boys and girls should have co-education till they are eight years of age.
2. Their education should mainly consist in manual training under the supervision of an educationist.
3. The special aptitudes of each child should be recognized in determining the kind of work he or she should do.
4. The reasons for every process should be explained when the process is being carried on.
5. General knowledge should be imparted to each child as he begins to understand things. Learning to read or write should come later.
6. The child should first be taught to draw simple geometrical figures, and when he has learnt to draw these with ease, he should be taught to write the alphabet. If this is done he will write a good hand from the very first.
7. Reading should come before writing. The letters should be treated as pictures to be recognized and later on to be copied.
8. A child taught on these lines will have acquired considerable knowledge according to his capacity by the time he is eight.
9. Nothing should be taught to a child by force.
10. He should be interested in everything taught to him.
11. Education should appear to the child like play. Play is an essential

part of education.

12. All education should be imparted through the mother tongue.
13. The child should be taught Hindi-Urdu as the national language, before he learns letters.
14. Religious education is indispensable and the child should get it by watching the teacher's conduct and by hearing him talk about it.
15. Nine to sixteen constitutes the second stage in the child's education.
16. It is desirable that boys and girls should have co-education during the second stage also as far as possible.
17. Hindu children should now be taught Sanskrit, and Muslim children Arabic.
18. Manual training should be continued during the second stage. Literary education should be allotted more time according to necessity.
19. The boys during this stage should be taught their parents' vocation in such a way that they will by their own choice obtain their livelihood by practising the hereditary craft. This does not apply to the girls.
20. During this stage the child should acquire a general knowledge of world history and geography, botany, astronomy, arithmetic, geometry and algebra.
21. Each child should now be taught to sew and to cook.
22. Sixteen to twenty-five is the third stage, during which every young person should have an education according to his or her wishes and circumstances.
23. During the second stage (9-16) education should be self-supporting; that is, the child, all the time that he is learning, is working upon some industry, the proceeds of which will meet the expenditure of the school.
24. Production starts from the very beginning, but during the first stage it does not still catch up with the expenditure.
25. Teachers should be paid not very high salaries but only a living wage. They should be inspired by a spirit of service. It is a despicable thing to take any Tom, Dick or Harry as a teacher in the primary stage. All teachers should be men of character.

26. Big and expensive buildings are not necessary for educational institutions.
27. English should be taught only as one of several languages. As Hindi is the national language, English is to be used in dealing with other nations and international commerce.

As for women's education I am not sure whether it should be different from men's and when it should begin. But I am strongly of opinion that women should have the same facilities as men and even special facilities where necessary. There should be night schools for illiterate adults. But I do not think that they must be taught the three Rs; they must be helped to acquire general knowledge through lectures, etc., and if they wish, we should arrange to teach them the three Rs also. Experiments in the Ashram have convinced us of one thing, viz., that industry in general and spinning in particular should have pride of place in education, which must be largely self-supporting as well as related to and tending to the betterment of rural life. In these experiments we have achieved the largest measure of success with the women, who have imbibed the spirit of freedom and self-confidence as no other class of women have done to my knowledge. This success is due to the Ashram atmosphere. Women in the Ashram are not subject to any restraint which is not imposed on the men as well. They are placed on a footing of absolute equality with the men in all activities. Not a single Ashram task is assigned to the women to the exclusion of the men. Cooking is attended to by both. Women are of course exempted from work which is beyond their strength; otherwise men and women work together everywhere. There is no such thing as *purdah* or *laj* in the Ashram. No matter from where she has come, a woman, as soon as she enters the Ashram, breathes the air of freedom and casts out all fear from her mind. And I believe that the Ashram observance of *brahmacharya* has made a big contribution to this state of things. Adult girls live in the Ashram as virgins. We are aware that this experiment is fraught with risk but we feel that no awakening among women is possible without incurring it.

Women cannot make any progress so long as there are child marriages. All girls are supposed to be duty bound to marry and that too before menstruation commences, and widow remarriage is not permitted. Women, therefore, when they join the Ashram, are told that these social customs are wrong and irreligious. But they are not shocked as they find the Ashram practising what it preaches.

Not much of what is usually called education will be observed in the Ashram. Still we find that the old as well as the young, women as well as men are eager to acquire knowledge and complain that they have no time for it. This is a good sign. . . . Real education begins after a child has left school. One who has appreciated the value of studies is a student all his life. His knowledge must increase from day-to-day while he is discharging his duty in a conscientious manner. And this is well understood in the Ashram.

The superstition that no education is possible without a teacher is an obstacle in the path of educational progress. A man's real teacher is himself. And nowadays there are numerous aids available for self-education. A diligent person can easily acquire knowledge about many things by himself and obtain the assistance of a teacher when it is needed. Experience is the biggest of all schools. Quite a number of crafts cannot be learnt at school but only in the workshop. Knowledge of these acquired at school is often only parrot-like. Other subjects can be learnt with the help of books. Therefore what adults need is not so much a school as a thirst for knowledge, diligence and self-confidence.

The education of children is primarily a duty to be discharged by the parents. Therefore the creation of a vital educational atmosphere is more important than the foundation of numerous schools. When once this atmosphere has been established on a firm footing the schools will come in due course (*History of the Satyagraha Ashram*, XI: Education, 11-7-1932, *CWMG* 50: 232-36).

National Gujarati School

For many years past, several friends and I have felt that our present education is not national and that in consequence people do not get from it the benefit they ought to. Our children languish as a result of this education. They become incapable of any great achievement and the knowledge they acquire does not spread among the masses — not even in their families. Nor do the young people have any aim in mind in taking this modern education except to get a job and make money. It is one of the fundamental principles of education that it should be planned with a view to the needs of the people. This idea finds no place at all in our schools.

Wherever I have travelled in India, I have discussed this question with the leaders and, without exception, almost everyone has admitted that our educational system must change.

To look to the government for this will be sheer waste of time. . . . But the best petition to the government will be an actual demonstration by us and this will also be the easiest way of cultivating public opinion.

It has accordingly been decided, in consultation with some educated gentlemen, to start a national school.

Education in the School

Basic principle: The education will be physical, intellectual and religious. For physical education, there will be training in agriculture and hand-weaving and in the use of carpenter's and blacksmith's tools incidental to these. That will provide sufficient exercise for the pupils.

In addition, they will be given drill, which is both an entertainment [and a practical utility] and, as part of this, they will be taught how to march in squads and how each one may work with quiet efficiency in case of accidents such as fire.

They will have instruction on how to preserve health and on home remedies for ordinary ailments, with as much of physiology and botany as may be necessary for the purpose.

For intellectual training, they will study Gujarati, Marathi, Hindi and Sanskrit as compulsory subjects. Urdu, Tamil and Bengali will also be taught.

There will be no teaching of English during the first three years.

In addition, the pupils will be taught Mathematics (Arithmetic, Algebra and Geometry). Instruction in multiplication tables, Indian book-keeping and the measures, weights, etc., currently in use will begin at once and the rest of the curriculum will be covered progressively.

There will be instruction in History, Geography, Elements of Astronomy and Elements of Chemistry.

By way of instruction in religion, pupils will be taught general ethical principles and we are hopeful that the teachers will demonstrate by their conduct that the essence of religion is good character.

All teaching will be through Gujarati, right up to the highest stage, and most of it will be oral during the first few years. The intention is to put across to the children, before they learn to read and write, quite a few things orally by way of stories, as was the practice in old days, and so help their minds to grow, and to give them some general knowledge as they play about, rather than repress them by doing nothing more than remarking, "O dear, dear! How dirty", and so on.

Explanation

The aim at present is that after a few years of such education, the student's equipment will approximate to that of a well-informed graduate. That is, he will have a reduced load by way of learning English and, during the time so saved, he will be given all the useful knowledge a graduate acquires. He will be freed from the fear of examinations. All the students will be tested from time to time, but that will be by the teachers of the school itself. The use to which the student puts his abilities after leaving school will be the true measure of the worth of his education. Every opportunity will be taken to rid his mind of the fallacious notion that the aim of education is to get employment. And, finally, every pupil joining this school is likely to develop such self-confidence in a few years that he will not be troubled with doubts or fears about how he will make a living. A pupil who has been in the school for five years will be fixed up, if he so desires, in some work in the school itself and be paid for it. The school will make arrangements with some factories, etc., so that they provide training in vocations and give a start to those who wish to set themselves up independently. If, after ten years of study, anyone wants to pursue a subject further, necessary arrangements for the purpose are left to the future.

Free Education

No fees will be charged in this school, the expenses being met from donations received.

Teachers

Paid teachers will be engaged and will be, all of them, grown-up men who have reached the college level or possess equivalent attainments. The idea is that children should have the best teachers in the early stages (National Gujarati School, after 18-11-1917, *CWMG* 13: 332-34).

Objects of School

1. To adopt a new method of education.
2. To pay special attention to character building, the aim being that 10 per cent of the pupils at any rate get trained for national service.
3. To raise the status of the Gujarati language.
4. To work for the spread of the national language, Hindi.
5. To open schools of the new pattern in every place, and make this school a model for them, and for government as well, to copy. The aim is to have teachers trained in this school who will then go to villages and run schools there.

6. To get the new pattern adopted by the government.

Requirements for Teachers

1. Knowledge of Hindi and Marathi
2. Proficiency in weaving
3. Well-preserved health
4. Travel in India
5. Readiness for other work besides that in the school, that is, for work in the Ashram or as secretary to Bapu.

Work to Be Attended to by Teachers, Apart from Teaching

1. Textbooks
2. Vocabulary of technical terms.

Co-Education

I am myself in favour of co-education, but I don't insist on it if the teachers hold a different opinion.

I am not in favour of common residence. Girls should not be kept in a hostel. I am of the view that they must live under the constant supervision of their mothers and nowhere else.

There should be holidays in summer and the school should be shifted to a cooler place. This, I believe, will enable the teacher and the pupils to work very much better at other times. The teachers and the pupils should spend the holidays together.

English should be an optional subject. One should know good, at any rate correct, English. It would be excellent if we could get an English teacher for the purpose, but I can think of no one at present except Miss Schlesin. If only she would come, we could want nothing better. She is a very capable person. A pupil of the school should be able to talk in English with any Englishman without being nervous.

Drawing will be taught not as a fine art but because the pupil should be able to draw for practical purposes, draw maps, for instance, and straight lines, have a good handwriting and should know memory drawing.

Rules should be framed for discipline in the school, but no compulsion should be used to enforce obedience to them; they [the pupil] should feel inclined to obey them on their own. One should keep a watch on them whether they do. If any of them does not, we should express our disapproval and advise him.

To start with, 100 pupils should be admitted to the school, all of whom can pay for their own expenses. Nothing may be spent from the School Fund for any of the pupils. If there is a good but poor student, we may secure help for him from one of our friends and beg of another for his fees; but the School Fund cannot be used for the purpose.

History, Geography, Science and Hygiene Can Be Part of Gujarati

We have necessarily to come into contact with people from the South, and this is to our benefit too; everyone should, therefore, know Marathi (Talk with Teachers of the National School, 23-6-1917, *CWMG* 13: 446-48).

True National Education

So long as education in the country is not imparted by men of integrity and conditions are not created in which the highest knowledge will be available to the poorest of Indians, so long as a perfect confluence of education and *dharma* has not taken place and education has not been brought into relation with conditions in India, so long as the intolerable burden imposed on the minds of the young by imparting education through a foreign medium has not been lifted, so long will there be no upsurge of national life; there is no denying this.

Purely national education should be imparted in the regional language. The teachers must be of high calibre. The school should be situated in surroundings where the student has fresh air and water, where he enjoys peace, where the building and the adjoining land are object lessons in healthful living; and the educational pattern must be one which will instruct [the pupil] in the main professions and religions of India (*Navajivan*, 21-9-1919; *CWMG* 16: 156).

Except during the first five years of a child's life, the rest of his education is given through a foreign language. Besides, in the first five years, which are in some respects the most useful and of the greatest importance, education is usually imparted by the most ordinary type of teachers. Then begins English. At this stage the boys pass as if into a different world altogether. The education which is given to them has no relation to the life at home. The boys who till then were quite happy to do their lessons sitting on the ground now have benches. At home, even today, the prevailing custom in most homes is to sit on the floor. Until then, the boy, if he was a Hindu, was content to wear a *dhoti*, a *kurta* and the *angarakha* and, if a Muslim, to wear the *payjama*s instead of the *dhoti*; but now he uses a coat and trousers. Until then, he could do with the homely *kalam*, but now he has a pen with a steel nib. Thus, many significant changes take place in his outer living and a wide gulf divides the home and the school. Gradually, but definitely, this change begins to enter his inner life too. How are these changes in the outer life and the inner mental make-up of the boy going to affect his home and the way his people live at home? His parents have no idea at all as to what sort of education the boy is getting and their faith in that education is negligible.

Parents only know that it will help the boy to earn money. And this satisfies them. If this situation lasts long, we might all become foreigners! What is worse even the *swaraj* for which we are struggling may become foreign in character when we finally get it, with the result that the very burden under which we are crushed today may continue even after *swaraj*. There is only one way to escape this danger. It is to change and overhaul our system of education. In the national education to be evolved:

1. Education must be imparted through the mother-tongue.
2. There must be accord between the education a child receives at school and the environment of the home.
3. It must be so planned as to meet the needs of the majority of the people.
4. The teachers in primary classes must be competent men of good character right from the first class.
5. Education must be free.
6. Overall control must be in the hands of the people.

Education must be imparted through the mother-tongue. It is a pity that we are required to prove this self-evident truth. If we had not been dazzled by the lure of English, there should have been no need to prove this most obvious truth. The advocates of English say:

1. It is through English that an awakening has been created in the country.
2. English literature is so rich and vast that to give it up would be a great misfortune. It is not possible to translate it all into our language.
3. We can achieve unity only through English. To try to encourage and promote the different languages of India would amount to disrupting this unity and retarding the growing feeling that we are one nation.

4. English is the language of the rulers.

These are the main arguments of the advocates of English. They have many other things to say, but they have no more substance or importance than is included in the above.

To say that all the awakening we see in the country has been brought about through English is only a half-truth. The fact is that all the education in the country is being imparted through English. And because the Hindus are not absolute blockheads they have imbibed and utilized the good they have found in it. And yet the overall result which this education has yielded has been disappointing. Everybody admits that the present system of education suffers from some grave defects. We have not received from it the results which we are entitled to expect of an education which has now lasted for more than fifty years. Why is it so? If it had been imparted from the beginning through the mother-tongue it would have produced much good by this time. What only a few English-knowing people know at present would have spread and reached crores of our people — who would have shown the spirit and the strength which is now shown only by the English-knowing handful. At present, our young men, when they pass out of the college, appear to be devoid of all energy and just wander about in search of jobs. Instead, if they had been educated through the mother-tongue, then having been spared the strain of cramming, they would have been stronger both in body and mind and would have therefore rejected government service as something inferior.

No one suggests that English literature should be given up. We should have translated what is precious in it into our different languages. Japan and South Africa have done it. In Japan, they taught German and French to some who then translated good books from German and French into Japanese. It is not that German has nothing to borrow from English. Even so, not all Germans learn English. No German receives his education through English. Only a few Germans learn English and then translate into German whatever they think will be of value to their nation, and thus serve their mother-tongue. We should do the same.

As to the assumption that we have received a sense of unity by using English, the fact is that we become sharply aware of the illusion of our separateness from one another only after this alien language was introduced into our country, though it may be admitted that once we had seen through that illusion we strove to throw it off and regain our national solidarity. We observe that in many countries the oneness of the people is not always due to the oneness of the language. There are two languages in South Africa. But the people are striving to achieve unity because their interests are the same. Similar is the case with Canada. In England, Scotland and Wales they still speak three different languages. Mr. Lloyd George is making great efforts to revive Welsh, the language of Wales. And, yet, in all the three parts of Great Britain there is a strong feeling that they are one nation. Development of the regional languages of our country will produce social, political and economic awakening amongst our people. They will have a better appreciation of their condition and position in the picture of the wider whole of the country. They will know that though belonging to different provinces they are sailing in the same boat. Thus they will forget differences of language, appreciate the unity of their interests and be ready to fight for it, and protect it from dangers. Besides, the better educated amongst us will have to learn Hindi — as the common medium of speech. The effort required to learn Hindi is as nothing compared to that needed to learn English.

That English is the language of the rulers proves nothing beyond the fact that some of us have to master this alien tongue. I do not dislike English; I am only pleading that it be put in its proper place. Then, we can truly appreciate its merits, and derive such benefit as we can. It cannot, however, continue to be the medium of our education; nor can it be the language of inter-provincial communication. In our schools and colleges we must provide for imparting even the highest education through the mother-tongue.

There must be accord between the education given in the school and the home. The reason for this is obvious. Today, there is no such accord between the two. In national education, we must see that such accord is achieved and maintained.

We will now pass on to the third attribute of national education, namely, that *it should be so designed as to meet the needs of the majority of the people.* The great bulk of our people are peasants. So, if our boys had been given, from the very beginning, a knowledge of agriculture and weaving and if they had cultivated an appreciation of the needs of these two classes, and if these classes had received the scientific training in these vocations, our peasants today would have been happy and prosperous. Our cattle would not have been weak and diseased as they are today. Our peasants would not have been crushed with the weight of debt — incurred by poverty. Our produce would not have first gone to foreign countries as raw material and then brought back to us in the shape of finished goods to drain us of wealth. Today, we feel ashamed of such a state of affairs. We could not have paid England 85 crore rupees a year for cotton cloth. The prevailing system of education has made slaves of us instead of masters.

In the lower stages of primary education teachers must be men of high character. There is a proverb in English: "The child is the father of the man." We have a similar proverb: "A child, even while in the cradle, shows signs of what he is going to be in the future." If we entrust our children, in their most impressionable years, to incompetent teachers, we have no right to expect that they will grow to be men of good and strong character. That would be as absurd as to sow the seeds of *kauvach* and expect from them the flowers of *mogra*. We must procure the best teachers for our children whatever it may cost. In ancient times, our children received their education from learned and wise *rishi*s and *muni*s.

The fifth requirement of national education is that it *should be free*. Education should not be made to depend *on money*. Just as the sun gives light to all equally and rain pours down for all, even so learning must be made available to all.

Lastly, *the people themselves must have control over the planning and carrying out of education*. In the exercise of this control lies education too. People will then have faith in the education meted out to their children, and feel their responsibility towards it. When this stage is reached and education occupies an important place in the life of our people, it will be possible for us to obtain *swaraj* with no trouble at all. Therefore, it is our duty to initiate such education. It is also our right to ask the government for it. But we can approach the government about this matter only after we set the ball rolling ourselves. However, it is beyond the scope of this article to discuss the steps we should take for organizing such a type of national education. Let people first accept the view expressed herein (*Atmoddhar* — a Marathi Monthly; *True Education*, pp. 40-44).

National Higher Education

I have done a good many things in my life; some of them I feel proud of, though some others I regret. A few of them were very responsible undertakings. But I should like to state here — I am sure I am guilty of no exaggeration — that nothing I have done so far can stand comparison with what we are about to do today. I am aware of a great risk in this undertaking, but not because I fear that it may prove harmful to the nation; what pains me, or rather the incongruity I feel, is this, that I am not fit for the task I have undertaken. I do not say this as a matter of formality, I speak from the heart. If I knew that the present undertaking related to education in the real sense of the term, this preface would not have been necessary. This Mahavidyalaya is not being established with the sole object of imparting education; it [also] aims at helping the student to acquire a means of livelihood and when, in this respect, I compare it with Gujarat College and other similar institutions, I simply shudder.

In this, too, I am not exaggerating. What comparison is possible between Gujarat College and other similar colleges, on the one hand, and this small Mahavidyalaya of ours? To my mind, of course, it is great, but I am afraid that in your eyes, as you compare this Vidyalaya with the colleges you have in India, this Mahavidyalaya probably appears an Anuvidyalaya. You are very likely thinking in terms of brick and mortar. Of this, to be sure, I see more in Gujarat College. . . .

Today, not an inch of the ground is ours. Everything belongs to the government. This land, these trees, everything belongs to the government, even this body, and I have now begun to doubt whether our soul also is ours. Placed in this pitiable condition, why go looking for good buildings to house our Mahavidyalaya? How can we afford to wait till we had found men of great learning? Even if the most ignorant of ignorant men, a mere simpleton, were to come forward and could succeed in convincing us that our *atman* had been starved, that this country had lost its light — its knowledge of things of the spirit — I would appoint him as the principal. I am not sure that you would be ready to appoint a shepherd as principal and so we have had to find Shri Gidwani. I have not been attracted by the position he occupied. Perhaps you do not know him apart from that position. I should, however, like you to adopt a different criterion, seek another touchstone, for judging the worth of this Vidyalaya. If you test it on the common touchstone, it will seem to be brass but it will be found to be gold if you test it on the touchstone of character.

The coming together of [talented] men for educational work here is like the holy confluence of rivers. We have men of character assembled here. Fine men from Sind, Maharashtra and Gujarat have banded together here. How could we have, ordinarily, secured this?

I shall first address my prayer to the sisters and brothers who have come here for the function. You are witnesses to the establishment of this Mahavidyalaya. If there are any among you who feel that what is taking place is a farce, I would ask them not to be so conscientious and sit through the function. They should remain only if they wish to give their blessings. With the blessings of you all, the Mahavidyalaya will earn a name as a great institution. But they should not be blessings merely uttered with the lips; bless it from your heart. This you can do only by offering your sons and daughters to the institution. People in India have plenty of capacity to contribute money. In no field is progress held up for lack of funds. It is held up for want of men — of teachers or leaders, or if a leader is forthcoming, for want of pupils, i.e., soldiers. It is my belief that, if the leader is worthy, there will be no lack of soldiers. A carpenter will not quarrel with his tools, however bad they may be. He will handle the bluntest of them with the utmost ease. Likewise, if the leader is a real artisan, whatever the quality of material, he will produce gold from it, will produce gold from the country's clay. This is my prayer to the principal.

You, principal and teachers, have been inspired by one ideal only in joining this institution. You have undertaken to secure freedom through the miracle not of learning but of character, secure it not by meeting the government, sword against its shining sword, but with peaceful, spiritual effort — howsoever imperfect it be — against its aggressive, Satanic way. We want just now to sow the seed of freedom and afterwards we will water the plant and rear it into a tree. This tree can be raised only through character, with pure, spiritual strength. So long as the principal and the teachers go on working with their eyes on this one aim, we shall never be put to shame. May God justify in your experience the faith which is mine. Were it not for this unshakable faith of mine, I would not at all have accepted the sacred position of chancellor. I am ready to live and die for this cause, thinking that to die in this cause is to live; it is because I know that this is also true of you that I live among you and have accepted this exalted position. . . .

We are establishing this Vidyalaya, not with an educational, but with a national aim in view. Advising that students be taught to cultivate strength and character, I have been saying everywhere that in the measure we succeed with them we shall make ourselves fit for *swaraj* in the country. *Swaraj* cannot be secured in any other way. No amount of money we can spend or strength of character we can employ to ensure the success of such colleges will be enough.

This is a time not for words but for action. I have placed my thoughts before you as they came. I asked of you what you could give. Now I shall ask something of the students as well. There is no doubt at all that they have in them the courage which takes risks. I shall not look upon them — upon those who have already joined — as mere students and, therefore, I will not treat them as being free from responsibility. Those who have registered their names here are half teachers. It is they who have provided the foundation for the Mahavidyalaya. It is on them that the structure of the institution has been raised. Had they not joined, this Mahavidyalaya could not have been started. They also, therefore, share equal responsibility. You are equal partners in this and, if you do not play your part well, no efforts on the part of the teachers will succeed or, at any rate, succeed completely. Students who have left their colleges should understand why they have joined here and what they should expect to gain. May God grant them the strength to go on with their work, no matter how long this grim war continues. If they do, I am sure that, even if they are a mere handful, this Mahavidyalaya will shine forth and be a model institution for the whole country.

The reason will not be that Gujarat has wealth or that it has learning; it will be, rather, that non-cooperation had its origin here. The seed was sown and watered here, the required *tapascharya* was performed here. Do not think from this that I am a conceited man to speak in this manner, or that all the *tapascharya* has been mine and the seed was sown by me. I merely gave the *mantra*, I fulfilled the function of a *rishi*, if a *vanik*'s son can do so.

I have done nothing more than this. The planting was done by my co-workers. It is because their faith was greater than mine that we have succeeded. I claim the knowledge which comes from direct perception. Even if the gods came down and tried to persuade me to the contrary, my faith would not be shaken. As surely as I see, with my eyes, the trees in front of me, so surely I know that there is no salvation for India except through nonviolent non-cooperation. As for my co-workers, however, they have believed this through logic or reasoning or accepted it on faith. . . .

My co-workers have laid the foundation. Many of them are Gujaratis; there are Maharashtrians, too, but, having been in Gujarat, they have become half or three-quarters Gujaratis, or, perhaps, more Gujaratis than the Gujaratis themselves. They have made this a weapon of shining strength. We have not yet seen all its miraculous power. Within six months, you will see more of the miraculous power of this programme for which young girls handed over their bangles to me. But the source of it all — the visible image — is this Mahavidyalaya. Hindus are worshippers of images and we are proud of being so. This image has its various limbs: one of them is the chancellor and that is myself. The teachers, the principal and the students are other limbs. I am, myself, an old man, a withering leaf, and busy with other work. The falling away of such a leaf as I am can do no harm to a tree. The principal and the teachers, too, are no more than leaves, though green leaves as yet. In a short while, they also will grow old and, perhaps, fall off. The students, however are the branches of this beautiful tree and it is on them that principals and teachers will grow as leaves.

I request them to put the same faith in their teachers as they do in me. Should they, however, see that the principal or any of the teachers is weak, let them burn him to ashes with the fire which was Prahlad's and go ahead with their work. This is my prayer to God and my blessings to the students.

I shall end with a prayer to God and I want you all to say "amen" to it. Join me in my prayer, all of you, with a pure heart, "God! Make this Mahavidyalaya of such worth that through it we may win the freedom for which we offer prayers day and night and grant it that, through that freedom, not only India but the entire world, in which India is but a dot, may be happy" (*Navajivan*, 18-11-1920; Inaugural Speech at the Setting Up of Gujarat Vidyapith, 15-11-1920, *CWMG* 18: 463-68).

National Institutions

A Gujarati correspondent has raised certain questions about national education. Some of them are summarized below:

> Since some of the staunchest supporters of non-cooperation have lost faith in it and since the numbers attending national institutions are dwindling, what is the use of holding on to these tottering schools and colleges and wasting good money after bad institutions?

My believing eye detects a flaw in this argument. My faith in non-cooperation remaining as staunch as ever, I can find it possible to reconcile myself to the existing national institutions even though the attendance may be reduced to half a dozen. For the half a dozen will be the makers of *swaraj* whenever it comes. When virgins are required to perform certain sacred ceremonies, others are not accepted as substitute if no virgin is found. And even one virgin if found is enough to save the situation. So will it be with the planting of the *swaraj* flag-post. The flags will be unfurled with the unsullied hands of those, be they ever so few, who have remained true to their creed.

I do not therefore regard it as waste of money to continue the national institutions. They are so many oases in the desert. They give the water of life to the souls thirsting for freedom. In writing this I cast no reflection upon those who attend or otherwise support government schools. They are entitled to hold the view if they choose that theirs is the only way or also a way to freedom. National institutions are meant for those whose thirst for freedom is not satisfied by the ones managed or patronized by the government. Few as they are, insignificant though they may appear, they supply a felt want and contain in them the seeds, as it appears to non-cooperators, of true and lasting freedom.

The final success of these institutions depends upon the worth of the teachers. "But they are deserting the national schools and colleges", says the critic. So some of them are. It tries the faith of the survivors. Have they the courage to stand alone? Are there enough monied men to support the surviving national institutions? On the correct answer to these questions depends the future of the national institutions and with them the freedom of the country, and so far as I can judge, there are teachers enough to stand the severest test and there are monied men enough to support them. I know no organization that has died for want of funds. Organizations die always for want of men, i.e., honesty, efficiency and self-sacrifice. And it is my certain knowledge that where there are teachers, pupils are not wanting.

But the pupils have perhaps the largest share of responsibility on their shoulders. The future depends upon their ability, integrity, application, and patriotism. The teachers cannot give what the pupils have not. The teachers can help to "draw out" in the pupils what they have. If it were otherwise, if the teachers were capable of putting something into their pupils, all the latter receiving instruction under them will be alike, whereas we know as a matter of fact that no two pupils have been yet known to be alike. The pupils must therefore have initiative. They must cease to be mere imitators. They must learn to think and act for themselves and yet be thoroughly obedient and disciplined. The highest form of freedom carries with it the greatest measure of discipline and humility. Freedom that comes from discipline and humility cannot be denied; unbridled licence is a sign of vulgarity injurious alike to self and one's neighbours (*Young India*, 3-6-1926; National Education, *CWMG* 30: 519-20).

Village Schools

GANDHIJI: The cruellest irony of the new reforms lies in the fact that we are left with nothing but the liquor revenue to fall back upon in order to give our children education. That is the educational puzzle but it should not baffle us. We have to solve it and the solution must not involve the compromise of our ideal of prohibition, cost whatever else it may. It must be shameful and humiliating to think that unless we got the drink revenue, our children would be starved of their education. But if it comes to it, we should prefer it as a lesser evil. If only we will refuse to be obsessed by the figures and by the supposed necessity of giving our children the exact kind of education that they get today, the problem should not baffle us.

QUESTION: Then would you really abolish what is called secondary education and give the whole education up to matriculation in the village schools?

A. Certainly. What is your secondary education but compelling the poor boys to learn in a foreign language in seven years what they should learn in the course of a couple of years in their own mother tongue? If you can but make up your minds to free the children from the incubus of learning their subjects in a foreign tongue, and if you teach them to use their hands and feet profitably, the educational puzzle is solved. You can sacrifice without compunction the whole of the drink revenue. But you must resolve to sacrifice this revenue first, and think of the ways and means about education later. Make the beginning by taking the big step (*Harijan*, 21-8-1937; Discussion on Prohibition, before 21-8-1937, *CWMG* 66: 59).

Intellectual Development

During my recent wanderings in Travancore and Madras I found that most of the students and "intellectuals" who came into touch with me were an instance of intellectual dissipation rather than intellectual development. The fault lies in the modern system of education which encourages this vicious tendency, misdirects the mind, and thereby hinders its development instead of helping it. My experiments in Segaon have only confirmed this impression. But they are as yet too incomplete to be cited as evidence. The views on education that I am now going to set forth have been held by me right from the time of the founding of the Phoenix settlement in South Africa in the year 1904.

I hold that true education of intellect can only come through a proper exercise and training of the bodily organs, e.g., hands, feet, eyes, ears, nose, etc. In other words, an intelligent use of the bodily organs in a child provides the best and quickest way of developing his intellect. But unless the development of the mind and body goes hand in hand with a corresponding awakening of the soul, the former alone would prove to be a poor lopsided affair. By spiritual training I mean education of the heart. A proper and all-round development of the mind, therefore, can take place only when it proceeds *pari passu* with the education of the physical and spiritual faculties of the child. They constitute an indivisible whole. According to this theory, therefore, it would be a gross fallacy to suppose that they can be developed piecemeal or independently of one another.

The baneful effects of absence of proper coordination and harmony among the various faculties of body, mind and soul respectively are obvious. They are all around us; only we have lost perception of them owing to our present perverse associations. Take the case of our village folk. From their childhood upward they toil and labour in their fields from morning till night like their cattle in the midst of whom they live. Their existence is a weary, endless round of mechanical drudgery unrelieved by a spark of intelligence or higher graces of life. Deprived of all scope for developing their mind and soul, they have sunk to the level of the beast. Life to them is a sorry bungle which they muddle through anyhow. On the other hand, what goes by the name of education in our schools and colleges in the cities today is in reality only intellectual dissipation. Intellectual training is there looked upon as something altogether unrelated to manual or physical work. But since the body must have some sort of physical exercise to keep it in health, they vainly try to attain that end by means of an artificial and otherwise barren system of physical culture which would be ridiculous beyond words if the result was not so tragic. The young man who emerges from this system can in no way compete in physical endurance with an ordinary labourer. The slightest physical exertion gives him headache; a mild exposure to the sun is enough to cause him giddiness. And what is more, all this is looked upon as quite natural. As for the faculties of the heart, they are simply allowed to run to seed or to grow anyhow in a wild undisciplined manner. The result is moral and spiritual anarchy. And it is regarded as something laudable!

As against this, take the case of a child in whom the education of the heart is attended to from the very beginning. Supposing he is set to some useful occupation like spinning, carpentry, agriculture, etc., for his education and in that connection is given a thorough, comprehensive knowledge relating to the theory of the various operations that he is to perform and the use and construction of the tools that he would be wielding. He would not only develop a fine, healthy body but also a sound, vigorous intellect that is not merely academic but is firmly rooted in and is tested from day-to-day by experience. His intellectual education would include a knowledge of mathematics and the various sciences that are useful for an intelligent and efficient exercise of his avocation. If to this is added literature by way of recreation, it would give him a perfect, well-balanced, all-round education in which the intellect, the body and the spirit have all full play and develop together into a natural, harmonious whole. Man is neither mere intellect nor the gross animal body, nor the heart or soul alone. A proper and harmonious combination of all the three is required for the making of the whole man and constitutes the true economics of education. To say that this kind of education can only be given after we have attained our independence would, I am afraid, be like putting the cart before the horse. The advent of independence would be incredibly hastened if we could educate millions of our people through an intelligent exercise of their respective vocations like this and teach them that they live for the common good of all (*Harijan*, 8-5-1937; Intellectual Development or Dissipation? *CWMG* 65: 72-74).

"Constructive Programme" for Students

I have always cultivated close contact with them. They know me and I know them. They have given me service . . . are the hope of the future. In the heyday of non-cooperation they were invited to leave their schools and colleges. Some professors and students who responded to the Congress call have remained steadfast and gained much for the country and themselves. . . . But such as the students are, it is from these young men and women that the future leaders of the nation are to rise. Unfortunately they are acted upon by every variety of influences. Nonviolence offers them little attraction. A blow for a blow or two for one is an easily understandable proposition. It seems to yield immediate result though momentary. . . . But I am myself a fellow-student, using the word in its broader sense. My university is different from theirs. They have a standing invitation from me to come to my university and join me in my search. Here are the terms:

1. Students must not take part in party politics. They are students, searchers, not politicians.
2. They may not resort to political strikes. They must have their heroes, but their devotion to them is to be shown by copying the best in their heroes, not by going on strikes, if the heroes are imprisoned or die or are even sent to the gallows. . . .
3. They must all do sacrificial spinning in a scientific manner. . . .
4. They will be *khadi* users all through and use village products to the exclusion of all analogous things, foreign or machine made.
5. They may not impose Vandemataram or the national flag on others. . . .
6. They can enforce the message of the tricolour flag in their own persons and harbour neither communalism nor untouchability in their hearts. . .
7. They will make it a point to give first aid to their injured neighbours and do scavenging and cleaning in the neighbouring villages and instruct village children and adults.
8. They will learn the national language, Hindustani. . . .
9. They will translate into their own mother tongue everything new they may learn, and transmit it in their weekly rounds to the

surrounding villages.

10. They will do nothing in secret, they will be above board in all their dealings, they will lead a pure life of self-restraint, shed all fear and be always ready to protect their weak fellow-students, and be ready to quell riots by nonviolent conduct at the risk of their lives. . . .
11. They will be scrupulously correct and chivalrous in their behaviour towards their girl fellow-students.

. . The effort will add to their equipment, mental, moral and physical, and they will have made even during their studies a substantial contribution to the freedom movement (Constructive Programme: Its Meaning and Place, 13-12-1941; *CWMG* 75: 162-64).

Nayee Talim

Self-Supporting Education (Discussion with an Educationist)

[GANDHIJI:] sounded a warning against the assumption that the idea of self-supporting education sprang from the necessity of achieving total prohibition as soon as possible.

Both are independent necessities. You have to start with the conviction that total prohibition has to be achieved, revenue or no revenue, education or no education. Similarly, you have to start with the conviction that looking to the needs of the villages of India our rural education ought to be made self-supporting if it is to be compulsory.

[THE EDUCATIONIST:] I have the first conviction deep down in me. Prohibition to me is an end in itself, and I regard it as a great education in itself. I should, therefore, sacrifice education altogether to make prohibition a success. But the other conviction is lacking. I cannot yet believe that education can be made self-supporting.

There, too, I want you to start with the conviction. The ways and means will come as you begin to work it out. I regret that I woke up to the necessity of this at this very late age. Otherwise I should have made the experiment myself. Even now, God willing, I shall do what I can to show that it can be self-supporting. But my time has been taken up by other things all these years, equally important perhaps, but it is this stay in Segaon that brought the conviction home to me. We have up to now concentrated on stuffing children's minds with all kinds of information, without ever thinking of stimulating and developing them. Let us now cry a halt and concentrate on educating the child properly through manual work, not as a side activity, but as the prime means of intellectual training.

I see that too. But why should it also support the school?

That will be the test of its value. The child at the age of 14, that is after finishing a seven years' course, should be discharged as an earning unit. Even now the poor people's children automatically lend a helping hand to their parents — the feeling at the back of their minds being, what shall my parents eat and what should they give me to eat if I do not also work with them? That is an education in itself. Even so the state takes charge of the child at seven and returns it to the family as an earning unit. You impart education and simultaneously cut at the root of unemployment. You have to train the boys in one occupation or another. Round this special occupation you will train up his mind, his body, his handwriting, his artistic sense, and so on. He will be master of the craft he learns.

But supposing a boy takes up the art and science of making *khadi*. Do you think it must occupy him all the seven years to master the craft?

Yes. It must, if he will not learn it mechanically. Why do we give years to the study of history or to the study of languages? Is a craft any the less important than these subjects which have been up to now given an artificial importance?

But as you have been mainly thinking of spinning and weaving, evidently you are thinking of making of these schools so many weaving schools. A child may have no aptitude for weaving and may have it for something else.

Quite so. Then we will teach him some other craft. But you must know that one school will not teach many crafts. The idea is that we should have one teacher for twenty-five boys, and you may have as many classes or schools of twenty-five boys as you have teachers available, and have each of these schools specializing in a separate craft — carpentry, smithy, tanning or shoe-making. Only you must bear in mind the fact that you develop the child's mind through each of these crafts. And I would emphasize one more thing. You must forget the cities and concentrate on the villages. They are an ocean. The cities are a mere drop in the ocean. That is why you cannot think of subjects like brick-making. If they must be civil and mechanical engineers, they will after the seven years' course go to the special colleges meant for these higher and specialized courses.

And let me emphasize one more fact. We are apt to think lightly of the village crafts because we have divorced educational from manual training. Manual work has been regarded as something inferior, and owing to the wretched distortion of the *varna* we came to regard spinners and weavers and carpenters and shoe-makers as belonging to the inferior castes and the proletariat. We have had no Cromptons and Hargreaves because of this vicious system of considering the crafts as something inferior divorced from the skilled. If they had been regarded as callings having an independent status of their own equal to the status that learning enjoyed, we should have had great inventors from among our craftsmen. Of course, the "spinning-jenny" led on to the discovery of water-power and other things which made the mill displace the labour of thousands of people. That was, in my view, a monstrosity. We will by concentrating on the villages see that the inventive skill that an intensive learning of the craft will stimulate will subserve the needs of the villager as a whole (*Harijan*, 18-9-1937; Discussion with an Educationist, before 18-9-1937, *CWMG* 66: 137-39).

Newness and Originality

It is necessary to understand the newness or originality in the *Nayee Taleem*. The new scheme of basic education will retain whatever was good in the old system. However, it will have newness in abundance. If there is something genuinely in it, it should result in hope taking the place of despondency, food of poverty, work of unemployment, unity of dissensions and in our boys and girls learning along with reading and writing some craft, for only through the latter will they gain the knowledge of the alphabet (*Harijanbandhu*, 29-1-1939; *Nayee Taleem*, 14-10-1938, *CWMG* 67: 438).

Education through Craft

The principle idea is to impart the whole education of the body and the mind and the soul through the handicraft that is taught to the children. You have to draw out all that is in the child through teaching all the processes of the handicraft, and all your lessons in history, geography, arithmetic will be related to the craft.

If such education is given, the direct result will be that it will be self-supporting. But the test of success is not its self-supporting character, but that the whole man has been drawn out through the teaching of the handicraft in a scientific manner. In fact, I would reject a teacher who would promise to make it self-supporting under any circumstances. The self-supporting part will be the logical corollary of the fact that the pupil has learnt the use of every one of his faculties. If a boy who works at a handicraft for three hours a day will surely earn his keep, how much more a boy who adds to the work a development of his mind and soul! (*Harijan*, 11-6-1938; Talks on Vocational Education, before 11-6-1938, *CWMG* 67: 114-15).

Craft and Curriculum

I have said that all instruction must be linked with some basic craft. When you are imparting knowledge to a child of 7 or 10 through the medium of an industry, you should, to begin with, exclude all those subjects which cannot be linked with the craft. By doing so from day-to-day you will discover ways and means of linking with the craft many things which you had excluded in the beginning. You will save your own energy and the pupils' if you follow this process of exclusion to begin with. We have today no books to go by, no precedents to guide us. Therefore we have to go slow. The main thing is that the teacher should retain his freshness of mind. If you come across something that you cannot correlate with the craft, do not fret over it and get disheartened. Leave it and go ahead with the subjects that you can correlate. Maybe another teacher will hit upon the right way and show how it can be correlated. And when you have pooled the experience of many, you will have books to guide you, so that the work of those who follow you will become easier.

How long, you will ask, are we to go on with this process of exclusion? My reply is, for the whole lifetime. At the end you will find that you have included many things that you had excluded at first, that practically all that was worth including has been included, and whatever you have been obliged to exclude till the end was something very superficial that deserved exclusion. This has been my experience of life. I would not have been able to do many things that I have done if I had not excluded an equal number.

Our education has got to be revolutionized. The brain must be educated through the hand. If I were a poet, I could write poetry on the possibilities of the five fingers. Why should you think that the mind is everything and the hands and feet nothing? Those who do not train their hands, who go through the ordinary rut of education, lack "music" in their life. All their faculties are not trained. Mere book knowledge does not interest the child so as to hold his attention fully. The brain gets weary of mere words, and the child's mind begins to wander. The hand does the things it ought not to do, the eye sees the things it ought not to see, the ear hears the things it ought not to hear, and they do not do, see, or hear, respectively, what they ought to. They are not taught to make the right choice and so their education often proves their ruin. An education which does not teach us to discriminate between good and bad, to assimilate the one and eschew the other is a misnomer.

Shrimati Asha Devi asked Gandhiji to explain to them how the mind could be trained through the hands.

Gandhi: The old idea was to add a handicraft to the ordinary curriculum of education followed in the schools. That is to say, the craft was to be taken in hand wholly separately from education. To me that seems a fatal mistake. The teacher must learn the craft and correlate his knowledge to the craft, so that he will impart all that knowledge to his pupils through the medium of the particular craft that he chooses.

Take the instance of spinning. Unless I know arithmetic I cannot report how many yards of yarn I have produced on the *takli*, or how many standard rounds it will make, or what is the count of the yarn that I have spun. I must learn figures to be able to do so, and I also must learn addition and subtraction and multiplication and division. In dealing with complicated sums I shall have to use symbols and so I get my algebra. Even here, I would insist on the use of Hindustani letters instead of Roman.

Take geometry next. What can be a better demonstration of a circle than the disc of the *takli*? I can teach all about circles in this way, without even mentioning the name of Euclid.

Again, you may ask how I can teach my child geography and history through spinning. Some time ago I came across a book called *Cotton: The Story of Mankind*. It thrilled me. It read like a romance. It began with the history of ancient times, how and when cotton was first grown, the stages of its development, the cotton trade between the different countries, and so on. As I mention the different countries to the child, I shall naturally tell him something about the history and geography of these countries. Under whose reign the different commercial treaties were signed during the different periods? Why has cotton to be imported by some countries and cloth by others? Why can every country not grow the cotton it requires? That will lead me into economics and elements of agriculture. I shall teach him to know the different varieties of cotton, in what kind of soil they grow, how to grow them, from where to get them, and so on. Thus *takli*-spinning leads me into the whole history of the East India Company, what brought them here, how they destroyed our spinning industry, how the economic motive that brought them to India led them later to entertain political aspirations, how it became a causative factor in the downfall of the Moguls and the Marathas, in the establishment of the English Raj, and then again in the awakening of the masses in our times. There is thus no end to the educative possibilities of this new scheme. And how much quicker the child will learn all that, without putting an unnecessary tax on his mind and memory.

Let me further elaborate the idea. Just as a biologist, in order to become a good biologist, must learn many other sciences besides biology, the basic education, if it is treated as a science, takes us into interminable channels of learning. To extend the example of the *takli*, a pupil teacher, who rivets his attention not merely on the mechanical process of spinning, which of course he must master, but on the spirit of the thing, will concentrate on the *takli* and its various aspects. He will ask himself why the *takli* is made out of a brass disc and has a steel spindle. The original *takli* had its disc made anyhow. The still more primitive *takli* consisted of a wooden spindle with a disc of slate or clay. The *takli* has been developed scientifically, and there is a reason for making the disc out of brass and the spindle out of steel. He must find out that reason. Then, the teacher must ask himself why the disc has that particular diameter, no more and no less. When he has solved these questions satisfactorily and has gone into the mathematics of the thing, your pupil becomes a good engineer. The *takli* becomes his *Kamadhenu* — the "Cow of plenty". There is no limit to the possibilities of knowledge that can be imparted through this medium. It will be limited only by the energy and conviction with which you work. You have been here for three weeks. You will have spent them usefully if it has enabled you to take to this scheme seriously, so that you will say to yourself, "I shall either do or die".

I am elaborating the instance of spinning because I know it. If I were a carpenter, I would teach my child all these things through carpentry, or through cardboard work if I were a worker in cardboard.

What we need is educationists with originality, fired with true zeal, who will think out from day-to-day what they are going to teach their pupils. The teacher cannot get this knowledge through musty volumes. He has to use his own faculties of observation and thinking and impart his knowledge to the children through his lips, with the help of a craft. This means a revolution in the method of teaching, a revolution in the teacher's outlook. Up till now you have been guided by inspectors' reports. You wanted to do what the inspector might like, so that you might get more money yet for your institutions or higher salaries for yourselves. But the new teacher will not care for all that. He will say, "I have done my duty by my pupil if I have made him a better man and in doing so I have used all my resources. That is enough for me".

Q. In training pupil teachers, would it not be better if they are first taught a craft separately and then given a sound exposition of the method of teaching through the medium of that craft? As it is, they are advised to imagine themselves to be of the age of 7 and relearn everything through a craft. In this way it will take them years before they can master the new technique and become competent teachers.

G. No, it would not take them years. Let us imagine that the teacher when he comes to me has a working knowledge of mathematics and history and other subjects. I teach him to make cardboard boxes or to spin. While he is at it I show him how he could have derived his knowledge of mathematics, history and geography through the particular craft. He thus learns how to link his knowledge to the craft. It should not take him long to do so. Take another instance. Suppose I go with my boy of 7 to a basic school. We both learn spinning and I get all my previous knowledge linked with spinning. To the boy it is all new. For the 70-year-old father it is all repetition but he will have his old knowledge in a new setting. He should not take more than a few weeks for the process. Thus, unless the teacher develops the receptivity and eagerness of the child of 7, he will end up by becoming a mere mechanical spinner, which would not fit him for the new method.

Q. A boy who has passed his matriculation can go to college if he wishes to. Will a child who has gone through the basic education syllabus too be able to do so?

G. Between the boy who has passed his matriculation and the boy who has gone through basic education, the latter will give a better account of himself because his faculties have been developed. He would not feel helpless when he goes to college as matriculates often do.

Q. Seven has been put down as the minimum age for admission of children to a basic education school. Is it to be a chronological or mental age?

G. Seven should be the average minimum age, but there will be some children of a higher and some of a lower age as well. There is physical as well as mental age to be considered. One child at the age of 7 may have attained sufficient physical development to handle a craft. Another one may not be able to do so even at 7. One cannot therefore lay down any hard and fast rules. All the factors have to be taken into consideration.

Many questions show that many of you are filled with doubts. This is the wrong way of going about the work. You should have robust faith. If you have the conviction that I have, that Wardha education is the thing required to give training for life to millions of our children, your work will flourish. If you have not that faith, there is something wrong with those in charge of your training. They should be able to imbue you with this faith, whatever else they may or may not give you.

Q. The basic education scheme is supposed to be for the villages. Is there no way out for the city-dwellers? Are they to go along the old rut?

G. This is a pertinent question and a good one, but I have answered it already in the columns of *Harijan*. Sufficient for the day is the good thereof. As it is, we have a big enough morsel to bite. If we can solve the educational problem of seven lakhs of villages, it will be enough for the present. No doubt educationists are thinking of the cities too. But if we take up the question of the cities along with that of the villages, we will fritter away our energies.

Q. Supposing in a village there were three schools with a different craft in each, the scope for learning may be wider in one than in the other. To which school out of these should the child go?

G. Such overlapping should not occur. For the majority of our villages are too small to have more than one school. But a big village may have more. Here the craft taught in both should be the same. But I should lay down no hard and fast rule. Experience in such matters would be the best guide. The capacity of various crafts to become popular, their ability to draw out the faculties of the student, should be studied. The idea is that whatever craft you choose, it should draw out the faculties of the child fully and equally. It should be a village craft and it should be useful.

Q. Why should a child waste 7 years on learning a craft when his real profession is going to be something else, e.g., why should a banker's son, who is expected to take to banking later on, learn spinning for 7 years?

G. The question betrays gross ignorance of the new scheme of education. The boy under the scheme of basic education does not go to school merely to learn a craft. He goes there to receive his primary education, to train his mind through the craft. I claim that the boy who has gone through the new course of primary education for seven years, will make a better banker than the one who has gone through the seven years of ordinary schooling. The latter when he goes to a banking school will be ill at ease because all his faculties will not have been trained. Prejudices die hard. I will have done a good day's work if I have made you realize this one central fact that the new education scheme is not a little of literary education and a little of craft. It is full education up to the primary stage through the medium of a craft.

Q. Would it not be better to teach more than one craft in every school? The children might begin to feel bored of doing the same thing from month to month and year to year.

G. If I find a teacher who becomes dull to his students after a month's spinning, I should dismiss him. There will be newness in every lesson such as there can be new music on the same instrument. By changing over from one craft to another a child tends to become like a monkey jumping from branch to branch with abode nowhere. But I have shown already in the course of our discussion that teaching spinning in a scientific spirit involves learning many things besides spinning. The child will be taught to make his own *takli* and his own winder soon. Therefore, to go back to what I began with, if the teacher takes up the craft in a scientific spirit, he will speak to his pupils through many channels, all of which will contribute to the development of all his faculties (*Harijan*, 18-2-1939 and 4-3-1939; Discussion with Teacher Trainees, 3/4-2-1939, *CWMG* 68: 372-77).

Basic Education

. . . Basic education has grown out of the atmosphere surrounding us in the country and is in response to it. It is, therefore, designed to cope with that atmosphere. This atmosphere pervades India's seven hundred thousand villages and its millions of inhabitants. Forget them and you forget India. India is not to be found in her cities. It is in her innumerable villages. . . .

Let us now glance at the fundamentals of basic education:

1. All education to be true must be self-supporting, that is to say, in the end it will pay its expenses excepting the capital which will remain intact.
2. In it the cunning of the hand will be utilized even up to the final stage, that is to say, the hands of the pupils will be skilfully working at some industry for some period during the day.
3. All education must be imparted through the medium of the provincial language.
4. In this there is no room for giving sectional religious training. Fundamental universal ethics will have full scope.
5. This education, whether it is confined to children or adults, male or female, will find its way to the homes of the pupils.
6. Since millions of students receiving this education will consider themselves as of the whole of India, they must learn an interprovincial language. This common interprovincial speech can only be Hindustani written in the Nagari or Urdu script. Therefore pupils have to master both the scripts (*Harijan*, 2-11-1947; Of New Universities, *CWMG* 89: 404-05).

Just Social Order

What kinds of vocations are the fittest for being taught to children in urban schools? There is no hard and fast rule about it. But my reply is clear. I want to resuscitate the villages of India. Today our villages have become a mere appendage to the cities. They exist, as it were, to be exploited by the latter and depend on the latter's sufferance. This is unnatural. It is only when the cities realize the duty of making an adequate return to the villages for the strength and sustenance which they derive from them, instead of selfishly exploiting them, that a healthy and moral relationship between the two will spring up, and if the city children are to play their part in this great and noble work of social reconstruction, the vocations through which they are to receive their education ought to be directly related to the requirements of the villages. So far as I can see, the various processes of cotton manufacture from ginning and cleaning of cotton to the spinning of yarn answer this test as nothing else does. Even today cotton is grown in the villages and is ginned and spun and converted into cloth in the cities. But the chain of processes which cotton undergoes in the mills from the beginning to the end constitutes a huge tragedy of waste in men, materials and mechanical power.

My plan to impart primary education through the medium of village handicrafts like spinning and carding, etc., is thus conceived as the spearhead of a silent social revolution fraught with the most far-reaching consequence. It will provide a healthy and moral basis of relationship between the city and the village and thus go a long way towards eradicating some of the worst evils of the present social insecurity and poisoned relationship between the classes. It will check the progressive decay of our villages and lay the foundation of a juster social order in which there is no unnatural division between the "haves" and "have-nots" and everybody is assured of a living wage and the right to freedom. And all this would be accomplished without the horrors of a bloody class war or a colossal capital expenditure such as would be involved in the mechanization of a vast continent like India. Nor would it entail a helpless dependence on foreign imported machinery or technical skill. Lastly, by obviating the necessity for highly specialized talent, it would place the destiny of the masses, as it were, in their own hands. But who will bell the cat? Will the city folk listen to me at all? Or, will mine remain a mere cry in the wilderness? Replies to these and similar questions will depend more on lovers of education like my correspondent living in cities than on me (*Harijan*, 9-10-1937; Primary Education in Bombay, *CWMG* 66: 169-70).

Manual Labour

One of the complaints that has been made by one of you is that too much emphasis is laid here on manual work. I am a firm believer in the educative value of manual work. Our present educational system is meant for strengthening and perpetuating the imperialist power in India. Those of you who have been brought up under it have naturally developed a taste for it and so find labour irksome. No one in government schools or college bothers to teach the students how to clean the roads or latrines. Here cleanliness and sanitation form the very Alpha and Omega of your training. Scavenging is a fine art you should take pains to learn. Persistent questioning and healthy inquisitiveness are the first requisites for acquiring learning of any kind. Inquisitiveness should be tempered by humility and respectful regard for the teacher. It must not degenerate into impudence. The latter is the enemy of receptivity of mind. There can be no knowledge without humility and the will to learn.

Useful manual labour, intelligently performed, is the means par excellence for developing the intellect. One may develop a sharp intellect otherwise too. But then it will not be a balanced growth but an unbalanced distorted abortion. It might easily make of one a rogue and a rascal. A balanced intellect presupposes a harmonious growth of body, mind and soul. That is why we give to manual labour the central place in our curriculum of training here. An intellect that is developed through the medium of socially useful labour will be an instrument for service and will not easily be led astray or fall into devious paths. The latter can well be a scourge. If you grasp that essential point, the money spent by your respective governments in sending you here for training will have been well-spent (*Harijan*, 8-9-1946; Address to Trainees of Basic Teachers' Camp, 23-8-1946, *CWMG* 85: 199-200).

3

Stages of Education

Infant Education

We should try to draw all the children towards us. We should admit that it is our fault if some do not come to us. They should all want to come to us.

We should treat those children who come to us as our own children. If their body and mind become sound and they acquire normal discipline, we should be satisfied that our purpose has been served.

I have taught many boys. I never allowed them to indulge in mischief. If they were under my care, I would educate them in such a way that they would learn from their very childhood that the desire to destroy was a very bad thing. Whatever they do, they should create something, produce something. There is an art in making anything and whatever they make should be artistic.

I do not believe that children are either good or bad from their very birth. Some tendency is there, but we have to mould them. This means that an infant starts learning right from the time of conception. At that time I would teach the mother. That would be a part of adult education. The training of the infant begins from that stage. We have to train the future generation on these lines. Till the child is separated from the mother, I would teach the mother. The infant is ever moving its hands and feet and is able to do something. If we are able to take under our care children of two or two and a half years of age and if they learn to move their hands and feet according to our method, I cannot set any limits to their progress.

If the child is put under our care, he will not destroy anything. He will feel hurt in doing so.

Whatever education we give to the children, it should be constructive and creative but never destructive.

When the child starts speaking, he starts learning a language. First you should teach him to distinguish different colours. Begin teaching him the letters of the alphabet only with the help of the pictures. Don't you have charts showing 1-2, A-B and so on? Reading, writing and arithmetic will come in due course of time and the child will not be overstrained. His education should be a form of play.

Whatever thing he makes should be useful. In this way his mind and hands and feet develop in coordination.

There are no distinctions between work and play in basic education. For a child everything is play. I would go so far as to say that thus his whole life becomes a kind of game. I have been doing this for many years now. I never feel that it is time for play and I should go and play. For me even writing is a game. Under basic education of my conception children will learn while playing (*Harijan Sevak,* 17-3-1946; Speech to Teachers, Sevagram, 17-2-1946, *CWMG* 83: 147-48).

Early Childhood Education

The subject of child education, which ought to be the simplest, appears to have become difficult or to have been made so. Experience teaches us that, whether we wish it or not, children do receive some education, good or bad. To many readers, this sentence may sound strange, but if we consider whom we can call a child, what education means and who can impart child education, perhaps we shall find nothing novel in the above sentence. A child means a boy or girl under the age of ten or anyone who appears to be of that age.

Education does not mean a knowledge of the alphabet. This type of knowledge is only a means to education. Education implies a child's learning how to put his mind and all his senses to good use. That is to say, he really learns how to use his hands, feet and other organs of action and his nose, ear and other organs of sense. A child who has acquired the knowledge that he should not use his hands for stealing or for killing flies, nor for beating up his companions or younger brothers and sisters, has already begun his education. He has started it, we can say, when he understands the necessity of keeping his body, his teeth, tongue, ears, head, nails, etc., clean and keeps them clean. That child has made good progress in education who does not indulge in mischief while eating and drinking, eats and drinks alone or in society in a proper manner, sits properly and chooses pure foodstuffs knowing the difference between pure and impure foodstuffs, does not eat like a glutton, does not clamour for whatever he sees and remains calm even if he does not get what he wants. Even that child has advanced on the road to education whose pronunciation is correct, who can recount to us the history and geography of the country surrounding him without knowing those terms and who understands what his country means. That child has made very good progress in his education who can understand the difference between truth and untruth, worth and worthlessness and chooses the good and the true, while rejecting the bad and the untrue. There is no need now to dilate on this point. The reader can supply other attributes himself. Only one thing needs to be made clear. In all this, one sees no need of a knowledge of the alphabet or of any script. To engage children in learning the script is tantamount to putting a burden on their mind and other organs and is like putting their eyes and hands to bad use. A child who has received true education easily picks up a knowledge of the alphabet at the appropriate time and in an interesting way. Today, knowledge becomes a sort of burden to children, their best time for development is spent uselessly, and in the end, instead of writing a beautiful hand and reading in a beautiful way, their handwriting is like the housefly's legs, and they read mostly what should not be read and even what they do read, they read wrongly. To call this education is blasphemy, or sacrilege. Before a child receives a knowledge of the alphabet, it should have received primary education. If this is done, one can be spared in this poor land the expenditure on many series of readers and primers and a lot of nonsense. If there must be a primer, it ought to be only for the teachers, and never for the children described by me. If we are not being carried away in the prevailing current, this matter ought to appear as clear as a lamp.

A child can receive the education outlined above even in the home and that too from the mother herself. Hence children receive elementary education from their mothers. If our homes are broken up and divided today, if the parents have forgotten their duty to their children, the children should, as far as possible, be educated under conditions providing a family-like environment. Only a mother can discharge this duty; hence child education should be placed in charge of women alone. A man has not generally till now been able to show the love and patience that a woman can. If all of this is true, the moment we tackle the question of child education, that of the education of women naturally stares us in the face. And until we have mothers capable of imparting education to children, I have no hesitation in saying that children will remain without education despite their attending hundreds of schools.

Now I shall give a sketch of child education. Let us suppose that five children have been placed in charge of a woman in the role of a mother. These children do not know how to talk or walk and they have running noses, they clean their nasal mucus with their hands and wipe it on their legs or their clothes. There is rheum in their eyes, there is wax in their ears and dirt in their nails. Even when asked to sit down properly they sit awkwardly, spreading out their legs, saliva drips when they speak, they say *hun* for *shun* and use the first person plural for the first person singular. They have no idea of east, west, north and south. They are wearing soiled clothes, their private parts are exposed, they toy with them and, if asked not to do so, they do it all the more. If their clothes have pockets, these are filled with some dirty sweets, which they eat from time to time, dropping some of these on the floor and making their sticky hands stickier. Their caps have become jet-black at the border and a bad odour issues from them. Only if motherly feelings spring up in the woman who looks after these five children can she teach them. The first lesson will certainly be to put them in good shape. The mother will give them a bath lovingly, she will do nothing but crack jokes with them for several days and in many ways, just as mothers have done till this day, just as Kausalya did with little Rama; she will bind them in the bonds of her love and train them to dance to her tune. Until the mother succeeds in this, just as a cow distractedly runs here and there for her lost calf, she will become anxious about those five children. She will not rest so long as the children have not learnt to be normally clean, their teeth, ears, hands and feet have not become clean, their stinking clothes have not been changed, and *hun* has not become *shun*. After gaining this much control over them, the mother will teach the children the first lesson of Ramanama. Some will call Him Rama, some will call Him Rahman, but it is all the same. Economics will surely come after religion. And so the mother will now start teaching them arithmetic. She will teach the children the multiplication tables and addition and subtraction orally. Children ought to know about the place where they reside; hence she will point out to them the adjoining rivers and channels, hillocks and buildings and while doing so give them an idea of the directions. And she will add to her own knowledge for the sake of the children. In this concept, history and geography can never be separate subjects. Knowledge of both can be imparted in the form of stories only. The mother cannot be satisfied with this much. A Hindu mother lets her children hear the sound of Sanskrit from their childhood and therefore makes them learn by rote verses in praise of God and trains the children in correct pronunciation. A patriotic mother will surely give them knowledge of Hindi. Hence, she will talk to children in Hindi, read to them from Hindi books and turn them bilingual. She will not at this stage impart to them knowledge of writing, but will surely place a brush in their hands. She will make them draw geometrical figures, straight lines, circles, etc. A mother will not at all concede that the children who do not draw a flower or a jug or a triangle, have received education. And she will not deprive children of music. She will not tolerate it if the children do not sing in chorus and in a sweet voice national songs, devotional songs, etc. She will teach them to sing in rhythm. If she is a good teacher, she places a one-stringed instrument in their hands, gives them cymbals and teaches them a dance with sticks in which both boys and girls join. In order to develop their bodies, she makes them do physical exercise, makes them run and jump. And because the spirit of service is to be inculcated in them and they are to be taught some craft too, she would teach them to pick cotton pods and break them open, to gin and card cotton and to spin it and the children would playfully spin for at least half an hour every day.

Most of the books we come across nowadays are useless for this curriculum. Her love will provide the books for every mother, because there will be different books of history and geography in every village and sums in arithmetic are of course to be set anew. A dedicated mother will prepare herself every day and will make up new stories and new sums in her notebook and teach them to the children.

It should not be necessary to prolong this curriculum. A quarterly course of studies can be drawn up from it, because the children have been brought up in different environments. Hence we can never have a uniform curriculum. We can draw up courses for them from time to time as and when the children come to us. Sometimes children come to us having learnt wrong things; we have to make them unlearn these. If a six-seven-year-old child is writing an indifferent hand or is in the habit of reading *ma bhu pa,* we have to make him forget it. Until the false notion that the child will gain knowledge through reading is removed from his mind, he cannot make headway. It can easily be conceived that even he who has not mastered a knowledge of the alphabet throughout his life may become unlearned.

I have made no use in this article of the word "teacher". A teacher is a mother. She who cannot take the place of a mother can never become a teacher. A child should not feel that it is receiving education. The child whose mother's eyes follow it everywhere is receiving education all the twenty-four hours. A child who sits six hours in a school may not be receiving any education at all. In this topsyturvy life, perhaps we may not find women teachers. It may well be that child education is practicable at present only through men teachers. Then the men teachers will have to acquire the noble status of a mother and ultimately the mothers will have to get ready for this job. But if my concept is right, any mother, if she has love in her heart, can become fit with a little assistance. And while preparing herself, she will prepare the children as well (*Navajivan*, 2-6-1929; Ideal Primary School for Children, *CWMG* 41: 5-9).

Montessori Education

I have no difficulty in agreeing with the scientific views of Madame Montessori. However, if they are propagated in their Western garb in Indian villages they are more likely to prove useless and might even prove harmful, because in that garb they will be too expensive for Indian villages and ill-adapted to the village atmosphere. It is possible the cities may not feel the expense so much and women influenced by Western ways may be receptive to the ideas presented in Western garb; but even so it will be of no use because India lives not in cities but in its seven lakh villages. Besides, scientific education with Western trappings might prove poisonous to the city dwellers because here education begins the moment the child is conceived and ends no one knows when. These days the cities are created by the foreigners to serve their ends and so they do not represent the villages. They do not protect the interests of the villagers but are becoming their exploiters (Note to Saraladevi Sarabhai, 12-4-1945, *CWMG* 79: 370-71).

Nursery Education

I saw the work done by teachers trained under Madame Montessori, and carefully observed the working of the Nursery School. Of course, the things were foreign and the poor teacher had not digested what she had been taught. What to speak of the children? They could not even observe normal discipline. I am not criticizing anyone. I have given the gist of my experience just for your information. Imbibe whatever you find useful and discard the rest. The conclusion I have drawn from this experience is that we shall be able to propagate scientific knowledge of child education only when our teachers are competent. They should have the will to become one with children. I am afraid I am not saying anything new in this. These things are certainly not beyond your range of experience but since I have come to know you and also love you I hope you will not find fault with me for saying the things you already know (Letter to Tarabehn Modak, 16-10-1945, *CWMG* 81: 364).

Primary Education

From many years of reflection and quite a few experiments, I have come to the conclusion that primary education should be given for at least a year without using any textbooks and even after that pupils should make the minimum use of them.

When a child is learning the alphabet, when he is trying to master the forms of numerals and letters, his senses remain dormant and his intelligence, instead of blossoming, becomes stunted. A child starts learning immediately after birth but it does so mainly through the eyes and ears. It learns language as soon as it starts speaking. Hence the child is as its parents are. If the latter are cultured, the child pronounces words correctly and imitates the right ways of the home. This alone constitutes his true education and were it not that our civilization has become so disrupted, children would be receiving the best education in the home itself.

But we are not yet in such a happy situation. There is no alternative to sending children to schools.

However, if children must go to schools, these should feel like homes to them and their teachers should be as parents. The education given also should be similar to that which is imparted in a cultured home. In other words, children must receive their primary education from teachers through the spoken word. By receiving education in this manner can a child gain in a year through his eyes and ears ten times the knowledge he can acquire through the alphabet.

The child will have got a general knowledge of history and geography in the first year through play and in the form of stories. He will have learnt some poems by heart with their correct pronunciation. He will have memorized his tables. Moreover, as the child will not be burdened with having to identify letters of the alphabet, his mind will be kept from withering and his eyes will not be misused.

The child's hand, instead of being used to form crooked letters on a slate and trying to understand the difficult symbols that are letters, would rather be engaged in drawing geometrical lines and recognizing pictures. This is the primary education of the hands.

And if we wish to impart primary education to the crores of children of Gujarat and of India, we shall not be able to do so in any other way.

Under the present circumstances, it is impossible for this country to see that books reach crores of children. I admit that if it is necessary to supply children with books in order to give them primary education, we should try to do so, whatever the cost. However, if books are regarded as superfluous and harmful, the practical argument may be put forward. What is unnecessary or harmful from an ethical standpoint is also found to be impractical. In a civilization that is free from flaws, the ethical and the practical are not opposed to each other and should not be.

It is clear that such education cannot be given by the teachers of present-day primary schools. These teachers may thrash the children and make them learn the alphabet and perhaps a few numbers. The poor teacher himself does not have the general knowledge which I visualize for the child in the first year. When the teachers themselves do not know how to speak the language in its pure form, how can the children learn it from them? (*Navajivan*, 13-5-1928; Primary Education – I, *CWMG* 36: 316-17).

Secondary Education

It is the duty and the right of the latter (National College) to find new methods in the field of education which would sustain the national cause. And in my humble opinion, we can take these methods in a very small measure from Europe and in an even smaller measure from the current trends in India. In every country education is for the preservation of its independence.

Hence we shall have to conduct new experiments in our education. In doing so, we may well make ourselves familiar with the experience in Europe; but we should not conclude that all that is found there is good or what is good under the conditions prevailing there will be good for us. One of the conclusions that emerges from this is that we should regard with suspicion the methods practised in the government schools. Since the education imparted by the government is fatal to *swaraj* as well as to our civilization, it is possible that if we follow the opposite methods in many matters we may find the right path. Let us take an example.

The medium of instruction there is English, hence we must conclude that the medium of national education cannot be English.

They put up huge expensive buildings in which to give education. We should realize that this is improper. Our school buildings should be simple and inexpensive. Stress there is purely on literary learning and India's industries are ignored. We know that this is improper.

In that form of education, teaching of religion, that is, religion not of any particular community but universal religion, has no place. We know that this leads to a negation of education.

The history that is taught in government schools is, if not false, written from the British standpoint. The very same facts have been interpreted differently by German, French and American historians. Contemporary events are interpreted by the government in one way and by the people in another, as in the case of the massacre in the Punjab.

The economics taught in government schools upholds the British system while we, on the other hand, view it differently. Government schools make a plea for the town civilization, whereas the villages are the soul of our national civilization.

In government primary schools, their teachers, with the minimum amount of knowledge, are employed without regard to their character and on the minimum salaries possible, whereas in national primary schools, the teachers being self-sacrificing and persons of character and learning (and not because they are in a sorry plight), should accept the smallest salaries.

We can now have an idea of the kind of education that should be given in the city schools.

Our pupils should live in villages, lend stability to village civilization, be familiar with the needs of villages, rid them of such faults as they may have, teach their children not to become city dwellers but to remain villagers, i.e., to become farmers. Hence so long as the existing system of education in the cities is not basically changed without fear, we shall not attain one of the basic ideals of the Vidyapith nor may we be said to practise it.

Let us take only one example: In Ahmedabad itself we are running a university, a new Gujarati school and a Vinay Mandir. We shall have the right to run them only when we attempt to make villagers out of the children who study in them, when we succeed in making them take interest in village life, when we make them understand the latter, and, finally, when those of them who are about to leave the Vinay Mandir or the University, spread out into the villages and start serving the villagers (*Navajivan*, 20-5-1928; Primary Education – II, *CWMG* 36: 327-29).

Rural Education

The problems of primary education or village education can be solved only when we thoroughly change the curricula of the Vidya Mandir and the University and when the teachers have understood my viewpoint.

Today we hesitate to effect certain changes for fear of losing pupils, for fear of public opinion or from a sense of false prestige. If we had no hesitation these Vidya Mandirs would produce a fine set of people who would serve the villages and this would somewhat atone for the sins of the cities.

The pupils of these Mandirs would become first-class spinners, carders and weavers; they would have the best knowledge of cotton growing, they would know carpentry to suit the needs of the village; in other words, they would know how to make good spinning wheels, they would know how to repair — if not make — bullock carts, ploughs, etc., they would know sewing enough for the needs of the village, their handwriting would be as beautiful as pearls, they would have a basic ability to write, they would know Indian multiplication tables, they would be familiar with ancient literature like the *Ramayana* and the *Mahabharata* and their modern spiritual meaning; they would know village games; they would be familiar with the rules of hygiene, they would be good home-doctors, i.e., they would be able to diagnose common ailments and prescribe remedies for them; they would know how to clean village dumping-grounds, ponds, wells and so on. In other words, education in these schools would be such that it enables the pupils to serve the villages in every way and the expenses incurred should be regarded as having been incurred on primary education. Only when we do so and are able to do so, can we be said to have truly entered the villages.

But directly such a question is raised, such a change brought about and such an ideal proclaimed, our Vidya Mandirs will become empty. Should such a contingency arise I would be willing to welcome it in the cause of truth. But so long as the ideal of the Vidyapith regarding village education remains what it is, not to do this would amount to untruth and betrayal.

However, it is my belief as well as my experience that if we remain steadfast in our objective, the public will in the end understand it and help in advancing it. If we looked into the causes of failures — so called or so considered — we would find that those who believed in the ideals were themselves disloyal, half-baked and half-hearted. He who doubts will perish, but people instead of taking his doom for what it is think that it was his ideal that was wanting in some way and so failed.

It is my firm belief that if our Vidya Mandirs had teachers with faith and a spirit of self-sacrifice, they would overflow with pupils. People can recognize a genuine thing. Often it seems to take time, but that is merely an illusion. It is a rule without an exception that the straight path is the quickest.

An institution which panders to people's weaknesses and their love of pleasure may fill in no time. So what? That certainly does not prove its success. One consequence may however flow from the acceptance of my viewpoint. Those pupils who have come in the hope of getting the same kind of education as is imparted in government schools, those who have come in the hope of acquiring fitness to lead a city life, would be disappointed and leave our Mandirs. But it would be as well. We as well as they would be saved from a false situation, would be able to render true service to one another.

I should like to close this series by dilating a little more on the idea with which I started it. And then I hope to discuss a few questions I have before me on this subject.

If the view that a knowledge of the alphabet should be totally avoided during the first year of primary education is correct, some of its desirable consequences ought to be apparent in the Vidya Mandirs and the University.

Nowadays the cult of bookish knowledge has increased a great deal. New books are being published every day. Anyone who has any command over language, anyone who has reflected even a little, becomes eager to put his ideas into print and believes that in so doing he is rendering national service. Consequently, an unbearable burden is placed on the brains of pupils and the pockets of their guardians. The pupil's intellect becomes confused. Their brains stuffed with a multitude of facts have no room for any original thought. And even facts instead of being properly arranged lie about in disorder in these brains like things in the house of an idle person. They are of no use either to themselves or to the public.

Hence in my opinion the numerous books that are published nowadays should not be given to the pupils. Even literate pupils should receive the larger part of their education orally from the teachers. They should read the minimum number of books but should reflect on what they read and while doing so translate into practice whatever they find acceptable. By doing so, the life of the pupils will become interesting, thoughtful, wise, steadfast, pure and energetic. Such education befits a poor nation and will prove useful to the pupils and the public. Hence the solution to the serious problem before the Vidyapith depends on the capacity of its present teachers to imbibe its ideals and to make a mighty effort to put them into practice (*Navajivan*, 27-5-1928; Primary Education – III, *CWMG* 36: 343-45).

4

Nature and Working of Universities

Higher Education

. . . I do hold very strong views on education in general, including what is called higher education. . . . I am always eager to discover them and more than eager to correct them.

Let me now state my conclusions held for a number of years and enforced wherever I had opportunity of enforcing them:

1. I am not opposed to education even of the highest type attainable in the world.
2. The state must pay for it wherever it has definite use for it.
3. I am opposed to all higher education being paid for from the general revenue.
4. It is my firm conviction that the vast amount of the so-called education in arts, given in our colleges, is sheer waste and has resulted in unemployment among the educated classes. What is more, it has destroyed the health, both mental and physical, of the boys and girls who have the misfortune to go through the grind in our colleges.
5. The medium of a foreign language through which higher education has been imparted in India has caused incalculable intellectual and moral injury to the nation. We are too near our own times to judge the enormity of the damage done. And we who have received such education have both to be victims and judges — an almost impossible feat.

. . . Thus I claim that I am not an enemy of higher education. But I am an enemy of higher education as it is given in this country. Under my scheme there will be more and better libraries, more and better laboratories, more and better research institutes. Under it we should have an army of chemists, engineers and other experts who will be real servants of the nation and answer the varied and growing requirements of a people who are becoming increasingly conscious of their rights and wants. And all these experts will speak not a foreign language but the language of the people. The knowledge gained by them will be the common property of the people. There will be truly original work instead of mere imitation. And the cost will be evenly and justly distributed (*Harijan*, 9-7-1938; Higher Education, *CWMG* 67: 159-63).

National University

The National University stands today as a protest against British injustice, and as a vindication of national honour. But it has come to stay. It draws its inspiration from the national ideals of a united India. It stands for a religion which is the Dharma of the Hindus and Islam of Mohammedans. It wants to rescue the Indian vernaculars from unmerited oblivion and make them the fountains of national regeneration and Indian culture. It holds that a systematic study of Asiatic cultures is no less essential than the study of Western sciences for a complete education for life. The vast treasures of Sanskrit and Arabic, Persian and Pali, and Magadhi have to be ransacked in order to discover wherein lies the source of strength for the nation. It does not propose merely to feed on, or repeat, the ancient cultures. It rather hopes to build a new culture based on the traditions of the past, enriched by the experience of later times. It stands for the synthesis of the different cultures that have come to stay in India, that have influenced Indian life and that, in their turn, have themselves been influenced by the spirit of the soil. This synthesis will naturally be of the *swadeshi* type where each culture is assured its legitimate place, and not of American pattern, where one dominant culture absorbs the rest, and where the aim is not towards harmony, but towards an artificial and forced unity. That is why the university has desired a study of all the Indian religions by its students. The Hindus may thus have an opportunity of studying the Koran and the Muslims of knowing what the Hindu Shastras contain. If the university has excluded anything, it is the spirit of exclusion that regards any section of humanity as permanently untouchable. The study of Hindustani, which is a national blend of Sanskrit, Hindi and Persianized Urdu, has been made compulsory. The spirit of independence will be fostered not only through Religion, Politics and History but through vocational training also, which alone can give the youths of the country economic independence and a backbone that comes out of a sense of self-respect. The university hopes to organize higher schools throughout the mofussil towns, so that education may be spread broadcast and filtered down to the masses as early as possible. The use of Gujarati as the medium of education will facilitate this process and, before long, the suicidal cleavage between the educated and the non-educated will be bridged. And as an effect of industrial education to the genteel folks, and literary education for the industrial classes, the unequal distribution of wealth and the consequent social discontent will be considerably checked. The greatest defect of the government universities has been their alien control and the false values they have created as regards "careers". The Gujarat University by non-cooperating with the government has automatically eradicated both these evils from its own system. If the founders and promoters stick to this resolve till the government becomes nationalized, it will help them to cultivate a clear perception of national ideals and national needs (Tagore, pp. 445-57; 17-11-1920; *Towards New Education*, by M.K. Gandhi, edited by Bhartan Kumarappa, 1953, Navajivan Publications, pp. 74-75).

College Education

I would revolutionize college education and relate it to national necessities. There would be degrees for mechanical and other engineers. They would be attached to the different industries which should pay for the training of the graduates they need. Thus the Tatas would be expected to run a college for training engineers under the supervision of the state, the mill associations would run among them a college for training graduates whom they need. Similarly for the other industries that may be named. Commerce will have its college. There remain arts, medicine and agriculture. Several private arts colleges are today self-supporting. The state would, therefore, cease to run its own. Medical colleges would be attached to certified hospitals. As they are popular among monied men they may be expected by voluntary contributions to support medical colleges. And agricultural colleges to be worthy of the name must be self-supporting. I have a painful experience of some agricultural graduates. Their knowledge is superficial. They lack practical experience. But if they had their apprenticeship on farms which are self-sustained and answer the requirements of the country, they would not have to gain experience after getting their degrees and at the expense of their employers (*Harijan*, 31-7-1937; Criticism Answered, *CWMG* 65: 451).

State Universities

Higher education should be left to private enterprise and for meeting national requirements whether in the various industries, technical arts, belles-lettres or fine arts.

The state universities should be purely examining bodies, self-supporting through the fees charged for examinations.

Universities will look after the whole of the field of education and will prepare and approve courses of studies in the various departments of education. No private school should be run without the previous sanction of the respective universities. University charters should be given liberally to any body of persons of proved worth and integrity, it being always understood that the universities will not cost the state anything except that it will bear the cost of running a Central Education Department.

The foregoing scheme does not absolve the state from running such seminaries as may be required for supplying state needs (*Harijan*, 2-10-1937; Questions Before Educational Conference, *CWMG* 66: 195).

Self-supporting Universities

I have pictured to myself an India continually progressing along the lines best suited to her genius. I do not, however, picture it as a third-class or even a first-class copy of the dying civilization of the West. If my dream is fulfilled, and every one of the seven lakhs of villages becomes a well-living republic in which there are no illiterates, in which no one is idle for want of work, in which everyone is usefully occupied and has nourishing food, well-ventilated dwellings and sufficient *khadi* for covering the body, and in which all the villagers know and observe the laws of hygiene and sanitation, such a state must have varied and increasing needs, which it must supply unless it would stagnate. I can therefore well imagine the state financing all the education my correspondent mentions and much more that I could add. And if the state has such requirements, surely it will have corresponding libraries.

What, however, according to my view the state will not have is an army of B.A.s and M.A.s with their brains sapped with too much cramming and minds almost paralysed by the impossible attempt to speak and write English like Englishmen. The majority of these have no work, no employment. And when they have the latter, it is usually clerkships at which most of the knowledge gained during their twelve years of high school and college is of no use whatsoever to them.

University training becomes self-supporting when it is utilized by the state. It is criminal to pay for a training which benefits neither the nation nor the individual. In my opinion there is no such thing as individual benefit which cannot be proved to be also national benefit. And since most of my critics seem to be agreed that the existing higher education, and for that matter both primary and secondary, are not connected with realities, it cannot be of benefit to the state. When it is directly based on realities and is wholly given through the mother tongue, I shall perhaps have nothing to say against it. To be based on realities is to be based on national, i.e., state, requirements. And the state will pay for it. Even when that happy time comes, we shall find that many institutions will be conducted by voluntary contributions. They may or may not benefit the state. Much of what passes for education today in India belongs to that category and would therefore not be paid for from the general revenue, if I had the way (*Harijan*, 30-7-1938; A Clarification, *CWMG* 67: 211-12).

New Universities

There seems to be a mania for establishing new universities in the provinces. Gujarat wants one for Gujarati, Maharashtra for Marathi, Karnataka for Kannada, Orissa for Oriya, Assam for Assamese and what not. I do believe that there should be such universities if these rich provincial languages and the people who speak them are to attain their full height.

At the same time I fear that we betray ourselves into undue haste in accomplishing the object. The first step should be linguistic political redistribution of provinces. Their separate administration will naturally lead to the establishment of universities where there are none. The province of Bombay absorbs three languages: Gujarati, Marathi and Kannada and, therefore, stunts their growth. Madras absorbs four: Tamil, Telugu, Malayalam and Kannada. Thus, there is overlapping also. That Andhra Desha has an Andhra University is true. In my opinion it does not occupy the place it would, if Andhra was a separate administrative unit, free from foreign control. India attained that freedom only two months ago. The same thing can be said of the Annamalai University. Who can say that Tamil has come to its own in that university?

There should be a proper background for new universities. They should have feeders in the shape of schools and colleges which will impart instruction through the medium of their respective provincial languages. Then only can there be a proper milieu. University is at the top. A majestic top can only be sustained if there is a sound foundation.

Though we are politically free, we are hardly free from the subtle domination of the West. I have nothing to say to that school of politicians who believe that knowledge can only come from the West. Nor do I subscribe to the belief that nothing good can come out of the West. I do fear, however, that we are unable as yet to come to a correct decision in the matter. It is to be hoped that no one contends that because we seem to be politically free from foreign domination, the mere fact gives us freedom from the more subtle influence of the foreign language and foreign thought. Is it not wisdom, does not duty to the country dictate, that before we embark on new universities we should stop and fill our own lungs with the ozone of our newly got freedom? A university never needs a pile of majestic buildings and treasures of gold and silver. What it does need most of all is the intelligent backing of public opinion. It should have a large reservoir of teachers to draw upon. Its founders should be farseeing.

In my opinion it is not for a democratic state to find money for founding universities. If the people want them they will supply the funds. Universities so founded will adorn the country which they represent. Where administration is in foreign hands, whatever comes to the people comes from top and thus they become more and more dependent. Where it is broad-based on popular will, everything goes from bottom upward and hence it lasts. It is good looking and strengthens the people. In such a democratic scheme money invested in the promotion of learning gives a tenfold return to the people even as a seed sown in good soil returns a luxuriant crop. Universities founded under foreign domination have run in the reverse direction. Any other result was perhaps impossible. Therefore, there is every reason for being cautious about founding new universities till India has digested the newly acquired freedom.

Then take the Hindu–Muslim question. The poison has assumed such dangerous proportions that it is difficult to forecast where it will land us. Assume that the unthinkable has happened and that not a single Muslim can remain in the Union safely and honourably and that neither Hindu nor Sikh can do likewise in Pakistan. Our education will then wear a poisonous form. If, on the other hand, Hindus, Muslims and all the others who may belong to different faiths can live in either Dominion with perfect safety and honour, then in the nature of things our education will take a shape altogether pleasing. Either people of different faiths having lived together in friendship have produced a beautiful blend of cultures, which we shall strive to perpetuate and increasingly strengthen, or we shall cast about for the day when there was only one religion represented in Hindustan and retrace our steps to that exclusive culture. It is just possible that we might not be able to find any such historical date and if we do and we retrace our steps, we shall throw our culture back to that ugly period and deservedly earn the execration of the universe. By way of example, if we make the vain attempt of obliterating the Muslim period, we shall have to forget that there was a mighty Jama Masjid in Delhi second to none in the world, or that there was a Muslim university in Aligarh, or that there was the Taj in Agra, one of the seven wonders of the world, or that there were the great forts of Delhi and Agra built during the Mughal period. We shall then have to rewrite our history with that end in view. Surely today we have not the atmosphere which will enable us to come to a right conclusion about the conflicting choices. Our two-months-old freedom is struggling to get itself shaped. We do not know what shape it will ultimately take. Until we know this definitely, it should be enough if we make such changes as are possible in the existing universities and breathe into our existing educational institutions the quickening spirit of freedom. The experience we will thus gain will be helpful when the time is ripe for founding new universities (*Harijan*, 2-11-1947; Of New Universities, *CWMG* 89: 402-04).

5

Medium of Instruction : The Question of Language
The Need for a National Language

The colonial education in India was imparted through English language, which is a foreign medium and hence was not in the reach of the common man. Hence, Gandhi always considered the mother tongue of a province as the best medium of instruction for an individual to enhance his knowledge.

In one instance he says: "I must cling to my mother tongue as to my mother's breast, in spite of its shortcomings. It alone can give me the life-giving milk" (*Harijan*, 25-8-1946; Speech at Education Ministers' Conference, 29-7-1946, *CWMG* 85: 88).

Throughout his tour in India, Gandhi opposed English education and advocated the use of vernaculars. Thus in his speech at the Banaras Hindu University he remarked:

> I am hoping that this University will see to it that the youths who come to it will receive their instruction through the medium of their vernaculars. Our language is the reflection of ourselves, and if you tell me that our languages are too poor to express the best thought, then I say that the sooner we are wiped out of existence, the better for us. Is there a man who dreams that English can ever become the national language of India? (Cries of "Never") Why this handicap on the nation? Just consider for one moment what an unequal race our lads have to

run with every English lad. I had the privilege of a close conversation with some Poona professors. They assured me that every Indian youth, because he reached his knowledge through the English language, lost at least six precious years of life. Multiply that by the number of students turned out by our schools and colleges and find out for yourselves how many thousand years have been lost to the nation. The charge against us is, that we have no initiative. How can we have any if we are to devote the precious years of our life to the mastery of a foreign tongue? We fail in this attempt also. "Was it possible for any speaker yesterday and today to impress his audience as was possible for Mr. Higginbotham? It was not the fault of the previous speakers that they could not engage the audience. They had more than substance enough for us in their addresses. But their addresses could not go home to us. I have heard it said that after all it is English-educated India which is leading and which is doing all the things for the nation. It would be monstrous if it were otherwise. The only education we receive is English education. Surely we must show something for it. But suppose that we had been receiving during the past fifty years education through our vernaculars, what should we have had today? We should have today a free India, we should have our educated men, not as if they were foreigners in their own land but speaking to the heart of the nation; they would be working amongst the poorest of the poor, and whatever they would have gained during the past fifty years would be a heritage for the nation (Applause). Today even our wives are not the sharers in our best thought. Look at Professor Bose and Professor Ray and their brilliant researches. Is it not a shame that their researches are not the common property of the masses?"

— *Speeches and Writings of Mahatma Gandhi*, pp. 318-20;
Speech at Banaras Hindu University, 6-2-1916, *CWMG* 13: 211-12

Foreign Medium

The foreign medium has caused brain-fag, put an undue strain upon the nerves of our children, made them crammers and imitators, unfitted them for original work and thought, and disabled them for filtrating their learning to the family or the masses. The foreign medium has made our children practically foreigners in their own land. It is the greatest tragedy of the existing system. The foreign medium has prevented the growth of our vernaculars. If I had the powers of a despot, I would today stop the tuition of our boys and girls through a foreign medium, and require all the teachers and professors on pain of dismissal to introduce the change forthwith. I would not wait for the preparation of textbooks. They will follow the change. It is an evil that needs a summary remedy (*Young India*,

1-9-1921; National Education, *CWMG* 21: 39-40).

Vernacular vs Foreign Medium

But for the fact that the only higher education, the only education worth the name, has been received by us through the English medium, there would be no need to prove such a self-evident proposition that the youth of a nation to remain a nation must receive all instruction including the highest in its own vernacular or vernaculars. Surely, it is a self-demonstrated proposition that the youth of a nation cannot keep or establish a living contact with the masses unless their knowledge is received and assimilated through a medium understood by the people. Who can calculate the immeasurable loss sustained by the nation owing to thousands of its young men having been obliged to waste years in mastering a foreign language and its idiom of which in their daily life they have the least use and in learning which they had to neglect their own mother tongue and their own literature? There never was a greater superstition than that a particular language can be incapable of expansion or expressing abstruse or scientific ideas. A language is an exact reflection of the character and growth of its speakers.

Among the many evils of foreign rule this blighting imposition of a foreign medium upon the youth of the country will be counted by history as one of the greatest. It has sapped the energy of the nation, it has shortened the lives of the pupils, it has estranged them from the masses, it has made education unnecessarily expensive. If this process is still persisted in, it bids fair to rob the nation of its soul. The sooner therefore educated India shakes itself free from the hypnotic spell of the foreign medium, the better it would be for them and the people (*Young India*, 5-7-1928; The Curse of Foreign Medium, *CWMG* 37: 22).

De-Indianizing Education

I find daily proof of the increasing and continuing wrong being done to the millions by our false de-Indianizing education. Those graduates who are my valued associates themselves flounder when they have to give expression to their innermost thoughts. They are strangers in their own homes. Their vocabulary in the mother tongue is so limited that they cannot always finish their speech without having recourse to English words and even sentences. Nor can they exist without English books. They often write to one another in English. I cite the case of my companions to show how deep the evil has gone. For we have made a conscious effort to mend ourselves.

It has been argued that the wastage that occurs in our colleges need not worry us if, out of the collegians, one Jagadish Bose can be produced by them. I should freely subscribe to the argument if the wastage was unavoidable. I hope I have shown that it was and is even now avoidable. Moreover, the creation of a Bose does not help the argument. For Bose was not a product of the present education. He rose in spite of the terrible handicaps under which he had to labour. And his knowledge became almost intransmissible to the masses. We seem to have come to think that no one can hope to be like a Bose unless he knows English. I cannot conceive a grosser superstition than this. No Japanese feels so helpless as we seem to do.

. . . The medium of instruction should be altered at once and at any cost, the provincial languages being given their rightful place. I would prefer temporary chaos in higher education to the criminal waste that is daily accumulating.

In order to enhance the status and the market value of the provincial languages, I would have the language of the law courts to be the language of the province where the court is situated. The proceedings of the Provincial Legislatures must be in the language, or even the languages of the province where a province has more than one language within its borders. I suggest to the legislators that they could, by enough application, inside of a month, understand the languages of their provinces. There is nothing to prevent a Tamilian from easily learning the simple grammar and a few hundred words of Telugu, Malayalam and Kanarese, all allied to Tamil. At the centre Hindustani must rule supreme. In my opinion this is not a question to be decided by academicians. They cannot decide through what language the boys and girls of a place are to be educated. That question is already decided for them in every free country. Nor can they decide the subjects to be taught. That depends upon the wants of the country to which they belong. Theirs is the privilege of enforcing the nation's will in the best manner possible. When this country becomes really free the question of medium will be settled only one way. The academicians will frame the syllabus and prepare textbooks accordingly. And the products of the education of a free India will answer the requirements of the country as today they answer those of the foreign ruler. So long as we the educated classes play with this question. I very much fear we shall not produce the free and healthy India of our dream. We have to grow by strenuous effort out of our bondage, whether it is educational, economical, social or political. The effort itself is three-fourths of the battle (*Harijan*, 9-7-1938; Higher Education, *CWMG* 67: 161-63).

State Languages

If the medium is changed at once and not gradually, in an incredibly short time we shall find textbooks and teachers coming into being to supply the want. And if we mean business, in a year's time we shall find that we need never have been party to the tragic waste of the nation's time and energy in trying to learn the essentials of culture through a foreign medium. The condition of success is undoubtedly that provincial languages are introduced at once in government offices and courts, if the provincial governments have the power or the influence over the courts. If we believe in the necessity of the reform, we can achieve it in no time (*Harijan*, 30-7-1938; A Clarification, *CWMG* 67: 212).

Richness of Dialects[1]

He deprecated the suggestion that it would need a lot of research and preparation to enable them to impart technical education through the medium of the mother tongue. Those who argued like that were unaware of the rich treasure of expressions and idioms that were buried in the dialects of our villages. In Gandhiji's opinion there was no need to go to Sanskrit or Persian in search for many expressions. He had been in Champaran and he had found that the village folk there could fully express themselves with ease and without the help of a single foreign expression or idiom. As an illustration of their resourcefulness, he mentioned the word *gadi* which they had coined to denote a motor car. He challenged university scholars to coin a more poetic expression than that for a motor car (*Harijan*, 18-8-1946; Speech at Seksaria College of Commerce, 9-8-1946, *CWMG* 85: 144).

National Language

As we have had to consider the question of the medium of education, so also is it necessary to consider that of the national language. If this is to be English, it must be made a compulsory subject.

Can English become our national language? Some of our learned men, good patriots, contend that even to argue that English should become the national language betrays ignorance, that it is already so. His Excellency the Viceroy in his recent speech merely expressed the hope that it would occupy this place. His zeal did not carry him as far as to say that it had already become our national language and that there could be no question about it. He believes, however, that English will spread

---

1. Extracted from Pyarelal's "Weekly Letter". The occasion was the inauguration of the change from English to Marathi as the medium of instruction.

in the country day by day, enter our homes, and finally attain the exalted status of a national language. On a superficial consideration, this view appears correct. Looking at the educated section of our population, one is likely to gain the impression that, in the absence of English, all our work would come to a stop. But deeper reflection will show that English cannot, and ought not to, become our national language.

Let us see what are the requirements of a national language:

1. It should be easy to learn for government officials.
2. It should be capable of serving as a medium of religious, economic and political intercourse throughout India.
3. It should be the speech of large numbers of Indians.
4. It should be easy for every Indian to learn.
5. In choosing such a language, considerations of temporary or passing circumstances should not count.

English does not fulfil any of these requirements.

The first point ought to have been placed last, but I have purposely reversed the order because it seems as though English fulfils it. Closer examination will, however, show that even at the present moment it is not for officials an easy language to learn or handle. The Constitution, under which we are being ruled, envisages that the number of British officials will progressively decrease until finally only the Viceroy and a few others are left here. Even now, the majority of people in government services are Indians and their number will increase as time passes. I think no one will deny that for them English is more difficult than any Indian language.

As regards the second requirement, I think that religious intercourse through English is an impossibility unless our people throughout the land start speaking English. Spreading English among the masses to this extent appears quite impossible.

English simply cannot satisfy the third requirement as it is not the speech of any very large number of Indians.

The fourth also cannot be met by English because it is not relatively an easy language for all our people to learn.

Considering the fifth point, we see that the status which English enjoys today is temporary; as a permanent arrangement, the position is that the need for English in national affairs will be, if at all, very slight. It will be required for dealings with the British Empire and will remain the language of diplomacy between different countries within the Empire; this is a different matter. It will certainly remain necessary for such purposes. We do not grudge English anything. We only want that it should not overstep its proper limits; this is all that we insist upon. English will remain the imperial language and accordingly we shall require our Malaviyas, our Shastris and our Banerjeas to learn it, confident that they will enhance the glory of India in other lands. But English cannot be the national language of India. To give it that position will be like introducing Esperanto into our country. To think that English can become our national language betrays weakness, as the attempt to introduce Esperanto would betray sheer ignorance.

Which language, then, fulfils all the five requirements? We shall have to admit that it is Hindi.

I call that language Hindi which Hindus and Muslims in the North speak and which is written either in Devanagari or Urdu script. There has been some objection to this definition.

It is argued that Hindi and Urdu are two different languages. But this is incorrect. Both Hindus and Muslims speak the same language in north India. The difference has been created by the educated classes. That is, educated Hindus Sanskritize their Hindi with the result that Muslims cannot follow it. Muslims of Lucknow Persianize their Urdu and make it unintelligible to Hindus. To the masses both these languages are foreign and so they have no use for them. I have lived in the north and have mixed freely with both Hindus and Muslims, and, though my knowledge of Hindi is limited; I have never found any difficulty in carrying on communication through it with them. Therefore, call it Hindi or Urdu as you like, the language of the people in north India is the same thing — basically. Write it in the Urdu script and call it Urdu, or write it in the Nagari script and call it Hindi.

There now remains the question of the script. For the present, Muslims will certainly use the Urdu script and most of the Hindus the Devanagari. I say "most" because thousands of Hindus even today write in Urdu script and some even do not know the Devanagari script. In the end, when Hindus and Muslims will have ceased to regard each other with distrust, when the causes for such distrust have disappeared, the script which has greater range and is more popular will be more widely used and thus become the national script. In the intervening period, Hindus and Muslims who desire to write their petitions in the Urdu script should be free to do so and these should be accepted at all government offices.

No other language can compete with Hindi in satisfying these five requirements. Next to Hindi comes Bengali. But the Bengalis themselves make use of Hindi outside Bengal. The Hindi-speaking man speaks Hindi wherever he goes and no one feels surprised at this. The Hindu preachers and the Mahomedan Maulvis always deliver their religious discourses in Hindi and Urdu and even the illiterate masses understand them. Even an unlettered Gujarati, when he goes to the north, attempts to speak a few Hindi words, but the man from the north who works as gatekeeper for the Bombay businessman declines to speak in Gujarati and it is the latter, his employer, who is obliged to speak to him in broken Hindi. I have heard Hindi spoken even in far-off Dravidian provinces. It is not correct to say that in Madras one needs English. Even there, I have used Hindi for all my work. In the trains, I have heard hundreds of Madrasi passengers speaking to others in Hindi. Besides, the Muslims of Madras know good enough Hindi. It should be noted that Muslims throughout India speak Urdu and they are found in large numbers in every province. Thus Hindi has already established itself as the national language of India. We have been using it as such for a long time. The birth of Urdu itself is due to the aptness of Hindi for this purpose.

Muslim kings could not make Persian or Arabic the national language. They accepted the Hindi grammar and, employing the Urdu script, used more Persian words. They could not use a foreign tongue in their dealings with the masses. It is not as if the British are unaware of this position. Those who know anything about military affairs know that they have had to adopt Hindi and Urdu technical terms for use with the sepoys.

Thus, we see that Hindi alone can become our national language, though the matter presents some difficulty to the educated classes of Madras.

For Maharashtrians, Gujaratis, Sindhis and Bengalis, the thing is very easy. In a few months they can acquire enough command of Hindi to be able to use it for all-India intercourse. It is not so easy for Tamil friends. Tamil and other languages of the south belong to the Dravidian group. The structure and the grammar of these languages are different from those of Sanskrit. There is nothing in common between these two groups except certain words. But the difficulty in learning Hindi is confined to the present educated classes only. We are entitled to trust their patriotic spirit and hope that they will make a special effort to learn Hindi. As for the future, if Hindi attains its due status, it will be introduced in every school in Madras and there will be increased possibilities of contact between Madras and other provinces. English has failed to reach the Dravidian masses, but Hindi will do so in no time (Speech at Second Gujarat Educational Conference, 20-10-1917, *CWMG* 14: 22-26).

Hindustani

Do not consider for one moment that you can possibly make English a common medium of expression between the masses. Twenty-two crores of Indians know Hindustani — they do not know any other language. And if you want to steal into the hearts of 22 crores of Indians, Hindustani is the only language open to you (*Young India*, 2-2-1921; Speech at Mirzapur Park, Calcutta, 23-1-1921, *CWMG* 19: 272).

Richness of the Hindi Language

You talk of the poverty of Hindi literature — you talk of the poverty of today's Hindi, but if you dive deep into the pages of Tulsidas, probably you will share my opinion that there is no other book that stands equal to it in the literature of the world in modern languages. That one book has given me faith and hope which no other book has given. I think that it is a book which can stand any criticism and any scrutiny alike in literary grace, in metaphor and in religious fervor (*Young India*, 9-2-1921; Speech at Opening of National College, Calcutta, 4-2-1921, *CWMG* 19: 322).

National Languages vs State Languages

A fear had been expressed, observed Gandhiji, that the propagation of *rashtrabhasha* or the national tongue would prove inimical to the provincial languages. That fear was rooted in ignorance. The present step of the Seksaria College was a living refutation of that suspicion. Provincial tongues provided the sure foundation on which the edifice of the national tongue should rest. The two were intended to complement, not supplant each other (*Harijan*, 18-8-1946; Speech at Seksaria College of Commerce, 9-8-1946, *CWMG* 85: 144).

Place of English

I do not dislike English; its riches are infinite. It is the language of administration and is rich with the wealth of knowledge. All this notwithstanding, I hold that it is not necessary for every Indian to learn it. But of this, I do not wish to speak more here. Students have been learning English and they have no option but to do so till some other system is devised and the present schools undergo a revolution. I shall, therefore, end this all-important subject of the mother tongue here, merely saying in conclusion that in their dealings with one another, and whenever possible, people should use only their mother tongue and that others, besides students, who are present here should strive their utmost to make the mother tongue the medium of education (Speech at Bihar Students' Conference, 15-10-1917, *CWMG* 14: 133).

English vs Mother Tongue

English is a language of international commerce, it is the language of diplomacy, it contains many a rich literary treasure, and it gives us an introduction to Western thought and culture. For a few of us, therefore, a knowledge of English is necessary. They can carry on the departments of national commerce and international diplomacy, and for giving to the nation the best of Western literature, thought and science. That would be the legitimate use of English. Whereas today English has usurped the dearest place in our hearts and dethroned our mother tongues. It is an unnatural place due to our unequal relations with Englishmen. The highest development of the Indian mind must be possible without a knowledge of English. It is doing violence to the manhood and specially the womanhood of India to encourage our boys and girls to think that an entry into the best society is impossible without a knowledge of English. It is too humiliating a thought to be bearable. To get rid of the infatuation for English is one of the essentials of *swaraj* (*Young India*, 2-2-1921; Notes, *CWMG* 19: 314-15).

English Language and Culture

My uncompromising opposition to the foreign medium has resulted in an unwarranted charge being levelled against me of being hostile to foreign culture or the learning of the English language. No reader of *Young India* could have missed the statement often made by me in these pages, that I regard English as the language of international commerce and diplomacy and therefore consider its knowledge on the part of some of us as essential. As it contains some of the richest treasures of thought and literature, I would certainly encourage its careful study among those who have linguistic talents and expect them to translate those treasures for the nation in its vernaculars (*Young India*, 1-9-1921; National Education, *CWMG* 21: 40).

English vs Hindi

I know this tussle between English and Hindi is almost an eternal tussle. Whenever I have addressed student audiences, I have been surprised by the demand for English. You know, or ought to know, that I am a lover of the English language. But I do believe that the students of India, who are expected to throw in their lot with the teeming millions and to serve them, will be better qualified if they pay more attention to Hindi than to English. I do not say that you should not learn English; learn it by all means. But, so far as I can see, it cannot be the language of the millions of Indian homes. It will be confined to thousands or tens of thousands, but it will not reach the millions (*Harijan*, 17-11-1933; Speech at Students' Meeting, Nagpur, 9-11-1933, *CWMG* 56: 204).

Literary Treasure in English

I must not be understood to decry English or its noble literature. The columns of *Harijan* are sufficient evidence of my love of English. But the nobility of its literature cannot avail the Indian nation any more than the temperate climate or the scenery of England can avail her. India has to flourish in her own climate and scenery and her own literature, even though all the three may be inferior to the English climate, scenery and literature. We and our children must build on our own heritage. If we borrow another, we impoverish our own. We can never grow on foreign victuals. I want the nation to have the treasures contained in that language, and for that matter the other languages of the world, through its own vernaculars. I do not need to learn Bengali in order to know the beauties of Rabindranath's matchless productions. I get them through good translations. Gujarati boys and girls do not need to learn Russian to appreciate Tolstoy's short stories. They learn them through good translations. It is the boast of Englishmen that the best of the world's literary output is in the hands of that nation in simple English inside of a week of its publication. Why need I learn English to get at the best of what Shakespeare and Milton thought and wrote? (*Harijan*, 9-7-1938; Higher Education, *CWMG* 67: 161).

English as an Optional Language

English is today admittedly the world language. I would therefore accord it a place as a second, optional language, not in the school but in the university course. That can only be for the select few — not for the millions. Today when we have not the means to introduce even free compulsory primary education, how can we make provision for teaching English? Russia has achieved all her scientific progress without English. It is our mental slavery that makes us feel that we cannot do without English. I can never subscribe to that defeatist creed (*Harijan*, 25-8-1946; Speech at Education Ministers' Conference, 29-7-1946, *CWMG* 85: 88).

Sanskrit and Education

My view is that Sanskrit should be used in all Hindu religious ceremonies. However good a translation, it cannot give us the meaning which lies in the sounds of certain words in the original. Moreover, by translating into regional languages, and remaining content with such translations, verses which belong to a language which has acquired a certain refinement over thousands of years and in which those verses have always been recited, we diminish the air of solemnity which attaches to them. But I have no doubt at all in my mind that the meaning of every verse and every step in the ceremony should be explained in their own language to the people for whose benefit they are being recited or performed. It is also my view that the education of every Hindu is incomplete without an elementary knowledge of Sanskrit. I simply cannot conceive the continued existence of Hinduism without a widespread knowledge of Sanskrit. The language has been made difficult by the type of curriculum we follow in teaching it, in itself it is not difficult at all. Even if it is, the practice of *dharma* is still more difficult and, therefore, to those who wish to follow it in life the means of doing so should seem easy, however difficult they may actually be (*Navajivan*, 28-3-1926; Some Questions on Religious Issues, *CWMG* 30: 195).

Sanskrit and Other Languages

It is the duty of every Indian student to learn Sanskrit. It certainly is the duty of the Hindus, but it is also the Muslims' because, in the final analysis, their forbearers too were Rama and Krishna and they ought to know Sanskrit in order to know them. However, to maintain contacts with the Muslims, it is also the duty of Hindus to learn the former's language. Today we run away from each other's languages because we have become mad. Take it for a certainty that an institution which teaches fear and hatred of others surely is not a national institution (Speech at National Educational Conference, Hardwar, 20-3-1927, *CWMG* 33: 170).

Sanskrit Scriptures

And remember that since you are in a vast majority, the responsibility rests on your shoulders to make Jaffna, and through Jaffna Ceylon also perfectly dry. Hinduism does not permit you to drink. And if the board of education will do its duty, you will encourage Sanskrit study in your schools. I regard the education of any Hindu child as incomplete unless he has some knowledge of Sanskrit. And so far as I have been able to see we have in Hinduism no book so compact and so acceptable all round as the *Bhagavadgita*. If you will, therefore, saturate your children and yourselves with the spirit of Hinduism, you will endeavour to understand the spirit of the teaching of the *Gita*. You should also cultivate a common knowledge of the *Mahabharata* and the *Ramayana* (Speech to Ceylon Hindus, Jaffna, 27-11-1927, *CWMG* 35: 337).

Sanskrit vs State Languages

. . . the study of Sanskrit is being sadly neglected. I belong to a generation which believed in the study of the ancient languages. I do not believe that such a study is a waste of time and effort. I believe it is an aid to the study of modern languages. This is truer of Sanskrit than of any other ancient language so far as India is concerned, and every nationalist should study it because it makes a study of the provincial languages easier than otherwise. It is the language in which our forefathers thought and wrote. No Hindu boy or girl should be without a knowledge of the rudiments of Sanskrit, if he will imbibe the spirit of his religion. Thus the Gayatri is untranslatable. No translation can give the music of the original which I hold has a meaning all its own. The Gayatri is but one example of what I have said (*Harijan*, 23-3-1940; Question Box, *CWMG* 71: 346).

Pronunciation

By all means study Sanskrit. The effort made for learning correct pronunciation will not be wasted. Chaste pronunciation is a requisite for [learning] any language. But perhaps for Sanskrit accuracy of pronunciation is imperative. It is not at all necessary for you to study English. Assimilate the knowledge you already have and add to it (Letter to Balvant Sinha, 21-10-1944, *CWMG* 78: 217).

Languages vs Composite Culture

Every cultured Indian will know in addition to his own provincial language, if a Hindu, Sanskrit; if a Mahomedan, Arabic; if a Parsee, Persian; and all, Hindi. Some Hindus should know Arabic and Persian; some Mahomedans and Parsees, Sanskrit. Several northerners and westerners should learn Tamil. A universal language for India should be Hindi, with the option of writing it in Persian or Nagari characters. In order that the Hindus and the Mahomedans may have closer relations, it is necessary to know both the characters (*Hind Swaraj*, Chapter XVIII: Education, *CWMG* 10: 56-57).

Language Chasm

Our love of the English language in preference to our own mother tongue has caused a deep chasm between the educated and politically-minded classes and the masses. The languages of India have suffered impoverishment. We flounder when we make the vain attempt to express abstruse thought in the mother tongue. There are no equivalents for scientific terms. The result has been disastrous. The masses remain cut off from the modern mind. We are too near our own times correctly to measure the disservice caused to India by this neglect of its great languages. It is easy enough to understand that unless we undo the mischief the mass mind must remain imprisoned. The masses can make no solid contribution to the construction of *swaraj*. It is inherent in *swaraj* based on nonviolence that every individual makes his own direct contribution to the Independence movement. The masses cannot do this fully unless they understand every step with all its implications. This is impossible unless every step is explained in their own languages (Constructive Programme: Its Meaning and Place, 13-12-1941, *CWMG* 75: 156-57).

Place for Languages in Curriculum

It is now my opinion that in all Indian curricula of / there should be a place for Hindi, Samskrit, Persian, Arabic and English, besides of course the vernacular. This big list need not frighten anyone. If our education were more systematic, and the boys free from the burden of having to learn their subjects through a foreign medium, I am sure learning all these languages would not be an irksome task, but a perfect pleasure. A scientific knowledge of one language makes a knowledge of other languages comparatively easy (*An Autobiography*, Part I, Chapter V: At The High School, *CWMG* 39: 19).

Multiplicity of Scripts

If we are to make good our claim as one nation, we must have several things in common. We have a common culture running through a variety of creeds and sub-creeds. We have common disabilities. I am endeavouring to show that a common material for our dress is not only desirable but necessary. We need also a common language not in supersession of the vernaculars, but in addition to them. It is generally agreed that that medium should be Hindustani — a resultant of Hindi and Urdu, neither highly Sanskritized, nor Persianized or Arabianized. The greatest obstacle in the way are the numerous scripts, we have for the vernaculars. If it is possible to adopt a common script we should remove a great hindrance in the way of realizing the dream which, at present, is of having a common language.

A variety of scripts is an obstacle in more ways than one. It constitutes an effectual barrier against the acquisition of knowledge. The Aryan languages have so much in common that, if a great deal of time had not to be wasted in mastering the different scripts, we should all know several languages without much difficulty; for instance, most people who have a little knowledge of Sanskrit would have no difficulty in understanding the matchless creation of Rabindranath Tagore, if it was all printed in Devanagari script. But the Bengali script is a notice to the non-Bengalis — "hands off". Conversely, if the Bengalis knew the Devanagari script, they would at once be able to enjoy the marvellous beauty and spirituality of Tulsidas and a host of other Hindustani writers. When I returned to India in 1915, I had a communication from a society whose headquarters were, I believe, in Calcutta, and whose object was to advocate a common script for all India. I do not know the activities of that society, but its object is worthy, and a great deal of substantial work can be done by a few earnest workers in this direction. There are obvious limitations. A common script for all India is a distant ideal. A common script for all those who speak the Indo-Sanskrit languages, including the southern stock, is a practical ideal, if we can but shed our provincialisms. There is little virtue, for instance, in a Gujarati clinging to the Gujarati script. A provincial patriotism is good where it feeds the larger stream of all India patriotism, as the latter is good to the extent that it serves the still larger end of the universe. But a provincial patriotism that says "India is nothing, Gujarat is all", is wickedness. I have selected Gujarat because it is the half-way house, and because I am myself a Gujarati. In Gujarat, somewhat fortunately, those who settled the principles of primary education decided to make Devanagari script compulsory. Every Gujarati boy or girl who has passed through a school, therefore, knows both the Gujarati and the Devanagari scripts. If the committee had decided upon purely Devanagari script, it would have been better still. No doubt, the research scholars would still have learnt the Gujarati script for deciphering old manuscripts, but the Gujarati boy's energy would have been spared for more useful labour, if he had to learn only one instead of two scripts. The committee that settled the education scheme for Maharashtra was more enlightened, and it simply required the Devanagari script. The result is that a Mahratta reads, so far as mere reading is concerned, Tulsidas with as much facility as he reads Tukaram, and Gujaratis and Hindustanis read Tukaram with equal facility. The committee in Bengal, on the other hand, ruled otherwise, with the result we all know and many of us deplore. The treasures of the richest Indian vernacular have been rendered most difficult of access as if by design. That Devanagari should be the common script, I suppose, does not need any demonstration — the deciding factor being that it is the script known to the largest part of India.

These reflections arise, because, I was called upon to solve, during my visit to Cuttack, a practical question. There is a tribe wedged between the Hindi-speaking people in Bihar and Uriya-speaking people of Orissa.

What was to be done for the education of its children? Were they to be taught through Uriya or through Hindi? Or were they to be taught through their own dialect and, if they were, was the script to be Devanagari or a new invention? The first thought of the Utkal friends was to absorb the tribe amongst the Uriyas. The Biharis would think of absorbing them in Bihar, and if the elders of the tribe were consulted, they would most probably and naturally say that their dialect was just as good as the Uriya or the Bihari, and that it should be reduced to writing. And for them it would be a toss whether the script to be adopted should be Devanagari or Uriya, if not even a newly invented script, as has happened in modern times in at least two instances I know. Endeavouring to think in terms of all India, I suggested to my friends that, whilst it was proper for them to strengthen the Uriya language among the Uriya-speaking people, the children of this tribe should be taught Hindi and, naturally, the script should be Devanagari. A spirit that is so exclusive and narrow as to want every form of speech to be perpetuated and developed is anti-national and anti universal. All undeveloped and unwritten dialects should, in my humble opinion, be sacrificed and merged in the great Hindustani stream. It would be a sacrifice only to be nobler, not a suicide. If we are to have a common language for cultured India, we must arrest the growth of any process of disintegration or multiplication of languages and scripts. We must promote a common language. The beginning must naturally be made with the script, and until the Hindu–Muslim question is solved, confined perhaps to Hindu India. If I could have my way, I would make the learning of Devanagari script and Urdu script, in addition to the established provincial script compulsory in all the provinces and I would print in Devanagari chief books in the different vernaculars with a literal translation in Hindustani (*Young India*, 27-8-1925; A Common Script, *CWMG* 28: 119-22).

One Script, Many Languages

Although it is my firm conviction that there should be one script for all the Indian languages, and that that script can only be Devanagari, I could not follow the correspondent's advice for the reasons stated in my note in *Navajivan*, and which I need not reiterate here. But there is no doubt that we ought to seize the opportunity that the great national awakening gives us, of not merely popularizing the idea but of doing something concrete in that direction. The Hindu–Muslim madness no doubt stands in the way of a thorough reform. But before the acceptance of Devanagari script becomes a universal fact in India, Hindu India has got to be converted to the idea of one script for all the languages derived from Sanskrit and the Dravidian stock. At the present moment we have Bengali script in Bengal, Gurmukhi in the Punjab, Sindhi in Sind, Oriya in Utkal, Gujarati in Gujarat, Telugu in Andhradesha, Tamil in Tamilnad, Malayalam in Kerala, Kanarese in Karnatak, not to speak of Kaithi in Bihar and Modi in the Deccan. If all these scripts could be replaced by Devanagari for all practical and national purposes, it would mean a tremendous step forward. It will help to solidify Hindu India and bring the different provinces in closer touch. Anyone who has any knowledge of the different Indian languages and scripts knows to his cost what time it takes to master a new script. For the love of his country, no doubt, nothing is difficult, and time spent in mastering the different scripts, some of which are very beautiful, is in no way idly spent. But this spirit of abandon is not to be expected of millions. National leaders have to make things easy for them. Therefore, we must have an easily adaptable universal script for all India, and there is nothing so adaptable and readymade as Devanagari script. There is, or there used to be, an all-India organization for this very purpose. I do not know what its activities are at present. But if the work has to be done, either the original association should be strengthened, or a new one should be formed for this purpose. The movement should in no way be confused with the spread of Hindi or Hindustani as the lingua franca. The latter work is going on very slowly, but steadily. Use of one script will facilitate the spread of one language. But the functions of the two run parallel only up to a point. Hindi or Hindustani is not designed to replace the provincial languages, but is intended to supplement them, and to be used for inter-provincial contact. And till the Hindu–Muslim tension lasts it takes the form either of Urdu written in the Persian script, and containing a preponderance of Persian or Arabic words, or Hindi written in Devanagari, and containing a preponderance of Sanskrit words. When the hearts of the two meet, the two forms of the same language will be fused together, and we shall have a resultant of the two, containing as many Sanskrit, Persian, Arabic or other words as may be necessary for its full growth and full expression.

But one script is undoubtedly designed to displace all the different scripts so as to render it easy for people belonging to different provinces to learn provincial languages. The best way of achieving the purpose is first to make the learning of Devanagari script compulsory at least for Hindus in all the schools, as it is in Gujarat, and second to print the important literature in different Indian languages in Devanagari script. Such effort has already been made to a certain extent. I have seen *Gitanjali* printed in Devanagari script. But the effort requires to be made on a large scale, and there should be propaganda carried on for the spread of such books (*Young India*, 14-7-1927; An All-India Script, *CWMG* 34: 168-69).

Devanagari and National Unity

The object of this conference is to collect gems from all provincial literatures and to make them available through Hindi. For this purpose I would make an appeal to you. Of course, everyone must know his own language thoroughly well, and he should also know the great literature of other Indian languages through Hindi. But it is also the object of this conference to stimulate in our people the desire to know languages of other provinces, e.g., Gujaratis should know Tamil, Bengalis should know Gujarati and so on. And I tell you from experience that it is not at all difficult to pick up another Indian language. But to this end a common script is quite essential. It is not difficult to achieve in Tamil Nad. For look at this simple fact: over 90 per cent of our people are illiterate. We have to start with a clean slate with them. Why should we not start making them literate by means of a common script? In Europe they have tried the experiment of a common script quite successfully. Some people even go the length of saying that we might adopt the Roman script from Europe. After a good deal of controversy there is a consensus of opinion that the common script can be Devnagari and none else. Urdu is claimed as a rival, but I think neither Urdu nor Roman has the perfection and phonetic capacity of Devnagari. Please remember that I say nothing against your languages. Tamil, Telugu, Malayalam, Kannada must be there and will be there. But why not teach the illiterate in these parts these languages through the Devnagari script? In the interest of the national unity we desire to achieve, the adoption of Devnagari as a common script is so essential. Here it is a question of just shedding our provincialism and narrowness, there are no difficulties at all (*The Hindu*, 27-3-1937; Speech at Bharatiya Sahitya Parishad Madras - I, 27-3-1937, *CWMG* 65: 27).

Universalizing Devanagari

I understand that some of the tribes in Assam are being taught to read and write through the Roman script instead of Devanagari. I have already expressed my opinion that the only script that is ever likely to be universal in India is Devanagari, either reformed or as it is. Urdu or Persian will go hand in hand unless Muslims, of their own free will, acknowledge the superiority of Devanagari from a purely scientific and national standpoint. But this is irrelevant to the present problem. The Roman cannot go hand in hand with the other two scripts. Protagonists of the Roman script would displace both. But sentiment and science alike are against the Roman script. Its sole merit is its convenience for printing and typing purposes. But that is nothing compared to the strain its learning would put upon millions. It can be of no help to the millions who have to read their own literature either in their own provincial scripts or in Devanagari. Devanagari is easier for the millions of Hindus and even Muslims to learn, because the provincial scripts are mostly derived from Devanagari. I have included Muslims advisedly. The mother tongue of Bengali Muslims, for instance, is Bengali as is Tamil of Tamil Muslims. The present movement for the propagation of Urdu will, as it should, result in Muslims all over India learning Urdu in addition to their mother tongue. They must, in any case, know Arabic for the purpose of learning the Holy Koran. But the millions whether Hindus or Muslims will never need the Roman script except when they wish to learn English. Similarly, Hindus who want to read their scriptures in the original have to and do learn the Devanagari script. The movement for universalizing the Devanagari script has thus a sound basis. The introduction of the Roman script is a superimposition which can never become popular. And all superimpositions will be swept out of existence when the true mass awakening comes, as it is coming, much sooner than any one of us can expect from known causes. Yet the awakening of millions does take time. It cannot be manufactured. It comes or seems to come mysteriously. National workers can merely hasten the process by anticipating the mass mind (*Harijan*, 11-2-1939; Roman Script vs Devanagari, *CWMG* 68: 380-81).

One Script for Sister Languages

The question of having one script for the Indian languages which are daughters of Sanskrit by birth or adoption has been before the public for a number of years. Yet in these days of aggressive provincialism, perhaps, any plea for one script will be regarded as an impertinence. But the literacy campaigns raging all over the country should compel a hearing for the advocates of one script. I have been one such for years. I remember having even adopted in South Africa Devanagari script for my Indian correspondence with Gujaratis in select cases. Interprovincial intercourse will be much facilitated by such adoption, and the learning of the various provincial languages will be made infinitely easier than it is today. If the educated people of the land were to put their heads together and decide upon one script, its universal adoption should be an easy thing. To the millions who are illiterate it is a matter of indifference what script is prescribed to them. If the happy consummation comes to pass, there will be only two scripts in India — Devanagari and Urdu — and every nationalist will deem it his duty to master the two scripts. I am a lover of all Indian languages. I have tried to learn as many scripts as possible. And if only I had the time, even at the age of seventy I have energy enough to learn more Indian languages. That would be a recreation for me. But in spite of all my love for the languages I must confess that I have not learnt all the scripts. But if the sister languages were written in one script, I should pick up a workable knowledge of the principal languages of the provinces in very little time. And Devanagari has nothing to be ashamed of in point of symmetry or beauty. I hope that those who are engaged in the literacy campaigns will give a passing thought to my suggestion. If they will adopt Devanagari script, they will save for the future generations tons of labour and time and earn their blessings (*Harijan*, 5-8-1939; Notes: One Script for Daughters of Sanskrit, *CWMG* 70: 46-47).

National vs International Language

English no doubt is the international language. But can it ever be our national language? The latter must be the common property of millions of our people. How can they sustain the burden of learning the English tongue? Hindustani is the natural national language, for it is already understood by 21 crores. The remainder of the population can also easily understand it. But English may be said to be the mother tongue of a mere handful — say, a lakh at the most. If India is a nation, it must have a national language. English will appropriately remain the international language with the Roman script. But the latter can never be the script of the national language (*Harijan*, 26-4-1942; Ten Questions Regarding the National Language, *CWMG* 76: 49).

6

Religious/Ethical Education

The Need for Religious Education

. . . we cannot do without it (religious education). India will never be godless. Rank atheism cannot flourish in this land. The task is indeed difficult. My head begins to turn as I think of religious education. Our religious teachers are hypocritical and selfish; they will have to be approached. The Mullas, the Dasturs and the Brahmins hold the key in their hands, but if they will not have the good sense, the energy that we have derived from English education will have to be devoted to religious education. This is not very difficult. Only the fringe of the ocean has been polluted and it is those who are within the fringe who alone need cleansing. We who come under this category can even cleanse ourselves because my remarks do not apply to the millions. In order to restore India to its pristine condition, we have to return to it (*Hind Swaraj*, Chapter XVIII: Education, *CWMG* 10: 57).

Dharma and Scriptures

This brings me to the subject of *dharma*. Where there is no *dharma*, there can be neither knowledge nor wealth, nor health, nor anything else. Where there is no *dharma*, life is devoid of all joy, is mere emptiness. We have had to go without instruction in *dharma*; we are in much the same position as the bridegroom's party at a wedding without the bridegroom. Students cannot have innocent joy without a knowledge of *dharma*. That they may have such joy, it is necessary for them to study the Shastras, to reflect over their teaching and bring their conduct in conformity with their ideals. Smoking a cigarette the first thing in the morning or idle gossip does good to nobody. Nazeer Akbarabadi has said that, even the sparrows as they twitter, sing the name of the Lord morning and evening, when we are still lying in our beds full-length. It is the duty of every student to acquire the knowledge of *dharma* in any manner he can. Whether or not *dharma* is taught in schools, it is my prayer to students who have assembled here that they introduce its essential principles in their life. What exactly is *dharma*? In what manner can instruction in religion be imparted? This is not the place for a discussion of this subject. But I shall give you this practical advice, based on my own experience, that you should take to the *Ramacharitamanasa* [of Tulsidas] and the *Bhagavadgita* in love and reverence. You have a real jewel in the latter; seize it. But see that you study these two books in order to learn the secret of *dharma*. The seers who wrote these works did not set out to write history but only to teach *dharma* and morals. Millions of people read these books and lead pure lives. They read them with a guileless heart and live in this world full of innocent joy. It never occurs to them even in a dream to ask whether or not Ravana was a historical figure or whether they might not kill their enemies as Rama killed Ravana. Even when face to face with enemies, they pray for Ramachandra's protection and remain unafraid. Tulsidas, the author of the *Ramayana* [*Ramacharitamanasa*], had nothing but compassion by way of a weapon. He desired to kill none. He who creates, destroys. Rama was God; He had created Ravana and so had the right to kill him. When any of us becomes God; he may consider whether he is fit to have the power to destroy. I have ventured to say this by way of introduction to these great books. I was, myself, a sceptic once and lived in fear of being destroyed. I have grown out of that stage and become a believer. I have thought it fit here to describe the influence which these books have had on me. For Muslim students, the Koran is the best book in this respect. I would counsel them as well that they study this book in a spirit of devotion. They should understand its true message. I feel, too, that both Hindus and Muslims should study each other's religious scriptures with due respect and try to understand them (Speech at Bihar Students' Conference, Bhagalpur, [1917], *CWMG* 14: 136-37).

Religious Instruction and the State

I do not believe that the state can concern itself or cope with religious education. I believe that religious education must be the sole concern of religious associations. Do not mix up religion and ethics. I believe that fundamental ethics is common to all religions. Teaching of fundamental ethics is undoubtedly a function of the state. By religion I have not in mind fundamental ethics but what goes by the name of denominationalism. We have suffered enough from state-aided religion and state Church. A society or a group, which depends partly or wholly on state aid for the existence of its religion, does not deserve or, better still, does not have any religion worth the name (*Harijan*, 23-3-1947, Letter to E.W. Aryanayakum, 21-2-1947, *CWMG* 87: 1).

Religious Education and the Teacher

You have rightly found place for religious instruction. I have experimented with quite a number of boys in order to understand how best to impart religious instruction and whilst I found that book instruction was somewhat of an aid, by itself it was useless. Religious instruction, I discovered, was imparted by teachers living the religion themselves. I have found that boys imbibe more from the teachers' own lives than they do from the books that they read to them, or the lectures that they deliver to them with their lips. I have discovered to my great joy that boys and girls have unconsciously a faculty of penetration whereby they read the thoughts of their teachers. Woe to the teacher who teaches one thing with his lips, and carries another in his breast (Speech at Mahinda College, Galle, 24-11-1927, *CWMG* 35: 306).

Liberal Education

I shall say to the 75 per cent Hindus receiving instruction in this college that your lives will be incomplete unless you reverently study the teaching of Jesus. I have come to the conclusion, in my own experience, that those who, no matter to what faith they belong, reverently study the teaching of other faiths broaden their own, instead of slackening their hearts. Personally, I do not regard any of the great religions of the world as false. All have served in embellishing mankind and are even now serving their purpose. A liberal education to all should include, as I have put it, a reverent study of other faiths, but I do not want to labour this point, nor have I the time to do so (*The Hindu*, 2-12-1927; Speech at Central College, *CWMG* 35: 343).

Religious Instruction

The other day, in the course of a conversation, a missionary friend asked me, if India was really a spiritually advanced country, why it was that he found only a few students having any knowledge of their own religion, even of the *Bhagavadgita*. In support of the statement, the friend who is himself an educationist told me that he had made it a point to ask the students he met whether they had any knowledge of their religion or of the *Bhagavadgita*. A vast majority of them were found to be innocent of any such knowledge.

I do not propose to take up at the present moment the inference that because certain students had no knowledge of their own religion, India was not a spiritually advanced country, beyond saying that the ignorance on the part of the students of religious books did not necessarily mean absence of all religious life or want or spirituality among the people to which the students belonged. But there is no doubt that the vast majority of students who pass through the government educational institutions are devoid of any religious instruction. The remark of the missionary had reference to the Mysore students, and I was somewhat pained to observe that even the students of Mysore had no religious instruction in the state schools. I know that there is a school of thought which believes in only secular instruction being given in public schools. I know also that in a country like India, where there are most religions of the world represented and where there are so many denominations in the same religion, there must be difficulty about making provision for religious instruction. But if India is not to declare spiritual bankruptcy, religious instruction of its youth must be held to be at least as necessary as secular instruction. It is true that knowledge of religious books is no equivalent of that of religion. But if we cannot have religion we must be satisfied with providing our boys and girls with what is next best. And whether there is such instruction given in the schools or not, grown-up students must cultivate the art of self-help about matters religious as about other. They may start their own class just as they have their debating and now spinners' clubs.

Addressing the Collegiate High School students at Shimoga, I found upon enquiry at the meeting that out of a hundred or more Hindu boys, there were hardly eight who had read the *Bhagavadgita*. None raised his hand in answer to the question, whether of the few who had read the *Gita* there was any who understood it. Out of five or six Mussalman boys all raised their hands as having read the Koran. But only one could say that he knew its meaning. The *Gita* is, in my opinion, a very easy book to understand. It does present some fundamental problems which are no doubt difficult of solution. But the general trend of the *Gita* is in my opinion unmistakable. It is accepted by all Hindu sects as authoritative. It is free from any form of dogma. In a short compass it gives a complete reasoned moral code. It satisfies both the intellect and heart. It is thus both philosophical and devotional. Its appeal is universal. The language is incredibly simple. But I nevertheless think that there should be an authoritative version in each vernacular, and the translations should be so prepared as to avoid technicalities and in a manner that would make the teaching of the *Gita* intelligible to the average man. The suggestion is not intended in any way to supplement the original. For I reiterate my opinion that every Hindu boy and girl should know Sanskrit. But for a long time to come, there will be millions without any knowledge of Sanskrit. It would be suicidal to keep them deprived of the teachings of *Bhagavadgita* because they do not know Sanskrit. (*Young India*, 25-8-1927; Students and the "Gita", *CWMG* 34: 394-95).

Religious vs Fundamental Virtues

To me religion means truth and *ahimsa* or rather truth alone, because truth includes *ahimsa*, *ahimsa* being the necessary and indispensable means for its discovery. Therefore anything that promotes the practice of these virtues is a means for imparting religious education and the best way to do this, in my opinion, is for the teachers rigorously to practise these virtues in their own person. Their very association with the boys, whether on the playground or in the classroom, will then give the pupils a fine training in these fundamental virtues.

So much for instruction in the universal essentials of religion. A curriculum of religious instruction should include a study of the tenets of faiths other than one's own. For this purpose the students should be trained to cultivate the habit of understanding and appreciating the doctrines of various great religions of the world in a spirit of reverence and broad-minded tolerance. This, if properly done, would help to give them a spiritual assurance and a better appreciation of their own religion. There is one rule, however, which should always be kept in mind while studying all great religions and that is that one should study them only through the writings of known votaries of the respective religions. For instance, if one wants to study the *Bhagavata* one should do so not through a translation of it made by a hostile critic but through one prepared by a lover of the *Bhagavata*. Similarly to study the Bible one should study it through the commentaries of devoted Christians. This study of other religions besides one's own will give one a grasp of the rock-bottom unity of all religions and afford a glimpse also of that universal and absolute truth which lies beyond the "dust of creeds and faiths".

Let no one even for a moment entertain the fear that a reverent study of other religions is likely to weaken or shake one's faith in one's own. The Hindu system of philosophy regards all religions as containing the elements of truth in them and enjoins an attitude of respect and reverence towards them all. This of course presupposes regard for one's own religion. Study and appreciation of other religions need not cause a weakening of that regard; it should mean extension of that regard to other religions.

In this respect religion stands on the same footing as culture. Just as preservation of one's own culture does not mean contempt for that of others, but requires assimilation of the best that there may be in all the other cultures, even so should be the case with religion. Our present fears and apprehensions are a result of the poisonous atmosphere that has been generated in the country, the atmosphere of mutual hatred, ill-will and distrust. We are constantly labouring under a nightmare of fear lest someone should stealthily undermine our faith or the faith of those who are dear and near to us. But this unnatural state will cease when we have learnt to cultivate respect and tolerance towards other religions and their votaries (*Young India*, 6-12-1928; Religious Education, *CWMG* 37: 254-55).

Religious Instruction Framework

Teachers who teach under a common administrative system have no right to impart religious instruction according to their own viewpoint.

As in the case of other subjects, religious instruction too must be given in accordance with the scheme provided by the administrative authorities. Every teacher will have his own method of teaching within that framework; however, such instruction may be imparted only in accordance with the ideals that have been laid down by the authorities with regard to religion. It is true that instruction in other subjects can be imparted by one who has read certain books on these subjects. That is not the case of religious instruction. It is never given through books. The method of imparting this instruction is quite different from that followed in the case of other subject. Whereas the latter is communicated through the intellect, the former can proceed from one's heart alone. Hence so long as the teacher is not steeped in religion, he should not impart religious instruction. Although in this manner the means of imparting religious instruction are different, nevertheless it is necessary to have a certain amount of understanding about the way in which it is to be done. In other words, one cannot impart education which would encourage violence where nonviolence has been accepted as the supreme *dharma*. Or, instruction antagonistic to other religions cannot be imparted where the ideal of love, tolerance and compassion towards all religions has been accepted as the ideal. In short, there can be no place for a state of anarchy with regard to religious instruction where its necessity has already been accepted (*Navajivan*, 10-6-1928; Questions on Education – II, *CWMG* 36: 383-84).

Satsang

It is true that we lack religious education in the country. Religious instruction can only be imparted through the practice of religion, not by exhibiting mere learning. That's why someone has said: What is there that *satsang* cannot do for a man? Who does not know the emphasis Tulsidas laid on the importance of *satsang*? This does not mean that there is no need to read and understand religious books. But the need for books, etc., arises only after a man has had *satsang* and has purified himself to a certain extent. If one starts studying religious books before this stage then instead of bringing peace this study could hinder the growth. This means that an intelligent man should put his religion into practice straightaway instead of worrying himself with all manner of questions. Then according to the maxim "as with the individual so with the world", one is bound to influence the other. If each one of us was to take care of one's self, nobody would need to worry about the others (*Navajivan*, 15-8-1929; Some Religious Questions, *CWMG* 41: 291).

Ethical Teaching in Schools[1]

Q. Should religious instruction form part of the school curriculum as approved by the state? Do you favour separate schools for children belonging to different denominations for facility of religious instruction? Or, should religious instruction be left in the hands of private bodies? If so, do you think it is right for the state to subsidize such bodies?

---

[1] Extracted from "Gandhiji's Walking Tour Diary".

A. As to this question he said that he did not believe in state religion even though the whole community had one religion. State interference would probably always be unwelcome. Religion was a purely personal matter. There were in reality as many religions as minds. Each mind had a different conception of God from the other. He was also opposed to state aid, partly or wholly, to religious bodies. For he knew that an institution or group, which did not manage to finance its own religious teaching, was a stranger to true religion. This did not mean that the state schools would not give ethical teaching. Fundamental ethics were common to all religions (*Harijan*, 16-3-1947; Speech at Prayer Meeting, 21-2-1947, *CWMG* 87: 5).

State and Religious Education

I do not subscribe to the view that the government should provide religious education. If there are some Mussalmans who want to give religious education of the wrong type, you cannot prevent it. If you try to do so, the result can only be bad. Those who want to give religious education, without expecting any remuneration for it, may do so on their own. We will only teach ethics based on the fundamental principles of all religions (*Harijan Sevak*, 9-11-1947; Discussion at Hindustani Talimi Sangh Meeting, 22-4-1947, *CWMG* 87: 332).

Religious Instruction

Religious instruction in the sense of denominational religion has been deliberately omitted. Unless there is a state religion it is very difficult, if not impossible, to provide religious instruction as it would mean providing for every denomination. Such instruction is best given at home. The State should allow enough time for every child to receive such instruction at home or otherwise. It is also conceivable that the State should provide facilities for private tuition by those denominations which may wish to instruct their children at school provided that such instruction is paid for by such denominations. . . .

As to the necessity of teaching equal regard for all religions, I personally hold strong views. Till we reach that happy state, I see no prospect of real unity among all the different communities. I regard it as fatal to the growth of a friendly spirit among the children belonging to the different faiths if they are taught either that their religion is superior to every other or that it is the only true religion. If that exclusive spirit is to pervade the nation, the necessary corollary would be that there should be separate schools for every denomination with freedom to each to decry every other, or that the mention of religion must be entirely prohibited.

The result of such a policy is too dreadful to contemplate. Fundamental principles of ethics are common to all religions. These should certainly be taught to the children and that should be regarded as adequate religious instruction so far as the schools under the Wardha scheme are concerned (*Harijan*, 16-7-1938; Some Objections, *CWMG* 67: 175).

Against Atheism

Amongst the students of today the spirit of atheism is gaining ground. I am deeply grieved that things should be so. Whenever I see Hindu students, I ask them to think of God, to pray, to repeat Ramanama. They ask me where is God, where is Rama and such other questions. When I see Mussalman youths and ask them to read the Koran, and to live the life enjoined therein, they also ask me similar questions. The education which leads to the negation of God cannot make for the service of the country nor of humanity. In your address, you have referred to my service to my country. Whatever I have been doing is done with a sense of my duty to God. And this I consider to be the right thing. God is not seated in the skies, in the heavens, or elsewhere. He is enshrined in the heart of everyone — be he a Hindu, Mohammedan, Christian or Jew, man or woman (*The Hindu*, 21-7-1927; Speech to Students, Mysore, *CWMG* 34: 203-04).

7

Adult Education

Importance of Adult Education

The primary need of those who are come of age and are following an avocation, is to know how to read and write. Mass illiteracy is India's sin and shame and must be liquidated. Of course, the literacy campaign must not begin and end with a knowledge of the alphabet. It must go hand in hand with the spread of useful knowledge. But municipal bodies should beware of trying to ride two horses at a time, or else they are sure to come a cropper (*Harijan*, 18-2-1939; Discussion with Representatives of Municipalities and Local Boards, 28-1-1939, *CWMG* 68: 341).

Indeed in my opinion what we have reason to deplore and be ashamed of is not so much illiteracy as ignorance. Therefore adult education, too, should have an intensive programme of driving out ignorance through carefully selected teachers with an equally carefully selected syllabus according to which they would educate the adult villager's mind. This is not to say that I would not give them a knowledge of the alphabet. I value it too much to despise or even belittle its merit as a vehicle of education. I appreciate Prof. Laubach's immense labours in the way of making the alphabet easy and Prof. Bhagwat's great and practical contribution in the same direction. Indeed I have invited the latter to come to Segaon whenever he chooses and try his art on the men, women and even children of Segaon (*Harijan*, 5-6-1937; Speech at Tithal, 22-5-1937, *CWMG* 65: 234-35).

Education for Life

Supposing I come across an old man who is dirty and ignorant. His village is his universe. It would be my job to teach him cleanliness, to remove his ignorance and widen his mental horizon. I need not tell him that I am to be his teacher. I will try to establish a living contact with his mind and win his confidence. He may reject my advances. I won't accept defeat, but continue my effort till I succeed in making friends with him. Once that is achieved, the rest must follow. . . .

Some work for adult education is being done in many places. It is mostly concentrated among mill-hands and the like in big cities. No one has really touched the village. Mere three Rs and lectures on politics won't satisfy me. Adult education of my conception must make men and women better citizens all round. To work out the syllabus and to organize the work of adult education is a more difficult task than preparation of the seven years' course for children. The common central feature of both will be the imparting of education through village crafts. Agriculture will play an important part in adult education under the basic scheme. Literary instruction must be there. Much information will be given orally. There will be books more for the teachers than the taught. We must teach the majority how to behave towards the minority and vice versa. The right type of adult education should teach good neighbourliness and cut at the very root of untouchability and communal problem.

The particular industry which is to serve as the medium of instruction will be determined by local conditions in each place. For instance, people in a village might tell you that they are interested in agriculture, but they are not interested in the spinning-wheel. In that case, you will choose the former as the medium of instruction. You could make a beginning by taking a census of its cattle. For instance, I find that almost everyone in Sevagram has a bullock and a bullock-cart. It seems wasteful. The villagers should be taught cooperation. Again, we must inculcate in them the right principles of relationship between men and women. Men get almost double the women's wages for identical work. Sometimes men sit lazily at home and smoke while the women toil the whole day. People should be made to realize that this is doubly wrong and ought to go. If you agree with me that the scope of basic education should be extended, you might have to change your constitution (*The Hindu*, 29-10-1944; Discussion with Representatives of Hindustani Talimi Sangh, before 27-10-1944, *CWMG* 78: 237-38).

Functional Literacy

The workers need not rack their brains at all. The lapse is bound to occur after the short courses that are given. The lapse can only be prevented by correlating the teaching to the villagers' daily wants. The dry knowledge of the three R's is not even now, it can never be, a permanent part of the villagers' life. They must have knowledge given to them which they must use daily. It must not be thrust upon them. They should have the appetite for it. What they have today is something they neither want nor appreciate. Give the villagers village arithmetic, village geography, village history and the literary knowledge that they must use daily, i.e., reading and writing letters, etc. They will treasure such knowledge and pass on to the other stages. They have no use for books which give them nothing of daily use (*Harijan*, 22-6-1940; Notes, *CWMG* 72: 180-81).

Self-supporting Adult Education

It is my firm belief that if Nayee Talim cannot become self-supporting, then the teachers do not understand what it is. In my view, amongst other characteristics self-reliance is the most important characteristic of Nayee Talim.

If this is so for the education of boys and girls, then adult education must also be self-supporting. If we believe that it is difficult to convince adults about the value of education, then I have to say that this is nothing but an old illusion. And the teaching of the three R's in adult education is no part of our Nayee Talim. The meaning of adult education is that we will give them, through their own language, all-round education of a pure and socially useful life. And if they do not easily become self-supporting, in my view there is some serious defect in that education. We should not also forget that complete cooperation should be the basis from the very beginning. Those who know the full meaning of cooperation will raise no doubts about self-reliance (Khadi Jagat, November 1945; Speech on Nayee Talim, *CWMG* 82: 143-44).

Knowledge of Alphabet

In the consideration of public education, knowledge of the alphabet takes a subordinate place. It can be said that knowledge of the alphabet has no place at all among the important aspects of life. *Moksha* is for us the final state to be desired. Who will deny that knowledge of the alphabet is not necessary for *moksha* here and hereafter? If we have to wait until crores of people have gained a knowledge of the alphabet in order to win *swaraj*, attainment of the latter will become almost an impossibility. Moreover, no one has claimed that the great teachers of the world like Jesus Christ had this knowledge.

Knowledge of the alphabet has been given the least important place in this series of articles. It is a means and not an end. It is a well-known fact that as a means it is very useful. However, when considering the type of knowledge that is required for crores of farmers who are engaged in their occupations and have reached a mature age, we find that there is much else that they should be taught before being given a knowledge of the alphabet (*Navajivan*, 15-12-1929; Diseases in Villages, *CWMG* 42: 281).

8

Women's Education

. . . As for illiteracy among the women, its cause is not mere laziness and inertia as in the case of men. A more potent cause is the status of inferiority with which an immemorial tradition has unjustly branded her. Man has converted her into a domestic drudge and an instrument of his pleasure, instead of regarding her as his helpmate and better half! The result is a semi-paralysis of our society. Woman has rightly been called the mother of the race. We owe it to her and to ourselves to undo the great wrong that we have done her (*Harijan*, 18-2-1939; Discussion with Representatives of Municipalities and Local Boards, 28-1-1939, *CWMG* 68: 341).

That India is very backward in the education of women is a fact that cannot be denied. But by admitting this, we do not mean to suggest that Indian women fail in their duty. We believe that, as there are in the world few men of any class who can compete with the Indians considered from all points of view, so are there few women anywhere in the world who can compare with Indian women. But this position can no longer be kept up in the present squalid, low and helpless state of India. The modern age is such that it does not allow anyone to remain in the same position. Those who do not want to go forward, or do not do so, must fall behind. In so far as this is true, we can see that Indian men have deliberately kept their women backward. Those who pose as reformers as also other well-to-do Indians, whether Hindu or Muslim, Parsi or Christian, either treat their women as if they were playthings or use them as they fancy for self-indulgence, with the result that they themselves become weak and help only to produce weaklings. And in this way they lead irreligious lives and still say, "It is God's will that prevails". If this state of affairs continues, India will remain in its present abominable condition even if she were to secure all her rights from the British government. In all countries where the people live a decent life, there is no disparity in the condition of men and women. It is easy to see how much the real wealth of India would be attenuated, if one half of her human beings remained ignorant and existed only as playthings of the others (*Indian Opinion*, 19-1-1907; Women's Education, *CWMG* 6: 282-83).

Yusuf Ali on Women's Education

Mr. Yusuf Ali's book on conditions prevailing in India is widely read. His views on the education of women as expressed therein are worth noting. He says that so long as Indian women do not get proper education, the condition of India is not likely to improve. Woman is known as the better half of man. If a half of one's body ceases to function, we call it paralysis and the person becomes unfit for any activity. Thus, if women in India are not employed as they should be, it can be said that the entire country suffers from paralysis. How is it surprising then that India is not able to keep pace with other countries? All parents should think of this in regard to their daughters, and all Indians should do likewise with regard to the womenfolk of India. We badly need thousands of women who can compare with Mirabai and Rabia Bibi (*Indian Opinion*, 22-6-1907; Yusuf Ali and Women's Education, *CWMG* 7: 51).

Equality of Rights for Women

We shall accept equality of rights for women, but I think their education should differ from men's, as their nature and functions do. In progressive countries, women receive the very highest education but, after it is over, they do not have to perform the same duties as men and in our country women have never to compete with men for a livelihood (*Prajabandhu*, 27-2-1916; Speech on Indian Women's University, 23-2-1916, *CWMG* 13: 246).

Education of Women vs Men

The education of women is as faulty as that of men. No thought has been given to the relations of men and women or to the place of women in Indian society.

Primary education for the two sexes can have much in common. There are important differences at all other levels. As Nature has made men and women different, it is necessary to maintain a difference between the education of the two. True, they are equals in life, but their functions differ. It is woman's right to rule the home. Man is master outside it. Man is the earner, woman saves and spends. Woman looks after the feeding of the child. She shapes its future. She is responsible for building its character. She is her children's educator, and hence, mother to the Nation. Man is not father [in that sense]. After a certain period, a father ceases to influence his son; the mother never abdicates her place. The son, even after attaining manhood, will play with the mother even as the child does. He cannot do that with his father.

If this is the scheme of Nature, and it is just as it should be, woman should not have to earn her living. A state of affairs in which women have to work as telegraph clerks, typists or compositors can be, I think, no good, such a people must be bankrupt and living on their capital.

Hence, just as, on the one hand, it is wrong to keep women in ignorance and under suppression, so, on the other, it is a sign of decadence and it is tyrannical to burden them with work which is ordinarily done by men.

There must be provision, therefore, for separate arrangements for the education of women after their attaining a certain age. They should be taught the management of the home, the things they should or should not do during pregnancy, and the nursing and care of children. Drawing up such a scheme presents difficulties. The idea is new. The right course would be to constitute a committee of men and women, of good character and well-informed, who would think further and arrive at conclusions, and ask them to produce a suitable plan for the purpose.

This committee should consider measures for the education of girls from the time that they cease to be children. There is, however, a very large number of girls who have been married off before puberty, and the number is increasing. Once they are married, they just disappear from the field. I have given my views on this in my foreword to the first book of the "Bhagini Samaj" series. I reproduce them here:

We shall not solve the problem of women's education merely by educating girls. Victims of child marriage, thousands of girls vanish from view at the early age of twelve. They change into housewives! Till this wicked custom has disappeared from among us, the husband will have to learn to be the wife's teacher. A great many of our hopes lie in women being educated on matters mentioned above. It seems to me that unless women cease to be a mere means of pleasure or cooks to us and come to be our life-companions, equal partners in the battle of life, sharers in our joys and sorrows, all our efforts are doomed to failure. There are men to whom their women are no better than animals. For, this sad state, some of the Sanskrit sayings and a well-known *doha* of Tulsidas may be held responsible. Tulsidas says at one place: "The drum, the fool, the Sudra, the animal and the woman — all these need beating."

I adore Tulsidasji, but adoration is not blind. Either this couplet is an interpolation, or, if it is his, he must have to the Sanskrit sayings, people seem to labour under the impression that every verse in that language was a scriptural precept. We must fight this impression and pluck out from its very root the general habit of regarding women as inferior beings. On the other hand, blinded by passion, many among us regard women as beautiful dolls to be adored as so many goddesses and decorate them with ornaments just as we have Thakorji dressed up in new finery every few hours. We must keep away from this evil also. Ultimately, however, there can be salvation for us only when — and not until — our women become to us what Uma was to Shankar, Sita to Rama and Damayanti to Nala, joining us in our deliberations, arguing with us, appreciating and nourishing our aspirations, understanding, with their marvellous intuition, the unspoken anxieties of our outward life and sharing in them, bringing us the peace that soothes. This goal can hardly be achieved in the immediate future merely by starting girls' schools. As long as we have around our necks the noose of child marriage, men have to be teachers to their wives, and that not merely to make them literate. Gradually, it should be possible to introduce women to the subjects of politics and social reform. Literacy is not essential for this. The man, in such a case, will have to change his attitude to his wife. If a girl were treated as a pupil till she came of age, the husband observing *brahmacharya* the while, if we had not been pressed down by the weight of inertia, we would never subject a girl of twelve or fifteen to the agony of childbearing. One ought to shudder at the very thought of it.

Classes are now conducted for married women and lectures arranged. All this is good as far as it goes. Those who are engaged in this work make a sacrifice of their time. This is to the credit side. It seems to me, however, that unless men simultaneously discharge the duty indicated above, these efforts will not produce much result. A little reflection will show this to be self-evident (Speech at Second Gujarat Educational Conference, 20-10-1917, *CWMG* 14: 31-33).

Woman, Like Man, Needs Education

But although much good and useful work can be done without a knowledge of reading and writing, yet it is my firm belief that you cannot always do without a knowledge thereof. It develops and sharpens one's intellect and it stimulates our power of doing good. I have never placed an unnecessarily high value on the knowledge of reading and writing. I am only attempting to assign its proper place to it. I have pointed out from time to time [that] there is no justification for men to deprive women or to deny to them equal rights on the grounds of their illiteracy; but education is essential for enabling women to uphold these natural rights, to improve them and to spread them; again, the true knowledge of self is unattainable by the millions who are without such education. Many a book is full of innocent pleasure and this will be denied to us without education. It is no exaggeration to say that a human being without education is not far removed from an animal. Education, therefore, is necessary for women as it is for men. Not that the methods of education should be identical in both cases. In the first place, our state system of education is full of error and productive of harm in many respects. It should be eschewed by men and women alike. Even if it were free from its present blemishes, I would not regard it as proper for women from all points of view. Man and woman are of equal rank, but they are not identical. They are a peerless pair, being supplementary to one another; each helps the other so that without the one the existence of the other cannot be conceived, and, therefore, it follows as a necessary corollary from these facts that anything that will impair the status of either of them will involve the equal ruin of them both. In framing any scheme of women's education, this cardinal truth must be constantly kept in mind. Man is supreme in the outward activities of a married pair and, therefore, it is in the fitness of things that he should have a greater knowledge there of. On the other hand, home life is entirely the sphere of woman and, therefore, in domestic affairs, in the upbringing and education of children, women ought to have more knowledge. Not that knowledge should be divided into watertight compartments or that some branches of knowledge should be closed to any one; but unless courses of instruction are based on a discriminating appreciation of these basic principles, the fullest life of man and woman cannot be developed.

I should say a word or two as to whether English education is or is not necessary for our women. I have come to the conclusion that, in the ordinary course of our lives, neither our men nor our women need necessarily have any knowledge of English. True, English is necessary for making a living and for active association in our political movements. I do not believe in women working for a living or undertaking commercial enterprise. The few women who may require or desire to have English education can very easily have their way by joining the schools for men. Introduction of English education in schools meant for women could only lead to a prolongation of our helplessness. I have often read and heard people saying that the rich treasures of English literature should be opened alike to men and women. I submit in all humility that there is some misapprehension in assuming such an attitude. No one intends to close these treasures against women while keeping them open for men. There is none on earth able to prevent you from studying the literature of the whole world if you are fond of literary tastes. But when courses of education have been framed with the needs of a particular society in view, you cannot supply the requirements of the few who have cultivated a literary taste.

Their needs can be met, after we are fully developed, by separate institutions as in Europe. When, through a well-planned scheme, large numbers of men and women begin to receive education and those who remain without it are looked upon as exceptions, we shall have plenty of writers in our languages to bring to us the pleasures of other literatures. If we seek the pleasure of literature always in English our languages will remain poor, which means that we shall remain a poor people. The habit of deriving enjoyment only from a foreign literature is, I must say, if you will pardon me the simile, like the thief's habit of deriving pleasure from stolen goods. The pleasure which Pope found in the Iliad he placed before the people in English of superb beauty. The pleasure which Fitzgerald derived from the *Rubaiyat* of Omar Khayyam made him render it in English of such power that millions of Englishmen keep his poem with them as they do the Bible. The *Bhagavadgita* filled Edwin Arnold with transports of joy; he did not ask the people to learn Sanskrit in order that they may have the same joy, but put the work into English which would stand beside Sanskrit or Pali, pouring his very soul into the language, and thus shared his joy with his people. Our being so very backward is a reason why such work should be undertaken among us on a much larger scale. This will be possible only when a scheme such as I have suggested has been formulated and is firmly adhered to. If only we can give up our infatuation with English and our lack of confidence in ourselves or in the capacity of our languages, the task is not difficult.

In asking our men and women to spend less time in the study of English than they are doing now, my object is not to deprive them of the pleasure which they are likely to derive from it, but I hold that the same pleasure can be obtained at less cost and trouble if we follow a more natural method. The world is full of many a gem of priceless beauty; but then those gems are not all of English setting. Other languages can well boast of productions of similar excellence; all these should be made available to our common people and that can only be done if our own learned men will undertake to translate them for us in our own languages (*The Hindu*, 26-2-1918; Speech at Bhagini Samaj, Bombay, 20-2-1918, *CWMG* 14: 206-08).

Higher Education for Women

I feel that teaching English to them under the circumstances would be like killing them. It will never be possible for hundreds of thousands of women to think or express their thoughts in English; and even if it were possible, it would be undesirable.

If the women for whom we are drawing up this plan are imparted higher education through the mother tongue, they could make their homes as bright and beautiful as gold. Not only that, they could also exert their good influence on their uneducated sisters and thus render valuable service to them as well (*Atmoddhar*, a Marathi Monthly, vol. II p. 135; *True Education*, pp. 157-58).

Education for the Modern Girls of India

I was really surprised to see the stride that education among girls had taken in the State of Travancore. It was a perfect eye-opener to me. The question has always occurred to me: "What will India do with its modern girls?" I call you modern girls of India. The education that we are receiving on these institutions, in my opinion, does not correspond with the life around us, and, when I say life around us, I do not mean the life around us in the cities but the life around us in the villages. Perhaps some of you girls, if not all of you, know that real India is to be found not here in the very few cities but in the seven hundred thousand villages covering a surface of 1,900 miles long and 1,500 miles broad. The question is whether you have any message for your sisters in the villages. Men do not need the message perhaps so much as the women, and I have long before come to the conclusion that unless women of India work side by side with men, there is no salvation for India, salvation in more senses than one. I mean political salvation in the broadest sense, and I mean economic salvation and spiritual salvation also (*The Hindu*, 25-3-1925; Speech at Women's Christian College, Madras, 24-3-1925, *CWMG* 26: 395-96).

Curriculum for Woman's Education

Women must learn as part of elementary education at least their own mother tongue, Hindi if it is not their mother tongue, enough Sanskrit to be able to understand the drift of the *Bhagavadgita*, elementary arithmetic, elementary composition, elementary music and childcare. Along with this, I think they should know well the processes up to the weaving from cotton. When a woman receives this education she should have an environment that will shape her character and enable her to see clearly the evils in society and to avoid them. I have not mentioned religious education separately as it is acquired by practice and would be covered by general reading. Truly speaking, it is a part of the elevating company of a teacher. This is about girls. The education of a widow or a married woman is of course a different matter (Letter to Anandibai, 22-8-1927; *CWMG* 34: 384).

Girls' Education

Today we have assembled for the opening of a girls' school. I have made a thorough study of child education. I could say the same thing about girls' education. But how can experts accept this? Today, even I cannot make that claim. In the prevailing state of affairs it is not easy to talk about girls' education. Everyone may well claim that he is capable of giving education to girls. I will however ask him whether he has imparted true education to his daughter or his wife. How can he who has not observed his *dharma* towards his wife, sister, mother or mother-in-law, set out to teach the daughters or sisters of others? They may well become B.A.s or M.A.s but I shall put them to the same test. I should like to know what kind of husbands and fathers those who write books on girls' education are (*Harijanbandhu*, 9-6-1935; Speech at Inauguration of Vithal Kanya Vidyalaya, Nadiad, 31-5-1935, *CWMG* 61: 118).

Co-education

In theory we are quite in favour of boys and girls receiving education together. But, in practice, it is impossible to ignore deep-rooted habits or prejudices. Experience has shown that Indian parents, as a rule, will not allow their daughters to mingle with boys at a school or elsewhere. And, whenever a forcible mixture takes place, the result "Let them", shouts the unthinking reformer. "They will soon be at home if left alone." But the parents will not wait for the process. They are not reformers and they will not allow experiments to be made at their children's expense (*Indian Opinion*, 19-8-1911; An Education Scandal, *CWMG* 11: 145).

Co-education not Compulsory

As for co-education, the Zakir Husain Committee has not made it compulsory. Where there is a demand for a separate school for girls, the state will have to make provision. The question of co-education has been left open. It will regulate itself according to the time-spirit. So far as I am aware the members of the committee were not all of one mind. Personally I have an open mind. I think that there are just as valid reasons for as against co-education. And I would not oppose the experiment wherever it is made (*Harijan*, 16-7-1938; Some Objections, *CWMG* 67: 175).

Sex Education

Sexual science is of two kinds, that which is used for controlling or overcoming the sexual passion and that which is used to stimulate and feed it. Instruction in the former is as necessary a part of a child's education as the latter is harmful and dangerous and fit therefore only to be shunned. All great religions have rightly regarded *kama* as the arch enemy of man, anger or hatred coming only in the second place. According to the *Gita*, the latter is an offspring of the former. The *Gita* of course uses the word *kama* in its wider sense of desire. But the same holds good of the narrow sense in which it is used here.

This, however, still leaves unanswered the question, viz., whether it is desirable to impart to young pupils a knowledge about the use and function of generative organs. It seems to me that it is necessary to impart such knowledge to a certain extent. At present they are often left to pick up such knowledge anyhow, with the result that they are misled into abusive practices. We cannot properly control or conquer the sexual passion by turning a blind eye to it. I am therefore strongly in favour of teaching young boys and girls the significance and right use of their generative organs. And in my own way I have tried to impart this knowledge to young children of both sexes for whose training I was responsible.

But the sex education that I stand for must have for its object the conquest and sublimation of the sex passion. Such education should automatically serve to bring home to children the essential distinction between man and brute, to make them realize that it is man's special privilege and pride to be gifted with the faculties of head and heart both; that he is a thinking, no less than a feeling, animal, as the very derivation of the word *manushya* shows, and to renounce the sovereignty of reason over the blind instincts is therefore to renounce a man's estate. In man reason quickens and guides the feeling, in brute the soul lies over dormant. To awaken the heart is to awaken the dormant soul, to awaken reason, and to inculcate discrimination between good and evil.

Who should teach this true science of sex? Clearly, he who has attained mastery over his passions. To teach astronomy and kindred sciences we have teachers who have gone through a course of training in them and are masters of their art. Even so must we have as teachers of sexual science, i.e., the science of sex control, those who have studied it and have acquired mastery over self. Even a lofty utterance that has not the backing of sincerity and experience will be inert and lifeless, and will utterly fail to penetrate and quicken the hearts of men, while the speech that springs from self-realization and genuine experience is always fruitful.

Today our entire environment — our reading, our thinking, our social behaviour — is generally calculated to subserve and cater for the sex urge. To break through its coils is no easy task. But it is a task worthy of our highest endeavour. Even if there are a handful of teachers endowed with practical experience, who accept the ideal of attaining self-control as the highest duty of man, are fired by a genuine and undying faith in their mission, and are sleeplessly vigilant and active, their labour will light the path of the children of Gujarat, save the unwary from falling into the mire of sexuality and rescue those who might be already engulfed in it (*Harijan*, 22-11-1936; Sex Education, *CWMG* 64: 61-62).

9

Physical Education

Sound Mind in a Sound Body

Exercise is just as essential to mankind as are air, water and food, though it is true that man cannot get on for a long time without air, water and food as he can without exercise. It is a fact of common experience, however, that one cannot enjoy really good health without exercise. We have to interpret exercise in the same way that we did "food". Exercise does not necessarily mean *moidanda*, football, cricket or going out for a walk. Exercise means physical and mental activity. Just as food is necessary for the mind as much as for bones and flesh, so also is exercise necessary both for body and mind. If the body has no exercise, it is sickly and, if the mind has none, it is dull. Stupidity should also be regarded only as a kind of illness. It betrays sheer ignorance to describe as healthy a wrestler who, though adept at wrestling, is mentally a boor. There is a saying in English that he alone is healthy who has a sound mind in a sound body.

What is this exercise? Nature has so arranged things for us that we can be continuously taking exercise in one way or another. If we but think calmly enough, we shall see that a majority of people in the world live on agriculture. All members in a farmer's family have some form of exercise. It is only if they work eight, ten or even more hours every day in the fields or elsewhere that they can get their daily bread. They need no separate exercise for the mind. A farmer cannot work without applying his mind. He must be able to test the nature of his soil, must watch changes of weather, must know how to manipulate his plough skilfully and be generally familiar with the movements of the stars, the sun and the moon. However clever a city-dweller may be, every time he goes to a farmer's house, he feels altogether out of his element. The farmer can say how seed should be sown; he is familiar with all the byways in the vicinity and knows all the men in the neighbourhood. By looking at the stars he can judge the direction even at night. He can make certain deductions from the voice and speed of birds; for instance, when certain birds cluster or sing together, he sees in it a sign of the approach of the monsoon or some other similar phenomenon. Thus, the farmer knows enough of astronomy, geography and geology to serve his needs. He has to feed his children and has, therefore, some idea of the duties of man, and, residing as he does in the vast open spaces of this earth, he naturally becomes aware of the greatness of God. Physically, it goes without saying, he is always sturdy. He is his own physician, when ill. Thus, we can see, he does have an educated mind.

But all men are not going to be farmers. Moreover, these chapters are not being written for the benefit of farmers. The question is, what should those who have gone into business or some similar profession do in this regard? The farmer's life has been described at some length in order that we may find a rational answer to this problem, that we who are not farmers can arrange our way of life somewhat on the pattern of his and that we may realize that, in so far as our manner of living differs from the farmer's, we would enjoy poorer health. We can conclude from a farmer's way of living that a man should do physical work for eight hours a day and that of a kind that would stimulate our mental powers in the very process of doing it. Now, merchants and others certainly obtain mental exercise in the course of their work, but this is one-sided. A businessman does not know astronomy or geography or history, as the farmer does. He may be able to judge about movements of prices and may be proficient in the art of salesmanship, but this is not enough to exercise fully his mental faculties. In this type of work, the body does perform some movements now and then, but they are too slight to be of any account.

In the West, they have invented games like cricket for such people.

Another way is to observe some days in the year as holidays, when more games are played, and to do some light reading by way of mental exercise. This is one method which we may consider. To be sure, spending time in sports does give some exercise to the body, but exercise of this kind does nothing to improve the mind. We can see the truth of this from numerous instances. What proportion of men of high intellectual calibre shall we find among those who regularly play cricket or from among the large number who play football? In India, what do we observe as regards the mental development of the princes who give their time to sports? Again, how many of those with well-developed intellectual powers are sportsmen? Experience shows that highly intellectual men are seldom sportsmen as well. The British nowadays are very much given to sports. Their own poet, Kipling, has described these sportsmen as enemies of the mind, and adds that they will also prove themselves enemies to their country. In India, our intellectuals seem to have found a different way. They provide exercise for their minds but relatively very little or none for their bodies. These people are lost to us. Their bodies are enfeebled by excessive intellectual work. They are continually pursued by some ailment or other and just when they have gained enough experience to be of real use to the country, they pass away. From this we may conclude that neither exercising the brain alone nor the body alone is enough and also that exercise which serves no useful purpose, namely, that derived from sports, has little meaning. Real exercise is that which trains, continuously, both mind and body alike. He alone who takes such exercise can preserve good health. The farmer is the only such person.

Then, what are those to do who are not farmers? The exercise obtained from sports such as cricket leaves much to be desired. We must, therefore, think of a form of exercise something like what the farmer gets. Businessmen and others similarly placed can make a garden round their house and regularly spend two to four hours a day digging there. Hawkers get exercise from their own work itself. If we are living in a rented room, we should not raise any difficulty about working in another's land, for that would indicate a small mind. We would derive nothing but benefit from working on land, whosoever's it might be. The appearance of our house would be improved and we would have the satisfaction of having looked after another's land. It is necessary to say a few words for those who cannot find an opportunity to work on land or who do not favour such work in any circumstances. Apart from working on land, the best form of exercise is walking. It has been truly described as the king of physical exercises. Our *fakir*s and *sadhu*s are very healthy.

One reason for this is that they do not use horses, carriages or other vehicles. Their journeys are always performed on foot. There has been a famous American writer named Thoreau, who has written a highly thought-provoking book on the subject of walking. According to him, the writings of one who refuses to leave his house on the excuse of lack of time and who undertakes no physical activity, are bound to be anaemic like himself. Speaking of his own experience, he says that when he wrote his best books he was doing his longest walking. He thought nothing of walking four or five hours at a stretch. Just as we cannot work when we are hungry, so it should be with exercise. We do not know how to measure mental work, therefore, we are not able to realize that mental work done unaccompanied by physical exercise will inevitably be dull and ineffectual. Walking results in rapid circulation of blood in all the parts of the body, promotes movements in every organ and strengthens it. One should remember that the arms move during walking. We obtain fresh air by going for a walk and behold the beauties of Nature. One should not take walks always in the same place or in narrow lanes but go out into fields and groves. We will then be able to appreciate in some measure the beauty of Nature. A walk of a mile or two can scarcely be called walking. A walk, to be worth the name, should cover ten or twelve miles. Those who cannot do this regularly can take long walks on Sundays. A certain patient, who used to suffer from indigestion, went one day to an experienced *vaidya* for some pills. The *vaidya* advised him to take short but regular walks. The patient protested that he was too weak. The *vaidya* realized that he was, in fact, a timid man. He thereupon took the patient with him in his carriage. On the way he purposely dropped his whip. The patient, out of politeness, had to get out to pick it up. The *vaidya* immediately drove off. The poor patient had to follow, panting hard for breath. The *vaidya* having made sure that the former had covered a fairly long distance, turned the carriage back, picked him up and told him that, since walking was the only medicine for him, he — the *vaidya* — had forced him to walk even at the risk of appearing cruel. By this time, however, the patient was ravenously hungry and had forgotten all about the whip episode. He thanked the doctor, went home and ate his fill. Those who are not in the habit of walking and suffer from indigestion and its accompanying ills should try the experiment (*Indian Opinion*, 12-4-1913; General Knowledge About Health [XV], *CWMG* 12: 22-25).

Walking Is the Best Exercise

We are as careless about exercise as about diet. To stroll one or two miles at a leisurely pace is no exercise. To hit a billiard ball one or two hundred times with a cue is also no exercise. When exercise is taken in this manner in a room with foul-smelling air, the effect is bound to be harmful. In our predicament, when no other form of exercise is convenient, walking is the best exercise. But exercise is worth the name only if one can walk six miles at a stretch in the morning and again in the evening. The walking should be done briskly, at a speed of four miles an hour. Thoreau used to walk for eight hours daily when he wrote his best book. Tolstoy testifies to the fact that while writing his best books he never used to sit at his desk before he had had plenty of exercise. He always used to work on a farm. [Some people say:] "I cannot spare a minute from the clients' work or from public work, and take exercise." Such talk is sheer vanity. It would seem to proceed from a belief that but for us public work would go to the dogs. The Grand Old Man of India, Dadabhai, has been observing all the general rules of hygiene and has never departed from his routine of exercise, etc. Hence, we see him alive to this day, and it would be in no way surprising if this *rishi* were to live a hundred years like those of old times (*Prajabandhu*, 23-4-1916; Letter to "Prajabandhu", 20-4-2016, *CWMG* 13: 270-71).

Indigenous Games

I include in the term "physical training" sports, games, etc. These, too, have been little thought of. Indigenous games have been given up and tennis, cricket and football hold sway. Admittedly, these games are enjoyable. If, however, we had not been carried away by enthusiasm for all things Western, we would not have given up our inexpensive but equally interesting games like *gedi-dado*, *gilli-danda*, *kho-kho*, *mag-matali*, *kabaddi*, *kharo pat*, *nava nagelio*, *sat tali*, etc. Exercises which provided the completest training for every bodily organ and the old style gymnasium where they taught wrestling have almost totally disappeared. I think if anything from the West deserves copying, it is drill. A friend once remarked that we did not know how to walk, particularly when we had to walk in squads and keep step. Silently to walk in step, by hundreds and thousands of us in twos and fours, shifting the directions from time to time is something we can never do. It is not that such drill is useful only in actual battle. It can be of great use in many other activities in the sphere of public service. For example, in extinguishing fire, in rescuing people from drowning, in carrying the sick and disabled in a *doli*, etc., [previous practice in] drill is a valuable aid. Thus, it is necessary to introduce in our schools indigenous games, exercises and the Western type of drill (Speech at Second Gujarat Educational Conference, Broach,

20-10-1917, *CWMG* 14: 30-31).

Inexpensive Exercises

Many students feel that it is not necessary to make any special effort for health. However, regular exercise is absolutely necessary for the body. What can be expected of a student who is not well equipped in health? Just as milk cannot be held in a paper container, so also education is not likely to remain for long in the paper-like bodies of our students. The body is the abode of the spirit and, therefore, holy like a place of pilgrimage. We must see that it is well protected. Walking regularly and energetically for an hour and a half in the morning and for the same period in the evening in open air keeps it healthy and the mind fresh. The time thus spent is not wasted. Such exercise, coupled with rest, will invigorate both the body and the intellect, enabling one to learn things more quickly. I think games like cricket have no place in a poor country like India. We have a number of inexpensive games of our own which afford innocent joy (Speech at Bihar Students' Conference, 15-10-1917, *CWMG* 14: 135-36).

Asanas and Pranayama

"In my opinion", Gandhiji remarked, "the physical training for our students should follow the old Indian system — that of *pranayama, asana*s, etc. I believe that the system of physical education developed by Müller and others in the West, who have written on this subject and also demonstrated the efficacy of their system through practical results, has its roots in the old Indian system. What these writers have done is to set it out in modern scientific language and perhaps to improve it in places. I am conscious that we have done very little work in this direction. Having gone through a course of training according to this old system, those who further want to learn the present-day wrestling, etc., may be given the facilities to do so. But training *lathi* and sword, etc., should not be considered necessary. I do not think that it is necessary to give *lathi* training, etc., to the boys. *Lathi* does not seem to have much to do with the toning up of the body or with the development of its different parts. It is not therefore a part of the physical training but a part of the training useful in one's defence or similar purposes" (Source not known. Probably from Madhpuda — the handwritten magazine of the Satyagraha Ashram School, date of writing approximately 1924-25).

Compulsory Physical Training

I was glad to hear that physical training and games have been made compulsory. Let us make compulsory for ourselves all that is good.

Gujarati and Sanskrit, etc., we consider good and necessary and therefore prescribe them as compulsory subjects. We did not consider physical training and games equally necessary and had left them to the choice of the students. Now that we have made them compulsory it means that we consider them as necessary as Gujarati. Restraints imposed upon us against our will tend to make slaves of us, but restraints willingly accepted augment our true independence (Source not known. Probably from Madhpuda — the handwritten magazine of the Satyagraha Ashram School, date of writing approximately 1924-25).

Brahmacharya and Physical Fitness

Our Shastras say that a boy who would keep his body fit and strong and make the best use of it should observe *brahmacharya*. I have travelled all over the country and one of the most deplorable things I have noticed is the rickety bodies of young men. So long as we labour under the curse of child-marriage, and so long as many members of our society are children of such marriages, so long much bodily exercise is an impossibility. Who will recommend physical exercise to consumptives? We should therefore lay the axe at the root of this curse, if we would see our young men and women strong and healthy and India on the path of vigorous and healthy growth. Manu has laid down that a student should observe *brahmacharya* up to his 25th year at least. All physical exercise will be futile so long as these conditions are not satisfied (*Young India*, 30-12-1926; Speech at Opening of Gymnasium, Amraoti, 21-12-1926, *CWMG* 32: 443).

Time for Exercise

I believed then and I believe even now, that, no matter what amount of work one has, one should always find some time for exercise, just as one does for one's meals. It is my humble opinion that, far from taking away from one's capacity for work, it adds to it (*An Autobiography*, Part III, Chapter XVII, *CWMG* 39: 189).

10

Education through Prayer, Music, Art and Culture

Prayer

As food is necessary for the body, prayer is necessary for the soul. A man may be able to do without food for a number of days — as MacSwiney did for over 70 days — but believing in God, man cannot, should not, live a moment without prayer. You will say that we see lots of people living without prayer. I dare say they do, but it is the existence of the brute which, for man, is worse than death. I have not the shadow of a doubt that the strife and quarrels with which our atmosphere is so full today are due to the absence of the spirit of true prayer. You will demur to the statement, I know, and contend that millions of Hindus, Mussalmans and Christians do offer their prayers. It is because I had thought you would raise this objection that I used the words "true prayers". The fact is we have been offering our prayers with the lips but hardly ever with our hearts, and it is to escape, if possible, the hypocrisy of the lip-prayer, that we in the Ashram repeat every evening the last verses of the second chapter of the *Bhagavadgita*. The condition of the "Equable in Spirit" that is described in those verses, if we contemplate them daily, is bound slowly to turn our hearts towards God. If you students would base your education on the true foundation of a pure character and pure heart there is nothing so helpful as to offer your prayers every day truly and religiously (*Young India*, 15-12-1927; Speech at Students' Meeting, Berhampur, 4-12-1927, *CWMG* 35: 361).

Prayer Meetings

Prayer is not an asking. It is a longing of the soul. It is a daily admission of one's weakness. The tallest among us has a perpetual reminder of his nothingness before death, disease, old age, accidents, etc. We are living in the midst of death. What is the value of "working for our own schemes" when they might be reduced to naught in the twinkling of an eye, or when we may be equally swiftly and unawares be taken away from them? But we may feel strong as a rock, if we could truthfully say: "We work for God and His schemes." Then all is as clear as daylight. Then nothing perishes. All perishing is then only what seems. Death and destruction have then, but only then, no reality about them. For death or destruction is then but a change. An artist destroys his picture for creating a better one. A watch-maker throws away a bad spring to put in a new and useful one.

A congregational prayer is a mighty thing. What we do not often do alone, we do together. Boys do not need conviction. If they merely attend in obedience to the call to prayer without inward resistance, they feel the exaltation. But many do not. They are even mischievous. All the same the unconscious effect cannot be resisted. Are there not boys who at the commencement of their career were scoffers but who subsequently became mighty believers in the efficacy of congregational prayer? It is a common experience for men who have no robust faith to seek the comfort of congregational prayer. All who flock to churches, temples, or mosques are not scoffers or humbugs. They are honest men and women. For them congregational prayer is like a daily bath, a necessity, of their existence. These places of worship are not a mere idle superstition to be swept away at the first opportunity. They have survived all attacks up to now and are likely to persist to the end of time (*Young India*, 23-9-1926; No Faith in Prayer, *CWMG* 31: 440-41).

Music

Nowhere do I find a place given to music. It exercises a powerful influence over us. We do not realize this vividly enough, otherwise we would have done everything possible to teach music to our boys and girls. The Vedic hymns seem to follow musical tunes in their composition. Harmonious music has the power to soothe the anguish of the soul. At times, we find restlessness in a large gathering. This can be arrested and calmed if a national song is sung by all. That hundreds of boys may sing a poem full of courage and the spirit of adventure and bravery and be inspired with the spirit of heroism is no commonplace fact. We have an example of the power of music in the fact that boatmen and other labourers raise, in unison, the cry of *Harahar* and *Allabeli* and this helps them in their work. I have seen English friends trying to fight cold by singing songs. Our boys learn to sing songs from popular plays in all manner of tunes and without regard to time and place, and try their hands on noisy harmoniums and other instruments, and this does them harm. If, instead, they were to be correctly trained in music, they would not waste their time singing, or attempting to sing, music-hall songs. Just as a trained singer never sings out of tune or at the wrong time, even so one who has learnt classical music will not go in for street music. Music must get a place in our efforts at popular awakening (Speech at Second Gujarat Educational Conference, 20-10-1917, *CWMG* 14: 30).

Music means rhythm, order. Its effect is electrical. It immediately soothes. I have seen, in European countries, a resourceful superintendent of police by starting a popular song controlling the mischievous tendencies of mobs. Unfortunately like our Shastras, music has been the prerogative of the few, either the barter of prostitutes or high-class religious devotees. It has never become nationalized in the modern sense. If I had any influence with volunteer boy scouts and Seva Samiti organizations, I would make compulsory a proper singing in company of national songs. And to that end I should have great musicians attending every congress or conference and teaching mass music (*Young India*, 8-9-1920; Democracy "Versus" Mobocracy, *CWMG* 18: 241-42).

Music and Other Arts

Our conversation having that morning centred round music, Mahatmaji told me in passing how fond he really was of music even though he could not boast of the power of any expert for analytic appreciation. He had said:

> I am so fond of music that once, while I was in a South African Hospital and ailing from a bruise on my upper lip, I felt greatly soothed as the daughter of a friend of mine sang the song "Lead, Kindly Light" at my request.

On my asking him if he knew any of the beautiful songs of Mirabai, he said:

> Yes, I have heard a good many of them. They are so beautiful. It's because they come from the heart and not from any desire to compose or to please a public.

I called the same evening at his request. After the music, I saw that it had affected him visibly. For I thought I saw his eyes glisten even in that none-too-bright light of the hospital.

"I feel" said I after a short pause, "that our beautiful music has been sadly neglected in the schools and colleges." Mahatmaji replied:

Yes, it has, I have always said so.

Srijut Mahadeo Desai who was present throughout our conversation corroborated this. "I am glad to hear you say so. Because I have been all along under the impression that you would be against all arts such as music."

I! Against music! Well, I know, I know. . . There are so many superstitions rife about me that it has become now almost impossible for me to overtake those who have set them afloat. As a result, my friends only smile at me when I try to lay any claim to being an artist myself.

"I am glad to hear this; because I have been given to understand that in your philosophy of life, which is one of unqualified asceticism, arts like music can hardly aspire to any place." Mahatmaji emphatically said:

But I maintain that asceticism is the greatest art in life.

"What I however meant by art just now is a somewhat different activity such as music or painting or sculpture for the matter of that. And I had thought that you would be rather opposed to them than otherwise." Mahatmaji said:

I, opposed to arts like music! Why, I cannot even conceive of an evolution of the religious life of India without music. I do say I am a lover of music as well as the other arts. Only, my values may be different from the accepted ones, that's all. I am doubtless against much that passes for art in these days. I do not for instance call that art which demands an intimate knowledge of its technique for its appreciation. If you go to the Satyagraha Ashram, you will find the walls bare. And my friends object to this. I admit I don't have paintings on the walls of my Ashram. But that is because I think that the walls are meant for sheltering us, and not because I am opposed to art as such. For have I not gazed and gazed at the wonderful vault of the starry sky — hardly ever tiring of the same? And I do say that I can never conceive of any painting superior to the star-studded sky in its satisfying effect on the mind. It has bewildered me, mystified me, sent me into the most wonderful ecstatic thrills imaginable. Side by side with this wondrous mystery of God's artistic handiwork, does not that of man appear to be the merest tinsel?

I said: "I agree with you when you say that Nature is a great artist, as also when you inveigh against the regrettable prostitution of art, which unhappily so often passes for art. I differ also from those artists who have acquired the habit of saying that art is even greater than life."

Exactly. Life is and must always be greater than all the arts put together. I go still further. For I say that he is the greatest artist who leads the best life. For what is art without the background and setting of a worthy life? An art is to be valued only when it ennobles life. I object emphatically only when people say that art is everything, that it does not matter even if life has to be held subservient to its (i.e., art's) fulfilment. I have then to say that my values are different, that is all. But fancy people saying that I am opposed to all arts on that account! (*The Bombay Chronicle*, 5-2-1924; Interview to Dilip Kumar Roy, 2-2-1924, *CWMG* 23: 192-94).

Music: A Divine Art

It is sad that the study of music is generally neglected in our country today. Without it, the entire educational system seems to me to be incomplete. Music brings sweetness to the individual and to the social life of the people. Even as *pranayama* is necessary for the regulation of breath, so is music for disciplining the voice. Dissemination of the knowledge of music among the people will greatly help in controlling and stopping the noise which is a usual feature of public meetings in this country. Music pacifies anger and its judicious use is highly helpful in leading a man to the vision of God. It does not mean shouting and shrieking a tune anyhow like a rigmarole, nor does it mean the singing of stage songs. I have already referred to its ordinary meaning above, but its deeper meaning is that our whole life should be sweet and musical like a song. It goes without saying that life cannot be made like that without the practice of virtues such as truth, honesty, etc. To make life musical means to make it one with God, to merge it in Him. He who has not rid himself of *raga* and *dvesha*, i.e., likes and dislikes, who has not tasted of the joy of service, cannot have any understanding of celestial music. A study of music, which does not take account of this deeper aspect of this divine art, has little or no value for me (*Navajivan*, 1-7-1928; Questions on Education – V, *CWMG* 37: 2-3).

Music and Harmony

There is a famous classical saying which has now become a proverb that the man "that hath no music in himself" is either an ascetic or a beast. We are far from being ascetics, and to the extent that we are devoid of music we are near allied to beasts. To know music is to transfer it to life. The prevalent discord of today is an indication of our sad plight. There can be no *swaraj* where there is no harmony, no music.

Where there is discord and everyone striking his own tune, there is bad government or anarchy. Work for *swaraj* fails to appeal to us because we have no music in us. When we have millions of people singing together in harmony or taking God's name in unison, making one music, we shall have taken the first step to *swaraj*. If we cannot achieve this simple thing, how can we win *swaraj*?

We have free music classes in Ahmedabad for the last three years conducted by one who is an expert. And yet we have to be satisfied today with a roll-attendance of 10 and a regular attendance of four. It is poor consolation indeed; but we live in hope and Dr. Hariprasad, who sees a ray of hope when he finds even one pol out of the hundreds in Ahmedabad clean and tidy, might well feel satisfied that we have at least four regular music lovers.

Where there is filth and squalor and misery there can be no music. It implies an atmosphere quite the contrary. If we put a broad interpretation on music, i.e., if we mean by it union, concord, mutual help, it may be said that in no department of life can we dispense with it.

Music today has been regarded to mean the vocal effort of a singing girl. We fight shy of sending our sisters and daughters to music schools. There seems to be a superstition that their voice is best when it is devoid of sweetness. That explains why Dr. Hariprasad has had to express satisfaction with an attendance of ten students.

Music, truly speaking, is an ancient and sacred art. The hymns of *Samaveda* are a mine of music, and no *ayat* of the Koran can be recited unmusically. David's Psalms transport you to raptures and remind you of the hymns from *Samaveda.* Let us revive this art and patronize the school of music.

We see Hindu and Mussalman musicians sitting cheek by jowl and partaking in musical concerts. When shall we see the same fraternal union in other affairs of our life? We shall then have the name of Rama and Rahman simultaneously on our lips.

I am glad some of you here are patronizing music. If many more send their children to the music class it will be part of their contribution to national uplift.

But to go a step further. If we would see music in millions of our poor homes, we should all wear *khadi* and spin. The music we have had today was sweet indeed but it is a privilege of the favoured few. The music of the spinning-wheel can be a free gift to all and is therefore sweeter. It is the hope and solace and mainstay of the millions, and for me therefore the truly good music (*Young India*, 15-4-1926; Speech on Music, Ahmedabad, 21-3-1926, *CWMG* 30: 159-60).

Music Fills the Soul

Music has given me peace. I can remember occasions when music instantly tranquillized my mind when I was greatly agitated over something. Music has helped me to overcome anger. I can recall occasions when a hymn sank deep into me though the same thing expressed in prose had failed to touch me. I also found that the meaning of hymns discordantly sung has failed to come home to me and that it burns itself on my mind when they have been properly sung. When I hear *Gita* verses melodiously recited I never grow weary of hearing and the more I hear the deeper sinks the meaning into my heart. Melodious recitations of the *Ramayana* which I heard in my childhood left on me an impression which years have not obliterated or weakened. I distinctly remember how when once the hymn "The path of the Lord is meant for the brave, not the coward" was sung to me in an extraordinarily sweet tune, it moved me as it had never before. In 1907 while in the Transvaal I was almost fatally assaulted, the pain of the wounds was relieved when at my instance Olive Doke gently sang to me "Lead, Kindly Light".

Let no one infer from this that I know music. On the contrary it would be more correct to say that my knowledge of music is very elementary. I cannot critically judge music. All I can claim is that I have a natural ear for good homely music.

I do not mean to suggest either that because the influence of music has been uniformly good on me it must act similarly on others. On the contrary I know that many people employ music to feed their carnal passions. To sum up, therefore, we may say that the influence of music will differ according to temperaments. As Tulsidas has sung:

The Lord of Creation created everything in this world as an admixture of good and evil. But a good man selects the good and rejects the evil even as the fabled swan is said to help himself to cream leaving the water in the milk (*Young India*, 10-1-1929; Influence of Music, *CWMG* 38: 90).

True Art is Expression of the Soul

[RAMACNANDRAN:] How is it that many intelligent and eminent men, who love and admire you, hold that you consciously or unconsciously have ruled out of the scheme of national regeneration all considerations of Art?

[GANDHIJI:] I am sorry that in this matter I have been generally misunderstood. There are two aspects of things — the outward and the inward. It is purely a matter of emphasis with me. The outward has no meaning except in so far as it helps the inward. All true Art is thus the expression of the soul. The outward forms have value only in so far as they are the expression of the inner spirit of man.

[R:] (Hesitatingly) The great artists themselves have declared that Art is the translation of the urge and unrest in the soul of the artist into words, colours, shapes, etc.

Yes, Art of that nature has the greatest possible appeal for me. But I know that many call themselves as artists, and are recognized as such, and yet in their works there is absolutely no trace of the soul's upward urge and unrest.

[R:] Have you any instance in mind?

Yes, take Oscar Wilde. I can speak of him, as I was in England at the time that he was being much discussed and talked about.

[R:] I have been told that Oscar Wilde was one of the greatest literary artists of modern times.

Yes, that is just my trouble. Wilde saw the highest Art simply in outward forms and therefore succeeded in beautifying immorality. All true Art must help the soul to realize its inner self. In my own case, I find that I can do entirely without external forms in my soul's realization. I can claim, therefore, that there is truly sufficient Art in my life, though you might not see what you call works of Art about me. My room may have blank walls; and I may even dispense with the roof, so that I may gaze out upon the starry heavens overhead that stretch in an unending expanse of beauty. What conscious Art of man can give me the panoramic scenes that open out before me, when I look up to the sky above with all its shining stars? This, however, does not mean that I refuse to accept the value of productions of Art, generally accepted as such, but only that I personally feel how inadequate these are compared with the eternal symbols of beauty in Nature. These productions of man's Art have their value only so far as they help the soul onward towards self-realization.

[R:] But the artists claim to see and to find Truth through outward beauty. Is it possible to see and find Truth in that way?

I would reverse the order. I see and find Beauty in Truth or through Truth. All Truths, not merely true ideas, but truthful faces, truthful pictures, or songs, are highly beautiful. People generally fail to see Beauty in Truth, the ordinary man runs away from it and becomes blind to the beauty in it. Whenever men begin to see Beauty in Truth, then true Art will arise.

[R:] But cannot Beauty be separated from Truth, and Truth from Beauty?

I should want to know exactly what is Beauty. If it is what people generally understand by that word, then they are wide apart. Is a woman with fair features necessarily beautiful?

[R:] Yes.

Even if she may be of an ugly character?

[R:] But her face in that case cannot be beautiful. It will always be the index of the soul within. The true artist with the genius of perception will produce the right expression.

But here you are begging the whole question. You now admit that mere outward form may not make a thing beautiful. To a true artist only that face is beautiful which, quite apart from exterior, shines with the Truth within the soul. There is then, as I have said, no Beauty apart from Truth. On the other hand, Truth may manifest itself in forms which may not be outwardly beautiful at all. Socrates, we are told, was the most truthful man of his time and yet his features are said to have been the ugliest in Greece. To my mind he was beautiful, because all his life was a striving after Truth, and you may remember that his outward form did not prevent Phidias from appreciating the beauty of Truth in him, though as an artist he was accustomed to see Beauty in outward forms also!

[R:] But, Bapuji, the most beautiful things have often been created by men whose own lives were not beautiful.

That only means that Truth and untruth often coexist; good and evil are often found together. In an artist also not seldom the right perception of things and the wrong coexist. Truly beautiful creations come when right perception is at work. If these moments are rare in life, they are also rare in Art.

[R:] If only truthful or good things can be beautiful, how can things without a moral quality be beautiful? . . . Is there truth, Bapuji, in things that are neither moral nor immoral in themselves? For instance, is there truth in a sunset or a crescent moon that shines amid the stars at night?

Indeed these beauties are truthful, inasmuch as they make me think of the Creator at the back of them. How else could these be beautiful, but for the Truth that is in the centre of creation? When I admire the wonder of a sunset or the beauty of the moon, my soul expands in worship of the Creator. I try to see Him and His mercies in all these creations. But even the sunsets and sunrises would be mere hindrances, if they did not help me to think of Him. Anything which is a hindrance to the flight of the soul, is a delusion and a snare; even, like the body, which often does hinder you in the path of salvation (*Young India*, 13-11-1924 & 20-11-1924; Discussion with G. Ramachandran, 21/22-10-1924, *CWMG* 25: 248-50).

Music and Painting

There is this difference between music and painting: While painting can be learnt only by a few who have a natural aptitude for it, music must be and can be learnt by all. In painting too, drawing of straight lines and the figures of animate and inanimate objects can be taught to all. It is certainly useful and necessary and I want it to be taught to every child before it is taught the alphabet (*Navajivan*, 1-7-1928; Questions on Education – V, *CWMG* 37: 3).

Global Culture

I do not want my house to be walled in on all sides and my windows to be stuffed. I want the cultures of all the lands to be blown about my house as freely as possible. But I refuse to be blown off my feet by any. I refuse to live in other people's houses as an interloper, a beggar or a slave. I refuse to put the unnecessary strain of learning English upon my sisters for the sake of false pride or questionable social advantage. I would have our young men and young women with literary taste to learn as much of

English and other world languages as they like, and then expect them to give the benefits of their learning to India and to the world, like a Bose, a Roy or the poet himself. But I would not have a single Indian to forget, neglect or be ashamed of his mother tongue, or to feel that he or she cannot think or express the best thoughts in his or her own vernacular. Mine is not a religion of the prison-house (*Young India*, 1-6-1921; Notes, *CWMG* 20: 159).

Cultural Diversity

Nothing can be farther from my thought than that we should become exclusive or erect barriers. But I do respectfully contend that an appreciation of other cultures can fitly follow, never precede an appreciation and assimilation of our own. It is my firm opinion that no culture has treasures so rich as ours has. We have not known it, we have been made even to deprecate its study and deprecate its value. We have almost ceased to live it. An academic grasp without practice behind it is like an embalmed corpse, perhaps lovely to look at but nothing to inspire or ennoble. My religion forbids me to belittle or disregard other cultures, as it insists under pain of civil suicide upon imbibing and living my own (*Young India*, 1-9-1921; National Education, *CWMG* 21: 40).

The Indian culture of our times is in the making. Many of us are striving to produce a blend of all the cultures which seem today to be in clash with one another. No culture can live if it attempts to be exclusive. There is no such thing as pure Aryan culture in existence today in India. Whether the Aryans were indigenous to India or were unwelcome intruders, does not interest me much. What does interest me is the fact that my remote ancestors blended with one another with the utmost freedom and we of the present generation are a result of that blend. Whether we are doing any good to the country of our birth and the tiny globe which sustains us or whether we are a burden, the future alone will show (*Harijan*, 9-5-1936; Hindi or Hindustani, *CWMG* 62: 385).

Either people of different faiths having lived together in friendship have produced a beautiful blend of cultures, which we shall strive to perpetuate and increasingly strengthen, or we shall cast about for the day when there was only one religion represented in Hindustan and retrace our steps to that exclusive culture. It is just possible that we might not be able to find any such historical date and if we do and we retrace our steps, we shall throw our culture back to that ugly period and deservedly earn the execration of the universe (*Harijan*, 2-11-1947; Of New Universities, *CWMG* 89: 403).

Western vs Eastern Culture

Of myself whilst I have freely acknowledged my debt to Western culture, I can say that whatever service I have been able to render to the nation has been due entirely to the retention by me of Eastern culture to the extent it has been possible. I should have been thoroughly useless to the masses as an Anglicized, denationalized being knowing little of, caring less for and perhaps even despising their ways, habits, thoughts and aspirations (*Young India*, 5-7-1928; The Curse of Foreign Medium, *CWMG* 37: 21).

European civilization is no doubt suited for the Europeans but it will mean ruin for India, if we endeavour to copy it. This is not to say that we may not adopt and assimilate whatever may be good and capable of assimilation by us as it does not also mean that even the Europeans will not have to part with whatever evil might have crept into it. The incessant search for material comforts and their multiplication is such an evil, and I make bold to say that the Europeans themselves will have to remodel their outlook, if they are not to perish under the weight of the comforts to which they are becoming slaves. It may be that my reading is wrong, but I know that for India to run after the Golden Fleece is to court certain death. Let us engrave on our hearts the motto of a Western philosopher, "Plain living and high thinking". Today it is certain that the millions cannot have high living and we the few who profess to do the thinking for the masses run the risk, in a vain search after high living, of missing high thinking (*Young India*, 30-4-1931; The Loin-Cloth, *CWMG* 46: 55-56).

11

Libraries and Textbooks

Library and Librarian

. . . let me set out the ideals I cherish about the library. Have the building of the library planned in such a way that when it expands into new departments, new structures could be annexed to the parent building without their looking hemmed in or without reducing the architecture to a monstrosity. While planning the building see that it can serve as a public lecture hall, a quiet place for students to read and study as also for research scholars. Our ideal should be to make it the largest and the best library in the world. . . .

Please see that the library makes progress day by day. It would be better if you get one or two persons who could give most of their time to the library. Do not have as your librarian a merchant who can only preserve your books but have someone who appreciates them and can select them. If no one volunteers for the task, offer higher remuneration. Allow the Harijans free use of the library and let them take books home. Please bear the loss if they soil or steal the books. They are lowest even among the poor. Allow this concession to all the poor if you can. That will bring credit to you (*Harijanbandhu,* 1-10-1933; Speech at Ahmedabad – II, 21-9-1933, *CWMG* 56: 16-17).

Textbooks

I have written a book called *Balpothi,* not much worth talking about. If I sit down to read it, I can finish it in five minutes. If I read it a little carefully, I would finish it in ten minutes. I have not read the comments on it which have been received. I know that many of these are not likely to please me much. There is no measure in the praise or censure generally showered on me and, therefore, either has little effect on me. However that be, the idea behind that book is great. It is that a teacher should impart education only by word of mouth; that he cannot do so with the help of books and textbooks. Who knows what stuff gets into the brains of children in countries where there are heaps of textbooks! The devil takes possession of them, the children's thinking power is reduced to nil. This conclusion of mine is based on my experience of countless children and on discussions with many teachers. I used to move about with wide-open eyes in South Africa. There was a conflagration in the country, and moving even in the midst of that I observed this thing. Let us compare two schools: one in which teachers are supplied with textbooks and another in which they have to teach without the use of a single textbook. The teachers in both are equally gifted. The one, then, which has no textbooks to use will be able to give more to the pupil; than the one which has them. I do not want children to have any textbooks. The teachers may, if they wish, read them. We may write as much for them as we choose. If you write for children, you will make the teachers mechanical and destroy their originality and initiative. . . .

You may ask me if I have worked as a teacher. My view is based on considerable experience and I have thought a great deal about education (*Navajivan*, 3-8-1924; Speech at National Education Conference, 1-8-1924, *CWMG* 24: 489-90).

Choking Load of Books

Our students are weighed down with cares and worries when they should really be "careful for nothing". They have simply to receive and to assimilate. They should know only to discriminate between what should be received and what rejected. It is the duty of the teacher to teach his pupils discrimination. If we go on talking in indiscriminately, we would be no better. than machines. We are thinking, knowing beings and we must in this period distinguish truth from untruth, sweet from bitter language, clean from unclean things and so on. But the student's path today is strewn with more difficulties than the one of distinguishing good from bad things. He has to fight the hostile atmosphere around him. Instead of the sacred surroundings of a *rishi* guru's *ashram* and his paternal care, he has the atmosphere of a broken down home, and the artificial surroundings created by the modern system of education. The *rishi*s taught their pupils without books. They only gave them a few *mantra*s which the pupils treasured in their memories and translated in practical life. The present-day student has to live in the midst of heaps of books, sufficient to choke him (*Young India*, 29-1-1925; Speech at Samaldas College, Bhavnagar, 9-1-1925, *CWMG* 25: 575-76).

Textbooks for Teachers

For India a multiplicity of textbooks means deprivation of the vast majority of village children of the means of instruction. Textbooks, therefore, in India must mean, principally and for the lower standards, textbooks for teachers, not pupils. Indeed, I am not sure that it is not better for the children to have much of the preliminary instruction imparted to them vocally. To impose on children of tender age a knowledge of the alphabet and the ability to read before they can gain general knowledge is to deprive them, whilst they are fresh, of the power of assimilating instruction by word of mouth. Should, for instance, a lad of seven wait for learning the *Ramayana* till he can read it? The results that we arrive at when we think of the few lakhs living in the cities of India are wholly different from those we obtain when we think in terms of the millions of rural India . . ., therefore, is fraught with important consequences (*Young India*, 16-9-1926; Notes, *CWMG* 31: 410).

Books vs Need-based Learning

I have, therefore, come to the conclusion that books are required more for the teachers than for the taught. And every teacher, if he is to do full justice to his pupils, will have to prepare the daily lesson from the material available to him. This, too, he will have to suit to the special requirements of his class.

Real education has to draw out the best from the boys and girls to be educated. This can never be done by packing ill-assorted and unwanted information into the heads of the pupils. It becomes a dead weight crushing all originality in them and turning them into mere automata. If we were not ourselves victims of the system, we would long ago have realized the mischief wrought by the modern method of giving mass education, especially in a case like India's (*Harijan*, 1-12-1933; School Books, *CWMG* 56: 295).

Craze for Changing Textbooks

The craze for ever-changing textbooks is hardly a healthy sign from the educational standpoint. If textbooks are treated as a vehicle for education, the living word of the teacher has very little value. A teacher who teaches from textbooks does not impart originality to his pupils. He himself becomes a slave of textbooks and has no opportunity or occasion to be original. It, therefore, seems that, the less textbooks there are the better it is for the teacher and his pupils. Textbooks seem to have become an article of commerce. Authors and publishers who make writing and publishing a means of making money are interested in frequent change of textbooks. In many cases teachers and examiners are themselves authors of textbooks. It is naturally to their interest to have their books sold. The selection board is again naturally composed of such people. And so the vicious circle becomes complete. And it becomes very difficult for parents to find money for new books every year. It is a pathetic sight to see boys and girls going to school loaded with books which they are ill able to carry. The whole system requires to be thoroughly examined. The commercial spirit needs to be entirely eliminated and the question approached solely in the interest of the scholars. It will then probably be found that 75 per cent of the textbooks will have to be consigned to the scrapheap. If I had my way, I would have books largely as aids to teachers rather than for the scholars. Such textbooks as are found to be absolutely necessary for the scholars should circulate among them for a number of years so that the cost can be easily borne by middle-class families. The first step in this direction is perhaps for the state to own and organize the printing and publishing of textbooks. This will act as an automatic check on their unnecessary multiplication (*Harijan*, 9-9-1939; Notes, *CWMG* 70: 153).

12

Message to the Teachers and Students

Section I — Message to the Teachers

A good teacher would never content himself with summarizing or explaining the meaning of difficult passages. Time and again, he would go beyond the textbooks and present his subject to the pupil in a vivid manner in the same way as an artist does. The best textbook may be compared to the best photograph. However, just as a painting by an artist although second rate is invariably superior to a photograph, similar is the case with a real teacher. A true teacher introduces the pupil to his subject, creates in him interest for the subject and enables him to understand it independently. In my opinion, one who explains difficult passages and prepares abstracts can never be regarded a good teacher. Our endeavours should be to turn out true teachers who could be infused with a spirit of service. It is not that stray instances of such teachers are not be found even today (*Navajivan*, 16-6-1928; Questions on Education – II, *CWMG* 36: 382-83).

The teachers will have to come together at least once a week to exchange ideas and make such changes as may be called for. The intelligent students should be consulted and their suggestions invited about methods of teaching.

The students' health is the collective responsibility of the teachers; the main responsibility, however, will rest on the teacher in charge of hygiene.

The teachers should read up the subjects in the curriculum which they do not know especially Hindi. I can see from my work here how very essential Hindi is. I find that I shall have to ask for volunteers from other places. Difficulties will arise about those of them who do not know Hindi. I see it proved every day that education is altogether incomplete without Hindi (Letter to Narahari Parikh, 17-5-1917, *CWMG* 13: 399).

Cultivate the Spirit of Sacrifice

As the second condition for the success of national education we need teachers of good character. I congratulate the head master and other teachers of this high school who have made a sacrifice for the sake of their *dharma* and their country, and I ask of them that in their work henceforth they show the same spirit which has prompted their self-sacrifice. Once you are absorbed in your work, money will come in of itself. Your executive committee will be able to raise funds with ease. Even if they have nothing else than clean ground to sit on, the boys of national schools will be able to hold their own against other boys and, if their teachers are men of character, will acquire a greater spirit of manliness than the pupils of the more pretentious government schools (*Navajivan*, 10-11-1920; Speech at Opening of Lokamanya National School, Ankleshwar, 2-11-1919, *CWMG* 18: 419).

Teachers to Develop Positive Outlook

. . ., teachers will not be valued according to their salaries and work. Teachers themselves will place more value on their teaching work than on their salaries. In short, teaching should be regarded as the teachers' *dharma*. The teacher who takes his food without performing that sacrifice should be looked upon as a thief. If that is done, there will be no shortage of teachers and yet they will be valued a million times higher than millionaires. By changing his outlook, every teacher can enjoy that position even today. . . .

If the teachers would forget the question of their livelihood and think only of their duty, the schools will come to have new vitality and become truly national, and then alone will they be of use to the national movement (*Navajivan*, 10-8-1924; Education Conference, *CWMG* 24: 542-43).

Make Teaching Absorbing

Experience shows that students' interest in a subject is sustained not by the subject matter but by the teacher. My own experience has been that one teacher used to bore me to sleep while teaching chemistry, whereas another teacher kept me wide awake and interested in the same subject. The former, who talked and talked without clarifying the topic, was not liked while, as the other teacher elucidated the theme, one wished that his period should never end. The topic was the same as well as the students. Instruction by one, however, was absorbing and by the other insipid. The spinning-wheel holds a jar of nectar (*Navajivan*, 17-8-1924; Teachers and Training in Spinning, *CWMG* 25: 5).

Build Heart to Heart Contact

I have felt that the teachers' work lies more outside than inside the lectureroom. In this work-a-day life where teachers and professors work for the wages they get they have no time to give to the students outside the classroom, and that is the greatest stumbling block in the development of the life and character of students today. But unless the teachers are prepared to give all their time outside the classroom to their students, not much can be done. Let them fashion their hearts rather than their brains. Let them help them to erase every word out of their dictionary which means disappointment and despair (*Young India*, 4-4-1929; Speech at Students' Meeting, Rangoon, 10-3-1929, *CWMG* 40: 120).

Freedom for All-round Growth

The students' minds must not be caged nor for that matter those of the teachers. The teachers can only point to their pupils what they or the state considers is the best way. Having done so they have no right to curb their pupils' thoughts and feelings. This does not mean that they are not to be subject to any discipline. No school can be run without it. But discipline has nothing to do with artificial restraint upon the students' all-round growth. This is impossible where they are subjected to espionage. The fact is that hitherto they have been in an atmosphere subtly anti-national where it has not been openly that. This should now be dispelled. The students should know that the cultivation of nationalism is not a crime but a virtue (*Harijan*, 18-9-1937; For Ministers of Education, *CWMG* 66: 141).

Develop Sense of Belonging

You can teach best by identifying yourself with your students. In order to do so, the teacher must prepare himself fully in the subject he has to teach (*Navajivan*, 11-4-1926; Assorted Questions [IV], *CWMG* 30: 322).

Develop Motherly Love

A teacher is a mother. She who cannot take the place of a mother can never become a teacher. A child should not feel that it is receiving education. The child whose mother's eyes follow it everywhere is receiving education all the twenty-four hours. A child who sits six hours in a school may not be receiving any education at all. In this topsy-turvy life, perhaps we may not find women teachers. It may well be that child education is practicable at present only through men teachers. Then the men teachers will have to acquire the noble status of a mother and ultimately the mothers will have to get ready for this job. But if my concept is right, any mother, if she has love in her heart, can become fit with a little assistance. And while preparing herself, she will prepare the children as well (*Navajivan*, 2-6-1929; Ideal Primary School for Children, *CWMG* 41: 9).

Develop Proper Relationship

To a question: "Should a teacher marry a girl who is his student? Likewise, should a boy marry a girl studying in his class?" Gandhi replied:

I at any rate would consider both very improper. A girl who is my student should be as safe [with me] as my daughter, and a girl in my class as safe as a sister. That pure brother-and-sister relationship is the only proper relationship between boys and girls studying together. This is all I should like to say in reply to this question, but it is an important enough question for a fuller discussion. I have no doubt in my mind about the correctness of my reply to the first question. With regard to the second, however, I see some difficulties in these modern times when thousands of boys and girls attend the same school. In any case, in every institution that I have managed I have insisted on the foregoing rule being followed and the results have always been happy (*Navajivan*, 20-10-1921; My Notes, *CWMG* 21: 328-29).

Teaching for the Love of It

The unfortunate position is that educated Indians take to teaching not for the love of it, but because they have nothing better and nothing else for giving them a livelihood. Many of them even enter the teaching profession with a view to preparing for what they regard as a better thing. The wonder is that in spite of this self-imposed initial handicap so many teachers are not worse than they are. By well-ordered agitation, no doubt, they may better their pecuniary prospects, but I see no chance even under a *swaraj* government of the scale of salary being raised much higher than it is today. I believe in the ancient idea of teachers teaching for the love of it and receiving the barest maintenance. The Roman Catholics have retained that idea and they are responsible for some of the best educational institutions in the world. The *rishis* of old did even better. They made their pupils members of their families, but in those days that class of teaching which they imparted was not intended for the masses. They simply brought up a race of real teachers of mankind in India (*Young India*, 6-8-1925; Teachers' Condition, *CWMG* 28: 34-35).

Be Affectionate

Students must not be given corporal punishment. But there should be such a rapport between the teacher and the taught that if the teacher punishes himself in some way the children, because of their affection for him, should feel sorry, their hearts should melt and they should change for the better. I am not talking in the air. This has been my personal experience. Mothers also can reform their children in the same way. In South Africa I had looked after Hindu, Muslim and Parsi boys and girls. During those days I remember having only once beaten a pupil. But it was my experience that my nonviolent method was more successful. If the children have affection for their teacher they are bound to feel sorry when they find the teacher suffering on their account. That would soften them. But if in spite of that there is a difficult pupil, we should non-cooperate with him. But that is another method. The former is the better method (Letter to a Teacher, 15-4-1947, *CWMG* 87: 283-84).

Teaching without Punishment

There is violence in punishing pupils and also in sending them to the headmaster in order that they may be punished. The correspondent has not asked whether a teacher is free to punish any pupil, but the question is implied in the one which he has asked. I myself can imagine a situation in which it becomes one's duty to punish a child who has done something wrong, knowing that it is wrong. Every teacher should think and decide for himself what his duty is. The general rule, however, is that a teacher should never inflict physical punishment on a pupil. If anyone should have this right at all, let it rest with the parents. A punishment is just only if the pupil himself accepts it as such. Such occasions are not frequent. Even when an occasion has arisen, the pupil should not be punished if there is any doubt about the punishment being justified. In any case, no one should be punished in anger (*Navajivan*, 27-9-1925; Some Questions, *CWMG* 28: 242).

In my opinion, it is simply improper to subject students to any form of punishment. By doing so, the feelings of respect and pure love that teachers should have for students disappear. The method of teaching students by punishing them is being progressively abandoned. I know that occasions do arise when even the best of teachers cannot but inflict punishment. However, this should be an exception and should not in any way be commended. If the best of teachers has to resort to beating, this should in fact be regarded as a drawback in his art. Although an individual like Spencer has looked upon every punishment as improper, he has not always been able to put his theory into practice. After replying to this question, I need not answer in detail the other questions.

Ordinarily, punishment is not compatible with nonviolence. Of course, I can conceive of instances in which punishment cannot be regarded as such. These, however, should be regarded as irrelevant so far as teachers are concerned. For instance, if a father who is extremely unhappy punishes his son, it is a case of punishment given out of love. The son, too, would not regard it as an act of violence. Or, when in some cases a delirious patient has to be smacked by the person nursing him, it is not a violent act but a nonviolent one. But these instances do not help teachers at all. A teacher has to develop the technique of teaching students and maintaining discipline amongst them without resorting to beating. We have before us instances of such teachers who have never beaten their students. Punishments other than corporal would be to make the student ashamed of himself, make him alternately sit down and stand up, make him hold his toes, abuse him, etc. I feel that teachers should discard all these methods.

To repent after punishing a student in order to improve him is no repentance at all. Moreover, teachers who believe and make their students believe that punishment leads to the latter's improvement, end up by making such a belief take root in society. And this belief creates the illusion that reforms can be brought about through violence. In my opinion, teachers of national schools who deliberately punish their students are indeed guilty of violating their pledge (*Navajivan*, 21-10-1928; My Notes, *CWMG* 37: 379-80).

I am quite clear that you must not inflict corporal or other punishment on your children or pupils. You can punish yourself, if you like and are qualified, in order to melt your children's or pupils' hearts. Many mothers are known to have corrected their children in this manner. I have on many occasions. I had to deal with wild boys in South Africa: Muslims, Christians, Hindus and Parsis. With one exception, I do not remember ever having punished a single boy. The nonviolent method invariably succeeded. When a bond is established between a teacher and his pupils, the latter will generally yield before their teacher's suffering for their sake. In the case of your "bully", if he has no respect for you, you can non-cooperate with him by sending him away from your school. Nonviolence does not compel you to keep in your school a student who does not carry our disciplinary rules (*Harijan*, 13-7-1940; Question Box, *CWMG* 72: 226).

Inculcate a Sense of Honour

We have to fall back upon the voluntary assistance of teachers, but when I look for teachers, they are very few, especially, teachers of the type wanted, in order to draw the best from the children through understanding, through studying their individuality and then putting the child on its own resources, as it were, on its own honour. And believe me from my experience of hundreds, I was going to say thousands, of children I know that they have perhaps a finer sense of honour than you and I have. The greatest lessons in life if we would but stoop and humble ourselves, we would learn not from grown-up learned men, but from the so-called ignorant children. Jesus never uttered a loftier or a grander truth than when he said that wisdom cometh out of the mouths of babes. I believe it, I have noticed it in my own experience that, if we would approach babes in humility and in innocence, we would learn wisdom from them (*Young India*, 19-11-1931; Speech at Montessori Training College, 28-10-1931, *CWMG* 48: 239-40).

Follow Golden Rule

Teachers develop secret relationships with their women students. That in some cases these relationships are given the form of marriage does not make them virtuous. It is my firm opinion that just as husband–wife relationship is not possible between brothers and sisters, so should it not be possible in the case of teachers and pupils. If this golden rule is not faithfully adhered to, educational institutions will eventually collapse; no girl will be safe from her men teachers. A teacher's position is such that students — both boys and girls — are constantly under his influence; they regard the teacher's words as gospel truth. So they do not entertain any doubts about any liberties taken by the teacher. Hence such relationships are regarded, and should be regarded, as uncondonable where the soul is respected as something apart from the body. When such relationship creeps into an institution such as the Harijan Sevak Sangh, it has far-reaching evil effects and ruins its activities (*Harijanbandhu*, 29-11-1936; One Enemy Alone, *CWMG* 64: 91).

Be a Student of Students

A teacher who establishes rapport with the taught, becomes one with them, learns more from them than he teaches them. He who learns nothing from his disciples is, in my opinion, worthless. Whenever I talk with someone I learn from him. I take from him more than I give him. In this way, a true teacher regards himself as a student of his students. If you will teach your pupils with this attitude, you will benefit much from them (*Harijan Sevak*, 15-2-1942; Talk to Khadi Vidyalaya Students, 29-1-1942, *CWMG* 75: 269).

Ideal Education

And when it is remembered that the primary aim of all education is, or should be, the moulding of the character of pupils, a teacher who has a character to keep need not lose heart (*Harijan*, 1-12-1933; School Books, *CWMG* 56: 296).

Teacher–Taught Relationship

I am a believer in *gurubhakti*. However, every teacher cannot become a *guru*. The *guru*-disciple relationship is spiritual and spontaneous, it is not artificial, it cannot be created through external pressure. Such *guru*s are still to be found in India. (It should not be necessary to warn that I am not speaking here of *guru*s who give *moksha*.) The question of flattering such a *guru* just does not arise. The respect towards such a *guru* can only be natural, the *guru*'s love is also of the same kind. Hence the one is always ready to give and the other is always ready to receive (*Navajivan*, 3-7-1928; Questions on Education – I, *CWMG* 36: 361).

Religious Instruction

If we wish to create among students respect, tolerance and love for every religion — which is indeed religion and not irreligion, we should certainly instruct them in their principles. I do not consider it very necessary to have a knowledge of the superstitions and rituals. In a country like India anyone who goes about with his eyes and ears open can see for himself the superstitions and rituals. If we wish to adopt that which is virtuous, we should not at all insist upon a knowledge of the superstitions and rituals of every religion. It is possible that a good deal of the students' time will be taken up by our insisting on their gaining a minute knowledge of whatever rituals and superstitions are to be found in our religion and trying to introduce any necessary reforms in them (*Navajivan*, 17-6-1928; Questions on Education – III, *CWMG* 36: 421).

Section II — Message to the Students

Many students feel that it is not necessary to make any special effort for health. However, regular exercise is absolutely necessary for the body. What can be expected of a student who is not well equipped in health? Just as milk cannot be held in a paper container, so also education is not likely to remain for long in the paper-like bodies of our students. The body is the abode of the spirit and, therefore, holy like a place of pilgrimage. We must see that it is well protected. Walking regularly and energetically for an hour and a half in the morning and for the same period in the evening in open air keeps it healthy and the mind fresh. The time thus spent is not wasted. Such exercise, coupled with rest, will invigorate both the body and the intellect, enabling one to learn things more quickly. I think games like cricket have no place in a poor country like India. We have a number of inexpensive games of our own which afford innocent joy.

The daily life of the student should be above reproach. He alone can experience true delight whose mind is pure. Indeed, to ask such a man to seek delight in worldly pleasures is to deprive him of the real delight which is his. He who has resolved to rise does indeed rise. Ramachandra, in his innocence, wished for the moon and he got it.

From one point of view, the world seems to be an illusion; from another, it seems real enough. For students, the world does indeed exist, for it is they who have to strive for great achievement in it. He who declares the world to be illusory without knowing what that really means, indulges in pleasures as the fancy takes him and then claims to have renounced the world, is welcome to call himself a *sannyasi* but in reality he is a deluded man.

This brings me to the subject of *dharma*. Where there is no *dharma*, there can be neither knowledge nor wealth, nor health, nor anything else. Where there is no *dharma*, life is devoid of all joy, is mere emptiness. We have had to go without instruction in *dharma*; we are in much the same position as the bridegroom's party at a wedding without the bridegroom. Students cannot have innocent joy without a knowledge of *dharma*. That they may have such joy, it is necessary for them to study the Shastras, to reflect over their teaching and bring their conduct in conformity with their ideals. . . . I shall give you this practical advice, based on my own experience, that you should take to the *Ramacharitamanasa* [of Tulsidas] and the *Bhagavadgita* in love and reverence. You have a real jewel in the latter; seize it. But see that you study these two books in order to learn the secret of *dharma*. The seers who wrote these works did not set out to write history but only to teach *dharma* and morals. . . . For Muslim students, the Koran is the best book in this respect. I would counsel them as well that they study this book in a spirit of devotion. They should understand its true message. I feel, too, that both Hindus and Muslims should study each other's religious scriptures with due respect and try to understand them.

From this most absorbing subject, I shall pass on to a topic of more worldly interest. It is often asked whether it is proper for students to take part in politics. I will let you know my opinion about it without going into the reasons. Politics has two aspects, theoretical study and practical activity. It is essential that students be introduced to the former, but it is harmful for them to concern themselves with the latter. They may attend political meetings or the sessions of the Congress in order to learn the science of politics. Such gatherings are useful as object-lessons. Students should have complete freedom to attend them and every effort should be made to get the recent ban on them removed. Students may not speak or vote at such meetings but may serve as volunteers if that does not interfere with their studies. No student can afford to miss an opportunity of serving Malaviyaji if one comes his way. Students should keep away from party politics. They should remain detached and cultivate respect for the leaders of the nation. It is not for them to judge the latter. Students easily respond to excellences of character, they adore them. They say it is the duty of students to look upon elders with reverence and respect their words. This is well said. He who has not learnt to respect others cannot hope for respect for himself. An attitude of insolence ill becomes students. In this respect, an unusual situation has come about in India. Older folk are careless how they behave, or fail to maintain their dignity.

What are the students to do in these circumstances? As I imagine, a student should have regard for *dharma*. Such a student, when faced with a moral dilemma, should recall the instance of Prahlad. Placed in circumstances in which this boy respectfully disobeyed the commands of his father, we can act in like manner towards elders resembling the latter. But any disrespect shown to them beyond this will be wrong. It will ruin the community. An elder is so not merely by virtue of his age, but by virtue of the knowledge, experience and wisdom which age brings. Where these are absent, the elder's position depends simply on his age. Nobody, however, worships age as such.

Another question is: How can students serve the country? The simple answer is that a student should study well, safeguarding his health meanwhile and cherishing the aim of using the fruits of his study in the service of the country. I am quite sure he will thereby serve his country. By living a purposeful life and taking care to be unmindful of our own interests and to work for others, we can achieve much with little effort. I want to tell you of one task of this kind. You must have seen my letter in the newspapers about the difficulties of third-class passengers. I suppose most of you travel third. These passengers spit in the compartment; they also spit out the remains of betel leaves and tobacco which they chew right in the carriage, and likewise throw the skins of bananas, etc., and other leavings on the floor of the carriage; they are careless in the use of the latrine and foul it. They smoke *bidis* and cigarettes without any regard for the convenience of fellow passengers. We can explain to the other passengers in our compartment the harm that results from their dirtying the place. Most passengers respect students and listen to them. They should not then miss these excellent opportunities of explaining the rules of hygiene to the masses. The eatables sold at stations are dirty. It is the duty of students, when they find the things dirty, to draw the attention of the traffic manager to the fact, whether he replies or no. And take care that you write to him in Hindi. When he receives many such letters, he will be forced to heed them. This is easy work to do but it will yield important results.

I have spoken about the habits of chewing betel leaves and tobacco. In my humble opinion, these habits are both harmful and unclean. Most of us, men and women, have become their slaves. We must be free of this slavery. A stranger visiting India will surely think that we are always eating something or the other. That the betel leaf, possibly, helps to digest food may be conceded, but food eaten in the proper quantity and manner is digested without any help from things like the betel leaf. Moreover, it does not have even an agreeable taste. And tobacco chewing must be given up as well. Students should always practise self-control. It is also necessary to consider the habit of smoking. Our rulers have set a bad example in this respect. They smoke cigarettes anywhere and everywhere. This has led us to consider smoking a fashion, and to turn our mouths into chimneys. Many books have been written to show that smoking is harmful. We call this age Kaliyuga. Christians believe that Jesus Christ will come again when selfishness, immorality, addiction to drugs and drink, etc., become rife. I shall not consider to what extent we may accept this as true. But I do feel that the world has been suffering a great deal from evils such as drinking, smoking, addiction to opium, *ganja*, hemp and so on. All of us are caught in this snare and so we cannot truly measure the magnitude of its unhappy consequences. It is my prayer that you, the students, keep away from them.

. . . The worth of your learning will be judged by your actions. Stuffing your brains with the contents of hundreds of books may bring its reward but action is of much greater value by far. One's stock of learning is of no more value than the action it leads to. The rest is an unnecessary burden. I would, therefore, always request you and urge you to practise what you learn and what appears to you to be right. That is the only way to progress (Speech at Bihar Students' Conference, 15-10-1917, *CWMG* 14: 135-39).

Students' Life

The student's stage of life is similar to the *sannyasi*'s and his life should, therefore, be pure and celibate. Today two cultures are competing for the students' attention — the ancient and the modern. Self-restraint was the keynote of the former. Ancient culture tells us that a man advances in the measure that he deliberately and with full knowledge reduces his wants. Modern civilization teaches us that man progresses by increasing his wants. The difference between self-restraint and self-indulgence is the difference between *dharma* and *adharma*. The ideal of self-restraint attaches less importance to the outward life than to the inner. There is a danger that in place of the ancient culture based on self-restraint, the modern civilization of self-indulgence will be accepted. Students can play decisive part in averting this danger. University students will be judged, not by their knowledge, but solely by their good conduct. Religious education and ethical conduct should be given the first place in this university. This requires the fullest cooperation from the students. Panditji himself is a man of piety and virtue. By bringing another man of similar qualities, viz., Anandshankar, he has provided an opportunity to the students. I should like them to make the best use of this opportunity and adorn their learning with *dharma*. These were the thoughts I placed before them on that morning. I have repeatedly expressed these ideas, in one form or another, at several places, and a summary of these same ideas which I explained to the students of Kashi University on getting this happy opportunity, I now lay before readers of *Navajivan* for them to think over. I am convinced that we cannot profit from political reforms unless we also give thought to religion. Religion will not be revived through these reforms. Rather, it is religion which will supply what the reforms may lack (*Navajivan*, 29-2-1920; Punjab Letter, *CWMG* 17: 57-58).

Students Must Have Faith in God

. . . in this world, we have to look only to God for help. None other could render any effectual help. There is no sin equal to that of disbelieving in Him, in denying Him. Amongst the students of today the spirit of atheism is gaining ground. I am deeply grieved that things should be so. Whenever I see Hindu students, I ask them to think of God, to pray, to repeat Ramanama. They ask me where is God, where is Rama and such other questions. When I see Mussalman youths and ask them to read the Koran, and to live the life enjoined therein, they also ask me similar questions. The education which leads to the negation of God cannot make for the service of the country nor of humanity. In your address, you have referred to my service to my country. Whatever I have been doing is done with a sense of my duty to God. And this I consider to be the right thing. God is not seated in the skies, in the heavens, or elsewhere. He is enshrined in the heart of everyone — be he a Hindu, Mohammedan, Christian or Jew, man or woman.

I consider that real service of the country and of God consists in serving the poor humanity, whom Deshbandhu Das rightly designated the Daridranarayana. Such service however must be whole-hearted (*The Hindu*, 21-7-1927; Speech to Students, Mysore, *CWMG* 34: 203-04).

No Intoxicants

I shall now proceed to say something about cigarette smoking and coffee and tea drinking. These are not necessities of life. There are some who manage to take ten cups of coffee a day. Is it necessary for their healthy development and for keeping them awake, for the performance of their duties? If it is necessary to take coffee or tea to keep them awake, let them not drink coffee or tea but go to sleep. We must not become slaves to these things. But the majority of the people who drink coffee or tea are slaves to them. Cigars and cigarettes, whether foreign or indigenous, must be avoided. Cigarette smoking is like an opiate and the cigars that you smoke have a touch of opium about them. They get to your nerves and you cannot leave them afterwards. How can a single student foul his mouth by converting it into a chimney? If you give up these habits of smoking cigars and cigarettes and drinking coffee and tea you will find out for yourselves how much you are able to save. A drunkard in Tolstoy's story is hesitating to execute his design of murder so long as he has not smoked his cigar. But he puffs it, and then gets up smiling and saying, "What a coward am I," takes the dagger and does the deed. Tolstoy spoke from experience. He has written nothing without having had personal experience of it. And he is much more against cigars and cigarettes than against drink. But do not make the mistake that between drink and tobacco, drink is a lesser evil. No. If cigarette is Beelzebub, then drink is Satan (*Young India*, 15-9-1927; Speech at Pachaiyappa's College, Madras, 7-9-1927, *CWMG* 34: 483-84).

Be Humble

. . . I would like to tell the students, boys and girls, that humility is the primary thing to be acquired. One who is not humble cannot put one's learning to proper use. What does it matter if he has obtained double first class or has stood first? One does not achieve everything by just passing an examination. It is possible that it may help in securing a good job or a good marriage alliance. But, if learning is to be put to proper use, if it is to be used only for the sake of service, one should acquire more and more humility every day. No service is possible without it. . . . I suggested to you how to put your education to the best use. I also told you that you must keep away from the evil custom of taking and giving [dowry] (*Harijanbandhu*, 22-7-1934; Speech at Dayaram Jethamal Sind College, Karachi, 10-7-1934, *CWMG* 58: 164-67).

On Costly Education

When it is difficult for millions even to make the two ends meet, when millions are dying of starvation, it is monstrous to think of giving our relatives a costly education. Expansion of the mind will come from hard experience, not necessarily in the college or the schoolroom. When some of us deny ourselves and ours the so-called higher education, we shall find true means of giving and receiving a really high education. Is there not, may there not be, a way of each boy paying for his own education? There may be no such way. Whether there is or there is not such a way is irrelevant. But there is no doubt that when we deny ourselves the way of expensive education seeing that aspiration after higher education is a laudable end, we shall find out a way of fulfilling it more in accord with our surroundings. The golden rule to apply in all such cases is resolutely to refuse to have what millions cannot. This ability to refuse will not descend upon us all of a sudden. The first thing is to cultivate the mental attitude that will not have possessions or facilities denied to millions, and the next immediate thing is to re-arrange our lives as fast as possible in accordance with that mentality (*Young India*, 24-6-1926; Sacrifice, *CWMG* 31: 45).

Importance of Self-Study

It is a gross superstition to suppose that knowledge can be obtained only by going to schools and colleges. The world produced brilliant students before schools and colleges came into being. There is nothing so ennobling or lasting as self-study. Schools and colleges make most of us mere receptacles for holding the superfluities of knowledge. Wheat is left out and mere husk is taken in. I do not wish to decry schools and colleges as such. They have their use. But we are making altogether too much of them. They are but one of the many means of gaining knowledge (*Young India*, 25-5-1931; Notes, *CWMG* 47: 60).

Importance of Learning Artisan's Work

The utterly false idea that intelligence can be developed only through book reading should give place to the truth that the quickest development of the mind can be achieved by artisan's work being learnt in a scientific manner. True development of the mind commences immediately when the apprentice is taught at every step why a particular manipulation of the hand or a tool is required. The problem of the unemployment of students can be solved without difficulty if they will rank themselves among the common labourers (*Harijan*, 9-1-1937; Notes, *CWMG* 64: 219).

On Students Going for Foreign Studies

I have never been an advocate of our students going abroad. My experience tells me that such, on return, find themselves to be square pegs in round holes. That experience is the richest and contributes most to growth which springs from the soil (*Harijan*, 8-9-1946; Why Go Abroad? *CWMG* 85: 238).

Reference

CWMG. (1958-94). *The Collected Works of Mahatma Gandhi* (100 vols.). New Delhi: Publications Division, Ministry of Information & Broadcasting, Govt of India (referred to as *CWMG* vol. no.: page no.).

On the Philosophy of Mahatma Gandhi*

M. Venkaiah Naidu

I am really happy to be here, in this prestigious, most beautiful, dutiful, purposeful institution, GITAM University and participate in this important international event Gandhirama today. I think this is the first time in my life, except once during emergency when I was in Visakhapatnam jail, I was outside my house on the day of the festival Sankranthi. On the three days of *Bhogi*, *Pedda Pandanga* and *Kanuma Pandaga*, I never go outside. That is the only thing I do for my wife and family. My wife always says, "my husband comes to our house once in a while". Because of my love, affection and respect for Prof. Ramakrishna Rao garu, I could not say no when he invited me to this conference.

I know Prof. Ramakrishna Rao garu from my student days. I admire him, because he is a treasure house of knowledge and he is an embodiment of our culture, our values. He has the character, calibre, conduct, discipline, dynamism, dedication and devotion — all in one. So, I respect him. As a professor, he used to be our role model at Andhra University. Even now at this age of 80 plus, he looks like 20 plus and he still wishes to create Gandhi Mandir and then has a plan and agenda for it. This means, he wants to live for another 20-30 years actively. I think he can. Because of his mental and physical discipline, he is able to function so effectively even now. He should be a role model to all of us.

Dr. M.V.V.S. Murthi was a Member of Parliament from my political community, but politics has not gone to his head. That is his greatness. See his vision of creating this university. Once you enter GITAM campus, the entire atmosphere changes. Your thoughts change and you get a sort of inspiration. He has created in this part of the country such a prestigious institution which has now won not only national but also international

---

* This is a transcript of the extempore lecture delivered by Shri M. Venkaiah Naidu, Hon'ble Minister for Urban Development, Housing & Urban Poverty Alleviation and Information & Broadcasting, Government of India at Gandhirama. Shri Naidu has approved the draft.

acclaim. I have every hope that GITAM University will become one of the most prestigious institutions in the entire globe with all its superb infrastructure, strong faculty and its spectre of natural beauty. In creating this outstanding institution, Dr. Murthi did not add any family members. In India the problem we all know is dynastic rule. Though in democracy dynasty is nasty, it is tasty to many people. People often ask me: Sir, what about your daughter? When is she coming into politics? They try to praise sons and sons-in-law and daughters and daughters-in-law also to the hilt. That is a weakness in our system. But Murthi garu did not have any family members in this institution. He has brought vibrant professionals. He has brought key people. That is why this institution is flourishing. What is required to build an institution is character, calibre and conduct; not caste, or the other consideration.

Manishiki paiki ravalante javasatvam kavali, varasatvam kadu. Varasatva lekapoyina javasatvam unte enta varakayina vellavachane vishayam mana mundu anekamaina udaharanalu unnayi. We have seen a paper-distributing boy become the President of India — Dr. A.P.J. Abdul Kalam. We have also seen a tea vendor's son, who was serving tea in railway stations, become the Prime Minister of India and creating waves across the world. Wherever he goes — to America, China, Germany, Japan, Malaysia, Singapore — people appreciate. Why? Because, people see India in him and people get energized due to his dynamism, dedication and developmental agenda.

What is the philosophy of Mahatma Gandhi? It is very simple. It is the philosophy of India. Mahatma Gandhi did not find anything new. He simply brought to the fore the core of classical Indian thought with contemporary idioms, focusing on its relevance. He brilliantly espoused our culture, heritage, knowledge system and practices which our forefathers had handed over to us. *Adi kalam nunchi, veda kalam nunchi, purana kalam nunchi, mana poorvikulu anubhavinchi, rangarinchi, melavinchi, manaki andinchina varasatvanni gandhi garu manakandariki ichchi, desaniki javasatvanni kalipinchadu.* Unfortunately, the country remembers Gandhi, but does not practise Gandhian ideals. That is the problem. People take Gandhi's name and also have his name, but do not act like him.

Gandhiji had given two advices immediately after Independence. The first advice was political. I do not want to elaborate on it. He asked to disband the Congress because the Congress was a platform, not a political party. It was a platform of all shades who had come together to fight the British and bring *swaraj*. He said: "The purpose is over, so disband it." Our people did not care for his suggestion. The second thing he said was to go back to the villages. But our great leaders have shown their back to villages and moved towards towns. That is why this urban–rural divide got widened. Now urbanization is a reality and you can't reverse it. See the irony. Even I have moved from rural development to urban development. Earlier, I was rural development minister; now I am urban development minister. Most of us are rural people. The other day I was seeing on television Vizag wearing a deserted look; Hyderabad too had a deserted look. Why? Many people had gone to their native places. Most of the people living in Vizag, living in Hyderabad and living in other cities are people from villages. So you have to take care of them. This is how the Prime Minister convinced me to be the Minister of Urban Development. My heart lives in villages even today. But the reality is that urbanization is moving at a greater pace. We have to take care of those people and we have to bridge the gulf between the urban and the rural. In the process we rejuvenate the urban as well as rural lives.

While unveiling the statue of Mahatma Gandhi in Germany our Prime Minister said that Gandhiji's teachings and principles are the appropriate remedies to challenges like terrorism and global warming that the world faces today. Gandhiji was a powerful man without power and showed that one can be powerful even without power. This is what we have to learn from Gandhi.

The shadow of terror is overcast upon humanity. In this situation, the ideas of nonviolence, *vasudhaiva kutumbakam* championed by Mahatma Gandhi are appropriate solutions to this challenge as Shri Modi specified on that occasion. The Prime Minister also referred to the global warming and said that the principles practised by Mahatma Gandhi can very well address the challenge. He said that Gandhi used to love and respect nature, even those days when there was no topic like climate change. He always used to refer to nature and respect it. In fact, the present government under the leadership of Shri Narendra Modi has explicitly acknowledged the relevance of Gandhiji's ideas and practices to the development of the country and in maintaining peace and harmony among the people of the world. Swachh Bharat programme is one of those programmes that has already caught the imagination of the people. Indians gained freedom under the leadership of Gandhiji but his dream of a clean India still remains unfulfilled. Mahatma Gandhi while visiting Banaras Hindu University one hundred years back said that sanitation is more important than independence. *Arogyame mahabhagyam, parisubhrate paramatmaku daggara ninnu cherustundi ani chepparu*. It is a powerful statement. He made cleanliness and sanitation an integral part of his way of living. His dream was total sanitation for all — sanitation in every sense — cleanliness of the body and mind. Keeping this in view, on 2 October 2014 Prime Minister Modiji launched the nationwide cleanliness campaign on the occasion of Mahatma Gandhi's birth anniversary. The concept of Swachh Bharat is to provide sanitation facilities to every family, including toilets, solid and liquid waste disposal systems, village cleanliness, and safe and adequate drinking water supply. We have to achieve this by 2019. *Mana gudi, mana badi, mana vollu, mana kallu, mana illu, mana irugu, mana porugu, veetannitini parisubhramga vunchukovalasina karathavyam mana andari paina vundi.* And it is a daily activity. *Nenu Swachh Bharatam, Gandhigari October 2 taareekhune chestanu, malli October 2 daka vuntanu ante, nuvvu sadhuvu laga ayipotavu. Roju geddam giyyadam ela avasaramo, pallu tomukovadamu ela avasaramo, parisubhramga vundatamu kuda anta avasaramane vishayanni Gandhigaru spashtamga cheppadam jarigindi.*

The United Nations designation of 21 June as an International Yoga Day is another event intended to promote global harmony, peace and all-round wellness of the people inspired by Gandhian vision. We are very happy and proud that the proposal of Shri Narendra Modi was accepted by 172 countries and 192 countries did observe Yoga on 21 June. This speaks of the values of what we have inherited from Mahatma Gandhi. Likewise were his programmes such as Antyodaya — uplifting the poorest of the poor. He always advised authorities to look at the last man in the queue because oppressed, suppressed, depressed, poorer people have to be taken care of and one has to show extra care for them. Keeping that in mind, the Prime Minister enunciated these new schemes of Jana Dhana Yojana, Jana Sree Bima Yojana, Atal Pension Yojana, Mudra Bank Yojana — all these social security schemes aimed at uplifting the poorest of the poor. Behind all these pogrammes Mahatma Gandhi is the inspiration.

Gandhiji preached and practised tolerance throughout his life. We have seen recently that there was a big debate over tolerance. India I can say is the first and the best place for tolerance in the entire world today, in spite of some political *pundit*s trying to blow out of proportion certain incidents and thus trying to tarnish the image of India. I don't know what sort of satisfaction they get — *rakshasanandamo, paisachikanandamo nakayithe telavadu kani, ee bharatadesamu yokka peru pratishtalu debbateesi vaallu anandanni pondutu vunnaru.* With 120 crore population, more than 30 states, different languages, different ways of living, there are bound to be some problems here and there. However, you see the country's history. India was never an aggressor against any country, because love and compassion, peace and altruism were our hallmarks and they still run in our blood. *Cheemaku chakkara petti, pamuku palu posi, chettuki dannam petti, pasuvuku namalu pettetatuvanti pavitramaina jaati manadi. Alanti desamlo sahanam ledani cheppi anukunte. . . .*

I recently had an occasion to meet Sadguru Vasudev. I asked him, "Guruji, why some people are returning the awards?" He said that their soul might have told them that they are unfit to get the awards. That is how they are answering to their soul. In this great country, there is always a difference of opinion. I respect and admire Mahatma Gandhi. But I feel sorry that why he had not chosen Sardar Patel as the Prime Minister of India. Of the 17 state presidents, 15 had suggested his name. But, he had taken a different decision. I am sure he had his reasons. I have my own view and I have my difference of opinion with regards to Gandhiji and the Khilafat Movement. But at the same time, the other contributions made by Mahatma Gandhi are so great — truth, nonviolence, *satyagraha*. *Satyagraha* is such a powerful tool which he had given to the entire humanity, particularly to the people of India to fight the British. *Satyaniki aagraham vaste, nigraham kolpokunda satyagraham cheyadam edaite vundo, adi ela vuntundanedi gandhigaru manaki chesi chubincharu*. That is the greatest contribution he has made.

Gandhi showed the way to simplicity, as to how people could happily lead a simple life with noble thoughts. *Swadeshi* or encouraging Indian goods, encouraging Indian spirit was his another great contribution. Self-reliance and self-respect were the two principles he put before us. He always advocated *Ramarajya* and also said: "*Ramarajya* is incomplete without *Gramarajya*". That shows the importance he had given to the villages. Every action he undertook and in all his preaching and teaching, there was a message for us. He learnt it from our forefathers and enriched it by his own experience. People have to change, though some people these days say that Gandhi means all old thinking. Of course, Gandhi is old. But old is also gold, one has to understand. Tradition and modernity have to go hand in hand. You cannot have all that past has given. Sometimes you have to change. We are now in the age of liberalization, privatization and globalization. So we have to adopt modern techniques without discarding our old values. The old values are the gold values. That is why Gandhiji's teachings and preachings are eternal. Gandhi was relevant yesterday, day before yesterday, is relevant today, will be relevant tomorrow, he will be relevant day after tomorrow, he will be relevant eternally. That is why the entire world and whoever has come to know of Gandhi admire him.

The life story of Mahatma Gandhi as a man is of great relevance to every human being, who aspires to rise above the average level and lead a meaningful life with the watchword from good to better. Man, the individual, is the centre of Gandhiji's system of thought. Its objective is the moral and spiritual development of man. *Kevalamu vyaktigatani gurinchi alochinchadamu kakunda, chitti na bojjaku sree rama raksha, desam sangati demuderuka, evaretta pote naku endukani alochiste paripoorna vyaktitvam kadu. Samajani gurinchi alochinchali, samajika spruha undala, samaja chintana undala, dharmika chintana undala. Mahatma gandhi garu cheppina prati matalo kuda alanti spoorthi manaku labhisrundi.* He believed in man's built-in potentiality to judge between good and evil, between what will help him in his evolution to higher levels of being and to what will obstruct his path. Gandhiji believed in the self effort and the path outlined through ethical, moral and spiritual discipline. He always advocated ethical, moral and spiritual discipline. This is the need of the hour. The public life in the country is facing so many challenges today.

When we talk of Gandhi, we must get back to his ideas and particularly the ethical, moral and spiritual discipline which he taught all of us. His thoughts need to be practised by one and all. That will be the greatest tribute to that great man. Gandhi's social philosophy boils down to *sarvodaya* which precludes the suppression or elimination of any class. His concept of *sarvodaya* is relevant even today. It is in this context I look at the new initiatives of the Government of India and of the Prime Minister. I see a new hope with a sense of justified optimism. However, I do recognize that the policies that we introduced are at a preliminary stage. We need to wait for their development and consequent results. All that we can say this time is we seem to be on the right track and hope that we will move without hurdles to reach the goal of *Ramarajya* that Mahatma Gandhi had visualized. Our country is at crossroads with relation to some of the issues such as religious conversions, untouchability, uniform civil code, caste politics and caste systems. Regretably, untouchability is practised in certain parts of the country even today. Great men like Kandukuri Veeresalingam Pantulu, Raja Rammohun Roy, a lot of others were born in this society and had sown the seeds of social change that we should continue to help grow.

On religious conversions, Gandhiji has said:

> Hinduism as I know it entirely satisfies my soul, fills my whole being. When doubts haunt me, when disappointment shocks me in the face and I see not a ray of light on the horizon, I turn to the *Bhagavadgita* and find a verse to comfort me and I immediately begin to smile in the midst of overwhelming sorrow.

If I had the power and could legislate, Mahatma Gandhi has said, I would stop all proselytization. In Hindu households the advent of conversion by missionaries has meant disruption of the family, coming in the wake of change of dress, manners, language, food and drink. This is what he said when some people asked him "why don't you convert?" There is nothing wrong if you are converting voluntarily. But if you are converted out of allurement or force, then it becomes a big challenge. We are facing that challenge today.

Gandhiji advocated Uniform Civil Code. He had said that we should get out of the miasma of religious majorities and minorities. To have a common bond of relationship among all of us we must try to have a common uniform civil code for all Indians irrespective of religion and caste. Religion is a way of worship. Government should not get into that. But when we talk of *dharma*, it is a culture; it is a way of living in matters of marriage, inheritance, divorce, maintenance, there should not be any discrimination on the basis of any religion at all. The law should be common to all but unfortunately we are not able to move forward in this direction. In spite of everybody quoting Gandhiji, reminding us of many things and accusing others that you are unGandhian and all. The core issues raised by Mahatma Gandhi are not receiving the serious attention they deserve.

Gandhiji represented simplicity. He was for prohibition, nonviolence and for Hindu–Muslim unity. He wanted all communities to live together in peace and harmony. He was against cow slaughter. Again some people are making cow slaughter also as a religious issue. The central tenet of Hinduism is cow protection. I quote Gandhiji:

> Cow protection to me is one of the most wonderful phenomena in human evolution. It takes the human being beyond the species. The cow to me means the entire sub-human world. Man through the cow is enjoined to realize his identity with all that lives. Why the cow was selected for the apotheosis is obvious to me. The cow was in India the best companion. She was the giver of plenty. Not only did she give milk, but she also made agriculture possible. Cow protection is the gift of Hinduism to the world and Hinduism will live so long as there are Hindus to protect the cow.

This is a powerful statement of Mahatma Gandhi, something we should all keep in perspective.

On *varnasrama dharma* and untouchability Gandhiji said:

> I do not want to be reborn but if I have to be reborn I should be born as an untouchable, so that I may share their sorrow, sufferings and the affronts levelled at them in order that I may endure to free myself and

> them from that miserable condition. I therefore prayed that if I should be born again I should do so not as a Brahmin, Kshatriya, Vaisya or Sudra but as an Atisudra.

This is a very powerful statement. It is atrocious to differentiate people on the basis of caste and then treat somebody as untouchable. Gandhi tried his best to get rid of this shameful practice. He himself suffered in South Africa the racial discrimination. So taking inspiration from what Mahatma Gandhi taught, we should see to it that this evil practice is put to an end totally at every level. And, at the end of it we must all strive, work hard to see that the caste system is totally eliminated. But now people are developing vested interest in the caste system. They are playing caste politics. Instead of playing calibre, capacity and conduct, they are playing caste cards. That is another threat to the unity and integrity of our country.

In post-British era, *Ramarajya* as a concept was first advocated by Mahatma Gandhi. He announced that *Ramarajya* would be brought once we are independent. *Ramarajya* was his concept of an ideal state. *Ramarajya* was not a religious state. *Sree rama chandrudu eka patni vratudu, satya vak paripalakudu, pitru vak paripalakudu, dharma parirakshakudu, adarsa paripalakudu; andukane rama rajyam kavalani mahatma gandhi garu chepparu. Ramarajya ante adi. Ramarajyam ante oka adarsa rajyam. Aakali dappulu leni, avineetiki jada leniyokka, akramalaku taavu leniyokka, asamanatalu toliginchetatuvanti rajyam yokka pere rama rajyam; alanti rajyam kavalani mahatma gandhi cheppadu. Aa rama rajyanni manamu duradrushta vasattu marchipothunnamu.* By using the *Ramarajya* slogan Gandhiji implied an ideal *rajya* where values of justice, equality, idealism, renunciation and sacrifice are practised. *Sree rama chandrudu valla tandrigaru maata isthe ventane anathi prakaram rendava alochana kuda cheyyakunda ventane aayana vana vaasaaniki valladu*. In every act of Rama, there is a powerful message to humanity. He has set models. *Kashtaalu anekamu anubhavinchadu, nashtaalenno chavichusadu, ayina manakentho aadarsamga nilichadu.* "By *Ramarajya*", Gandhiji said, "I do not mean Hindu Raj. I mean by *Ramarajya*, a Divine Raj, the kingdom of God. For me, Rama and Rahim are one and the same deities. I acknowledge no other God but the one God of Truth and Righteousness." *Manamu anekamandi aneka rakala devullanu pujisthu untamu. Devullaku devatalaku mana desamlo korathe ledu. Inkoka iddaru devullu extra cherataarante manaku vachina ibbandi emundi cheppandi daniki. Anduke bharata desamu eppudu andarini aahvaninchindi, andarini aalinganamu chesukundi andarini manalo kalupukundi. Ee desanikunnatuvanti goppa tanamu ade. Prapanchamulo evvaru vachina sare andarini mana desamulo kalupukune prayathnamu manamu chesamu. Evari paina eppudu kuda denini vathidi cheyyaledu*. Whether Rama of my imagination ever lived or not on this earth, the ancient ideal of *Ramarajya* is undoubtedly a true democracy in which the meanest citizen could be sure of swift justice without an elaborate and costly procedure. *Ee nyaya vyavasthalo ippudu roju choosthunnamu manamu okkasari case vesthe, vadu poyindaka nadusthu vuntundi mamuluga, ani manamu andaramu badha padutu vuntamu. Vistruthamayinanti okka, procedure lekunda, chaala telikaga, suluvuga, satvaranga nyayanni andichetatuvanti rajyanni rama rajyam ga aayana cheppadu.*

On *Gramaswaraj* Gandhiji gave the clarion call of back to villages, as he wanted to see each village as a little republic, self-sufficient in its vital wants, organically and non-hierarchically linked with larger spatial bodies, enjoying the maximum freedom of deciding the affairs of the locality. Gandhi wanted political power to be distributed among the villages in India. He said *Ramarajya* is incomplete without *Gramarajya*. We have to empower the village. We have to empower the local bodies. But unfortunately in spite of 73rd and 74th constitutional amendments, 29 subjects which were supposed to be devolved to local bodies are not fully done. They are only partly done so far. We must all commit ourselves to Gandhi's ideal of *Gramaswaraj* while we are discussing about the philosophy of Mahatma Gandhi. But now globalization has taken over; urbanization appears to be inevitable. But what we can do now is adapt the ideals of Gandhiji to present conditions, create such infrastructure in both rural and urban areas so as to make them self-sufficient. That is why, our government has mooted the idea of Sansad Adarsh Gram Yojana, Smart City Mission, (1) Atal Mission for Rejuvenation and Urban Transformation (AMRUT), (2) Heritage City Development and Augmentation Yojana (HRIDAY), (3) Pilgrimage Rejuvenation and Spirituality Augmentation Drive (PRASAD), etc., schemes.

Satyagraha was the most powerful weapon that Gandhiji gave to mankind. Truth and nonviolence were his *mantras*. Self-reliance, self-respect were the catchwords. The relevance of Gandhiji's message of nonviolence to the troubled world today, traumatized by terror, is all too obvious. See, the other day in spite of all the provocations and what is happening between India and Pakistan our Prime Minister suddenly, while coming back from Afghanistan, landed in Pakistan and met its Prime Minister. People have questioned as to why he suddenly went there. But, see the amount of moral pressure on Pakistan now; the amount of moral pressure from the international community on Pakistan. This is the Gandhian method. See, in one way, you can't even think of talking with Pakistan, with the way Pakistan is aiding, abetting, funding, training terrorism. But at the same time, they are our neighbour. It is a fact we must live with. We were together once upon a time. We were all one country. We were all the part of Akhanda Bharat earlier. So, keeping that in mind we have to see that the tensions are removed. If there is tension on the border, we cannot tend to many of our internal issues and development agenda. So the tension has to be curtailed, if not eliminated fully. This is what Mahatma Gandhi has said. The best way is again *satyagraha*, throwing the ball in the other man's court. Now Pakistan is trying to act in some way. Let us hope that they will realistically take some steps. If Pakistan removes this irritant menace of terrorism, both the countries can together become powerful, can grow together. That is the wish of our people. Geographically we are divided, for administrative convenience. But at the same time, our original race is one and the same. So we have to think on those lines.

Mahatma Gandhi's message of nonviolence to the troubled world, traumatized by terror, is all too obvious. However, less understood and more significant are Gandhiji's message and the methods he experimentally designed and actually practised in life, deriving from his basic philosophical premises inlaid in Indian tradition and his understanding of human nature. Whatever, he said, again as I told you, is inlaid in Indian tradition. Dr. Martin Luther King Jr, the Nobel Prize winner of USA came to India as a pilgrim in 1959. After a month's sojourn in the land of Gandhi, on the eve of his departure, he was asked a cynical question at a press conference in Delhi. There are many people in India who always ask cynical questions. "Where is Gandhiji today?" he was asked, ". . . we see him nowhere". Dr. King's reply was that Gandhi was inevitable. "If humanity has to progress, Gandhi is inescapable. He lived, thought and acted inspired by the vision of humanity evolving towards a world of peace and harmony. We may ignore him only at our risk." So our people, the namesake people, only talk about Gandhi but they do not walk. We all have to think about it seriously and see that of what he preached, whatever is suitable to the present time we all practise it and we all walk on the path shown by him. We revere Mahatma as the Father of the Nation, because he was the principal architect of the Indian freedom struggle. Besides paying due respects on his birth and death anniversaries, unfortunately we could not do enough, we could do only little to implement various constructive programmes Mahatma Gandhi championed, the essential ingredients in the country's desired development.

In this context, it is very refreshing to note that the Center for Gandhian Studies, GITAM Institute of Management is organizing events such as Gandhirama in order to heighten awareness by highlighting Gandhian thought from different perspectives. I had an occasion just to go around and see what has been created by GITAM University — the exhibition, the museum, the photo gallery, the thoughts of Gandhiji — all these are very inspiring. I really compliment GITAM University and also, particularly Prof. Ramakrishna Rao for creating such a centre here. Because the moment you enter the new generation, the younger generation only know namesake Gandhis. They have not seen Mahatma Gandhi's philosophy or ideology. It is high time that we must make them visit Gandhiji's life, try to understand the preachings and teachings of Mahatma Gandhi and try to follow his footsteps. For that you need statues, temples and other memorials, to remind you Gandhiji, just as temples remind you of God. Same is the case with statues. The statues are created to give you inspiration and this photo museum is also to give an insight into how Gandhiji acted; what Gandhiji preached and all such things. This would be very useful in inspiring the younger generation. Nowadays you see, people are creating institutions. Some people start it as a mission and end up with commission. But I am happy that Murthi garu is taking this mission forward, in the larger interests of the country. I was just telling him that Visakhapatnam has got a bright future. It is going to be a destination because Visakhapatnam city has a unique beauty and God's blessings. In addition to this, the focus is also on the development made now and one of the great additions to Visakhapatnam is GITAM University. People from abroad, people from across the country whoever comes to Visakhapatnam shall also visit GITAM University to see, to understand how an important institution, a beautiful institution has come here and how the pious atmosphere is maintained here. A concerted effort in this direction is needed to arouse interest in the person and philosophy of Gandhi. Let me repeat a concerted effort in this direction is much needed to arouse interest in the person and philosophy of Gandhiji. Gandhiji is an icon of hope to inspire humankind tormented by terror and troubled by the menace of conflict. His philosophy, as I told you, is the philosophy of India. It is eternal. His message of peace, love, nonviolence and altruism has much to offer and help humankind to address current challenges. I compliment GITAM Institute of Management and particularly Prof. Ramakrishna Rao garu for I admire him as one of the finest human beings and an intellectual for conceptualizing and implementing the noble idea of Gandhirama.

Nowadays people are starting institutions in the name of their fathers or forefathers or in the name of the leaders who can give them something. We are all politicians. You know some of the politicians are now trying to make their own statues also, because they are sure nobody is going to make their statue afterwards, once they are out of power, or die. In such a situation, focusing on Mahatma Gandhi, his life, his teachings and preachings and preserving a great culture to pass on to the next generation is really a laudable objective. Ramakrishna Rao garu is having a great vision of having a Gandhi Mandir on the top of Kailasagiri. His philosophy is already on Kailasagiri. You have to take it there physically. There is no other philosophy which can match Gandhiji's philosophy, because as I told you Gandhiji's philosophy is Indian philosopohy. We will all try to work hard to see to it. I will talk to the chief minister of Andhra Pradesh and ask him also to cooperate in this project. Recently, we had that Telugu cultural museum there, thanks to Indira Dutt and Lakshmi Prasad and many people who have all joined together. I am hopeful in the coming days this Gandhi Mandir also will become a reality. Recently, I have been to Gandhinagar. Prime Minister had suggested me that whenever I go to Gandhinagar, I should visit Dandi Kutir, which is built in the memory of Dandi Salt Satyagraha. I went. From the outside it is like a bundle of salt. But inside, it is a four-storey building. The entire life of Gandhi from birth to death was conceptualized and put live and then they have made it in such a modern way that, when you enter every room, whatever picturization is there, there is a running commentary in Hindi, English and Gujarati. You can wear the headphone, whatever language you want you can switch it to and hear in that language. It is very inspiring. I was suggesting Murthi garu also to take a team of his people to Gandhinagar and see that Dandi Kutir also, because Murthi garu has got a large heart and also has a large area of land here and he has the potency to take up such projects. That will also be an important addition to the great city of Visakhapatnam.

To conclude, the need of the hour is shaping values among the younger generation. Community spirit and living together without conflict, promoting good education are also the prime needs. Inspiring values that come from the national pride — you must feel proud of your nation, your heritage, great leaders who fought for you. Patriotism, unity, self-confidence are all as important as the infrastructure development. This is what the Prime Minister has said. *Ee desamlo manamu portlu, airportlu, jaatiya rahadarulu, sthaniya rahadarulu, alage aneka rakala okka nirmana projectlu nirminchadamu entha mukhyamo, daanitho patu viluvalanu, adarsalanu, samskaranni kooda mana yuvathaku andichadamu chaala avasaramu. Andukani manandaram kuda ee gandhirama ane project edayite vundo, deenni, marintha munduku teesukellenduku vaaru chesthunna krushiki manandaram kuda sahakarinchalsina avasaramu entho vundi.* I once again would like to compliment Prof. Ramakrishna Rao garu and his team of people and the boys and girls who have joined this endeavour. Foreign delegates have also come. I am confident that through discussion and debate over the coming days, we will be enriched further, new ideas will come, new facets of Gandhi's life will also come to the fore. That is the great expectation. My colleague Shri Mahesh Sharma could not make it today. But I can assure you I will definitely make him visit this institution and bless this Gandhi Mandir project. I told Haribabu that once we go to Delhi I will tell Mahesh Sharma to visit this institution and know about its activities. When he sees this, I am sure, he will be inspired. Thank you very much. *Namaskar*! *Jai Hind*!

Gandhi's Favourite Bhagavadgita

Hermeneutical Disaster, Profoundly Insightful, or Invitation for Creative Reconstitution?

Douglas Allen

Abstract: The *Bhagavadgita* is Gandhi's favourite text, his guide to daily living, and its *karma-yoga* is his primary moral and spiritual path. Scholars and Hindu followers of the *Gita* have found Gandhi's readings and commentaries of *karma-yoga* and the *Gita* surprising, inadequate, and a hermeneutical disaster. What distinguishes Gandhi's interpretation of *karma-yoga* is his emphasis on the status of the karmic world of relative truth with the necessity for non-egoistic selfless action to focus on alleviating the suffering of others. What is really remarkable is Gandhi's interpretation of the central message of the *Gita* as a gospel of *ahimsa* (nonviolence). How can Gandhi justify such a seemingly bizarre claim? I examine the usual interpretations of this claim that one must not take the *Gita* or other scriptures literally, but must instead read and interpret them as highly symbolic, mythic, allegorical texts. More significantly, I attempt to analyse Gandhi's approach and dramatic nonviolent interpretations by regarding the *Gita* as a dynamic open-ended text and as involving a key, creative, insightful hermeneutical move of the greatest relevance today.

M.K. Gandhi repeatedly avows that the *Bhagavadgita* is his favourite text, his moral and spiritual guide to daily living.[1] He expresses the following personal sentiments:

> when doubt haunts me, when disappointments stare me in the face, and when I see not one ray of light on the horizon, I turn to the *Bhagavadgita*, and find a verse to comfort me; and I immediately begin to smile in the

1 A shorter version of this essay was presented at Gandhirama 2016, held at GITAM University, Visakhapatnam, 16-21 January 2016. I would like to thank Prof. K. Ramakrishna Rao, Prof. B. Sambasiva Prasad, and others at the GITAM School of Gandhian Studies for their assistance. A longer version of this essay will appear in my forthcoming book on Gandhi.

> midst of overwhelming sorrow. My life has been full of external tragedies, and if they have not left any visible and indelible effect on me, I owe it to the teachings of the *Bhagavadgita*.

He later writes:

> As for myself, I run to my Mother *Gita* whenever I find myself in difficulties, and up to now she has never failed to comfort me. It is possible that those who are getting comfort from the *Gita* may get greater help, and see something altogether new, if they come to know the way in which I understand it from day-to-day.[2]

The *Bhagavadgita* is Gandhi's greatest resource for formulating and living his primary moral, philosophical, and practical approach of *karma-yoga*. In his commentaries, theoretical analyses, and practices embracing his understanding of the *Gita*, what is most distinctive is Gandhi's identification with and primary emphasis on the path of *karma-yoga*.[3]

In his formulations, Gandhi is consistent with most previous interpretations of renunciation and its approach in *karma-yoga*: an action-oriented approach of renunciation in action in which the *karma-yogin* fulfils one's *dharma*, consistent with one's *karma*, with an attitude or spirit of complete nonegoistic attachment to the results of one's action.

In his interpretation of the *Bhagavadgita* as a whole, its central message of renunciation, and its specific treatment of *karma-yoga*, Gandhi is influenced by traditional Indian and more specifically Hindu sacred texts and philosophical and religious traditions in their approaches to the karmic world and liberation or *moksha*. In his approach to the *Gita*'s renunciation and *karma-yoga*, Gandhi is certainly influenced by Jain, Buddhist, and other Indian sources, and by Christian and other Western sources, but one must appreciate how the radically non-traditional Gandhi is deeply influenced by traditional philosophical and religious Hindu sources.

The *Gita*, consistent with other classical Hindu texts, emphasizes the

---

2 M.K. Gandhi, *Young India* (6-8-1925), p. 274 and *Young India* (13-11-1930), p. 1.

3 The major treatment of *karma-yoga* is chapter 3, the Yoga of Action, in the *Bhagavadgita*. Gandhi's translations and commentaries on the *Bhagavadgita* can be found in various pamphlets and in M.K. Gandhi, *The Collected Works of Mahatma Gandhi* (*CWMG*, New Delhi, Publications Division, Ministry of Information and Broadcasting, Government of India), especially *CWMG* 32 (Discourses on the Gita): 94-376 and *CWMG* 41 ("Anasaktiyoga", published in English under the title *The Gita According to Gandhi*): 90-133. In this essay, I primarily use Mahatma Gandhi, *The Bhagavad Gita According to Gandhi*, ed. John Strohmeier (Berkeley, CA.: North Atlantic Books, 2009), which is taken almost entirely from "Discourses on the Gita" in the *Collected Works*.

goal of self-realization, which is impossible without self-control, which is impossible without the control of the senses, the mind, desires, and attachments. Although it is difficult to perfect, *yoga* allows one to stabilize the mind, control the senses with their sense-object attractions, desires, and attachments to allow the higher Soul or Self (*Atman, Purusha,* untouched by change) to control the lower karmic unstable self (Chapter 6, verses 34-36).[4]

For Gandhi, this ideal of the perfected *yogi*, the ideal moral and spiritual human being, is best expressed in the last part of the *Gita*'s chapter 2, verses 55-72, upon which Gandhi meditates every day. These eighteen verses present the ideal, which provides Gandhi with daily practical guidance, of the *sthitaprajna*, the person of steadfast wisdom, of self-controlled and self-disciplined mind, with no ego attachment to results, with control of senses, of desires, of thoughts, and living a life full of equanimity, peace, truth, reality, and joy.[5]

What is it that makes Gandhi's approach to *karma-yoga* so distinctive, self and world transformative, and potentially revolutionary for our contemporary world?

What differentiates Gandhi's *Gita*-informed *karma-yoga* from many past philosophical and religious interpretations is his greater emphasis on the significance of the karmic world of relative truth. More specifically, this involves Gandhi's major focus on selfless service, self-discipline, self-renunciation, and self-sacrifice (*yajna*), in which one sacrifices the ego-self with its desires and attachments so that one realizes the moral and spiritual Self that necessarily includes the karmic world of unfree and suffering others.

What renders Gandhi's approach to the *Gita* so idiosyncratic, controversial, and seemingly bizarre is his claim that it is also a gospel of nonviolence. As Gandhi writes,

> Let it be granted that, according to the letter of the *Gita*, it is possible to say that warfare is consistent with renunciation of fruit. But after 40 years' unremitting endeavour fully to enforce the teaching of the *Gita* in

---

4 *Bhagavad Gita According to Gandhi*, p. 98.

5 Ibid., pp. 26-32. In his interpretation and application of the lessons of the *Gita* as central to decades of struggle in India's Independence movement, Gandhi focuses on the *sthitaprajna*, the person of steadfast wisdom, as necessary for renunciation with no ego attachment to results, and he uses this to organize his *satyagrahas*. In the Freedom Movement, Gandhi thus emerges as the exemplary *satyagrahi*, and the lessons of the *Gita* are used to organize individual and mass *satyagraha*.

> my own life, I have, in all humility, felt that perfect renunciation is impossible without perfect observance of *ahimsa* [nonviolence] in every shape and form.[6]

How is it possible for Gandhi to provide his dramatic, seemingly bizarre, nonviolent interpretation of the true meaning of the *Gita*? After all, the dramatic setting for the *Gita* is the battlefield, and Krishna instructs the morally challenged, conflicted, and indecisive Arjuna to engage in battle, fulfilling his *dharma* as a warrior, based on his karmic self-knowledge, but renouncing any attachment to the fruit of his action. In order to convince Arjuna to fulfil his *dharma*, Krishna provides him with a variety of responses as to why he should not be attached to such inevitable results as winning or losing the battle and killing other human beings.

For example, in the powerful and terrifying chapter 11 of divine revelation, verses 33-34, Krishna instructs Arjuna to arise and win glory. Defeat the foes and enjoy a thriving kingdom. The enemies have already been destroyed by Krishna, and Arjuna as an archer, skilful with either hand, will be no more than Krishna's instrument. The warrior chiefs have already been killed by Krishna, and Arjuna should now slay them. Do not hesitate. Fight! Victory is yours over your foes on the battlefield.[7]

It seems not to have occurred to the classical philosophers, the nineteenth-century Hindu revivalists, the twentieth-century Indian nationalists, who wrote influential commentaries on the *Gita*, or to the hundreds of millions who have identified with the *Gita*, that this could possibly be a text with Gandhi's essential message of *ahimsa*.[8]

Critics, examining how Gandhi uses occasional passages in the *Gita* to justify his interpretation that it is a scripture with its essential meaning of *ahimsa*, assert that Gandhi's nonviolent interpretation is a hermeneutical disaster. It has nothing to do with a rigorous objective interpretation of the meaning of the actual text. Gandhi's readings and commentaries may reveal a lot that is of autobiographical and biographical interest, his own personal idiosyncrasies, his contextual history, and his own moral and spiritual values. However, his imposed nonviolent interpretation does violence to the actual nature of the real text. As is well known, others, usually Gandhi defenders, who see value in Gandhi's commentaries, often

---

6 *Bhagavad Gita According to Gandhi*, pp. xxiii-xxiv.

7 Ibid., pp. 48-49.

8 In the longer version of this essay, I provide many references to nonviolence in the *Bhagavadgita*, although Gandhi goes far beyond these in his interpretation of the *Gita*'s essential message of *ahimsa*.

use Gandhi's own writings on the *Gita* to assert that Gandhi is offering an allegorical, highly symbolic reading that cannot be taken literally.

Symbolic, Mythic, Allegorical Interpretation

As just stated, Gandhi's commentaries on the *Gita* often present an allegorical, highly symbolic reading and interpretation of the essential meaning of the sacred text. Others most frequently uphold Gandhi's claim that the battle is not some actual, historical, or literal warfare.[9] Instead, the *Gita* directs us to the battle within each of us when we are confronted with moral conflicts and when we are full of doubt as to how to deal with our internal forces of good and evil. Gandhi, in his translation and interpretation, repeatedly upholds such a symbolic approach to the dramatic setting and message of the *Gita*.[10]

For example, Gandhi submits that he does not regard Krishna as some historical human being, who literally appears at some specific time in history as the charioteer, as the battle is about to commence, in order to advise the warrior Arjuna. Instead, in his symbolic approach, Gandhi submits that the *Gita*'s Krishna is a creation of our imagination. When we encounter exceptional moral and spiritual beings in our actual experiential world, they inspire us to use our imaginations to create an ideal of perfection, just as we may imaginatively construct and then imperfectly live ideals of perfect Nonviolence, perfect Truth, perfect Ethics, and perfect Religion. Through the imaginative creation of this Krishna ideal of the perfect being, we are then able to realize the Krishna (God, Self, *Atman*, *Brahman*, Truth, etc.) within each of us.[11]

Gandhi certainly intends to offer a symbolic, mythic, and allegorical interpretation of the *Gita*, but to make this claim does not resolve the serious hermeneutical issues and debates. After all, we have a long tradition, going back at least to Aristotle, in which myths and mythologies

---

9 In *Young India*, 12-3-1925 (published in *CWMG* 26 (1925: 289), Gandhi writes: "The fact is that a literal interpretation of the *Gita* lands one in a sea of contradictions." Gandhi is responding to a correspondent and others who claim that the *Gita* advocates and teaches violence.

10 See, for example, *Bhagavad Gita According to Gandhi*, p. xvii.

11 Ibid., pp. xvii-xviii. Gandhi continues by interpreting this approach to divine incarnation, how we experience perfected beings in this world, as intended to bring out self-realization, the central subject of the *Gita*. Gandhi grants that the author did not write the scripture to establish that doctrine. Nevertheless, the *Gita* shows Gandhi the most excellent way of attaining self-realization through renunciation, right knowledge, devotion, and especially desireless action and service renouncing all attachment to the fruits of action.

are analysed as works of fiction. They may be highly imaginative, fascinating, and have great aesthetic value, but they have nothing to do with critical, rational, objective, scientific, and philosophical accounts of truth and reality. This is reflected in the history of philosophical and other scholarly approaches in which the scholar must demythicize and critique the mythic or simply ignore it if the scholarly focus and goal are to formulate and justify claims to truth and reality. This approach is reflected in the most common meaning of myth in everyday discourse, as in "5 myths about Bollywood stars": people believe such myths, but to describe something as a myth is to expose it as false.

There is a radically different sense of truth and reality of the mythic and the allegorical for those who believe in and live the mythic and allegorical and for some phenomenological, hermeneutical, and other scholarly approaches that examine such phenomena. It seems non-controversial to assert that for the mythic person, the mythic is much more than some subjective fictional story. Just the opposite: the mythic reveals an existential orientation, an experiential way of being in the world, in which the narrative is experienced as an exemplary true story, allowing one to live the myth and realize its truths and realities. Certainly, this is what Gandhi intends when he describes and interprets the meaning of the devotional and other dramatic stories that so impressed him in his childhood or his identification with the *Gita*'s powerful narrative. He is doing more than simply sharing his own personal story.

However, Gandhi intends much more than the descriptive phenomenological and hermeneutical claim that the *Gita* has such meaning for the believer, who accepts the moral and spiritual truths of the narrative. For Gandhi, his symbolic, mythic, and allegorical approach to the *Gita* reveals profound truths and realities about our human existential mode of being in the world. Such an approach reveals profound insights about our false and limited, materialistic and consumerist, egoistic and ego-attached relations today and about our inauthentic and alienating, violent and destructive, modern mode of being in the world. His symbolic reading and interpretation of the *Gita* provides a radical critique of dominant values, but it also opens up a new approach for constructive nonviolent resistance and for self and world transformation. Such a process of transformation is necessary for more meaningful, authentic, moral relations of peace, harmony, and true human development.

Nonviolent Interpretation of Bhagavadgita as Open-ended Dynamic Text

While such allegorical, mythic, and symbolic interpretations are invaluable for understanding Gandhi's approach to the *Gita*'s narrative, they do not by themselves leave us with Gandhi's most important moral, spiritual, and hermeneutical claim in his nonviolent interpretation. After all, one could grant almost everything said above about an allegorical and mythic approach to the *Gita* while rejecting an interpretation of the *Gita* as a gospel of nonviolence. One can back this up with the obvious observation that myths, allegories, and other symbolic narratives throughout history are often extremely violent.

What has generally been overlooked is Gandhi's surprisingly complex, nuanced, and insightful methodological claims about texts, contexts, the interpretation of meaning, and a dynamic, open-ended approach to formulating and applying the values and principles of the *Bhagavadgita* and other texts. Gandhi grants that earlier formulators and interpreters of the *Gita* did not view it as a gospel of nonviolence. The *Gita*, the *Mahabharata* and the *Ramayana*, and the traditional religious and philosophical texts reveal profound moral and spiritual values and meanings, but they are often full of violent narratives or simply marginalize or are completely silent on questions of *ahimsa*.

In Gandhi's approach, earlier formulators, interpreters, and devotees of the *Gita* were often situated in contextual worlds defined by psychological, linguistic, economic, political, and cultural violence. They were socialized through language acquisition not expressing *ahimsa*, that then shaped their experiences, and through which they communicated their understanding of the message of the *Gita*. Therefore, Gandhi grants that in earlier readings and interpretations of the moral and spiritual truths of the *Gita*, including the path of *karma-yoga*, the *Gita* is not regarded as a scripture of nonviolence.

As previously mentioned, Gandhi, for all of his admirable simplicity, has a surprisingly complex, nuanced, and insightful methodological approach with a symbolically expressed, but often hidden, epistemological and ontological framework for uncovering and interpreting meaning. The three components — the *Gita* as a narrative text, the contexts within which the *Gita* is read and understood, and the diverse interpretations of meaning of the *Gita* — are always integrally related in Gandhi's dynamic open-ended approach. In an actual experiential world of how we are presented, relate to, understand, and apply or practice the *Gita*, none of the three components can be abstracted, objectified, and reified, as if it had any separate, self-defined and self-sufficient, independent existence in reality. Each is integrally related to the others as part of our actual dynamic process of experiential realization.

To provide a revealing, contrasting, personal anecdote, during one of my research sabbaticals in India, I engaged in work in comparative philosophy with different philosophical approaches to self and self–other relations. I gave a Philosophy Department Lecture at Banaras Hindu University (BHU) focusing on four approaches: the *karma-yoga* analysis of the *Bhagavadgita*, the *anatta* analysis of the Buddha in the Pali Canon, the dialectical analysis of self-alienation and self-realization by Karl Marx, and the existential feminist analysis of the patriarchal self by Simone de Beauvoir. After delineating each approach, I attempted to analyse their similarities and differences, their relative strengths and weaknesses, and to bring them into dialogue in order to explore what new formulations and meanings might develop.[12]

My commentator was a senior, influential philosopher of Advaita Vedanta at BHU. He was clearly exasperated by my approach and analysis. He began his response with a very emotional outburst: "When it comes to the *Bhagavadgita*, Professor Allen knows absolutely nothing!" He did not say that I had misinterpreted the text, that my analysis was inadequate, but rather the startling assertion that I knew absolutely nothing. He then went on: "The *Bhagavadgita* has nothing to do with women", by which he meant that the overt or actual text did not address the status of women, male–female relations, and patriarchal structures. He had other comments on how I did not understand the real or true *Gita*. As an aside, the next day he told me that his wife had chastised him for being so rude and told him to apologize to me. Since I had not personalized this, I was able to maintain the collegial relationship I had had with him.

My response to this attack was to acknowledge that when I first studied the *Bhagavadgita* in my youth, as taught to me by T.R.V. Murti and other distinguished Advaita Vedantins at BHU, I would have taken the same position toward the text that my commentator did. I would have agreed that there was one, essential, decontextualized, actual *Gita*, the real *Gita*, and that Shankara and his followers had formulated the most profound and most accurate interpretation of the true meaning of the text.

I then responded that I now rejected my earlier position as inadequate and that is why I now approached the *Gita* as a complex open-ended text. It is a text with hidden meanings in need of disclosure and new meanings that need to be constituted and formulated. Even the apparent silence of

---

12 This is formulated in "Social Constructions of Self: Some Asian, Marxist, and Feminist Critiques of Dominant Western View of Self", in my edited *Culture and Self: Philosophical and Religious Perspectives, East and West* (Boulder, CO.: Westview Press/Harper Collins, 1997), pp. 3-26.

questions of, say, the status of women, gendered relations, and hierarchical patriarchal structures is poignant with significant meaning. Textual omissions, silences, and marginalizations are most relevant in understanding how texts are constructed and what they reveal of the contextual worlds in which they have been formulated, read, interpreted, and applied.

Therefore, the *Gita*, including Gandhi's *Gita*, should not be approached as one, decontextualized, nonhistorical, permanent text, as if our philosophical or religious objective is to uncover and argue for the one true *Gita*. Instead, we should always be asking: Which *Gita*? The *Gita* of the *jnana*-privileged Advaitins or the *Gita* of the *bhakti*-devotional masses? Shankara's *Gita*? Rammohun Roy's *Gita*? Vivekananda's *Gita*? Tilak's *Gita*? Aurobindo's *Gita*? Gandhi's *Gita*? Indeed, one should not necessarily rule out the possibility that there may be several Gandhi philosophies and several Gandhi *Gita*s expressing different stages in his personal, moral, political, and spiritual development.

This is not to confuse Gandhi's approach with many, modern, fashionable approaches that would reduce such an acknowledgement of the wide diversity of *Gita*s to some position of complete subjectivism and unlimited relativism. Just as Gandhi, unlike some of traditional Indian philosophy and spirituality, is a philosophical realist to the extent that he takes very seriously the existence of a real world of violence and suffering, he accepts that there is a *Gita* text that actually exists. There is a real *Gita*, with actual independent existence, that exists independently of Gandhi's readings and surprising nonviolent interpretations.

However, even while affirming the *Gita* as a text with some significant independent status in real existence, we need to make sense of the wide diversity in how Gandhi and others have approached the *Gita* as text. We cannot understand this without appreciating how this textual diversity is necessarily related to the diverse, changing, contextual situations within which Gandhi and others read and relate to the *Bhagavadgita*. There can be no, absolutely decontextualized approach. For over 2,000 years, Indians and others have lived under complex, diverse, changing linguistic, economic, cultural, political, religious, hierarchical, caste, class, gender, and other violent and nonviolent contextual variables and structures. They have mediated and filtered their readings, receptiveness, expressions, and understandings of the *Gita* through such contextual situatedness. Just as we must ask which *Gita*, we must always relate this to the question of asking which contextual situatedness.

Therefore, in trying to understand how Gandhi could read the *Gita* and interpret its message of selfless action as a gospel of nonviolence, we must analyse how Gandhi was one of the most fascinating human beings, being shaped negatively and positively by numerous changing contextual variables, experimenting with truth in ways that appreciated much of his traditional world and its *Gita* and introducing radically new contextual breakthroughs and new contextual worlds of meaning with his new formulations of the *Gita*.

Gandhi would not have read the *Gita* narrative as symbolically expressing an essential message of *ahimsa* if he had not been exposed to Jainism and other influences in his childhood and to Tolstoy and other influences after he was first exposed to the *Gita* while a student in England. He would not have read the *Gita* narrative as nonviolent if he had not developed an appreciation for the incredible violence of "modern civilization", much of which he has earlier embraced, the violence of British colonial rule, and the violence in traditional Indian contexts toward *dalit*s or untouchables, lower classes and castes, women, and other suffering beings.

In short, without understanding these multiple contexts with their variables and influences, both within the contextual worlds in which Gandhi was raised and socialized and also the new contextual worlds which he played a major part in creating, we cannot understand how Gandhi gradually developed his philosophy of *ahimsa* and how he could regard the *Gita* as a scriptural text of nonviolence.

In developing the dynamic, interrelated, open-ended relations between texts, contexts, and interpretations of meaning, we must recognize that even on the seemingly simple level of what is presented or given to us as the *Gita*, what is received by Gandhi and by us, is a text that is already constituted and structured in contextually complex ways. In our broader and deeper hermeneutical approach, what is presented to us at the first stage of experience is not some simple, given, actual *Gita* narrative that then requires our contextually shaped reading, interpretation, evaluation, and application. At the first experiential stage, what is recognized as the given *Gita* text, as violent or nonviolent, what captures our attention or is marginalized or completely silenced and omitted, what is given priority and strikes us as meaningful or what is devalued, must be analysed as integral to a dynamic process of experiential realization.

A second personal anecdote will illustrate this hermeneutical claim. Twenty years ago, a young man, wearing a conservative suit and with a very conservative appearance, visited our campus, told me that he was deeply involved in studying and lecturing on the message of the

Bhagavadgita, and asked if he could give his presentation to my Philosophy of Hinduism class, which was then reading the *Gita.* There was no indication in his appearance or in anything he said that he was a very intelligent devotee of the International Society for Krishna Consciousness (ISKCON) movement, with A.C. Bhaktivedanta Swami Prabhupada as its founder and *acharya.* For this movement, Bhaktivedanta's version of the *Gita* serves as a foundational text.[13] The young man gave his articulate lecture for about forty minutes, with his complete focus on the *bhakti-yoga* path as "the" message of the *Gita.* When it came to questions, one of my students, influenced by what we had been studying, asked: "What about *karma-yoga* which you never mentioned?" His revealing response was the following: "Oh, yes, *karma-yoga* is mentioned in the *Bhagavadgita,* but it is a minor and insignificant approach!"

It would be hermeneutically inaccurate to charge that this Krishna Consciousness devotee was dishonest or even that he misinterpreted the true message of the *Gita* that had been given to him. In his received *Gita,* a specific approach to *bhakti-yoga* is the essence and true reading and message. Diverse *karma-yoga* readings and interpretations, including Gandhi's preferred nonviolent reading and interpretation, are omitted or are devalued as nonessential in this given *Gita* text.

This is not to deny that when reading the entire *Gita,* the *bhakti-yoga* devotional approach with devotees focusing on Krishna is certainly the most emphasized *yoga* in the scripture. This has led to numerous Krishna *bhakti* approaches that present this devotional emphasis in their translations and specific commentaries. However, the *Gita* is not one unified coherent text. Its tremendous appeal for 2,000 years has been that diverse approaches, different philosophies and religions, can read the *Gita* in diverse ways. This is reflected in the diverse translations and commentaries about the true meaning of the *Gita.* Diverse philosophical and religious approaches always recognize all of the other yogic approaches, but they then usually privilege one of them.

For example, many influential philosophers privilege their *jnana-yoga* focus of the knowledge-based experiential realization of *Brahman–Atman* as expressing the highest attainment of truth and reality. They cannot avoid acknowledging the numerous *bhakti-yoga* chapters, but they typically analyse them as expressing easier approaches, more accessible to ordinary people, and at a lower level of self-knowledge and self-realization.

---

13 *Bhagavadgita As It Is,* with translations and elaborate purports, by His Divine Grace A.C. Bhaktivedanta Swami Prabhupada (New York: Bhaktivedanta Book Trust, 1972).

In a similar way, Gandhi certainly recognizes and is deeply influenced by *bhakti-yoga* in the *Gita*, as well as the need for *jnana-yoga*. However, what is so unusual in his translation and commentaries is how he privileges his specific action-oriented, renunciatory approach of *karma-yoga* and especially his interpretation of this as revealing its deepest message of *ahimsa* at the highest experiential level of truth and reality.

The Key Hermeneutical Move in Gandhi's Interpretation of the Bhagavadgita as a Gospel of Nonviolence

This brings us to the key hermeneutical move in Gandhi's approach in which the *Gita* is not some gospel of nonviolence in some fixed, essentialized, nonhistorical and decontextualized true reading of the true meaning of *Bhagavadgita*. As we have seen, Gandhi acknowledges that the original author, earlier formulators, and earlier interpreters of the *Gita* did not view it as a gospel of nonviolence. In his translation and commentary on the *Gita*, there are many similar acknowledgements.[14]

In his radical hermeneutical move, Gandhi claims that the *Gita* is a gospel of nonviolence for him (and for us today) because he and we can purify and develop the text in more moral and spiritual ways. We can and must do a re-reading of the *Gita*, reformulating it, reapplying it, in dynamic, open-ended experiments with truth. This involves embracing the traditional insights of renunciation, *karma-yoga*, and other *yoga* paths, but that addresses our contextual situatedness, living in a contemporary world of so many violent relations, in how we relate to our self, other beings and nature.

In such a hermeneutical approach, we recognize that Gandhi exists in a complex dynamic world of texts, contexts, and interpretations of

---

[14] In the longer version of this essay, I illustrate Gandhi's dramatic key hermeneutical move by showing in great detail and with extensive documentation how he expands and develops his understanding of *yajna* as sacrifice in the *Gita*. Gandhi critiques earlier Hindu formulations of *yajna*, including those by Vyasa, and claims that there is no harm in expanding and introducing new meanings of *yajna*, even if they never occurred to Vyasa in his *Gita* formulations. As we become more enlightened, the meanings people attach to "sacrifice" and other words become more morally and spiritually enlightened, so that we realize that true *yajna* as selfless sacrifice and service can never involve inflicting suffering on others. In citing many passages and providing his creative developed interpretations, Gandhi rejects traditional caste-based interpretations of *yajna*, including attitudes towards the labour of *dalit*s. He submits that only *yajna* as nonviolent selfless service allows for the control and transcendence of ego-based desires and attachments and for the realization of *Brahman*, *Atman*, and other formulations of ultimate reality.

meaning. Born on 2 October 1869, Gandhi first reads the *Gita* through Sir Edwin Arnold's English translation, *The Song Celestial or Bhagavadgita*, during 1888-89. How Gandhi receives, reads, and relates to the *Gita* is shaped by his lived world consisting of his personality and cultural upbringing and socialization, shaped by a long history of cultural, linguistic, political, social, religious, and other determinants. These include diverse past expressions, readings, and interpretations of the *Gita* and other formative texts in his life.

Gandhi offers his first focused series of talks on the *Gita* at his *ashram* from 24 February until 26 November 1926. In explaining why his translation and understanding of the *Gita*, including his claim that it is a gospel of *ahimsa*, seems so different, Gandhi submits that unlike other translators, he has been actively engaged for 40 years in transformative practice in living the *Gita*. Through his experiments with truth and action-oriented transformative engagements, Gandhi then transforms his life world, including his radical interpretations and applications of *karma-yoga* and other paths in the *Gita* as expressing a more moral and spiritual message of *ahimsa*.

At the same time, in such a hermeneutical approach, we recognize that we today exist in a very different, complex, dynamic world of meaning with new relations of texts, contexts, and interpretations of meaning. Although Gandhi's moral approach and profound insights into truth and nonviolence speak in the most significant ways to our contemporary values and crises, we cannot decontextualize, worship, or uncritically appeal to the Mahatma, his philosophy of truth and nonviolence, and his interpretation of the message of the *Bhagavadgita*. We must reject a kind of Gandhi fundamentalism or decontextualized essentialism in which Gandhi has already given us the infallible blueprint with all of the clear solutions to our problems. In fact, such an uncritical authoritarian approach would violate the experimental spirit and lessons of Gandhi's own life and his moral and philosophical formulations.

In analysing how we receive, read, and relate to the *Bhagavadgita*, we exist in our own, developing world of texts, contexts, variables, structures, and meanings. Our new, actually lived world has been shaped by Gandhi's remarkable readings and interpretations of how we can develop nonviolent interpretations and applications of *karma-yoga* and the *Gita*. We can now appreciate how Gandhi's innovative approach provides us with invaluable resources for addressing our contemporary violent, moral, philosophical, social, economic, cultural, educational, and environmental crises.

Thus we have multiple interconnected but also different perspectives, horizons, or worlds of meaning — Gandhi's and our own — that are highly complex, sometimes with values and meanings that are transparent and coherent and at other times hidden and contradictory, open-ended and resisting any final closure. Our hermeneutical challenge is to connect, mediate, or fuse Gandhi's contextually structured understanding and interpretation of the meaning of the *Gita*'s text, including his radical claim that it is a scripture of nonviolence, with our contemporary, contextually structured approaches to the text.

First, in connecting our perspective with Gandhi's, we may decide that Gandhi is insightful in claiming that the ego is *necessarily* violent. Our construction and functioning of the false, untruthful, violent ego necessarily limits our realization of non-attachment and nonviolence with its separation of the I–me ego self, its ego-desires and possessive attachments, and its generation of conflict, war, hatred, greed, and relations of disharmony toward other beings and toward nature. Therefore, a morally and spiritually developed *karma-yoga* approach today necessarily involves a commitment to non-attachment that necessarily involves a commitment to *ahimsa*. It may be granted that Indian philosophers for thousands of years have made connections between the ego and violence, but Gandhi develops his *karma-yoga* nonviolent approach in new action-oriented transformative ways that can be reconstructed to address our violent contemporary world.

Second, in his reading and interpretation of the *Gita* and *karma-yoga* as nonviolent, Gandhi adopts a cause–effect, means–ends moral approach in his formulation of a kind of law of *karma*. Stated briefly, violent immoral causes, structures, and conditioning factors lead to immoral violent and untruthful effects, which then become new immoral causes and conditioning factors. We thus become entrapped in relative, immoral, untruthful, violent cycles. *Karma-yoga*, as a morally developed approach, allows us to control and decondition those violent interconnected causes and conditions and to introduce more moral nonviolent causes and conditioning factors. Only by addressing the basic violent causes and conditions and engaging in nonviolent transformation, through the developed *karma-yoga* understanding of *ahimsa*, will we be able to break the causal links in the cycles of violence. Only then will we develop as self-realized nonviolent beings, relating with love, compassion, and justice, as moral beings integrated with a morally unified interconnected world.

Third, Gandhi's moral approach, illustrating and justifying his nonviolent reading of *karma-yoga* and the *Gita*, is grounded in his ontological view of truth and reality. This also provides an ontological framework of our previously analysed approach to the dynamic, interconnected, open-ended relations of texts, contexts, and the interpretation of meaning. We can develop an understanding today in which we realize that violence, including violent interpretations of *karma-yoga,* not only leads to violent immoral consequences, but it also separates us from truth and reality.

Put briefly, Gandhi repeatedly upholds an organic, holistic view of the interconnected unified nature of truth and reality. Violence separates us from truth and reality. It is based on a primary ontological distinction that the other — whether individual, social, ethnic, caste, class, gendered, race, national, etc., other — is othered as fundamentally different from me, my caste, my religion, my gender, my nation, etc. *Ahimsa,* by way of contrast, is the active transformative love-force, truth-force, soul-force, nonviolent force that brings us together in nonegoistic, compassionate, loving, meaningful, unified, interconnected relations. This involves the purification and development of the self-realization of our basic unity with a respect for legitimate perspectival differences. In other words, a developed Gandhian approach today would be grounded in the underlying ontological philosophy and practice which maintains that only a nonviolent interpretation of *ahimsa* is commensurate with truth and reality.

Finally, these claims and issues lead to key unresolved challenges for Gandhi's reconstituted nonviolent readings, interpretations, and applications of the *Bhagavadgita*. These challenges can be related to Gandhi's insightful, often non-traditional, and often controversial claims about his inclusivistic, pluralistic, perspectival approach; the status of relative truth in which we are always attempting to move from one relative truth to greater truth closer to the Absolute ideal; and his moral, epistemological, and ontological view of the organic, interconnected, unifying nature of truth and reality.

In his tolerant approach involving real respect for the views of the other, Gandhi repeatedly affirms a contextualized pluralism and diversity, often using such images as the many branches on the tree or the many paths ascending the mountain. He repeatedly asserts that what may be true and real for him may not be true and real for the other. Gandhi upholds the necessity for numerous, legitimate approaches expressing diverse relative truths and different paths to developing greater relative truths. We must respect that the other must develop her or his legitimate approach to truth, that is commensurate with one's karmic personality and contextualized situatedness, and we can even learn from the diverse other in developing our own moral and spiritual self-transformation and realization.

This all sounds very admirable, especially when dealing with so much intolerance, hatred, conflict, and multidimensional and structural violence in our contemporary world, but such an approach faces serious questions and challenges. In the above images and claims, Gandhi submits that there are diverse legitimate paths climbing to the same mountaintop; that there are diverse relative truths that express our incomplete realizations of the same, unifying, nonviolent, truthful Absolute ideal. In his moral, epistemological, and ontological view of truth (Truth), Gandhi submits that we only have partial, incomplete, perspectival, temporary "glimpses" of the unified, meaningful, interconnected, harmonious, moral, and spiritual nature of reality.

In his approach to the *Gita* in general and *karma-yoga* in particular as a gospel of nonviolence, how does such a Gandhi-informed interpretation meet the challenges of many Muslims and Christians, dominant post-Enlightenment approaches, secular political and scientific thinkers, those focusing on contemporary violence and terrorism, and others who may recognize but reject the legitimacy of many or all diverse paths and claims to relative truth? Who may reject Gandhi's view that they are climbing the same mountain with the shared goal of reaching the same mountaintop or that they share the same Absolute ideal? Who may reject Gandhi's moral and ontological view of reality? Who may be devout Hindus embracing the *Gita*, but who reject his interpretation of it as a gospel of nonviolence as inadequate and even immoral? These, of course, are challenges that Gandhi faced during his lifetime and that continue to challenge his claims about the *Gita* as a nonviolent text today.

My own view is that Gandhi's approach to the *Gita* and *karma-yoga*, as an evolutionary developmental reformulation expressing the key message of *ahimsa*, is of the greatest significance for us today. In such a Gandhi-inspired approach, we are challenged to rethink our basic assumptions, theories, paradigms, and practices in developing deeper and broader nonviolent approaches. This means selectively appropriating and reconstituting what is insightful from Gandhi's interpretation of the *Gita* and integrating this with complementary non-Gandhian approaches and insights. Gandhi has valuable answers to the key questions and challenges that confront us, but he does not have all of the answers.

In his nonviolent reading, interpretation, and application of the *Bhagavadgita*, Gandhi invites us to engage in developing more nonviolent theories and practices. In this complex, dynamic, open-ended process of nonviolently transforming ourselves and our world, we are able to develop more moral, spiritual, and pragmatically effective ways for addressing our contemporary ethical, social, economic, cultural, religious, educational, and ecological crises.

Perpetual Peace:
A Philosopher's Pipe Dream?

K. Ramakrishna Rao

Abstract: Matters relating to the possibility of perpetual peace, as discussed by one Western philosopher (Kant) and one Indian philosopher (K.S. Murty) are discussed along with M.K. Gandhi's contributions. It is contended that Gandhi's analysis is more profound and goes much deeper.

From Kant's perspective, there are two sides to human nature, perilous egoism and rational commitment to lawful social order. Gandhi adds a spiritual dimension to man's morality; Kant locates morality in reason itself seen from its practical side. There is thus a significant difference between Gandhi and Kant. Kant does not rule out violence and physical force to maintain law and order within the state, while forbidding violence to settle inter-state disputes. For Gandhi, violence has no place in the resolution of inter-state as well as intra-state conflicts. Thus Gandhi goes beyond Kant. Unlike Kant, an arm-chair thinker, who had no direct political experience, Gandhi grew up amidst political turmoil.

In his studies of peace, Murty draws from Western scholars as well as Eastern systems equally. However, in his later years there is a transition from his earlier secular and Western perspective of peace to the Indian spiritual approach. He goes on to suggest that peace is to be obtained through self-control and a vision of Transcendence — which are basic concepts in the Indian tradition. Murty points out that the Indian tradition from Upanishads and Buddhism until the time of Gandhi the control of the ego and selfishness and spiritual transformation of the person are the true way to peace. Though Murty discusses some of Gandhian ideas of peace and nonviolence, he falls short of discussing the spiritual perspective of Gandhian thought as it relates to the issues of peace and war. This paper is an attempt to fill this gap and bring out the relevance of Gandhi's ideas to perpetual peace.

The humankind is longing for peace because the world is in turmoil.

Homicide and suicide, terror and violence have become frequent news items. Aggression, exploitation, greed, intimidation, cruelty, and viciousness are all in the air as if they are part of our daily lives. Even though we are spared of World War III so far, all reasonable people are troubled by the very thought of it because of its destructive potentialities. Further, war as a phenomenon is conspicuous by its ubiquitous presence in one part of the world or another. It is frightening that wars are no longer limited to conflicts between states but perpetuated by non-state actors and pursued by groups operating beyond national boundaries. They are often linked to religious, ethnic, and other identities, which are generally believed to bring people together rather than divide them. Religions generally stand for peace and harmony among people. They are known to promote virtues of love and compassion. Instead we find something very different. It is no longer an uncommon sight to witness destruction of life and property in the name of religion. There is a general despair on the horizon; and painful and desperate longing for peace in the minds of thoughtful men around the world. Given the current spectacle, is perpetual peace a pleasant dream or a possible ideal? Is there any hope for and are there any possible means of achieving perpetual peace? Where do we begin? How do we proceed?

These are the kinds of questions I wish to address. These are not fresh issues. Philosophers both in the East and the West dealt with these matters and left behind many insights from which we can learn much. It is not possible to review here the views of many thinkers who reflected on the subject of peace. I will limit myself to one Western philosopher and one Indian scholar to highlight the issues involved with the backdrop of classical Indian tradition and then round off the discussion drawing from Mahatma Gandhi's paradigm of nonviolence and his ideas on peace.

Immanuel Kant on Perpetual Peace

When we talk of perpetual peace, the foremost name that comes to mind is the German philosopher Immanuel Kant (1724–1804). He is clearly the most prominent among modern Western philosophers, who wrote about perpetual peace and pleaded for it. Kant shared Rousseau's view that war is an intolerable evil that needs to be avoided and eliminated completely in all human societies. He also saw like Rousseau the insurmountable difficulties in conceiving a federal structure that could function in practice without war between states. Unlike Rousseau, however, Kant was more optimistic and felt that, while there are great difficulties in finding appropriate solutions to eliminating as deeply rooted a political evil as war, the notion of perpetual peace is something that we should entertain and cherish as a desirable and achievable goal in the long run. He published in 1795 his celebrated pamphlet *Perpetual Peace*, which pleads not merely for permanent peace but goes on to suggest some ways of achieving it. Several writers saw in it an important precursor of the idea of the League of Nations (Hobsbawm, 1962).

Perpetual Peace has three sections and two appendices added in the second edition. The first section contains a number of Preliminary Articles of Perpetual Peace between states. The Preliminary Articles include pledges by the signatory states to abjure any secret treaties, renounce acquisition of any state by another by purchase, gift or inheritance, disallow maintenance of standing armies, refrain from any interference with the constitution of another state, and abandon all subversive acts such as assassination that harm and preclude peaceful relations between states. The second section contains what Kant called Definitive Articles. They describe the political presuppositions and safeguards the states participating in the perpetual peace initiative need to subscribe. They include: (a) the states should have the benefits of a representative constitution, and (b) their joining of the federation makes them to commit only to repudiation of war-making acts against each other, while enjoying complete freedom within their own territories to enforce their laws on matters that are of immediate concern to them. The third section deals with Guarantee of Perpetual Peace. This section contains Kant's thoughts on the factors that possibly help realize the long-term goal of perpetual peace.

Kant subscribes to the Aristolean view that man is a rational animal. As such there are two sides to him. One is the *animal*, which makes him inherently egoistic. The other is the *rational*, which helps him to go beyond the ego dictates and compulsions. While the animal brings the person closer to self-destruction, and is the cause of the perils and dangers he faces, the rational endows him with ingenuity and inventiveness, and gives insights to overcome the negative effects of animal instincts and the egoistic tendencies. Reason is behind one's respect for justice and his law-abiding nature, whereas the animal makes him ruthless, irresponsible, and war-prone. Therefore, in order to have a stable social order, it is necessary to tame the natural egoism in people by enforcement of necessary laws by the state. Rule of law requires that the state has the irresistible power and that the citizens consider the exercise of that power in their own collective best interests. The state is thus vested with coercive power to ensure that the citizens comply with its laws meant for harmonious and peaceful living.

The use of such coercive power, according to Kant, should be limited to use within the state for enforcing the laws of the state for the welfare of its citizens. However, when conflicts arise, the egoistic tendency often spills over into inter-state relations and becomes the prime cause of wars. However, Kant is unequivocally against the use of force of violence to settle inter-state differences and disputes, while he concedes the necessity of exercising force by legitimate governments to maintain the state's laws. So, as W.B. Gallie (1978) aptly observes, "Kant had come to believe, there is a fundamental asymmetry between establishing and maintaining a just constitution within a state and in establishing and maintaining a just relationship between states" (p. 24). We depend heavily here on the interpretation provided by Gallie.

Kant emphatically rejected the notion that peace between nations may be sustained by coercion and force as absurd on logical as well as practical grounds. He believed that an international order can only be conceived as a cooperative understanding between like-minded states who are committed to abjure their right to go to war. Such an understanding cannot be forced but can be initiated by the voluntary consent of the states.

Kant considers war as the greatest evil embellishing human societies. Indeed, war is seen as the mother of all evils and the root cause of moral corruption. Kant unequivocally condemns any act of aggression against another state as patently unjust and unwarranted by law. Therefore, there can be no just wars to make or maintain peace. While Kant concedes the right of a state to defend itself by force, when attacked, he does not consider such an attempt as contributing to peace. Peace and coercion/violence cannot coexist in relations between states. The first step towards perpetual peace is a pledge by a few sovereign states of voluntary commitment to non-aggression and their total compliance with it. Therefore, in Kant's view, it is necessary for governments to voluntarily abjure their right to engage in war and join together as a federation by legally signing the mutual non-aggression pledge. Perpetual peace calls for a global international order created by signing of a non-aggression treaty by the participating states. Such a non-aggression treaty, Kant suggests, would become practical only when the states involved adhere to the principle of non-interference in the internal affairs of other states and each state remains sovereign and autonomous in its functioning.

Kant's proposal for perpetual peace thus begins with an attempt to replace the natural lawlessness inherent in man's animal nature by a legally binding relationship prompted by his Reason that calls for mediation and arbitration instead of armed intervention to settle differences, disagreements, and disputes between states. While there is an immediate moral demand for "action now" to create a global confederation of like-minded states, Kant is realistic in recognizing that it is an uphill task that can only be accomplished by a long and continuing process. What is needed now is to take the first steps by inaugurating this peace initiative by two or more states subscribing to this view. This would constitute the embryonic cell of a legal set-up that could gradually grow into a global order. So the beginning point is the conception of "peace-intended-to-be-perpetual", starting with a few states forming a federation, which it is hoped would cover in due course the entire world. The reason behind the hope is the growing cost of war and its destructive potential. Man can ill afford a future war which portends great peril to humankind. Our Reason makes this abundantly clear and calls for action to prevent it.

There are two conceivable aspects in the functioning of the states signing the permanent mutual non-aggression treaty. One is that the states joining the federation would legally pledge that they would not engage in any acts of aggression against each other and that all disputes and differences between them would be settled by mediation and arbitration. The aim is then one of perpetual peace between the signatory states. The other aspect is that the conceived confederation of states would also offer common defence against aggression by outsiders directed at any of the member states of the federation. Many see that the true strength of the confederation rests in the second aspect. Gallie in his perceptive analysis of Kant's thinking in *Perpetual Peace* writes, however, that the real strength of Kant's proposal "lies in its capacity to maintain and extend peace among a number of like-minded powers. In this way, it will demonstrate both that arbitration is the only morally acceptable way in which states can secure their rights, and that marked non-aggression *pays* — in a quite material sense — in a world where war is becoming ever more costly and destructive" (p. 25). Gallie goes on to argue persuasively that Kant's conviction, that "war is no way in which to pursue one's rights", makes better sense when we consider that the governing principle of perpetual peace is the observance of non-aggression and not the strength of mutual defence. The latter may become necessary and unavoidable, but it will not contribute to the cause of perpetual peace. Kant is very clear that peace cannot be enforced or maintained by threat of war.

The proposed confederation of sovereign states in Kant's view does not make it an international state. Since it excludes the right of the state to enforce peace when differences between states arise, we may ask, how can the member states stay together when inevitable differences arise at some point? What is it that guarantees peace between them? Kant finds the answer in man's Reason. As war becomes more menacing with increased costs and destruction, it becomes more urgent that man rises above the animal urges and moves toward perpetual peace, beginning with the acceptance of the Preliminary Articles by a few states and eventually extending to all states. This will not be easy. However, the threat of destruction posed by war would sustain Reason's demand to abjure violence and war. In Kant's formulation, Reason has two aspects — the theoretical and the practical. The theoretical aspect of reason is directed at finding unity, synthesis, order, and lawfulness in the world outside. The consequence is the development of science. We are quite successful in using Reason towards this end. Practical Reason is directed at understanding and control of the self. This is the area in which we are less successful. However, Kant believes along with Rousseau that even the modest achievements in this area have profound implications in man's political and moral spheres. Now, it is in the sphere of Practical Reason that Kant finds the guarantee of perpetual peace.

Perpetual peace in Kant's terms is a categorical imperative. That mankind is a single moral community implies and warrants the assumption of perpetual peace. Justice between men and between states presupposes peace. Reason demands that men form governments and support them to enforce justice. However, peace between states rests on an entirely different principle. It may not be enforced by forming a super-state or organizing an international police system. The realization of the impossibility of achieving a secure global system to ensure peace among states by force makes the moral necessity of perpetual peace more relevant and urgent. The threat of cost and destruction posed by war makes men realize that war is morally and economically ruinous and consequently intolerable. Any attempt to enforce peace only means renewal of war. Thus, the pursuit of perpetual peace without coercion, however difficult, becomes imperative and inescapable.

In Kant, perpetual peace appears to be more an ideal than an actually realizable state, given the perils and the crises of animal behaviour characterizing man. Peace intended-to-be-perpetual will always remain an intention prompted by man's reason than a reality of actual life. As we all know, reason is admirably ingenious and creative but utterly powerless. Men often fail to put the dictates of reason in practice. Kant's reference to "Nature's secret plan" remains quite unconvincing to guarantee perpetual peace.

The above weakness in Kant's scheme to bring about perpetual peace may be highlighted also by pointing to the asymmetry mentioned earlier between the state's principle behind governance vis-à-vis, its citizens, where the state exercises the power, physical force to control, and the principle underlying international relations forbidding the use of force. The former follows from the paradigm of violence and the latter implies the paradigm of nonviolence. The same human beings involved as citizens and statesmen cannot be reasonably expected to follow one line in one context and a completely opposite line in another context. Again, from the perspective of the state, it is equally difficult to assume that the state used to govern by the threat of force would actually abjure force in its relations with other states.

K.S. Murty on Causes of War and Bases of Peace

K. Satchidananda Murty is one among the very few Indian philosophers who wrote extensively and passionately about war and peace (Murty and Bouquet, 1960; Murty, 1986). In a scholarly survey of the causes of war, Murty (1986) discusses psychological, sociocultural, economic, and demographical factors and examines whether war is rooted in human nature and man's instincts. He further evaluates what he describes as "tension theory" of war and the sociocultural approach of philosopher John Dewey and anthropologist Ruth Benedict and briefly refers to economic and demographical factors as causes of war. He comes to the conclusion that "it is difficult to have peace in a world organized on the principle of sovereign nation states" (p. 171), and goes on to suggest that "only a new world view, a new system of values and restructuring of societies in all countries would save mankind from wars" (p. 170).

Regarding the psychological factors believed to be relevant to the institution of war, Murty rules out the possibility that war is rooted in human nature on the ground that human nature appears to differ from one civilization to another and that "in modern civilization many men seem not to want wars" (p. 144). Murty examines the views of William James, William McDougall, Sigmund Freud and others, and concludes that there is no sufficient evidence to prove that aggression and violence or pugnacity are innate instincts. First, anthropological studies have shown that there are some cultures in which aggression and competitiveness are conspicuously absent. Second, there is some psychological evidence that competitiveness is more a learned behaviour than inherited. Third, Freud's views were discounted by even some of his early associates like C.G. Jung and Erich Fromm. Fourth, there is good deal of evidence in support of frustration–aggression hypothesis of John Dollard and Neal Miller that frustration leads to aggression in people.

Murty approvingly refers to H.J. Eysenck's remark "the view that men are the play things of uncontrolled unconscious forces, which irresistibly drag them on to wars and which cannot be influenced by reason, is as much an exaggeration as the other view that men are *entirely* subject to rational considerations" (p. 156).

All the above make abundant sense that there is no one psychological theory at present that reasonably accounts for war as an institution rooted in human nature. However, it does not follow that there are no psychological factors that are contributory causes of war. On the contrary, they are as relevant for understanding conflicts and wars just as there are other socio-economic matters triggering wars. In fact, in recent years, there has been a great deal of psychological data relevant to war and peace. It is not possible to review them here, except to note that while there is no overall psychological theory that would account for all wars, there is indeed significant psychological data relating to aggression that throws bright light on factors relevant to violence and war (Rao, 2010). Psychology of peace is a growing area with increasing interest for those interested in peace studies.

Murty dismisses tension theory of wars as inappropriate, even though he acknowledges that the UNESCO appears to favour this approach for understanding wars. In a nutshell, according to the tension theory, economic inequalities, insecurities, and frustrations tend to create tensions between groups and states. Such tensions may bias perceptions and lead to conflicts which end up ultimately in wars (Krech & Crutchfield, 1948). Murty argues that tensions happen to take place in individual minds. However, an understanding of individual minds and their experiencing tensions and engaging in hostile behaviour does not help us to understand antagonisms between states. Individual frustrations are insufficient causes of war which involves groups and states and not simply individuals. Further, tension theory, according to Murty, assumes that war is a pathological condition reflecting the aberrant behaviour of those responsible. Murty suggests that most wars result from careful planning and rational thinking of national leaders and are not a consequence of a pathological state of mind of people behind a war. He concludes that "modern warfare among great states does not seem to be mainly the effect of tensions either in leaders or in peoples. Modern wars are carefully planned over a period of years by men who clearly know what they want and who have equally clear ideas as to how to get it" (p. 161).

Raising the question whether overpopulation or economic distress are causes of war, Murty answers in the negative. He sees "no necessary connection between overpopulation and war mentality" (p. 168). Similarly, he concludes that "economic distress does not necessarily lead to wars, nor will economic prosperity prevent nations from going to wars" (p. 170). These observations make good sense even though, they are also on occasion become contributing factors for precipitating wars.

Murty appears to find some merit in the sociocultural approaches to understand war. He considers the views of John Dewey on human nature and concludes (a) that much of man's behaviour is culturally determined, (b) that wars do not have their origin in human nature but are a function of social institutions, and (c) that a reorganization of social institutions is necessary to prevent wars. Citing that in some cultures there is no place for war, Murty suggests that cultural diversity renders the view that proneness to war is rooted in human nature an antiquated idea. He concludes that though war is a social institution in some cultures, "It is not the effect of the evil in human nature, or the necessary product of a biological instinct; nor is it the result of group tensions" (p. 166).

While Murty is correct in concluding that neither the psychological dispositions of individuals, nor any of the biological factors, economic and demographic conditions are necessary and sufficient to account for wars, it would be unwarranted to conclude that they are not relevant to understanding wars and how they might be prevented. In fact, one could argue that sociocultural factors are also some of the contributory factors though not sufficient to account for all wars. In Murty's view, however, the primary factors responsible for the lack of harmony among people in the world today are "class hatred, nationalism and the principle of self-determination". But all of them have their origin in human mind!

Examining the bases of peace, Murty describes five types of pacifism and finds them all inadequate to guarantee peace. He concludes that a new vision is needed to pave the way for peace. His incisive analysis of the so-called "golden ages" of peace in human history suggests three concepts which are likely responsible for producing peace. They are "*Homonia*, Tolerance, and Universal Ethics".

Homonia is a concept that evolved in Greece. It stood for "being of one mind together". With Alexander the Great it came to mean brotherhood of all men. Murty credits Alexander the Great to have arrived at that intuition after his contacts with other races and cultures, including Indians during the years of his conquest. It was, however, the stoic philosopher Zeno who conceived that harmony and empathy bind all men in a rational universe. Murty believes that "the Stoic doctrine of human brotherhood reinterpreted and enriched so as to suit the modern mind can provide a basis for the world community, of which all peace lovers are in search" (p. 189).

Murty traces the concept of "tolerance" to the Indian King Ashoka, who saw fundamental commonalities among all religions that were in vogue at the time, which included Hinduism, Jainism, and Buddhism among other minor faiths. Therefore, Ashoka desired that all religions should coexist and learn from each other. This required that one practice avoiding praise of one's own faith and contempt for other's learning, and control his speech and irrelevant talk. The virtue of such tolerance is widespread in the West as well. Murty discusses the views of Baruch Spinoza, Gottfried Wilhelm Leibniz, and John Locke and arrives at the conclusion that tolerance implies the assertion of freedom in three respects — (1) freedom to think and hold beliefs that appeal to one, (2) freedom to lead one's life as he chooses with no harm intended to others, and (3) freedom to associate oneself with others in pursuing his goals without transgressing the notion of human brotherhood. Murty pleads for all the three types of freedom in a tolerant society, contributing for peace to prevail.

Finally, the third concept "universal ethics" flows from the other two. The basic element underlying universal ethics is the recognition that each man is an end in himself and therefore the criterion of morality has to be its universal applicability. Here Murty commends Kant's universal ethics. While the precepts of universal ethics are centred around the person, the groups and states are equally bound by the same ethics. Inasmuch as the state is an association of people it is bound by the same principles that govern individuals. Further, it follows, according to Murty, that "citizens have an absolute obligation to obey their state is unsustainable" (p. 189). Consequently, Murty favours the promotion and propagation of universal culture as a prelude to perpetual peace. He writes:

> If a consistent world view could be evolved in consonance with (if not based upon) these three concepts, through the cooperative efforts of the intellectuals of all cultures, and if they take pains to make it fashionable among all peoples, a universal culture may evolve, and make permanent world peace a possibility. — p. 199

Murty concludes his *Quest for Peace* with two suggestions for possible ways of working for world peace. One of them is working towards what he calls Respublica Litteraria, a voluntary association of the outstanding scholars and scientists around the world as citizens in the republic of letters committed to creating a general will for global peace transcending local, regional, and national loyalties. "Scientists and scholars", writes Murty, "should feel it their duty to influence politics and the shaping of events. There should be continuous interchange of ideas on academic matters as well as things that concern good life — freedom, well-being, peace — among men of learning, cutting across national boundaries" (p. 205). Such an association comprises of "men who can put the interests of truth, justice, and humanity above the interests of their countries and races, and who have voluntarily come together in a missionary spirit animated by the same ideals" (p. 206). The community of such scholars and scientists should endeavour to generate "intellectual universality" which would pave the way for "political universality". Murty pleads for an organization of such men committed to promote harmony, goodwill among nations and cultures in every country of the world and thus to help create an intercultural system conducive to global peace.

One could argue that the so-called "intellectual universality" cuts at the very roots of pluralism and leads to some kind of fundamentalism. However, what Murty means here is not the uniformity of ideas but of criteria for good conduct and righteous behaviour — universality of values and shared ethics and not ideological uniformity.

The second suggestion involves working towards "expression of world conscience". Here Murty pleads for democratic countries with independent foreign policies to take on themselves "the function of becoming the world conscience". In order to serve this function, these countries should go beyond defending particular ideologies as opposed to others and give up the notion that peace can be secured by deterrent strength. When nations begin to take such a role to promote world conscience and speak out their minds without fear or prejudice even at the risk of courting displeasure from some powerful countries, then, there would be bright prospects for global peace.

Murty's proposals are no less utopian than others such as those envisaged by Kant. Of course, there is nothing intrinsically wrong with an utopian idea, if it serves as the ideal to strive for. However, D.P. Chattopadhyaya (1995) brings to our attention several difficulties with Murty's proposals. First, scientists and scholars are not particularly known to be people who can help generate the will-for-world-peace. In fact, several philosophers have been ideologues of some of the known enemies of peace. Further, we find that people who mould public opinion are often political leaders and not the learned *pundit*s. Chattopadhyaya thinks that intellectuals are generally pro-establishment. He writes: "Among the scholars, scientists, technologists and professionals, only a few stand firm in their genuine intellectual commitment, the rest are for self-promotion and more or less indifferent to the public interest" (p. 218). Finally, in human history, the people who contributed most to promotion of peace in the world are not known for their scholastic achievements or scientific discoveries. Rather, like the Buddha, Christ, and Confucius, the champions of peace were driven by moral and spiritual force.

Murty is a versatile scholar, equally familiar with Eastern and Western philosophies. His philosophical roots are, however, in the classical Vedantic tradition. In his studies of peace, though Murty draws from Western scholars and Eastern systems equally, his surmises and suggestions appear more in line with the Western approach. Despite the fact that he notes in his Prologue that peace issues "are not just political, for Peace is a spiritual category" (p. xvi), the rest of the book does not appear to be inspired by the spiritual perspective of peace characteristic of Indian tradition.

In the Indian tradition peace has an exalted place. Its pursuit is the goal of life. The world is one family (*vasudhaiva kutumbakam*). Therefore, we wish all people to be blessed with happiness (*sarvejanah sukhino bhavantu*). Ultimate happiness consists in realization of peace (*shanti*). The world we live in is a place of turbulence surrounded by suffering. Therefore, the goal of human endeavour is to overcome suffering by experiencing authentic peace. Authentic experience of peace involves self-realization. Self-realization is again the authentic self-experience, which consists in apprehending and appreciating the similarity and the identity of one's *self* with others. This in turn generates empathy, altruism, compassion, happiness, and of course peace. It is considered a state of bliss (*ananda*), free from all turbulence and filled with tranquillity and equanimity.

Such a state of bliss and peace can be cultivated. There are well-known ways of cultivating it. They go in the name of *yoga*. There are various types of *yoga* such as *jnana-yoga*, *bhakti-yoga*, *karma-yoga*, and *dhyana-yoga*. The essence of all of them consists in gaining control over one's wandering mind. Control of the ego is the key to gaining control of the mind. Elimination of the ego, by realizing that it is not one's true self, is the necessary condition for self-realization; and self-realization is basic to experiencing authentic peace.

Peace thus has its origin in the mind of the individual. Peace of mind is the foundation of perpetual peace. It is *self*-driven; and is truly in the domain of the spiritual. It follows that sustained peace may not be imposed by external manipulations involving physical force; or secured by simply signing peace treaties between nations, but can be cultivated and guided by moral force and personal development and transformation. This in a nutshell is an outline of peace in the Indian tradition, as I understand it.

It is reasonable to think that Murty himself has moved significantly closer to the Indian conception of peace in his later years. Let us recall that the bulk of his book *The Quest for Peace* is a reprint of what he wrote in *Studies in the Problems of Peace*, which he coauthored with A.C. Bouquet and published in 1960. The only thing new in *The Quest for Peace* is the Prologue written in September of 1986. The intervening quarter century between the two books shows a significant transition from his earlier secular and Western perspective of peace to the Indian spiritual approach. In the Prologue of 1986, Murty sees "transformation of man" as a necessary condition for peace and that peace is in the domain of the spiritual. These two points are basic to the Indian approaches to peace.

Murty makes two important points in the Prologue. While reviewing "the three great indigenous classical philosophies of India" — Vedanta, Buddhism, and Jainism — Murty notes that they "consider 'analogy with oneself' (*atmaupamya*) as the basis of *ahimsa*" (p. xx). All of them, Murty points out, assert that "Peace is to be won through self-control and a vision of Transcendence" (p. xxiii). Shankara in his commentary on the *Gita* writes, for example, that he who recognizes that all beings desire happiness, as one does, and that they equally shun suffering cannot in any way act in a manner to hurt others. The realization of the likeliness, if not the identity of all beings, and the respect for the right of all to live are the foundational principles underlying the practice of *ahimsa*, according to Shankara. In Advaita philosophy, we have the metaphysical foundation for nonviolence and peace.

Again, in Jainism, *ahimsa* (nonviolence) is the cardinal virtue, the foundational base of all values. *Ahimsa* is considered an inviolable duty of all because every being has the right to live. Murty quotes from *Acharangasutra*: "He who ignores or negates other beings ignores or negates one's self; he whom you wish to kill or control or on whom you wish to inflict suffering is yourself." Thus, a Jain perceives killing of another person as killing of oneself. Compassion shown towards others is compassion towards oneself. In the same Sutra, we find the following definition of *ahimsa*. *Ahimsa* is "not to cause pain or tend to cause pain or destruction to any living being by thought, speech or conduct" (*Acharangasutra* II.15). Self-control is a necessary condition for observing *ahimsa*. Without self-restraint it is difficult for one to restrain from harming others. The basic characteristic of *ahimsa*, according to Jain thinkers, is spiritual purity.

Buddhism shares the Jain view of *ahimsa* as a cardinal virtue; but it goes beyond it in some ways. The foundational base of the Buddha's conception of *ahimsa* is that hatred cannot be appeased by hatred but by non-hatred, compassion, and love. Hate and ill will arise from the false conception of the self. The notions of "I" and the "other" are mere linguistic conveniences, and they have no basis in reality because there is no permanent self or soul underlying the continuing change of interconnected events we experience. Peace and happiness presuppose absence of suffering. Suffering is ubiquitous in the world. It cannot be isolated and confined. It is indivisible and inseparable inasmuch as everything is interconnected. Consequently, one man's suffering is equally the suffering of others. There can be no peace when there is suffering even on the part of one person. Therefore, the Buddha sought to end suffering everywhere by preaching unbounded compassion (*karuna*) and by practising charity (*dana*), right conduct (*sila*), and right intention (*bhavana*).

The concluding section of the Prologue focuses on peace leading to *nirvana*.

> The path of peace, Buddhism maintains, leads to Nirvāṇa, i.e. immortality, peace and happiness. Santimaggameva brūhaya, nibbāna sugatena desitam (*Dhammapada*, 285). Nirvāṇam paramaṁ sukham. Peace has, Vedānta also teaches, Nirvāṇa as its end. Śāntim nirvāṇa paramāṁ (*Gītā*, 6.15). Peace, Śaṅkara explains, is liberation (mokṣa); Nirvāṇa is liberation (mokṣa) and to approach peace is to become the Absolute (*Gītābhāṣya*, 2.70; 6.15; 2.71). Śāntim adhigacchati brahmabhūto bhavati (Śaṅkara). Peace or Nirvāṇa, according to Śaṅkara, is the complete cessation of all suffering. The *Gītā* teaches us that it is not to be obtained by "desiring desires", but through non-Myness and non-I-ness and through wisdom and abandonment of fruits of actions (*Gītā*, 2.70-1; 4.39; 5.12). Gandhi was true to this tradition when he taught that peace is to be obtained only when desire for material prosperity is given up, and there is "a living faith in a living God". — Murty, 1986: xxii

Thus Murty leads the way from Upanishads and Buddhism to Gandhi to show that the control of the ego and selfishness and spiritual transformation of the person are the ways to peace. He goes on to refer to and cites A.N. Whitehead and Albert Einstein from the West in support of the above.

Mahatma Gandhi on Peace

Though he discusses some of Gandhian ideas of peace and nonviolence in the main text of the book, Murty falls short of discussing the spiritual perspective of Gandhian thought as it relates to the issues of peace and war. The only reference to Gandhi in the Prologue is in the paragraph quoted above. I will now try to fill this gap and bring out the relevance of Gandhi's ideas on perpetual peace.

Gandhi's conception of human nature is very relevant to his views on peace and violence. Human beings are animal like, according to Gandhi, but they also contain a streak of divine in them. The latter is more intrinsic and human even if less obvious. The divine is the spiritual. To be spiritual is to be altruistic. To be altruistic is to see oneself in others and others in oneself. Self-realization is the goal of the person, which is none other than extending oneself beyond the ego to include others. In Gandhi's terms it is reducing oneself to "zero", nothingness.

In Gandhi's writings spiritual stands for different things at different levels of discourse. When Gandhi says that man is spiritual, he means that (a) he is intrinsically altruistic, even when he behaves as if the ego is the centre of his being, (b) he has access to trans-rational forms of knowing and acting, even though he is basically dependent on his sensory-motor system, and (c) one's identity goes beyond self in that all of us are interconnected in a significant sense by sharing the *self* at a deeper level of being. Gandhi's belief in God and religion has an important pragmatic element. He asserts repeatedly that faith in God and religion gives one the needed strength, courage, and determination to pursue what one considers to be true even in extremely adverse circumstances.

In Gandhi's conception, man is thus both good and evil. There is the divine and the devil in him as we noted. The divine enables him to realize God, Truth in his being. Inasmuch as God is Truth, the struggle to realize God is embedded in his striving to realize truth. God-realization is truth-realization; and truth-realization is self-realization. The beast in man drives him to indulge in sensory gratification. The ego emerges as the mechanism to channel the demands of sensory gratification in acceptable ways in the surrounding reality. Truth then gets distorted in one's perception. Morality takes the back seat as pleasure seeking comes to the front. The beast in man makes him a slave to habits. It makes him bound and conditioned. The animal in him struggles for existence. Man then is mired in competition, exploitation, and consequent violence.

The divine enables man to exercise his volition to cultivate virtues. The divine seeks liberation; it sets one free; and makes him altruist in pursuit of serving others instead of being self-seeking. "Man's estate is one of probation", observed Gandhi. "During that period he is played upon by evil forces as well as good. He is ever a prey to temptations. He has to prove his manliness by resisting and fighting temptations" (*Harijan*,

April 1936). Here manliness represents for Gandhi the spiritual aspect as distinguished from the brute in him. Each person has to choose for himself whether to follow the "law of the jungle" or "the law of humanity". Gandhi draws attention to "how repugnant it must be to invoke the beast in any human being" (*Young India*, October 1931). The divinity in a person manifests in proportion to the realization of the true human within. Altruism is the *sine qua non* of the spiritual in humans. Gandhi wrote:

> Man is worse than the brute, so long as he is selfish, and indifferent to the happiness of others. He rises above the level of the brute, when he begins to work for the welfare of his family. He rises higher in the scale when he comes to look upon the whole community or race as his own family. He becomes greater still when he begins to regard even the so-called barbarous races as the members of his own family. In other words, man becomes great exactly in the degree in which he works for the welfare of his fellow-men.
> — 1922: 58

The ego creates artificial identity, which is among the prime sources of conflict. Altruism enables one to expand one's identity beyond the ego-bound self to the common self that binds us all as humans. Consequently, egoism is basic to man's experience of turbulence, suffering, and lack of peace; and altruism is the foundation of peace. Spiritual in Gandhi refers to the divine aspect of human being. It manifests in altruistic behaviour when one transcends the ego and extends his *self* to include others.

The Gandhian dialectic of the animal and human in man is an interesting psychological model for understanding human development. The animal instincts and human aspirations are the two opposing structures that underlie human development. Man's volition can profoundly impact the emerging synthesis arising out of their conflict. More importantly, the model as developed by Gandhi has lessons for moulding development in desirable ways to help promote the survival and happiness of human species. What is truly original in Gandhian dialectics is that the two opposites do not contradict but coexist to evolve a cogent synthesis. Such a coexistence of contraries, a magical synthesis of them in the spiritual realm, is again a very special feature of Indian psyche.

Now, Gandhi differs from Murty who seems to share the views of John Dewey on human nature. In Gandhi, man is prone to violence and aggression and consequently to war because of his animal instincts. Here, there is a similarity between the views of Gandhi and Kant. The latter also conceives man as an animal endowed with rationality.

From Kant's perspective, there are two sides to human nature, the perilous egoism and rational commitment to a lawful social order. Gandhi explicitly adds a spiritual dimension that is behind man's morality, whereas Kant locates morality in reason itself seen from its practical side. In a sense, Kant's practical reason is an inadequate substitute to Gandhi's conception of the spiritual in man. Again, both Gandhi and Kant seek perpetual peace. While acknowledging that violence is a part of man's nature, they rule out violence/war as a means of securing peace between nations. There is, however, a significant difference between Gandhi and Kant. Kant does not rule out violence and physical force to maintain law and order within the state, while forbidding it to settle inter-state disputes. For Gandhi, violence has no place in inter-state as well as intra-state conflict resolution.

In Kant, the state occupies the pivotal position in maintaining peace within and between states. It is the state which controls the citizens and ensures that they comply with its laws. The movement is from the top to the bottom, from the authority of the state to the compliance by the citizens. Again, in international relations it is the state that is groomed to maintain peace. Now, Gandhi is deeply suspicious of the state. He considered the state as an institution based on power, and power implies violence. In Gandhi, the individual is supreme and not the state. It is the people and their grass-root organizations that are fundamental in maintaining and experiencing peace and enjoying its fruits. In Gandhi's system, peace is grounded in morality; and true morality is not driven by law but by conscience. In order to change the social order one should first change himself. Change should begin with self. Roots of peaceful social order are grounded in the individual whose neglect or subordination to the state has serious adverse consequences to peace and social stability.

Treaties, however legally binding are ineffective to bring lasting peace. Laws cannot enforce permanent peace. It is cultivation of consciousness and building up of the needed conscience among people that will bring perpetual peace to the person individually and collectively. Laws may be useful; but respect for and voluntary compliance with them have their origin in morality. Therefore, morality is primary, and laws are secondary. Morality constitutes, according to Gandhi, the spiritual side of the person. It has its origin in the divine component in the human being. Thus, Gandhi goes beyond the legalism of Kant. While sharing Kant's concern with the animal aspect of man, his egoism and consequent evil, Gandhi does not subscribe to the view that this evil aspect should be tamed and curbed by physical force sanctified by the laws of the state.

In Gandhi, the only successful way to tame, control, conquer, and permanently subdue the animal in man is by cultivating consciousness, developing the spiritual side of the person and bringing about self-realization. All this involves altruism; and service to others becomes the nucleus of social action. It is what Gandhi labelled as *anasakti-yoga*.

Unlike Kant, an ivory-tower thinker, who had no direct political experience, Gandhi grew up amidst political turmoil. He had first-hand participatory experience in the unfolding of significant political events around the world. Consequently, even when his ideas sometime sound utopian, he was a man with his feet firmly on the ground and was never without realistic assessment of human situation. Himself a lawyer by training and practice, and yet champion of mediation and arbitration as important means to end all kinds of disputes, Gandhi was fully aware of the limitations of legalist approach to resolve conflicts, national as well as international.

Gandhi firmly believed in the possibility of perpetual peace. "Not to believe in the possibility of permanent peace", wrote Gandhi, "is to disbelieve in godliness of human nature. Methods hitherto adopted have failed because rock-bottom sincerity on the part of those who have striven has been lacking." He goes on to add, "I have been taught from my childhood, I have tested the truth by experience, that primary virtues of mankind are possible of cultivation by the meanest of the human species. It is this undoubted universal possibility that distinguishes the human from the rest of God's creation" (*Harijan*, 16 May 1936). Perpetual peace is thus inherent in human nature and therefore a realizable goal; but the path to it is not legal but moral. It is not the binding legal treaties, but moral dictates that ensure permanent peace. Morality is not something to be legislated by the state but cultivated by the person. Perpetual peace may be built on a value base and sustained by preserving those values that prompted it. The quest for peace must begin with the individual. It is the individual who in the final analysis makes and maintains peace, because it is he who breaks it. Peace is abstract at the state level; it is concrete in the person. In fact, peace is more than absence of war. It is wholesome experience of tranquillity, contentment, and composure. It is the state of the person described as *sthitaprajna* in the *Gita*. In Gandhi's view, morality is more than rational. It is rooted in spirituality, but articulated and systematized by reason.

Since the individual is the key, the focus should be on him. It is the individual person, joining with others, who makes, and keeps, or breaks peace. More significantly, peace is what the individual seeks, experiences, lives, and longs for. Therefore, the seeds for peace should be planted in the minds of men. The training must begin with them. The states are secondary within the paradigm of nonviolence where the individual is salient. However, they are primary when one subscribes to the paradigm of violence. Gandhi's emphasis on individual peace as against the state enforced peace reminds us of Nietzsche. Friedrich Nietzsche (1844–1900) wrote, "real peace . . . must always rest on a peace of mind: whereas the so-called armed peace, as it now exists in all countries, is the absence of peace of mind" (p. 204).

Kant and Gandhi agree that egoistic tendencies need to be checked and controlled for the reason to prevail. However, for Gandhi unlike Kant, the checks and controls are things to be cultivated at the individual level and not imposed by the state in order that they be truly effective. Gandhi's recipe is that the individual reduce himself to a zero and get rid of the ego. It is only then that the person enjoys authentic peace. In the final analysis, it is the authentic peace enjoyed by increasing numbers of people that ensures perpetual peace. Indeed this is the message of classical Indian tradition to which Gandhi subscribes.

This is the central thesis of Gandhi in interpreting the *Gita* as *anasakti-yoga*. *Anasakti* is non-attachment. Non-attached action is "selfless action". Selfless action is action delinked from the ego. Delinking the ego from action and deliberate refraining from enjoying the fruits of action is reducing oneself to a zero or nothingness. To repeat, practice of non-attached action, action performed without concern for its fruits, is Gandhi's method for eliminating the ego. Elimination of the ego is a necessary condition for self-realization which is the goal of human endeavour. Self-realization is truth-realization; and truth-realization is God-realization.

The way for truth-realization and the divine ascent from man's animal origins is nonviolence. Therefore, nonviolence becomes a binding virtue and not an expedient policy; and when nonviolence is a spiritual force driving human thought, passion and action in place of physical force of violence, there would be perpetual peace. In other words, authentic peace experienced at the level of the individual is a necessary condition for perpetual peace. Then, the individual and not the state takes the central place.

Gandhi shares with Jainism that nonviolence is a cardinal virtue that we need to practise by refraining from causing injury to others. Gandhi also shares the activist conception of *ahimsa* of the Buddha that nonviolence is more than abstaining from causing injury and that it also involves unbounded compassion and love for others to alleviate suffering in the world. Gandhi goes further into the causes of suffering and finds exploitation to be the main source of causing injury to and suffering in others. Therefore, the thought and action of Gandhi were primarily directed at ending exploitation at all levels. Gandhi's economics, his social *dharma*, his political activism, and his constructive programmes are all his insights into and recommended remedies for removing exploitation in all walks of life. It is unique in its comprehensiveness and all-encompassing rationale consistent with the ethic of nonviolence.

Equally important is that Gandhi was able to transform nonviolence, an individual virtue, into a social virtue, an individual initiative into group action and thus bridge the chasm between the individual and the other and show the correct way to achieve authentic peace and self-experience and at the same time help make and keep peace in the world. In this context, we may recall Gandhi's distinction between weak nonviolence and strong nonviolence. Weak nonviolence is passive, whereas the strong nonviolence is active. The latter generates the "soul-force" or "truth-force", which has the power to transform the self as well as others around. Strong nonviolence is a spiritual act, unlike weak nonviolence which is refraining from physical violence. It is in some ways repressive. Strong nonviolence is spontaneous, free-flowing, and spiritual. In Gandhi's life, we have examples of such spiritual force, for example when he undertook fasting to bring about communal harmony in Calcutta and Delhi, when they were boiling with communal riots.

Perpetual peace may never be reached. In that sense, it may remain a pipe dream. However, like Truth it is an ideal. As an ideal, it is real even if it is never fully realizable. In Gandhi, as in Kant, perpetual peace is an ideal; but their ways to achieve it are different. The question is not whether the ideal is realizable in practice; but it is about its value to promote peace. In both Kant and Gandhi, perpetual peace is not a pipe dream but a practical course that would have useful ramifications for positive peace when faithfully followed. Kant left it to states to initiate the process of perpetual peace by a confederation of sovereign states wedded to nonviolent international relations. Gandhi through his *yoga of nonviolence* brought it down to the level of the person. At the same time, he was able to show also how nonviolence, a personal virtue, can lead to social action. Gandhi's contribution is more than theoretical. He carried out significant experiments to test his theories.

Kant had full faith in reason. Gandhi also was committed to reason; but his approach goes beyond reason to embrace spirituality. Gandhi's notion of spirituality is no more mysterious than practical reason in Kant.

Both are moral forces. Morality is central to peace. Gandhi's *yoga of nonviolence* is a spiritual exercise. It consists in taming and controlling the ego and promoting altruism. Perpetual peace is possible in spiritual space, where contraries coexist without creating conflict. Man can indeed exist in that space because spirituality is a part of his being. Change begins with oneself. So does peace. This is Gandhi's *dharma*.

In a significant sense, Gandhi's views on peace reflect the quintessence of Indian tradition. Kant's notion of perpetual peace is an important strand in Western thought. Murty has attempted some kind of synthesis of the best in the East and the West. A wholesome synthesis or amalgamation of all traditions, I believe, is a vain goal. Eastern and Western traditions are distinct with their own interesting identities, and they will remain so. What we may profitably look for is their complementarity and not synthesis. Again, this is something we find in Gandhi — an identity of the Indian tradition that does not gloss over differences, but reflects their complementary aspects.

References

Āchārānga. (1906). *Acharanga Sutra* (2 vols.). Rajkot: Rajkot Printing Press.

Chattopadhyaya, D.P. (1995). Murty on Peace, in S. Bhattacharyya & A. Vohra (Eds.). *The Philosophy of K. Satchidananda Murty*. New Delhi: Indian Council of Philosophical Research.

Gallie, W.B. (1978). *Philosophers of Peace and War: Kant, Clausewitz, Marx, Engels and Tolstoy*. Cambridge: Cambridge University Press.

Gandhi M.K. (1922). *Ethical Religion*. Madras: S. Ganesan.

Hobsbawm, E.J. (1962). *The Age of Reason*. London: Weidenfeld & Nicolson.

Kant, I. (1903). *Perpetual Peace: A Philosophical Essay* (Tr. Mary Campbell Smith). Crows Nest: G. Allen & Unwin.

Krech, D. & Crutchfield, S.R. (1948). *Theory and Problems of Social Psychology*. New York: McGraw-Hill.

Murty, K.S. (1986). *The Quest for Peace*. New Delhi: Ajanta Publications.

Murty, K.S. & Bouquet, A.C. (1960). *Studies in the Problems of Peace*. Bombay: Asia Publishing House.

Nietzsche, F. (1986). *The Wanderer and His Shadow in Human All Too Human:* Including Assorted Opinions and Maxims and "The Wanderer and His Shadow", Cambridge: Cambridge University Press.

Rao, K.R. (2010). *Violence, Identity and Gandhi*. Visakhapatnam: GITAM University Press.

Book Review

ASHWIN DESAI and GOOLAM VAHED, *The South African Gandhi: Stretcher-Bearer of Empire*, Stanford University Press, 2015, 344 pp.

Majority of Gandhian scholars observe Mahatma Gandhi's legal and political battles in South Africa (1893–1914) as a prelude to the remarkable role that he played in reshaping the strategies of Indian freedom struggle against the British Empire. However, the above book presents a different account of Gandhi's life and work. It is not a hagiography of Gandhi but an attempt to critically examine the work that he did during his stay in South Africa time span. In the introductory chapter the authors express the key ideas of the book:

> This book shows that Gandhi sought to ingratiate himself with Empire (*sic*) and its mission during his years in South Africa. In doing so, he not only rendered African exploitations and oppression invisible, but was, on occasion, a willing part of their subjugation and racist stereotyping. This is not the Gandhi spoken of in hagiographic speeches by politicians more than a century later. This is a different man picking his way through the dross of his time; not just any time, but the height (*sic*) of colonialism; not through any country, but a land that was witness to three centuries of unremitting conquest, brutality and racial bloodletting (pp. 22-23).

There are twenty-one chapters in the book, covering the entire canvas of Gandhi's stay in South Africa, viz., first day of his arrival and farewell; and the incidences (like he was thrown off a train at Pietermaritzburg station en route to Pretoria, in May 1893), and activities and movements that he led there in between these years. This study basically focuses around four of Gandhi's campaigns – the Boer War (1899), the Bhambatha Rebellion (1906), mobilization against fingerprinting in the Transvaal (1907), and significantly the 1913 strike that resulted in Gandhi's South African stay being narrated as a successful one. The authors with their intensive research work and exhaustive references show that in all these four campaigns Gandhi worked mainly as a facilitator and a sympathizer of the British government and hardly had any concern for the rights of African natives. During the Boer War, he worked as a "stretcher bearer" (nursing the sick and wounded soldiers) of the British Empire citing the reason that Indians were "British subjects, . . . (so they should) render some service" (p. 50). Gandhi was very eager to offer his service to the Empire during the Boer War and sent his request to serve several times. After the war he raised the issue of the "Queen's Chocolate" that had been given as a gift to white soldiers. The Natal Indian Congress organized a public meeting on 14 March 1900, to "demonstrate their loyalty to the Crown". It was presided by John Robinson (former prime minister of Natal), under whose rule a spate of anti-Indian laws were passed. The letter of invitation for the meeting bore the headings "Long Live Kaiser-I-Hind" with a picture of Queen Victoria and three British generals. At the end, Gandhi thanked whites for attending in such large numbers and said:

> It was the Indians' proudest boast that they were British subjects. If they were not, they would not have had a footing in South Africa (p. 57).

What is very shocking in this entire episode is that Gandhi did not utter a single word about the British atrocities against the Boers. During this war the British interned Boer women and children in concentration camps and thousands died of malnutrition as well as diseases. Rather than denouncing these atrocities, about two decades later in his book *Satyagraha in South Africa* Gandhi tried to justify the death of thousands of Boer women as an example of *satyagraha* because "real suffering bravely borne melts even a heart of stone" (p. 61). This interpretation of *satyagraha* is not convincing because the precondition for a *satyagraha* movement is that the *satyagrahi* must have a choice. But here, women who died in concentration camps did not choose to suffer in order to melt the hearts of the enemies. They had no choice. Those who have read Gurcharan Das' *The Difficulty of Being Good* (Penguin, 2012) will find a striking similarity here, when Das criticizes Gandhian *ahimsa* by referring to George Orwell's *Reflections on Gandhi*.

During the Bhambatha Rebellion (also known as the Second Zulu War, 1906) around four thousand Zulus were killed, ten thousand rendered homeless, and their Chief Bhambatha was also killed, while white causalities were trifling. This rebellion was an expression of rage against new taxes and cruel labour conditions imposed by the Natal government. According to Nelson Mandela this rebellion inspired generation of South Africans. The South African government awarded "The Order of Mendi for Bravery in Gold" to Bhambatha posthumously in 2006. But in this rebellion too Gandhi worked as a stretcher bearer of the Empire. As he writes in his Autobiography (p. 350):

> A genuine sense of loyalty prevented me from even wishing ill of the Empire. The rightness or otherwise of the "rebellion" was therefore not likely to affect my decision.

This time, he even went ahead from being just a stretcher bearer to requesting Indians to join as "colonial militia bearing arms". According to the authors, *it is perhaps fortuitous that Gandhi's request . . . was turned down. One shudders to think what would have been the consequences of such a scheme* (p. 117).

Despite British brutality to quell this rebellion, "Indian Opinion" embraced the patriotism during Empire Day celebration on 24 May 1906. An American published a report in the Zulu newspaper *Izwi Labantu*, which stated that Africans would not forget that "Indians had volunteered to serve with the English savages in Natal who massacred thousands of Zulus in order to steal their land" (p. 115). It demands a serious debate whether the recent "relocation" of the statue of Gandhi gifted by President Pranab Mukherjee from University of Ghana Campus is right because of the pressure from the academicians that Gandhi was a "racist" (*The Hindu*, New Delhi edition, 8 October, 4 December 2016), but it gives us a reminiscence of the past and forces us to examine the role that Gandhi played in Africa during native African revolts against the British Empire.

The Black Act of 1906-07 (also known as Transvaal Asiatic Law Amendment Act) required "Indians to register with a full set of ten fingerprints to establish who had a right to reside in the Transvaal – thereafter, there would be no further Indian immigration and the £3 tax would be dropped" (p. 120). The aim of this act was to control illegal immigration of Indians. Gandhi opposed this act on two grounds: first, it denied Indians the equality they deserved as British subjects; and second, their status would be reduced to that of Africans. In spite of Gandhi's strong protest this Act was passed on 11 May 1907. Gandhi called it a "murderous law" and announced that Indians would resist it. He was arrested with other protesters on 28 December 1907. Even in this crucial situation he tried to prove that Indians were British subjects and they should not be lodged with the *kaffirs*, African prisoners, and others (p. 131). He hardly showed any concern at the plight of Africans. According to Henry Polak "the oppression of Africans, like their humanity, was scarcely recognized" (p. 146).

The 1913 Third Immigration Bill, came as a "rude shock" to Gandhi and other Indians. According to this bill, now Indians were not allowed to enter into the Orange Free State (OFS); and Hindu, Muslim marriages would not be recognized. The aim of this Bill was to exclude and dominate all who were not white. Resolutions were passed to launch a massive "passive resistance" to oppose this Bill. What was more noticeable in this resistance was the mass-level participation of women led by Valliamma Munuswami and Bai Fatima. Gandhi, Polak, and Kallenbach were arrested. Gandhi was arrested three times in four days. Perhaps, "it is a sign that the government was not sure how to deal with him" (p. 206). Gandhi was sent to Bloemfontein Jail for nine months in OFS (19 November 1913). This is an irony because Indians were forbidden from entering this state. African miners also participated in this strike. These developments show the leadership qualities of Gandhi, which culminated during the freedom struggle of India. Because of mounting pressures, Gandhi, Polak, and Kallenbach were released on 18 December. After release, these persons addressed a gathering of around 6,000 people in Durban. This is the first time Gandhi appeared publicly wearing *lungi* and a knee-long *kurta*, the dress of indentured Indians. The authors have described it as a "born again" Gandhi, shorn of his suit and tie (p. 245). Gandhi was very much pained by the death of some protesters during the strike and pledged to live on one meal per day. Finally, on the basis of the Solomon Commission recommendation £3 tax was repealed, registration of monogamous marriages started; but Indians were still not allowed to enter OFS. Various incidents which happened during this movement prepared the way for the new *avatar* of Gandhi before his final *adieu* from South Africa.

The 19th chapter of the book "Goodbye Mr Gandhi" starts in a very unique way. Describing the contrary role and nature of Gandhi, the authors write:

> Gandhi's long sojourn in South Africa was coming to an end, . . . The journey saw him in various roles that often overlapped and sometimes clashed. He was a lawyer and lawbreaker, journalist and propagandist, a loyal subject of Empire and agitator, a fighter against discrimination and a racist, a man of principle and a dealmaker, and a passive resister yet a sergeant major (p. 269).

These descriptions reflect the "unusual" nature of Gandhi regarding his work in South Africa. Several farewell functions were organized for Gandhi across South Africa. He attended many of them. One organized by Montford Chamney and Hajee Habib in Pretoria on 10 July 1914, needs specific attention here. Chamney was the same Transvaal immigration officer, whose removal Gandhi had demanded in 1907 and who arrested Gandhi in 1913 during the march across the Natal border. But Gandhi did not show any personal ill will towards him. This shows his virtue of forgiveness.[1] But, I wish to add one point here. During the President's election of Indian National Congress in 1939 when Gandhi's preferred candidate Pattabhi Sitaramayya was defeated by Subhas Chandra Bose, Gandhi described it as "my personal loss". It is another matter that he conferred the title of "Netaji" on him. This exhibits the foibles of Gandhi's nature.

What is very "surprising" was that in all farewell functions Gandhi was hosted by *white mayors or their representatives*. In most speeches he praised the British Empire saying that "Englishmen and Indians have been knit together . . . though Empires have gone and fallen, this Empire perhaps may be an exception and that this is an Empire not founded on material but on spiritual foundations. That has been my source of solace all through" (p. 277). Native Africans did not get any mention during his farewell speeches too "except as people who had to be kept in *their* place in the lowest rungs of society" (p. 278). As expected neither the South African Native National Congress, forerunner of the ANC, nor individual personalities like John Dube (neighbour of Gandhi) and Sol T. Plaatje hosted Gandhi, nor did Gandhi deem it necessary to address Africans in any way (ibid.). The authors comment: "Was not this the kind of recognition that he had craved from the very beginning?" (ibid.). According to the authors, Gandhi behaved like an Anglophile (p. 72) during his South Africa stay. Gandhi himself wrote on 23 July 1914 that during his final years "the white people, too, made an excellent demonstration of their affection. During the final days, we drank the cup of their love also full to the brim" (ibid.).

This book narrates several incidents where Gandhi showed his loyalty towards the British Empire. When Queen Victoria died on 22 January 1901, Gandhi not only organized a march in Natal to pay homage, but also sent telegrams to other parts of South Africa requesting "please have

[1] About the nature of forgiveness, there is an example from a different field but an interesting one to mention here. In one of his interviews with the question, "what is the saddest day in your cricket career"? Sachin Tendulkar replied "it was when I am batting at score 194 at Multan, and captain Rahul Dravid called me back declaring the innings"; but, he continued "this does not mean that I have any personal grudge towards Dravid, it may be a team decision; he is still my good friend". During the inauguration of his autobiography (*Playing It My Way*, pp. 247-51, 2015) he invited Dravid also as well as V.V.S. Laxman and Sourav Ganguly.

something similar there. Note that all business should be entirely stopped tomorrow" (p. 59). In another place he showed his gratitude for British Raj's "blessings" by saying that "We fully realize the blessing of the munificent British rule. It is because we are in the folds of the all-embracing Union Jack that we have a footing outside India" (ibid.). He founded BIA (British Indian Association), the aim of which was to show loyalty to the Crown whenever British interests are in threat.

When Britain declared War on Germany on 4 August 1914, Gandhi was on the way to London to visit Gopal Krishna Gokhale (his political *guru*). Gandhi decided "for the sake of Motherland and the Empire to place services unconditionally during this crisis". He appealed to Indians to take up arms to prove that they were worthy "partners in the Empire" (p. 72). He offered the services of Indians in writing to Lord Crewe. He mailed to his third son, Ramdas: "If you had been here and had agreed, I would have sent you to the war" (p. 290). This is just opposite to his ideology of *satyagraha*, which worked as the foundation of his freedom struggle in India. These developments "shocked" Gandhi's liberal friends like Elizabeth Monteno, Emile Hobhouse, and Olive Schreiner. James Hunt wondered about this attitude of Gandhi:

> How remarkable that the man of peace, the follower of Tolstoy, the pioneer of *satyagraha*, should be moved by the spectacle of devoted service more than by the terrible carnage that was about to unleashed! Not a word does he utter be . . . throughout his entire London visit of the horrors of war or of the folly of the European nations in their descent into barbarism (p. 281).

According to Gandhi helping empire would *accelerate* home rule. If we do not understand this truth, then in his own words, it would be *national suicide* (p. 289). But, according to Gandhi home rule is not getting rid of the British, rather Indians wanted to become partners in the British Empire. These attitudes of Gandhi reflect the ambivalent nature of his concern about the freedom of India. That is the reason, according to George Orwell, "he (Gandhi) could be regarded as *our man*". These attitudes had been severely challenged by Lal, Bal, Pal trio and also by Aurobindo Ghosh, as he wrote in 1914:

> We gain nothing by preaching an unconditional loyalty to the government. . . . Gandhi's loyalism is not a pattern for India. . . . What Gandhi has been attempting in South Africa is to secure for Indians the position of kindly treated serfs . . . Our position is different and our aim is different, not to secure a few privileges, but to create a nation of men fit for independence and able to secure and keep it (p. 267).

Gandhi's policy was to demand racial equality with Europeans on the basis of Indians being Aryans and to claim equal citizenship rights for Indians as "British subjects". It is ironical that Gandhi kept separated the Indian freedom struggle from native Africans who were equally denied civil and political rights on the basis of colour and could also "lay claim to being British subjects". Socialist leader Ram Manohar Lohia disagreed with Gandhi on this issue. Lohia wanted South African Indians to be designated as "Indians" not as "British Indians" and he wanted to launch a common cause with Africans and the coloured people. Gandhi rejected it, saying that "Indians cannot make common cause with them" (p. 303).

Having studied Gandhi's various writings, petitions, and speeches in a comprehensive way for the "past ten years" the authors differ with the evaluation of Ramachandra Guha and Nelson Mandela. Guha describes Gandhi as one "who led the first protests against the racial laws" and he should really be recognized as being among apartheid's first opponents (p. 305)." And Mandela claims Gandhi "taught that the destiny of the Indian community was inseparable from that of the oppressed African majority" (ibid.). Desai and Vahed conclude their writings by disagreeing with Guha and Mandela:

> At a time when there is a resurrection of Gandhi in South Africa — given that 2014 marked a hundred years of him leaving South Africa — it is worth taking cognizance of what it is that we remember of his years there. He was a man of Empire (*sic*) . . . while bowing to Empire (*sic*), he did raise universal demands for equality and dignity. However, there are often blind spots in activists who present themselves as messiahs to the world. An anti-imperialist may be terribly sexist or a "feed the world" campaigner may evade taxes. The Mahatma too averted his saintly gaze from some "untouchables" (p. 306).

Those who have studied Ramachandra Guha's *Gandhi Before India* (Penguin, 2013) have found that Guha did not describe these aspects of Gandhi's work done in South Africa. Rather, he tried to rationalize Gandhi's loyalty to the Empire during the Boer War by quoting historian Peter Warwick that African volunteers "believed or hoped that a British victory would bring about an extension of political, educational and commercial opportunities for black people" (p. 60). This argument is not justified because an atrocity is an "atrocity". It can't be justified because it brings prosperity to the victims. In a similar vain Jean-Paul Sartre criticized the French government's outrageous activities towards the Arab people of Algeria, differing from Albert Camus, who said that "Arabs should not be deprived of such benefits of French citizenship as its educational system had enabled a poor youth like himself to escape poverty".

Apart from the core emphasis on Gandhi's "loyal" role towards Empire there are several other descriptions which make this book academically valuable, like the objective of starting the newspaper *Indian Opinion*; impacts of various thinkers like Leo Tolstoy (*The Kingdom of God Is Within You*), Henry Thoreau (*An Essay on Civil Disobedience*), John Ruskin (*Unto This Last*), and William Salter (*Ethical Religion*) on Gandhi; establishment of Phoenix settlement and Tolstoy Farm; the huge participation of women in various movements; and the analysis of the inconsistencies of "Hind Swaraj" by Jonathan Hyslop. The minutely organized lifestyle of Phoenix *ashram*, is also described where people practise simple living, do collective work manually, but selflessly reflect the new atmosphere of collective living, a lifestyle that people wish to emulate in present nuclear and techno-centric families. Gandhi was so obsessed with discipline in this *ashram* that he slapped his own face when he knew that "his son Devdas illicitly ate lemons and failed to confess for fear of being slapped" (p. 74). This reflects the eccentric nature of Gandhi.

Some very extreme expressions could be avoided in this book while evaluating Gandhi, like, he "was a powerful tool of the Empire (p. 295); the title of chapter 15: "The Rajah Is Coming" (*Rajah* denotes here Gandhi, p. 213), etc. We may disagree with Gandhi on several issues but he hardly behaved like a *rajah* in his life. It denotes a feudalism in Gandhi's attitude, which is foreign to his nature. Further, the view of Patrick French that "Gandhi's blanking of Africans is the black hole at the heart of his saintly mythology" is also an inordinate comment and could be omitted (p. 304).

In the last chapter of the book the authors express their dissension with Guha's citation of his last chapter of *Gandhi Before India* where he quotes the statement of his South African friend — "You gave us a lawyer; we gave you a *mahatma*." According to Desai and Vahed "this, of course, is wrong. *Mahatma* (great soul) is an honorific believed to be conferred on Gandhi by Rabindranath Tagore" (p. 296). My understanding is that this is also incorrect. As far I know, it was the people of India who called Gandhi, *mahatma* informally (I could not get any primary source rather secondary sources like *The Cambridge Companion to Gandhi* edited by Judith Brown and Anthony Parel, p. 31, 2011; and *Time Warps* by Ashis Nandy, pp. 223-24, 2002). It is Tagore, who made this title "formal". First time, I read about this title on a wall of the *National Gandhi Museum*, Rajghat, New Delhi, around seven years back, while going to the upper storey of the museum. It is a quotation of Tagore. I found it very riveting and noted immediately. It is:

> He (Gandhi) stopped at the thresholds of the huts of the thousands of the dispossessed, dressed like one of their own. He spoke to them in their own language; here was living truth at last, and not quotations from books. For this reason "MAHATMA" the name given to him by the people of India, is his real name. Who else has felt like him that all Indians are his own flesh and blood?

There may be various arguments and counterarguments regarding the loyalty of Gandhi towards the British Empire. Many historians and scholars will present their thoughts in different ways after reading this book. But one can't ignore the issues which have been raised by Desai and Vahed in this well-researched work. It is very surprising as to how the majority of scholars overlooked the "ingratiate nature" of Gandhi towards the Crown when he himself said:

> In my humble opinion, no Indian has cooperated with the British government more than I have for an unbroken period of twenty-nine years of public life in the face of circumstances that might well have turned any other man into a rebel . . . I put my life in peril four times for the cause of the empire (p. 280).

Actually Gandhi's work and contribution to India are unquestionable and beyond any doubt. His method of nonviolent resistance has been adopted and successfully practised by so many social reformers, freedom fighters, and politicians across the world. They have shown their indebtedness and gratitude to Gandhi for this. Among these, Nelson Mandela[2] (Autobiography — *Long Walk to Freedom*, pp. 98, 107, 220-22, 7-43, 347-48, 407, London: Little Brown, 2010); Dalai Lama (Autobiography — *Freedom in Exile*, pp. 127-30, London: Abacus, 2009); Aung San Suu Kyi (Autobiography — *Freedom from Fear*, pp. 105-08, 121-23, 183-84, 281, 321-25, 355, London: Penguin, 1995); Anwar el-Sadat (Autobiography — *In Search of Identity*, pp. 12-13, 330, Dehradun: Natraj Publishers, 1983), and Martin Luther King Jr (*Stride Toward Freedom*: *The Montgomery Story*, pp. 84-93, London: Victor Gollancz, 1959 and *A Testament of Hope*, pp. 7, 16-18, 86, 164, 485-86, 583, New York: Harper San Francisco, 1991) are prominent figures. All of them fought their struggle against all types of exploitations, racial discriminations, and injustices using completely

---

2 Nelson Mandela himself often cited Gandhi as an inspiration and claimed the Indian leader as a son of South Africa. In a meeting with Sachin Tendulkar, Mandela said: "You are fortunate that you are from the land of Gandhi. He has had a profound impact on my life." Cf. "Invoking Eternal Images . . ." by Sachin Tendulkar in Raghunath Mashelkar's edited book, *Timeless Inspirator: Reliving Gandhi*, p. 287, Sakal Publications, 2010.

nonviolent means. But what he had done in South Africa in around twenty years time span raised questions about his idea of human equality, dignity, and solidarity. His "reluctance" with regard to the rights of native Africans who were equally facing discriminations and subjugations is doubtable. One can accept these aspects of Gandhi's works without any unreasonable liking or disliking and there is no harm in it. This book reflects the South African phase of Gandhi's life in a comprehensive way. It is a must read work for academicians and also for those who have a general interest in the life and work of Gandhi. Brad Jenkins expresses his views about this book in following words:

> Many people will take this book as a scathing review of Ghandi's (*sic*) whitewashed past (pun intended), . . . What this book shows is that NOBODY is perfect, no matter how infallible they appear. Once we can actually grasp that concept, we will stop holding certain people to such a high degree . . . Ghandi (*sic*) did a lot of good for the Indian people throughout his entire life . . . there's no argument there. The problem is when you go back to his time in South Africa when he had a chance to throw his support behind the native people and help pull them out of the depths of English persecution . . . he refused. Ghandi (*sic*) actually went out of his way to distance Indians from Africans, using the argument that only Indians and English should be on equal standing. With this stance, Ghandi (*sic*) was shoehorned into supporting the whitewashing of South Africa. . . . Does this make Ghandi (*sic*) a bad person? Does this diminish the accomplishments he made later in life? Does this mean we must rethink Mahatma Ghandi (*sic*), the person? After reading this book, I can give you an unequivocal vote of confidence in the negative to all of these questions. Ghandi (*sic*) was a great man and I will never take that away from him . . . but he wasn't perfect. Nobody is.

This book challenges in a very rational way those notions about Gandhi that have been engraved in the minds of the majority of scholars as well as laypersons.

Satyendra Kumar Srivastava
Assistant Professor
Dept of Philosophy
Hans Raj College
University of Delhi
Delhi - 110007
e-mail: satyendrasrivas@gmail.com

Contributors

Anand, Y.P., has been Director, National Gandhi Museum and Library, Rajghat, New Delhi for ten years from 1996 to 2006. He has written numerous papers and compiled books on various Gandhian subjects. His books include *The Essential Relationship between Netaji Subhas Bose & Mahatma Gandhi* (1997); *Birth of Free India's National Anthem: A Gift from Netaji Subhas Bose* (1997); *Mahatma Gandhi and the Railways* (English and Hindi, 2002); *Mahatma Gandhi and Art* (2003); *Mahatma Gandhi and Satyagraha: A Compendium* (2006); *Albert Einstein and Mahatma Gandhi: The Centenary of Physics, War, Satyagraha and Peace* (2006/2010); *Mahatma Gandhi's Works and Interpretation of the Bhagavad Gita* (2 vols) (2009); *Gitapadarthakosha* (by Mahatma Gandhi), translated into Hindi (2010); and *Historical Background to the Imposition of SALT TAX under the British Rule (1757–1947)* and *Mahatma Gandhi's SALT SATYAGRAHA* (1930-31) (2014, published by Ministry of Culture). He attended seminars on Gandhian subjects in USA, Canada, and Italy. He is now working on the subject: "Tolstoy and Gandhi". e-mail: <ypanandindia@yahoo.co.in>.

Aruna Pariti, is the Head, Department of History, Nizam College, Osmania University, Hyderabad and Academic Counsellor in History for IGNOU. Prior to this, she worked as a Research Fellow at GITAM Center for Gandhian Studies, GITAM University. She also served as Guest Faculty in the University of Hyderabad. She worked as a Research Assistant in the Ford Foundation-funded project on "Historical Atlas of South India" and in the Salar Jung Museum. She did her PhD from the University of Hyderabad in 2005. Dr. Pariti has published two books: *Genealogy, Time and Identity: Historical Consciousness in the Deccan (Sixth Century* CE *– Twelfth Centure* CE*)* and *State Formation in the Eastern Deccan (7th Century* AD *– 13th Century* AD*)*. She has also contributed a number of papers for reputed journals and chapters in History for BA and Intermediate Textbooks (in English and Telugu), published by Telugu Akademi, Government of Telangana. e-mail: <arunapariti@gmail.com>.

Douglas Allen, is Professor and former Chairperson of Philosophy at the University of Maine, USA. He served as President of the Society for Asian and Comparative Philosophy and is Series Editor of *Lexington's Studies in Comparative Philosophy and Religion*. He is author and editor of fifteen books and 150 chapters and scholarly articles. He has written several books on Mahatma Gandhi and is finishing a new Gandhi-informed book in 2017. He has been awarded Fulbright and Smithsonian grants to India, Maine Presidential Research and Creative Achievement Award, and Distinguished Maine Professor Award. A peace and justice scholar-activist, he has been active in Civil Rights Movement, Vietnam/Indochina Antiwar Movement, and other struggles resisting violence, war, class exploitation, imperialism, racial and gender oppression, and environmental destruction. He has been a recipient of "Hands of Peace Award" in Maine and "Scroll of Peace International Award for Peace Research" in India. During his 2015-16 sabbatical in India, he was based at the Indian Institute of Technology Madras and was selected as the first Distinguished Scholar Chair of Gandhian Studies at the Indian Institute of Technology Bombay. e-mail: <dallen@maine.edu>.

Ramakrishna Rao, K., is a philosopher, psychologist, and educationist with international expertise in the areas of Indian psychology, consciousness, and Gandhian Studies. He has published over 200 research papers and sixteen books. His most recent books are *Cognitive Anomalies, Consciousness and Yoga* (Matrix Publishers), a thousand-page volume that brings together the wisdom from different disciplines for building a unified psychological model of the person, and *Gandhi and Applied Spirituality*. Prof. Rao has served as the Executive Director of the Foundation for Research on the Nature of Man in USA. He has been the Founder, Head, and Professor of the Department of Psychology and Parapsychology, and Honorary Director of the Institute for Yoga and Consciousness, at Andhra University. He has held various other major executive and advisory positions including Vice-Chancellor of Andhra University, Chairman of the AP State Commission of Higher Education, and Chairman of the Indian Council of Philosophical Research (ICPR). He is currently the Chancellor of GITAM University. e-mail: <krrao007@gmail.com>.

Sambasiva Prasad, B., is ICPR Senior Fellow at GITAM School of Gandhian Studies, GITAM University, Visakhapatnam. Earlier, he was the Director, Center for Gandhian Studies, GITAM University, Visakhapatnam. His current areas of interest include Gandhian Philosophy and Peace Studies. He has published about forty research papers in reputed journals and anthologies. Some of them were published in *JICPR, IPQ, Gandhi Marg,* and *GITAM Journal of Gandhian Studies*. He has presented about seventy research papers at national and international conferences. He has edited the book *Consciousness, Gandhi and Yoga: Interdisciplinary, East–West Odyssey of K. Ramakrishna Rao* (2013). He is the Executive Editor of *GITAM Journal of Gandhian Studies*. Currently he is working on the socio-economic philosophy of Mahatma Gandhi. e-mail: <b.sambasivaprasad@gmail.com>.

Venkaiah Naidu, M., a zealous and visionary leader of the masses, was born on 1 July 1949 at Chavatapalem, Nellore, Andhra Pradesh. A law graduate from Andhra University, he started his career as a student leader of the Akhil Bharatiya Vidyarthi Parishad (ABVP) and played a prominent role in the Jai Andhra Movement and in the anti-emergency movement led by Jayaprakash Narayan in the 1970s. From 1977-80, he was President of the Bharatiya Janata Party (BJP) Youth Wing. He was elected as Member of Legislative Assembly (MLA), Andhra Pradesh, from Udayagiri constituency, Nellore in 1978 and 1983. A Rajya Sabha MP from Karnataka in 1998, 2004, and 2010 and from Rajasthan since 2016, he also served as BJP President during 2002-04. As the Union Minister for Rural Development in the Vajpayee government, he was known for his aggressive rural development initiatives. He is currently the Union Minister of Housing and Urban Poverty Alleviation, and Information and Broadcasting in the Modi cabinet. Shri Venkaiah Naidu's Swarna Bharath Trust in Nellore is dedicated to the service of the underprivileged. He has a passion for educating the masses and has written widely on various subjects.

Index